INSIDE PHOTOSHOP® CS

BY
Gary David Bouton
Mara Zebest
Gary Kubicek
Dave Huss
Christian Verhoeven

SAMS

800 East 96th Street, Indianapolis, Indiana 46240 USA

Inside Photoshop® CS

International Standard Book Number: 0-672-32644-2

Library of Congress Catalog Card Number: 2003112584

Printed in the United States of America

First Printing: May 2004

06   05   04   4   3   2   1

Trademarks

All terms mentioned in this book that are known to be trademarks or service marks have been appropriately capitalized. Sams Publishing cannot attest to the accuracy of this information. Use of a term in this book should not be regarded as affecting the validity of any trademark or service mark.

Warning and Disclaimer

Every effort has been made to make this book as complete and as accurate as possible, but no warranty or fitness is implied. The information provided is on an "as is" basis. The authors and the publisher shall have neither liability nor responsibility to any person or entity with respect to any loss or damages arising from the information contained in this book or from the use of the CD or programs accompanying it.

Bulk Sales

Sams Publishing offers excellent discounts on this book when ordered in quantity for bulk purchases or special sales. For more information, please contact

U.S. Corporate and Government Sales
1-800-382-3419
corpsales@pearsontechgroup.com

For sales outside of the U.S., please contact

International Sales
+1-317-428-3341
international@pearsontechgroup.com

Acquisitions Editor
Betsy Brown

Development Editor
Lorna Gentry

Managing Editor
Charlotte Clapp

Project Editor
Andy Beaster

Copy Editor
Chuck Hutchinson

Indexer
John Sleeva

Proofreader
Wendy Ott

Technical Editor
Mara Zebest

Publishing Coordinator
Vanessa Evans

Multimedia Developer
Dan Scherf

Cover Designer
Gary David Bouton

Page Layout
Julie Parks
Brad Chinn

Contents at a Glance

Table of Contents

2 The Critically Important Color and Gamma Calibration Chapter   71

Part II   A Hands-On Reference for Creating and Editing Photoshop Images

4   Layers and Channels   197

Part III   Image Acquisition Basics

8   Loading Digital Images into Photoshop CS from Digital Cameras, Photo CDs, Scanners, and More   375

Part V   Ambitious Image Editing

14   Retouching a Group Scene by Creating a Composite Image   559

15   Creating a Dream Image from a Hopeless Snapshot   589

18 Replacing the Main Elements in an Image   739

Part VI Illustration, Page Layout, and Photoshop

19 Restoring a Historic Poster   765

Part VII   Working for the Web with ImageReady

22   Animations and Rollovers   881

About the Authors

Gary David Bouton is an illustrator/writer/all-around-nice guy who lives with his wife in a cozy hamlet in upstate New York. Mr. Bouton has authored 14 books on Photoshop; several other books on the Internet, CorelDRAW, and modeling applications; and some freelance columns relating to computer graphics for photography and digital art publications. Gary holds four international awards in DTP and graphics. He is also moderator of the 3D forum at `TalkGraphics.com` and a moderator of the (Photoshop) "Inside Track" at `http://www.photoshopgurus.info/forum/viewforum.php?f=13`. Gary can usually be reached at `Gary@TheBoutons.com`.

Mara Zebest is a graphic artist who lives with her family in Folsom, California. Besides satisfying the needs of numerous commercial clients by designing brochures, newspaper and magazine ads, and a variety of other graphics, Mara also spends part of her schedule supplying people in her area with computer training and technical support for software and troubleshooting issues. Mara also occasionally donates her time to a local school by designing T-shirts and offering consultation on image-related areas. This is Mara's third time as a contributing author and technical editor for the *Inside Photoshop* series.

Gary Kubicek has been a contributing author for 8 books on Photoshop; he has also been a technical editor for 12 books. A professional photographer for more than 20 years, Gary was an early adopter of Photoshop and the "digital darkroom" as an extension of the self-expression he finds in his traditional photographic work. Gary is also a digital imaging consultant. And when he's not pushing pixels, he is playing his Strat and trying to learn how to play some of his favorite Stevie Ray Vaughan tunes.

Gary can be reached at `gary@garykubicek.com`. His Web site address is `www.garykubicek.com`.

Dave Huss has authored 15 books on all aspects of digital imagery that have been translated into six languages. A popular conference speaker, Dave has taught classes throughout the U.S. and Europe. His digital montages have won awards at national competitions, and he has been interviewed on both CNN and TechTV.

Christian Verhoeven is a Belgian freelance artist, photographer, and painter who is passionate about Photoshop, which opened for him new doors of creativity and new fields of experience in graphic arts. Christian is currently living in East Asia.

Dedication

This book is dedicated to my father, Jack Orvin Bouton,
March 17, 1926–August 15, 2002.
I loved him a lot and miss him.

—Gary Bouton

Acknowledgments

Getting this book into your hands took not only the talents of a writing consortium, but also the skills and patience of the publishing professionals at Sams Publishing and the support of many throughout the graphics industry.

I want to thank all of them from the bottom of my heart:

- First, I want to thank Betsy Brown, acquisitions editor, for moral support (directed toward a guy who *has* no morals, mind you :)), a string of critical back-and-forths almost every other day over the telly and email—which kept this book organized along the road from idea to printed page—and mostly for allowing us to show each other that we're human, we catch colds, we get tired sometimes, we fall off the roof hanging Christmas ornaments. Betsy, thanks. I mean it.

- Thanks to Lorna Gentry, development editor, for letting me tell the story my way. The *Inside Photoshop* series is FAR from being a "formula" book, and it's always eggshells you walk on when you break conventions and rules. Thanks for being a "good egg" (OUCH!), Lorna.

- A thousand thanks to Andy Beaster for keeping the author reviews a'comin' in a timely, easy-to-digest fashion.

- Thank you and a tip o' the hat to Chuck Hutchinson, copy editor, who kept my pronouns in a row and organized my gerunds, and actually thought a picture or two in the book were funny! Thanks, Chuck.

- Thanks to Marc Pawliger and Chris Cox at Adobe Systems for answering all my questions, and then some, during the beta cycle. Also thanks to John Nack, for letting us participate in the creation of this product through suggestions and the beta cycle channels. Special thanks to Adobe Systems Beta Coordinators Le Dang-Ho and Stacey Strehlow, for accommodating our special needs during the writing of this book. You folks were incredibly responsive and helpful. We needed that in order to write this book.

- Thanks to my wife, my friend, and my Talent Liaison (or more appropriately, Talent Wrangler—she handled the mail and the calls so I could write). Barbara, we have a long history with Pearson, and I know we have a longer one with each other. Thank you, mate.

- Thanks to Wendy Biss for her chapter on home renovations. This was a student project that grew into a chapter under her skilled hands. Thank you, Wendy!

- Thanks to Sue Messruther for the cover photo of the pelicans!

- Thanks to Atlas at Spiral Graphics for allowing us to include a demo version of Genetica on the companion CD.

- A million thanks to Don McClure at Digital Element for allowing us to include Verdant and Aurora 2.

- Thanks to Eric Wijngaard at Shinycore for allowing us to include Path Styler.

- Thanks to Jan Esmann for letting us include the demo to Power Retouche.

- Many, many thanks to Mark Goodall of Xara, Ltd. Mark made it possible at the last moment for Windows users to get a trial edition of Xara X on the companion CD (no slight here; it's a Windows-only program). See the ad in the back of the book for an incredibly low-priced offer on a program I have been using for five years to get stuff like book covers and annotations and charts and technical drawings done. And I've done fun stuff, too, that's on the gallery at www.xara.com. Mark, thank you for listening to me, and I realize that you've probably lost huge clumps of hair as a result of reading email from me that started out with the sentence, "Mark, wouldn't it be neat if Xara did...." You and Kate Moir have been the most responsive business contacts I've ever had the privilege to know. Thank you both.

- Thanks to technical editors Doug Nelson and Kate Binder for their support of the chapters Mara did not handle. You people kept it tight, informative, and more than anything, correct for our readers. I'd tip my hat to you, except it's a straw summer hat that got stains on it from mowing the lawn.

- Thanks go to Software Specialist Dan Scherf for mastering a CD that is accurate, despite how complex we made it for you!

- Thanks to Bill Sawyer for the use of his image in this book; a million thanks to our families and friends for putting up with having a camera stuck in their faces; and particular thanks to Craig, Drew, Julian, Jake, Josh, and everyone else who showed up at the birthday party so we could document it.

- Thanks to Mara Zebest, Gary Kubicek, Dave Huss, and Christian Verhoeven for their invaluable contributions to this book. Dear reader, these ladies and gentlemen have, pardon the phrase, *really busted* to bring to the world information because they love the arts or communication and content creation, and they also love to share.

Mara Zebest would like to thank her friends and family members for their support and encouragement. I would like to give a special thanks to my kids, David and Leah, who constantly keep it real (for me) with their never-ending supply of laundry and their endearing personalities. I would also like to thank my friend and neighbor, Valerie Myers, who has taken the time to listen to my daily tales and has helped me through my frustrations and cheered me on through my successes. And a big *thank you* to Robert Stanley, an infinitely wonderful and extraordinary person, who has always been by my side with encouragement and has inspired me to think outside the box on many occasions.

Gary Kubicek thanks his father, Bill Kubicek, for instilling in him a love for reading. Dad, I'm glad that I could make you proud by doing what you have always wanted to do—write a book. Well, Dad, this is the eighth book I've contributed to!

Gary also thanks Mary Ellen Sims for signing a model release for a photo that I shot way back in 1995. Who knew that you'd be in two Photoshop books! Thanks for…um, standing around in the Everson Museum! Gary also thanks Candace and Mike at the local Target store for providing a lot of answers to a lot of questions that helped make Chapter 11, "Working with Picture CD Pictures," an informative chapter. Thanks, guys!

Christian Verhoeven would like to thank his wife Gracianne, who agreed to be a model in the book. Her viewpoint on my work is particularly noticeable and pushes me to go always further in my work. I thank her for sharing all my fantasies and for never losing patience when faced with my mood swings!

A very special thanks to Gary David Bouton who, with great generosity and incredible confidence, allowed me to express myself in his book. In him, I also found a friend, which is more and more rare in this world of hard competition and jealousy.

We Want to Hear from You!

As the reader of this book, *you* are our most important critic and commentator. We value your opinion and want to know what we're doing right, what we could do better, what areas you'd like to see us publish in, and any other words of wisdom you're willing to pass our way.

You can email or write me directly to let me know what you did or didn't like about this book—as well as what we can do to make our books stronger.

Please note that I cannot help you with technical problems related to the topic of this book, and that due to the high volume of mail I receive, I might not be able to reply to every message.

When you write, please be sure to include this book's title and author as well as your name and phone or email address. I will carefully review your comments and share them with the author and editors who worked on the book.

Email: graphics@samspublishing.com

Mail: Mark Taber
         Associate Publisher
         Sams Publishing
         800 East 96th Street
         Indianapolis, IN 46240 USA

Reader Services

For more information about this book or others from Sams Publishing, visit our Web site at www.samspublishing.com. Type the ISBN (excluding hyphens) or the title of the book in the Search box to find the book you're looking for.

Introduction

Not New, and Not Wonderful!

How's that for a provocative, controversial lead-in? :) What I mean by this headline is that I've been writing Photoshop books for more than 10 years now, and in the first book I was fairly gushing over what a marvelously new, useful, almost mystical tool Photoshop was. Well, it's still magical, but I now hesitate to call it "new." My dentist, my astrologer, and the three guys who work on my car will all attest, "Oh, yeah, Photoshop. You retouch pictures with it. My brother-in-law uses it." So although Photoshop CS introduces new features that we'll thoroughly document in this book, em, calling Photoshop "new" is sort of like calling something a secret that everyone on the earth knows about.

Similarly, I'm not going to write about how "wonderful" Photoshop CS is. That, too, would be gushing, and besides, you're going to find out firsthand exactly how wonderful Photoshop is on your own, or gather a profound, in-depth appreciation for its wonder if you play with Photoshop in combination with the exercises we've provided in this book.

Okay, so what's this *book* going to mean to you, the phrases "new" and "wonderful" mercifully reserved? Well, to the beginner, this book is going to turn you into a bona fide journeyman with Photoshop skills that you will find deeply rewarding, regardless of the type of assignment before you. You're going to understand why a pixel acts as it does, what resolution you need for outputting to the Web and to an inkjet printer, and how to accomplish that special visual trick you saw in a magazine. A snowball effect will take place: Photoshop the Pastime will become Photoshop the Hobby; you'll start thinking of ways you can spruce up Christmas cards, calendars, and correspondence; you'll start strolling down the paper aisles at Staples looking for the right card stock—your life as an *imagist* will take root and blossom.

If you're already a journeyman, this is the right book for professional advancement as well. How many newspaper ads have you seen for "average knowledge of Photoshop a must"? Never, right? As Photoshop has grown into the *de facto* image editing program, the market for skilled Photoshoppists has become crowded. You cannot afford to maintain a "passing knowledge" of this killer application. Imagine walking into an interview, sitting down at the company's graphics workstation, calibrating the monitor in 3 minutes, setting up preferences in another 2 minutes, and then casually editing wings onto a horse to create a Pegasus in less time than it takes to go to the canteen for coffee? Quit imagining now! *Inside Photoshop CS* is your one-stop resource for both the technical information and the low-down on how to accomplish mind-blowing and salary-garnering effects. Do what nobody else out there is doing. Use Photoshop as naturally as you would hold a pencil in your hand.

Okay, I'm Hooked. What's Behind the *Content* of the Book?

Inside Photoshop CS is a fully guided tour of the behind-the-scenes magic this program can produce. My coauthors and I take you through comprehensive steps in each chapter to show you how to produce award-winning work, photo-realistic or otherwise. Our approach is a straightforward and simple one: It is our belief that every attention-getting image has to begin with a *concept*. The user then chooses the tools to complete the goal and, through a set of procedures, finishes the work. It is our intention to show you a task, to examine what needs to be done, and then to provide the steps needed to bring the piece to completion. By structuring the book in this way, we make it possible for you to be able to apply the "methodology" shown in this book to a *multitude* of personal and professional assignments.

An Omnibus Approach Provides Help for All Classes of Designers

As the theme of the book goes, *everyone* is new to Photoshop CS; it's an adventure for the pro and the beginner alike, and we didn't want to leave out anything in the steps, the notes, the text, or the discovery process. Do not take the attitude "Yeah, yeah, I know about the Lasso tool, so I'll skip this section." There are new features on the Lasso tool flyout on the toolbox, and you'll be missing out on valuable information if you "gloss" a chapter. We didn't presume anything, so as a reader, you shouldn't either!

Taking the Road to Adventure

Let us make learning Photoshop CS an excursion, an adventure. As most adventures go, you must pack a few things first, such intangible things as a positive attitude, a concept, a proficiency with your computer, and an eagerness to learn. And last but not least, you should have a map, so you can instantly find your way from Point X to Point Y, while ignoring entirely Point A. We have *provided* the map (it's called "this book"!), and the following sections describe this map, by way of explaining some of the conventions of *Inside Photoshop CS*.

Push Down and Twist: The Directions for Accessing This Book

Most of the examples described in the book are documented in a step-by-step format. If you follow along, your screen should look exactly like this book's figures, except that your screen will be in color. Each chapter leads you through at least one set of numbered steps, with frequent asides explaining why we asked you to do something. The figures show the results of an action, and we explain what the effect should look like.

Most of Photoshop CS's tools have different, enhanced functions when you hold down the Shift, Alt, or Ctrl keys (Shift, Opt, ⌘ Command keys, for Macintosh users) while you click with the mouse or press other keyboard keys. These *modifier keys* are shown in the steps as Ctrl(⌘)+click, Alt(Opt)+click, Ctrl(⌘)+D, and so on. *Inside Photoshop CS* is a multiplatform documentation of the application; Windows key commands are shown first in the steps, followed by the Macintosh key equivalent (enclosed in parentheses). The primary difference in Photoshop CS across platforms is the "look" each operating system lends to interface elements.

Note

What's the difference?   Okay, here's a list of the *real* differences in features between the Windows and the Macintosh versions of Photoshop CS:

- When you are in full-screen mode without the menu or title bar on an image, in Windows, you can still access the menu because a flyout button appears on the top of the toolbox.

- The Document Sizes field and the Zoom Percentage field on the Macintosh version of Photoshop are located on the bottom of the current image window. In Windows, the Document Sizes and Zoom Percentage fields are on the status bar at the bottom of the screen, where you can also see options displayed for the currently selected tool.

- As of this writing, the Adobe Gamma control panel automatically loads upon installing Photoshop CS on the Macintosh. You can find this utility under the Apple menu, Control Panels. As of this writing, the Adobe Gamma control panel might or might not automatically load during installation while running Windows Me, NT, 2000, or Windows XP. Be sure to check out the (Photoshop5), Goodies, Calibration folder if Adobe Gamma didn't load into the system control panel. You will find instructions in the Calibration folder on how to manually install Adobe Gamma. (Hint: Do it; it's the best global gamma adjustment utility you can find for your computer, and it's free.)

To show you how easy it is to follow along in this book, we tell you how to access the Feather command like this:

1. Press Ctrl(⌘)+Alt(Opt)+D (Select, Feather), and then type **5** in the Pixels field. Click on OK to apply the feathering.

The translation? You hold down the first key while you press the second and third keys (then release all three keys to produce the intended result), or you can access the command the "hard way" through the menu commands enclosed in parentheses. We are trying to get you comfortable with modifier keys rather than menu commands because this constant reinforcement, highlighted throughout the book, will eventually make you work more efficiently in Photoshop CS. Function keys appear in this book as F1, F2, F3, and so on.

If the steps in an application that's available in both Windows and Macintosh formats are significantly different, we fully explain the steps used in this book.

The figures in this book were taken in Windows XP; there simply isn't room in this book to show all the versions of Windows, Unix, and Macintosh interfaces! Again, where there is a significant difference in the way something is accomplished on a specific platform, this book details specific steps to be used.

Terms Used in This Book

The term *drag* in this book means to hold down the primary mouse button and move the onscreen cursor. This action is used in Photoshop to create a marquee selection and to access tools on the toolbox flyout. On the Macintosh, dragging is also used to access *pull-down menus*; Windows users do not need to hold the primary mouse button to access flyout menus and main menu commands.

Hover means to move your cursor onscreen without holding a mouse button. Hovering is most commonly used in Photoshop with the Magnetic Pen and Magnetic Lasso tools, and also with the Eyedropper tool when seeking a relative position in an image and the color value beneath the tool (the Info palette, F8, must be displayed to determine the values the Eyedropper reads).

Click means to press and release the primary mouse button once.

Double-click means to press quickly the primary mouse button twice. Usually, you double-click to perform a function without the need to click an OK button in a directory window. Additionally, when you double-click on a tool in Photoshop's toolbox, the Options palette appears.

Shift+Click means that you should hold down the Shift key while you click with the primary mouse button.

Special (Not Ordinary) Things We Used in This Book

Throughout this book, we used several conventions to clarify certain keyboard techniques and to help you distinguish certain types of text (new terms and text that you type, for example). These conventions include the following:

Special Text

Information you type is in **boldface**. This rule applies to individual letters, numbers, and text strings, but not to special keys, such as Enter (Return), Tab, Esc, or Ctrl(⌘).

New terms appear in *italic*. Italic text is used also for emphasis, as in "*Don't* unplug your computer at this point."

We Use Nicknames for Well-Known Products

Inside Photoshop CS would be an even larger book than it already is if every reference to a specific graphics product or manufacturer included the full brand manufacturer, product name, and version number. For this reason, you'll occasionally see Adobe Photoshop CS referred to as simply "Photoshop" in the text of this book. Similarly, Adobe Illustrator is referred to as "Illustrator," and other products are mentioned by their "street names."

Sams Publishing and the authors acknowledge that the names mentioned in this book are trademarked or copyrighted by their respective manufacturers; our use of nicknames for various products is in no way meant to infringe on the trademark names for these products. When we refer to an application, it is usually the most current version of the application, unless otherwise noted.

Some Special Information in Special Features

Throughout *Inside Photoshop CS*, you'll find special pieces of information added to help you understand how to use both Adobe Photoshop CS and this book. Those features include:

Note

> **Notes supply extra information.** When we want to tell you about something useful but not necessarily essential to the current "conversation," we'll add it in a note.

Tip

> **Tips offer helpful hints.** Shortcuts, workarounds, productivity boosters, and other forms of expert advice are collected in the tips you'll find scattered throughout this book.

Caution

> **Look out when you see a Caution!** When we want to point out a potential pitfall or pothole in your path to Photoshop mastery, we'll shout out the warning in a Caution.

Sidebars Offer Interesting Diversions

> When we have a relevant story to tell about some Photoshop CS success, an interesting use of a Photoshop technique, an alternative approach, a little-known Photoshop fact, or other alarms and diversions, we'll lay it all out for you in a sidebar. These items make for good reading and (sometimes) a well-earned break in the action.

Insider

> When you're working through any of the stepped procedures in this book, you're likely to run across one or more of these helpful features we call Insiders. When you read these bits, imagine you're hearing the voice of the authors whispering in your ear, helping you over potentially tricky steps in learning and using the techniques we teach you in the book. Insiders also give you important advice and guidance about alternative approaches, and they explain why we're telling you to do the things we're telling you to do. It's the next best thing to having all of us crowded behind you while you work—without all the noise and shoving!

Inside Photoshop CS User's Guide

We recommend that you use *Inside Photoshop CS* as a reference guide, but it was also written as a string of hands-on tutorials. And this means that you might benefit most from the information in the book by reading a little at a time. We are aware, however, that this is not the way everyone finds information—particularly in an integrating graphics environment such as Photoshop's, where one piece of information often leads to a seemingly unconnected slice of wisdom. For this reason, most chapters offer complete, self-contained steps for a specific topic or technique, with frequent cross-references to related material in other chapters. If you begin reading Chapter 4, for example, you will learn a complete area of image editing, but you can build on what you've learned if you thoroughly investigate Chapter 16, as well.

Part I: The Basics So You Don't Get Headaches Later: Pixels, Color Spaces, and the Universe

We believe that the best way to get off on the right foot with Photoshop is to understand the basics first. First you walk, and then you fly, in a manner of speaking. Part I is a necessary part of your education, and if you read it first, you'll work more quickly through the rest of the book. Here's what's in this part of the book:

- **Chapter 0: Answers to the Most Important Imaging Questions**—This chapter was designed to get you up and running on imaging terminology and to dispel a myth or two about resolution and pixels. Check into this chapter, and you'll check out with a fistful of terms and notions that'll come in handy as you peruse the remainder of the book.

- **Chapter 1: Producing Awesome Images from the Start**—This is the "fun" chapter; you'll get your feet wet using many of Photoshop's tools without ever having used them before. Under expert tutelage, you'll retouch an image—admittedly a *silly* image—gain confidence in your image editing prowess, and hey, who doesn't like getting results right away from a book? :)

- **Chapter 2: The Critically Important Color and Gamma Calibration Chapter**—If you are after color-critical work, this chapter is a MUST, and you should probably read it before any of the other chapters. Why? Because your system's calibration will affect every other example and tutorial in this book.

- **Chapter 3: Setting Preferences, Customizing, and Optimizing Photoshop CS**—Photoshop works for you, and not the other way around. Chapter 3 shows you all the little neat things spinning around the interface—and beneath and behind it—and we offer suggestions on the smartest, most time-efficient, and friendly way to "mold" your own interface. Photoshop will work faster and you'll be happier with the results after reading this chapter.

Part II: A Hands-On Reference for Creating and Editing Photoshop Images

This part of the book focuses on the most important features in Photoshop. Hands-on tutorials guide you through working with paths, selections, layers, channels, and more. Part II includes:

- **Chapter 4: Layers and Channels**—What is a layer? What is an alpha channel? All questions are answered in this comprehensive and fun chapter. Don't miss out on some of the core features of Photoshop. Mark this chapter as one to dive into post haste!

- **Chapter 5: Harnessing the Power of Selections**—We'll take you around the virtual block with a potpourri of selection techniques because one selection method does not fit all. Find out what to use on what type of image or painting to accurately and invisibly separate areas upon which you want to work.

- **Chapter 6: Using the Pen Tools**—Paths are non-printing vector shapes that can assist you in making precise selections. The only problem? You need to learn how to use the Pen tools! This chapter is a wall-to-wall treatise on how to get the most out of Photoshop's vector tools.

- **Chapter 7: Filters**—Filters are a good thing, but what are they good *for*? This chapter covers some of the more popular filters in Photoshop and shows you unique uses for them. Additionally, we'll take a survey of the third-party filters out there that'll knock your virtual socks off.

Part III: Image Acquisition Basics

Naturally, before you can retouch a picture, you have to get it into your computer! The chapters in this part cover the basic strategies for digitizing real-world images so you can work with them in Photoshop.

- **Chapter 8: Loading Digital Images into Photoshop CS from Digital Cameras, Photo CDs, Scanning, and More**—This chapter covers the means by which an image can be made digital. Scanning, Picture CDs, digital photography, and other methods are discussed.

- **Chapter 9: Digital Photography and Photoshop: A Checklist for Better Imaging**—How does a traditional camera differ from a digital one? What are the things you need to watch out for with a digital camera? What are the advantages of a digital camera? We answer these questions and more in this indispensable chapter.

Part IV: Correcting, Restoring, and Retouching Images

This part of the book concentrates on the essence of Photoshop's power—the capability to mold and shape digital images to express anything you have in mind. Here's what you get in this part:

- **Chapter 10: Color Correction and Selections: Creating Beautiful Hands**—Hands can be as beautiful and as expressive as the human body or the human face. Come take a look at how the pros optimize a photo of a pair of hands to make them look positively magical.

- **Chapter 11: Working with Picture CD Pictures**—Picture CD pictures are more popular than ever. However, how do they stack up against a digital camera photo? What do you need to watch out for in terms of image resolution? And how do you retouch a Picture CD photo? The answers lie at your fingertips in this chapter.

- **Chapter 12: Curves and Adjustment Layers**—Curves and Adjustment Layers go hand in hand. If you haven't tried out these Photoshop features, you owe it to yourself to check out this chapter and then start retouching like the pros.

- **Chapter 13: Keeping Up Appearances: Techniques for Retouching Images**—A house is as likely a candidate for a makeover as a person. What if you need to portray a cozy summer cottage, but it's the middle of the winter when you need to take the picture? This chapter takes you through the improvements you can add to the image we provide you, or to pictures of your own.

Part V: Ambitious Image Editing

As the book progresses, so does the intricacy of the tutorials. This part of the book deals with more sophisticated, involved image editing. Part V includes:

- **Chapter 14: Retouching a Group Scene by Creating a Composite Image**—Take a dozen unruly kids at a birthday party, take a bunch of photos, and then check out this chapter, as you learn how to seamlessly stitch together the best of each photo to arrive at a picture-perfect celebration.
- **Chapter 15: Creating a Dream Image from a Hopeless Snapshot**—Sometimes great images are not "born." Sometimes your subject needs a lot of help from Photoshop. Learn how to use Photoshop CS to rescue a really bad image.
- **Chapter 16: Color Balancing and Adjustment Layers: Creating a Cover Girl Image from an Average Picture**—There's nothing wrong with the photo in this chapter's assignment. It just needs a little help to evolve from an average picture to an outstanding one. Learn all kinds of secrets in this chapter.
- **Chapter 17: Surrealistic Photoshop**—There's perhaps nothing more fun than creating a scene that's photographically accurate but at the same time totally impossible. Come learn the secrets to creating surrealistic images in this chapter.
- **Chapter 18: Replacing the Main Elements in an Image**—Taking something as prominent in an image as a guitar and gifting the guitarist with a different one sounds impossible, right? Wrong! See how to replace the main element in a photo in this chapter.

Part VI: Illustration, Page Layout, and Photoshop

Photoshop isn't only all about photographic retouching. This part of the book shows you some fancy typography tricks, how to restore a 60-year-old poster, and more! Here's what you'll learn in this part of the book:

- **Chapter 19: Restoring a Historic Poster**—Learn how to sample colors; use paths to re-create shapes; and use a new font to replace crooked, inexpert typography in a historic WPA poster. It's all right here in this chapter.
- **Chapter 20: Typography and Page Layout in Photoshop**—Learn how to choose fonts based on their characteristics, and get a grasp on how to create a stunning

page layout. Heck, we'll even show you how to create a *garage sale* sign in this chapter!

- **Chapter 21: Output**—We discuss, in *human* terms, the best way to acquire an image, your alternatives, the number of samples you need to take of an image or physical art to make it print correctly, and a formula or two that you should tuck in your back pocket before you go off photographing or scanning things.

Part VII: Working for the Web with ImageReady

ImageReady picks up where Photoshop leaves off with respect to Web-sized images and animation. The two programs complement each other, and this part of our book shows you the ins and outs of creating Web media in these two chapters:

- **Chapter 22: Animations and Rollovers**—This chapter leads you through—with great results—the adage "make every pixel count on the Web." We've whipped up a healthy serving of tips, innovative approaches, and just plain good advice from a voice of authority about these sorts of things. Your Web buttons will animate, your images will be small but beautiful, and you'll have learned yet another aspect of successful electronic communications.

- **Chapter 23: Optimizing Your Images for the Web and Email**—You want that snapshot of your new kid to look as good as possible when you email it to your folks, right? Well, dive right into Chapter 23, and learn how to decide on file formats, optimization techniques, and more.

Part VIII: Working Smarter and Quicker in Photoshop

Photoshop is not an island. Noop, plenty of programs work well with it, and this part of the book offers a glimpse or two at the possibilities of working cross-application. The chapters in this part include:

- **Chapter 24: Ten Photoshop Tricks**—This chapter is a potpourri of useful, inventive tricks and techniques that, quite frankly, didn't merit an entire chapter on their own! :) Learn how to create some amazing effects using Photoshop alone or in combination with a filter or an additional program or two.

- **Chapter 25: Using Photoshop with Quark, Illustrator, XARA, and Other Programs**—Working between applications doesn't have to be hard. This chapter gets right down to the nitty-gritty and shows you the options for moving copies of Photoshop work into Illustrator and other programs…and back again.

- **Chapter 26: Where Do We Go from Here?**—It's not about Photoshop. It's about *you.* How do you feel about a career in graphics once your head has stopped spinning from this book? How do people get into the business? Can you make a good living? What should you expect, and what's the most important thing to hold in your mind as you walk out into the sunshine and start looking at the real world and all the commercial trappings that go with it?

Amazingly, we provide all that info and advice in about five pages. It's the least we could do for our readers.

Part IX: The Back O' the Book

Don't you hate reaching the end of a good book, only to find that the authors skimped on the research they put into it?! Everyone who works with a computer has a natural curiosity about where to learn more, where to find the best sources for more tools, and what stuff means when they read it out of context.

This is precisely what the *Inside Photoshop CS Companion CD* is all about. On the CD, you will find a number of important resources for your continuing adventures in Photoshop, long after you've poured through the pages in this book:

- Resource files for the chapter examples. We recommend that you work through the steps shown in this book, using files (carefully prepared by the authors) that demonstrate specific procedures and effects. The files, located in the Examples folder on the companion CD, are platform-independent and can be used on any Macintosh or Windows system with Photoshop CS installed. Sorry, Photoshop CS itself is *not* included on the companion CD! You need to bring *some* ingredients for imaging fame and fortune to the party yourself!

- The *Inside Photoshop CS* eGlossary. This Acrobat PDF file contains color examples, shortcuts, definitions, and other material pertaining to this book, to Photoshop, and to computer graphics in general. We recommend that you install the OnLine Glossary on your system and then launch Adobe Acrobat Reader when you need a quick explanation of something. Acrobat Reader comes on the Adobe Photoshop CD.

- Fonts, textures, and scenes in Windows and Macintosh formats. We have produced a fairly extensive collection (in our opinions) of frequently needed items for Web pages, traditional publication, and other types of media construction. Check out the Boutons folder on the companion CD; these are completely unique Photoshop-oriented files and programs.

- Shareware, demo versions of working programs, and utilities provided on the companion CD are hand-picked items we have used and that we recommend. Certain restrictions are placed on some of the shareware, so please don't confuse "shareware" with "freeware." If you find something on the companion CD that is useful in your professional work, please read the Read Me file in the folder where you found the utility or file, and register (pay a small fee) to the creator of the program.

- The mark of a well-written book is only as good as its index. Sams Publishing has the best indexers in town, and if you can't wait to thumb through the pages for something, check the Back O' the Book.

- Last, but certainly not least, don't overlook the special discount offers you'll find at the back of the book. These offers can save you hundreds of dollars!

Hey. It's So Complex, It's Simple.

Electronic imaging is such a magical thing that it's impossible to keep the child in us quiet. For that reason, many of the examples in this book are a little whimsical—they stretch reality a tad, in the same way you'll learn to stretch a pixel or two, using Photoshop. We want to show you some of the fun we've had with a very serious product and hope that perhaps we will kindle or fan the flame of the creative spark in you as well.

Part I

The Basics So You Don't Get Headaches Later: Pixels, Color Spaces, and the Universe

Chapter 0

Answers to the Most Important Imaging Questions

In this chapter, you'll learn

- How pixels convey color in Photoshop images
- The difference between bitmap and vector graphics
- How to work in color modes

The oddity of a Chapter 0 is bound to attract some attention, so let's put this attention to good purpose. Before you think of cranking up Photoshop, you need to understand some very important

0

definitions, because like a snowball rolling downhill, gathering speed and size, so will your talents and powers in Photoshop build as you read this book. But misunderstanding the basics can get your snowball off to an uneven start and hamper your ability to master the use of Photoshop.

Therefore, the following is not so much a list of definitions as it is a contextual explanation of various terms and concepts that will guide your snowball across the finish line and into the arena of imaging professionals.

What Is a Pixel?

The term *pixel* has been used and abused for so long that it is practically meaningless. And that's a shame, because every image before you on a monitor is made up of pixels; you can't get more basic than a pixel. So here goes the studied explanation.

A Pixel Is a Placeholder

A pixel is the building block of raster graphics. And a *raster graphic* is the type you typically see on a monitor or TV set—also called a *bitmap graphic*. Photoshop enables you to subdivide a pixel; you can specify .7 pixels, for example, as a filter setting. But for all intents and purposes, a pixel—short for *pic*ture *el*ement—is as small a unit of image graphic as you can use.

What does a pixel consist of? *Color*. A pixel is merely a placeholder for a color value. For example, the description "Red equals 168, Green equals 192, and Blue equals 170" is a pretty good definition of a medium plum-colored pixel. Red, green, and blue are primary additive colors—colors that when combined at full strength in equal amounts create white.

Note

Measuring colors   You can measure and define the amount of component colors in a pixel in two ways: percentages and a scale from 0 to 255. In this book, you'll frequently see the 0-to-255 scale used because it is technically more precise. Color channels (this is covered a little later) are typically 8 bits in color capacity, and because a bit of information is either on or off and 2 to the 8th power is 256, the exact number of brightness values that can be had lies between 0 and 255.

Tip

Pixel shape   Besides color, a pixel also has a shape. For the purposes of this book, we'll assume that a pixel is square, although rectangular pixels do exist, mostly in broadcast, motion picture, and 3D rendering arenas.

In Figure 0.1, you can see four pixels, with their color values written inside them (because this book is in black and white).

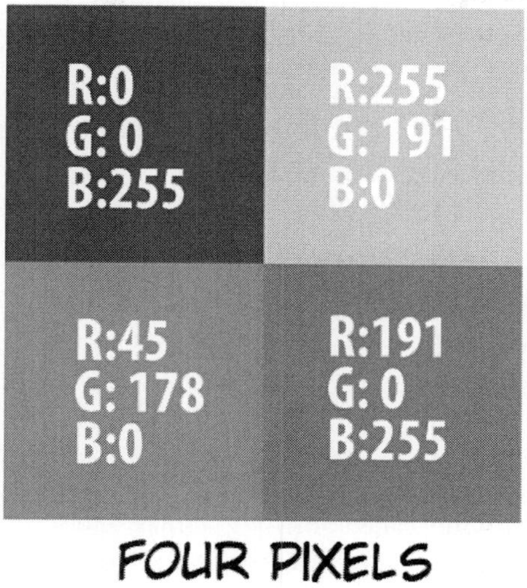

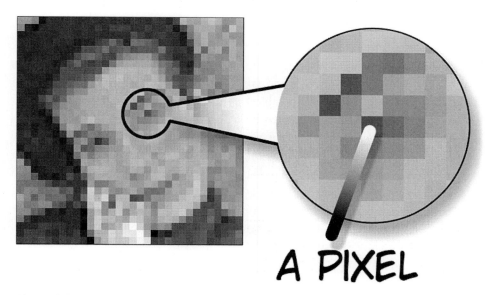

Figure 0.1   A pixel is a placeholder in a mesh of other pixels.

Understandably, a single pixel cannot express very much art, so we work with groups of pixels, arranged in rows and columns in a grid-like pattern, each pixel holding a unique color value. In Figure 0.2, you can see a low-resolution image of a woman and a magnified section, where you can clearly see the building blocks of bitmap imagery—pixels.

Figure 0.2   A bitmap image of low resolution offers a clear view of its component pixels.

0

Now, Photoshop handles two different types of graphics. In the section to follow, we'll cover the different graphics types, and you'll see the advantages and disadvantages of each.

Bitmap and Vector Graphics

Okay, we've tossed the word *resolution* into the discussion of pixels twice so far, and it's time now to provide an explanation of the term…

In Photoshop, the term *resolution* refers to the number of pixels-per-inch used to portray an image; a high-resolution image contains a lot of pixels, whereas a low-resolution image carries relatively few. Typically, the more pixels in an image, the finer the level of detail the image conveys.

Bitmap Graphics

Raster graphics are commonly called bitmap graphics, and so shall we, because a graphic of this type is literally a *map* of *bits* of information. The identifying characteristics of a bitmap are photographic quality, occasional visible jaggy edges due to insufficient viewing resolution, the capability to show camera focus and blurriness, and other image phenomena similar to an image displayed on television. You see bitmap images daily; both JPEG and GIF format images belong to the bitmap family of computer graphics.

Bitmap graphics are also called "resolution dependent" graphics, because if you try to scale one up, you distort (read *mess up*) the original resolution of the image. More on resolution in a moment.

Vector Graphics

Vector graphics are "resolution independent"; you can scale a vector graphic as large as a Winnebago or as small as a snail, and none of the design information is lost. Why? Because strictly speaking, a vector graphic is not made up of pixels; it's not a bitmap but instead a "recipe" for how a graphic can look. This recipe is full of information such as fill color and math equations for how a vector should travel across a page and look. The advantage to using vector graphics is that all you're telling an application such as Illustrator (and even Photoshop with its Paths features) is to multiply or divide the math used to describe the vector design. Typically, vector designs are called products of "drawing" programs as opposed to the "paint program" moniker that is ascribed to programs such as Photoshop. "Stroke and fill" is a common term used in vector graphics, because that's all a vector graphic is composed of.

In Figure 0.3, you can see a hollow circle painted in Photoshop (and magnified with a grid laid over it) and a drawing of a circle done with a vector program. Notice the differences: The bitmap's entire visual description of the circle is done with pixels—the outline, the size of the hole in the center, the width of the outline, the whole shebang. And the bitmap circle looks jaggy because not enough pixels were used to visually describe it. In contrast, the vector circle will be smooth regardless of how you scale it because all it consists of is a formula describing the circle, fill and stroke properties, and its position on the page.

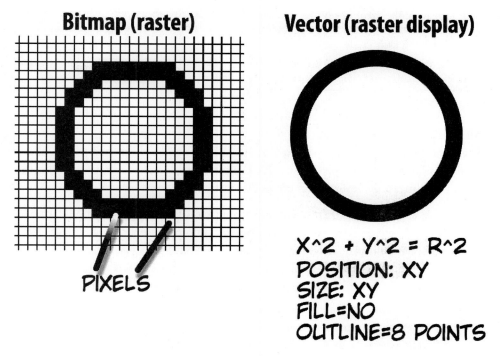

Figure 0.3   Bitmap images create visual content by using pixels, whereas vector graphics create images by way of a math formula.

There is no compelling reason to have to make a choice as to what type of graphic to stick with; as you can see, each graphics type has its advantages and disadvantages. Perhaps the most compelling reason we use Photoshop is that bitmap graphics can portray a photographic image, while it's hard to impossible to convey an image with photographic feeling in a vector application such as Illustrator.

Okay, we know that bitmap graphics are resolution-dependent, so now is a good time to discuss what *resolution* means in your Photoshop work.

0

Note

> **Understanding the truth about vectors**   This is a NOTE because there's no rea-
> son to confuse the body of this chapter with the following information. A vector graphic
> can't really be *seen*. Huh? You can't "see" math equations as a design—vector graphics
> have to be written to the screen before they can be seen—and a monitor is a raster
> device, so the vector has to be displayed as a bitmap. Illustration programs have to
> update screen data on-the-fly so you can see what you're designing. Moreover, when you
> print a vector design, it then becomes resolution-dependent; you cannot resize the physi-
> cal result. Photoshop shows vector paths as lines on your screen, but you cannot print
> these lines; you must stroke or fill the paths to create something you can print.
>
> The only time a vector graphic remains a vector graphic is when you save it to file.
> When you do that, the drawing application saves math data about the design; you cannot
> peer into the file and see the design.
>
> This is the truth about vectors, and I'm presenting this information to clarify rather than
> to cloud the nature of vector graphics.

Resolution: Pixels Per Inch

There must be a way to measure pixels, right? Well, yes and no: The bad news is that a
pixel does not have a fixed size because it's a color placeholder, not a unit of distance. So
how do you measure the size of an image file? In three different ways:

- As an absolute measure of the number of pixels—for example, 800 by 600 or 640
  by 480. These descriptions give you the exact number of pixels in an image (by
  multiplying the pixel height by the pixel width) but fail to give you a measurement in inches (or picas or centimeters; for the purpose of this chapter, we'll use
  inches) because a pixel has no fixed size. It's only a placeholder for color.

- The measurement of an image as expressed in bytes. This, too, is an imprecise
  measurement because two files having the same file size as saved to disk can have
  different aspects (2 by 4 is different than 4 by 2, for example), they could have
  different color capabilities (more on this soon)—one could be grayscale and the
  other in color—and even compression used on a file could make it appear the
  same size as a smaller file. But there is one advantage to measuring an image
  using file size: You can be certain that an image has not been resized if its beginning file size and finished file size (after using a Photoshop command or two) are
  identical.

- The most common way of evaluating the size of a bitmap image is expressed as a
  fraction: pixels per inch (pixels/inch). It is by this fractional amount that we can
  judge an image's resolution.

Let's see how we can evaluate some small images according to resolution. As you'll note in Figure 0.4, the tiny bitmap image (and by tiny, I mean that it is of small resolution...you can see the jaggy edges in the image; high-resolution images almost never show off their pixels) is 32 pixels wide and 32 pixels in height, for a total of exactly 1,024 pixels. Without changing this image in any way, it will always have 1,024 pixels. And it will always be 32 pixels high and 32 pixels wide.

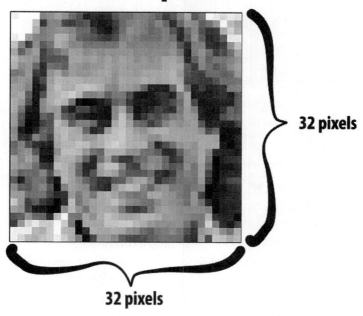

Figure 0.4   Bitmap images are of fixed resolution; you can't add or remove pixels without making a fundamental change to the visual content of the image.

Here's how the fractional equation becomes meaningful. In Figure 0.5, you can see that the image has been resized, but not fundamentally changed. The resolution of the image at left is 32 pixels per inch. The resolution of the image at right is 64 pixels per inch, so the image at right has twice the resolution—but half the size in inches, as you can see—as the image at left. But both images have 1,024 pixels in them. We can come to this conclusion:

> **Image resolution is inversely proportional to image size, as measured in inches, centimeters, picas, and so on.**

0

32 PIXELS PER INCH   64 PIXELS PER INCH
1,024 total pixels   1,024 total pixels
LOSSLESS RESIZING

Figure 0.5   Resizing an image changes the size and resolution.

This little truth is going to keep you out of trouble later. If you want to size an image up without changing the image in any way, you'll have to lose some resolution. Here's another neat little fact: The proper resolution for writing a file to an inkjet printer is approximately 1/3 the true output capability of the inkjet. So let's do a little math here: Let's say your inkjet printer has a true (not interpolated) resolution of 720 dots per inch. One third of 720 is 240; 240 pixels per inch therefore is the maximum resolution you need to print a picture. Let's further suppose that you have an image that is 4 inches by 5 inches high at 480 pixels per inch. To print the image, you would use Photoshop's Image Size command (without resampling the image) to increase the image dimensions to 8 inches wide by 10 inches high, decreasing the resolution to 240 pixels per inch. You have not changed the number of pixels (the pixel count) in the image, but merely traded off the image dimensions as measured in inches for image resolution.

See?

Let's take the other case here; let's actually change the number of pixels in an image to change its dimensions. What happens when you change the number of pixels in an image?

- The image loses focus, because Photoshop has to reassign colors to the new number of pixels, and each pixel is going to have a slightly different color, and the image gets 100% of its visual information from the original arrangement of pixel colors.
- The resolution changes, without the benefit of the image dimensions being accordingly and inversely changed.

In Figure 0.6, you can see an image at left. It has 32 pixels per inch. The image at right looks larger and coarser, doesn't it? That's because it is only 16 pixels per inch, but has the same 1 inch squared dimensions. It has fewer pixels, it has been resampled, and if you do this in your own work, generally, the resulting image will look coarse and fuzzy.

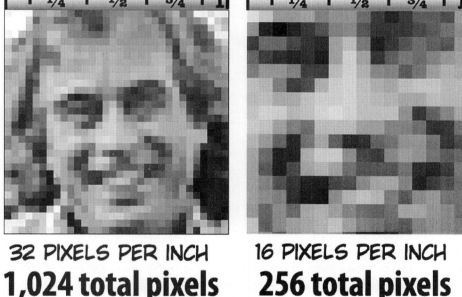

32 PIXELS PER INCH   16 PIXELS PER INCH
1,024 total pixels   256 total pixels
LOSSEY RESIZING

Figure 0.6   Resampling an image ruins the focus of an image.

Generally speaking, when you have the choice, it is not a good idea to resample an image (changing the resolution without changing the physical dimensions). But rules are meant to be broken, and you'll see a number of occasions in this book when resampling is necessary, but always to a minor extent. Usually, you use image sharpening after resampling to restore some of the image's focus.

0

Besides height and width of bitmap images, there's sort of a third dimension, too, called *color depth*, also known as *color capability*, and in Photoshop, *color mode*. In the section to follow, we'll explore color capability and what it means to your work.

Working in Color Modes

It wasn't that long ago that you were lucky if your computer's video card had 1MB of memory. Due to the physical constraints of that memory, a lot of applications would show you a screen with diffusion-dithered graphics. Color depth is inversely proportional to image resolution; for example, with 1MB of graphics card memory, a screen resolution of 1,024 by 768 could not be shown in true color, but instead had to be a limited palette of colors with dithering displayed to "fake" the colors that could not be shown. You'll find more information on this phenomena in Chapter 2, "The Critically Important Color and Gamma Calibration Chapter." Thank goodness, we don't have to worry about video card memory in these times.

Note

> **The dithering process**   *Dithering* is the placement of available colors in a given color mode in a pattern, to express colors that lie outside its range. GIF images are typically dithered because the GIF image format can hold only 256 unique colors.

But the color mode commands in Photoshop still remain, not because of memory constraints but because we sometimes want to get a little creative with the use of a design in a limited color mode. And because the GIF file format, popular as it is, has a limited color capability. Let's take a look at various color modes in Photoshop.

Bitmap Mode

At the low end of color capability lies the *bitmap* color mode, also called *line art*, and *1 bit/pixel* art. As you might imagine, with a color capability of but a single bit of information per pixel, your creative endeavors are severely hampered. A bit of information can be an *on* signal or an *off* signal. In graphics, this translates to an image whose areas are either black or white. This might seem like a color mode you would never use, but wait a minute. Weren't the daily comic strips in newspapers in black or white and no one complained? Aren't graphics on signs black or white a lot of times? And if you need to make a poster from a laser printer, yup, you're usually going to be confined to a halftone of an image, which is made up of tiny dots of black on a white paper.

So, yes, you do encounter situations in which the black or white color mode serves your purposes. And although this is covered in Chapter 7, "Filters," stochastic screening (the type of screening you used to see on the pages of the *Wall Street Journal*) can provide crisp, clean, exciting-looking graphics with only one bit per pixel.

Note

> **Adding punch**   Flaming Pear's India Ink Filter and Andromeda Software's Cutline plug-in can provide line and stochastic screening that will positively add punch to any bitmap mode graphic.

Entering the Grayscale Color Mode

Although Grayscale is a color mode that Photoshop supports and that we all have an intuitive understanding of, there's more than meets the eye (pun intended) with this color mode. Grayscale is a "special" color mode, unlike Indexed color (discussed real soon here); Grayscale can express any image you desire using 256 levels of brightness, without dithering.

It's very easy to show you an example of a grayscale image in this book because the book itself shows stuff in Grayscale mode! Grayscale mode has a higher color capability than bitmap mode because the color depth of bitmap mode is 1 bit per pixel, or 2 to the 1st power (2). Grayscale, on the other hand, has a color depth capability of 2 to the 8th power, or 256 levels.

Indexed Color Mode

Photoshop does not support an Indexed color mode, but Indexed color mode exists anyway, and you will use an indexed palette of colors in your work if you're interested in Web design work.

A long time ago (in computer years) there were many strategies for making an image as small as possible because it had to travel across the Internet or to services such as CompuServe at impossibly sluggish modem speeds, such as 9600 baud. And so was devised the Graphics Information Format (GIF). The GIF file format limited the possible available colors to 256 (2 bits to the 8th power), and so reduced the overhead of an RGB mode image, which can contain 16.7 million unique colors.

How does indexing of an image work? You start with a full-color image and then use Photoshop to apply a different selection of dithering options to reduce the number of available colors. For images that are *monotonous* (*having a predominant shade*, I don't mean *boring* here), creating an indexed color version is a snap. Take a sunset, for example. It looks glorious, right? But in actuality, a sunset has only a few thousand unique colors, so averaging only a few thousand colors into a 256-color "bucket" generally displays very few unpleasant side effects. This is particularly true when you do not have the original image to compare to the Indexed color cousin.

0

So where's the "indexing" part of an indexed color image? Instead of explicitly declaring values for every pixel, such as, "Yo—the third pixel from the top left is Red equals 45, Green equals 219, and Blue equals 135," a reference is made to a color lookup table embedded within the image that tells a browser how to read the 256 possible unique colors in the image. The image then sort of tells the image browser, "The third pixel from the top left is indexed color #19. Go look it up." This scheme makes for speedy deciphering (display) of the image, but again, the palette of colors is limited, even taxed sometimes, when a faithful rendering of a full-color image is desired.

In Photoshop, you can work with an Indexed color image, but chances are you would be unhappy with the results because a lot of tools and features will just not work with an Indexed color image. Your best bet is to convert the image to RGB color mode (Image, Mode, RGB Color) and then save it to this new color mode. Better still, leave GIF images alone; don't perform image editing on them, but instead try to track down the original RGB image and edit *it*.

Introducing the RGB Color Mode

RGB color mode is the mode we commonly use in Photoshop when creating and saving image files. RGB color mode is made up of three color channels—red, green, and blue— each having 8 bits per channel to make up a 2 to the 24th power (24-bit) image whose color capability is 16.7 million possible unique colors. RGB color mode is usually the best color mode in which to save other color mode images you've been editing (or intend to edit). Most file formats are available and can hold an RGB image; TIFF, Photoshop's Native PSD, JPEG, and Targa (TGA) are commonly used as color mode "vessels."

As of Photoshop 7, RGB color mode can also be assigned 16 bits per channel instead of 8 bits, for a total of 281,474,976,710,656 (281 trillion), or 2 to the 48th power, possible colors. Later in this book, you'll learn why 16-bit RGB images can help with image editing. For now, 24-bit RGB images are commonly used because monitors can display only 24-bit RGB images and printers commonly express even fewer colors.

In Figure 0.7, you can see four examples (they're in black and white, unfortunately) of the color modes we've covered.

Figure 0.7   Color capabilities describe how many different colors can be displayed in a particular image.

Color Spaces

Like color modes, *color spaces* describe the color capability of a certain device, such as a monitor, an inkjet printer, and even the human eye. A little knowledge about color spaces is a good thing, especially when you're wondering why an inkjet print doesn't look as lively as the same image on the monitor.

Let's begin with the largest color space: CIELAB. The LAB color space is tongue-shaped because visible light is broken down into uneven amounts, with green being predominant, as shown in Figure 0.8. Our eyes are more sensitive to greens than to blues or reds—hence, the distortion in the shape of a color space. In the color section in this book, you'll find an image (a color image, natch') of the CIELAB color model in two dimensions and three dimensions. It also shows how Adobe RGB (1998)—our recommendation for working spaces—neatly fits inside the gamut of the LAB space.

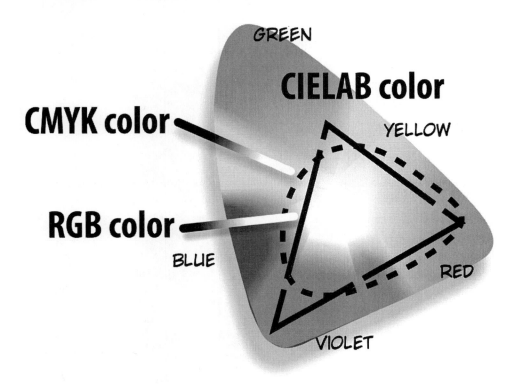

Figure 0.8   The color space of CIELAB encompasses both RGB and CMYK color spaces.

LAB color is equivalent to what the human eye can see. Within this color space is RGB color. RGB color displays handsome, vibrant colors, but as you can see, RGB color space is not nearly as large as the spectrum of human eye color capability. Also, CMYK, the color space of inkjet printers, overall, is smaller than the RGB color space, but an inkjet can produce slight areas that an RGB monitor cannot reproduce.

In future chapters, we'll convert images to different color spaces. In doing so, we always change an image's color space to LAB because LAB engenders all other color spaces, and a translation between color spaces does not suffer any information loss when you go from a lesser to a greater color capability. It helps to think of color spaces as vessels such as glasses and buckets. If you pour a glass-full of liquid into a bucket, there is no loss of liquid. Then you can, in a controlled atmosphere, pour from the bucket to a different glass. But if you pour from a glass to a different glass, some of the liquid (visual information) can get spilled.

Summary

We've covered a lot of ground in this chapter, and we hope that your process of assimilating all this stuff hasn't led to a sustained headache or anything. Suggestion? Mark this chapter with a fluorescent sticky note; it's a good reference chapter when you get stuck with output and grayscale images and things.

The most important point you should take away from this chapter is this:

> **Everything is conditional.**

The only hard-and-fast answers you can get to your questions must be derived from a little math and a little science. This is why I can't tell you, Mr. Buster Ogilvy (official Photoshop user), what the optimal resolution for your scanner is. You need to think about what device you're outputting to before you scan. Similarly, you cannot simply be handed the ideal resolution for your inkjet printer; as mentioned before, you need to divide the true resolution by three, and then there are resolution considerations to make as to what physical dimensions you need for output. But the good news is that you have a lot of the math formulas and definitions tucked under your belt now.

- Don't be misled by things you may have heard "on the streets" about resolution and pixels and things. This book is a studied exploration of the mysteries of digital imaging, and the material presented is not off the streets.

- Build on what you now know as you travel through this book. I guarantee that once you understand all the information in this chapter, you will sally through the rest of the book with a sense of confidence and purpose.

It's time for a healthy dose of fun mixed in with all the learning! What say we create a multi-layer composition and use selection tools to create a totally ridiculous composition? You'll be amazed at how much you can learn when you're not pressured to produce! Just turn the page!

Chapter 1

Producing Awesome Images from the Start

Personal experience has reaffirmed the

belief that there are two types of people:

In this chapter, you'll learn

- How to work with Photoshop fonts
- How to add new elements to existing images
- How to edit image contents using paths, masks, and other tools
- How to merge layers
- How to add text to images
- How to save edited text in images

- People who are fastidious to a fault. They open the same end of a roll of Life Savers time after time, they eat their vegetables before eating dessert, they never sneak ahead and read the last page of a mystery novel, and they irk me.

And then there's...

- The enlightened ones who don't mind asking directions at a gas station, believe that the shortest path is a straight line, and want to produce stuff using Photoshop and this book right from the get-go.

Note

> **People**   Samuel Clemens originally wrote that there are two types of people: those who divide the world into two types of people and those who don't.

Because "getting to the point"—that is, diving right into a Photoshop adventure before explaining all the important stuff to follow in this book—is key here, an overly long introduction would defeat the purpose. Let's just leave it at this much:

You can actually have fun and produce some decent work, working in Photoshop, even though you might not have a clue at this point as to many of the finer workings of this magnificent program. This "test drive" chapter is the place where you have the opportunity to get a feel for how the major controls behave, where they are located, and what they are good for. You'll discover tons of advanced features later in this book, but for now you'll work with the stuff the advanced procedures build on, and soon come to appreciate how easily you can build a complex image without doing any heavy lifting.

Besides, how often do you get to purely experiment with images, without a deadline, a goal, a paycheck looming over your brow? Not often enough is a fair guess!

So without further ado, let's get our creative juices flowing and experience the power and the joy that working with a fine tool like Photoshop brings. Building the whimsical "For the Birds" image using a whole bunch of cool images is well within your reach when you follow along and perform the steps that follow. As with every tutorial in this book, you will find all the resource files you need on the companion CD, so dig that out if you haven't already done so.

A Brief Diversion into Fonts

If you're going to use a typeface in Photoshop, you can't load it while you have Photoshop running. And it would be a stone-cold drag to have to quit Photoshop in this chapter to load one measly font, so here's the story before you go and get creative in this chapter.

Meet Nick and His Fonts

Nick Curtis is a dashingly handsome and terribly creative guy. He makes fonts, and I am even on a first-name basis with him. Because Photoshop is so typographically oriented, I asked Nick to lend us a few of his original font creations to be used in examples in this book. They are wonderful fonts, and I want you to dig into the Examples/Chapt01 folder of the companion CD right now and install GuinnessExtraStoutNF.otf before you launch Photoshop. This font is bi-platform, so Mac users, load the font in your System/Fonts folder, and Windows users, load the font in the Control Panel, Fonts folder.

And now we're all set to hunker down with fonts, fun, and fotos.

Creating a Layered Image

There is one big trick to making something you add to a photograph appear as if it were there when the picture was taken: *Match the lighting and camera angle of the original image.* That means that if an image was taken from waist height and lit from the left, for example, the image you paste into the scene should also have been taken with light from the left and at waist height. The more attention you pay to matching lighting, camera focus, angle, position, and other attractions in the insert photo, the better your chances are of creating a seamless and plausible composition.

"Playing detective," analyzing an image before you start making changes to it, is a recurring theme in this book. The more you notice about the qualities of the target image, the better you'll be able to spot, photograph, and/or manipulate an additional photo to fit into the scene.

Studying a Host Image for "Clues"

Let's begin at the beginning with the host image for this chapter's assignment. Open the ForTheBirds.tif image from the Examples/Chap01 folder on the companion CD. Then save it to your hard drive as ForTheBirds.psd (Photoshop's primary native file format), and keep the image open. See Figure 1.1.

What do you see here? Besides ducks, you can see that the image was taken by someone of average height standing up (look at a similar scene through the viewfinder of your own camera to affirm this). Also, the depth of field is great; everything is in focus, as you would expect with a sunny outdoors picture. Finally, the light is being cast into the scene from the upper left: It's a morning picture.

Okay, the images you'll add to this picture don't need to be some you've taken. They're provided for you on the companion CD; this is a fun chapter, and you shouldn't have to go out duck hunting to complete the assignment! However, there are indeed hurdles you'll encounter in the assignment (or else it wouldn't be an assignment), but fortunately, you can successfully clear them all using Photoshop.

Figure 1.1   This image will serve as the host to other images.

Adding a Branch of Birds

The first addition to this image is a branch of birds, brightly colored and created in a 3D modeling program. Naturally, the birds don't look as real as the fowl in the image, but we are not setting out to "improve" a documentary photograph or even produce a photorealistic image. We're here to learn, have fun, and maybe even create a piece of art.

Let's see how to integrate the birds with the host, the main image:

Manipulating an Image into the Host Scene

1. Open the 3BirdsOnnaBranch.psd image from the Examples/Chap01 folder on the companion CD. Press Ctrl(⌘)+the minus keyboard key to reduce the view of the 3Birds image so you have a full view of both the ForTheBirds image and the 3Birds image.

2. On the Layers palette, with the 3Birds as the foreground image in the workspace (click on its title bar to make sure it's in the foreground), drag the Curly, Larry, & Moe Layers palette title into the ForTheBirds image window, as shown in Figure 1.2. Press F7 if the Layers palette is not onscreen.

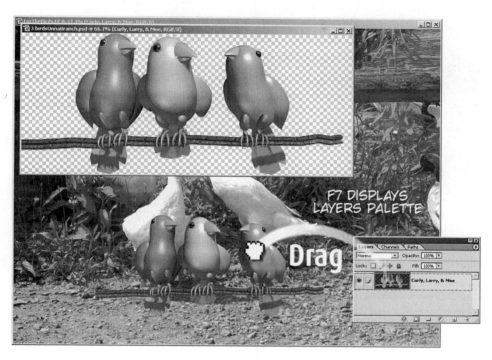

Figure 1.2   Drag the title of the layer into the other window to copy the layer.

3. Now, as you can see, the light on the birds is coming from the right—WRONG for the background scene! Press Ctrl(⌘)+T to display the Free Transform box around the birds.

4. Right-click (Macintosh: hold Ctrl and click) and choose Flip Horizontal from the contextual menu. See Figure 1.3.

5. Double-click inside the Free Transform box to confirm the change in the birds that you've made (or press Enter). The birds are now facing the right way, and the branch upon which they're sitting can exit from the right of the frame.

6. The birds appear to be photographed nearly from the photographer's head height; therefore, they should appear toward the top and right of the image. Press **V** (Move tool), and then drag the birds up and to the right until the branch falls out of frame. Use your artistic eye for the exact height within the image.

Figure 1.3   The Flip Horizontal command mirrors the selection from left to right.

7. Close the 3BirdsOnnaBranch file.

8. Press Ctrl(⌘)+S; keep the main file open.

Just a few quick pointers here before we move on. First, you'll notice that the ForTheBirds image has a new layer in it; check out the Layers palette. And lo and behold, this new layer has a name—specifically, the name it has in the 3BirdsOnnaBranch file! So we can deduce that if you name a layer before copying it, the name will stick. File this truth; you'll want to use it momentarily.

Also, Photoshop CS has a new feature called *Bicubic Sharper*. Great—what's that mean? Well, *Bicubic interpolation* is a mathematical method for ensuring that when pixels are removed from an image area due to resizing (you can't make a bitmap image area smaller without removing picture elements, *pixels*), the image area retains sharpness. Whenever you resize an image or an image area, pixels are removed and remaining pixels have to take on a blend of existing and removed color values, and this inevitably results in some loss of focus. Bicubic Sharper helps retain focus, thus eliminating the need, most of the time, to use a sharpen filter after scaling down an image or image area.

File the preceding nugget of wisdom away for a moment, too, for we'll tap into the power of Bicubic Sharper in the following set of steps.

Adding a Wicker Duck and Shadow to the Scene

A challenge isn't a challenge unless it gets a little harder as you go along! The next winged thing you'll add to the ForTheBirds composition is a wicker duck. You're going to have fun with this addition, because

- The wicker duck is far too large in scale with the rest of the image.
- And the wicker duck has a shadow on a separate layer. If you look carefully at the ForTheBirds image, the ducks are casting shadows; therefore, so must the wicker duck.

Are you ready for this new addition? I can see that you are! :)

Copying a Shadow and a Wicker Duck

1. Open the WickerDuck.psd image from the Examples/Chap01 folder on the companion CD. You'll notice, on the Layers palette, that the Wicker Duck has a title, but the shadow layer is basically unnamed.

2. Double-click on the layer 1 title; this opens the title name for editing. Type **Wicker Duck shadow** in the field, and then click outside the name field to finalize your editing of the name or press the Enter (Return) key.

3. Press Ctrl($\mathcal{H}$)+the minus key to zoom out your view and the image window so that you can see both the image window and the ForTheBirds image window in the workspace.

4. Drag the Wicker Duck shadow title on the Layers palette into the ForTheBirds image window. The shadow is copied to the ForTheBirds image. See Figure 1.4.

5. Make sure the WickerDuck image window is in the foreground in Photoshop's workspace by clicking on its title bar. Now drag the Wicker Duck title on the Layers palette into the ForTheBirds image window. You dragged the shadow in first so the wicker duck would be on top of the shadow (although later you'll learn how to reorder layers on the Layers palette).

Insider

Notice that the two layers for the WickerDuck image are linked together on the Layers palette. Because they are linked, you can move both layers at once (if you choose to do so). With the Move tool as the active tool, click in the WickerDuck image window and drag the shadow into the ForTheBirds image (instead of dragging from the Layers palette). You'll see both layers appear on the palette in the ForTheBirds image, and they will remain linked together in the new image as well. This linking of layers gives the additional benefit of moving both items around in the image window together (as one).

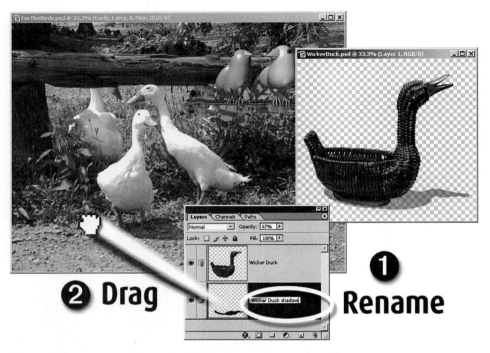

Figure 1.4   Rename and copy the shadow layer to the ForTheBirds image.

6. Press **V** to access the Move tool, and then make sure that the Wicker Duck layer is the active layer (only one layer at a time can be active in an image, unless the layers are linked). You can make this layer active by right-clicking (Macintosh: holding Ctrl and clicking) over the wicker duck in the image and choosing Wicker Duck from the pop-up contextual menu (or by clicking on the layer's title in the Layers palette).

7. Drag the WickerDuck image to its place on top of its shadow. Now click on the box at the left of the Wicker Duck shadow title on the Layers palette. A tiny chain link appears in the box; this symbol means that the current editing layer, the Wicker Duck, and the shadow are linked. You can now move the duck and shadow and scale them as one.

8. Press Ctrl(⌘)+T to access the Free Transform box around the duck and shadow. Carefully grasp a corner handle of the Free Transform box, and while holding Shift (to constrain the proportions of the selected image areas), drag toward the center of the wicker duck and shadow (and the Free Transform box), as shown in Figure 1.5. If necessary, you can move the wicker duck and shadow by clicking inside the Free Transform box and dragging it to a new position in the document window.

Figure 1.5   Scale the wicker duck and shadow down so that they are smaller than the real ducks in the image.

9. Once you've scaled down the wicker duck and shadow to believable proportions with regard to the other ducks in the image, double-click inside the Free Transform box, or press Enter (Return) to finalize the scaling.

10. With the Move tool, move the wicker duck and shadow to the left of the image, over the gravel, until it looks like it belongs in the scene.

11. Press Ctrl(⌘)+S; keep the file open.

A little later in this chapter, we're going to delve into properties of shadows such as transparency, and you'll even get to create your own shadow. For joy! But for now, we're going to stray into some unknown, exciting territory: selecting an image area and copying the contents of the selection to the birds scene.

A Brief Lesson in Photoshop Paths

Although Chapter 6, "Using the Pen Tools," gets you into the thick of some very important selection tools, there's no reason you can't get a little taste of the power of paths right here, in this experimentation chapter. We have a tiny toy stuffed chick that you'll add to the ForTheBirds image, and it has a path around it, but the path is imperfect.

In the steps to follow, you'll correct the path around the chick, base a selection on the path, and then copy the contents of the selection to the ForTheBirds image.

Note

Understanding selections   In Photoshop, a selection is not the same as the *contents* of a selection. That is, you can move a selection around in the image without disturbing the underlying image in any way. That is why we use the Move tool for copying the *contents* of a selection, and the selection tools in Photoshop only *describe* a space over the image. Tough concept, admittedly!

A Primer on Paths

1. You can close the WickerDuck.psd image at any time now and open the Chick.psd image. Surprise! There's a background all around the chick, unlike the wicker duck and the three birds! What to do now?

2. Click on the Paths tab on the Layers palette, and then click on the Chick Path title. A thin outline will appear around the chick, with an awkward, inexpertly created bulge featured at the right. I did this on purpose and rarely color outside the lines in my spare time.

3. Choose the Direct Selection tool, as shown in Figure 1.6, and click on the path. The anchor points are revealed. Click on the anchor point of the bulge, and then drag that anchor back so it conforms to the outline of the chick.

4. Now let's turn this perfect outline into a selection. The Direct Selection tool should still be active, so click anywhere in the document (outside the path area) to deselect the points on the path. Click on the Load path as a selection icon on the bottom of the Paths palette, as shown in Figure 1.7.

Tip

Using open paths   As you grow more proficient with Photoshop and paths, you'll see that a path does not have to be closed to convert it to a selection. An open path will convert to a selection with the open edge closed by a straight line, the shortest route between two anchors.

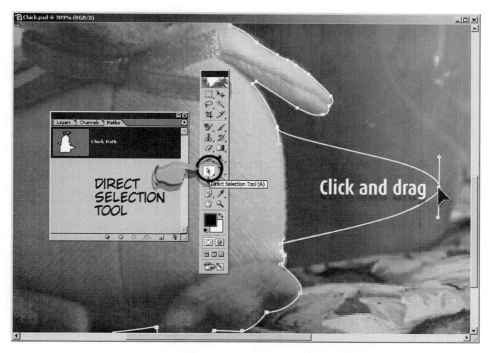

Figure 1.6   A path is a non-printing Photoshop element that is easy to create, and the shape can be applied to a selection marquee's shape.

Figure 1.7   You can convert any path, closed or not, to a selection marquee.

5. Let's stray from the main objective for just a moment because I want to show you
    something real cool. Now that the selection exists, it would be a good idea on
    certain occasions to save the selection for calling up later. How to do this? Click
    on the Channels tab of the palette, and then click on the Save selection as chan-
    nel icon, as shown in Figure 1.8. Your selection might or might not look exactly
    like that shown in Figure 1.8; it might be a white silhouette on black, but its
    appearance makes not a whit of difference at this moment. Preferences determine
    the black-and-white scheme of a saved selection. For now, the only important
    thing to know is that saved selections are stored in image channels.

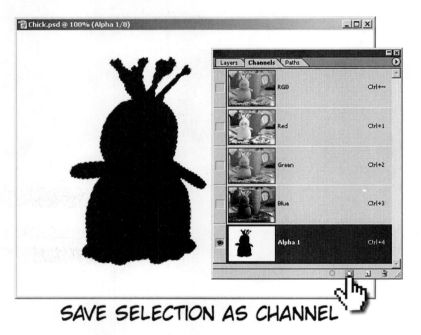

Figure 1.8   Although you don't need to save right now, it's good to know that any selection
can be saved in a channel in Photoshop.

6. Back to work! Click on the Layers tab. If necessary, press Ctrl(⌘)+the minus key
    to zoom out your view and the image window so that you can see both the
    image window and the ForTheBirds image window in the workspace. Using the
    Move tool, drag the chick selection from the Chick.psd image window into the
    ForTheBirds image.

7. You can close the Chick.psd image now without saving.

8. Hmmm. We don't have a shadow for the chick, so the next best thing (always be
    a detective and the resourcefulness will come to you) is to plunk the chick down
    in an area that already has a shadow. Technically, the shadow in the image would
    extend to the chick and hide it, but this is supposed to be a fun chapter, and

waves shouldn't be made at this point! Move the chick into a duck's shadow, as shown in Figure 1.9. Oh, and you might want to press Ctrl(⌘)+T, right-click (Macintosh: hold Ctrl and click), and choose Flip Horizontal from the contextual menu. Press Enter (Return) to apply the transformation. This gives the impression that the lighting is from the left for the chick, too.

Figure 1.9   It's not a problem that the chick has no shadow. Just move it to an area where a shadow already exists.

9. Press Ctrl(⌘)+S; keep the file open.

We're going Great Guns now! Stay tuned for the section to follow, where I actually let you create a selection all on your own!

Using the Layer Mask Feature

The Layer Mask feature in Photoshop doesn't really have a physical equivalent. In a nutshell, when you add a layer mask to an image layer in Photoshop, painting on the layer with black will hide areas of the image. They disappear! And when you paint over those hidden areas with white, the areas reappear. The layer mask is not destructive, though; you only hide areas and reveal them ad nauseum until you feel prepared to actually delete the hidden areas. And that's how you can make a very refined selection around a duck, a car, or whatever your photographer's eye leads you to capture.

And if a professional had to describe Photoshop in a single sentence, it would be, "Photoshop work is powerful and undetectable because of its refined, sophisticated selection tools." Trust me on this one.

In the steps to follow, you'll use some tools to mask away "everything that's not a duck" in the tutorial image and then add the duck to, um, the flock in ForTheBirds.psd.

Layer Masking the Duck

1. Open the JustAnotherDuck.psd image from the Examples/Chap01 folder on the companion CD. You'll notice that some of the work has been done for you: It's a loose selection around the duck, and the background checkered pattern tells you that these areas are transparent.

2. Unfortunately, the Indian Runner duck (that's the breed) is white, and so is the white checkered pattern, so selecting the duck might be a futile and aggravating task. Press Ctrl(⌘)+K to access preferences.

3. Click on the drop-down menu button next to General and then choose Transparency & Gamut. Click on the white-colored square and then choose a medium red from the Color Picker. Now click on the gray square and choose a similar color, as shown in Figure 1.10. Now, wherever you create a transparent area using the Layer Mask feature, the background will turn red and will be obvious to spot.

Figure 1.10   Photoshop's transparency indicator should be set to a solid color for this assignment, a color that clashes with the scene's color.

4. Choose the Brush tool and zoom in on the duck's head. You can do this by pressing Ctrl(⌘)+the plus keyboard key, and then by pressing the spacebar to toggle to the Hand tool and panning (dragging in) the window. When you release the spacebar, you still have the Brush tool selected. Wow, you accessed three different tools! Don't underestimate the power of the keyboard when using Photoshop.

5. Right-click (Macintosh: hold Ctrl and click) to access the Brushes palette. Choose the 19-pixel brush tip, but also drag the Master Diameter slider so that you now have a 45-pixel (in diameter) tip. You're doing this because the 19 pixel is a hard tip, and you want a brush tip that is both hard and 45 pixels across.

6. Click on the title bar to close the Brushes palette without accidentally making a stroke on the image, and then click on the Add layer mask icon on the bottom of the Layers palette. See Figure 1.11.

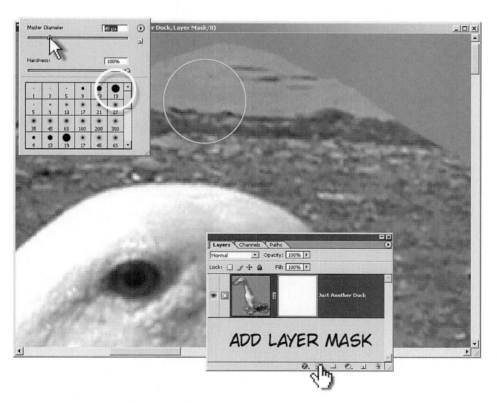

Figure 1.11   Create a layer mask "over" the image of the duck.

Tip

Identifying icons   If you hover your cursor over the icons on the Layers palette (as well as the toolbox), you'll get a good description of what that tool or feature does.

7. Press **D** (for default colors; the toolbox will feature a black foreground and a white background color). Start painting with black to erase everything but the duck. You can see the brush size onscreen. Trim carefully around the duck's head first. See Figure 1.12 for an approximation of the effect; the hidden areas show red on the image.

Insider

If you make a mistake, press **X** to switch white to the foreground color and paint to correct the mistake. Press **X** again to switch black to the foreground color and continue painting to hide the areas around the duck. Repeat this process as necessary.

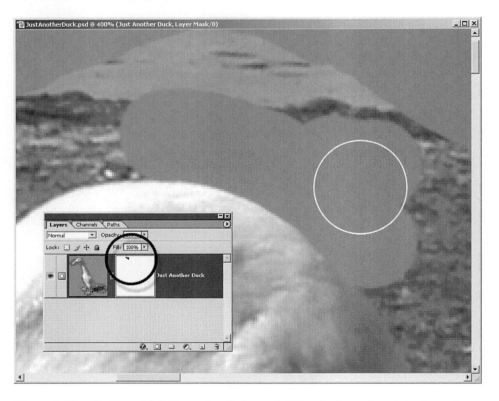

Figure 1.12   The Layer Mask feature is called a *mode*. When the image layer is in the mask mode, stroking black will hide selected areas.

8. Keep scrolling down the window (by holding down the spacebar to toggle to the Hand tool). You can see more areas where the outside of the duck needs hiding. You will eventually come to the tail feathers area and find that your current brush tip is just too large to remove the areas between feathers. Right-click and reduce the size of the tip, as shown in Figure 1.13. Press Enter (Return) to dismiss the Brush palette. Continue until you reach the shadow beneath and slightly to the right of the duck.

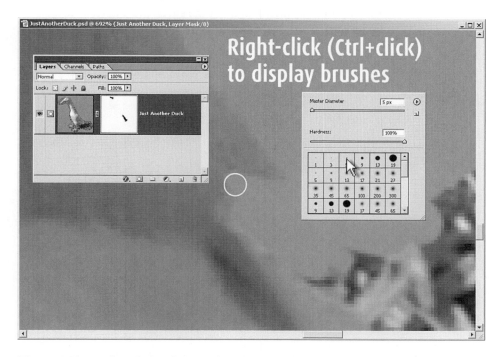

Figure 1.13   Reduce the brush size and mask around the tail feathers.

9. Press Ctrl(⌘)+S; keep the file open.

10. Return to the Transparency & Gamut dialog box and reset the transparency option to a checkerboard.

This exercise is going to propel you into the advanced section of Photoshop beginners! In the next section, you're going to mask around the duck's shadow and save the selection.

Using Quick Mask

Now, it makes no sense to continue layer masking the duck's profile when there's a perfectly good shadow to use in the image below him (or her, or it). This calls for a quick switch of modes from layer masking to quick masking.

What is quick masking? It's the application of a tinted overlay to image areas using the Brush or other tools, to indicate the future site of an image area selection. This process is easier to work through than to explain, so why don't we dive right into the next steps?

The Quick Mask Mode and a Duck

1. Click on the Create new layer icon on the bottom of the Layers palette, to keep your layer masking work separate from this brief foray into quick masking.

2. Click on the Quick Mask icon on the toolbox; see Figure 1.14. The new layer should be your current editing layer. Click on its title if it is not.

3. Paint over the shadow very carefully. Change brush sizes if necessary.

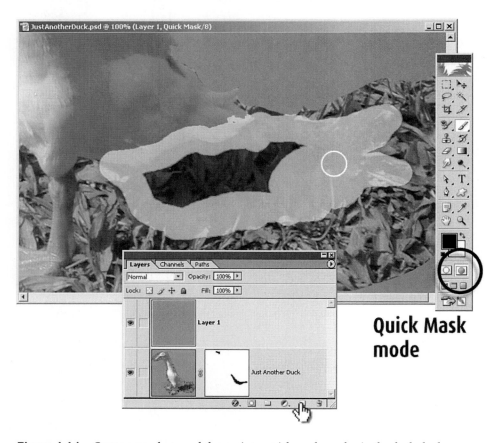

Figure 1.14   Create a new layer and then paint a quick mask overlay in the duck shadow area.

4. Once you've painted the duck shadow, click on the Standard Editing mode button, the one directly to the left of the Quick Mask button. The mask turns into a selection marquee, and yep, you do want to save this selection, so click on the

Channels tab on the palette, and then click on the Save selection as channel icon. Then press Ctrl(⌘)+D to deselect the selection.

5. Click on the Layer Mask thumbnail (shown in Figure 1.15), and you're back to layer masking. You probably have a big chunk of background you want to hide, and it's plain silly to paint it out with the Brush tool. Make sure black is still the foreground color. Choose the Lasso tool from the toolbox, encircle the unwanted background with the tool, and then press Alt(Opt)+Delete (Backspace). This floods the selection marquee with foreground color.

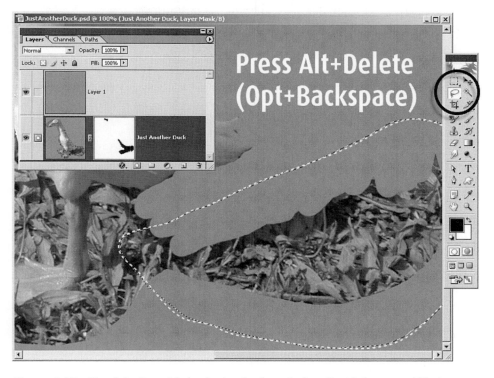

Figure 1.15   Flood the Layer Mask selection (and *not* the layer!) with foreground black to hide what's underneath.

6. There's one last generalized instruction in store for you: If you hid an area you did not want to hide, press **X**; this reverses foreground and background colors. You can then unhide a hidden area by painting white over the area.

7. Once you've worked your way completely around the duck's outline, it's time to delete the layer mask and remove the hidden areas for keeps. Drag the Layer Mask thumbnail from the Layer palette and deposit it in the tiny trash icon on the palette. You'll get a confirmation box that asks whether you want to apply the

mask, discard (your masking work and return the layer to normal), or to cancel this editing move. Choose Apply, as shown in Figure 1.16.

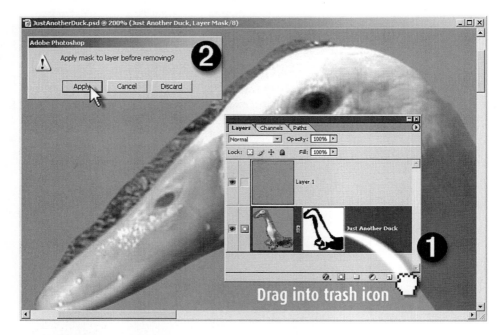

Figure 1.16   Trash the Layer Mask thumbnail, and then tell Photoshop to apply your edits to the layer.

   8. Press Ctrl(⌘)+S; keep the file open.

You should now have a trimmed duck in the image window. Neatness is of little concern in this chapter because

- You haven't yet learned about more precise selection tools (and there are a lot of them).
- Plus, this is a chapter on exploration, and you aren't getting paid for your work yet!

Next up: creating a shadow for the duck.

Creating a Shadow for the Duck

You might well ask, "Hey, Bouton, why did you tell me to delete the shadow area when I'll need it later?" The answer: You need only the geometry of the shadow, not the image area where it fell. And you've saved this geometry. And you're going to apply color to it in a moment.

Using a Saved Selection

1. Click on the Channels tab on the palette, and then Ctrl(⌘)+click on the Alpha 1 title. Doing this loads the selection you saved of the duck shadow.

2. Click on the layer above the duck (the one you created), and then double-click on its title and type **Just Another Duck** (or some other evocative name) in the text field. Press Enter (Return) to commit the new title to the layer. Remember, you're going to move the shadow to the ForTheBirds.psd image, and you want to be able to track your layers.

3. Using the Brush tool and with black as the foreground color, paint inside the selection marquee, or simply press Alt(Opt)+Delete (Backspace).

4. Press Ctrl+D to deselect the shadow layer, and then drag the layer thumbnail beneath the duck layer, so the shadow is below (or behind) the duck.

5. With the Brush tool, paint legs (and one foot) connecting the shadow to the duck, as shown in Figure 1.17. This is easy!

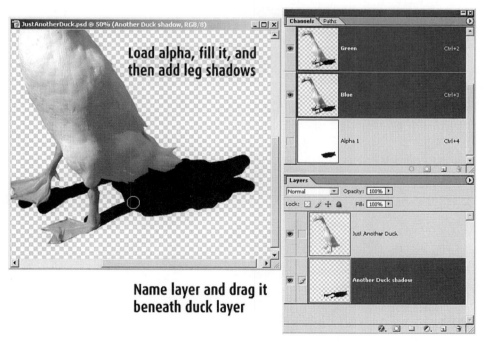

Figure 1.17 Choose your layer, load the alpha, fill it with black, and then add legs to the shadow.

6. Choose the ForTheBirds image by clicking on its title bar, and then click on the Wicker Duck shadow title. Now, when you copy over the Just Another Duck and its shadow, they will be behind the wicker duck (layer) in the image.

7. Click on the JustAnotherDuck title bar to make this image the active window again. On the Layers palette, the duck shadow layer should be the active layer. Click on the column to the left of the duck layer to link these two layers together. Press **V** to switch to the Move tool. Position the JustAnotherDuck window so that you can see both image windows in the workspace. Click in the JustAnotherDuck image window, and drag the duck and shadow into the ForTheBirds image window. You can then close the JustAnotherDuck.psd file without saving it.

8. Press Ctrl(⌘)+T to display the Free Transform box around the duck and shadow, hold Shift (to constrain proportions), and then drag toward the center of the duck to scale down the duck. See Figure 1.18. Stop dragging when the duck is in scale with the other (real) ducks in the image, and then double-click inside the Free Transform box.

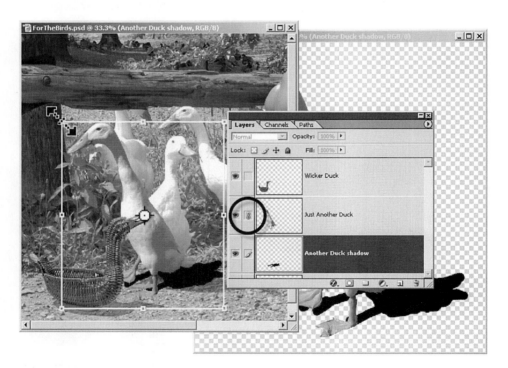

Figure 1.18   Scale down both the duck and its shadow by linking layers.

9. The duck's shadow is way too dark. Click on the duck shadow layer, and reduce the opacity of the layer (the control's at the top of the Layers palette) to about

45% or whatever you think looks right. Finally, move the duck and shadow to a location on the road in the image where you think they look good.

10. Press Ctrl(⌘)+S; keep the file open.

Coming up is a quick lesson in using the Clone Stamp tool.

Introducing the Clone Stamp Tool

If you haven't heard already, Photoshop sports a tool that enables you to paint on an image using a different part of the image. It's called the *Clone Stamp tool*. You'll need this tool shortly because the duck you copied to the ForTheBirds image looks as though it's floating on top of the picture and not truly part of the picture. To anchor the duck, you'll add a little of the road on top of part of its webbed feet.

Here goes:

Cloning Dirt onto the Duck's Feet

1. Zoom into the duck's feet. You can do this by choosing the Zoom tool (the magnifying glass icon on the toolbox) and dragging diagonally across the duck's feet area to suggest a rectangle.

2. Choose the Clone Stamp tool, the little rubber stamp icon on the toolbox.

3. Click on the JustAnotherDuck layer on the Layers palette to make this the current editing layer, and then check the Use All Layers check box on the Options bar. You need to sample from the Background layer but paint on the current editing layer.

4. Right-click (Macintosh: hold Ctrl and click), and then choose a brush tip similar to the size shown in Figure 1.19.

5. Alt(Opt)+click on an area of the dirt away from the duck's foot. This is called the *sampling point*. The sample area travels as you move the Clone Stamp tool and deposits image areas where you stroke. Stroke over the foot that's on the ground a little.

6. Press Ctrl(⌘)+S; keep the file open.

Next, you'll cure a plastic duck of a mallardy (sorry). This duck is covered with green spots and presents the perfect, contrived opportunity to introduce a new tool!

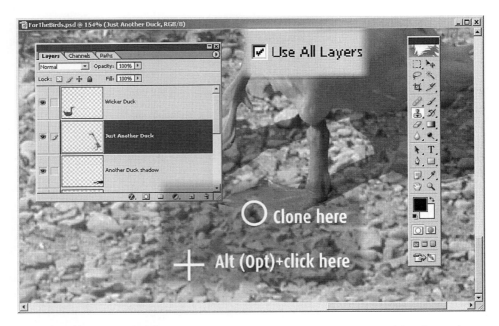

Figure 1.19   Clone over the webbed foot just a little to suggest that the duck has dug its foot into the ground.

Working with the Color Replacement Tool

Photoshop CS has a new tool that essentially takes the tedium out of creating a new layer, setting the layer to Color mode (don't worry about this; I'll explain it later in the book), and then painting a color into a layer area. Instead, the Color Replacement tool enables you to sample a color and then paint over an area with the sample color.

This procedure is as simple as it sounds, and in the following steps, you'll remove the green spots from the plastic duck and then copy it to the ForTheBirds image:

Replacing Color in an Image

1. Open the Pipsqueak.psd image from the Examples/Chap01 folder of the companion CD.
2. Choose the Color Replacement tool from the toolbox. It's the fourth from the top-left side of the toolbox.
3. Alt(Opt)+click on a bright yellow part of the duck. Doing this toggles your tool to the Eyedropper tool, and you've just made the color with which you'll paint a bright yellow. Check out the foreground color swatch on the toolbox to reaffirm this color.

4. On the Layers palette, check the Lock Transparency check box (see Figure 1.20). Doing this prevents you from "coloring outside the lines." Choose a good-sized tip for the Color Replacement tool (adjusting the diameter to around 40 pixels might work), and paint away those unsightly green spots. Resample colors if necessary.

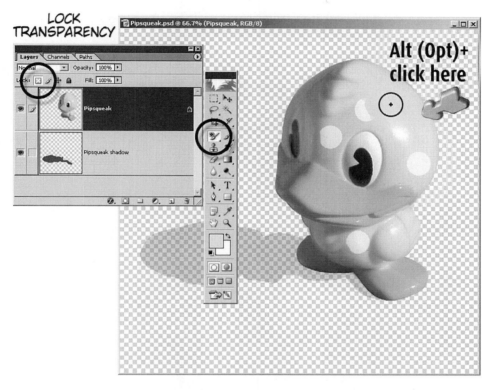

Figure 1.20 Sample the right color, and then paint over the spots using the Color Replacement tool.

5. Here comes the part that you can easily perform, due to steps you've memorized in previous examples. Link the Pipsqueak layer to the Pipsqueak shadow layer. Switch to the Move tool and drag the Pipsqueak from the image window into the ForTheBirds image. You can close the Pipsqueak image without saving at any time.

6. Oh, oops. Pipsqueak is facing the wrong way. Press Ctrl(⌘)+T to display the Free Transform box, then right-click (Macintosh: hold Ctrl and click), and choose Flip Horizontal from the contextual menu. While you're at it, hold down the Shift key and drag in a corner of the bounding box to resize Pipsqueak and the shadow to a smaller and more manageable size. Double-click inside the Free Transform box to finalize these edits.

7. The shadow doesn't seem to be the correct intensity, so you'll adjust it but also apply something called a *layer blending mode* to the shadow. Multiply mode treats anything you put on a layer as though it were a stain, like a magic marker drawn repeatedly across a piece of acetate. And this is exactly the mode you need to make a convincing Pipsqueak shadow in the composition. In Figure 1.21, you can see that the shadow layer is the current editing layer (so click on the layer title to make it so), and the blending mode is changed to Multiply. Do this and then increase or decrease the Opacity until the shadow looks as though it belongs to the little duck and the overall image.

Figure 1.21   Use the Multiply blending mode to make the shadow dense and realistic.

8. Press Ctrl(⌘)+S; keep the file open.

You've worked hard, so the upcoming section is a "breather"—it's extremely easy and helps to finish off all the elements you added to the composition.

Adding a Final Duck

Besides all the wonderful things you can do when you load Photoshop, there are still some traditional considerations that are important to obey, such as artistic composition.

Yes, the scene is crowded by now, but the image still has an area that looks lonely and empty. The bottom-right corner could use a duck, too.

In the steps to follow, you'll add the last duck to the image. You already know the techniques needed, so simply follow the steps. I guarantee the image will be completed in no time.

Adding a Sailor Duck to the Image

1. Close the Pipsqueak image, and open the TheDuck.psd image from the Examples/Chap01 folder on the companion CD. Surprise! The duck's shadow is already attached to the duck, so you don't need to copy both duck and shadow layers to the ForTheBirds image.

2. Press **V** (Move tool), and then drag the title The Duck from the image window into the ForTheBirds image. See Figure 1.22. Then, using the Move tool, position the duck in the lower right of the image. Close the TheDuck.psd image without saving changes.

Figure 1.22   Move a copy of the duck to the ForTheBirds image.

3. Press Ctrl(⌘)+S; keep the file open.

Now, the bigger the image, the better it will print, but also the slower you might find you're working in Photoshop. In the following section, you'll see how to optimize the composition so it's as small as it can be.

Merging Layers

Each layer in a Photoshop composition adds to the overall saved file size, and it's a crying shame to save layers when you don't really need them. Let's look at our example: Do we really need all the ducks and their shadows on separate layers, after we're happy with where they're positioned? (Audience responds with a resounding, "No!")

In the steps to follow, you'll merge the ducks with their shadows. You can still move the ducks around until the cows come home, but their shadows will be anchored to them, and the saved file size will be smaller for the composition.

Merging the Ducks with Their Shadows

1. Expand the Layers palette by dragging the edges away from the center of the palette. Can you see all the layer titles now?

2. First, click on the Just Another Duck layer title to make it the current editing layer. Then click on the tiny circular button with the right-facing arrow on it, at the top right of the palette. A menu, called a *flyout menu*, flies out, and you choose Merge Down, as shown in Figure 1.23. Note also that you can use a keyboard shortcut for this stuff: the shortcut is Ctrl(⌘)+E.

Figure 1.23   Use the Merge Down command to merge the duck with its shadow and also to conserve file size.

3. You can repeat step 2 as many times as you see fit. There is only one caveat: You should make sure that the shadow is directly beneath the duck in the stack of

layers, or you'll be merging unwanted layers. To reorder the layers—for example, to put the Wicker Duck's shadow directly beneath the Wicker Duck—drag the title upward on the Layers palette. It's easy, it's fun.

Tip

> **Preserving names**   To preserve the names you've created for the layers, link two layers before you merge them, and then use the Merge Linked command on the flyout menu.

4. Press Ctrl(⌘)+S; keep the file open.

Let's get back to the power of layer masking next, eh?

Revisiting the Layer Mask Mode

The Layer Mask mode gives you a chance to renege on your editing before you apply it, and that's why we typically prefer it over the Eraser tool. Here's an opportunity to make the chick in the image look as though it's getting a ride in the Wicker Duck basket.

Here's how to move and edit the chick:

Masking Part of the Chick

1. With the Move tool, right-click over the chick in the image. Surprise! Photoshop provides you with names of the layers over which you've clicked. Choose the Chick layer to make it the current editing layer.

2. Move the chick to the wicker duck, and try to place it in the basket. I know, I know; this doesn't work because the Chick layer is on top of the Wicker Duck layer. Instead of reordering layers, let's mask the bottom of the chick.

3. Click on the Add a Layer mask icon on the bottom of the Layers palette. Choose the Brush tool and a medium-sized brush tip, and then stroke over the bottom of the chick, stopping when you've reached the lip of the wicker duck basket, as shown in Figure 1.24.

4. Drag the Layer Mask thumbnail into the trash icon, and choose Apply in the dialog box that asks you whether you're playing for keeps in this editing move.

5. Press Ctrl(⌘)+S; keep the file open.

Whew! Your editing work is finally finished. Now, if you really want to, you can choose Flatten image from the Layers palette's flyout menu. This will really bring down the saved file size, but if you have the RAM and the hard disk space, you might want to keep all the ducks on separate layers to play around with later. The rule is: If you put a lot of effort into editing work, preserve it on separate layers.

Figure 1.24 Use the Layer Mask mode to hide the parts of the chick that would not be in front of the wicker duck.

Adding Text to the Image

I'll bet you were wondering when we'd get around to Nick's font! In the steps to follow, you'll see how to "skwunch" a typeface that's too wide for an available image area and how to make the text look as though it's on a roller coaster ride.

Using the Type Tool and the Warped Text Features

1. Press **D** for the default colors and then press **X** to switch white to the foreground color. Choose the Type tool from the toolbox.

2. Click an insertion point in the upper left of the image. A new layer icon appears on the Layers palette.

3. Type **For The Birds!**

4. Press Ctrl(⌘)+Enter (or click on the check mark icon at the upper-right side of the Options bar) to commit the text to a layer.

5. On the Options bar, choose GuinnessExtraStoutNF from the list of available fonts on your system.

6. Press Ctrl+T; the Free Transform box surrounds the text.

7. Drag on the corner handle, dragging in the center of the box to move it to the desired position. Do not use the Shift key (because you want to distort the text and not preserve proportions). Then check out Figure 1.25 to see what's going on.

Figure 1.25   Disproportionately scale the text so that it comfortably fits in the space at the top left of the image.

8. Double-click inside the text to finalize your edit of its size and width.

9. Click on the Warp Text tool on the Options bar. Choose Flag, as shown in Figure 1.26, and then drag the Bend slider until the text looks funky.

10. Click on OK to apply the change, and then press Ctrl(⌘)+S; keep the file open.

But wait! The excitement continues as you make the text look 3D in the following section.

Figure 1.26   Use the Warp Text tool to add movement and excitement to the text.

Using the Pillow Emboss and Stroke Commands

The text would not only look cooler, but also more legible if you did two things to it at this point: add a Pillow Emboss (a soft emboss), and then score the outline of the text. It should be noted that if you need to edit the text, you can still highlight the text and make corrections right now, even though the text is wavy.

Embossing and Highlighting the Text

1. With Text as the selected layer on the Layers palette, click on the **f** icon at the bottom left of the Layers palette, and then choose Bevel and Emboss.

2. In the Layer Style box, choose Pillow Emboss, as shown in Figure 1.27. Then drag the Depth slider to around 820, and drag the Soften slider to about 15. Uncheck the Use Global Light option, and adjust the Angle and Altitude settings as shown in Figure 1.27. Finally, drag the Shadow Mode Opacity slider to 100%.

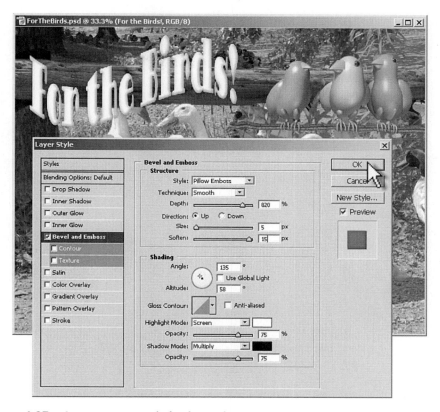

Figure 1.27   Create a custom style for the text by accessing Style controls for a layer.

3. Click on OK to make the text appear to bulge.

4. Ctrl(⌘)+click on the text layer title to load the text as a selection marquee, and then click on the Create a new layer icon at the bottom of the Layers palette. You will stroke the selection marquee without damaging the text and actually make the text look more legible now.

5. Choose Edit, Stroke, and then choose 8 pixels as the width of the stroke and Outside as the stroke location. Click on the color swatch in the dialog box, and choose black as the color for the stroke. Click OK to exit the Color Picker. Click OK again to exit the Stroke dialog box, and then press Ctrl+D to deselect the selection marquee. See Figure 1.28.

6. Press Ctrl(⌘)+S; keep the file open for anyone within three city blocks to come and gawk at!

LOAD THE TEXT SELECTION ON A *NEW* LAYER
AND *THEN* STROKE THE SELECTION

Figure 1.28   Stroke the text's outline, the selection marquee, with foreground color.

Terrific! You're done, and the composition probably looks like that shown in Figure 1.29, except yours is in color.

Take a long gander at your finished composition, and I promise to stop making puns. Did you ever think you would create such a complex image right from the start of Photoshop and this book? Did you think you would get hands-on with so many of the tools? Congratulations to you, hard-working reader! This image is a real feather in your cap!

Summary

Briefly, we covered layers, Layer Mask mode, Quick Mask, at least four or five toolbox tools including the very important Type tool, a Style filter, the Free Transform tool, and others. That's quite a lot for an "up and running" chapter, eh? Actually, there was an ulterior motive to piling on the tutorials in this chapter, which was that a lot of the tools and features you used here, you'll use again and again in Photoshop and in the examples in this book. And now, we can move more quickly, pick up the pace in this book, as you take on more and more fantastic assignments.

Figure 1.29   It was a fowl job, but it was also everything it was quacked up to be, and now that you have your ducks in a row, you can send the client the bill....

Chapter 2 is a departure from working with Photoshop; it's about color calibration. But before you say, "Yuck" or "Borrrring," think about this: You have a whole book before you and a whole career of editing and saving images as well. What if you bought a truckload of audio cassettes, but your tape player played them all at the wrong speed? What if you won the Publishers' Clearing House contest and got 5,000 DVDs, but your TV set was out of whack and showed Harrison Ford as having a blue face?

Unpleasant thoughts, right? Now, what happens when your monitor isn't calibrated and you make all these wonderful images, and your friends and your boss all have calibrated monitors and your work looks awful in front of them?

'Nuff said. I'll tell you what to do in the next chapter to manage colors on your system so every image you post, print, or share is picture perfect.

Chapter 2

The Critically Important Color and Gamma Calibration Chapter

Everyone likes surprises, such as being treated to breakfast in bed on an ordinary day or winning the 12 million dollar state lottery. But there are some surprises that *no one* wants to receive, like having uninvited relatives permanently bond themselves to your sofa at the exact same moment that your special someone is about to arrive for a romantic evening, or chomping into a wax pear thinking it's the real thing.

The unpleasant surprise that haunts graphic artists' and photographers' dreams usually involves color. Specifically, the problem is "color-gone-wrong." No one wants to spend hours staring at the monitor getting the delicate blush on a model's face just right, or tweaking the color of this month's Sweater of the Month Club sweater only to have the model's blush look like a rash and the sweater take on a royal blue hue instead of a regal purple one when printed. But just about the only way to avoid the unpleasant and often expensive problem of color-gone-wrong requires the help of a workable color management system (CMS).

The purpose of a color management system is to supply users with tools that can control the colors in images so that they remain as true as possible all through the process—from acquisition to final output. Ideally, such a system should work effortlessly and flawlessly and should be constrained to producing color-perfect output by the laws of physics itself.

Ideally, the photo of a pear you scanned should be the same color on your monitor and the same color when printed, and in a perfect world, the scanner's output should look like the physical pear.

Guess what? The world is not perfect, and neither is any color management system that was, or is, available. But it *did* get a whole lot better, and even worth using on an everyday basis when Adobe introduced a new, comprehensive color management system in Photoshop 6. The Adobe CMS works pretty much the same in professional Adobe products such as Photoshop, Illustrator, and InDesign. And because the Adobe system is based on the use of an international standard for creating ICM (color) profiles (descriptions of how a device handles color), color-managed files from Photoshop work as expected with other manufacturers' software and hardware.

So why are we rehashing a Photoshop 6 feature in a book on Photoshop CS? Simple—because color management is very important and because it is not the most intuitive or easy thing for most people to understand and embrace. Many Photoshop users just skipped over the feature as best they could and continue to work in a graphics world where color is more likely to go wrong than right. Also, it's possible you never read this chapter in our version 6 book.

If you were one of the brave and became a whiz at managing color consistency using Adobe CMS in Photoshop 6, you probably have more time to spend doing the things that you love to do. Learning how to use Photoshop's color management tools is not only for folks whose day gig is in a studio, either. If you have a digital camera and you like to retouch family photos or create and print your own holiday cards, you've already found out how much time and how many pieces of expensive inkjet photo paper it takes to produce *one copy* that has colors you anticipated.

What you are going to learn in this chapter is the most important thing you can learn about Photoshop: how to get predictable, consistent output and how to make your scanner, monitor, and printer display approximately the same thing. This is the graphic artist's dream, but it doesn't come without a price, and that price is this—a very serious, very technical chapter.

Our advice up front is that you take two or three days to digest what we teach in this chapter. We also realize that the other chapters in this book are light and occasionally humorous when compared to this chapter. So, keeping in mind that you're human and need a break when involved in anything serious, we present to you Figure 2.1. Now, this is a funny picture. Any time you find your attention drifting from this chapter, turn back to this page.

Aren't you glad we authors have a sense of perspective?

Figure 2.1   Return to this page and this image any time you're reading this chapter and find you're in over your head.

Understanding Photoshop's Color Management System (CMS)

Up 'til now, establishing a color-managed workflow was something attempted only by large organizations with big, fat budgets for equipment and dedicated color management technicians. And it didn't always work, even for them. Photoshop 5 introduced a color management process for the individual desktop, and Photoshop 5.5 improved upon that beginning. But those efforts fell short of being impressive; and most users, including us, continued to run, screaming, for the exits. Even talking about color management was too horrible to contemplate.

Well, times have changed. Adobe's new color management system (also referred to as CMS) is probably the single most important feature in Photoshop CS, in Illustrator 10, and in every other new Adobe product coming down the pipeline. Adobe deserves a lot of credit, but so do Apple and Microsoft and a whole bunch of other companies that make up the International Color Consortium (ICC). All these companies have made a serious commitment toward making color management work. It is now possible for mere mortals to understand and use color management. This is great news!

Having a usable system for managing color is a big deal. It is headline news. It is worth writing home about. Why? Because after you have set up your system to use color management and you've learned how to use these new color management tools, you'll never have to play the "What color is it, really?" game again. The colors you see on your monitor will be surprisingly close to what will come streaming out of a high-speed printing press or tumbling out of your desktop inkjet printer.

Adobe has made a splendid CMS that works the same in all of its products. Apple and Microsoft have done their part by providing operating system–level support for color management so that every program, even non-Adobe programs, can use color management. Equipment manufacturers have made descriptions of the color capabilities of their products available so that the information can be "plugged into" the CMS. Now you can master the concepts of color management and take up the new tools that have been placed at your disposal.

Coming to Terms with Color Management

To be frank, color management is still not an easy topic to understand, and you can't master it by reading a few paragraphs. But we promise you that it *is* possible to learn, that it is worth the effort, and that if you take your time going through this chapter, you will be able to use Adobe's CMS and still have enough brain cells left to do creative, artistic work.

In this section, we look at some of the key terms used in talking about color management. Along the way, you'll catch a little of the history of how this newest CMS evolved.

Color Spaces and Color Gamut

Throughout this chapter, you frequently are going to see the terms *color spaces* and *color gamut*, as coarsely described in Chapter 0, "Answers to the Most Important Imaging Questions." *Color space* is a model for representing color in terms of values that can be measured, such as the amount of red, green, and blue in an image. CMS works with standard color spaces, including RGB (Red, Green, Blue), LAB (L for relative lightness, A for relative redness-greenness, and B for related yellowness-blueness), and CMYK (Cyan, Magenta, Yellow, Black). *Color gamut* refers to a contiguous range of colors describing the limitations of a device or image. Color gamut might be called *color capability* when referring to a specific color space. "How many colors can this model represent?" is the question put forth by color gamut.

Life would be very boring and one-dimensional if the universe and every man-made device had only one color space. That's not the case, however, and so the issue of color gamut is a big concern for anyone involved in color-critical work. Here's a quick summary explaining why:

- Every device—monitor, printer, printing press, camera, film, ink, and media combination—can produce only a limited number of colors.
- No two devices or processes have the exact same color gamut.
- Even two printers or monitors of the same make and model vary from each other, although new generations of desktop printers with built-in densitometer (color-measuring device) and automatic self-calibration tend to be reliable from printer to printer.
- A device changes in its color-rendering capability because of age, lighting, or other operating conditions.

Ugh. These varying factors drive digital artists and production people up a virtual wall!

Color Calibration

Before you explore the Adobe CMS further, you need to calibrate your devices. What do we mean by the term *calibrate? Calibration* is the process of bringing a device, such as a printer or monitor, to an absolute standard to ensure consistency over time and across devices of the same make and model. That is, you are attempting to make the color gamut and characteristics of a physical device adhere to some empirical, mathematically perfect standard.

Calibration is critical when you want accurate color output on a monitor. A good place to start is to match the white point and gamma from monitor to monitor, using monitor calibration software such as Adobe Gamma, or third-party software and hardware when available.

Working Space

Time for a new term: *working space*, which includes RGB and CMYK color spaces. A *working space* is the pool of possible colors available when you edit a file. In the early days of color management, the monitor's color capability (color gamut) was the same as the space in which you worked with your image (the working space). If there were only one monitor in the world, and it never changed, you could consider the color gamut and the working space to be the same. But such is not the case, and a CMS shouldn't assume it is.

A much better idea is to assign actual numbers to specific color values (sometimes referred to as *data*) and then reference and manipulate the data within the context of an ideal, standard working color space, rather than use the settings of a fallible and limited physical device. How is such an ideal, a standard, established, when the world is full of so many different types of monitors, printers, scanners, and other devices? Read on!

Commission Internationale de l'Eclairage (CIE)

CMS creators needed a uniform way to describe the color space of devices and standard color spaces. They also needed to define a standard set of rules that govern the way information about color values is exchanged between color spaces that do not overlap.

In the 1930s, the Commission Internationale de l'Eclairage (CIE), based in France, began the task of establishing color standards by assigning numbers to every color visible to the human eye. The color spaces the CIE defined, such as CIELAB, form the foundation of device-independent color for color management. However, the group's work was only a beginning; it did not resolve the color management issues encountered in electronic publishing. Who had InDesign in 1930 :) ?

International Color Consortium (ICC)

In 1993, the International Color Consortium (ICC)—a group of companies recognized as leaders in the fields of electronic publishing, software development, and digital pre-press—formed a committee to establish standards for *electronic* color publishing. The ICC based its standardized color information on the CIELAB color space, and developed device profiles that would easily transfer color information from one device to another and from one computing platform to another.

Here is the problem the ICC tackled: Each printing device, scanner, digital camera, and monitor has its own way of *rendering* a color (that is, assigning a meaning to a color). This meaning is called the device's *color space*.

Monitors, for example, specify colors as values of red, green, and blue (RGB). The values R:100, G:20, B:30 specify a certain shade of red on a particular monitor. These values are said to be *device-dependent*; if these values are sent to a second monitor with different colored phosphors, a different color red will be displayed. If they are sent to a printer that describes colors as percentages of cyan, magenta, yellow, and black (CMYK), yet another different red will be printed.

Which is the correct color? The color seen on the first monitor? The color seen on the second monitor? Or the color printed on the printer?

Photoshop CS Color Working Spaces

Fast forward to today. To enable Photoshop to provide uniform ways of describing color space, Adobe needed to offer several different standard color working spaces. Thanks to the foundation laid by the CIE and the ICC, Adobe was able to do so. For RGB images Photoshop offers sRGB, Adobe RGB 1998, Apple RGB, and Colormatch RGB working spaces. For CMYK working spaces, Photoshop offers US Web Coated SWOP, US Web Uncoated, US Sheetfed Coated, US Sheetfed Uncoated, Japan Standard, Euroscale Uncoated, and Euroscale Coated.

Establishing these color working spaces wasn't enough. How could that information be *exchanged* between devices?

Enter ICC profiles.

ICC Profiles

ICC profiles are an essential element of the color management equation. Because no device can be brought into perfect calibration, and because no two devices—monitors, printers, or scanners—perform identically even if they are the same make and model, profiles are created to *document* the ways a specific device strays from the standard. What kind of documentation is this? Well…

The Adobe CMS uses ICC standard device profiles to ensure that colors are accurately converted across devices. *Profiles* are data files that record all the relevant information for a particular device, including its color space, capabilities, and limitations. Each profile relates a device's color space to the CIE-referenced color space. By doing so, a profile assigns an absolute meaning to each color that a device can produce.

When you transfer an image between two devices that have ICC profiles, a *Color Management Module* (CMM) compares the ICC profile of the source device (such as the monitor) with the ICC profile of the destination device (such as the printer) to create consistent color results. With the information contained in the ICC profile, the CMM transforms colors in image files to produce consistent color simulation on the monitor and the proofing device. For every RGB value in the monitor color space, for example, the color transformation produces a similar CMYK value in the printer's color space. If a color space specified on one device falls *outside* the color gamut of another device, the

CMS may automatically reassign the actual values put out from the devices to preserve the *relationship* of colors from one device to another. The CMS in effect *remaps* colors that fall outside the other device's gamut, *but…*it does so in a way the human eye accepts.

> **Note**
>
> **In Windows it's ICM**   Because the Windows operating system had already assigned the ICC suffix to another system component, Windows refers to ICC profiles as ICM. The suffixes ICC and ICM are interchangeable in the language of CMS.

2

How do you *get* ICC profiles? Adobe and your operating system offer generic profiles for popular brands of monitors. Adobe also offers Adobe Gamma, which creates a custom ICC profile the Adobe CMS can use to understand how your monitor handles color. (Hang on. We cover Adobe Gamma next.)

Even if one of the generic profiles fits your monitor, we recommend that you create a custom ICC profile. It is *not* recommended (at least, not by us) to use preset monitor profiles. They are of little value, due to aging and varied viewing conditions of the devices that the profiles describe. Custom profiles are always better. After all, would you rather have a picture of an ideal family or a picture of *your* family?

> **Note**
>
> **Profiling**   When you create an ICC profile for your monitor, you are making a *system-level* adjustment. This means that *any* program that is color management–capable uses the ICC profile you've created for your monitor.

You can (and should) have multiple ICC profiles for printing devices—one profile for one specific working condition. *But use only one profile at a time.* Also, be careful that you are using the correct profile for the current condition. For example, you may have one profile for your inkjet printer that you use with the manufacturer's standard glossy paper, and another that you use with a third party's glossy paper.

In addition to performing regular calibration (hey, stuff ages) and profiling of the monitor, an artist should try to maintain consistent lighting conditions. The monitor needs to be calibrated and profiled at least once a month. Of all the devices that require ICC profiles, the monitor loses its calibration the quickest.

Translation, Please

The Color Management Module (CMM), mentioned earlier, is a color transformation engine that translates data from one device's color to another via an independent color space. The CMM receives the necessary information from the profiles so that it can accurately transform a color from one device to another. The CMM interprets the data and, in essence, says to the monitor, "The file data says to display a blue that has the RGB values of 66, 66, 150, but I've looked at your profile and you always make things too red. You will display RGB value 60, 66, 150 so that it *looks like* the ideal 66, 66, 150. *Photoshop doesn't have to know about our arrangement.* When it does something to the color 66, 66, 150, use the color in the file data."

When Photoshop performs an operation that requires it to calculate a new color value, that color must be contained in the current working space. The working space's color mode and the position and size of the color gamut of the working space are determined by the ICC profile. Successfully moving color values from one color space to another is a difficult problem because color spaces do not generally share the same color gamut. How is this conversion done?

To bring all the possible color spaces into a common space where accurate color translation becomes possible, a very large device-independent color space is needed. For example, to translate monitor colors to printer colors, a space must exist that is large enough to encompass all *device-dependent spaces* (spaces that are unique to a specific device) as well as standard color spaces. At the heart of Adobe's Color engine is a Profile Connection Space (PCS) that is device-independent and has a large enough color gamut to hold both the source and the target color spaces. That PCS is based on the CIELAB color space.

Figure 2.2 shows a representation of LAB color space. It is tongue-shaped because visible light is broken down into uneven amounts, with green being predominant. Our eyes are more sensitive to greens than to blues or reds—hence, the distortion in the shape of a color space. In the color section in this book, you'll find an image (a color image, natch') of the CIELAB color model in two dimensions and three dimensions. It also shows how Adobe RGB (1998)—our recommendation for working spaces—neatly fits inside the gamut of the LAB space.

In the illustration, the working space is Adobe RGB 1998. This color space, larger than anything your monitor can show you, fits within the translation color space making it possible for every point in the space to be mapped—without color loss—to the translation space (LAB). The colors in printer space, whether it's a commercial press or an inkjet, are CMYK. They represent a smaller space than RGB color and have a few areas that RGB cannot reproduce. Fortunately, the translation layer *can* reproduce those colors. That is why, in the illustration, the printer space eclipses the monitor space slightly, but overall, fits within the working space.

2

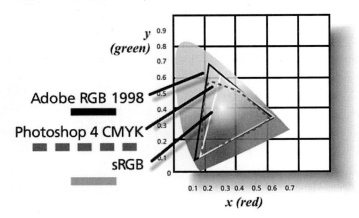

Figure 2.2   Different color spaces often fit inside one another and often overlap.

Note

> **When to use sRGB**   Less expensive digital cameras use the sRGB color space, and
> this throws a monkey wrench into our argument for Adobe RGB 1998 as a default
> working space. When you use a digital camera that uses the sRGB color space, you
> might choose to edit the image in sRGB and print to an inkjet whose gamut is within
> the sRGB color space. Check your manufacturer's documentation.

Adobe Gamma

Note: At the time of this writing, Adobe Gamma is available in Photoshop CS only for
Windows. Macintosh users might want to skip this section, but you *should* refer to the
ColorSync information that came with your OS.

The term *gamma* is the error measured between a straight, linear mapping of voltage
applied to your monitor's circuitry and brightness you see on your monitor. Huh? Okay,
example time:

Suppose you were holding a lever that applied voltage to your monitor's blue phosphors.
In theory, the screen would be black at zero voltage, medium blue (half blue) at half
power, and as bright a blue as possible at full voltage. This is a linear plotting of voltage
versus brightness, and it *does not exist*. There is a *sag* in the midrange of the voltage versus brightness graph, which is why we perform gamma correction.

Note

> **Gamma settings debate rages on**   You may have heard that Windows gamma is 2.2, and 1.8 for the Macintosh. Do not be confused by the Control Panel's default settings for gamma; don't argue with them. Monitor gamma is different than the gamma of working spaces. Some CMS experts tend to favor 2.2 for both platforms. You very well could have a profile for your monitor that is 2.2 but find that Photoshop's working space displays images with deeper midtones than you would expect.

When you installed Photoshop, the setup program installed a feature called Adobe Gamma in your Control Panel(s) folder. In Windows, the Control Panel is under Start, Settings, Control Panel. You can use this Adobe Gamma Control Panel and your eye to calibrate your monitor or adjust its gamma.

The Adobe Gamma Control Panel actually does more than just adjust your monitor's gamma. It also builds an ICC profile of your monitor that your operating system CMS can use instead of the default one that was installed when you installed your monitor or operating system. In fact, the Adobe Gamma Control Panel provides a much better profile, one that is tailored to the way your monitor actually operates, and not just what the engineering specification for the monitor said should be happening.

Note

> **Use third-party software if your work is color critical**   If your work is color critical, you may want to use a more precise, less subjective method to calibrate and profile your monitor. Third-party folks like Monaco, X-Rite, and Gretag Macbeth all offer special color measurement hardware and software that produces a more precise result, but a result that can cost anywhere from $300 to tens of thousands of dollars. For most people, however, the Adobe Gamma software does good enough profiling for the monitor. And the price certainly can't be argued.

For most computers, Adobe Gamma's control of the monitor's white point and gamma affects your view of everything and every program displayed onscreen, whether it uses color management or not. (The *white point*, or *highlight*, is the lightest part of the picture; it is the point along the range of tones in an image after which light tones appear white.)

In some situations, Adobe Gamma doesn't have full control: Windows NT 4 and some Windows 95 machines with video cards do not allow software to manipulate display hardware on a global basis. If you use Windows NT 4 or Windows 95 and have one of the stubborn video cards, you're not totally out of luck; Windows allows programs, such as Photoshop and PageMaker that "understand" color management, to alter the display and use the information Adobe Gamma provides (along with the info in the ICC profile) to adjust the information sent to the display, even if *every* program and the system itself do not permit that alteration and adjustment. On the Windows NT 4 operating system, the ICM must reside in the Color folder within the System32 folder to be available to graphic applications that support system-level profiles.

The *good* news is that Adobe Gamma works under Windows 2000 and Windows XP.

Warning

> **Watch out for double color management**   If you use Adobe Gamma to calibrate and set the gamma of your monitor, don't use another program's software to do the same thing. Pick one system and use it.

Color Clipping

You now know that, for physical reasons, every device—monitor, printer, camera—is limited in the number of colors it can access. The group of colors available to a device—its *color space*—differs from that of other kinds of devices (monitors and printers, let's say). When one color space can express 10 shades of green, for example, you will see nice transition or good detail in parts of the image that use green. But what happens when you ask a different device to display the same image, and that device has a smaller color space or one with less variety in the number of greens available to it? What if it can express only two shades of green? All 10 of the greens will have to be expressed as one or the other of the two available greens in the new color space. The result will be a poster effect—areas of flat, saturated color where lots of different colors (green, in this example) used to be. This posterization of color is called *color clipping*. The way a color that is clipped is mapped into the new gamut is called *rendering intent*. We talk more about rendering intent later.

Color clipping can happen when you move an image between standard color spaces, such as RGB and CMYK. Color clipping also can occur when you move between subsets of each color space (Adobe RGB to sRGB, for example), or between the color gamuts that different inks or dyes can produce. The color management engine uses the ICC profiles for the different devices and color gamuts to determine the best way to resolve the differences in color capability.

If you're striving for a lighter color or a more saturated one and nothing seems to work, you've reached the greatest possible parameters for such a color when it is output using the media and methods you've chosen. To get the color you want, you would have to step outside the image's color gamut. In the CMYK print world, that usually means adding an extra ink, a *spot color*. A *spot color* is a custom ink that is prepared to represent a color that's unavailable in the CMYK color space. It is applied as a separate color plate, in addition to the cyan, magenta, yellow, and black printing plates.

Preparing to Create a Custom Profile

Before we start building custom profiles and plugging them into the system, let's look at other issues that impact color management. Getting these issues squared away will make your custom profile more accurate.

Check Out Yourself, Your Environment, and Your Equipment

All the color profiling and monitor calibration on earth won't help you achieve color consistency across devices if you don't get your physical working conditions in order. Here are a few questions you should ask yourself:

- Have you been to the eye doctor lately?

- Are you taking cold medication? If so, it will really affect your color perception.

- Have you cleaned the smudges off your eyeglasses? Your glasses aren't tinted, are they? Did you remember to park your sunglasses at the door?

- Have you wiped the monitor screen clean lately? You aren't using a glare filter or one of those polarizing privacy screens, are you?

- Is the monitor warmed up? Has it been on for at least 30 minutes before you use it for color work or before you create a new profile?

- Do you work in a windowless room or one with heavily draped windows? You should, because the constantly changing qualities of natural light make it impossible to achieve accurate consistent color.

- Is your artificial lighting even? No bare bulbs peeking out from under their shades? No hot spots reflected in the monitor, or shadows cast across it?

- Is your lighting a neutral, subdued white? Or is the light in your workspace too blue because it is lit with fluorescent tubes, or too yellow because incandescent lamps provide your lighting. See whether you can get your boss to install professionally color-balanced lighting, or at least try to get the fluorescent tubes that profess to have fuller frequency ranges to mimic daylight. If you are using fluorescent bulbs, the next time they need replacing, change them to 5000K bulbs, available at most home improvement stores.

- Are your walls, furniture, curtains, posters, paintings, and plants all a nice neutral, medium gray? Probably not. Be aware that light reflecting off everything in the room can change the color of the light in the room and alter your perception of the colors on your screen and the output from your printer.

- Did you know that even the color of your clothing can make a difference? If your work is color critical, put on a light gray lab coat or artist's smock when you sit down to work. Who knows; your customers might be so impressed with your "technical" uniform that you could charge more. Or more likely, if you pay attention to everything on this list and in this chapter—your color work will be so dead on, your customers will *beg* to pay you more. Wouldn't that be nice (this is a rhetorical question)?

- Have you extended the neutral gray color scheme to your desktop wallpaper, Windows title bars, and other screen elements? Let the color live in your work and not in your immediate surroundings.

> **Tip**
>
> **Neutralize your desktop**   Ideally, a 50% gray desktop would help you evaluate colors without influence. However, cursors tend to disappear at R:128, G:128, B:128.
>
> Go a little lighter or darker with your desktop so it is still color-neutral, but you can make out your cursors.

We know you're eager to get to the fun stuff, creating something in Photoshop or ImageReady, and that you would like to finish all this hardware, techie stuff ASAP. But just as you have to do your exercises if you want to keep fit and trim, you have to put in some time now to get your *system* in shape so you can enjoy the good life of a successful Photoshop user.

Read Your Monitor Manual

Before you start to calibrate and create a profile for your monitor, using Adobe Gamma or any other calibration device, you need to find out on what color temperature your monitor bases its display. A monitor's temperature, also called its *white point*, is a value, measured in degrees Kelvin, that describes the point at which white light is produced from equal amounts of red, green, and blue light. Monitors are designed to operate at a white point that matches one of the standard illuminant temperatures defined by the CIE standards body. Some monitors offer a selection of operating temperatures from which the user can pick, while others offer only one fixed setting.

As you can see in Table 2.1, the default white point setting for Windows monitors is 6500 degrees Kelvin. This may be referred to as 6500K, D65, or daylight. The Macintosh OS default color temperature is 9300K (D93, or Cool White). The color temperature most often used in the publishing (to paper) community is 5000K (D50 or Warm White, Page White, or Paper White) because it produces a view that more closely resembles material printed on white paper. Other common white point settings are 5500K and 7500K. One of the latest trends among the CMS gurus is to use 6500K for both platforms.

Table 2.1   Default White Point Settings

Environment	Default White Point	Standard Abbreviation	Commonly Referred To As
Windows	6500K	D65	Daylight
Macintosh	9300K	D93	Cool White
Publishing to Paper	5000K	D50	Warm White, Page White, or Paper White

Check your monitor's manual, its onscreen help, or the manufacturer's Web site to see whether your monitor offers a user-definable color temperature and how to make that selection. If your monitor does offer a choice of color temperature or white point, you should choose based on the work you do most often. If your work centers around print, use the monitor's controls to set the white point at 5000K. If you design mostly for Web or onscreen presentation, you could set your white point to the default temperature of the operating system used by most people who view your work. Or you could split the difference and set your hardware temperature to 7500K, if your monitor offers that choice (my monitor doesn't). Or you could set it to match the default setting for your operating system.

Older monitors may not offer user-definable color temperature, but you should still see what the fixed temperature of the monitor is. Whatever type of monitor you have, find out what the current white point setting is, change it if you can and want to, and then write it down. You will need this value handy when you use Adobe Gamma to calibrate and make an ICC profile for your monitor.

If you are unable to find any of this information, don't panic. Adobe Gamma has a measurement feature that will provide an approximate value for your monitor's white point.

Setting the color temperature and gamma when calibrating and profiling the monitor can be referred to as "setting the *target*." In work environments with more than one monitor, it is important always to use the same target when you're trying to achieve consistent color from one workstation to another.

Install the Latest Drivers for Your Equipment

Before you begin to set up your system and Photoshop to use color management, make sure that you have installed all the latest drivers for your equipment. Monitor, video card, scanner, and printer manufacturers often update their drivers to fix bugs and to add or update the ICC profiles they have created for their products. These default manufacturer profiles are what you'll use if you don't create custom-made profiles for your equipment. In addition, they are often used by products that profile things, including Adobe

Gamma, as a basis for the custom profile. So, fire up your Internet browser or give customer service at each place a call, and get the newest drivers the equipment manufacturers have to offer. Follow their instructions for installing the drivers on your computer.

Creating an ICC Profile for a Monitor

Okay—gamma, brightness/contrast, and other parameters lie ahead of us. Follow these steps to create an ICC profile for your monitor, using Adobe Gamma:

Profiling Your Monitor

1. If you haven't done so already, go to the monitor manufacturer's Web site and download the most recent driver, and then follow the instructions there to install it for your monitor.

   Insider

   By installing the latest drivers, you ensure that the Adobe Gamma will base its work on the most accurate information available about your monitor.

2. With Photoshop and other applications closed, open the Control Panel(s) (folder), and double-click the Adobe Gamma icon.

   The Adobe Gamma Control Panel opens. You can choose to work with a single dialog box that has a number of different tasks, or use a step-by-step method that involves a Windows Wizard.

3. Click to set the Control Panel option, and then click Next. We'll show you how the single dialog box version (shown in Figure 2.3) of this application works, but you're free to switch to the step-by-step method at any time by clicking the Wizard button.

   In the Description field, you should see one or more profiles listed for your monitor. These profiles are already installed on your system and assigned to your monitor. If there are two, one was probably installed when you installed your operating system, and the other is the one you just downloaded and installed from the monitor manufacturer. Unless you told the install program differently, the last installed profile is the one currently in use.

4. Highlight the profile you just installed in step 1, and type a meaningful name, like **Downloaded 11-14-03**, to indicate that you downloaded it on November 14, 2003. This will make it easier to pick the profile from a list (if you choose to use this profile at a later date).

   Adobe Gamma will base the new profile being created on the highlighted profile in the Description field.

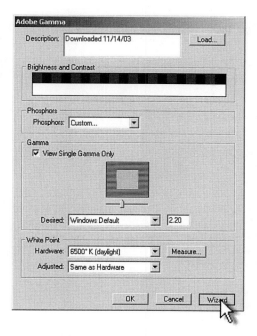

Figure 2.3   If you want to walk through the process of using the Adobe Gamma Control Panel screen by screen, click the Wizard button.

5. Click the Load button if you want to base the new profile on a profile other than the one currently in the field.

6. Using the controls on your monitor, increase the Contrast to 100%, or set it as high as the control will go. With your eye on the Brightness and Contrast section of the Adobe Gamma Control Panel, use the monitor's brightness control to adjust brightness up or down until the gray squares in the gray-and-black checkerboard strip are almost black (see Figure 2.4). The goal is to end up with an almost black-and-black checkerboard strip above a crisp, bright white strip. If the white gets dirty, be sure to increase the brightness. If your monitor has onscreen controls, fiddle with them the same as you would do with on-monitor knobs.

Warning

> **Changes to contrast and brightness will affect profiles**   If you change the monitor's contrast and brightness settings later in the profile-making process, or at any time in the future, the profile will no longer be accurate and you will have to create a new profile. If your monitor has external knobs that adjust brightness and contrast, you should use duct tape—or stronger—to tape them down so they can't be changed by accident.

Figure 2.4   Use your monitor's brightness and contrast knobs or onscreen controls to make the gray squares in the Adobe Gamma Control Panel almost black.

7. Change the Phosphors setting only if you are absolutely certain that what is shown is wrong. If you are certain it is wrong, but you don't know what the right setting is, the best guess would be Trinitron.

   Adobe Gamma sets the Phosphors properties based on information from the manufacturer's profile. If you installed the latest driver and profile from your monitor's manufacturer, you probably won't have to make any changes with the Phosphors drop-down list. For many users, the setting will be Custom; you should leave it alone and move on to the fun control: Gamma.

8. Make sure that the View Single Gamma Only option is checked. Then lean back and squint, and drag the slider to the left or to the right until the solid tone in the center has the same apparent tone as the stripes outside the box.

   You just defined gamma by using a composite control that applied the same gamma setting to each of the three RGB channels. This "one-gamma-setting-fits-all-channels" method works just fine for most people. However, if you want greater control or if you think that your monitor's RGB channels are a little out of sync with each other, clear the View Single Gamma Only option and, one by one, drag the slider under each box until the center box fades into the striped frame around it. Then move on to the next step.

Note

> **Older Windows operating systems**   If you are using Windows NT 4 or Windows 95 with certain video cards, you will not have the option of choosing a setting from the Desired drop-down list, as shown in the next step. This is a limitation imposed by the operating system, not by Adobe Gamma. Some Windows 95 users and all Windows 98, ME, 2000, and XP users will have the option available to them and should follow the advice in the next step.

9. Choose Windows Default, Macintosh Default, or Custom from the Desired drop-down list. These are the options as of this writing; however, as we mentioned earlier, Adobe has no plans to implement Adobe Gamma on the Macintosh platform. I chose Windows Default (see Figure 2.5) because I'm working on a Windows computer. If you choose Custom, you will need to enter a value in the field next to the drop-down. We don't recommend choosing a custom setting unless you are very experienced in color management and have a very compelling reason to do so.

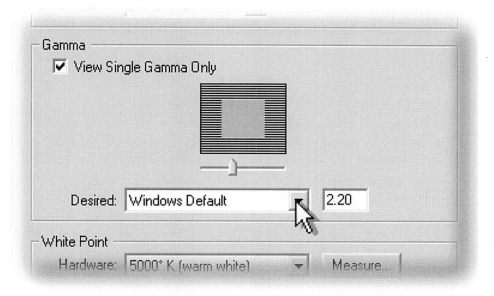

Figure 2.5   Choose from the (Gamma) Desired drop-down list. Your choice should match your operating system.

Insider

> In the White Point area of the Adobe Gamma Control dialog box are two drop-down lists. The first refers to the actual hardware setting of your monitor.

2

10. Click on the Hardware drop-down list and choose the color temperature your monitor actually uses. Earlier in the chapter, this is the value you set or determined in the "Read Your Monitor Manual" section.

11. If you were unable to determine the hardware setting, or if your monitor is old and you think it might not be operating as well as it used to, click the Measure button next to the Hardware drop-down list. Follow the onscreen instructions carefully. Removing all ambient light means the room should be dark. You may even want to wait until night to do this if your workspace has windows. Click the center square when you are done. The entry in the Hardware drop-down list will now read Custom.

    The Adjusted drop-down box offers the same color temperature choices as the Hardware drop-down list did. Adobe Gamma can override the hardware settings and force the monitor to display other standard white points.

Note

> **Use consistent lighting**   The lighting conditions present when you're calibrating and profiling the monitor should be maintained when you use that profile. If you use other lighting conditions, you should recalibrate and reprofile. In other words, don't calibrate your new computer in the store and expect the profiles to hold true when you get the machine home.

12. If you ever need to use a nonstandard white point, choose Custom from the list, and enter the values that describe the custom white point.

    If your monitor can display the color temperature you want to use, choose Same as Hardware from the Adjusted drop-down list. If your monitor has a fixed color point of 9600K, for example, and you want to use a 5000K white point to more closely mimic paper, choose 5000K from the Adjusted drop-down list, as shown in Figure 2.6.

13. Click OK, and then in the Save As dialog box, give a descriptive name to your monitor's custom profile. On the Macintosh, the file extension would be .pf; in Windows, it's *.icm.

    For example, I'm calling the settings for one of my machines Win XP machine 11-14-03.icm. In this way, I can tell how recently I profiled the monitor.

14. Click Save, and then click OK in the Gamma Control Panel to finish calibrating and profiling your monitor.

It probably took longer to read how to calibrate and profile your monitor than it took to actually *do* it! This is a good thing, because if you want to keep your colors consistent, you really should recalibrate and reprofile your monitor at least once a month, even if nothing noticeable has changed in the environment. Recalibrate and reprofile right away if something *does* change in the environment. Changing a light bulb or repainting the room both qualify as events that should cause you to open Adobe Gamma and run through it one more time.

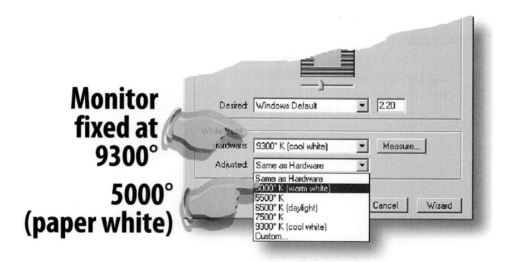

Figure 2.6   Choose a color temperature in keeping with the way you view your final output in Photoshop.

Now that every color management–aware piece of software on your system has a target profile for your monitor, it will be easier to establish color consistency when you print or do Web work in Photoshop. The next thing to do is to set up a working color space for Photoshop.

Photoshop and the CMS look in specific folders for profiles. The location of the folder that stores profiles depends on the operating system you use. Table 2.2 shows where you should save profiles you've created or obtained if you want to make them available for use.

Table 2.2   Required Locations for ICC Profiles

Operating System	Installed Location of ICC Profiles
Windows NT version 4	WinNT\system32\Color
Windows 2000	WinNT\system32\spool\drivers\color
Windows XP	WinXP\system32\spool\drivers\color
Macintosh OS using ColorSync, earlier than version 2.5	System Folder, Preferences, ColorSync Profiles
Macintosh OS using ColorSync version 2.5 or later	System Folder, ColorSync Profiles

To recap: You've profiled your monitor, and the operating system has assigned that pro-file to your monitor. Now it is time to open Photoshop and start setting up the rules for the way it should do its part in the color management process.

Setting Photoshop's Color Management Defaults

Setting Photoshop Color Setting defaults doesn't take much time, but it does require a little thought to make them work best with the kind of work you do most. These settings can be changed at any time. These are defaults; Photoshop will use these settings unless you tell Photoshop to do something else. You can always override default settings on a per-file basis; when you find that you frequently are overriding the default settings, just press Ctrl(⌘)+Shift+K and set new defaults.

To make matters even simpler, Adobe has come up with different collections of settings that suit common needs of different types of work: printing to U.S., European, or Japanese printing presses; creating graphics for the Internet; working in the color spaces of Photoshop 4; or even turning off color management. If one of the default settings is good for your kind of work, your stay in this dialog box will be brief. But if the defaults don't cut it for you, or you just want greater control over things, there are lots of choices you can make. In the next sections you'll discover what all the choices are, and I'll offer some recommendations for what you should choose.

Most of my recommendations are based on the premise that you are looking for a good, general-purpose workspace profile—one that enables the monitor's color capability to show through, one that embraces most other color output spaces and gives a reasonably accurate view of images that come from different color spaces. Some images might be RGB, some might be LAB color, while others might have been saved in CMYK mode. It all depends on where you work!

A Word on Your "Out of the Box" Experience

You haven't ruined anything if you ran Photoshop for the first time, and you answered No to Photoshop's offer to help determine Custom color settings. You just need to press Ctrl(⌘)+Shift+K and change one or two things in the Color Settings box to get a better color space than the default going in Photoshop. More importantly, we have selected the Adobe RGB 1998 color space when saving most of images on the companion CD. You will get annoying, confusing dialog boxes when you open every image on the CD if you do not go with our recommendations concerning color space.

In a nutshell, as of this writing, Adobe has chosen sRGB as the default color space in Photoshop (meant for the Web and inexpensive digital camera images), and we disagree. We feel you should be working most of the time in Adobe RGB 1998 color space. Read on!

The Color Settings Dialog Box, or Laying Down the Rules

This section takes you to color management central, the Color Settings dialog box. We won't cover this as an exercise with lots of numbered steps because we don't know what the best choices for you will be. That's up to you to decide. But we do want to explain what all the choices mean and translate the parlance of color management into more understandable and accessible terms. Here's what we'd like you to do, to make following along easier:

> Open Photoshop (you do not need an image to be open), and then choose Edit, Color Settings, or press Ctrl($\mathcal{H}$)+Shift+K.
>
> The Color Settings dialog box pops up onscreen, where you can refer to it as you proceed through the following sections.

The Color Settings dialog box on your screen (and in Figure 2.7) has two major functions. It is used to define the default working color space that will be used when you create an image and to "tag" the image with the ICC profile of the workspace. The workspace tag is kind of like a short biography that tells what color space the file was born in and where it currently lives. The tag is also used to set the rules or Color Management Policies for what happens when you work with files that don't have workspace tags or have tags that don't match the default space you've set. Your work is not harnessed to the profile, however. When you choose File, Save As, you can uncheck the ICC profile box, and Photoshop will protest a little in the form of a warning, but this is cool.

Now, for most folks, the choices shown in Figure 2.7 should be perfect for getting right down to work in Photoshop. If your screen doesn't look like this figure, manually select the options so that your screen matches what you're reading here. As mentioned earlier, we cannot adopt Adobe's decision to make the default space the teensy, Web-friendly sRGB color space; we need more room if we're going to create something good.

The Settings Drop-Down List

You use the Settings drop-down list to choose either a preset collection of settings or to select independently the various settings in the dialog box. Adobe has provided some very useful presets, and you, of course, can also create your own presets and choose them from this drop-down list. When you choose one of the presets in this drop-down list, the preset specifies and sets all the other fields and options in the dialog box for you. If none of the shipping color setting files meet your needs, for example, go through the dialog box, make your choices, and then save all the changes you've made to a new color setting file. From then on, you can access your custom settings with the convenience and precision of the shipping presets. You can even share these settings with other people by giving them the file that was created.

2

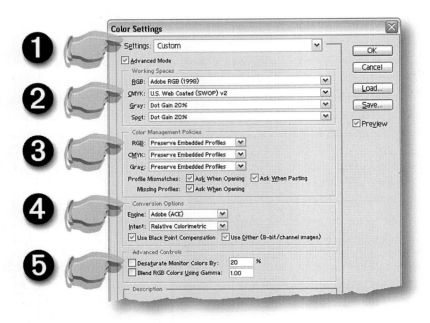

Figure 2.7   You need to set five areas in the Color Settings dialog box to make the workspace foolproof and easy to work in.

If you click the arrow for the Settings drop-down list, you'll see that Adobe has provided the following presets:

- **Color Management Off.** As good as using color management is under most circumstances, sometimes you definitely want to turn it off. The most common reason for turning off color management is to create graphics that in their finished version will be viewed only onscreen, by users with different monitors and operating systems, or for video work. Examples of such material would be onscreen help files, reference material, and multimedia presentations.

- **Emulate Acrobat 4.** If you use the Acrobat file format to send to your commercial printer, you might want to use this setting. This is the "traditional" CMYK-based color management default. If you have no intention to print images to a commercial press, do *not* use this option.

- **Emulate Photoshop 4.** Photoshop 4 was the last version of Photoshop that did not have any color management features. Internally, both Macintosh and Windows versions of Photoshop 4 (and earlier versions) used a working space based on the characteristics of a Macintosh monitor. Choose this preset if you are working with files created in early versions of Photoshop, files you used successfully in projects of that era, which you might need to reproduce. Choose this preset also when you are working with older graphics and DTP software that does not have color management features.

- **Europe Prepress Defaults, Japan Prepress Defaults, and U.S. Prepress Defaults.** Each of these three separate presets defines conditions suitable for common commercial press conditions of the specific region. These generic conditions are good as a starting point for creating a custom definition for the area of the world and the kinds of press/ink sets and paper conditions you typically use.

- **Photoshop 5 Default Spaces.** This preset lands your Photoshop working space back in the sRGB mode, which we tell you is only good for screen presentations and Web work. Make this your preset only if you did oodles of work in Photoshop 5, and you have no business that requires photographic realism when going to print.

- **Web Graphics Default.** The settings specified by this preset are optimal for creating graphics that will be viewed on the Web or on an intranet through ICC-aware Web browsers.

- **ColorSync Workflow (Macintosh OS only).** Choose this setting if you are using ColorSync version 3.0 or higher, and you are using the ColorSync Control Panel to choose profiles.

Working Spaces

The settings in the Working Spaces section of the Color Settings dialog box (shown as item 2 in Figure 2.7) determine which of the many ICC profiles is the default working space profile assigned to newly created files. It's critical to understand here that when you convert from—say RGB to CMYK—the resulting color space that the CMYK image is saved to is not necessarily the CMYK space you want. The image will default to the current CMYK working space in the Color Settings dialog box. Unless you have only one output device, and you've chosen the profile for that device in the Color Settings dialog box, you will get more accurate results by changing color mode using Image, Mode, Convert to Profile instead of depending on the Image, Mode colors listed in the main menu.

The Working Spaces section of the Color Settings dialog box contains four drop-down lists labeled RGB, CMYK, Gray, and Spot, respectively. The working space for each color mode is defined by the ICC profile you want to attach automatically to new documents that use the same color space: RGB, CMYK, Grayscale, or Multichannel.

When the Advanced Mode option is checked, the ICC profiles available at the system level are displayed. Those are the ones in the ColorSync folder (Macintosh) or Color folder (Windows). If you have loaded profiles in these locations and you need to access them, you should activate the Advanced Mode.

Choosing from the RGB Working Spaces Drop-Down List

When you click the down arrow to expose the choices offered by the RGB drop-down list, you may find a *huge* list of profiles from which to choose. The number of profiles in the RGB drop-down list depends on the number of RGB profiles loaded at the system level and whether the Advanced Mode is activated. If Advanced Mode is not activated, the list is rather short. The profiles are grouped into the following categories:

- **Custom.** (Available in Advanced Mode only.) At the top of the list is Custom RGB. If you choose this option, you can define your own custom RGB space. Unless you are an expert in color management trying to solve a particular problem, we strongly recommend that you avoid the potential masochism in creating your own RGB workspace. That said, the only reason ordinary Photoshop users might use this feature would be to create a profile for BruceRGB.

- **Load RGB and Save RGB.** (Available in Advanced Mode only.) These two commands are found in the second section of the drop-down list. Load RGB enables you to cruise your hard disks for an ICC profile that's not in the system-level Color folder; oddly, this is not an option when Advanced Mode is not checked. Photoshop can convert the monitor setup file (*.AMS) into an ICC profile if you save it by using the Save RGB command after you've loaded it with the Load RGB command. Save RGB will save any currently chosen RGB workspace profile to any location on your hard disk, which is handy when you need to share a custom profile with another Photoshop user.

- **Other.** This section contains any profile you've created with the Custom command but have not yet saved with the Save RGB command.

- **Monitor RGB.** This is a straightforward choice to use Adobe's sRGB space. Although the colors on your screen will look lush on your monitor and on the monitors of others who visit your site, it's a limited color space and not good for much other than Web graphics.

- **Standard Working Spaces.** This part of the list contains the profiles that are the best as default working spaces. Unless you are working under unusual conditions, you should choose one of the profiles in this section. The profiles are Adobe RGB (1998), Apple RGB, ColorMatch RGB, and sRGB IEC61966-2.1 (commonly referred to as sRGB).

  - **Adobe RGB (1998).** A good all-around RGB working space with a color gamut large enough to produce decent RGB or CMYK printed output. This is our recommendation as a default working space.

  - **Apple RGB.** A good working space if your finished work will be seen only on Macintosh OS monitors, or if you are using older software that is not capable of color management. This working space is used by the Emulate

Photoshop 4 preset. I use Apple RGB space on a Windows XP machine occasionally to work between Apple and Windows systems, for comparison's sake.

- **ColorMatch RGB.** A working space that corresponds to the color space of the Pressview monitor. A small color space, it is sometimes used for images that will be output to a CMYK commercial printing press. Many prepress experts prefer to use a larger space than this for print work.

- **sRGB IEC61966-2.1.** The working color space of choice for the creation of Web graphics. If you think you will use an image on the Web and also in print, choose Adobe RGB (1998) as your working space instead. sRGB is too narrow for print work, even on RGB inkjet printers.

Note

> **Mac's ColorSync RGB**   On the Macintosh, ColorSync RGB is also available as a standard working space. The actual working space used when Macintosh ColorSync is chosen depends on what you've chosen in the Apple ColorSync Control Panel.

- **More RGB Profiles.** (Available in Advanced Mode only.) The last section of the list contains all other RGB profiles available in your computer's system-level Color folders. You'll see all kinds of default device profiles for monitors, printers, scanners, and cameras, as well as profiles installed by RGB equipment you own. A few standard working spaces are listed here also: They include NTSC (1953) and PAL/SECAM,SMPTE-C, which refer to TV and video color spaces; CIE RGB and Wide Gamut RGB, which are both very wide, large color spaces that are *not* recommended unless you are working with files that are 16 bits per channel.

Adobe RGB (1998) is the best overall choice for working with or creating images that will output in a variety of ways. Logos, for example, typically are used in print, on the Web, in videos, and on product packaging. If you want to be able to set and forget your workspace profile, Adobe RGB (1998) is the one to choose because it is the most flexible workspace. If you want to tweak images from the moment the first pixel is laid down, you should choose one of the special-use profiles that will work best for your intended output.

Note

> **Meet BruceRGB**   One other standard RGB space, BruceRGB, is worth mentioning. Bruce Fraser, a prepress guru and writer, felt that Adobe RGB was too large a color space and that ColorMatch was too small for most prepress work. BruceRGB has become one of the accepted standard working spaces in the prepress world. Unfortunately, Adobe doesn't install the BruceRGB profile along with the other standard RGB working spaces. You can use the Custom RGB feature described earlier, however, to create this profile. To obtain the values, you must enter them in the Custom RGB dialog box to create the profile.

Choosing from the CMYK Working Spaces Drop-Down List

The profile you choose in the CMYK drop-down list is the profile that will be applied to new CMYK images you create. You should be aware that what you specify as your default working CMYK space is also the default space when you use the View menu's proofing feature. Unless a custom proofing space is specified, the default CMYK working space is used for the soft-proof view, even when the image being proofed is an RGB image or has a different CMYK working space. The structure of the drop-down list parallels that of the RGB list:

- **Custom.** When you click on the CMYK Custom option, you'll see a dialog box that will be familiar if you ever looked at or changed the CMYK settings in Photoshop 5.5. If you need to tweak the settings of an existing profile or create one of your own, this is the place to do it. But if you are trying to re-create a custom setting you created and saved in an earlier version of Photoshop, it's easier to use the Load CMYK and Save CMYK options instead.

- **Load CMYK and Save CMYK.** Use these two commands to load new ICC profiles you may have obtained, or to load CMYK Setup files (*.API) or Separation Setup files (*.ASP) you may have created in previous versions of Photoshop. Use Save CMYK to save a loaded ICC profile to disk or to convert and save a CMYK Setup file or Separation Setup file you've loaded to the now-standard *ICC profile* that Photoshop CS uses.

- **Other.** This section contains any profile you've created with the Custom command and have not yet saved with the Save CMYK command.

- **Standard CMYK Work Spaces.** This section contains the profiles you'll use most. These standard profiles were designed to describe the colors that can be printed using various kinds of presses and papers under print conditions typical in the U.S., Europe, and Japan. You should choose for your default the profile that matches the CMYK press conditions you most often use. If you are working with files from Photoshop 4 or earlier, or files that will be used in older publishing programs that are not capable of color management, you may prefer to choose a standard profile—the Photoshop 4 Default CMYK or Photoshop 5 Default CMYK profile—from the next section on the list instead. On the Macintosh, ColorSync CMYK is also available as a standard working space. The actual working space used when Macintosh ColorSync is chosen depends on what you've chosen in the Apple ColorSync Control Panel.

  Generally, the CMYK ICC profile you use for soft-proofing would be the same one you use for conversion from RGB or LAB to CMYK.

Choosing from the Gray Working Spaces Drop-Down List

By now you've surely (and correctly) guessed that the Gray drop-down is used to specify which profile is used by default with grayscale images. This one has a twist: It has a few custom commands:

- **Custom Dot Gain.** (Available in Advanced Mode only.) Choose this command to display the Custom Dot Gain dialog box, where you can enter values or click points and drag on the curve to create a profile that matches the way dot gain occurs at different halftone percentage points when printed. *Dot gain* is the amount by which a printed halftone dot increases or decreases in size when the ink, dye, toner, or other pigment is applied to the printed surface. To determine how to construct the curve, you should use a densitometer to take readings from a gradient bar that actually used the same inks, media, and output device you will ultimately use. For example, if the densitometer produces a reading of 16% when it reads the 10% portion of the gradient tint bar, you would type **16** in the 10% field of the Custom Dot Gain dialog box. If you do not have access to test prints, ask the folks who run the press which values you should use.

- **Custom Gamma.** (Available in Advanced Mode only.) With this command you can create a profile for grayscale images that mimics their display on a monitor that has a custom gamma setting. Gamma determines the contrast of the midtones in an image. If you want to use a profile that reflects the gamma settings for Macintosh and Windows monitors, use either the Gray Gamma 1.8 or 2.2 settings at the bottom of the list.

- **Load Gray and Save Gray.** (Available in Advanced Mode only.) Use these commands to load custom gray ICC profiles you may have obtained but that are not installed, or to save a custom setting you've created.

- **Other.** This section contains any profile you've created with the Custom command but have not yet saved with the Save Gray command.

- **Standard Gray Working Spaces.** The balance of the list contains standard profiles that reflect dot gains of 10, 15, 20, 25, and 30%. Typically, you obtain this sort of information by asking the pressman who is familiar with the (device-dependent) physical printing press. This dialog box section also contains standard profiles called Gray Gamma 1.8 and Gray Gamma 2.2. Gray Gamma 1.8 mimics the default gamma of a Macintosh OS monitor and also corresponds to the default grayscale setting used in Photoshop 4 and earlier versions. Gray Gamma 2.2 corresponds to the default gamma of a Windows OS monitor. Choose the default setting that most closely matches the behavior of your most common grayscale output.

2

Choosing from the Spot Working Spaces Drop-Down List

The default choice you make in the Spot working spaces drop-down list differs from the others in that it governs the way spot color channels and duotones display. These profiles are the only ones that are not attached to files themselves, as you would embed other types of profiles in saved files. The choices here are identical to those offered in the Gray Working Spaces drop-down, except that Custom Gamma and the two Gray Gamma choices are not available here. You create custom dot gain profiles and choose between standard default profiles based on the same information and concerns you would for dot gain in the Gray Working Spaces. If the system-level Color folder holds custom Grayscale ICC profiles, another section (the custom Grayscale set) will appear after the Standard set.

Color Management Policies

The default working spaces profiles you just went through apply primarily to newly created files. But what happens when you open a file that doesn't have a color management profile attached to it, or that has a different working space profile attached to it than the default profile you've selected? Similarly, what happens when you cut from and paste into images that have different working spaces? The Color Management Policies section in the Color Settings dialog box (see item 3 in Figure 2.7) takes care of situations in which profiles are mismatched. Adobe calls the actions taken by Photoshop to reconcile color mismatches and missing profiles the *Color Management Policies*.

Each of the three drop-down lists—RGB, CMYK, and Gray—offers the same three Color Management Policy options:

- **Off.** This setting doesn't exactly mean no color management at all. It means that an ICC working space will *not* be assigned to newly created files. This is not to say that the working spaces you have designated are not affecting the soft-proofing capabilities while working on a newly created file in Photoshop. Very large gamut RGB working spaces usually create printed output that is prone to excessive clipping, so a choice here other than Off might be the solution when you aren't happy with the output.

  Off also means that profiles attached to documents that are opened will be ignored, and they will be discarded if they do not match the default working space. On the other hand, if the profile of the opened document matches the current default profile, the profile will be preserved.

  And Off means that when part or all of an image is pasted into another image, the colors will be added based on their absolute numeric value.

Note

> **Perception versus numerical value in color conversion**   When the numerical value of a color takes precedence in determining how colors are translated from one color space to another, the perceived color often changes, and many observers would not think it a faithful translation. The reason is that the perceived color of inks and dyes is greatly affected by the surface to which they are applied. For example, when a numerically specified color (RGB 97, 176, 224) is applied to newsprint, it appears darker and duller than the same color printed on glossy coated cover stock.
>
> When the perceived appearance takes precedence over the numerical value of a color, the goal is to create a color that appears to be the same on newsprint as on cover stock, even though the actual ink or combination of inks used is wildly different. Maintaining perceptual color fidelity is very important when you are working with corporate colors or most photographic material.

- **Preserve Embedded Profiles.** This Color Management Policy means that profiles attached to open documents are used and preserved. When material from one file is copied into another and the working space profiles of the two do not match, this policy attempts to maintain perceptual color values when the receiving image is an RGB or grayscale image, and will use absolute numeric color values when the receiving image is a CMYK image.

- **Convert to Working.** When this policy is in effect, the default behavior is to convert all opened images to the current working color space regardless of whether they have a profile attached. Additionally, when image data is copied from one file into another, the appearance of the color always takes precedence, regardless of the color mode of either image.

We recommend that you use the Preserve Embedded Profiles Color Management Policy for all three color modes. You can always change the profile that is attached to an image, but we believe that is a decision you should make consciously and not have happen on a default basis.

Second Guessing Default Color Management Policies

The default policies are useful but they are not always what you really want to have happen. For this reason, Adobe has provided you with the option of asking Photoshop to notify you whenever a mismatch occurs between image profiles when documents are opened or created, and when you open an image that doesn't have a profile. We recommend that you always keep the Profile Mismatches and Missing Profiles options checked so that you are able to make these critical color decisions.

Having Photoshop notify you of mismatches or missing profiles when you open a document is a good idea if your workflow has only a few workstations and the artist is trained to make such choices. In a high-volume workflow with many workstations, how-ever, such on-the-spot decision making can really slow things down.

Advanced Color Settings Options

We've now covered all the Color Settings options that Adobe thinks most people need to make. But other options are available in the Color Settings dialog box. If the Advanced Mode option in the upper-left corner of the dialog box is checked, the dialog box expands to reveal *additional* important color management settings. Even if you don't want to change these default settings, you should read on because the choices offered in the section on Conversion Intents are those you are asked to make when you convert an image's profile, when you choose a custom soft-proofing profile, and when you assign a print profile.

Check the Advanced Mode option in the Color Settings dialog box if it is not already checked, and then let's move on to the next section.

Conversion Options: Which Engine to Use

Now we'll look at the Conversion Options section of the Color Settings dialog box (item 4 in Figure 2.7). The default color management engine used in new Adobe products is ACE (*Adobe Color Engine*). Windows 2000 and XP users can choose to use the Microsoft ICM engine instead of Adobe's engine, and Macintosh users can use the ColorSync engine instead, if they prefer. All three engines are similar because all three are based on Linotype AG's LinoColor Color Management System.

At first glance, the Adobe engine provided in all new Adobe products seems like a great choice because having the same engine available on both Macintosh and Windows makes trading files between the two operating systems entirely compatible. But because the Adobe ACE engine can be accessed only by Adobe products, you might not want to use Adobe's color management engine. Color management engines really should belong to the operating system so they are available to *all* programs that use color management.

In the ideal world, we'd all be 125 pounds, blonde, rich, never flame a jerk in a news-group…and only one color management engine would be used, and it would work exactly the same on any operating system. But we haven't reached—and are not likely ever to find ourselves in—such a world. Unless you count Hollywood as a "world."

So what engine should you use? Use the one that is used by the most people who will handle the file. If you, your colleagues, clients, service bureaus, and printers use only Windows ME or higher, choose the Microsoft ICM system; if everyone in the chain uses Macintosh OS systems, choose the ColorSync engine. If your files move across platforms now, or may in the future, your best bet is probably to choose the Adobe ACE engine because Adobe graphics products are the leading products on both platforms and the ACE engine works identically on both platforms. What you want to strive for is *consistency*. For the purposes of this book, we will assume that you are using the Adobe ACE engine.

Conversion Intents

Intent, in the context of color management, is not exactly what it sounds like. It does *not* mean what your plans are. Instead, it asks, "What overall rules do you want to use when you're moving an image from one color gamut to another?" Whenever you change the profile an image uses, the color management engine must somehow decide how the numbers that define the colors are changed, or how the interpretation of those numbers changes to fit within the confines of the new profile. Exactly how this conversion takes place is governed by the source and destination profiles. When the source and destination profiles are created, they usually are assigned a default rendering intent. This default intent can be overridden by applications capable of designating rendering intent, like Photoshop.

Four intents have been defined by the ICC: *Perceptual* (sometimes called Image), *Saturation* (sometimes called Graphic), *Absolute Colorimetric*, and *Relative Colorimetric*. These four intents are used by all color management engines. Only one of the four intents can be applied during a conversion, but any one of the four could be specified. Which rendering intent you choose as the default intent depends on which qualities of your original image you want to preserve during a color transformation from one gamut to another. As mentioned earlier, it is important to understand what these intents do because you are asked to choose an intent whenever you convert an image's color space, when you choose a custom soft-proofing profile, and when you assign a print profile. A brief description of each of the four intents follows.

Perceptual Intent

Perceptual intent is usually the best choice for working with photographic images. When Perceptual is chosen, the white points of the source and the destination color spaces are matched to each other. Then all the colors in the source space are shifted to new color values that maintain the original relative difference between colors. This means that the actual color values (the numbers) are changed in a way that preserves the overall look of the image rather than preserving the actual colors.

Because photographic and photorealistic images most often are moved from a large RGB editing working space to a smaller RGB or CMYK printing space, either source colors have to be clipped, or the gamut of colors needs to be compressed. The Perceptual intent avoids having to clip colors, which would result in loss of image detail, by desaturating the colors in common between both spaces. Desaturating the common colors produces the room needed to assign color slots to colors that would otherwise be clipped. Consequently, using Perceptual rendering *sacrifices* absolute color fidelity to preserve detail and the overall look of the image. Perceptual's strategy of using desaturation works particularly well for photographic images that are making the large-to-small color space transition because the human eye doesn't notice the desaturation of colors as much as it notices color clipping or posterization.

When images are being converted the other way around, from a small color gamut to a destination with a larger color gamut, the Perceptual intent would not be the best choice for a photograph or photorealistic image. Because almost all the colors will fit within the new, larger space, desaturation of common colors is no longer necessary to avoid excessive loss of detail due to clipping. Consequently, conversions of photographic and continuous tone images from smaller to larger color spaces usually turn out better if the Relative Colorimetric is chosen for the conversion intent.

It is also important to note, since Perceptual intent maintains the relationships between colors by remapping most, if not all, colors in an image by compressing them to fit into the new gamut, Perceptual would not be the correct choice when the destination gamut is very small—a flexographic newsprint press, for example. In that instance, it would be better to take the clipping hit and try to remap manually the colors that have turned to mud.

Saturation Intent

Saturation is a good intent to choose for images in which the actual color (hue) is not as important as the purity or distinctiveness of the color. The Saturation intent is most often used for business graphics, such as bar graphs, pie charts, and presentation graphics. These kinds of graphics typically don't require precise color matching; rather, they need non-subtle, easily distinguishable color that makes reading data easy or that doesn't wash out when projected. The rules inherent in the Saturation intent essentially tell the conversion process to focus on producing distinctive colors rather than maintaining an exact color specification. The Saturation intent is also good for re-creating psychedelic posters of the 1960s and for producing cartoons.

Absolute Colorimetric Intent

Absolute Colorimetric is the conversion intent most often used when the most important goal is to ensure that as many colors as possible in the source image are matched exactly in the destination image. Colors that cannot be matched exactly in the destination space will be clipped. White points in the source and the destination color gamuts are not matched.

Color clipping (total saturation of an area in an attempt to render a specific color) will occur during a move from a profile with a large color gamut to a profile with a smaller color gamut, but the colors that do fall within the output gamut are faithfully preserved. When a color is clipped, it is generally moved to the edge of the new gamut, which generally translates as "muddy." Clipping can also take several dissimilar colors and assign them to the same color in the new gamut. With the power of preview soft-proofing, the artist has the opportunity to manually remap those colors that will be clipped before the change occurs. This intent is the best one to use when you are working with corporate logos, spot colors, or other specific colors that must be used in an image.

Relative Colorimetric Intent

Relative Colorimetric intent is our pick for best overall choice, and we're sorry if we made you muddle through the other options—but to be a Photoshop guru, ya gotta know this stuff. Relative Colorimetric intent maps the white point (the hottest point in an image—absolute white) of the source profile to that of the destination profile and then shifts all the colors so that they maintain the same relative position to the white point. Source colors that fall out of gamut in the destination profile's color space are clipped (changed to the nearest color in gamut). Resorting to clipping colors (reducing the number of unique colors) instead of preserving the absolute number of different colors by desaturating some of them is what makes Relative Colorimetric intent different from Perceptual intent.

Relative Colorimetric intent is a good choice if the destination space is capable of producing almost all the colors or if you have done a lot of tweaking to bring colors into the destination's gamut. Examples of this would be if you turned on gamut warning and then used color correction techniques to bring the color used in the image into the CMYK gamut, or if you used only Web-safe colors when creating the image. You should base your default rendering intent on the nature of the images you work with and the kind of output to which these images typically are sent.

The Conversion Options section of the Color Settings dialog box contains two other options, which we'll look at next.

Black Point Compensation

The tonal range of an image is determined by the number of intermediate grays the image contains between pure white (the white point) and pure black (the black point). ICC profiles have rules that govern how and when white points are matched to each other when conversions take place, but surprisingly, they don't have rules about how black points should be matched. When black points are not considered during an image's color space conversion, the translation between color spaces does *not* always look as good as it should or would if the black points had been evaluated. Adobe has developed a fudge factor, called *black point compensation*, that evaluates source and destination black points and then makes corrections to help ensure that the blacks in the converted file aren't blocked in or washed out. But like most workarounds, it doesn't suit all situations. The rule of thumb commonly used is that the Use Black Point Compensation option should be enabled when you're converting an image from RGB to CMYK or from one CMYK profile to another, and that it should not be enabled when you're converting from one RGB space to another.

2

> **Note**
>
> **Controlling contrast**   The human eye is more sensitive to tonal changes in the low end of the spectrum than it is to changes approaching the white point. This is another reason it is important to control the contrast of darker tones.

Black point compensation should also be avoided when the conversion from RGB has a destination gamut in which the paper and inks used have a low black density, such as CMYK newsprint, which has a washed-out black.

Use Dither (8-Bit per Channel Images)

Dither refers to a process (dithering) that uses different colored dots, shapes placed close to each other, or patterns made up of different colors, to fool the viewer's eye into seeing a color that is not actually there. When small specks of colors are intermingled, the brain blends the viewed colors together and interprets them as the color that would be produced if the colors were actually mixed together. This phenomenon of human vision is what makes both the painting style of Pointillism and CMYK halftone printing work. Activating the Use Dither (8-bit per channel) option enables profile-conversion processes to use dithering to reduce the perceived amount of banding that is caused by color clipping. This is a good option to use, but it will increase file size and make file compression techniques less effective.

Advanced Controls

The last set of options in the Color Settings dialog box is Advanced Controls, consisting of Desaturate Monitor Colors By and Blend RGB Colors Using Gamma (item 5 in Figure 2.7). Adobe recommends that only advanced users use the first option, but we're not sure that it is useful even for advanced users. Desaturating the monitor colors by a user-definable percentage could, if you have a really good imagination, give you a general idea of what colors that cannot be displayed on the monitor might look like when output. The second option, Blend RGB Colors Using Gamma, is more useful than desaturating your monitor, but only if a specific image will be created and output from Photoshop. The default gamma setting of 1.0 for this option produces slightly better color choices on the edges of sharp color transition in RGB images. You probably shouldn't bother to enable either of these options.

Wow! We've looked at *all* the options in this dialog box. You might want to recalibrate your *eyeballs* now! The only other thing to do is to click the Save button to save a color settings file if you've made changes that aren't the preset color settings files. And that, Fellow Photoshoppist, brings us back to where we were before we started looking at the settings in this dialog box.

Choosing Between Assigning and Converting to Profile

Although you have specified the default color settings and set the Color Management Policies in the Color Settings dialog box, it is not the only place where you can assign profiles to images. The Image, Mode menu is another. It has two very important entries, Assign Profile and Convert to Profile, that perform very different functions. And it is *quite* important that you understand the difference.

When we look at an image we've created and saved, it is irresistible not to imagine that an *actual* image of some sort exists inside the file image—a cyber version of a photographic print. In actuality, the image is just a bunch of numbers that represent the individual flecks (pixels) of color. Photoshop reads these numbers, figures out what to do with them in terms of color, and then puts them onscreen. Our eyes and our brain then take in all the bits of color and decide what they represent, what they look like. Is it a representation of a loved one or just a splash of color?

Some of the rules Photoshop uses to figure out what to do with the numbers it finds in image files are found within Photoshop's own program code. This part of the process of making an image out of numbers is out of Photoshop users' hands. It reflects the logic, decisions, and preferences of the programmers who wrote the Photoshop application. If a CMS is used, Photoshop's actions are guided and modified by an additional set of rules: the rules laid out in ICC profiles that are used in concert with the image. You decide which profile rules are associated with an image file.

Assigned Profile

Photoshop uses ICC profiles in two ways. It looks to an *assigned profile* for instructions on how to interpret or change the numbers in the file. Assigning a profile to an image tells Photoshop how to interpret the numbers in an image file. When you use the Image, Mode, Assign Profile command to assign to an image a profile other than the default one you designated in the Color Settings dialog box, you are telling Photoshop to look at the numbers as though they had been changed to fit the requirements of some other color space. But the numbers, the data in the file, have not really changed.

An assigned profile instructs Photoshop how to *interpret* the numbers. The assigned profile is similar to a statement that might be associated with or assigned to this paragraph, a statement that says, "The groups of letters that form this paragraph are to be thought of as being English words that are arranged in a way that makes sense to English language readers. Additionally, if any modification (editing) takes place, interpret that in the same way you interpret the original paragraph."

But a new profile could be assigned to take the place of the first one; the new one could say to interpret the groups of letters in the paragraph according to the rules and grammar of the German language. This new interpretation might not be very pleasing or be the best way to interpret the current order and grouping of the letters, but it would let you know how much or little of the intended communication would be understood if "output" to a German language speaker. In both cases, the only things that change are the *interpretation* instructions (assigned profile), and not the actual letters, their grouping, or their sequence.

Changing an assigned profile is a game of "what if…." What would this data, these colors, look like if they were transferred to another color space? The color space could be anything for which you have an ICC profile—another monitor, a television, an Epson inkjet print, an HP inkjet print, a press using newspaper, or a Matchprint.

This is the important point to remember: Assigned profiles tell Photoshop and other color management–aware programs how to *interpret* the data.

But sometimes you want to *change the data*, not just its interpretation. To use the English-German analogy, sometimes we want to change the letters and their order, translate the data so that it is useful in another context, so that the paragraph makes sense to a German reader. In color management terms, that means that the data within the file, the *numbers themselves*, must be *changed*. The way that is done is covered in the next section.

Insider

> **Changing Your View**   Dr. Alvy Smith, who founded PIXAR and is partially responsible for inventing the HSB color model, has a profundity that would seem to fit right in here:
>
> > Change your *view* of the data before you change the data.
>
> In other words, when you change your view, and you've been shown plenty of examples of how to change image view, you are not disrupting original data. Nor are you making the potentially false presumption that your monitor is calibrated perfectly and the system of the person who did the artwork was off.
>
> When you make *physical* changes to image data, you can almost never get back to the original's content. It's kinda like a turnstile in a subway station: Try exiting from a turnstile that is used for entrance. Manipulating the colors in an image, similarly, is a one-way trip. Choose to change your view as a first, second, and third measure for viewing a file accurately.

Using Profiles to Change the Color Mode of an Image

As stated before, profiles are sets of rules, definitions of color spaces, which programs use to interpret color data. But profiles are also used to provide some of the rules on how to actually *change the data* in the file to make all the colors fit within a particular color space. The intent—Perceptual, Saturation, Absolute Colorimetric, or Relative Colorimetric—chosen for the conversion also provides rules to guide the conversion process.

To continue with the English-German language analogy, a bilingual person who acts as the translator (the CMS) would look at the letters (the numerical color data), consult the rules of the German language (the destination profile) and the German language dialect that is desired (the intent), and then change the letters (the data) so that the data would actually be transformed from something that could be *translated* into German—to something *already written* in German.

If you want to permanently change the data in an image file, use the Convert to Profile command on the Image, Mode menu. Read the previous sentence out loud once or twice; it is an *important* concept.

This is not the only way to change the data in an image file. Photoshop users have been changing file data for years whenever they changed an image's color mode, from RGB to CMYK, for example. You still can go the traditional route, using the Color commands at the top of the Image, Mode menu, but you will give up the ability to fine-tune the process. When you use the Convert to Profile command, you choose which ICC RGB profile or which ICC CMYK profile you want to use. The traditional color mode commands use the default ICC profile settings you set in the Color Settings dialog box.

Note

> **Precise conversion**   Internally, Photoshop uses the LAB color model as the heart of the conversion engine when going from one Image, Mode to another. So, the conversions are still fairly good, but not as precise as choosing Convert to Profile.

Putting Theory into Practice

If your head hurts from trying to assimilate all this data, you're in good company (refer to Figure 2.1 again). Color management is *not* a topic to digest the first or even the second time around. But when the light bulb goes on in your head and you shout, "Eureka! I really understand how this works!" you will have moved a long way from hoping your print jobs go okay, to *knowing* what they will look like before you see the finished results. So let's put into action the concepts of color management we've discussed. We'll start by creating a custom Color Settings preset file and then practice assigning and converting profiles.

2

Creating a Custom Color Settings File

1. Launch Photoshop, if it is not already open.

2. Press Ctrl(⌘)+Shift+K to display the Color Settings dialog box. Make sure the Advanced Mode and Preview options are checked. Make the changes specified in the following four steps, if the options are not already set that way.

3. Set the RGB working space to Adobe RGB (1998); the CMYK working space to U.S. Web Coated (SWOP); the Gray and Spot working spaces to Dot Gain 20%.

4. Set all three Color Management Policies to Preserve Embedded Profiles. Check both Ask When Opening options and the Ask When Pasting options.

5. In the Conversion Options section, set the Engine to Adobe (ACE). Set the Intent to Relative Colorimetric. Check both the Use Black Point Compensation and the Use Dither options.

6. Make certain that the options in the Advanced Options section are not checked.

7. Click the Save button. In the Save dialog box that appears, use the Save In drop-down and other controls to navigate your way to the folder in which the other color setting files are saved, if you are not already there. Then type **IPCS** in the File name field, and click Save.

8. In the Color Settings Comment dialog box that appears, type something that describes these settings, such as **Set used for exercise in Inside Adobe Photoshop CS book, that definitive guide**—um, you get the picture. Click OK.

   IPCS now appears as the selected setting in the Settings drop-down list.

9. Click OK to put these settings into use.

You can now choose the IPCS set of custom settings just as you would the ones that Adobe provided.

Now that you have the IPCS defaults set, you will be sure to get the same results as we do in the exercises that follow. As promised, the next set of steps gives you hands-on experience with assigned profiles.

Color Management Policies in Action

1. Choose File, Open, and open Vision.tif from the Examples/Chap02 folder on the companion CD. This file has no profile attached, so a warning box should appear.

2. In the Missing Profile dialog box that appears (see Figure 2.8), choose the Assign Working RGB: Adobe RGB (1998) option. Click OK to open Vision.tif.

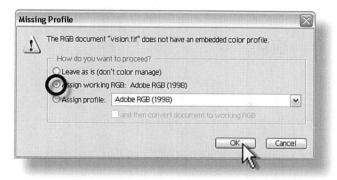

Figure 2.8   The Missing Profile dialog box appears when you open files to which a color management profile is not attached. Use its options to assign a profile.

Insider

You could choose any working space by selecting one from the drop-down list, but because you don't know which working space this file was created in, and you haven't decided on a use for this file, the best choice is to assign Adobe RGB (1998). If you knew this file would be used for Web use only, choosing sRGB would also be okay. Remember—at this point you are deciding only how Photoshop should *interpret* and show the file to you; you have *not changed* any of the numerical *data* in the file.

If you had chosen the third option, Assign Profile, and picked from the pop-up list the same profile as the default working profile *and* checked the "and then convert the document to working RGB" option, you would have done two things at once. You would have set the interpretation of the data to Adobe RGB (1998) and *changed* the data (the word *convert* is the clue) to data that fits in Adobe RGB (1998) space. If you chose to assign some other profile, you would have made your view of the file that of the assigned profile, but with the option checked, the data would have been converted to the working space profile Adobe RGB (1998). It is usually not a good idea to create a mismatch when you open a file; doing so distorts your view and can lead to unexpected color shifts when the assigned profile is eventually matched to the data profile.

3. Press Shift+Ctrl(⌘)+S to open the Save As dialog box. Note that toward the bottom of the dialog box, in the section labeled Color, the option ICC Profile: Adobe RGB (1998) is checked (see Figure 2.9).

Insider

If you leave this option checked, the profile you assigned and noted here will be embedded in the file. This will become the profile that always governs your view of the file until you either assign a new profile or convert to another profile. If you remove the check from the profile, the file will not be color managed. Until you close the file, however, your view of the file will be from the perspective of the Adobe RGB (1998) profile.

2

Figure 2.9   The Color section of the Save As dialog box has options for embedding profiles in images.

4. Find a place on your hard disk to save the file, and then click Save. In the TIFF Options dialog box under Image Compression, choose NONE, and choose the Byte order of your choice (PC or Macintosh). Do *not* check the Save Image Pyramid box. Click OK and leave the image open.

To recap, you've opened an image that did not have a color management profile attached to it and assigned a working profile to the file. You then embedded the profile in the file by saving the file to disk with the profile option checked. But how do you change the assigned profile for a file that already *has* a profile? In the next section, you'll seek out the rather obviously named Assign Profile command.

Changing the Assigned Profile

1. With Vision.tif open in Photoshop's workspace, choose Image, Mode from the menu. Note at the top of the Image menu that RGB is checked. From this section of the menu, you could change the file to an entirely different color mode, like Grayscale or CMYK, but you can't change to a different RGB color space.

2. Choose Assign Profile from the Image, Mode menu. In the Assign Profile dialog box that appears (see Figure 2.10), be sure the Preview option is checked. As you can see, this dialog box offers three choices: Don't Color Manage This

Document, Working RGB: Adobe RGB (1998), and a Profile drop-down list that contains the standard RGB working spaces as well as every other RGB profile that has been made available to the CMS.

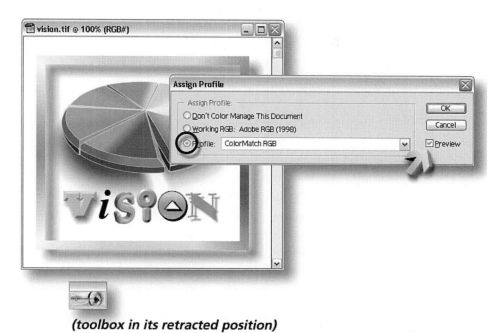

(toolbox in its retracted position)

Figure 2.10   With the Preview option checked, you can see how different assigned profiles would look.

3. Now let's see the effect on the document when we convert to a narrower color gamut such as CMYK. Click Cancel to close the dialog box without changing the Assigned profile. Go to the Image menu and choose Mode, CMYK Color. Notice that the colors in Vision.tif become duller: You've gone from a wide color gamut to a fairly narrow one, and the nuances of the Vision picture are being discarded. If you now choose Assign Profile from the Image, Mode menu, you will see that the Assigned profile in the dialog box is US Web Coated (SWOP) v2. This is what the file would look like in the editing window *if* you were to keep this profile. But remember, as long as you don't save these changes, you are changing only the interpretation, your *view* of the data, and not the data itself. (But this is what the data would look like if you *did* convert it.) Choose other profiles to see how they affect the view of Vision.tif. Then click Cancel to close the dialog box without changing the Assigned profile. Go to the File menu and choose Revert (to revert to the file settings when last saved). Again, notice the shift in colors as you return to the Adobe RGB (1998) color space. Leave Vision.tif open in the workspace.

Okay, let's say a client calls to say her company has decided it really wants to use the Vision.tif file on the Web, but that the company has decided not to use it for its print campaign. So you figure that now's the time to get this image prepped, and one of the first steps toward doing that is to move the file to the preferred color space of the Web, sRGB IEC61966-2.1. To move the file to that color space, you need to do more than simply change the assigned profile; you need to change the data in the file to ensure that all the colors in the image are within the smaller color space the Web uses. To change the data, you must convert the profile, and you'll see how to do that in the next set of steps.

2

Converting a Profile Means Changing the Data

1. Press Shift+Ctrl(⌘)+S to open the Save As dialog box. Choose the As a Copy option and then click Save. Because converting profiles involves changing the data, this is the right time to make a backup copy of Vision.tif. You or the client may change your mind at some point about the way you want to use this file.

2. With Vision.tif open in Photoshop's workspace, choose Image, Mode, Convert to Profile from the menu. The Convert to Profile dialog box opens (see Figure 2.11). Position the dialog box so that you can still see most, if not all, of Vision.tif, and make sure the Preview option is checked.

Insider

The Convert to Profile dialog box is divided into three sections. The first lists the profile of the Source Space. This corresponds to the working color space profile. In the middle section, Destination Space, you choose a profile that defines which color space and color mode the CMS will change the data to fit inside. The last section, Conversion Options, should look familiar; it involves options, such as Intent and color management engines, that you learned about earlier in the chapter.

3. Click the arrow next to the Profile drop-down list. Notice that in addition to the standard RGB color spaces you saw in the Assign Profile dialog box, this list includes profiles not only for RGB but also for other color modes.

4. Choose sRGB IEC61966-2.1 from the Profile drop-down list. Notice that the image got brighter, not duller as it did in the previous example, because the dialog box opens with a CMYK profile chosen, instead of the current working profile. And CMYK is always duller than RGB, and even sRGB.

5. While watching to see how the image changes or doesn't change, try each of the four rendering intents. You'll notice that for this image, little if any change occurs in the image preview when you change the rendering intent. For some images there would be noticeable changes.

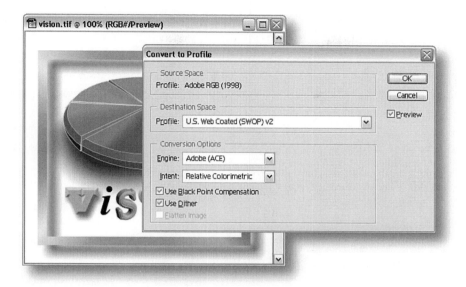

Figure 2.11   Use the Convert to Profile dialog box to convert from one color profile to another in the same color mode, or to one in an entirely different color mode. This is the preferred way to change from RGB to CMYK.

Insider

Based on the earlier discussion of Intents, Relative Colorimetric is probably the best choice. This is not a photograph, and with the full spectrum gradient at the edges, maintaining the white point, and then using absolute values where possible, this will most likely produce the best conversion of values.

6. Choose Relative Colorimetric from the Intent drop-down list. To see what will happen if you choose Relative Colorimetric, you can look at the preview if you have that option selected (see Figure 2.12). Leave the Engine option set at Adobe (ACE), leave Use Dither checked and uncheck Use Black Point Compensation. As mentioned in the Color Settings section of the chapter, the rule of thumb is to turn off Black Point Compensation when you're converting from one RGB profile to another.

7. Click OK. Press Alt(Opt)+Ctrl(⌘)+Z three times, pausing between clicks to see what effect the Convert to Profile has on the image colors. The shift in color is particularly noticeable in the greens. This is not surprising because Adobe RGB (1998) has a lot more greens in its color space than does sRGB IEC61966-2.1. By the third Step Backward, the image should be back in Adobe RGB (1998) mode; leave it there and leave the image open in Photoshop's workspace.

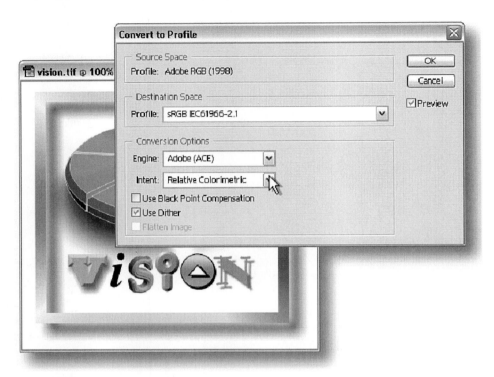

Figure 2.12   With the Preview option checked, you can see how different Intent choices change the look of the image.

Tip

Look to the status bar for clues   If you ever become confused as to which profile is currently the assigned profile, look at the bottom of the Photoshop interface (on the status bar). If you don't see a status bar, go to the Window menu and choose the Status Bar option. On this bar, you have access to information (including the current viewing magnification of a document in the lower-left corner). You'll also see a right-facing arrow (on this status bar). Click on the arrow and choose Document Profile from the context menu list, and the status bar will now display the currently assigned profile for the active document.

In fact, knowing that this information is available at your fingertips, you might want to consider choosing the option to "Leave as is (don't color manage)" when opening a document that prompts a Missing Profile dialog box to appear. By choosing not to color manage, you can then see what profile is assigned to the image (simply by observing the status bar). If you want to assign a different profile, you can still do so within the Photoshop interface. This method of waiting to change a color profile gives you more control over the results. Here's why: If you make a profile change when opening the document, there are no previews to see the effects of that change. But once the document is open, you can then access the Assign Profile dialog box within Photoshop, and with the Preview option selected, you can see (for yourself) the effects of any profile changes (as we have demonstrated in the exercises from this chapter).

Seeing how the image changes depending on which profile you assign or convert to might have given you the idea that whenever you want to see how a particular image will look when it's output to the Web or to print you could or should change the image profile. *Don't!* There is a much easier, safer, and more elegant way to do it. It's called *soft-proofing* an image. Read on, and you'll find that Adobe has tucked this time-, money-, and fingernail-saving feature in the View menu.

Soft-Proofing, or Seeing Onscreen What an Image Will Look Like When It's Printed

Because Adobe's soft-proofing feature is driven by ICC profiles, it is a very good idea to collect ICC profiles for every device you use in your work and for every output device your work will be sent to. Getting your local commercial printers to give you an ICC profile for their press, let alone for their press using the exact paper and ink you want to use, is next to impossible. What *is* possible is to get ICC profiles for traditional hard-proofing materials, such as Matchprints. Most printers will set up their presses to produce results that match the color of an agreed-upon hard-proof. What is also possible is to obtain the ICC profiles of the wonderful new inkjet printers that many folks are using for short-run printing.

Additionally, you already may have noticed that Adobe and your operating system have gifted you with generic ICC profiles for many proofing devices and conditions, as well as default ICC profiles for standard press conditions. Generic ICC profiles are never as precise as custom-made ICC profiles, which is why we showed you how to create a custom ICC profile for your monitor instead of using the default one. But using generic profiles with a CMS is better than not using any CMS at all. So hop on the Web, go to the manufacturers of the equipment you and your customers use, and download the profiles for the devices. It is worth your while to collect ICC profiles for some of the more popular inkjet printers made by Epson, HP, and others. If you don't own one of these printers now, you really should put it on your wish list. Install the profiles, and then move on to the next example.

Note

> **Printer profiles and paper color**   Most ICC printer profiles are based on a specific paper color, generally a neutral bright white.

Soft-Proofing and Color-Correcting an Image

1. Vision.tif should still be open in Photoshop's workspace. In the last example, we converted the profile associated with the image from Adobe RGB (1998) to sRGB IEC61966-2.1, and then used the Undo command to cancel the conversion of the data and the assignment of a new working profile.

2. Choose Window, Arrange, New Window for Vision.tif. A new window opens containing an additional view of the original image, not a new copy of the image. Arrange the two image windows so you can see each image.

3. Choose View, Proof Setup, Custom. In the Profile drop-down list, choose the profile for the inkjet printer you have installed. In the Intent drop-down list, leave the entry as Perceptual, check Use Black Point Compensation, and check Simulate: Paper White, as shown in Figure 2.13. Click OK.

Insider

If you don't have any inkjet or other desktop color printer profiles installed, use the Euroscale Coated profile.

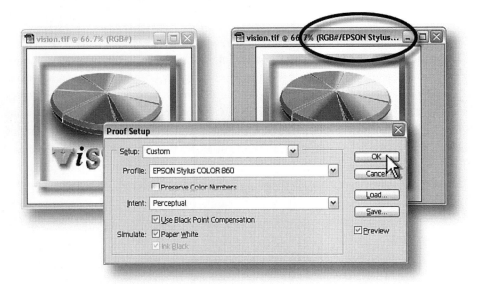

Figure 2.13   In the Proof Setup dialog box, choose the output device to which you want to print, and Photoshop will display the document more or less as it will print.

4. Notice that the title bar of the inactive window remains the same but that the active image title bar now reads RGB/Epson Stylus Color 860 (your title bar will read whatever you've loaded as a profile). The Epson Stylus Color 860 part corresponds to the Epson printer picked in step 3 and is your soft-proof view. Your title bar will probably say something different because you chose a different output profile. Notice also that the colors in the RGB/Epson Stylus Color 860 window are duller than in the original RGB window. The data hasn't changed; only your view has. Think of it as looking at the RGB/Epson Stylus Color 860 image with Epson glasses on.

Chances are 100% that the image in the soft-proof window is not everything you hoped it would be. The solution? Edit the image. Because these two windows are different views of the same image, any edits you make will be reflected in both windows. It doesn't matter which window is the active window when you make the edits. To improve this image for printing to the inkjet printer, move on to the next step.

5. Click the Create new fill or adjustment layer icon at the bottom of the Layers palette (fourth icon from the left). Choose Color Balance from the menu. The Color Balance dialog box appears. Drag it off to one side so you can see the images. Make sure the Preview option is checked.

The neutral background in the soft-proof window shows an unwanted color cast. Because you've most likely chosen a different printer to soft-proof to than we have, you may not have a color cast or it may be different from ours. Make your adjustments to suit your image. For the purposes of this example, we'll report what works according to our setup and what looks good to us.

Insider

Although you have set up and are using the CMS in Photoshop, you should not abandon the use of the Info palette for color feedback (correcting by the numbers). Your experience with your intended target device, combined with the Photoshop CMS, will yield better results than using either CMS or experience/Info palette alone.

6. Keep your eyes on the soft-proof window; that is the window you want to look good. The problem appears to be mostly in the midtones. Preserve Luminosity should be checked. Drag the Cyan slider toward Red (right) to a value of +7; drag the Magenta slider toward Green (right) to a value of +14; drag the Yellow slider toward Yellow (left) to a value of −3, as shown in Figure 2.14. Click OK.

Insider

Now the soft-proof window doesn't have a color cast, but the original window does. That is okay. An image often looks terrible onscreen but prints beautifully. That happens because the monitor and the printer have different color spaces. If you want good printed output, don't get hung up on how it looks onscreen in the working space. Pay attention to the soft-proof view.

2

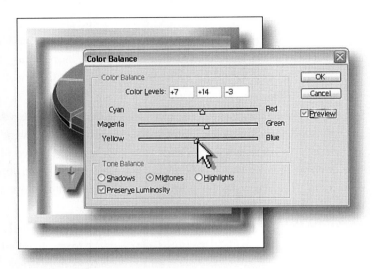

Figure 2.14   Use a Color Balance adjustment layer to remove an unwanted color cast that will develop when the image is printed to the inkjet.

7. Click the Create new fill or adjustment layer icon at the bottom of the Layers palette. Choose Levels from the menu. The image lacks punch because it doesn't really have a good white or black point. Drag the White point slider to around 226. Drag the Black point slider to around 13, and drag the Midpoint slider left to about 1.14, as shown in Figure 2.15. Click OK.

8. Take a good look at the preview window. If you like what you see, flatten the image by choosing Flatten Image from the Layers palette menu.

9. Choose File, Save As. In the File name field, enter **Vision for Inkjet**. Notice that the image still has the original profile listed in the Color section, and not the inkjet profile you proofed to. That happened because the proof view was a view, and not a conversion of the data to a new color space. You did change data when you edited, but it was changed in the context of the working space, not the proofing space of the inkjet. Click Save.

When it comes time to actually print the image to the inkjet printer to get the results you saw in the proof, you will want to change the data. You can do that by using the Convert to Profile command you experimented with in a previous example, or you can choose to do it as part of the print process. (We'll take a closer look at this route in Chapter 21, "Output," on custom halftone schemes.)

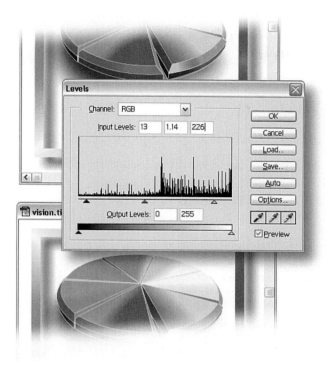

Figure 2.15   Use a Levels adjustment layer to create a better tonal range.

Bear in mind that while it takes fewer steps to specify the conversion from the print dialog boxes, you don't get a chance to preview the different Intent options. Consequently, we recommend that you use the Convert to Profile command to change the data in the image and assign the same profile you used for soft-proofing.

Summary

That's it! If you've followed along, you've just joined the ranks of color management specialists. And you probably need to focus on postcards of Hawaii to rest your eyes for a week or so. We realize that you may hold the title of designer a little closer to your heart than that of color management specialist, but it will look great on your résumé. It will signal to all that you are an artist who can produce work that can be counted on to look fabulous in any and every media.

Resources

`http://www.apple.com/colorsync/`

Apple's ColorSync site has a lot of information on its color management engine.

`http://www.cie.co.at/cie/`

Commission Internationale de L'Eclairage (CIE)

`http://www.inkjetmall.com/store/`

Inkjetmall.com, a division of the famous Cone Editions Press, is a great place to buy ICC profiles for Epson printers. These profiles not only profile the printer, but also specific paper and ink combinations. The site even offers a few free profiles.

`http://www.color.org`

International Color Consortium (ICC)

`http://search.microsoft.com/`

Microsoft has lots of information on color management available, but it is not neatly organized in one place. Your best bet is to do a search on its site, using the keywords "color management" or "ICC profiles."

`http://www.praxisoft.com`

Good information on color management is available on the Praxisoft site. The company also sells a reasonably priced (under $100) program called WiziWYG that can create good custom ICC profiles for your scanner and for printers.

`http://www.xrite.com/`

X-Rite, Inc., makes all kinds of hardware tools for measuring color and calibrating devices. Most of its solutions are rather high-end, very precise, and geared in price toward large, big-budget operations.

C h a p t e r   3

Setting Preferences, Customizing, and Optimizing Photoshop CS

Okay, so you needed a new set of wheels

and you picked this century's hottest car,

the BMW Mini Cooper S. This popular

auto mixes a little bit of the past and a little

of today's car style and engineering. But

In this chapter, you'll learn

- How to set Photoshop CS General preferences
- How to set Photoshop's File Handling preferences
- How to customize Display & Cursor settings
- How to choose Transparency & Gamut settings
- How to choose Units & Rulers settings
- How to set Guides, Grid & Slices preferences
- How to determine which screen elements will be hidden
- How to customize and allocate system resource usage
- How to use the Preset Manager
- How to group palettes
- How to customize the Shapes feature
- How to set up and use Brush presets
- How to copy and rename layers
- How to use the Tool Presets palette
- How to customize the assignment of keyboard shortcuts
- How to set Selection and Mask modes
- How to set up Photoshop's spell-checking feature
- How to use the Palette Well

3

wait, as long as you're spending half your trust fund, you might as well add a pair of fake fur cheetah fuzzy dice to the mirror. And your MP3 file collection on CDs deserves a Blaupunkt stereo system with JBL speakers.

Then you wake up. "What have I done?" you ask. The answer lies in this chapter's title (clever segue, huh?). You've just customized and specified preferences to an awesome piece of machinery. In this chapter, you learn to make the same kinds of "tweaks" to your installation of Photoshop CS. We're going to show you how to customize Photoshop so you can work with it more quickly (and with better results) than if you simply drove Photoshop CS right off the lot.

Photoshop CS has so many preferences from which to choose, you might want to set aside a whole afternoon with PS CS and this chapter.

Accessing Photoshop's Preferences Settings

The good news is that there's an entire menu of preferences in Photoshop; all you need to do to display it is press Ctrl(⌘)+K. The not-so-good news, however, is that some of the useful stuff on the Preferences menu is "logically opaque" (in other words, unfathomable) to beginners and even some intermediate users. So our best advice is to follow our lead about which preferences to select. We'll show you examples and perhaps a mini-tutorial or two, and then you can decide for yourself what you're going to hold and what you're going to fold.

In Photoshop, press Ctrl(⌘)+K now so you can get started on the following section.

General Preferences

The first page you come to in Photoshop Preferences relates to the broadest changes you can make. Photoshop's General Preferences settings determine how Photoshop displays, hides, or reveals things in the interface. The General Preferences page is shown in Figure 3.1. Let's take the tour.

Put your thumb or a paper clip on this page so you can refer to it as we proceed and illustrate some of the General Preferences choices.

Color Picker

The Color Picker appears when you click on the foreground/background color swatches on the toolbox. The Preferences dialog box enables you to choose from two options. We recommend selecting Adobe's Color Picker, shown as item a in Figure 3.2.

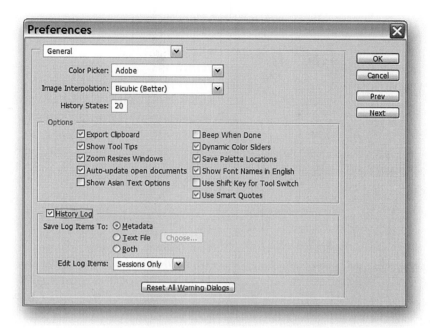

Figure 3.1   On the General Preferences page, you select settings that determine how elements are displayed in the Photoshop interface.

Why do we recommend Adobe's Color Picker? Because you can configure it in many different ways, and at least one is sure to fit your work style. In Figure 3.2, you can see the default Windows Color Picker and the Macintosh Color Picker. The Macintosh has a more robust selection of color modes for color choosing, but there is a flaw in its design: It specifies color components between 0 and 100% in RGB color mode, whereas Photoshop, most other programs, and Windows use the 0-to-255 increment. So you need to translate the values (and that means—ugh—*math*) to communicate color specifications to Photoshop users who use Adobe's Color Picker.

In contrast, Photoshop's Color Picker, as shown in Figure 3.3, supports the mapping of its color field by each component of four color models (RGB, LAB, CMYK, and HSB). For example, you can click on the *S* in the HSB area, and the color field changes its configuration. The Adobe Color Picker also supports more than a dozen color-matching specifications, including the legendary PANTONE. So when a client says, "Hobkins, I want the label on the can to be PANTONE 1485c," you can access the PANTONE collection of swatches by clicking on Custom in the Adobe Color Picker, typing the PANTONE number until it appears, and clicking on OK to use this color in an image window…and, while you're at it, tell the guy your name is not Hobkins.

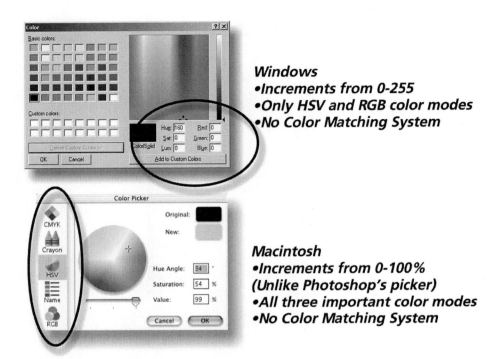

Windows
- **•Increments from 0-255**
- **•Only HSV and RGB color modes**
- **•No Color Matching System**

Macintosh
- **•Increments from 0-100%**
- **(Unlike Photoshop's picker)**
- **•All three important color modes**
- **•No Color Matching System**

Figure 3.2   Windows and Macintosh color picking choices are limited and are best used by applications whose programmers didn't feel like making a program Color Picker.

Okay, let's leaf back to Figure 3.1 and the General Preferences menu. Or better yet, why not sit in front of your computer, open Photoshop, press Ctrl(⌘)+K, and read along?

Image Interpolation

An easy way to remember what the Image Interpolation setting is all about is to remember the word *interpretation*. When you command Photoshop to stretch or shrink an image, it has to calculate (take a guess at—interpret) additional pixels to fit into the image, or it must decide which pixels to remove to make a smaller image.

Whether you are shrinking or stretching an image, it will have some detail loss because Photoshop has to make an estimate of the number of pixels to add or remove.

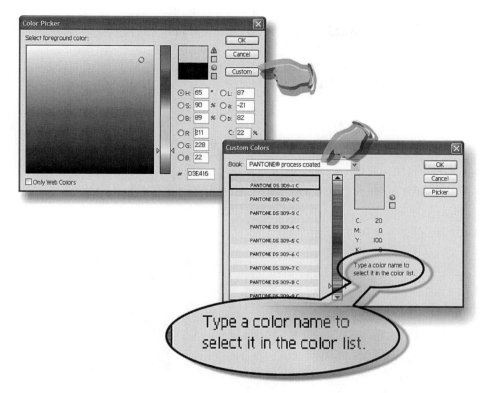

Figure 3.3   Many of your would-be clients will insist on exact color matching. And no program does it better than Photoshop.

Fortunately, Photoshop (and very few other applications) uses bicubic "guesstimating" when removing or adding pixels. This is the most accurate math method for evaluating which pixels go where. bicubic sampling searches across, up, down, and diagonally to the target pixel that's being added or deleted. The process then uses a weighted average of pixel colors to color in the new region if you're shrinking a file, or it creates new pixels using a weighted average if pixels need to be added to the new image. This means that if, say, the region of an image is primarily green, you can expect bicubic sampling to make the region mostly green, with a very minor color influence from only one or two pixels that are not green.

Bicubic Smoother is typically used when you want to scale an image up, and bicubic Sharper can be used when scaling an image down (making it smaller).

Your other choices are bilinear (Photoshop looks in only two directions for neighboring pixel colors) and Nearest Neighbor, which is not an interpolation method at all. Nearest Neighbor simply puts the neighboring color next to a pixel when an image is enlarged.

Nearest Neighbor is a phenomenally inaccurate choice for interpolation. However, if you need to increase the size of, for example, a screen capture of a palette (as we do in this book), Nearest Neighbor is terrific. The process simply makes the horizontal and vertical dimensions twice as large, resulting in an image area that's four times larger than the original—with no smoothing or averaging or fuzzy text.

To make this fairly lofty concept more "creative-person friendly," check out Figure 3.4. This dot has been resized using the three different choices.

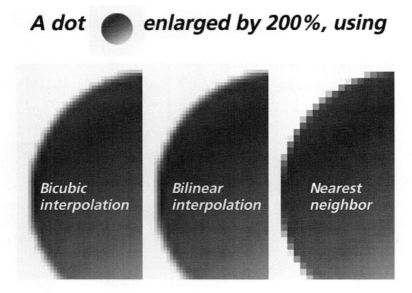

Figure 3.4   Stick with bicubic interpolation. Your new 6000MHz muscle machine with 1GB RAM can handle the calculations in a flash.

History States

The History States setting determines how many steps back in a file (how many undo times) you can tap into. Each History State requires a hunk of RAM to store the undo data, so the number of states you enable is a balancing act between how big a safety net you want and the amount of RAM you have installed on your computer. The default number of History States is 20. This means that you can undo the previous 20 commands or tool strokes you made. After you make your 21st command or stroke, the undo state for the first command or stroke is deleted to allow room to undo the most current command or tool stroke.

So, even though you would probably like to set this option to a thousand—*don't*. If you have 192MB of RAM installed on your computer (the minimum amount of RAM that

Photoshop requires to run), 10 is probably a reasonable setting for History States. If you have 256MB of RAM (the amount you *really* need to run Photoshop so you don't feel as though you're working underwater), 20 History States is a good figure. If you have lots and *lots* of RAM, you can probably bump up the number some. But whatever number you set for this option, if your system acts sluggish or if Photoshop pops up a warning that available memory is low, you probably have too many History States set. Besides, if you plan on making more than 20 mistakes at a time, you don't belong in Photoshop—you belong in government work.

Options

Ah, now we come to the Options settings in the General Preferences dialog box. Some of these options are useful features; others matter not a whit. Some commands are vestigial organs from a time when a Macintosh Classic or an i386sx was considered a fast machine.

Please take a look now at the preferences on your monitor; we are going to have you change some of the defaults:

- **Export Clipboard.** Yes, by all means. Now this means that you must also "flush" the Clipboard after you've pasted a Photoshop piece into a different application, because holding anything on the Clipboard takes up system resources. To perform Clipboard flushing, choose Edit, Purge, Clipboard from the main menu.

- **Show Tool Tips.** Um, these balloons that pop up when your cursor lingers over a toolbox icon aren't exactly tips. In other words, the pop-ups won't tell you nearly as much about a chosen tool as the status bar will (we recommend that you always have Window, Status Bar checked). What Tool Tips *will* do is name the tools on the toolbox for you, provide the shortcut key, and occasionally tell you what a button is supposed to do on the Options bar. We recommend leaving Tool Tips on for your first few months working with PS CS. As you memorize and familiarize, you may find the tips to be a distraction, so you can turn them off by unchecking the box.

- **Zoom Resizes Windows.** This sounds like a bizarre tabloid headline, doesn't it? Actually, you can zoom in and out of an image window in many ways. One of the first ways that experienced, ancient Photoshoppists like myself used to short-cut the zooming process (without using the toolbox tool) was to press Ctrl(⌘) and then press the plus and minus keys on the numerical keypad. We recommend that you keep this check box checked because it doesn't make much sense to zoom into an image and then have to resize the window. This option is your one-stop shop for image navigation.

- **Auto-update open documents.** If you are in a studio, or even working remotely over the Internet on a collaborative piece, you want to check this option. Why? Because PS CS's Workgroup feature enables several people to work with the same image. This capability is a boon to desktop publishing professionals because Larry in Seattle can be composing the page while Phil in Delphia can be color correcting the image. If you don't auto-update the file, you will not keep current with the revisions going on within your workgroup. Leave this one checked unless you run a standalone computer.

- **Show Asian Text Options.** There's really no reason for showing Asian text options unless you or someone you are collaborating with is Chinese, Japanese, or Korean. When this option is enabled, Asian text options appear on the Paragraph and Character palettes. Asian characters use a double-byte character system, whereas English and West European characters are single-byte in complexity.

- **Beep When Done.** This option causes you to run around the office making beeping sounds after you've finished an assignment. O*nnnnnnly* kidding! Actually, this is another vestigial organ in Photoshop. There was a time when you would apply a Gaussian blur to a 3MB image, and you had time to go out for lunch, get a haircut, and have your taxes done. And Photoshop's beep after a tediously long operation was welcome because it woke you up so that you could proceed with your editing. I personally have not heard Photoshop beep ever since processor speed increased to around 500MHz or so. Uncheck this option, and if you're a fan of beeping, drop your money on the ground at a drive-through that has a lot of folks behind you who are in a hurry. In addition to beeping, you'll learn some new words, too.

- **Dynamic Color Sliders.** Check this option. There's no way to get an accurate idea of the result of mixing colors on the Color palette without seeing how one component of a color affects the color range of a different component. This option doesn't slow you down at all, and watching the sliders change color is kinda fun.

- **Save Palette Locations.** Check this option unless several other people use your computer at work. With this option selected, the location of your palettes stays put after closing and rebooting Photoshop. (If other people use your computer, everyone can use the Window, Workspace, Save Workspace menu item so that each setup can be quickly accessed.)

- **Show Font Names in English.** Again, Chinese, Japanese, and Korean fonts are unlike your garden variety Georgia TrueType or Type 1 Garamond. If you want to use double-byte fonts such as these, and you were brought up with the alphanumeric system of Europe and the U.S., check this option. It'll make finding the font you need on your machine a lot easier.

- **Use Shift Key for Tool Switch.** This is a safety feature. If you do not check it, you can make mistakes in choosing tools if you're a keyboard kinda guy or gal. Unchecked, for example, pressing **G** will toggle the Bucket tool with the Gradient tool. Do you want this to happen? If not, check this option. Then tools assigned to that button will alternate only when you hold Shift and press **G**.

Tip

> **Toolbox shortcut keys**   My advice is that, when editing in Photoshop CS, you invest a moment to choose the tool you want to use from the toolbox. I'm not sold on memorizing toolbox keyboard shortcuts (there are *plenty* of other, more productive shortcuts in this program to memorize, believe me!), and the Use Shift Key for Tool Switch option will *not* activate a tool with no shortcut letter next to it in a group. For example, the only way to get to the Convert Point tool is to hold on the Pen tool until the flyout does its thing, and then you choose the Convert Point tool.

- **Use Smart Quotes.** This means that you can use *smart* quotes from people like Ben Franklin, Samuel Clemens, and John Cleese. Dumb quotes abound in our times…okay, I'm pulling your leg here. "Smart quotes" is a PlainTalk phrase for "typographer's quotes" or "Curly Quotes." If you check this option, the text you create in Photoshop will look more professional, and you will not have to look up the scan code (for example, a left typographer's quote in Windows requires that you remember, and type, **0147** while holding the Alt key). Wotta trial! Thank you, Adobe, and leave this option checked. (The only exception to this is the case in which you want to express something in inches. If that's the case, you need to turn off smart quotes and type the symbol ".)

History Log

History Log is a new and valuable feature if you need to record your edits. You have the option to save the list of edits in the image file as metadata, as an external text document, or both. This feature is especially useful in a training environment (because taking notes is no longer necessary) and in a collaborative setup when someone else needs to know any edits you have applied.

Photoshop offers three choices of what exactly to record. Sessions Only records when Photoshop is opened, when each file is opened and closed, and then when Photoshop is closed. If you need to track time, you'll love this option. Concise records the Sessions Only information and the edits listed in the History palette. Detailed records both the Sessions Only and Concise information, plus text that appears in the Actions palette.

Reset All Warning Dialogs

The Reset All Warning Dialogs option, the last in the General Preferences pane, is pretty self-explanatory. Photoshop has some warning dialog boxes, most of which have to do with color management profiles that you can prevent from displaying ever again by checking an option on the face of the dialog box. But if the dialog box never again shows its face, how are you ever going to get a chance to uncheck the option if you change your mind and want to be warned?

Simple: Press Ctrl(⌘)+K and click on the Reset All Warning Dialogs button at the bottom of the General Preferences dialog box.

And that's the end of the General Preferences settings. Congratulations! You just finished exploring the longest of the Preferences pages.

File Handling Preferences

You get to the next page of the Preferences dialog box by clicking the Next button. This page is all about file handling, as you see in Figure 3.5. The settings on this page handle how you create thumbnails of images, how you save TIFF and PSD files, and whether you want to collaborate with others in a workgroup using Version Que. Let's begin.

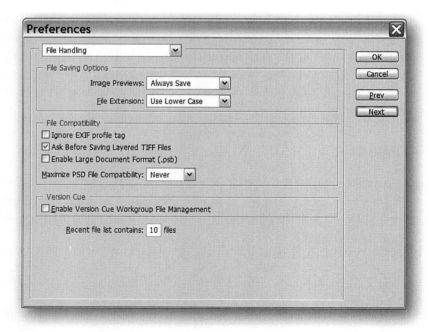

Figure 3.5   The File Handling Preferences dialog box.

File Saving Options

Image previews are miniature pictures of the actual image contained in a file. These miniature versions of the file are also sometimes called *thumbnails*. Image Previews is one area in Photoshop where operating system differences between Windows and Macintosh are evident. The biggest difference is that the Mac OS supports more image previews and that it does not, by default, use file extensions to indicate the kind of file or program that can be used to open the file.

The default setting for the Image Previews drop-down list, Always Save, is the setting we recommend you use. Your other choices are Never Save and Ask When Saving. These settings do exactly what they say. Saving an Image Preview is particularly useful for files saved in Photoshop's PSD file format. Photoshop PSD files, when saved with a preview image, show up as little thumbnails of the file on your desktop and in folders (when the viewing mode is Large Icons). If you choose the Always Save option, Photoshop's Open dialog box and File Browser will display thumbnails of all image files, which makes it very easy to spot the file you want to open.

File Extension, the next option in the File Saving Options area, allows you to choose the letter case of file extensions. Use Lower Case is the default. Unless you have an in-house rule that says all filenames have to be in uppercase, leave Use Lower Case selected. Who on earth wants a file extension shouting at them from a long list of files?

File Compatibility

The File Compatibility area of the Preferences dialog box contains four options. Top on the list is Ignore EXIF Profile Tag; when this option is selected, Photoshop disregards the information that digital cameras write to each picture file (camera settings, for example). Leaving this item unchecked preserves a lot of information that you might find useful later. Therefore, we recommend that you leave the Ignore EXIF Profile Tag option unchecked.

Ask Before Saving Layered TIFF Files, on the other hand, should be checked. Adobe is sort of hamstrung between still-image artists who want the TIFF format to remain the same as it's always been so that Photoshop users on both platforms can access an image in this format. Also, those who do not own Photoshop usually can view a TIFF. But the digital video industry has been pleading for a TIFF version that can contain layers since…well, since digital video editing has been around. For the user, you need to pay attention and not accidentally save a layered image to the TIFF format.

> **Tip**
>
> **Clean up those files!**   The problem caused by layers in a TIFF file you send to your client isn't the only headache you can cause with image files that can contain special features. Get rid of those paths in your image before you send it to press or for placement in a DTP (Desktop Publishing) document. Once we accidentally included a path that acted like a clipping path when we sent the TIFF to the printer!
>
> Learn from our mistakes, eh?

The third item in this section, Enable Large Document Format (.psb), enables you to save files in this new format that, at the time of this writing, only Photoshop CS supports. The PSB format can handle documents up to 300,000 pixels in both dimensions—almost a life-size image of Godzilla—plus up to 56 channels. If your machine has the RAM and you have the need for big monster images, you'll want to put a check in this field.

Ah, now for the last option in this section, Maximize PSD File Compatibility. Each new version of Photoshop comes with tons of new features. The downside to all the new features is that older versions of Photoshop, as well as other programs that can import Photoshop files, don't *know* about the features. At best, these programs will ignore stuff in the file that they don't understand (type layers, effect layers, layer sets, and so on). And, at worst, these programs may not be able to open the newer version Photoshop files at all. Backward-compatibility issues have always focused on Photoshop's native file format, PSD files. But now, because Adobe has enhanced the capability of the TIFF and PDF file formats, you need to watch out for backward-compatibility problems with files saved in these formats as well.

When this option is set to Always, extra information is saved along with the TIFF, PDF, and PSD images, creating flattened versions of the file. Doing so allows the programs that don't know about the latest version of Photoshop to open those files. Be aware, however, that saving this extra version of the file within the saved file increases the file's size noticeably.

It's really your call. Our recommendation is that if you are in an enterprise where there are many licenses for Photoshop, all different versions, you bite the bullet and use backward compatibility. But for small groups of users who all have version CS, why needlessly plump up the saved file size? Use the extra disk space for MP3 files!

Version Cue

Version Cue is the new workgroup feature and installs only with Adobe Creative Suite (refer to Figure 3.5). If you do not have Creative Suite installed and are working on a standalone computer, leave the Enable Version Cue Workgroup File Management option unchecked.

If you are in a workgroup and collaborate with others on an assignment across the room, on an intranet, or over the Internet, and Version Cue is installed, be sure to select this option.

Recent File List Contains

The Recent File List Contains option allows you to enter the number of recently used files you would like to have quick access to. These file titles will be listed in the File, Open Recent option. Most Windows applications have included this feature in the past, but now not only do both platforms have this option under the File menu, but you can also set the number of files you want to retrieve. Many of my programs limit me to the last four used files, but Photoshop CS will let you crank it up to the *last 30* used files!

You'll never lose your file on your hard disk again, even if you use the default of only 10 of your most recent files. This feature requires *no* additional memory usage.

The Macintosh File Handling Preferences Box

You have slightly different choices on the File Handling page of the Preferences dialog box on the Macintosh, so here's the scoop on the different options.

Image Previews

As with Windows, you have a choice of Always Save, Never Save, and Ask When Saving the image previews (see Figure 3.6), but there's also a sub-choice here. Do you want to save to Icon, Macintosh Thumbnail, Windows Thumbnail, and/or Full Size?

- Icon size displays the picture at 32×32 pixels on the desktop and in folder windows. This is a very sensible option to check and adds practically nothing to the saved file size.

- Macintosh or Windows Thumbnail size is the image you see in preview boxes. The image is larger than an icon thumbnail and smaller than a Winnebago. Check this option if you want the saved file size to be a little larger than the icon option but want to have an easier time previewing files before you load them. Your choice of Windows and/or (you can choose both) Macintosh thumbnail has to do with the final destination for the file. Are you a Macintosh user who sends work to a Windows service bureau? Then make your preview choice here.

- Full Size may seem redundant, but it's not. What we mean here is that some applications such as Quark can place and link at full page preview at 72 pixels/inch resolution. The actual picture might be the same size in inches, but its resolution could be something such as 266 pixels/inch. Yes, this option does, indeed, increase the size of your saved file significantly, but you will work more quickly in Quark when the on-page image links out to the 72 pixel/inch preview for display.

3

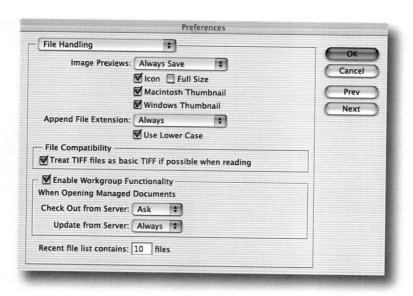

Figure 3.6   The Macintosh dialog box for File Saving Preferences contains options that are different from those in Windows.

Append File Extension

The choices in the Append File Extension option are Never, Ask When Saving, and Always. If you design for the Web, browsers insist on file extensions. Many, many Web servers use Unix as the operating system, and GIF, JPEG, and HTML files *must always* have the file extensions (*.gif, *.jpg, and *.html, respectively) appended to a document name for the server to successfully pass the correct image type to the visitor's browser. And even if there weren't a Web, multiplatform companies are out there, and sharing your work with Windows users is that much more difficult if neither of you know the file format.

The rest of the preferences are the same as in Windows, so we're essentially done with this Preferences box.

It's time to move on to the Display & Cursors page of the Preferences dialog box.

Setting Display & Cursors Preferences

The Display & Cursors page of the Preferences dialog box enables you to choose how cursors, image channels, and images themselves are presented onscreen. Look at Figure 3.7.

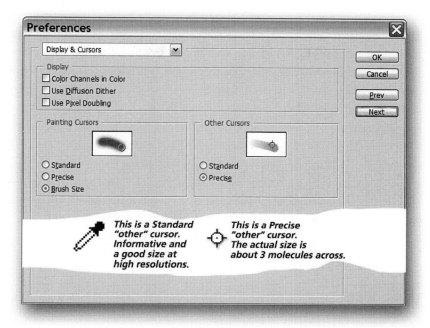

Figure 3.7   The Display & Cursors page of the Preferences dialog box.

Display

In the Display area, you can set three options:

- **Color Channels in Color.** We've been puzzling about this one for a long time and have concluded that to show, for example, a blue channel in shades of black and blue would simply be a visual reminder that you are working in the blue channel. We recommend that you turn this novelty *off* and work with color component channels in *grayscale* because this is the way color information is stored—as varying amounts of tones (grayscale): the whitest being full contribution of the component color to the color composite (RGB) image, while 100% black indicates no contribution. Additionally, you can easily lighten or darken the channel with a number of toolbox tools and commands to refine a component of an image.

- **Use Diffusion Dither.** This option applies only to users whose video card has something like 20KB of video memory—as well as to many laptop users. Seriously, you will almost never work on a system today that doesn't support 24-bit color, so you can leave this box unchecked. This option will dither images that are beyond the video capacity of your system settings for video.

- **Use Pixel Doubling.** Enable this? Not really, unless you want to view your movements on an image at half the image area's resolution. It's disconcerting to see an image area move at low resolution and then go to normal resolution after it's been moved. Today's processors usually remove any need for this fancy screen mapping while you edit.

Painting Cursors

In the Painting Cursors area (refer to Figure 3.7), you have three choices for the display of a painting cursor: Standard, Precise, and Brush Size. These cursors include the Brush cursor and the Clone Stamp tool—in other words, tools that apply paint, as opposed to editing, selection, annotation, and other cursors. We recommend the Brush Size option. This option shows you the outline of the tip of your current painting tool brush, which is darned handy when you have, say, a 300-pixel diameter brush defined; you can see exactly what you're going to hit and what you'll miss while editing an image.

Other Cursors

When you get around to choosing Other Cursors, we recommend you choose Standard cursors for two reasons. First, a Standard cursor will show you onscreen exactly which tool you are using; and with as many new tools as Photoshop has, this is a blessing. The callouts in Figure 3.7 show a magnified view of both cursors.

The second reason we recommend the Standard "other" cursor is that the Precise cursor is *small*, especially on 1,024×768 and higher screen resolutions. However, if you need pin-point accuracy to change a single pixel onscreen, you want the Precise (crosshair) cursor. And you know what? You don't have to come to this Preferences dialog box to access a Precise cursor for *any* tool. Simply press the Caps Lock key on your keyboard, and poof!—you've toggled to a Precise cursor.

Let's tackle the invisible now—Transparency & Gamut preferences. Click on Next. Onscreen, of course—not in this book.

Understanding How to Choose Transparency & Gamut Settings

It's funny, but the correct choice on the Transparency & Gamut page of the Preferences dialog box depends entirely on the color content of the image at hand. Figure 3.8 shows the Transparency & Gamut Preferences page. Transparency settings determine what the pattern is for areas that are transparent. In other words, a large pink and black checkerboard could be used to denote transparent regions in an image; so could small gray-on-white checkerboard patterns. The option is yours to make. Gamut (actually, "out of gamut") tells you where in an image the color threshold has been exceeded. In PlainSpeak, if an area is out of gamut, it contains color or a percentage of color that cannot be reproduced on paper.

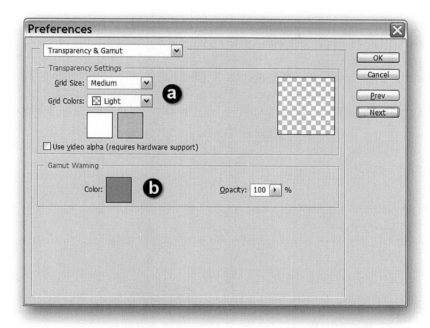

Figure 3.8   The Transparency & Gamut page of the Preferences dialog box.

The default Transparency Grid Colors setting is Light checkered. But, what if the image area you are editing has a light checker pattern to it? As you can see at the top of Figure 3.9, in that situation, the transparency default is about as worthwhile as going to sea in a tea strainer.

Note

> **The Video Alpha setting**   The Use Video Alpha option will probably interest only a small percentage of Photoshop users. If your video board enables images to be laid on top of a live video signal and you will be working with video in Photoshop, place a check in the Use Video Alpha box.

As far as the Gamut Warning color goes, if you want Photoshop to display a tinted overlay in areas in your image that cannot be faithfully reproduced in CMYK colors, you would usually press Ctrl(⌘)+Shift+Y or choose View, Gamut Warning. The default for this is gray at 100% opacity. So here's the obvious question now: How can you tell whether something's out of gamut if the original picture contains a lot of grays, as shown in Figure 3.9?

Figure 3.9   You must choose—and rechoose—colors for CMYK gamut saturation and for transparency design, depending on the specific image you are editing.

The default checkerboard transparency pattern does a fairly good job at helping you to determine the location of opaque pixels in the image. But you will inevitably run into situations in which a solid color does a better job at showing the transparent areas.

In the following set of steps, we'll demonstrate the problem of using a transparency color that is too close to the colors in the image and then show you how to fix it using four keystrokes:

Changing Transparency Display

1. Open the visible.psd image from the Examples\Chap03 folder on the companion CD. Zoom to the word *visible* in the image to do the editing.

2. Display the Layers palette by pressing F7 if necessary, and click on the Add Layer Mask icon (the icon is a circle within a rectangle, to the right of the *f* icon) on the bottom of the Layers palette.

3. Choose the Brush tool, choose the 20-pixel tip from the Options bar, and press **D** (default colors). If necessary, press **X** to make black the foreground color. Make sure Opacity is set to 100%, and then start hiding the image background by painting over it. Carefully work your way to the edge of the *v* in *visible*. Stop when you think you've trimmed around the outside edge of the *v* to see what you are supposed to be masking (see Figure 3.10). It's very hard to tell where the transparent background ends and the graphic begins, isn't it?

Figure 3.10   Add a layer mask, and then start painting around the *v* to remove the background.

4. Press Ctrl(⌘)+K, click the top drop-down list in the Preferences dialog box, and choose Transparency & Gamut.

5. Click on the foreground color swatch, choose green from the Color Picker, click on OK, and then click on the other swatch for the grid and make it the same color green, as shown in Figure 3.11. Click on OK to apply the changes.

6. Use the Zoom tool and zoom in to the area you are editing to 500%. Hold the spacebar and drag in the window until you see the area where you were editing, if needed (see Figure 3.12).

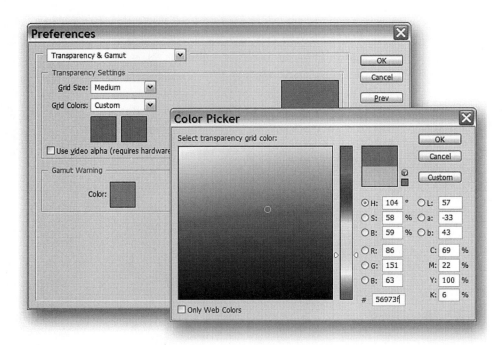

Figure 3.11   If you want a good view of the edges to mask in this image, choose a color not found in the image—a strong green.

Wow! There are unedited areas you didn't even see, aren't there? However, now that you've defined a different color transparency grid, you can accurately trim around the lettering. The Polygon Lasso tool helps you work around the straight edges.

The point's been made here, so you really don't need to completely edit around the lettering. But if you want the experience of working with the Brush tool, choose a tip that is two sizes smaller for going around the lettering. When the white background is completely gone, right-click (Macintosh: hold Ctrl and click) on the layer mask thumbnail, and choose Apply Layer Mask. For those of you who would like to return the swatches back to the default checkerboard colors in the Transparency & Gamut page, simply return to the dialog box, and use white for the first swatch (RGB values set to 255 each) and a pale gray for the second swatch (RGB values set to 203 each).

7. You can save visible.psd to your hard disk, or simply close it without saving. Keep Photoshop open.

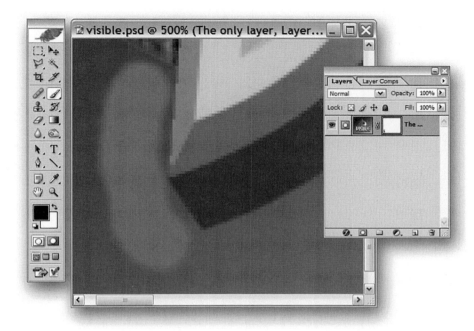

Figure 3.12   Well, oops. Your view of both the transparent regions and the foreground design are important to perform accurate masking.

Setting Units & Rulers Preferences

You can specify units for rulers two different ways in Photoshop. Whenever you press Ctrl(⌘)+R, rulers pop up to the left and top of the document window. Besides enabling you to measure things, the rulers are the only interface elements that enable you to drag guides from them (which means that if you need to place a guide, you need the rulers visible). The Units & Rulers Preferences page is shown in Figure 3.13.

> **Tip**
>
> **Units & Rulers Preferences**   To go directly to the Units & Rulers Preferences page, press Ctrl(⌘)+R to display the rulers, and then double-click on a ruler.

The Units area of the Units & Rulers Preferences dialog box includes settings that determine the Ruler and Type measurement units your screen will display. In the Rulers dropdown list, we suggest that you specify Pixels (unless you work somewhere that uses centimeters or picas), and choose Points for Type (and every once in a while picas). As you can see in Figure 3.13, you also can set the rulers to inches on the Info palette (press F8 if it's not already visible). A plus sign appears in the lower-left area of the Info palette, and if you click on it, a context menu allows you to quickly change the measurement increments.

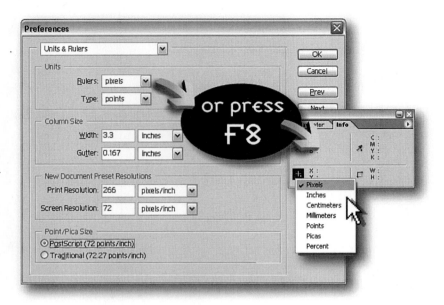

Figure 3.13   Make choices that make sense to your working methodology in the Units & Rulers Preferences dialog box.

In Figure 3.14, pixels have been chosen as the units of measurement. Every command that uses units of measurement, such as the Canvas Size command shown here, displays image attributes in pixels.

Why pixels and not inches for the rulers? Pixels are an absolute measurement, but inches depend on the resolution of the image file.

The settings in the Column Size area are for desktop publishing. You might change these settings, for example, when your client needs a photo that runs across the gutter or simply fits in one column. The gutter is set to inch values here although Photoshop ships with the default measurement of picas. We put these values in because they are the column and gutter width settings for a default PageMaker page. Hey, why not? For best results, get the specs from your client before goofing with the column and gutter distances.

Photoshop gives you the option of saving print and display settings you want to apply to all the images you create. You make these choices in the New Document Preset Resolutions area. Here, you can choose the print and screen resolution at which the image is printed and displayed. Here are our recommendations for these settings:

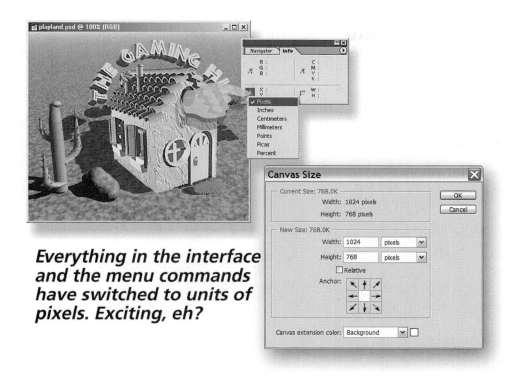

Figure 3.14   Your clients will give you "exotic" units of measurement. Trust us—you're equipped to handle that with the Units & Rulers Preferences dialog box.

- **Print Resolution.** The default for printing, 300ppi (pixels per inch, not dots per inch), is fanciful. Later in this book, we'll cover commercial printing and the math behind it. A coffee table book, a luxurious item, is printed at about 2,540 dots per inch. This translates to 266 pixels per inch for a 1-to-1 printing. Using 300 pixels per inch is too large a capture for most Photoshop users' needs.

- **Screen Resolution.** Although some Windows products, and Windows itself, set screen resolution at 96 pixels per inch, this is not the commonly adopted standard. It's 72 pixels per inch (which, comfortably, is the same measurement as a typeface point—72 per inch). Leave this setting at 72.

In the Point/Pica Size area, the PostScript (72 points/inch) setting should be checked. We are creating electronic documents and using PostScript technology in Photoshop, so the Traditional (72.27 points/inch) standard is not of use to us.

What do you say we check out the Guides, Grid & Slices Preferences next?

Checking Out the Guides, Grid & Slices Preferences

The settings on the Guides, Grid & Slices Preferences page, shown in Figure 3.15, control how guides, a grid, and HTML slice guidelines appear on an image in Photoshop.

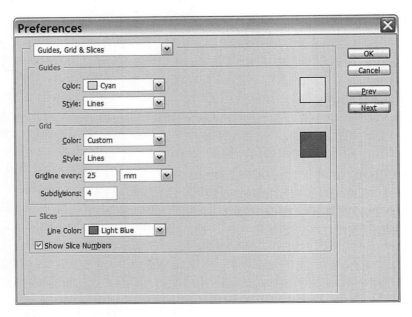

Figure 3.15   The Guides, Grid & Slices Preferences dialog box.

Here is some essential information about these features and the settings that control them:

- **Guides.** For those of you who are new to Photoshop, *guides* are non-printing screen elements that you pull out of rulers (press Ctrl(⌘)+R) to help you align vertical and horizontal elements. You can hide guides, but it's a better idea to put them back into the rulers—to avoid embarrassing presentations (or choose View, Clear Guides). Any tool can be used to pull guides out of the rulers; however, only the Move tool can be used to put 'em back.

  Guides were introduced in Photoshop 4 and are a big hit for users. The only possible gripe is that the default color of medium blue for guides is probably too dark for richly colored images. We suggest, at your discretion, that you click on the color swatch on the right side of the Guides area of the Guides, Grid & Slices Preferences page, take a ride to the Color Picker, and choose a lighter color.

  You are given a choice of either a solid line or a dashed line from the Style dropdown. Solid is the default because solid works best for most images.

- **Grid.** Again, the Photoshop Grid is another non-printing element that assists in accuracy and alignment of areas on layers and so on. You set the increments and subdivisions of the Grid in the Grid area of this Preferences page. Grid increments are set independently of the Units & Rulers specifications. (Can you imagine Units & Rulers getting into a fight with Guides, Grids & Slices?)

  We see nothing wrong with the conventional ruler layout for the Grid—a tick every inch with four subdivisions. It all depends on the way you work. If you work on the Web, for example, you might want to set the Gridline Every option to 10 pixels with, say, 5 subdivisions every tick to ensure precise Web media placement (the Web is one place where *every pixel* counts in design work).

  From the Style menu, you can choose Lines, Dashed Lines, or Dots. As we recommend for the Guides Style, Lines is most useful. Also, if needed, you can change the color of the grid by using the Color Picker to locate a color that contrasts the colors in your image.

- **Slices.** Slices are actual pieces of an image file that you create with the Slice tool. (You'll learn about slices and Web page creation in Part VII, "Working for the Web with ImageReady.") In the Slices area of this Preferences page, you can choose the color of the indicator of the slice boundary (again, non-printing and invisible on the Web). I find that electric orange works nicely with almost any image.

  The Show Slice Numbers setting gives you the option of showing the slice numbers. The numbers become part of the filenames of the slices, so it's probably a good idea to leave this option checked. Who knows; later you might decide to edit a slice of an image without the hassle of locating it or creating the sliced image a second time.

Getting Some Control Over Screen Appearances of Elements!

Okay, in terms of non-printing screen elements, we've covered the guides, the grid, and the slices. Coming up soon will be selection edges (affectionately known as *marching ants*), Target Paths (which involve using the Pen tools, discussed in Chapter 6, "Using the Pen Tools"), two gandarks, a swozzle, and a pnuph. Okay, I'm exaggerating toward the end there; however, it's not funny when you've ganged up a bunch of screen aids and want to hide them from view in one fell swoop.

Adobe calls these screen elements "extras." To choose which of these extras will appear on a screen near you, choose View, Show, Show Extras Options to display the dialog box shown in Figure 3.16. (The figure also shows the shortcut key you can use to hide these elements.) The Show Extras Options dialog box lists the screen elements that you can hide if you choose.

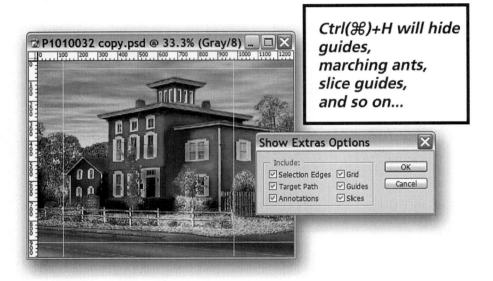

Figure 3.16   Uncheck the boxes of screen elements that are non-essential to your work. Elements that remain checked are displayed onscreen unless you turn them off by digging into the View menu.

If you uncheck an item, you cannot use the Ctrl(⌘)+H shortcut to hide and show extras. So we recommend that you leave checked every screen element you regularly use. Then a simple Ctrl(⌘)+H toggles the visibility and invisibility of the screen elements. Remember that by hiding a screen element, you are *not* deleting it; you're *hiding it from view.*

Let's hop over to Plug-Ins & Scratch Disks next.

Optimizing Photoshop's Performance with the Plug-Ins & Scratch Disks and Memory & Image Cache Preferences Settings

Photoshop handles memory very elegantly, but it doesn't know the memory and hard disk specs of your system. Therefore, the next two Preferences dialog boxes are where you find the *real* control—how to fine-tune Photoshop's performance. The following sections discuss the settings on the Plug-Ins & Scratch Disks Preferences page and the Memory & Image Cache Preferences pages.

Choosing Plug-Ins & Scratch Disks Preferences

The settings in the Scratch Disk area of the Plug-Ins & Scratch Disks Preferences page are probably as important in Photoshop as color settings are for the workspace. Photoshop needs hard disk space in which it saves history pieces, Clipboard pieces, multiple copies of an active file for Undo purposes, and more. If you do not give it enough hard disk space, your work could come to a grinding halt even with gigabytes of RAM on your system. The Plug-Ins & Scratch Disks Preferences page is shown in Figure 3.17.

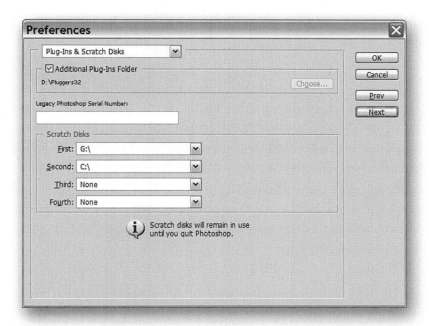

Figure 3.17   You can specify up to four temporary locations on your system's hard disk(s) where Photoshop can store parts of files, multiple undo images, and other things.

Let's get the trivial preferences here out of the way so that we can talk memory management with you:

- **Additional Plug-Ins Folder.** Plug-ins, those third-party enhancers from Alien Skin, Andromeda Software, and others can be installed to Photoshop's Plug-Ins directory. Now, here's the catch: What if you also own, say, Painter and want to use the same plug-ins in Painter? No problem. You create a folder on one of your drives, plunk your third-party plug-ins in the folder, and then point Photoshop toward this folder as an additional place to look for plug-ins. To do this, you need to check the Additional Plug-Ins Directory option and then specify the plug-ins location in the Browse for Folder dialog box that appears. This way,

Photoshop will go looking the next time you start it. Changes to folder locations for plug-ins don't take place until you restart Photoshop.

- **Legacy Photoshop Serial Number.** Some plug-ins will not work without a legitimate Photoshop serial number. Well, the sequencing of the registration number changed back with version 7 of Photoshop, and this might keep third-party plug-ins from working. So, put in your registration number from a previous version of Photoshop if your plug-ins aren't plugging in.

Okay, memory management…

Choosing Scratch Disks Preferences to Dole Out System Resources

New users might be surprised to learn that Photoshop doesn't use that nice hunk of temporary space you set away for applications to use. Nope, Photoshop wants its *own* space that no other application's going to touch while it is running—and it wants it to be as large as possible. Adobe, like virtually no other company, knows how to handle memory. This means where other applications might gag and crash handling a 40MB image file, Photoshop can do it—*if* you set up memory and scratch disk allocation the way it wants.

As a rule of thumb, Photoshop wants to work with three to five times the size of a saved image file. This means that if you are working on a 15MB file, you need to have 45 to 75MB free of both scratch disk space and physical RAM. If you have less scratch disk space than RAM, Photoshop will not use any more RAM than it has access to scratch disk space. Therefore, if you have 1GB of RAM and have assigned Photoshop 200MB of scratch disk space, Photoshop will use only 200MB of that huge RAM amount you have installed.

You can specify up to four scratch disks. In the Scratch Disks area of the Preferences page shown in Figure 3.17, you can see that I specified two drives for scratch disk space. When the hard disks were partitioned, drive G (the First drive) was created to be used only by Photoshop. Hard disks are cheap—image work is much larger than it used to be—and I felt that 3GB was plenty of room in which Photoshop could play. The Second drive, drive C, is simply a drive with a lot of room on it.

> **Tip**
>
> **Big recommendation here**   Windows ME and later versions defragment drives while you're not watching so that the drives are always optimized. This is not true on the Macintosh. Macintosh users should defragment and optimize their scratch disks regularly using a utility, such as those made by Symantec.

Beginning in 2002, both Windows and the Mac OS began to handle memory in similar ways. This means that the memory handling techniques you'll read about in the following section apply equally to Macintosh and Windows users.

Scratch Disk Assignment and RAM Requirements

Windows and the Macintosh dynamically resize the memory pool to allow applications to extend their use of RAM while you work. But it's still a good idea to devote hard disk space to as many drives as you can afford in the Plug-Ins & Scratch Disks page of the Preferences dialog box. Good candidates to which you can assign a scratch disk location are these:

- **A drive that has a lot of free space.** I've gone overboard with my own system, but even 1GB is not unreasonable, and naturally, you get this space back after you close Photoshop.

- **A drive that does not use a compression scheme.** Microsoft DriveSpace is *not* cool on the drive to which you assign the primary scratch disk. Compressed drives shouldn't even exist in 2004. Get a big hard disk instead of compressing.

- **A drive that has been defragmented.** As mentioned before, use the Disk Defragmenter utility to optimize any drive to which you assign scratch disk status if your OS doesn't have native clean-up features.

Your first choice should be the drive that happens to have the most free, uncompressed space. If you have any other drives that have a lot of free space, you can assign them as second, third, and fourth drives. Photoshop *honestly needs* this kind of hard drive space to enable you to work quickly and flawlessly. You might even want to rethink running other applications while Photoshop is loaded to give maximum memory support to Photoshop.

Warning

> **Don't put a scratch disk on your C drive**   It is not a good idea to put a scratch disk on your C drive. Not only is this usually the drive where your operating system is located, but it's also where temp folders for other applications are placed. If you attempt to dynamically resize a space on a drive on Windows that's been assigned as a scratch disk, you will have system problems.

If you look at the Preferences dialog box again and click Next now, you see the Memory & Image Cache settings.

Setting Memory & Image Cache Preferences

Cache setting for images helps speed up their display in the same way that caching on your system helps speed up display of frequently used screen areas. The default Cache Levels setting is 4, and we see no need to change this because it is a good trade-off between snappy display and overall system performance. The Memory & Image Cache Preferences page for a Windows system is shown in Figure 3.18.

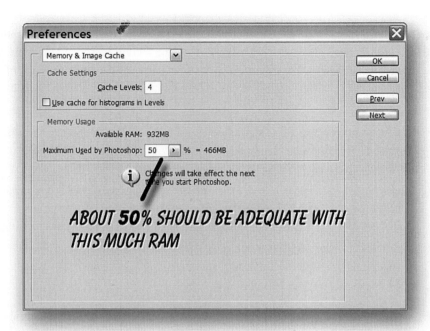

Figure 3.18   Set the Maximum memory used by Photoshop to at least 96MB; 128 is better; and 256MB is better still.

Use Cache for Image Histograms in Levels is not really a preference you want to choose. We recommend that you leave this option unchecked. Even if you have the system resources to dedicate to caching histogram information, caching is performed on a *sampling* of pixels in the image, instead of *all* the pixels in the image.

The Available RAM you dedicate to Photoshop depends on how much total RAM your machine has. As you can see in the Memory Usage area of the Preferences page shown in Figure 3.19, the Macintosh computer in this example has 384MB of RAM. Adobe suggests at least 128MB of RAM for Photoshop, so math tells us that, in this example, about 50% of available RAM can be used by Photoshop, with a matching amount of scratch disk space.

Note

Choosing the Efficiency display   If you click on the triangle on the status bar (Mac: on the bottom scrollbar) and choose Efficiency from the pop-up, you will be in constant touch with how much RAM Photoshop is actually using (the indicator will read 100%). You will also be able to see whether Photoshop is swapping out to hard disk. If the Efficiency drops to 58%, for example, you should (1) save and close the file, and/or simplify it by merging unused layers, and (2) buy more RAM!

Tip

> **System resources**   If, by chance, your editing work exceeds the RAM and scratch disk space, Photoshop will begin to swap in and out elements it needs to complete your work, and this really drags your system down.
>
> Also, you can set Maximum memory usage to 100%, but doing this is sort of a fairy tale. You aren't actually committing 100% of your system's resources to Photoshop; the Windows OS will not allow this. The OS needs resources of its own and will hang onto whatever it needs.
>
> Strong hint: Buy RAM, and keep a large space on one or more of your hard disks free.
>
> You actually decrease Photoshop efficiency as the RAM dedicated approaches 100%. This happens because the Windows system itself can use software caching, and Photoshop and Windows will fight over how much RAM is actually available.

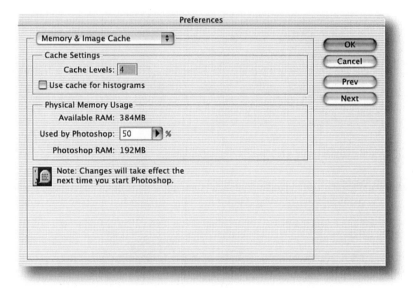

Figure 3.19   The Macintosh handles memory differently and much better for Photoshop users, with the introduction of OS X.

Let's move on to the next (and last) page in the Preferences, File Browser.

Choosing File Browser Preferences

The File Browser Preferences page, which is new in Photoshop CS, enables you to customize the functionality of the File Browser. The File Browser is very handy when you need to see thumbnails of the images within a particular folder, and it's especially useful if you need to sort through your images using keywords, for example. So, if you'll be using the File Browser, you'll want to understand your options on this Preferences page (see Figure 3.20).

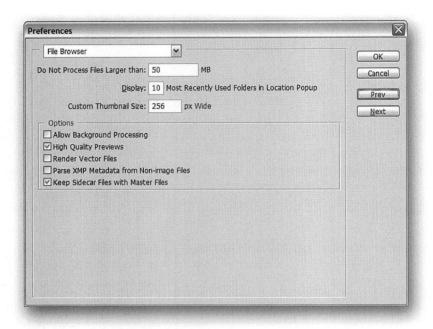

Figure 3.20   The File Browser Preferences page is new in Photoshop CS.

Check out the figure as we look at each of the options:

- **Do Not Process Files Larger Than.** The default value of 500MB is quite large. The File Browser processes and generates a thumbnail of each of the images in the folder that you point the Browser to open. The more images you have and the larger those images are, the more processing power—and time—required of Photoshop. If you have images that are in the three-digit MB range, you might want to enter a smaller number like 100 or even 50.

- **Display.** This option sets the number of most recently viewed folders that will appear in the Recent Folders section of the Location drop-down. You can enter any number from 0 to 30.

- **Custom Thumbnail Size.** The default setting, 256, is good for most users. However, you might find a smaller or larger size more practical for your use. For example, say you have your screen resolution set to 800×600 but would like to see more thumbnails at one time in the File Browser. You could type a value smaller than 256, such as 128, thus making the File Browser generate smaller thumbnails so that twice as many could fit in the Browser preview window.

Within the Options field, you can select the following check boxes:

- **Allow Background Processing.** Click to put a check in this box. The File Browser can be quite slow when processing a large number of files. So, unless you enjoy waiting for Photoshop to complete a task, having this item checked will speed up the process. Background processing employs extra processing power to pre-generate the cache information.

- **High Quality Previews.** Again, processing power and time are the concerns here. If you prefer high-quality thumbnails and have a fast machine, we recommend leaving the default check in this box. Otherwise, if your machine bogs down when the File Browser is generating the thumbnails, uncheck this item for faster processing.

- **Render Vector Files.** Check this item if you need to see vector image files, such as Illustrator files.

- **Parse XMP Metadata from Non-image Files.** With this option checked, the File Browser will show a thumbnail of non-image files, such as text files, and enable you to edit the metadata. Unless you have a need for this option, leave the check box unchecked. That way, if the folders where you are browsing contain any non-image files, you won't be wasting processing power and time generating thumbnails of those files.

- **Keep Sidecar Files with Master Files**. Photoshop gives you the choice of maintaining the photos of the passenger car of a motorcycle. Okay, not really. But maybe a brief explanation is needed here. A *sidecar file* is an .xmp or .thm file that is generated from another (master) file and is used to help other applications process the metadata associated with that master file. (For example, many digital cameras create a .tmb file when a TIFF file is created.) And because the File Browser enables you to move, delete, or copy files from within the browser window, you have a choice of whether you want those sidecar files to tag along with their master image file. We recommend that you check this box. After all, what good is a sidecar without a motorcycle?

Whew! Do you feel like you've been locked in a (Preferences) box for around a week? Okay, come out in the sunshine now. You've optimized all the base-level stuff in Photoshop, and now it's time to make your preferences in the *working space*. Make Photoshop's workspace truly your own.

More Choices and More Control with the Preset Manager

Photoshop CS is *just about* everything to everyone. This means that whatever type of graphics you are interested in creating, Photoshop's got your number, so to speak. However (and this is a BIG "however"), Photoshop sort of keeps things you might or might not need hanging out there in the interface. Additionally, there's some quasi-hidden stuff with which you should acquaint yourself.

Let's start with the master control panel for Photoshop's collections of neat stuff. Technically, it's called the Preset Manager.

The Preset Manager (Edit, Preset Manager) is your "one-stop shop" for accessing exactly what you need when you pick up a tool (see Figure 3.21). After you have displayed the Preset Manager, click the drop-down list (item 1) for Preset Type, and then choose from categories by clicking that tiny arrow button (circled in Figure 3.21). As you can see, you also can choose how the members of a category are presented on palettes (we recommend, for example, Small Thumbnail for the Brushes collection, at least for the default brushes).

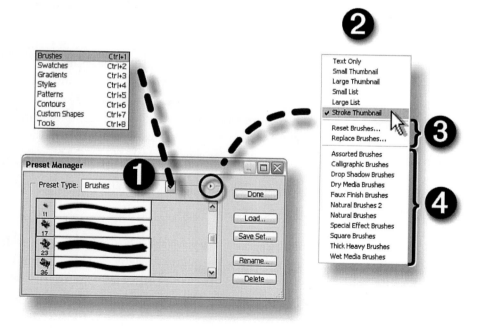

Figure 3.21   The Preset Manager gives you complete control over eight creative elements found within Photoshop.

To briefly explain a fairly intuitive selection process, follow the bouncing bullets in Figure 3.21:

1. Clicking the down button on the Preset Type field displays the eight types of palettes from which you can customize the appearance and choose from Photoshop's collection. Brushes have been chosen here.

2. Clicking the encircled icon in Figure 3.21 opens the menu for the Preset Manager. For the default brushes, you can get away with a Small Thumbnail display on the Brushes palette, but for exotic stuff such as the Wet Media brushes, you will probably want a Stroke Thumbnail display.

3. Here, you see the Reset Brushes and Replace Brushes. What's the diff'? Resetting the Brushes returns the Brushes palette to the "normal," round, hard, and soft-tipped brushes—ideal for image editing. Replacing the Brushes leads you to a directory box, where you must scout (needlessly) for a brushes palette file.

4. The items bracketed here are the reason you really don't need to use Replace Brushes (marked by bullet 3). You can find all of Photoshop's brushes' collections here. Now, if you or someone else has created a Brushes palette, you would either want to put the file in with the other Brushes files (in the Adobe Photoshop CS\Presets\Brushes folder) or go through the hassle of tracking down the file every time you want to use it. The choice is obvious, eh?

You can perform the same customizing with Styles, Patterns, and so on—and you do it all the way we've shown you with the Brushes palette.

Who Wants So Many Palettes in a Group?

As you've noticed if you've worked much with Photoshop, palettes are grouped such that Adobe considers to be a practical and logical way to work. If you like this arrangement, leave it, but you are not limited to keeping the palettes grouped in this way, don'cha know.

Our recommendation for a happier, less cluttered desktop is shown in Figure 3.22.

Allow us to explain the construction work going on in this figure:

*   The History palette is useful, but if you remember Ctrl(⌘)+Alt(Opt)+Z, this is the shortcut for a "History Backward" command. This means you don't really need the History palette in the Layers group; you can call it when you need it from the Window menu.

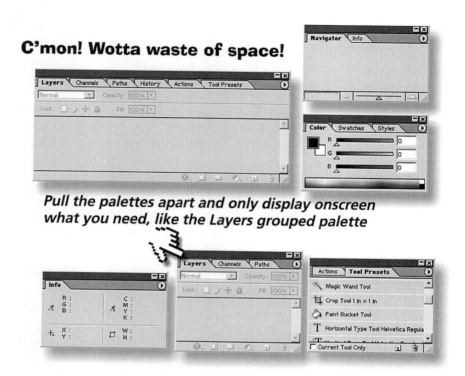

Figure 3.22   For 99% of your daily palette needs, simply remember F6, F7, and F8.

You click and hold on the title of a palette, and then drag to pull it free from a palette group. Conversely, you drop a palette on top of a group title bar to add it to the group.

- Actions and Tool Presets seem to work well together, and you don't need them onscreen all the time, so why not group them together and close the palette? Besides, you can access the Tool Presets from the Options bar (more on them later in this chapter—it's a wonnnnnnn-derful feature).

- The Navigator palette surely has to be about the least useful innovation as of Photoshop 4, but it's still around. Harsh criticism? No. You can use the Hand tool to bop around an image without the need for a palette, regardless of the image size. And you can zoom in and out, too…to replace what the Navigator palette does. Still, if you're attached to it, leave it together with the Info palette. I have the Info palette on my machine set up as a standalone group of one palette.

- Similarly, the Color, Swatches, and Styles fit together nicely. This is the default configuration; we suggest you leave it this way.

Terrific! Now, no grouped palette has more than three members, and they are configured logically. Here are the magic keys to make your workspace even more user-friendly:

- F6 toggles the Styles, Color, and Swatches palette on and off.

- F7 toggles the Layers, Channels, and Paths palette on and off. You will probably want this palette in the workspace all the time, however. The Options bar and the Layers/Channels/Paths palette account for around 85% of my design work.

- F8 toggles the Info palette on and off. This shortcut key is a very quick first step to changing the unit of measurement, as described earlier in this chapter. This palette can also be a very useful tool for RGB values while color correcting (see Chapter 12, "Curves and Adjustment Layers," for more examples of how this is done).

Wait. We're not done yet. More customizing ahead!

Customizing the Shapes Feature

Shapes were introduced way back in Photoshop 6. They are vector designs on a palette, and typically, you create a vector mask layer when you create a shape in an image window, as is being done in Figure 3.23. Don't worry about Shapes right now; they are covered in Chapter 4, "Layers and Channels." What we're doing here is showing you how to access different shapes.

Replace Shapes is selected in Figure 3.23. The reason? We've put some really inventive Shapes palettes on the companion CD, and to access them, you need to choose either the Replace Shapes or Load Shapes command. Then again, as you can see in the figure, Photoshop ships with a bunch of different shapes themes, which are listed at the bottom of the palette menu.

To try your hand using different shapes, do this: Click on the down arrow next to the Shapes icon on the Options bar. Then click on the menu flyout button and choose Replace Shapes. Navigate to the Examples\Chap03 folder on the companion CD. Click on Icons.csh, and then click on Load.

Open a new image window, and click on the Shape layers icon on the Options bar. Select a shape, and then marquee drag the shape in the image window (hold Shift to constrain proportions of the shape). Fun, eh? And best of all, shortly you'll learn how to make a shapes palette of your own.

If you click on the down arrow to the right of the Shapes icon, the Custom Shapes Options appear (see callout a in Figure 3.24). This dialog box enables you to choose options for the shapes you create. If you toggle off the link icon (callout b in the figure), whatever the shape allows to peek through under the layer will *not* move in sync if you choose to move the shape on the layer.

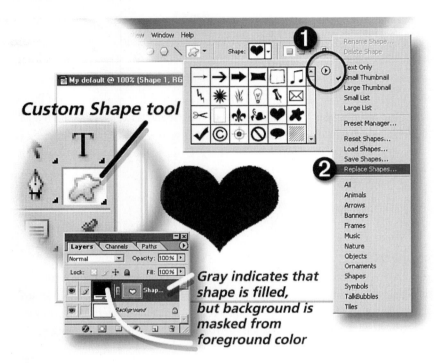

Figure 3.23   Choose the Custom Shape tool, and then on the Shapes palette, choose Replace Shapes.

Finally, callout c shows that no style has been chosen for the shape. A style is a combination of different effects that produce gem-like or stone-like qualities. With no style, what shows through the shape is the underlying foreground color. Double-click on the left thumbnail on the Layers palette, and you will see that you can change layer colors by making the change in the Color Picker.

Shape Styles and Their Components

In Figure 3.25, you can see that a shape has been given a style, specifically one of the Glass Button collection styles. All you do to add a style to a shape is click on the style icon; either select it from the drop-down palette on the Options bar or from the Styles palette (F6).

Why don't you create a shape now in a new image window? That way, you'll see what goes into a style.

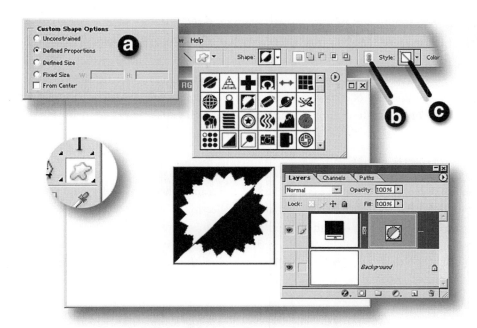

Figure 3.24   Use your own shapes with Photoshop's Shapes feature.

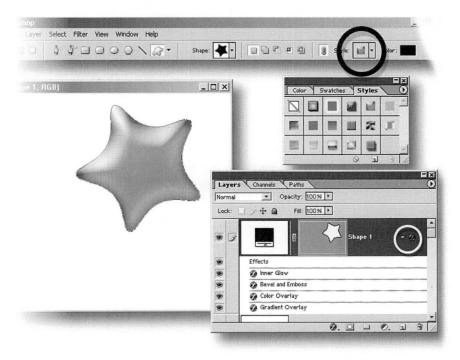

Figure 3.25   You can drag a style icon and drop it on top of a shape, or you can simply click on the style icon.

As you can see in Figure 3.25, a down arrow appears to the right of the Shape thumbnail on the Layers palette. Click on the triangle, and all the effects that go into making the current style are revealed to you. You can change any aspect of the style that has been applied by double-clicking on a style effect and then changing the default settings. Changing a component of a style applies only to what you added it to in the image window; a style on a palette cannot be changed unless you explicitly delete or otherwise modify the style.

Adding Your Own Shape to Photoshop

So far, we've touted the Shapes tools as the best thing since those wash-off tattoos; however, we didn't tell you that you, too, can make a collection of shapes and use them. Now, we assume that you have not read Chapter 6 yet, and therefore, you are not familiar with the Pen tool. That's okay; this chapter is on customizing. The working knowledge of tools comes later. But now, we're going to walk you through the process of using the Pen tool to create a simple shape, so you can learn how to add your custom shape to Photoshop CS.

Start by clicking on the Pen tool. Draw anything you like—a doodle is fine—and close the path by clicking on its origin point, the point you started with. If you're not familiar with the Pen tool, attempt a simple shape for now, such as a rectangle, by clicking at the points that make up the corners.

You can now add the shape to the current shapes palette in two easy steps:

1. Choose Edit, Define Custom Shape.
2. In the Shape Name dialog box, type the name of the shape, as shown in Figure 3.26. Done!

You might want to use the Blank.csh file in the Examples\Chap03 folder to populate a palette with your own designs. This palette has only one shape that you can delete after adding at least one of your own creations (palettes have to have at least one object).

If you're wishing now that you had the same control over defining brush tips as you do now with vector shapes, well, you *do!*

Come on—let's take a trip to the brush tip controls.

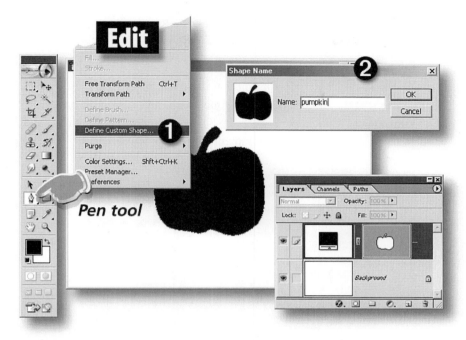

Figure 3.26   Creating a new shape on a Shapes palette is as easy as 1-2-3, without the 3.

Exploring Near-Infinite Brush Variations and Creating Custom Brushes

If the heading to this section were true, you would have to plod through a near-infinite chapter! Fortunately, we've collected for your enjoyment the really interesting variations-on-a-brush tips and presented them in this section. We've also provided you with only necessary explanations of the less-than-spectacular controls so you can go off and experiment on your own.

Levels of Brush-Building Complexity: Part I

You can dig into two areas with the Brushes controls; you need to be careful not to mistake the Brush Preset picker for the Brushes palette. The Brush Preset picker is the place where the saved brush tips are offered up for you to use. But when you want to truly customize a brush or build your own, the Brushes palette is "Shape Central." Without further diversions, let's look at how you can build one of your own brushes with the Brush Tip Shape controls—the less elaborate and confusing of the controls.

Here are the steps you need to create a unique tip for the Brush tool:

Creating a Custom Brush

1. Click on the menu icon on the Options bar (item a in Figure 3.27). A menu drops down into the workspace with way too much information for mere mortals to understand. Click on the Brush Tip Shape button to simplify things and avail yourself of only the tools you immediately need.

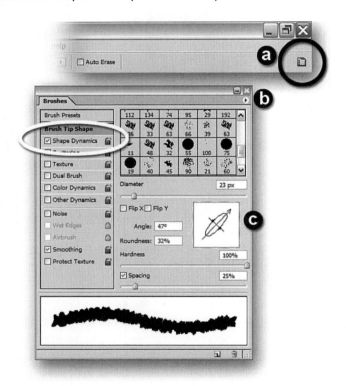

Figure 3.27   The Brush Tip Shape controls enable you to create a rudimentary custom brush that could be ideal for photo-retouching.

2. Round brushes are the staple of Photoshop; you can't retouch images without them. However, each round brush is based on an existing one, so click on the 19-pixel hard brush on the Brushes palette within this menu box. Then click on the arrow inside a circle at the top right of the menu (item b in Figure 3.27), and choose New Brush Preset from the flyout menu. If the Brushes palette is docked in the well, the arrow for this menu is located on the tab to the right of the Brushes tab title, or you can click on the Brushes tab and drag the palette away

from the Options bar to get a better look at the arrow location. When the Brush Name dialog box appears, name the new brush **23 Elliptical Hard** and press Enter (Return).

3. Drag the diameter slider over to the right so it reads 23 px, or type this number into the Diameter field and then press Enter (Return).

4. Drag one of the dots in the brush tip proxy box (near item c in Figure 3.27) closer to the center of the brush; the brush shape becomes elliptical. Don't worry about the Angle and Roundness fields; we're experimenting here, and if you want to be precise, you can always come back to these controls.

5. Drag the arrow in any direction you choose. As you can see in the preview window, a stroke will now become thicker or thinner depending on the direction in which you stroke.

6. We'll get to the Hardness slider in a moment. For now, leave it and the Spacing slider alone. You now have a new brush with the name you have given it at the end of the currently loaded Brushes palette. Keep Photoshop open; there's more in store.

It is important for you to understand—and I guess right now is a good time—that Photoshop has brush tips that fall into two different classes: those that are based on math (and can be squished and have hardness altered) and those that are built from a captured bitmap design. We haven't touched the bitmap sort yet, but we will soon. With both math-based and bitmap brush tips, you have the option of increasing Spacing. Spacing is the distance between one paint daub and the next. When you drag the Brush tool, you are actually making oodles of individual daubs that are spaced so closely together that it appears to be—and for all purposes, *is*—a continuous line.

You do not need a tutorial to walk you through Spacing, but you can take a moment and experiment on your own. Choose a small hard round tip, and increase the Spacing for it on the menu (see Figure 3.28 for an example). You'll see the continuous stroke break up into individual dots, and if you paint with the setting you've chosen, you can make a path of dots. Spacing is much more useful when the individual paint daubs represent something such as stars or other mini-designs on the Brushes palette. Painting with dots wears thin in the amusement department fairly quickly but could come in handy if you need to make a dotted line with evenly spaced dots.

The next set of steps will be the world's shortest tutorial because you will play with only one control—an important one—Hardness.

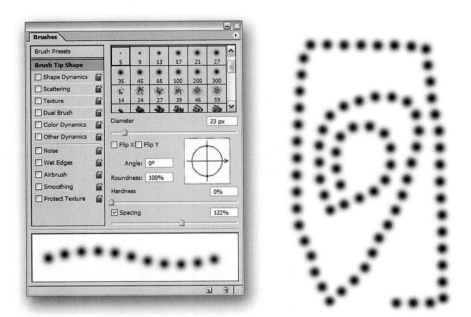

Figure 3.28   Spacing is the control that can break up a continuous stroke a brush makes into its components.

Using the Hardness Control

1. Click the 19-pixel hard tip brush on the palette, and choose New Brush Preset from the palette flyout menu. Name the brush **23 pixel soft tip, round**. Click on OK. Do not goof with the Angle and Roundness controls this time.

2. Drag the Hardness slider all the way to the left.

3. Check out the preview window at the bottom of the menu (see Figure 3.29).

4. You now have a small brush that is ideal for retouching using the Brush or other painting tool (such as the Clone Stamp tool). And let's face it—professional retouching requires a lot of subtlety, and a totally soft round brush is very hard to detect in a finished piece of retouching. It's a bit harder than the airbrush option, but softer than using the Pencil tool.

Tip

Changing brush tip size   At any time, you can change the size of your brush tip without leaving the scene of your retouching or designing efforts. Right-click (Macintosh: hold Ctrl and click) when a painting tool is chosen, and up pops the Brush Preset picker with a Master Diameter control at the top. A changed brush is not a saved brush, but you can save a setting very quickly by adding the configuration—even the present foreground color—to the Tool Preset picker, the top-left icon on the Options bar; then click on the page icon on the palette to save the tool as a preset.

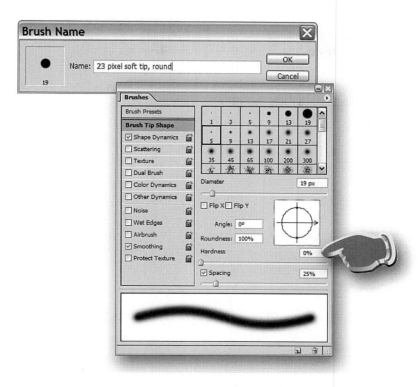

Figure 3.29   Create a soft brush of the diameter you like for special occasions such as image retouching.

So you say you want more control over brush tips? We hear you, and the following sections will take you on a (pleasant) roller coaster ride of options you can put at your mouse tip.

Tip

> **Using a digitizing tablet**   A digitizing tablet is really an enhancer to these new brushes in Photoshop. This type of tablet gives you more control than a point-and-click device, and Photoshop is able to recognize pressure-sensitive input, which means you'll get more work that appears genuinely hand-drawn. Hint: Wacom's Graphire 3 tablet and stylus come with Painter Classic, a wonderful graphics arsenal addition and frequently a helpful mate to Photoshop.

Using Brush Presets: A First Look

We're not going to dig too deeply in this section because *every* option on the Brushes palette has at least three sub-options. If you need a simple solution for the "round-tip, soft" blahs, however, this section will show you how just a few clicks can take you to an arresting new look for painting.

Let's do it in tutorial format, just because my publisher told me to:

Oh, Those Brush Presets

1. Click on the Brush Presets tab on the Brushes palette. Now, before we go changing stuff (not to worry—changes here are not permanent, although we'll discuss how to make permanent changes shortly), why don't you click on some of the weird new brush tips on the Brushes palette to see which properties suddenly have a check mark next to them.

2. Okay. Let's stop clowning around while we're learning. Click on the 19-pixel hard brush tip, and then draw a stroke on an empty canvas. Hmmm, round on both ends of the stroke and fairly unremarkable. Click on the Scattering check box, marked as item a in Figure 3.30. Now drag the brush. Wowee! The page looks like a marbles championship! Keep Figure 3.30 handy because we'll be referring to it for a few more steps.

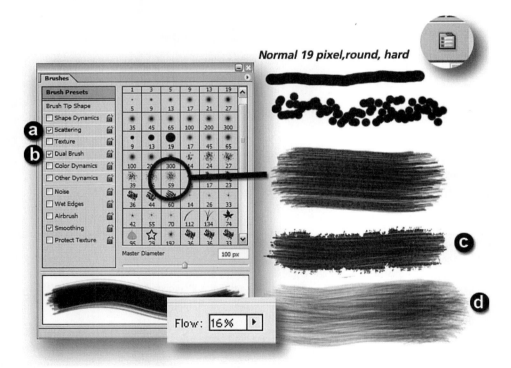

Figure 3.30   Permutations are piled upon permutations in the Brush Presets area. Chances are, you can design a brush tip no one has even thought of yet.

3. Choose the 59-pixel brush tip (circled in the figure) that looks like a splatter. Stroke it across the canvas. Pretty neat, huh? It looks like an actual, physical brush stroke. How can we improve its realism? Click on the Dual Brush check box (item b in the figure), and make a stroke (item c in the figure). Okay, perhaps this is not what you had in mind, but an explanation might help things here. Dual Brush means that all four sides of a brush stroke display the ends of the stroke—the unevenness, or whatever the effect of a particular brush tip may be. Not all brushes will make such a pronounced effect; in fact, round tip brushes are a total dud when used in combination with Dual Brush. Uncheck Dual Brush.

4. You can use a brush tip enhancer that isn't even in the Brushes menu: It's called Flow and it's on the Options bar. Crank Flow down to about 16%, as shown in Figure 3.30, and make a stroke with this 59-pixel splatter tip (item d in the figure). Now, you can see the hairs on the brush, and the stroke looks a lot more realistic.

Keep Photoshop open because we're really going to turn this customized brushes stuff on its ear in the following section.

Noise, Wet Edges, and Color Dynamics

In the steps that follow, you will experiment with far more interesting effects (although I'm sure you feel that the ones you've been using are already thrilling!). So, to pile superlative upon superlative before getting to the point, let's do some knock-out stuff:

More (and More Complex) Brush Presets

1. Get out a new, blank, white image window, or erase what you've been using. Choose the Brush tool and a 100-pixel, soft-edged tip from the palette, as marked by callout a in Figure 3.31.

2. Check the Noise check box (callout b in Figure 3.31), and make a brush stroke (callout c). Wild, eh? It looks like a horizontal cat's tail in a marsh, or something. This stroke is neither soft nor hard. Think about stroking a path using a brush this size or smaller.

Insider

Again, not all brush tips work as well as the one we've recommended here for the Noise filter. Soft edges produce the most attention-getting effect. If you still have the Flow set to 16% on the Options bar (from the last exercise), try a few brush strokes with it turned back up to 100%.

3

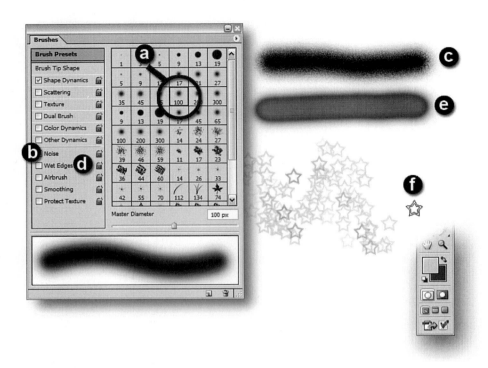

Figure 3.31   These are the Noise, Wet Edges, and Color Dynamics modifiers for brush tips.

3. Click in the Wet Edges check box (callout d in Figure 3.31). Make a stroke; it looks like finger painting, right? A visual example is marked e in the figure.

4. Color Dynamics is one of my favorite parameters. Choose the hollow star or the leaves tip from the Brushes palette, and then click on Color Dynamics to select it and view the options. Now set the Foreground/Background Jitter to a number greater than 0% (for example, try starting with 50%). Then set the color swatches on the toolbox to diametrically opposing colors. Green and blue will do. Now stroke away. You can't see it in Figure 3.31 (callout f), but the individual components of the stroke cycle colors from green in the spectrum to blue.

Now let's look at how the rest of the modifiers change brush shapes. And we'll even show you how to build a really interesting new brush shape of your own.

Brush Dynamics, Textures, and Making Your Own Sophisticated Tip

Guess what? There's a "trap door" in the Brushes menu that we haven't opened yet. Right now, check the Shape Dynamics check box, and then click on its title. Wow! A whole new world of strange new options has taken the place of the Brushes palette. Things like Control and Jitter and Angle are listed. Whatever do they mean?

Well, first, unless you have a pressure-sensitive digitizing tablet, you aren't going to get much out of the Control drop-downs. This is not to say you can't experiment, but the Fade option seems to cause the most apparent change in the behavior of the brush tip.

Second, we're going to run down the terms found in this "Fine-Tuning Center" so that you can adjust the parameters quickly and confidently on your own:

- **Jitter.** Means randomness, straying from the default. Therefore, if you set Roundness Jitter up high, you get a brush tip that produces thick and thin strokes (thin where the random Roundness decides to be un-round, elliptical).

- **Shape Dynamics.** Should be the first place you stop when designing a custom brush tip. This area on the menu has controls for size (and variation in size as you paint), Angle (with variations—Jitter), and Roundness (also with variations).

- **Texture.** This area gives you a big chance to mess with the look of the brush stroke. Shortly, when we run down a mini-tutorial, you will add a predefined texture to the brush stroke. When a brush tip already looks as though it's a captured bitmap and has texture, adding texture makes the tip look more complicated. And because nature is a very complex place, the more complex a brush tip, the more natural it looks.

- **Other Dynamics.** These are Opacity and Flow controls, and you can easily access more of them from the Options bar. However, when Flow is used at a low setting (in other words, your digital pen is slightly clogged), you can simulate paint build-up by stroking over areas a different number of times.

The Noise, Wet Edges, and other options at the bottom of the palette have no secret door to variations, and their purpose is self-explanatory. However, the Protect Texture check box is of great interest to us brush-builders. When you have the ultimate texture to tip into the brush recipe and then decide to change parameters, you might wind up with a different texture in the Texture dialog box. Click on this option (under Texture) to retain the texture while you design your brush tip.

Ready to test drive the Brushes controls with a little back-seat driving? Of course, you are!

Making a Sophisticated Brush Tip

1. Press Ctrl(⌘)+N to open a clean image window (callout 1 in Figure 3.32). Choose White for the Background Contents color, and its size can be as small as 1" square, 72 ppi, and Grayscale. Click on OK.

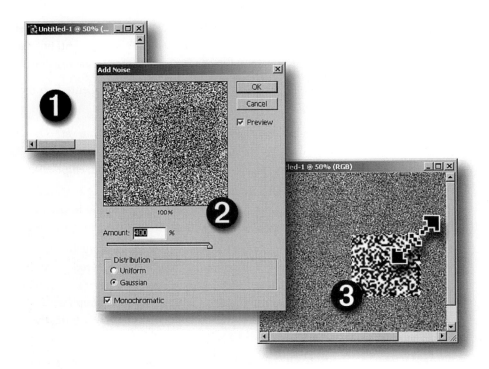

Figure 3.32   Create a noisy image, and then enlarge a section to become your brush tip (at least the *beginning* of it).

2. Choose Filter, Noise, Add Noise. Crank up the Amount to 400%. Choose Gaussian Distribution. Here, the Monochromatic option is irrelevant because this is a grayscale image (see callout 2 in Figure 3.32). Press Enter (Return) to apply the filter.

3. With the Rectangular Marquee tool, hold down the Shift key to restrain the tool to a perfect square, and drag a small rectangle (a quarter inch is more than fine). Press Ctrl(⌘)+J to copy the selected area to a new layer. Now press Ctrl(⌘)+T to put the rectangle in Free Transform mode (callout 3 in the figure). Drag a corner away from the center of the selection until you can clearly see the dots of the noise.

4. Press Enter (Return) or click the check mark on the Options bar to execute the enlargement of the selected section.

5. On the Layers palette, drag the Background layer to the trash icon so that you can see more clearly what you have to work with on Layer 1.

6. Switch to the Eraser tool. Then use a 35–pixel brush tip, click on the Airbrush icon from the Options bar, and soften the edges of the dotted rectangle on the

layer (see Figure 3.33, callout 1). Choose Edit, Define Brush Preset, and then in the dialog box, name the brush tip something you'll remember, such as **My First Brush tip**. Switch to the Brush tool, and select your new brush from the Options bar (it should be located at the end of the list on the Brush Preset palette). On a new canvas, make a stroke or two, first with the Flow at 20% and then with Flow turned up to 100% (callout 2 in Figure 3.33). What a difference Flow makes, eh?

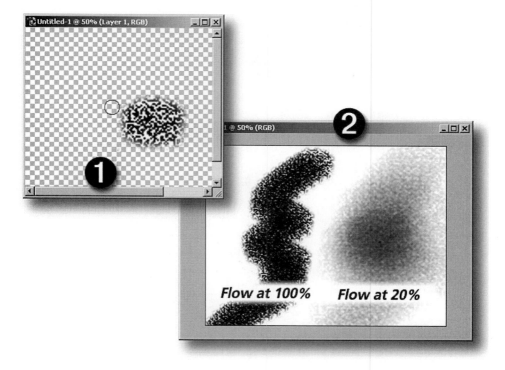

Figure 3.33   The Flow control allows more detail to become visible and also enables you to build up a texture using multiple strokes.

7. Okay, now you're ready for the big time. Click on the Brushes menu on the Options bar, and to be cool, use only the Shape Dynamics. You can see the settings and an example of the stroke in Figure 3.34.

8. Okay, it's boogie time. Click the Texture title, specify 100% Depth (see Figure 3.35), and then choose one of the preset textures from the drop-down box. Use Hard Mix, and then drag the brush around the canvas. It's a pretty interesting, organic-looking brush stroke, eh? Ooops—make sure Flow is still at 20% on the Options bar, or your strokes will look too heavy and be lacking in character. You might want to remember to return your Flow setting to 100% when you're finished.

Figure 3.34   Using only the Shape Dynamics controls, you've turned an interesting brush art tip into a *very* interesting one!

Figure 3.35   Wow! Did *you* create that? You bet, with a little guidance and Photoshop's new Brushes controls.

9. You might want to save this brush now in a more accessible place. Click on the Brush on the far left of the Options palette, and add it—with your own inspired name—to Tool Presets. You can close the working canvas at any time. Keep Photoshop open.

So now you have total control over how brushes and shapes appear within the work-space. Next, let's see how to make a palette obey your beck and call.

Customizing Layers

Layers are Photoshop's most powerful feature, and if there's any one thing you need to learn about Photoshop, learn all about layers and especially how to customize them.

The technique for leveraging layers in your work is a topic covered in future chapters. For now, we're just going to show you how to *manage* them because, after all, this is the *reference* section of this book.

Photoshop is most decidedly "layer-centric"—if you're working efficiently (in other words, if you read this book!). You will find layers indispensable, and almost every editing move (or perhaps every other editing move) somehow involves using layers.

Take out the icons.psd image from the Examples\Chap03 folder on the companion CD. You're going to learn some tricks here and now!

Naming and Propagating Layer Content

1. With the icons.psd image open, press F7 if the Layers palette isn't already open in your workspace. If it is, sit there for a moment.

2. As you can see, the top layer containing the icon is labeled "Gluntwerp," a dumb and useless name for the purposes of this assignment. Double-click on the name and, surprise, fellow Photoshop users, Photoshop finally lets you rename a layer in place. Type **icon** in the space to rename the layer title, and then press Enter (Return) to apply the new name (see Figure 3.36).

3. Click and hold the layer title on the Layers palette, and drag the layer title onto the Create a new layer icon at the bottom of the Layers palette. Repeat this proce-dure two more times, as you can see in Figure 3.37. What is the lesson here? Well, there are two: First, a copy of a layer is always placed precisely over the original; so in this case, you cannot see that there are four images of that icon from look-ing at the image window. Second, because you duplicated the layers in this way, they are conveniently numbered for you on the Layers palette.

Double-click on current name, then type in the name you want

Figure 3.36   You can rename a layer (or channel or path) simply by double-clicking the current name and entering the new name in the text field.

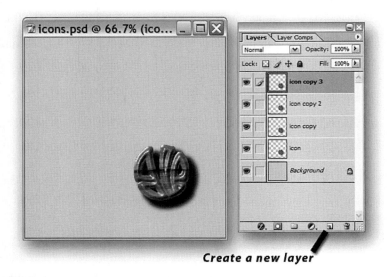

Create a new layer

Figure 3.37   Duplicated layers are numbered automatically if you drop the desired layer onto the Create a new layer icon.

4. Press **V** to switch to the Move tool, and right-click (Macintosh: hold Ctrl and click) on the image window. As you can see in Figure 3.38, any layer that has content (non-transparent pixels) is listed on the context menu. Note that this works only if you click directly on the desired image element. Now, because we

have all these icons stacked up, let's separate them a little. Choose icon copy from the context menu, and this layer becomes highlighted on the Layers palette, indicating that it is the new editing layer.

Insider

By the way, if you've chosen Auto Select Layer on the Options bar, you've ruined step 4! When Auto Select Layer is checked and you click in a document window, this feature will automatically select the top layer under your cursor after you click using the Move tool. It's our recommendation that you uncheck this option. This feature can get you into tons of editing trouble. And then, of course, you'll be late delivering your assignments, and you will most likely starve. When the Move tool is active, it's a much better solution to use the feature on demand by simply holding down the Ctrl(⌘) key to temporarily toggle the feature on when you need to select the layer for an object quickly.

Figure 3.38   Right-click (Macintosh: hold Ctrl and click) with the Move tool active to bring up the context menu, where you can choose to activate any layer with content on it directly beneath your cursor.

5. Aw, why not choose icon copy from the context menu? Now, with the Move tool (and only the Move tool), you can scoot the icon copy visual contents up and to the left of the stack of icons. If you have been fooling around with other features for a while and need a quick reminder of which icon you just moved, right-click (Macintosh: hold Ctrl and click), as shown in Figure 3.39, and click the only logical choice (the choices are Icon copy and Background).

The pop-up menu tells you which layers are under your cursor.
Click on a title, and you will make that layer the
active layer.

Figure 3.39   This context menu is very handy, when used in combination with the Move tool, to quickly identify areas on the image.

6. Move a few more icons out of the way of the original one. Oh, okay—we'd be remiss if we didn't show you the Auto Select Layer option. Click the check box on the Options bar, and then click on an icon. You will see the Layers palette changing the highlight for the current editing layer, as shown in Figure 3.40. You can close the file without saving changes.

Insider

Remember that Auto Select Layer is an option, but again, this option of auto-selecting can work against you because it's so easy to accidentally click a different image area after you've auto-chosen the layer you need. It's best to leave this option turned off and more efficient to select this feature on demand by simply Ctrl(⌘)+clicking on an object with the Move tool.

Let's drift back to those custom brushes to show off a new feature only hinted at so far: the Tool Presets feature.

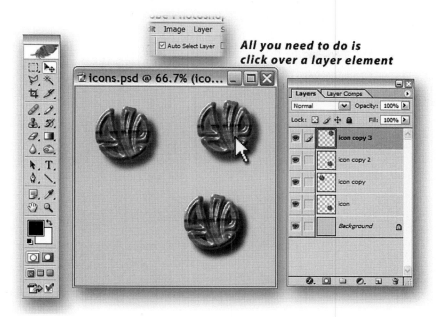

Figure 3.40   The Auto Select Layer feature puts layer choosing—and inadvertent mistakes—at your fingertips.

Using the Tool Presets Palette

Of the scores of innovations Adobe Systems has brought to Photoshop, the one we're most impressed with is the Tool Presets palette. The Presets palette is always up there on the Options bar, and it's a good, *quick* way to save a configuration for any tool. And to add the icing on the cake, you can sort saved presets so the palette presents only the tool you want to use and the permutations you've created and saved. This means, for example, that if you want the orange-tipped square 43-pixel brush tip, you don't have to wallow through presets that refer to Lasso customizations or Eraser tools.

In the steps to come, you'll create a brush, specify a color for it, work on a design, and then pretend you take four months off to go to Barbados (*in your* dreams!), only to come back to a layout that needs the exact same brush, color, and all. Oh, what to do? What to *do*?

You do the following steps:

Working with the Tool Presets Palette

1. Create a brush tip you can call your own (or pick a different name than "your own"), and pick a color, any color, for the foreground color swatch on the toolbox. See Figure 3.41; you remember this stuff from the previous section.

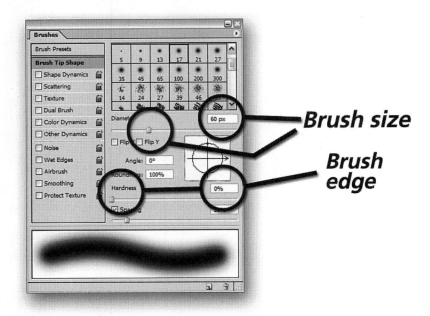

Figure 3.41   Create a brush tip that you're certain you will totally forget about after rest and recreation.

2. Click on the Tool Presets picker (it's the first icon on the left in the Options bar). Click on the icon that looks like a page of paper with a corner partly turned over. In the resulting New Tool Preset dialog box, type a name for the brush (such as **Sunny soft brush**), check the Include Color check box, and press Enter (Return) to close the dialog box.

3. Open the icons.psd image from the Examples\Chap03 folder on the companion CD, and then make a pathetic design, such as the one I created, using the brush, as shown in Figure 3.42.

4. Dash off on vacation, leaving no one responsible for watering your office flowers; then come back to the office, totally relaxed, blood pressure on the floor someplace, barely a pulse; and then discover that the sunny icon design you made needs revision. Blood pressure rises.

Figure 3.42   This is more than just a custom brush you're using; it also is a saved brush, for use a little later or after your vacation in Barbados.

5. Open the Tiffletrom.psd image from the Examples\Chap03 folder of the companion CD. Mr. Tiffletrom now owns the company, and instead of a round logo, he wants a square one with the sunny paint strokes. Oh, wow…big changes, huh?

6. Click on the Brush tool, click on the Tool Presets icon (you remember where it is after vacation?), check the Current Tool Only check box, and choose Sunny soft brush, as illustrated in Figure 3.43.

7. Complete the design, as shown in Figure 3.44. Mr. Tiffletrom is so impressed with your stamina, sheer raw talent, and vigor that he gives you a promotion and makes you the head of the Barbados office.

    End of Fairy Tale.

Let's move on to the Actions palette. We have some good news for users who need the Brightness/Contrast menu but are sick and tired of going to the main menu and then doing the sub-menu shuffle to reach this command.

Figure 3.43   Photoshop has an excellent memory. So do elephants, but elephants don't come with a Tool Presets palette.

Figure 3.44   Your custom brush could be just the ticket to Happily Ever After!

Using Actions to Add Keyboard Shortcuts

After some tough Photoshop artistic challenges, you might already know how valuable keyboard shortcuts are—especially ones such as F7, which is used to hide and display the Layers palette.

Well, Contrast/Brightness was demoted a few versions ago, and I use it a lot for special effects, such as those found in some of these screen figures. The drawback is that I could have a birthday while wading through Image, Adjustments, Brightness/Contrast... accessing it from the main menu just takes me too far away from my work.

The good news is that Photoshop CS now lets you assign your own keyboard shortcuts to items that don't currently have keyboard shortcuts (from the main menu, choose Edit, Keyboard Shortcuts). The bad news is that very few keyboard shortcut combinations are available because just about every possible shortcut combination is already in use for one feature or another. You can attempt to wade through all the possible combinations until you find one that doesn't display a warning that it's already in use, or you can consider making an Action as an alternative solution.

So let's invent a Photoshop Action that assigns Brightness/Contrast to the F11 key—a key few people use in Photoshop.

Actions for Keyboard Shortcuts

1. Open the Actions palette from the Window menu. Click on the menu flyout button (circled in Figure 3.45), and then choose New Action. In the New Action dialog box, type **Brightness/Contrast** in the Name field, leave Set at its default, assign the action a function key (F11), and then click on Record.

Figure 3.45   Record an action that is activated with a function key.

2. Click on the menu flyout button again on the Actions palette, and then choose Insert Menu Item, as shown in Figure 3.46. The dialog box stays onscreen.

Figure 3.46   Later in this book you'll learn to create really fancy Actions, but for now, we want Brightness/Contrast to pop up at a keystroke!

3. Follow the numbered callouts in Figure 3.47. The first step is to reconfirm the Insert Menu item. As you can see in this figure, you need to mouse your way to the desired command. Choose Image, Adjustments (callout 2 in the figure).

4. Click on Brightness/Contrast (callout 3), and then click on OK in the Insert Menu Item dialog box (callout 4).

5. Finally, click on the STOP button at the bottom of the Actions palette (callout 5). You're done. In fact, you can close the Actions palette now, and the command will work!

Coming up: Selections versus masks. Don't put your money on a winner yet....

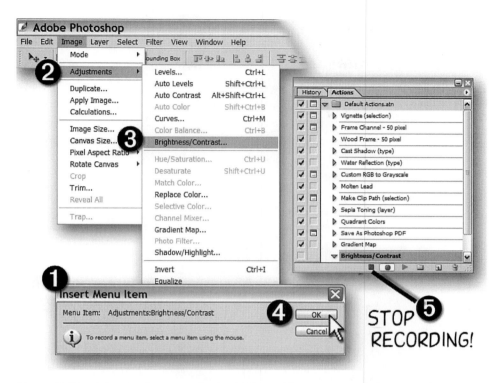

Figure 3.47   A few simple steps make the Brightness/Contrast command pop up when you press F11.

Setting Selection and Mask Modes

Adobe Systems sometimes leaves me speechless because of the way things are named. For example, a Quick Mask, which is an overlay you paint on image areas to declare "I want this area selected," can mark either a selected area or a masked area.

It really doesn't matter that Photoshop has tacked the word *mask* onto at least 15 things that can produce selections in addition to masking. Quick Mask can both protect the area you mask over from editing (in which case, it's truly a Quick Mask) or make areas you tint on top of the image *available* for editing (in which case, you are defining a selection and not a mask).

Let's perform a short series of steps to make sure that when you want a selection, you get a selection, and when you want a mask, you get a mask. You will thank me for this later if you're just coming to Photoshop.

Quick Masking...and Quick Selecting

1. Open the Daisy.tif image in the Examples\Chap03 folder on the companion CD. Press **D** for the default colors to make certain that the foreground color swatch on the toolbox is black.

2. The top right of Figure 3.48 shows a magnified view of the Quick Mask icon located on the toolbox below the color swatches. To the left of the Quick Mask icon is the Edit in Standard Mode icon, the button that will most frequently be selected as you work. Double-click on the Quick Mask icon, and the Quick Mask Options dialog box appears.

Standard editing mode button.
You see selection lines (marching ants) in this mode.

This means the areas you tint will become selected

Double-clicking on the Quick Mask icon produces this dialog box

See?

Figure 3.48   With the Quick Mask tool configured this way, it's actually a "Quick Selection" tool.

3. Click on the Selected Areas button in the dialog box, and then press Enter (Return). Now, only places where you apply tint over the image will be selected when you return the image to Standard editing mode (the act of double-clicking on the quick Mask icon automatically puts the image into Quick Mask mode after the dialog box is closed).

4. Get out a small round, soft tip brush to tint the daisy. (Precision is not an issue here. We're not master maskers yet; we're only exploring our way around Photoshop options.) Paint over the daisy, and then click on the Edit in Standard Mode icon on the toolbox (or press **Q** to toggle Quick Mask on and off). A marquee appears around the daisy. Click on the Move tool on the toolbox, and then you can move the daisy around. Stop when the novelty fades.

5. Okay. Choose File, Revert (and start fresh again). Alt(Opt)+click the Quick Mask icon. As you can see in Figure 3.49, the icon reverses coloration, so the *outside* of the circle has a tinted tone (you've changed the preference to "Masked Areas"). In Selected Areas mode, the circle had a tinted tone on the icon.

Figure 3.49   In "true" Quick Mask mode, everywhere you tint is protected from editing.

6. Paint away again, filling the daisy with tint. After you've finished, click on the Edit in Standard Mode icon (or press **Q**). You will see the daisy outlined with marching ants, but the edge of the image has ants, too. This means the background is selected, and the daisy truly is masked.

   Wanna prove it to yourself?

7. Choose the Gradient tool, and then choose a nice, complex, Chrome preset gradient. Then drag the tool in the image window. Surprised? Hope not. The background accepts the gradient while the daisy is still all nice and neat because it was *not* selected.

Pin the daisy on your lapel or on a bucket hat and keep Photoshop open.

We need to make one last step to consider thorough our examination of things that can be changed to suit your tastes. Guess what? Photoshop has a spell checker now.

Spell Checking and Photoshop

Photoshop's spell checker is sort of like a tasting spoon at Baskin-Robbins. The checker is serviceable, but for heavy-duty text formatting, spell checking, and other word processor tasks, you should use a word processor.

Still, it's nice to be able to do spot checks in Photoshop, and the following steps will show you how to check the spelling in your creations and add your own custom spellings to the spell-checker's dictionary.

Spell Checking and Increasing the Number of Words

1. Open the GrandFunc.tif image from the Examples\Chap03 folder on the companion CD.

2. Choose white for the foreground color. Choose the Text tool, and click in the image to deliberately mistype **Grand Func Railway** (two lines of text and a 48-point ornamental font will do fine).

3. Highlight Func and then choose Edit, Check Spelling. A box pops up suggesting word alternatives. Pick the correct spelling from the Check Spelling dialog box, and then click on Change, as shown in Figure 3.50. Click on OK when a dialog box notifies you that the spell check is complete.

4. You receive a call. The band has changed its name to The Brawloney Bros. Fair enough. You type this name in the image window, and as part of a well-oiled routine, you summon the spell checker. Guess what? *Brawloney* is not in the spell checker, mostly because it's not a word. But you're going to be doing business with the band for a while, so you can add *Brawloney* to the spell checker for future checking (see Figure 3.51).

Keep Photoshop open and go see the Brawloney Bros.—or whatever they're calling themselves this week. I hear they're opening for McCartney in Chicago in a few months....

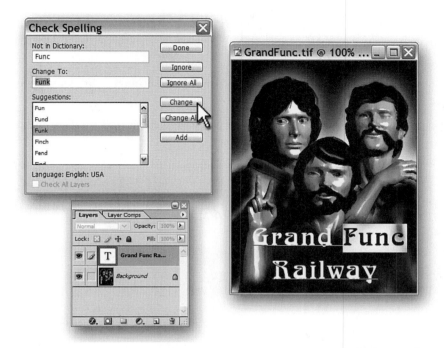

Figure 3.50   Photoshop's spell checker can prevent large mishaps unless the *Oxford English Dictionary* is your "light reading" at bedtime.

Figure 3.51   Customizing Photoshop's spell checker is easy.

Customizing Your Workspace with the Palette Well

The Palette Well expands your capabilities to customize your Photoshop workspace.

If you're comfortable with 800×600 video resolution, you may never see Photoshop's Palette Well. It's on the far upper right of the screen at 1,024×768 and higher, and it's a place where you can drop palettes.

Palettes stay neatly arranged, and you can display a palette from the well by clicking on its title (see Figure 3.52).

Figure 3.52   The well is available only at 1,024×768 video resolutions and higher.

Summary

Well. I believe we've come to the end of the preferences, options, and customization of Photoshop. Most importantly, we took a look at all the settings in the Preferences where most of the program settings are stored. Then we moved on to the options and customization of specific features such as palettes, shapes, brushes, and layers. Admittedly, it was a quick look, but you have your hands on important stuff that you need to complete a lot of the tutorials in this book. What you learned here will also help you work quicker, smarter, and with a greater sense of self-satisfaction.

We created this chapter for you so Photoshop tasks would go more smoothly. Yes, we are opinionated, but a strong point of view is always beneath reproach :). The number of sections we covered are too numerous to recap here, but if you take away a sense of confidence after reading this chapter (or if you even refer to it as you plunge into the later parts of the book), then the effort has been as worthwhile to you as it's been writing it.

Part II

A Hands-On Reference for Creating and Editing Photoshop Images

Chapter 4

Layers and Channels

Within every image you look at or edit in Photoshop lies the potential for the image to be a composite of "stacks" of images, and they are called *layers*. Similarly, colors and saved selections can also be part of a saved image file, although you might never see them onscreen, and they are called *channels*.

The purpose of this chapter is to get you comfortable working with layers and channels. To a newcomer, or even one who has experience with an image editor different than Photoshop, these two features, along with their sub-features, beg for some verbal organization.

Examining the Flexibility of Layers

Layers have been a Photoshop feature since version 3.0 (shortly after electricity was discovered). In passing years, Adobe has made the layers feature so powerful that today, it almost overshadows Photoshop's most used feature, the cartload of different ways you can select image areas.

In the sections that follow, you will become familiar with Layer modes, layer locking, layer linking, clipping groups, clipping paths, layer sets, layer ordering, layer deleting, layer comps, and layer effects. Is learning *all* this stuff necessary? Yes, most certainly so; once you make layers a part of your Photoshop knowledge, you will work at least twice as fast as the next (uneducated) guy or gal.

First, we felt you would benefit the most from a potpourri-style tutorial, where you'll learn exactly what you need to know about a *number* of different layer tools and features. You'll see how efficiently you can work to perform complicated image editing.

Introducing the "Pocket Contents" Image

If someone were to ask you to empty the contents of your pockets on a table

- You're probably being booked for a crime, and…
- You'll notice that from an artistic standpoint, the composition formed by dumping your pockets is dimensional. Everything is *not* neatly ordered and distributed, but the pile could be considered to constitute *layers* of things. Your keys might be above some folding money, and the folding money partially hides some pocket change.

The point here is that realistic image composition inherently has a depth of field; things go in front of and behind other elements. This is where Photoshop layers come in handy. They can help imitate real-world compositions by enabling you to rearrange the layers of things in your images.

Now imagine you're Jim Carrey—a comedian whose appearance and belongings are as predictable as a Chinese New Year celebration—and you're asked to dump out your pockets on a table. The contents would probably be like the contents of the Pocket.psd image you'll work with in a moment.

The image looks like any other table-top scene, except this scene was rendered in a modeling program, and everything is on different layers. FYI, shadows are attached to everything using the glow and shadow technique you'll become familiar with later in this book. Let's start off slow and easy as you learn how to manipulate the ordering of layers.

Investigating Layer Order

1. Open the Pocket.psd image from the Examples/Chap04 folder on the companion CD, and save it to your hard disk using the same name and file type. This image is 600 by 800 pixels, with a resolution of 72 pixels per inch. Zoom in or out of the image if necessary to see all the contents of the image window.

2. Press F7 to display the Layers/Channels/Paths grouped palette. Press **V** to switch tools to the Move tool.

Insider

And remember this shortcut: When the toolbox is partially hidden or closed, pressing **V** selects the Move tool directly, saving you the trouble of looking through the toolbox for the tool you need.

3. Right-click (Macintosh: hold Ctrl and click) over the 15 ball in the image. As you can see in Figure 4.1, the context menu offers two layers presently underneath your cursor, called the 15ball and the Background. Click on the 15ball choice, and you will see that the 15ball layer on the Layers palette is highlighted. You've made the 15ball layer the current editing layer.

Note

Selecting Layers   When the Move tool is selected, the Options bar offers a check box for Auto Select Layer. We don't recommend using this option. When the option is checked, if you click anywhere in the image (with the Move tool active), you immediately move to the layer that was underneath your cursor. Can you imagine how this option can be both confusing and hazardous to your work?

You can take a safer route to select a layer quickly (when the Move tool is active). Simply Ctrl(⌘)+click on an object (in the document window) to move to a specific layer that contains that object. This enables you to change layers when it's *convenient* and avoids the accidental layer jumping that would occur if Auto Select were enabled.

Right-click
(Macintosh:Ctrl+click)
to move to the layer that contains
the shape

Figure 4.1   Move directly to a layer you want to edit by right-clicking (Macintosh: holding Ctrl and clicking) over the area you want to edit.

4. In the document window, drag the 15ball downward so it is between the dart and the ice cream. Let's say we want the 15ball to play a more predominant role in the composition. No problem. On the Layers palette, drag the layer title for the 15ball up *between* the Soft Ice Cream layer and the Dart title, as shown in Figure 4.2. This puts the 15ball layer between the dart and ice cream layers. Like me, you might not hit the "sweet spot" on the palette on your first try. If you release the layer title *on top of* a layer, it then resides *directly beneath the layer* upon which you dropped it. This technique might be worth a few practice strokes on your own.

Note

Using shortcuts to change the position   We acknowledge that we are cramming your head with stuff here, but if you feel you have the memory (the carbon-based, organic kind), you can make use of a keyboard method to change a selected layer's position in the stack of layers. Press Ctrl(⌘)+] (right bracket) to move the chosen layer up on the Layers palette. And as you might expect, to demote a layer, press Ctrl(⌘)+[(left bracket), to move the layer downward in the stack.

Photoshop uses the same ordering commands for layers as Illustrator and PageMaker do for objects.

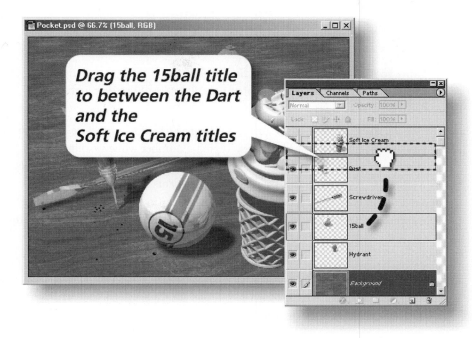

Figure 4.2   Move the order in which layers are organized to place an object in front of another.

5. Play around with the position of the 15ball as much as you like. There's no exam at the end of this chapter. It's sort of fun to see how the shadow and pool ball cover different layer items. Keep the image and Photoshop open.

A Photoshop layer has more than one property. A layer is not only a container in a stack of other layers; it also can be changed with respect to opacity and the way the layer's contents blend with layers underneath it. Come explore layer properties in the following section.

Changing the Appearance of a Layer

If you change a property of a layer in Photoshop, you also change the same property of whatever is on that layer. You can do eight things to a layer, *without* mixing a layer with an additional, modifying layer (covered later in this chapter). The sections that follow introduce you to these different properties.

Opacity

You can change how apparent a layer and its contents look by doing the following:

- Planting your cursor in the Opacity field and typing. Highlight the current Opacity setting and type a new number to replace the old setting with the desired Opacity setting.

- Typing a number value when your cursor is *anywhere* in the interface. This, too, affects the opacity of the current layer. Typing a number while working in a channel and inadvertently changing the opacity of a layer might be a little unsettling, though. If you type a single digit, this represents 10 times the opacity applied. In other words, type **5**, and 50% will appear in the number field. A zero (0) represents 100% opacity. Typing two numbers, one right after the other without pausing, will enter these two numbers in the number entry field. Typing **5** and then **7**, for example, will make the opacity 57%.

- Using the hands-on method for changing the opacity. Here's how it works: Click on the Soft Ice Cream layer title, click and hold on the palette's Opacity flyout button, and drag the Opacity slider down to 57%, as shown in Figure 4.3.

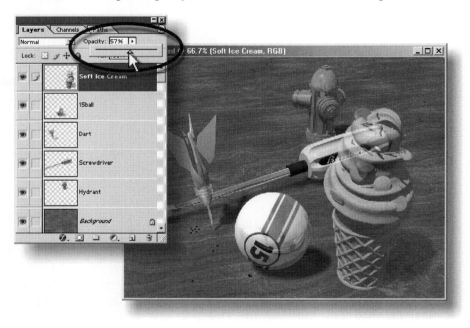

Figure 4.3   Create semi-transparent objects on a layer. Assign the layer partial opacity.

The Modes Drop-Down List

In Photoshop, you can paint using a certain mode you choose from the Options bar, and you also can put an entire layer's contents into most of the same modes. Photoshop has 23 modes, which means that you have 23 different ways to blend a layer into the underlying layers.

After using layer modes in several versions of Photoshop, I have discovered that there are actually four modes you'll use regularly: Normal, Multiply, Screen, and Overlay. Yes, you will experiment on your own and find the perfect blending mode for your own images, but let's cover the "basic four" here and now:

- **Normal.** Normal is the default mode, and the blend between the target layer and the layer(s) underneath is simple math. For example, if a layer is 50% opaque, and the image underneath is 100% opaque, the resulting image at any point will be a color combination of 50% layer and 50% background image. Try making a bright blue background and a bright red layer, and then tune the red layer down to 50% opacity. The resulting color, in Normal mode, will be a deep purple.

- **Multiply.** This is a terrific blending mode for working shadows into images, so it should come as no surprise that this layer mode is grouped with the modes that operate by "darkening" the image when interacting with layers below. Multiply mode replaces colors with a combination of layer colors that is subtractive in regions that are less than 50% in brightness. Huh? Okay, think of staining something light in color with a blue marker pen. Only the target area gets darker. Now imagine a white marker. Writing across the surface of something with the white marker causes no difference in the surface's color—due to the fact that no subtractive color process is going on with a light color and a light target in Multiply mode. In other words, the "darkening" modes—such as Multiply—compare the active layer to the underlying layers and allow only the darker areas to interact. The lighter colors such as white tend to drop out.

- **Screen.** If Multiply mode is like staining something, Screen mode is like bleaching something; it's the exact opposite effect (and grouped with the other modes that result in a "lightening" effect). In Screen mode, lighter colors become more intense, while deeper colors drop out (and again, 50% brightness is the break point for what Photoshop considers light and dark). Try out Screen mode on the Pocket image, on the partially visible Ice Cream Cone layer. As you can see in Figure 4.4 (and *much* better on your own monitor), Screen mode really brings out the whites of the vanilla ice cream. And the deeper shadow areas on the cone seem to vanish.

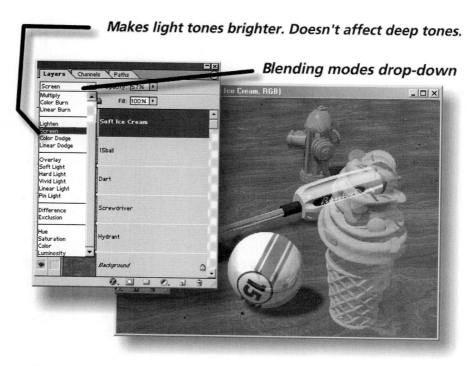

Figure 4.4   Screen mode is very useful if you have a layer with light colors that you want to separate from a dimly lit background.

- **Overlay.** This mode produces an effect somewhat similar to placing a colored gel over an image. Overlay is grouped in the list with "contrast" modes, in which the 50% gray areas drop out. With Overlay, colors are screened if they are more than 50% in brightness, and colors are multiplied if the image's original color is less than 50% bright.

You can change the appearance of a layer in two more ways, and you can find both controls located on the Layers palette.

Fill

The Fill slider on the Layers palette enables you to achieve two different kinds of opacity on a single layer. This Fill option was once buried in the Layer Effects dialog box (back when Layer Effects were first introduced in version 5.5), and few knew about it. But since Photoshop 7, Adobe decided to make this function more overt and obvious to users by placing the option on the Layers palette as well. So what's the difference between Opacity and Fill? Not much if the layer contains *no* layer effects. Remember, this function used to be buried in the Layer Effects dialog box (and can still be found there now). When no layer effect is applied to the layer, the layer will appear to respond to the Fill slider in the same way it responds to the Opacity slider. But—and this is an important "but" folks—when you apply a layer effect, the Fill slider allows you to lower the opacity to the objects on the layer *without* lowering the opacity to the layer effect.

Try this trick with our Pocket image (we're going to trash this image through the course of the chapter, so don't worry about messing it up). Click on the Soft Ice Cream layer; then click on the Add a Layer style icon at the bottom left of the Layers palette, and choose Bevel and Emboss from the list. When the dialog box opens, accept the default settings by clicking OK. Now, with opacity at 100%, drag the Fill slider down to 0%. Ooooh, ghostly ice cream! You can no longer see the ice cream cone, but you can see the Bevel and Emboss effect surrounding it. Now, if you were to drag the opacity down to 0% as well, everything on this layer would disappear (including the layer effect).

Why not use the History palette (Window, History) to restore the image to the point before the Bevel and Emboss was applied (by clicking on the title above Bevel and Emboss)? We have more to do with this image, and you can always mess with the Fill feature on other layered images later.

Visibility and Editability Icons

To the left of any layer, you will see two columns on the Layers palette:

- The visibility icon, in the leftmost column, is pretty self-explanatory. If there's an eye in the box, this means you can see the contents of the layer. If you click on the eye, the content of the layer disappears, and so does the visibility (and editing) of the layer's content. One way Photoshop users have been leveraging the power of the visibility icon for years is by turning off the visibility of a layer, so no accidental editing can happen to the layer.

  Also, the Lock feature has an option for painting. If you click the brush icon, you'll get one of those international "do not" symbols if you try to paint on this layer.

- The column to the right of the visibility column is called the Layer Link mode column, and the appearance (or absence) of a link icon tells you whether a layer is linked. But you may actually see a few different icons in this column, depending on which state the layer is in.

There are four possible states into which you can toss a layer. These states and their associated icons include

- Target Layer state, indicated by a paintbrush icon
- Layer Mask state, indicated by an icon that resembles a shaded rectangle with a circle inside it

- Layer Link mode, indicated by a chain icon
- Layer Lock mode

Target Layer State

You can paint on only one layer at a time in Photoshop, and you choose that layer by either keyboarding your way to a layer or by clicking on its title on the Layers palette. When the layer is highlighted, it is called the *target layer*. A paintbrush icon in the Layer Link mode column's box indicates that this layer is the target (current editing) layer. The title bar on the image also lists the current layer.

Layer Mask State

Later in this chapter, you will edit the Pocket composition, using the Layer Mask. The quickest way to put a layer into the Layer Mask state is to choose the layer and then click the icon second from left on the bottom of the Layers palette (the shaded rectangle with the circle inside it). When a layer is in Layer Mask mode, you see the same icon in the Layer Link mode column next to the Layer title.

What's this state *do*? Layer masks enable you to control the parts of a layer you want to hide or reveal. Not to worry! We're getting ahead of ourselves here, and you *will* play with the Layer Mask state later in this chapter!

Layer Link Mode

You'll be doing a step-by-step procedure with the Layer Link state later in this chapter, too. If you click in the second column box when the paintbrush icon (target layer) isn't there, this layer turns into a *linked* layer, and a tiny chain appears in the box. This layer is linked to the target layer, and if you use the Move tool to move the target layer's contents, the linked layer's contents move correspondingly. This is a terrific feature when you have two objects aligned on different layers and you want to move them both, but you do not want to merge the layers. A click in a box that contains the link icon unlinks the layers.

Layer Lock Mode

As the name suggests, Layer Lock mode locks the layer from editing. This mode is very useful when you want to prevent accidental editing of a layer when you are working across layers.

We've saved the least critical three controls for layers for last. Don't worry if you find you are not using them daily in your work.

The Lock List

You've had a taste of the Lock feature with the Lock Image Pixels (that teeny brush icon). This horizontal list above the top layer title is probably used most often by intermediate to advanced users, primarily because these users are the ones who create intermediate to advanced *problems* in an image, and locking features are art-savers.

We have no tutorial to show you how the Lock choices work, so you might want to open a new image and add a layer to it now. To do this, click on the folded page icon directly to the left of the trash icon on the bottom of the Layers palette. Then use the Brush tool to paint something, any color, on the layer.

The default setting for the Layer Lock feature is Lock Nothing. This means that *no* part of the layer is protected against accidental editing. You can paint over the first strokes you've made in the image window, and you also can paint over empty areas of the layer.

Set the Lock feature by clicking Lock Transparent Pixels, the first icon next to the word *Lock* (see item 1 in Figure 4.5). Areas on that layer that have even 1% opacity (it's doubtful any of us can see a 1% opaque area) cannot become more opaque, regardless of what tool you use to paint with. Needless to say, a layer with some completely transparent areas cannot be painted into.

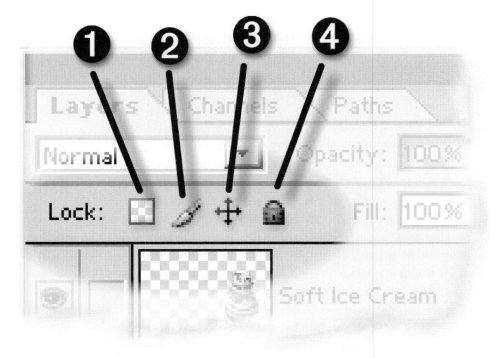

Figure 4.5   The Lock feature can disable painting over areas, prevent moving areas on a layer, and completely prevent editing on the target layer.

The next icon, Lock Image Pixels, shown as item 2 in Figure 4.5, as mentioned earlier keeps you from painting on the layer. Item 3 in Figure 4.5, Lock Position, stands for "no moving stuff, pal." With this icon selected, you cannot use the Move tool to accidentally or intentionally move any non-transparent areas on a target layer. Finally, item 4, Lock All, stands for "you cannot do anything to this layer; it is locked against *everything*."

These are definitely more options than you'll use in your first months with Photoshop, but it's nice to have them and know what they do. Let's get back to our Pocket masterpiece and explore more layer features.

Layer Sets

The Layer Set feature enables you to pack away multiple layers so that they can be organized in the image and therefore can't be seen cluttering up your Layers palette. And just as you can do with the individual layers, you can turn on and off the visibility for Layer Sets as well. Now let's continue messing up the Pocket.psd image.

Packing Away Layers You Don't Need

We'll let you in on the ending of the Pocket.psd story here: Eventually, you will be editing only the dart and the 15ball against the background. This means the tiny hydrant, the screwdriver, and the ice cream cone serve no purpose other than to distract us.

Here's how to pack the three layers away in a Layer Set. You no longer need to delete superfluous layers, only to find later on that they weren't superfluous!

Using the Layer Set Feature

1. On the Layers palette, click on the menu flyout triangle near the top-right of the palette.

2. Choose New Layer Set from the menu (item 1 in Figure 4.6). A dialog box pops up (item 2 in Figure 4.6). Type **Unused Pocket items** in the Name field, and because this is our first time using this feature, make the color of the Layer Set violet. Pass Through is the default mode assigned to Layer Sets. This means that any of the contents of the Layer Set that are activated (to activate, the visibility or eye icon is toggled on for the layers) will appear in Normal mode. You also can do some weird stuff like assigning Color mode to the Layer Set, which causes every activated layer in the Layer Set to take on the "parent" Blending mode. Leave the mode at Pass Through and then click on OK. Onscreen, the closed set entry on the Layers list will be violet…very easy to locate.

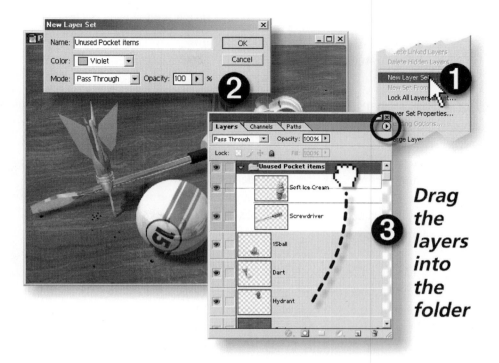

Figure 4.6   Create a new Layer Set—a container for layers—as easily as you create new layers.

3. Drag the Hydrant, Screwdriver, and Soft Ice Cream layers into the Unused Pocket Items title on the Layers palette (item 3 in Figure 4.6). The layers will appear under the Layer Set title and will also reflect the violet color in the two columns next to the left of the layer title thumbnails.

4. Close the Layer Set title by clicking on the down triangle to the left of its name; the triangle then faces right. Hide the images in the Layer Set by clicking the eye icon to the left of the Unused Pocket items folder and title on the Layers palette.

5. Press Ctrl(⌘)+S and keep the image and Photoshop open.

Tip

> **View hidden layer contents**   You can see the contents of a hidden Layer Set in the image window by clicking on the Layer Set title's eye icon. If you click on the Layer Set title's triangle so that it faces down and the title expands to show thumbnails of the contents of the Layer Set folder, you can edit layers in the Layer Set exactly as you would do with layers outside the set. You must, of course, have the eye icon and the brush icon enabled for the selected layer title before you can do any work with that layer's contents.

Let's do something that's impossible in the real world. In the following section, you'll work with the Layer Mask feature to make it look as though the dart is harpooning the 15ball. And you'll do it without the need for woodshop tools.

Using the Layer Mask Feature

A layer mask does something a little more substantial and dramatic than the name suggests. When you put a layer into Layer Mask mode, you can erase and restore image areas using selection or painting tools, but none of the changes are permanent. You can refine the edge of an object on a layer, save the file, and open it up in a week, and still the changes you've made are *proposed* ones. Nothing you see is permanent until you remove (apply) the layer mask. Let's get to the example of the layer mask, the dart, and the 15ball in the Pocket image.

Creating a Unique Composition Through Layers

You need to do two things to make the dart look as though it was thrown at the 15ball by a small explosion. First, you need to move the dart to the top layer. Second, you need to remove part of the dart's tip and part of its shadow, combine the two dart pieces, and position them over the 15ball.

That's the plot. Let's start hatching....

Pinning Down a 15Ball

1. Drag the Dart layer title on the Layers palette to the top of the individual layers. Or, if you remember the key commands for this technique, click on the Dart title to make it active and press Ctrl(⌘)+] (right bracket) until you can see the Dart title above the 15ball title.

2. Move the dart closer to the 15ball by dragging on the Dart layer using the Move tool, as shown in item 2 of Figure 4.7.

3. Zoom in (Ctrl(⌘)+plus sign) so you have a good view of the tip of the dart, and place that dart tip on the upper left of the pool ball. As you can see in Figure 4.8, a 100% viewing resolution does the trick. Now click on the Add layer mask icon with the Dart layer as the active layer. Weird stuff is going to happen when you start to apply the Brush tool and the foreground color!

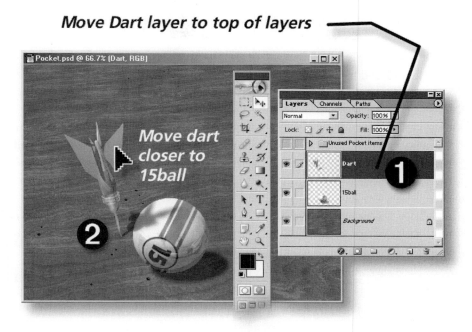

Figure 4.7 The dart should be in front of the 15ball, and the two objects should be close to one another.

Figure 4.8 When a layer's layer mask is in place, you are editing the visibility of areas; you are not moving or painting them.

4. The colors on the toolbox should now show black as the foreground color and white as the background color. If this is not the case, press **D** for the default colors, and if you need to swap black to the foreground color, press **X**. Choose the Brush tool, and then right-click (Macintosh: hold Ctrl and click) to produce the Brushes palette over your work. Click on the 19-pixel hard round tip (this is the *default* palette of tips from which you're working); then press Enter to commit your choice and make the floating palette disappear. Also, check the Options bar and make sure that the Opacity and Flow (for the Brush tool) is set at 100% and the Mode is on Normal. Drag the Brush cursor over the tip of the dart, shortening the tip by about 50%. Do the same to the tip on the shadow of the dart.

Insider

> Black hides objects on a layer, and applying white restores the hidden areas. So if you make a goof, press **X** to swap foreground and background default colors, and paint with white to restore what you wiped out. Press **X** to return the foreground color to black and continue your work.

5. When you finish editing (the image should look pretty much like item 1 in Figure 4.9), drag the *right* thumbnail on the Dart layer title into the trash icon. Make sure you're trashing the one on the *right* side; this is the layer mask thumbnail (see item 2 in Figure 4.9). If you drag the left thumbnail into the trash, you delete *the entire layer.*

6. Next, the "last chance" attention box pops up (see Figure 4.10). When you trash a layer mask, Photoshop asks whether you want to apply the mask (permanently deleting hidden image areas), cancel (think twice about trashing the hidden areas), or discard (throw away your masking work and return everything to the way it was).

   Go for it. Click Apply with a swift, definitive keystroke.

7. As you've probably noticed, there's a gap now between where the shadow of the dart ends and where the dart tip begins. This is a tad unrealistic, no? Let's press Ctrl(⌘)+S at this point, keep the image and Photoshop open, and we'll show you a trick in the following section for the precision union of dart and shadow.

A long time ago Adobe used the term *floating selection* to identify an image area that was floating *on top of* the current editing layer. Adobe has dropped this term in recent versions and doesn't even tell you what's going on when you float an image area; however, that's okay. In the next section, we are going to show you how to create a floating selection and make it work for you.

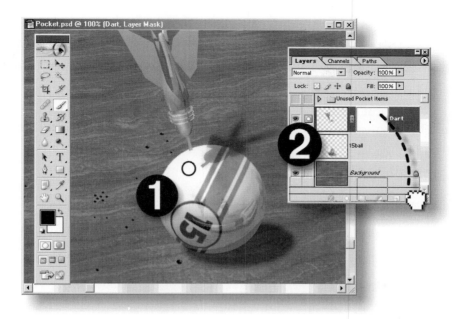

Figure 4.9 Dragging the layer mask thumbnail into the trash means that you're serious about what you've painted to hide, and you want to permanently delete the hidden areas from the file.

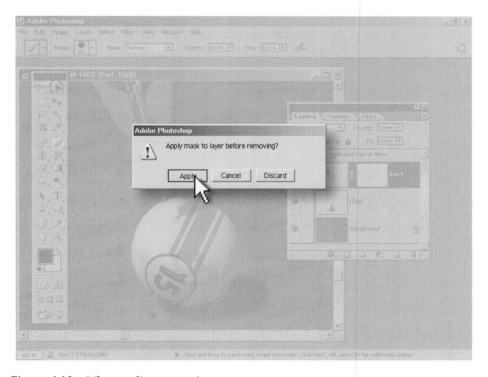

Figure 4.10 What a polite program!

Floating and Aligning the Dart with Its Shadow

As of version 4 of Photoshop, selection tools were redesigned to create selections, but they could not move the *contents* of the selection. Now the Move tool takes care of such feats as moving image areas on layers.

By using a shortcut key and the arrow keys on your keyboard, you can define a pretty broad selection around the dart and still place it precisely where you want it in the image.

Let's try out a new technique:

Finishing the Weird Composition

1. With Dart as the target layer (I think there was an unintentional pun in there someplace), choose the plain Lasso tool, and drag a selection marquee around the dart, as shown in Figure 4.11. Be careful not to select any of the dart shadow.

Figure 4.11   The selection might seem broad, but in reality, you are selecting only the non-transparent pixels on the layer—the dart.

2. With the Lasso tool still chosen (and the Feather setting at 0 px on the Options bar), place your cursor inside the selection marquee and then hold down the Ctrl(⌘) key. The cursor turns into a tiny Move tool with a pair of scissors

hanging off it. This means that if you move the marquee right now, the action will cut the selected area's contents from the layer. Nothing but transparency surrounds the dart, so this action is not destructive—*and* the dart selection is now hovering above the Dart layer.

3. While holding the Ctrl(⌘) key, press the down- and right-arrow keys until the dart meets the tip of its shadow, as shown in Figure 4.12. You'll notice also that as soon as the marquee selection is moved, the marquee changes shape to conform to the non-transparent areas within the selection. This is a nice visual confirmation that you are moving the right thing on a layer.

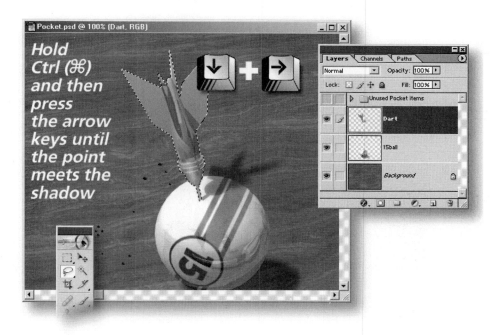

Figure 4.12   Hold Ctrl(⌘) and then use the keyboard arrow keys to nudge the selection toward the tip of the shadow.

Tip

> **Power nudging**   Just in case "power-nudging" sounds like fun to you, let us tell you what it is. You can hold Shift while you press the arrow keys to nudge a selection by 10 pixels instead of by 1. This makes your fingers all twisted but can save time when you need coarse movement editing, followed by precise movements.

4. Press Ctrl(⌘)+D to deselect the marquee, use the Move tool to reposition the dart so that it looks like it's piercing the 15ball, and you're done!

In Figure 4.13, you can see the finished piece. I'm going to frame my copy and put it in the game room (right next to the conservatory...*in my dreams*).

Keep Photoshop open, save the Pocket image, and keep it open, too.

4

Figure 4.13   Reality is what you make it in Photoshop.

For the super fussy-at-heart, there is a mistake in the finished dart and pool ball image—in the shadow of the dart. Right now, the shadow extends in a linear fashion away from the dart tip, when, in reality, if a dart happened to get stuck in a pool ball, the shadow on the pool ball would be curved, and then it would be linear as soon as the shadow hit the table top.

You know what? Who's going to notice? I am *exceptionally* nit-picky on aspects of photorealism in Photoshop pieces, but this is one inaccuracy that you can afford to let go. Why? Because the shadow of the dart is at such a steep angle that it is severely distorted, and the average viewer will not notice that the shaded part of the pool ball doesn't shade it with an arc.

The sub-lesson here is that if you create an image that is dramatic and striking and appealing and all that, most viewers will skip over the small flaws.

Coming attractions: You're going to use an Adjustment Layer to enhance the tones in the Pocket image.

Imagine Color Correction by Painting It On

I hope this title is a catchy one. For the most part, you change the color and tones of object areas in Photoshop by selecting them, applying feathering so the transition between edited and original areas is not severe (or noticeable), and then get out that Curves or Levels command.

You don't actually need to create a selection to perform color and tone corrections. Adjustment Layer fills enable you to paint on a layer that is above your target layer, and instead of applying paint, you're applying tone, color, or other corrections.

Adjustment Layers

Adjustment Layers were a hands-down boon to photographers using Photoshop because they provided the photographers with a preview of one or more different tone or color corrections. And this previewing could be done without touching the digitized image.

Photoshop's Adjustment Layers include the useful correction commands found on the Image, Adjust drop-down menu. Also (although we don't have an assignment that shows off this feature), *everyone*—even non-photographers—can play through "what if" scenarios without damaging the goods. In addition to Adjustment Layers, non-photographers can experiment with the Fill Layer feature. (To use this feature, you choose Layer, New Fill Layer and then click OK. You are presented with the current set of patterns. Then you choose which pattern you want to use from a pop-up dialog box. Remember from Chapter 3, "Setting Preferences, Customizing, and Optimizing Photoshop CS," that you can always change the offerings of a palette by using the Presets Manager.)

And like the layer mask, the tone of the color you apply to the Adjustment Layer determines how predominant the effect is. White shows off the effect at 100%, black doesn't show the effect at all, and you have 254 other levels of gray to use to bring out a little or a lot of the Adjustment Layer effect. Adjustment Layers change the appearance of every layer underneath them, not only the closest layer underneath.

In the following example, you are going to decrease the brightness of the pool ball and dart while holding the brightness of the table top. With layers, this task is a lot easier than it sounds.

Applying a Dynamic Fill Layer

1. Create a link between the Dart and the 15ball layer, as shown in Figure 4.14, and then with the Move tool, move the pair up in the picture a little so that the two objects are vertically centered in the image. (This procedure has nothing to do with Adjustment Layers. This step simply didn't fit into the preceding set of steps).

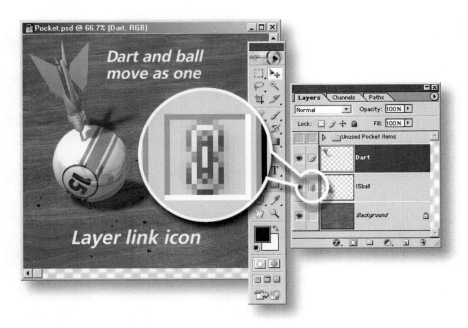

Figure 4.14   The Layer Link feature is on the Layers palette. Click in an empty box in the right column next to the layer thumbnail to link a layer to the current editing layer.

2. At the bottom of the Layers palette, click on the Create new fill or adjustment layer icon (the half moon icon next to the New layer icon), as shown in Figure 4.15, and choose Brightness/Contrast from the list. Note that we've moved the list over in this figure so you can see both the Create new fill or adjustment layer icon and the pop-up menu.

3. In the Brightness/Contrast box that pops up, drag the Brightness slider to –20, as shown in Figure 4.16. Click OK. All layers in the Pocket image lose brightness, and a new title appears on the Layers palette: Brightness/Contrast.

4. Let's simply play here for a moment. Choose a medium-sized tip for the Brush tool; to do so, right-click (Macintosh: hold Ctrl and click) on a tip from the palette (or use the 19-pixel brush tip from the previous exercise), and then press Enter to close the palette. With black as the foreground color, make a few strokes on the wood area of the image. As you can see on your screen, and in Figure 4.17, when you apply black to the Adjustment Layer (the chosen layer on the Layers palette), you are negating the brightness change you specified, and wherever you stroke, the wood becomes its original color.

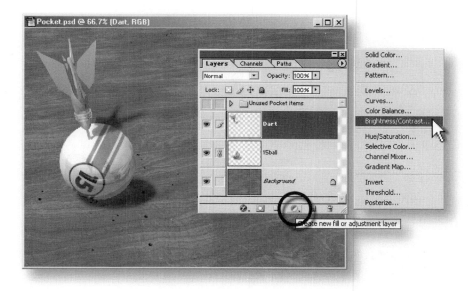

Figure 4.15   Choose Brightness/Contrast from the many Adjustment Layer selections.

Figure 4.16   With the Adjustment Layers Brightness/Contrast, you begin tuning the brightness of the picture with a −20 setting (the final brightness you want for unedited areas of the image), and add color (using a brush or a fill) to bring parts or all of the image back to the original brightness.

**Foreground black color restores original wood brightness.
So does a good furniture polish.**

Figure 4.17   Look at the Adjustment Layer fill (mask) thumbnail on the Layers palette. Wherever you apply black in the image, the image takes on its original brightness, and the thumbnail shows where you applied color.

5. Okay, let's do what we came here for. Hold Ctrl(⌘) and click on the Dart layer title on the Layers palette (to load a selection), and then hold Shift+Ctrl(⌘) as you click on the 15ball's Layer palette title to add the ball's layer to the selection (see Figure 4.18).

6. Press Shift+F7 (or Ctrl(⌘)+Shift+I; they both produce the same result) to invert the selection marquee in the image so everything except the dart and the ball are selected.

7. Make certain when you created the selections you did not change target layers! The Adjustment Layer should be the present editing layer (if it isn't, click on this layer to make it the active layer again). Also, black should still be the foreground color. Press Alt(Opt)+Delete (Backspace), and then press Ctrl(⌘)+D to deselect the marquee. You've filled the Adjustment Layer mask with black—except where the objects are—and the wood table top in the image takes on its original brightness. Now let's lighten the objects by half the brightness by which they were decreased.

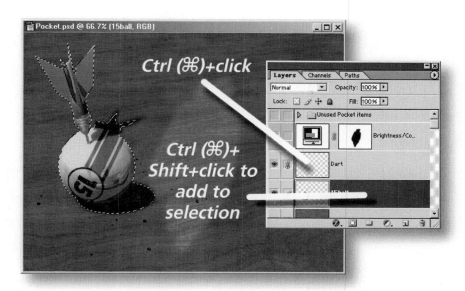

Figure 4.18   Create a selection marquee in the image by adding one shape's outline to another on a different layer.

8. Perform step 5 again, but do not invert the selection. The ball and dart are now selected. Be sure the Adjustment Layer is still the active layer, and apply 50% black to brighten these objects by half. To accomplish this, choose Fill from the Edit menu (or press Shift+F5).

9. The Fill dialog box pops up. Choose Foreground color from the Use drop-down list, and then type **50** in the Opacity box, as shown in Figure 4.19. Click on OK. Press Ctrl(⌘)+D to deselect.

Insider

If you look carefully at the Adjustment Layer thumbnail icon, or if you press Alt(Opt) while clicking on the mask thumbnail to open a view of the masking in the image window for the Adjustment Layer, you'll see that the entire layer is black (no effect) and the shapes are 50% black (50% of the effect). You can accomplish this "half bright" editing move by choosing a 50% black foreground color and then stroking in the selection, but filling it was quicker, right? You now know two ways to change an Adjustment Layer's effect. To go back to image view in the image window, Alt(Opt)+click again on the mask thumbnail to toggle the display back to the image with the Adjustment Layer affecting it.

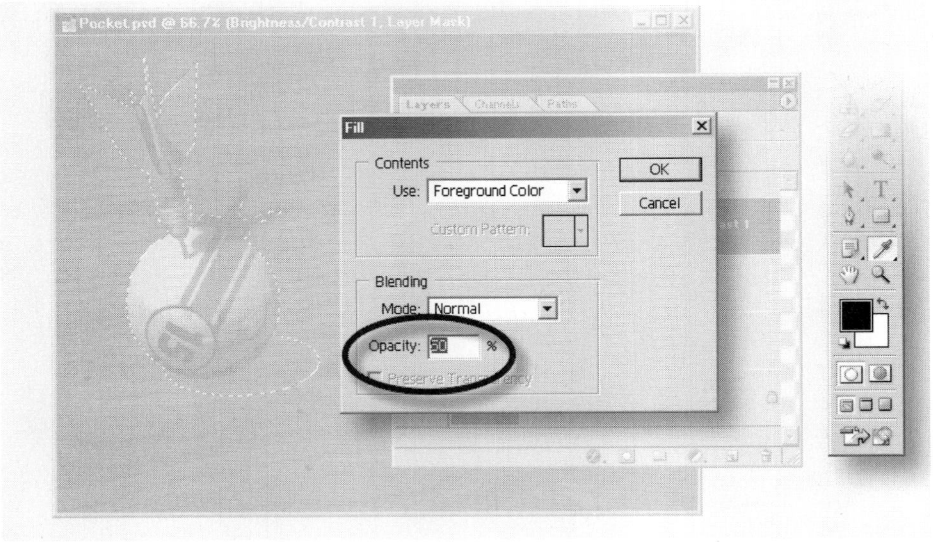

Figure 4.19   To make the selected area halfway between its current and its original brightness, fill the selection with 50% black.

10. Let's pretend you are servicing a client in these steps. The client looks at the tone changes you made and decides that he likes it better the way the image originally was. Clients, right? You drag the Adjustment Layer title into the trash icon. Or if you feel you might want it back for future work, simply click on the eye icon to turn the visibility off for the Adjustment Layer. If your client is less of a pain and likes your tone adjusting work, you can keep the image with an Adjustment Layer on it or flatten the image to make your editing changes permanent. Flatten Image is located on the Layers palette menu flyout.

Insider

If this were a real assignment, you would want to save the image with all its layers intact (as a PSD file) to give yourself the flexibility of returning to the file for future adjustments. Then you could flatten the image and save this flattened version under a different name or as a different file format (such as a TIFF file—for the client to view).

11. You can close the image at any time after saving it. Keep Photoshop open. It's time for a diversion, and we'll now move on to Layer comps.

Layer Comps

The Layer comps feature is new to Photoshop CS, and it is a boon to every designer who has an uncooperative, non-understanding client (where do we find this in real life?). A *comp*, short for *composite*, is a working design with all the elements loose so that you can shuffle them around according to the whims of others. Sure, you've been able to do this with layers, but how have you kept track of *multiple versions* of the comp? Aha! That's exactly what Layer comps offer you, and exactly what the following example is all about.

First, let's assume that you've typed in two headlines (we've done this for you) and because you might not have the same fonts as we do, we've used the Layer, Rasterize, Type command so everyone can start at the same place. If you want to, you can type in your own slogans in the steps to follow. Ready? Here goes:

Using Layer Comps

1. Open the lemon bangers.psd image from the Examples/Chap04 folder on the companion CD.

2. Click on the Bang On! title on the Layers palette to make it visible. If the visibility for the Add a Lemon Bang layer is turned on, click the eye icon to the left of this layer to off toggle the visibility.

3. Choose Window, Layer Comps (or click on the Layer Comps tab in the Palette Well at the upper-right corner of the Options bar). While you're working with this palette, it may help to drag the Layer Comps tab away from the Palette Well. If, at any time, you want to return the palette to the Palette Well, simply drag the palette back into the Well.

4. Click on the Create a New Layer Comp icon at the bottom of the Layer Comps palette (it's the page icon).

5. In the New Layer Comp dialog box, type **Bang** in the Name field, check the Visibility and Position options, and type an evocative description of the layer condition (the arrangement of the file vis-à-vis layers) if you would like in the Comments field (see Figure 4.20). Click OK.

6. Click on the visibility icon to the Bang On! layer to hide it and then click on the Add a Lemon Bang layer title on the Layers palette to make it active and visible (if it's not already visible).

7. Click on the Create New Layer Comp icon at the bottom of the Layer Comps palette and name this layer comp **headline top**, as shown in Figure 4.21. Make sure the Visibility and Position options are checked and click OK.

8. With the Move tool, drag the headline (or rather the Add a Lemon Bang layer) to the bottom of the layout, and then save this version of the design as a layer comp called **headline bottom**.

4

Figure 4.20   Name the first layer comp and give it a comment if you like.

Figure 4.21   Create a layer comp called headline top.

You're done. Now pretend that the client is breathing over your neck and cycle through the different layouts you've created (on the Layers Comp palette). Click on the forward arrow, as shown in Figure 4.22, to see all the variations on the design.

Figure 4.22   Layer comps show their importance when you cycle through the various designs you've created and saved.

You're now a master of Layer comps! Use them when you have a killer design or two and want to show them off. BTW, you can also save a Layer comp composition by choosing File, Scripts, Layer Comps to PDF, for a more permanent record of your efforts. Save this file to PSD format, and the file will retain the Layer Comp information. Neat!

Shapes and Clipping Paths

Adobe Systems wants *every* user to get with the program and start using the power of vector paths in Photoshop, right from Day One. Okay, suppose it's Day Two or Three with you and Photoshop; we are still going to show you the easiest way to start using vector paths. Paths travel under the guise of something called *shapes* in version CS; they are pre-made paths that you can fill, stroke, base a selection upon, and so forth. And shapes are simply a way to start understanding the relationship between vectors and designs that are filled with pixels. Shapes are a sort of vector container for the bitmap rendering you do in Photoshop.

So without further ado, let's play with some pre-made shapes we've created for you on the CD (they're really cool), and discover the different relationships vector graphics have with Photoshop CS features.

Building Upon a Simple (but Cool) Shape

Okay, here's a perfect chance to show you a relationship between a vector design and layers in Photoshop. In the steps to follow, you will copy a path from a collection of shapes on the Companion CD, fill it to turn it into the base layer of a clipping group, load the selection, and then pile on some layer effects to create stunning artwork in less than five minutes.

By the way, the shapes you'll see in this section were all taken from the BOUTON Logos typefaces on the Companion CD. And if you decide you like creating art using the steps to follow, there are plenty more shapes where these came from.

Here's how to create a shape on a layer from a path shape:

Copying and Using Paths

1. Open the Shapes.tif image from the Examples/Chap04 folder on the companion CD.

   Insider

   > Although this does not affect the way you use this file in any way, we've filled the vector shapes onto a layer, so when the file is opened, the shapes are visible to you even though the vector shapes on the Path palette are hidden. This way, you can still see the designs we put into this document.

2. Click on the Paths tab of the Layers/Channels/Paths/Tra La La palette, and then click on the Shapes by Bouton title. All the paths will appear in the image window.

3. Choose the Path Selection tool, and then marquee drag on the train stencil in the Shapes.tif image window, as shown in Figure 4.23.

4. Press Ctrl(⌘)+C to copy the path to the Clipboard.

   Insider

   > You can use the Path Selection tool to drag a copy of a path to a different image window, but we don't have a new window yet. Just a tip here.

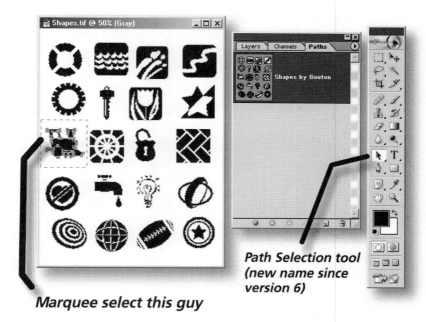

Marquee select this guy

**Path Selection tool
(new name since
version 6)**

Figure 4.23   Technically, all the designs are one big, composite path because they are stored under one title, one name. The Path Selection tool enables you to select only the train paths from all the rest in the image window.

5. Press Ctrl(⌘)+N to create a new image window; make it 3 inches by 3 inches at 72 pixels/inch, RGB color mode, and Contents: White. This image window is a tad larger than the train, but we'll be adding special effects to the train, so we'll leave a little elbow room in the new document. Click OK.

6. Press Ctrl(⌘)+V to paste the path in the new document window. On the Paths palette, double-click the Work Path title to rename the work path **Train**.

Insider

If you do not rename the Work Path title, the path is at risk of being replaced if you do any future path work in the file (using any of Photoshop's path or shape tools). Any new paths created with these tools will automatically replace the path currently on the Work Path title. By renaming the Work Path title, you permanently save a record of the path into the file and eliminate the risk of accidentally losing the path.

Note

Scaling paths   You have the opportunity to scale the train at any time now, which you might want to do if you feel the train is too small, or if you played with scale trains as a child, like I did. You marquee select all the paths using the Path Selection tool, press Ctrl(⌘)+T, and then hold Shift while dragging a corner of the bounding box away or toward the center of the bounding box. Then press Enter to "nail" the path (to make the changes permanent), or press Esc and return to the path's original size.

7. On the Layers palette, create a new layer, leave it as the current editing layer, and press **D** (default colors). On the Paths palette, click on the Fill path with foreground color icon, as shown in Figure 4.24. Then click on an empty area of the Paths palette (under the path title list area) to hide the path. Congratulations! You've just created a shape on a layer that can now be used for a number of things, not the least of which is the base layer for a clipping path.

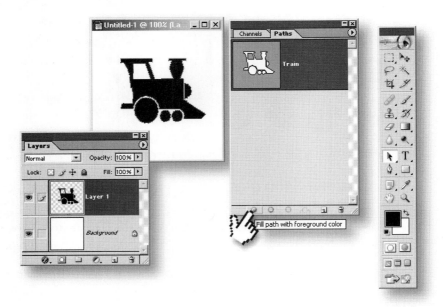

Figure 4.24   Fill the selection (shape) with foreground color.

8. Save the design as Train.psd in Photoshop's native format, and keep Photoshop open.

Here come the fireworks. Now that you've created a "stencil" of the train on a layer, you can fill this stencil, move it around, and add layer effects to it.

Introducing Clipping Groups

I think within the context that Adobe uses *clipping* in Photoshop, we can consider it the opposite of *masking*. Instead of everything outside a selection being opaque, the *inside* of a shape is a container for whatever you choose.

Clipping groups can be very useful when you have dozens of different patterns, for example, and want to see what they look like on a shirt pattern. You make the shirt pattern the base of a clipping group, and then anything you toss on top of this layer—on different layers—becomes the fill. And you can move the container around and the pattern will travel, too.

Let's walk through the following steps to demonstrate the power of clipping groups:

Creating a Clipping Group

1. Click on the Create a new layer icon at the bottom of the Layers palette (it's the folded page icon next to the trash icon). By default, this is named Layer 2.

2. Choose the Gradient tool from the toolbox. On the Options bar, choose the Linear Gradient option, and then from the drop-down list of preset gradients, choose the yellow/violet, orange, blue preset. Press Enter (Return) after you click on the icon to let Photoshop know you are sincere in your selection.

3. Drag the Gradient tool from the top to the bottom of the image window. The gradient now covers the train shape. If you hold down the Shift key while you drag, the gradient will be constrained to a perfectly vertical line.

4. Hold Alt(Opt) and then click right between the two layer titles on the Layers palette. As you can see in Figure 4.25, your cursor turns into a very novel design, and after you click, the top layer is clipped to fill only the train shape. We call the top layer the *clipping layer* and the train shape the *base layer*. Heads up for the note that follows.

Insider

> If there was any transparency on the gradient layer, you could add another layer, and it, too, could be viewed only through the portal that the train design has become.

Note

> **The Options bar options**   The Options bar contains three options when the Gradient tool is active, and they're kinda obscure. First, the Reverse check box enables you to quickly reverse the order of colors in the current gradient. Dither should be unchecked if you're composing artwork for the Web. If you are designing for color printing, you should probably check Dither because dithering is noise; if you add noise to a gradient destined for print, the noise will disguise the *banding* that inevitably occurs when you move an RGB image to the smaller color space of CMYK printing. Transparency is an option relating to any transparency that might be in a gradient you use or create. Keep this option checked unless you want your gradient to fill 100% of a layer, with no transparent areas.

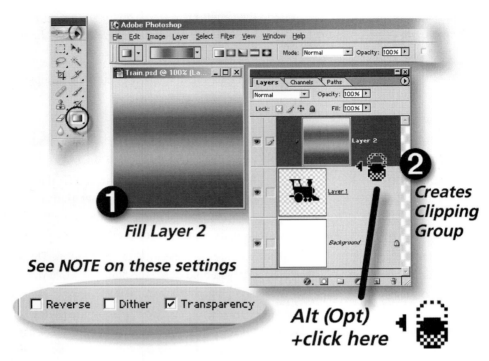

Figure 4.25   The thumbnail of Layer 2 on the Layers palette has shifted to the right, telling you that you've successfully made the base layer a host for the visual contents of Layer 2.

5. For fun, click on the Layer 1 title (it's underlined now because it is a base layer for a clipping group). Then, with the Move tool, move the train around. You will see different areas of the partially concealed gradient layer. Now click on the box in the second column, to the left of the thumbnail on the gradient layer. A chain link appears, and now the base layer and gradient layer are linked. Try dragging the train around. You'll notice that the contents remain static within the stencil of the train. This happens because the base layer is linked to the gradient.

6. For even *more* fun, let's try something else. First, move the Train.psd image to the top left of the screen so that you can preview effects as you modify them. With Layer 1 (the base clipping group layer) as the active layer, click on the **f** icon at the bottom of the Layers palette, and choose Bevel and Emboss. Doing this brings up a huge options palette called Layer Style. Drag the Depth slider to about 500% (for a default emboss that's really noticeable and deep in shading). Now click on the Drop Shadow title (on the left side of the palette) to select and view the Drop Shadow options. Play with the sliders, as shown in Figure 4.26, until you get a soft, but noticeable shadow. Click on OK.

Insider

> You can add as many effects as you like in the Layer Style palette by clicking on the effect title (at the left). Only when you click on OK are the effects permanently applied to the layer in your image. And even then, you can change your mind and delete them by dragging an effects title into the Layers palette's trash icon.

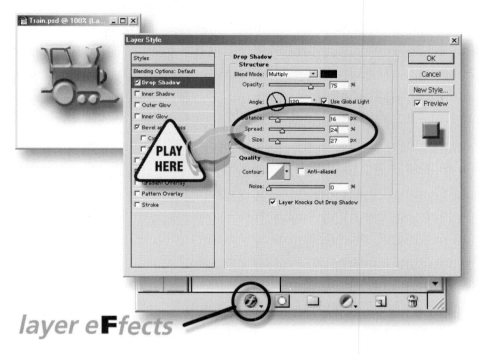

Figure 4.26   You can "mix and match" effects to be applied to the target layer using the Layer Style palette.

7. As you can see in Figure 4.27, you've created something of a mini-masterpiece, without even calling on your drawing prowess. Why not save this file to your hard disk, come back to it some other time, and paint the train different colors? You can close the image at any time, but keep Photoshop open.

It should be pointed out here (at this writing) that Adobe ships with 13 Shape palettes that you access from the Options bar when you choose the Custom Shape tool. On the Options bar, click on the down arrow to the right of the shape icon. Then click the triangle (contained within a circle) in the upper–right corner of the palette and choose one of the Shape categories from the many listed near the bottom of the context menu (to load a different Custom Shapes set). A dialog box will ask you to click OK if you want to replace the current shapes with the new set, or to click Cancel if you have changed your mind, or to click on Append if you prefer to add the chosen list to your existing shape set. Then scroll through the shapes available in the palette and click on one of the shapes to choose it.

Figure 4.27   You do not have to be a born artist to create striking visuals for a Web site, a greeting card for an inkjet printer, or whatever. Simply use Adobe's (or Bouton's) preset shapes, and add a few layer effects.

To add the chosen shape to an image window, simply click in the image window and start dragging. You might prefer to hold down the Shift key (to constrain proportions) while dragging diagonally in the image window. Doing so creates, by Photoshop default, a Shape Layer (which uses a vector mask—containing a path or paths like the ones you would create using the Pen tools). You have to admit that preset shapes are quick to implement. Later in the chapter, we'll show you how to create a Custom Shape palette of your own.

Now it's time to take a look at the most simple of paths to create—vector masks. What are they good for? How do you convert them to other types of image objects? You're going to find the following section to be a very integrating experience.

Working with a Vector Mask Layer (Shapes)

A Vector Mask layer has some nice options for enhancing your work. At the same time, many things you've learned about Photoshop features are not available to a Shapes layer.

The best way to get a feel for shapes is to experiment. The following steps take you on a fairly thorough investigation of these vector masks.

Note

> **Defining a shape**   Before we get too far into the game, we need to clear up an ambiguity of terms Adobe has bestowed on the Shapes tool. Technically, only the Shapes Layer tool creates a shape because, hey, that's what it's called, and it produces distinctly different results in an image window than the Paths option (which results in a path only of the shape—no fill color) or the Fill Pixels mode on the Options bar (which fills the shape with foreground color, leaving no editable path behind).
>
> However, all three modes on the Options bar use the Shapes tools. I think we can all keep a little more of our hair where it belongs if we accept the term *shapes* to mean a design that's a result of using any of the Shapes tools, regardless of whether the Shapes tool produces a vector mask, a simple path, or foreground colors (in the shape of a check mark or a speech balloon or whatever).

Creating a Shapes Layer

1. Press Ctrl(⌘)+N to open a new image and choose Default Photoshop Size from the Preset Sizes drop-down list in the New dialog box. Choose RGB color mode and White as the contents. Press Enter.

2. Click on the foreground color selection box (marked as item 1 in Figure 4.28), and choose a light purple as the color to paint with and also the color that will be peeking through the shapes on the Vector Path layer.

3. Drag on the face of the Shapes tool to view the flyout menu on the toolbox and then choose the Polygon tool (item 2 in Figure 4.28). Immediately, the Options bar sprouts new choices for you to make, and (as of this writing) the far-left tool (item 3 in Figure 4.28) is the active shapes mode—called, fairly enough, Shape Layers. Check the following Note for other choices you can make whenever you choose the Shapes tool.

4. Now, after you've created your first shape, the Boolean buttons on the Options bar (subtract from, add to, and so on) will become active. Because we want to draw oodles of shapes, click the Add to shape area icon (item 6 in Figure 4.28). Now, every shape will be on the same layer and will *not* create a new layer (try managing 47 layers!) when you create your second shape.

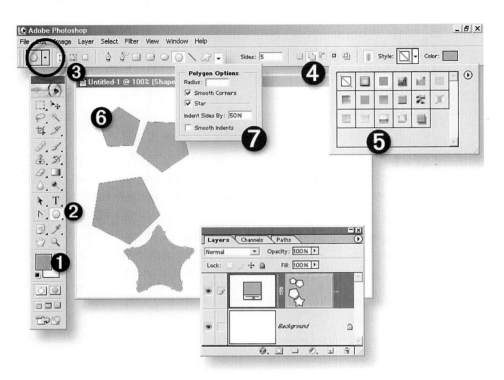

Figure 4.28   When you choose the Shapes tool, many options are available for creating a shape, its contents, and what is shown in non-path areas.

Note

Shape creation modes   The other modes for Shape creation are the Path option and Fill Pixels option. These modes pop up on the left side of the Options bar the moment you choose a Shapes tool. If you click the Fill Pixels icon (or option), the shapes you drag are filled with foreground color and are plain pixels against the current layer or background. For comparison here (this is a new topic), the Shape Layers option (which is grouped with the other two icon options) produces a shape on a new layer when you drag with the tool. You can turn off the vector outline if you like by clicking on the right thumbnail on the new layer.

If you choose the Path icon, every shape you draw will be a vector shape, but it will not clip the layer underneath it, nor will it have a color fill. With the Path option active, the shapes become just as the name implies—paths—plain and simple (which can be useful if you want to use a preset shape as a starting point and then alter the path to your needs).

Once you've thoroughly pored through this chapter and Chapter 6, "Using the Pen Tools," you might find that using the Path mode in combination with the Shapes tool is the way to work. For now, we'll keep digging through stuff for you.

5. The default Style on the Options bar should be set to None. If it's not, click on the Layer Style drop-down list button (item 4 in Figure 4.28), and then click on the Style None (a square with an international slash symbol through it). Now, when you create a polygon, its foreground will simply be purple with no layered effects on it. You can add effects later; you'll see how momentarily.

6. Click+drag in the image window to make the first shape (item 5 in Figure 4.28). Click on the Add to shape area icon and then start click+dragging in the image window to create more shapes. Create polygons of different sizes. If you want to create variations on the polygon, click on the Options down button to the right of the Shapes button (on the Options bar). Every preset shape (such as the Polygon, the Rounded Corner Rectangle, and so on) has different parameters you can change at any time. You can turn the Polygon into a star, with any degree of sharpness between points. Check it out; item 7 in Figure 4.28 marks the Polygon Options used to create the unusual star in this figure. Next to this option is Sides. Change this number to increase or decrease the number of sides for your polygons.

Tip

Repositioning a shape   Don't forget: You can press the spacebar to reposition your shape while you drag.

7. Stop when you've created about four or five polygons. You will see an unusual thumbnail for this layer on the Layers palette. Paths are shown in miniature in the thumbnail, and the thumbnail looks quite a lot like a Layer Mask thumbnail (giving you a clue as to what to expect we can do with this layer soon).

8. Keep the image window open and keep Photoshop open.

Tip

Using the presets button   See the circle around the shape icon in the upper-left corner of Figure 4.28? That's the presets button. If you go through the trouble of designing a really neat polygon (such as a purple rounded-edge star) and think you want to use it months from now, save yourself the steps of replicating the effect by clicking the down arrow to expose the Tool Presets palette. Click the triangle (contained within a circle) in the upper–right corner, and choose New Tool Preset. Give the preset an interesting name in the dialog box, and you can recall the tool and its customized options from the palette at any time in the future. You can even choose whether you want to save the foreground color that you used with the tool.

Earlier, we mentioned restrictions on editing a Shapes layer. Let's be a little more positive and explore next what you *can* do with Shapes layers.

Editing Clipping Path Layer Components

Although you cannot fill a Shape layer with a photograph, pattern, or unique gradient fill, you *can* edit the container shape using the Direct Selection tool, you can move shapes using the Path Selection tool, and you can add *styles*. But most importantly, you can *change your mind* about any of the edits mentioned here. Nothing is carved in stone on a Shapes layer until you choose Layer, Rasterize (change to pixels from a vector), and then click on Shape.

So let's play a little with some properties of the Shape layer. Um, your image might not look like mine (because we are not the same person), but you will get the general idea of the flexibility of Shapes layers.

Manipulating a Shapes Layer

1. Make sure a Shapes tool is chosen (or else you won't see a Styles box on the Options bar). Click the down arrow to the right of the international "no" symbol. This extends the Style palette, which you can see marked as item 1 in Figure 4.29. The palette might seem hidden, but if you click the down arrow to reveal it, and then click on the encircled triangle (at the upper right), you have several more palettes from which to choose. (To replace the current collection, click one, and then click OK.) Glass Buttons produces a neat effect. But *don't* do that yet. Click on Sunset Sky (item 2 in Figure 4.29), and immediately every polygon on that layer turns to multicolor glory…as not seen in Figure 4.29 because this darned book is in black and white.

Note

> **Shapes on a single layer**   We've taught you a non-standard way of applying many shapes to a single layer. The only drawback? All the shapes have to have the same fill. If you want different fills for different shapes, you should leave the Booleans selections to the far left, the simple rectangle, and not the Add icon/button.

2. Click on the down triangle to the right of the Shapes thumbnail on the Layers palette to display the list of Layer Effects (item 3 in Figure 4.29).

Caution

> **Making the symbols more visible**   We used the Dodge tool to make the triangle apparent in Figure 4.29, because at the time of this writing, the triangle and the effects' symbols are black against the dark blue of the Windows Millennium, Windows 2000, and Windows XP Windows Classic interfaces. To fix this problem, you need to right-click on the Desktop, choose the Appearance tab, and in the Scheme drop-down, pick Spruce or Rose.

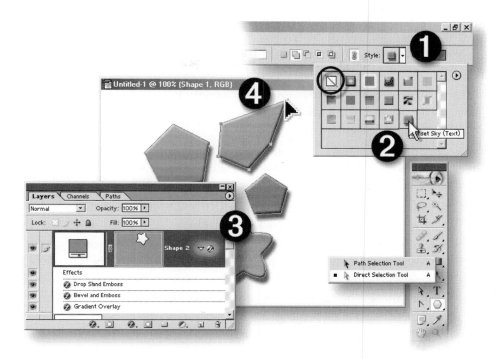

Figure 4.29   You apply a style to the entire layer. Anything within a path takes on the layer's style.

Note

> **Accessing the Styles palette**   The Options bar is not the only place from which you can access the Styles palette. It is grouped with the Colors and Swatches palettes and can be called by choosing Window, Styles. We simply think you don't need this palette out all the time, and accessing it from the Options bar is, um, *tidier*.

Insider

> Suppose you want to change the style of this layer. You can do so by clicking on a new style on the Styles palette. Suppose, on the other hand, you want to change a component of the Style; this is why we have a drop-down list of Effect titles beneath the Layer title that the effects were applied to. Double-click on one of the effect titles, and you're off to change the component upon which you clicked. You can also add a component by clicking on the Effects button (the icon with an *f* inside a circle) on the bottom of the Layers palette and then choosing a component. And, natch, you can get rid of a style component by dragging the unwanted effect title into the trash icon at the bottom right of the Layers palette.
>
> By the way, you are affecting the art in the image window by doing any/all of the above. You are not changing a style on the Styles palette at all.

In addition to coloring the shape, you can distort it and move it. As you continue with this exercise, you'll see how to rearrange stylized vector paths. That sounds almost scientific, doesn't it?

3. Click on the Direct Selection tool on the toolbox. It might be hidden right now; if so, click and hold on the Path Selection tool and choose the Direct Selection tool from the tool flyout.

4. Click on any polygon to select it; then click on an anchor point and drag it, as shown in Figure 4.29 as item 4. Notice that regardless of where you relocate a point, the fill extends to accommodate the new shape.

5. Switch to the Path Selection tool, and notice that if you still have a shape selected, all the anchor points also become selected (solid). With a shape selected, move a polygon. Surprise! Even though these paths have the same fill and were created on the same layer, the Path Selection tool enables you to individually sort and move these shapes! And if you want all the shapes to move as one, you can use the Combine button on the Options bar (although it is not shown in the figure).

6. Okay, let's say we're getting bored using the Sunset Sky style for all our polygons. Double-click the solid color thumbnail on the left of the layer title on the Layers palette. When the Color Picker appears, choose a light purple, and press Enter (Return) to define this new color. Now click on the international "no" swatch on the Styles palette. Woweeee! Everything inside the shapes is the color of purple you specified.

7. Now let's say we've grown weary of looking at all the straight edges. Choose the Convert Point tool from the Pen tools flyout on the toolbox. Click on a shape to select it, and then click+drag on one of the anchor points on the polygon. As you can see in Figure 4.30, clipping path layer elements obey the same rules as a regular path. You can move path elements, reposition their anchor points, bend path segments, and even use the Add Point and Delete Point on the clipping paths.

8. Click on the f icon on the bottom left of the Layers palette. Choose Bevel and Emboss from the pop-up list, and then click on OK in the Layers Style dialog box to accept the default properties for the embossing. In your own work, you should spend time in this dialog box to fine-tune the effect you want to apply. Feedback for your tuning is immediately shown onscreen, but if you are running less than 800 by 600 video resolution, the art probably is obscured by the Styles dialog box. The effect also can be seen in a square toward the lower right of the dialog box.

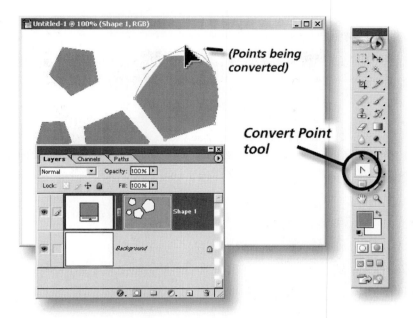

Figure 4.30 The subpaths in a Vector Mask (Shapes) layer can be changed using the Pen tools and selection tools.

9. Click on the **f** icon, and choose Drop Shadow. Again, click on OK in the dialog box to accept the defaults, and you are returned to the image.

10. This image is pretty dull without a background. Click on the Background layer to make this the active layer (on the Layers palette). By making this the active layer, we ensure that our new background will be positioned correctly when it is added to the Layers palette (since new layers are, by default, added above the current active layer). Open Paper.tif from the Examples/Chap04 folder on the companion CD.

11. With the Move tool, drag the title on the Layers palette into the image window with the shapes (as shown as item 1 in Figure 4.31). By holding down the Shift key (while you drag), you center the image in the shapes document (see the following Insider).

Insider

You can also drag an image in an image window into another image window to copy it, but dragging the title on the Layers palette is sometimes easier. An image window can cover another window, but a Photoshop palette will not.

Tip

Positioning copied contents   If you want the contents you are copying from one
window to land in the center of a different image window, hold Shift while you drag. This
feature is particularly nice if you want to duplicate the contents of a layer and you want
the contents positioned exactly as they are in the original image.

12. Right-click (Macintosh: hold Ctrl and click) over the path thumbnail on the
    Layers palette, and then choose Rasterize Vector Mask, as item 2 shows in Figure
    4.31. The effect you've created is that the paths no longer exist on the clipping
    path layer, and it's not a clipping path layer anymore. Now it's a *layer mask*.

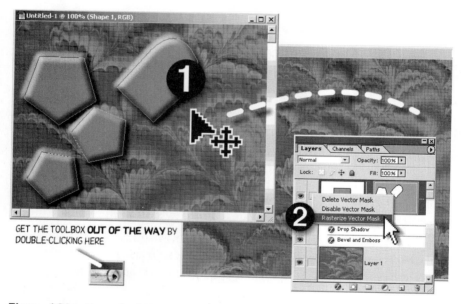

Figure 4.31   Copy a background to the target image window, move it to the bottom layer, and
then convert the Vector Mask layer to a layer mask.

13. Choose Layer, Rasterize, and then choose Fill Content. The shapes are no longer
    linked to the layer fill (the left thumbnail on the Shape title on the Layers
    palette).

14. Click the right (the right, the *right*, not the left!) thumbnail on the title, and drag
    it into the trash icon. A dialog box pops up asking whether you want to apply
    the mask before removing? Click Apply. You now have your embossed, drop-
    shadow images on a transparent layer on top of the tapestry background layer.

15. You can save this image to your hard drive, if you want. Close this image and the
    Paper.tif image at any time, but keep Photoshop open.

Pretty neat, huh? Do you realize that you've created a wonderful design without picking up the Brush tool? You've been taking full advantage of Photoshop's features, both old and new.

Whew! We've nary exhausted all the types of layers you can avail yourself of in Photoshop! It's time to move to a close cousin of layers, *channels*, in our next section.

Channels: A Definition and the Keys to Mastering Them

Let's pretend we can revisit grade school and are listening in on a lecture concerning how light is broken down into components. The professor whips out a prism, places it near sunlight (which is very close to absolute white), and ker-blooey…the white light is broken down into its components.

Although all this is very illuminating, it does not describe the *principle* of additive primary colors—the colors your computer monitor uses to make up all the colors you can imagine. What we need to do in our imaginary trip back to 4th grade is to come up with an equally imaginary device—a perverse prism—that will allow us to do the exact opposite of what a prism does. In Figure 4.32, you can see my own personal perverse prism. It's being fed red, green, and blue components on the left, and white light comes out the right side. What does this image tell us? That three components—*channels*, we shall call them henceforth—are the primary additive components that together at full intensity create white.

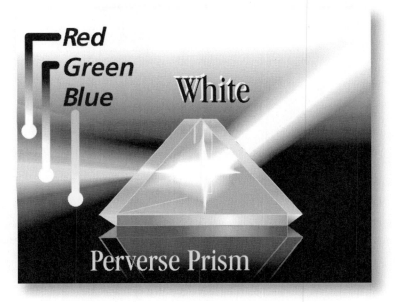

Figure 4.32   If a prism gathered components of white light and blended them, the action would essentially be what your monitor and video card do to create *additive color*.

Searching for More Colors

A good question right now is, "Hey, how do you get colors *other than white* using additive colors?" The equally good answer is in this bulleted list:

- You combine less than all three primary color channels at maximum brightness. For example, if you do not use green or red at all, the resulting color is blue. And if you mix green and blue together and ignore red, you arrive at the color cyan.

- You do not use the full brightness of a primary color in the mixture of additive colors. Orange, for example, is the result of mixing the red channel at full intensity, and the green channel at 50% intensity.

Figure 4.33 shows what happens when the first part of my answer is demonstrated using stage lights. Yes, I know the book is in black and white, but if you own stage lights (or even three flashlights with primary color cellophane over them—*hint, hint*), you will see the secondary additive colors where two colors converge. Cyan, magenta, and yellow are called *complementary colors*, in the additive color system, because they are a result of two neighboring colors in the color spectrum.

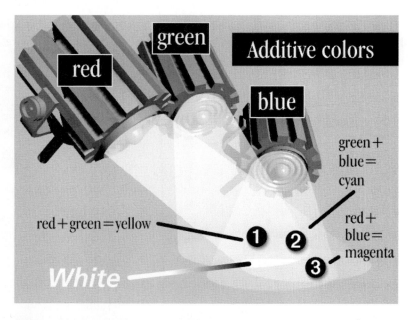

Figure 4.33   Additive colors have secondary, or complementary, colors. Add two primary colors to get a secondary color.

We're not done yet, and we cannot get to the fun assignments that follow unless we digress briefly into subtractive colors. You'll thank us some day for this discussion; it ties together a lot of cosmic color theory stuff.

Understanding Subtractive Colors

Most of us didn't get the straight story from our grade school teacher concerning primary colors. In fact, some readers out there might argue with me that red, blue, and yellow are the primary colors because Mrs. Griswell said so before you were old enough to reach a steering wheel.

Well, it is true that red, blue, and yellow are primary colors, but *not in the additive color model.* You probably didn't get to fool around with primary colored lights in grade school, and chances are the instructor used to pass out crayons as art materials. Pigments, such as crayons, house paint, artist's oil paints, and clothing textile paints, are all part of the *subtractive* color system. Instead of getting white when you mix all pigments together, you get black (see Figure 4.34).

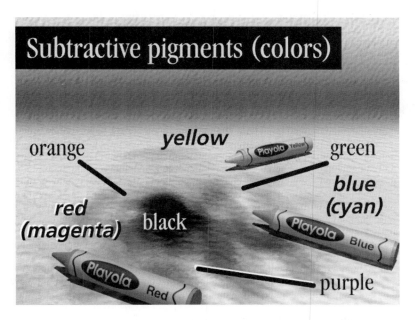

Figure 4.34   If you mix two subtractive colors together, you get a complementary color. All three colors added together at full intensity equals black.

Here's the interesting part: Commercial printing presses use subtractive colors, and the colors used to make up a composite (full-color original) picture are cyan, magenta, and yellow. Cyan is mighty close to blue, and magenta is close to red, so you can see now how your grade school crayons were fairly close to what is used commercially to produce *process color.* We call this *CMYK color.* The *K* is sort of unexpected in the abbreviation for cyan, magenta, and yellow. The *K* stands for **k**ey or black. A key plate is used in printing to complete the visible range of whatever you are printing. Let's make life easy and simply call it the black plate. A black plate is added to the cyan, magenta, and yellow printing plates because pigments are not totally pure; some light is absorbed into the art material instead of being bounced back at you. So the average of all three intensities of colors on the color plates is used to generate this black plate, and color printing is not only possible, but pleasing to look at. Without that fourth printing plate, you would wind up with sludge-like browns in areas that should be black.

The topic of color separations (C, M, Y, and K color plates) is dealt with in a more comprehensive tone in the printing chapter of this book. Why? Because printing your own color separations at this phase in your Photoshop career would be futile and heart-breaking; color printing-press printing is a science. But this was a good place to explain to you about both additive and subtractive colors, right?

In the section to follow, you will get hands-on work with channels to visually demonstrate the additive light system, but also to have a little fun in Photoshop. Some erudite (fancy-talking) individuals in the computer graphics field will call the following section *ChOps*—short for *channel operations*. I will simply call it "learning and having a ball by goofing around with some features in Photoshop."

Working with Color Channels

With the exception of the Macintosh Color Picker and a few applications, the intensity in each (primary) color channel that makes up an image goes from 0 (black) to 255 (white). This makes good sense when you consider that what we often call a 24-bit/pixel image (also called a TrueColor image, when referring to it as displayed on a monitor) has three channels—red, green, and blue. Therefore, each channel gets 8 bits of color expression to the channel: 8 times 3 equals 24.

Eight bits of color intensity (or *tone*, or *brightness*) in a channel means that there are 2 to the 8th power of different brightness possibilities in each channel… or (we did the math for you; it only took an hour) 256 unique tones. And it's no coincidence that 256 (one channel's color capability) brought to the 3rd power (there are three channels) equals 16.7 million possible total colors (or 2 to the 24th power).

In the example to follow (whew…thank goodness Bouton is going to shut up with this theory stuff for a while!), you are going to add a green pear to a scene—*not* by painting it into the composite color channel, but instead by first masking all three channels (producing a black pear in the scene—no color channel is making a brightness contribution), and then adding a white pear shape to the green channel. The result will be a green pear. Why? Because the green channel will be the only channel that contributes brightness to the overall scene (aka the *color composite*, or *RGB color channel*; this channel is shown at the top of the Channels palette).

Plop that companion CD into your system's CD player, locate Chap04 in the Examples folder, and let's get sailing.…

Painting a Picture Using Channels

1. In Photoshop, open both the Basic.tif image and the Pear.psd image found in the Examples/Chap04 folder on the companion CD. Arrange both image windows so that you have a clear view of both images.

2. Press F7 if the Layers/Channels/Etc./Etc. palette isn't currently onscreen. Click on the Channels tab.

Insider

If this is one of your first times out with Photoshop, you might want to click on the fly-out menu on the Channels palette, choose Options, click on the largest icon on the Options palette, and then close the Options box. This ensures that even if you're running at a high screen resolution, you will be able to see the magic that is about to take place.

In Figure 4.35, notice the callouts that show which color channels contain brightness, and therefore contribute to the overall color scene, and which areas in which channels do not. For example, in the blue channel, the entire top of the channel thumbnail is white. Do you know why? It's white because the color composite of this image has a pure blue sky; 100% brightness (white) is needed to create pure blue in the color composite. Take a moment to review this figure.

Figure 4.35   All color scenes are made up of color components—channels. And within the channels are tones that tell Photoshop how much of a particular primary color contributes to an overall scene.

3. With the Move tool chosen, drag the black pear into the RGB view of the Basic.tif image, as shown in Figure 4.36. Then press Ctrl(⌘)+E to merge the layer that contains the black pear with the background design. This editing move is not mandatory; it simply makes this assignment easier to follow if we aren't messing around with layers.

Note

> **Choosing channels**   If you're uncertain of how to see the color composite image in an image window, press Ctrl(⌘)+tilde (~). Most intermediate users switch channels by clicking on the channel thumbnail on the Channels palette. The channels are clearly labeled.
>
> I switch channels with a remote control.

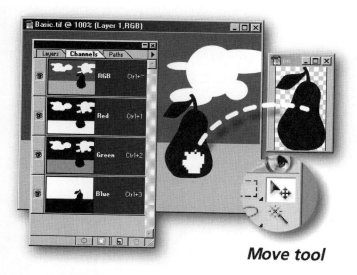

Move tool

Figure 4.36   Drag the black pear into the RGB channel of the Basic.tif image. Leave it to the right of the composition.

Insider

> Notice that every component channel turns black (0 color contribution) when you drag the pear into Basic.tif.

4. Guess what comes next? Yup. You need to turn the black pear shape into a white pear shape, so it can contribute 100% brightness (full color channel intensity) to the Green channel. Click on the title bar to the Pear.psd image to make it the active image window in the workspace. Now press Ctrl(⌘)+I. This is the keyboard shortcut for inverting colors in an image. Ya got a white pear now.

5. With the Basic.tif image as the active (foreground) image in the workspace, click the Green channel thumbnail to make this the active channel. Now click on the Pear image to make it the active editing image. (It does not matter what your channel view of the pear shape is; all channels, including the RGB composite channel, contain a white pear.) Press Ctrl(⌘)+A to select all of the pear shape, and then with the Move tool, drag the pear shape into the Green channel view of the Basic.tif image window, as shown in Figure 4.37. With the Move tool, align the pear shape with the black pear outline that's in the Green layer. Surprise! You will see a green pear emerge in the RGB color thumbnail of the image on the Channels palette!

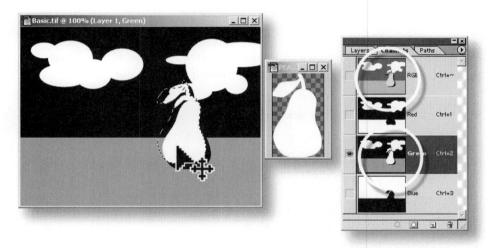

Move an inversed copy of the pear shape into the silhouette of the first pear using the Green channel

Figure 4.37   Adding 100% brightness to the Green layer will result in a green object within the RGB color composite view (the view we normally use) of the image.

6. Click on the RGB channel thumbnail on the Channels palette to see a full-size version of your new composition in the image window. Okay, pears don't get this green except in wax fruit stores, but you've just learned an invaluable lesson for future channel editing in Photoshop. Class dismissed. You can close the Pear and the Basic images at any time without saving.

We simply showed you a principle in the preceding assignment. We did not mean to teach you how to paint or edit, for there are quicker ways to put a green pear into a scene. Now that you're getting a feel for this "goofing with channels"—or *gotcha*, as I, the non-erudite author, call this stuff—let's progress to editing an image that would be somewhat hard to color correct without digging into a channel.

Nice Picture, Crummy Weather

We live in a less-than-tropical weather zone that gets an average of about five sunny days a month. It's a photographer's nightmare; all the skies in the images look like the color of lint. Not to worry; overcast skies are simply a combination of red, green, and blue colors mixed in equal amounts. A neutral shade of black is the result of red, green, and blue being applied in equal amounts, at less than full strength.

Let's get inventive here. Hmmm…if skies are supposed to be shades of blue, why not accentuate the blue channel in a picture, and play down the green and red channels? Now, we frequently "goose" a screen capture here and there to bring out a property we want you to see, to exaggerate a result. But we were shocked when we saw how much hidden detail in the sky emerged when the green and red were reduced in the image you're about to work with.

Using a nice picture of an art deco building with little or no sky detail, here's how to add visual interest to the image by re-working the colors in the channels:

Revealing Scene Objects by Manipulating Channels

1. Open the Mohawk.tif image from the Examples/Chap04 folder on the companion CD. (The image is the Niagara-Mohawk power company building here in town; that explains the filename.)

2. Click on the Magic Wand and then click on the Red channel layer in the Channels palette. Okay, you should notice a mild amount of tonal variation in the red channel, but it's all basically off-white. Set the Tolerance on the Options bar to 32 (a number I came to through trial and error; 32 out of a possible 256 tones is a moderately narrow tolerance for selecting pixels).

3. Click on the Anti-Aliased check box on the palette to make a smooth selection edge, and finally, click on the Contiguous check box. If you don't select these options, *every* instance of the color the Magic Wand selects will be chosen in the picture—including the interior of the building!

4. Click the Magic Wand tool as shown in Figure 4.38. As you can see, the sky is selected, and the building has no selection marquees inside its silhouette.

5. Press Ctrl(⌘)+L to display the Levels command. This feature can re-tune the brightness values in an image according to three zones: highlights, midtones, and shadows. In the Input area, drag the black point and the midtone sliders to the right, as shown in Figure 4.39. What you're doing here is telling Photoshop that the channel's black point exists at much more than 0 on a scale of 0–255. The black point, which is the slider control farthest to the left, is currently set at 51, and the midtone slider is set to .16, as you can see in the Input Levels fields in the

figure. You can use these settings if you like or come up with something that suits you better.

The effect? The channel's visual contents become darker. Then, on the Output scale, reduce the white point to about 203, as shown in Figure 4.40. Click OK. Again, you are telling Photoshop that white in this image actually starts at 203 on a scale of 0–255. So, although you've lied to Photoshop in only one step, you will notice that the color thumbnail of the sky is taking on a cyan color. This happens because although you've eliminated the red, there is still a dollop of green in the total area of the sky in the image.

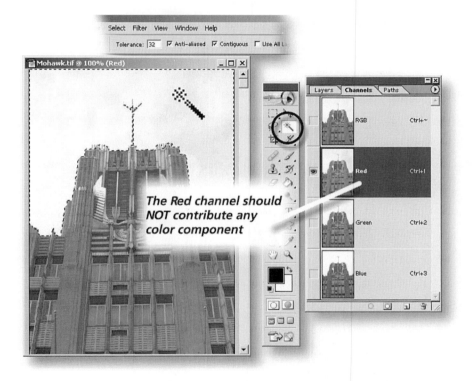

Figure 4.38   Select the part of the channel that is making more of an overall color contribution than it should.

Caution

Moderate midtones   Don't go too far to the right with the midtone slider, or you won't see white clouds in the picture. Instead, you'll see only shades of blue when you've finished this assignment.

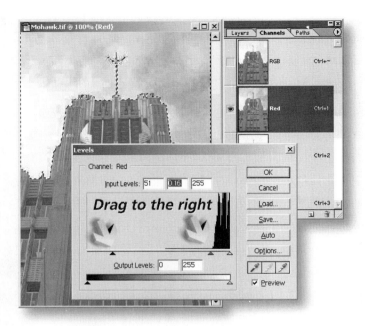

Figure 4.39   Except for sunsets, there usually isn't any red in the sky. Remove this unwanted primary color. Use the Levels command on part of the channel to make it darker (reduce its overall contribution to the RGB image).

4

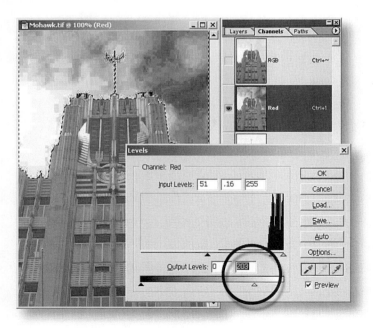

Figure 4.40   Negate any pure (255 brightness scale) contributions to the red channel by lowering the white point Output level.

6. Perform step 5 on the Green channel, as shown in Figure 4.41, except adjust only the midtone slider for the Input Levels to .13. As you can see in the image and the thumbnail, just sliding the midtones control to the right really makes the sky come alive. Click on OK to apply the changes and return to the workspace.

Make the Green channel dense by increasing the midpoint

Figure 4.41   When you darken the red and green channels, the image is left with brightnesses in the blue range, and this produces a mottled, realistic sky in the picture.

7. Click on the RGB color channel thumbnail on the Channels palette. You will see a sky with different tones (but no white clouds because white requires red, green, and blue at full intensity). Figure 4.42 *suggests* the results; hey, it's a black-and-white book, and we even exaggerated the tones in this figure to give you a better idea of the picture after experimenting with channels.

8. You can choose to save the image at this point (TIFF is a good format), or close it without saving it. Now that you realize the point of the assignment, there's no real need to keep the product.

Changing the tone in one channel of an image is only one way to bring out qualities that the original picture did not show. Let's get creative in the next section and *add* detail to the image that was never there.

Figure 4.42   Emphasizing a channel while playing down the others is a good method for bringing out the detail of the image as your human eye envisions it. Forget about what photography taught you; it's the aesthetics of the image that count!

Filtering a Channel

By this late date (in other words, five minutes after you've installed Photoshop!), you must surely have experimented with the filters and your favorite (or least favorite) photo. Photoshop is well known for its special effects prowess; more than 100 filters ship with the program.

Let's choose a particular filter, and instead of applying it to the photo, we'll apply it to a single channel and see how artistically we can mess up an image. Hey, *New Media* runs stuff like this all the time:

Applying a Filter to a Color Channel

   1. Open the Big_Dip.tif image from the Examples/Chap04 folder on the companion CD. Double-click on the Zoom tool to move your viewing resolution of the image to 100%, and then drag the window borders away from the image, if necessary, to see the whole image onscreen.

   2. Click on the Channels tab of the Layers/Channels/Blah/Blah palette, and then click on the Green channel title to make this channel active and appear in the

image window. Why are we doing this? Because we want to mess up the image a little, not a lot. And as you can see in Figure 4.43, the Green channel contributes some but not all of the component colors.

Green channel is fairly dim. This means it makes a so-so color contribution to the overall image.

Figure 4.43   If you want to make minor color changes to an image, find a channel that has very little visual information. The more dense the tones, the less contribution to the overall image this channel makes.

3. Choose Filter/Artistic/Colored Pencil. In Figure 4.44, you can see that the Colored Pencil filter *really* messes around with original tones! The Green channel's filtered tones will create a very different type of image. Click on OK to apply the filter and return to the workspace. Click on the RGB channel to view the full results.

4. In Figure 4.45, you can see a grayscale version of the finished image. You can choose to save the file to the TIFF format, or simply close it without saving— that's what *I* do to keep my hard drives clear of experiments that aren't of the artistic quality of the Mona Lisa. Keep Photoshop open. There's more fun with channels ahead.

Figure 4.44   By changing tones in the channel, you're actually mixing new amounts of red, green, and blue in the image to make a dramatic effect.

We tend to take it for granted that the component colors onscreen (and in slides) are aligned. In other words, we hardly think (or worry) that, for example, the Red channel will be misaligned with the two other channels. In fact, many monitors have a convergence feature that keeps the cathode guns in the back of the monitor aligned to hit exactly the same area of phosphors on the screen.

Hey, part of art is whimsy and going against convention. In the following section, we'll see how art is achieved by deliberately misaligning the visual information in channels.

Using Offset Channels to Create an Effect

You can use any image you like for the following steps, but we've provided you with a perfectly good one: a hand-drawn cartoon in color. The trick we're going to show you generally works best with cartoon figures, pictures of people you don't like, and simple, colorful objects such as billiard or croquet balls and informal dinnerware (Pier 1 stuff).

Over the years the Sunday newspaper's color funnies have gained a rightfully sorry reputation of printing inks that are out of register. I've seen colors fall at least 1/4" out of their target on a bad day. However, this mis-registration effect has become somewhat of an artistic icon. And here's how to reproduce it digitally:

Figure 4.45   Sorry that this figure is in black and white! If you perform the steps, on your screen, you'll see an image that appears to have been taken under fluorescent lighting about 50 years ago, at sunset, with mild solarization (similar to inverting tones in an image). And all you did was filter a single channel!

Creating Misaligned Channels

1. Open the Geek.tif image from the Examples/Chap04 folder on the companion CD. Or use a picture of your boss.

2. Open the Channels palette (press F7), and then choose the Move tool. You need to choose this tool because you cannot use the keyboard arrow keys to nudge when any other tool is chosen. And you will be nudging. Figure 4.46 shows the players in this assignment.

3. Click on the Green channel title on the Channels palette. Nudge the Green channel up by 2 pixels (by tapping twice on the keyboard's up arrow), and then nudge the channel to the left by 2 pixels (by tapping twice on the keyboard's left arrow), as shown in Figure 4.47.

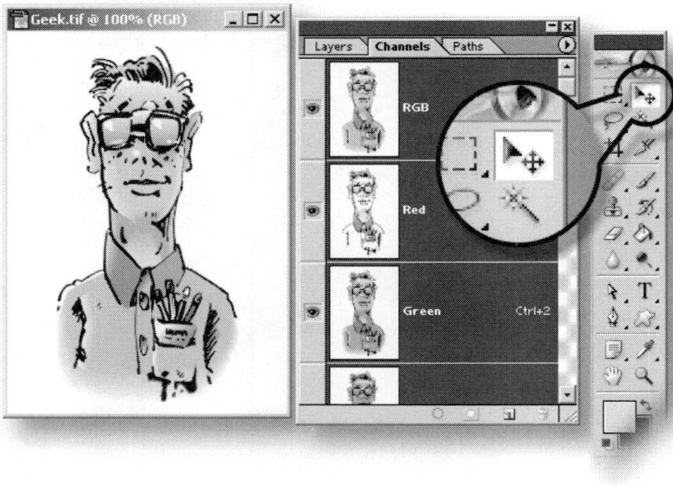

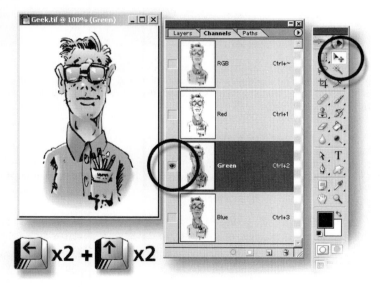

4

Figure 4.46   An image, the Channels palette, and the Move tool are all you need to create a comic book effect in Photoshop.

Figure 4.47   You're knocking the alignment of the Green channel's contents away from the other channels by tapping the arrow keys when the Move tool is chosen.

4. Click on the Red channel to make it the active editing channel. Nudge the channel down by 2 pixels and to the right by 2 pixels.

5. Click on the RGB title on the Channels palette's list. Yeah, yeah, Figure 4.48 is in black and white, but it should give you a fair idea of the wonderful effect caused when the three component channels in an image don't line up. For larger images, nudge the channels away from the center by more than 2 pixels; use your own artistic taste.

Figure 4.48   A comic book look can be achieved simply by throwing the color channels in an image off-center.

6. If you used your own image in these steps, you might want to save the image to your hard drive in the TIFF file format. Similarly, if you really like this weird version of one of my cartoons, save it. If you see the potential of this trick in your work and have no need for a test image, close it without saving.

Coming up next is a technique for adding text to an image *without* disturbing the graphic arrangement of the image. You'll *create* a channel, add some text, and...we don't want to spoil this now—read on!

Alpha Channels: Storage Space for Special Information

So far, we've played with what an image can provide—a number of color channels that together make up a color image. CMYK images have four channels, and Duotone images have two color channels. CMYK is a necessary color space because printing inks cannot capture RGB colors completely with fidelity. So cyan, magenta, yellow, and black simulate computer art colors. And Duotone is a color mode that uses a color plate in addition to a grayscale plate to make the gray tones look more rich. Truth be known, black ink doesn't provide total coverage on paper of the design you create. But Duotones are another story, covered later in this book.

In addition to the channel information that makes up an image, you can *add* a channel of grayscale visual information to an image for purposes we'll discuss in a moment. The Targa format can hold one extra channel, as can the Macintosh PICT files. TIFF images can hold several extra alpha (information) channels, and Photoshop's native PSD file format can hold up to 32 channels (a ridiculously luxurious amount). Before Photoshop refined the Layers feature, alpha channels were a must, because this is the place you could store and retrieve selection areas you created with the Lasso tool or the Quick Mask tool. Suppose you were in the middle of some real intricate selection work, and Mom called you for dinner. No problem; you saved your work to an *alpha channel*.

Using an Alpha Channel to Store Typography

As you will see in this section, alpha channels can be used to store selection information such as an area or the outline of text, and also to save texture images to be used with the Lighting Effects filter. Alpha channels are handy enough that we should take some steps toward mastering them. And those steps are as follows:

Creating a Type Effect Using an Alpha Channel

1. Open the Flowers.tif image from the Examples/Chap04 folder on the companion CD.

2. Press **D** for the default colors, press **X** to switch white to the foreground color, and choose the Type tool from the toolbox.

3. On the Options bar, click on the menu icon (toward the right of the Options bar) to access the Character and Paragraph palettes (item 1 in Figure 4.49). Choose a pretty font from the Character palette (item 2), and either experiment with the right font size for this image or take our word for it that 110 points will be a good size. At the top of the Options bar, click on the Left align icon. Click in the lower-left corner of the document window, and type **FLOWERS** on the image. Hold down the Ctrl(⌘) key to toggle to the Move tool, and reposition the text in the image if necessary (see item 3 in Figure 4.49 to get a good idea of the position and what is being described here).

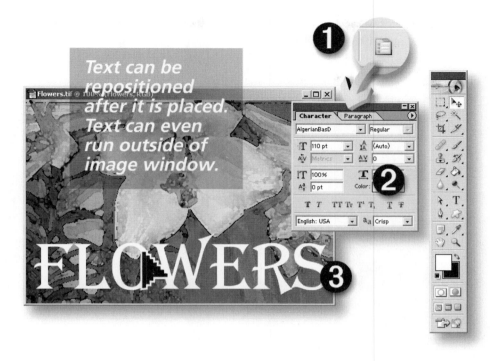

Figure 4.49   Create text that has ornamental features and scale it in the Type tool dialog box so that it will fit nicely on the background.

4. Press Ctrl(⌘)+Enter (Return) to commit the text to a layer. If necessary, you can enter a different point size (in the Character palette) to adjust the text size. You can also hold down the Ctrl(⌘) key to toggle to the Move tool if you're not completely satisfied with the position of the text—and want to tweak it further. So what did this have to do with channels? Wait a sec and you'll see. On the Layers palette, Ctrl(⌘)+click on the text layer title to create a marquee selection around the lettering.

5. On the Channels palette, Alt(Opt)+click on the Save selection as channel icon at the bottom of the Channels palette. When you use the Alt(Opt) modifier key, an options dialog box pops up before you save the selection of the text to a new alpha channel. Here's where you can make life easy on yourself. Although native color component channels all work on the "black contributes no color, white contributes a lot of color" principle, alpha channels can skip this rule because alpha channels are not pictorial information channels. In Figure 4.50, you can see the Alt(Opt)+click (item 1) that brings up the options dialog box (item 2), where you should check Color Indicates Selected Areas. Do you know why? Because it's

far more intuitive to write with black on white than it is to perform a "black-board" thing, where you have to draw using white on a black alpha channel to define selections.

Click on OK to add the lettering outline to the new alpha channel, and press Ctrl(⌘)+D to deselect the selection marquee. Click on the Alpha 1 channel title to make it active, if you would like to get a view of this channel in the document window.

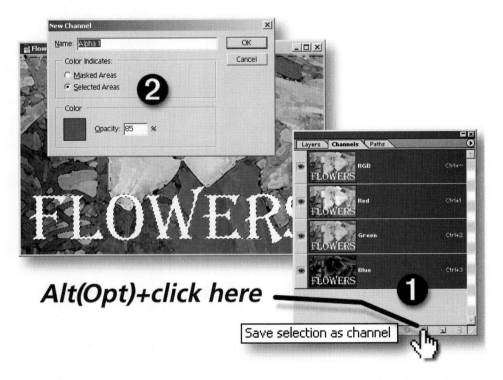

Figure 4.50   Alt(Opt)+click on the Save selection as channel icon, and then choose whether you want to work black on white or white on black in the new alpha channel.

6. Okay, the lettering has been saved as black on white in the alpha channel. How do you get it to work as a selection marquee? Glad you asked! Either hold down the Ctrl(⌘) key and click on the Alpha 1 title on the Channels palette list, or (more conventionally) click on the Load channel as a selection icon (see Figure 4.51).

Figure 4.51   Load the visual information stored in the alpha channel as a selection marquee.

7. Here's the really fun part: On the Layers palette, click on the Background layer to make it the active editing layer (and to return to the normal view of the document if necessary). Next, click the eye icon to the left of the Text layer's title to turn off the visibility for this layer. Then press Ctrl(⌘)+L to display the Levels dialog box.

8. Again, carefully arrange the image window so that when the Levels dialog box pops up, it doesn't cover the picture. As shown in Figure 4.52, drag the white point and the midpoint slider close to the left of the Input Levels scale. Doing this lightens the area inside the selection marquee, but the visual content—the flowers—is still quite visible. Can you think of, oh, about a million situations in which you need to add a title without disturbing the image? Here's the ticket (okay, here's one of *many* tickets). Click OK. Press Ctrl(⌘)+D to deselect the text.

9. There's no big need to hang on to this assignment, so close the image without saving.

So far, we've covered using color channels, saving to alpha channels, and loading selections from channels. Channels and selections seem to be irrevocably intertwined as Photoshop features go. And as you've seen, culling selections from layer information is as easy as Ctrl(⌘)+clicking.

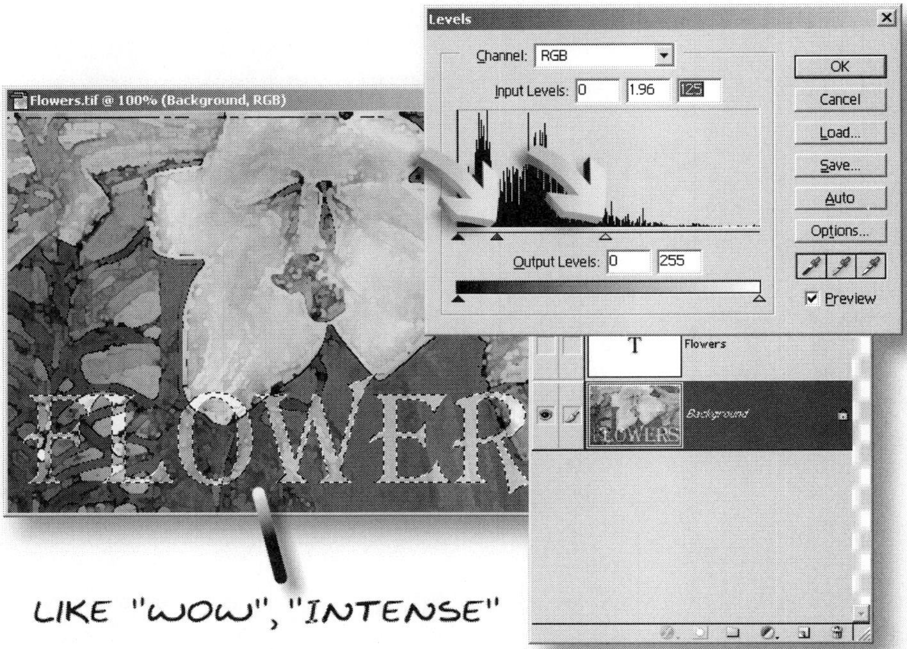

Figure 4.52   By moving the midpoint and white point sliders to the left, you are assigning pixels lighter colors than they originally had. The effect is an eye-pleasing one, and one you can use on many occasions.

Summary

Layers, Adjustment Layers, clipping layers, layer comps, channels, alpha channels—heady stuff, but you'll agree that there are associations galore *between* all these features, right? If you understand only the basics, your adventures in Photoshop will definitely be more rewarding, and you'll work quicker and more expertly with the knowledge of these niceties tucked firmly under your belt.

Coming up: all the ways you can create, save, and manipulate selections. You already know where selections are saved (answer: channels), but did you know that the core of Photoshop's power lies in the ways you can choose a selection? Better image editing and seamless, believable photo-trickery are yours for the asking, if only you turn the page!

Chapter 5

Harnessing the Power of Selections

All photo-editing work can be lumped into two general categories: You are working on an entire image (removing a color cast, cropping, rotating, and so on), or you're working on a portion of an image (perhaps removing backgrounds from people or

In this chapter, you'll learn

- How to perform basic selections in Photoshop
- How to use the Marquee tools and options
- How to use the Lasso tools to select image areas
- How to use the Magic Wand tool to select areas containing similar colors
- How to use a layer mask
- How to make the best selections—fast
- How to combine selection methods
- How to save and load selections
- How to use a number of selection tools to replace an overcast sky with one you've created in Photoshop

objects, creating special effects like a soft focus background, or doing any host of other common tasks). Photoshop provides an assortment of tools for selecting the portion of the image with which we want to work.

Basic Selections 101 with Lab

As I just said, Photoshop has a large number of different tools whose only purpose is to define the part of the image upon which we want to work. The area that is defined is called a *selection*, and all the tools that you use to make the selections are known as *selection tools*. If you are new to Photoshop, don't let the large number of selection tools with their strange-sounding names overwhelm you. We are going to learn this one step at a time, beginning with a look at what a selection actually is.

The concept of selection is something we work with all the time—perhaps without knowing it. If you have ever used a stencil, you have used a selection. The stencil enables you to apply paint to one part of the material while it protects the rest. Another example of a selection that is closer to home (literally) is using masking tape to mask off the parts of a room where you don't want to paint (which for me would be the whole room). Selections in Photoshop act just like a stencil or masking tape when it comes to applying an effect to a selected part of an image. Now that you understand the concept, let's look at the most basic of the selection tools—the Marquee tools.

5

Introducing Marquee Tools

The Marquee tools, shown in Figure 5.1, are used to create selections in the shapes of rectangles, ellipses, and one-pixel wide rows and columns.

The best way to see how these tools work is to use them to create some neat stuff. So, let's jump right in and make a poster for the National Wildflower Center in Austin, Texas. Our theme for this program is centered on the World of Texas Bluebonnets, and to make such a world, we'll use the Elliptical Marquee tool.

Creating a World of Flowers

1. Open the file BluebonnetField.tif from the Examples/Chap05 folder on the companion CD.

2. Select the Elliptical Marquee tool from the toolbox by placing the cursor over the marquee tools icon and clicking on the small black triangle in the lower-right corner of the button to open tool selection.

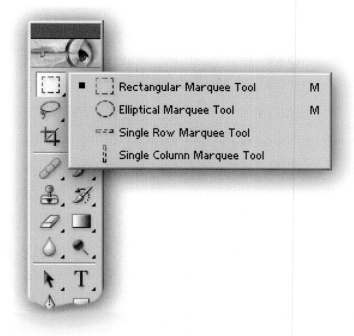

Figure 5.1   The Marquee tools provide the basic building blocks for many selections.

Insider

For this next step, make sure the Info palette is visible. If not, go to the Window menu and choose Info. As you perform step 3, you can watch the Width and Height numbers in the lower-right corner to help guide you. Your circle doesn't have to be the exact same amount, but the circle I created was about 286 (pixels), which gives you a general idea of the size. If your measurements aren't in pixels, you can click on the plus sign at the lower-left side of the Info palette to choose Pixels.

3. Place the cursor near the center of the photograph. Click and hold down the mouse button, and press the Alt(Opt)+Shift keys while dragging the mouse outward to form a circle roughly in the position shown in Figure 5.2. When the circle looks about the right size, let go of the mouse button and release the keys. The edge of the selection is marked by a flashing black-and-white marquee that has come to be called "marching ants."

4. Press Ctrl(⌘)+J to copy the selection to a new layer. *Only* the contents of the image inside the selection will be copied to the new layer (and the selection marquee will disappear).

Insider

> Holding down the Alt(Opt) key while making a selection (with the Marquee tools) will start the selection in the center and move outward from the center. Adding the Shift key constrains the Marquee tool to a perfect circle (or a perfect square in the case of the Rectangular Marquee tool). If you have enough fingers, holding down the spacebar lets you reposition the selection while you're still creating it. You can move the selection to a better position once the creation process is completed. Just click and drag it to relocate the selection (or use the arrow keys to nudge it). This trick works only as long as the Marquee tool (or any other selection tool) is active.

Figure 5.2   Hold down Alt(Opt)+Shift and drag out a circle. The figure has the selection highlighted to make it easier to see, but your own selection will not have this highlight.

5. If it is not already showing, open the Layers palette (F7) to see the new layer. Since we are going to need the selection that was lost when we used the Layer via Copy command, go to the Select menu and choose Reselect to re-open the marquee. We need this selection to be in place before applying the next filter, or the shape of the sphere will distort.

Insider

> You could also Ctrl(⌘)+click on Layer 1 to get the selection back, but it comes in handy to know that this Select, Reselect menu option exists. The Reselect option will reactivate a marquee selection for the last active selection used. And, like everything else in Photoshop, this option is not without a keyboard shortcut. Ctrl(⌘)+Shift+D will *reselect* (the opposite of Ctrl(⌘)+D, which will *deselect*).

6. Now go to the Filter menu and choose Distort, Spherize, and use the default setting of 100%. The bluebonnets have been distorted as if they were in a glass ball (as shown in Figure 5.3).

Figure 5.3   The selection allows the Spherize filter to be applied to the top layer without distorting the shape.

7. Press Ctrl(⌘)+H to temporarily hide (or turn off) the visibility of the selection marquee to make this next step a little easier.

Insider

> Sometimes the "marching ants" can become distracting. When you press Ctrl(⌘)+H to hide a selection, the selection is still active. If you need to see the selection again (to reassure yourself that it is still there), just press Ctrl(⌘)+H again to toggle the visibility back on.

Tip

> **Deselecting a selection**   Always remember that when you are done with a selection (whether it is hidden or not), you need to deselect it (Ctrl(⌘)+D). This is a common problem when hiding a selection. There's the tendency to forget that an active selection exists when it is hidden.

8. Select the Dodge tool from the toolbox. Right-click (Macintosh: hold Ctrl and click), and then choose the soft 100-pixel brush, set the Range to Midtones, and set the Exposure to **50%**. To make this look like a glass sphere, we need to lighten the edges. The trick to this effect is to apply just the edge of the brush inside the selection edge. Because we expect to see a little more light reflected near the upper-left part of the sphere, apply additional strokes with the Dodge tool here (see Figure 5.4).

Figure 5.4   Applying the Dodge tool along the edges defines the edge of the selection.

9. Press Ctrl(⌘)+D to deselect. (Remember, even though the selection is hidden, it is still active. So you need to deselect it when finished with the selection.) On the Layers palette, click on the Background layer to make it active. Go to the Filter menu and choose Blur, Gaussian Blur with a Radius of 2.0. Click OK. Click on Layer 1 to make it the active layer. Press **V** to switch to the Move tool, and drag the wildflower sphere to the right of the image, as shown in Figure 5.5.

Figure 5.5   You can use the Move tool to position the finished "wildflower world" anywhere in the image.

10. On the Layers palette, click on the Background layer once more. Click on the Create new fill or adjustment layer icon at the bottom of the Layers palette and choose Hue/Saturation. In the Hue/Saturation dialog box, check Colorize and change the settings to Hue **36**, Saturation **25**, and Lightness **0**, as shown in Figure 5.6. Click OK. Now you should have a brightly colored sphere of bluebonnets on top of what appears to be a sepia-tone photograph. If you would like to add just a slight amount of color back to the Background layer, lower the Opacity for the Hue/Saturation adjustment layer to **60%**.

    Now you'll place a title on this poster.

11. Press **D** for default colors. Press **X** to switch white to the foreground. Choose the Horizontal Type tool from the toolbox. On the Options bar, choose Impact as the font at 48 points, and select Right align text. Click in the document and type **A World of TEXAS Bluebonnets** (pressing Enter after typing the word *of* and again after the word *TEXAS*). Hold down the Ctrl(⌘) key to toggle to the Move tool, and reposition the text if needed (see Figure 5.7). When the text appears the way you want it, press Ctrl(⌘)+Enter (Return) to commit the text to a layer. Click on the triangle in the upper-right corner of the Layers palette, and choose Flatten Image.

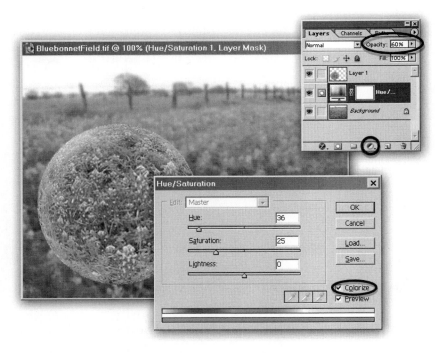

Figure 5.6   The Hue/Saturation command makes the background look like a sepia print.

5

Figure 5.7   Add text and then flatten the image to prepare for the next step.

12. Go to the Filter menu and choose Render, Lens Flare. In the Lens Flare dialog box, choose the default settings of 100% for Brightness and 50-300mm Zoom for Lens Type. In the Flare Center preview box, drag the marker to position it, as shown in Figure 5.8.

Figure 5.8   You can add a hint of reflection using the Lens Flare feature.

Tips and Tricks Using Marquee Tools

So what did you just do in the preceding set of steps? You used several key combinations to extend the use of the Marquee tools. These combinations are referred to as *modifier keys.* This is what they do:

- **Shift key**—When you press Shift *after* you press the mouse button, it constrains the Ellipse tool to a circle and the Rectangle marquee to a square. If you don't do this, it is next to impossible to get a pure square or a pure circle-shaped selection.

- **Alt(Opt) key**—Pressing the Alt(opt) key *after* you press the mouse button makes the marquee expand outward from the center. If you don't use this option, the marquee is created diagonally from the upper-left side down to the lower-right side. Centering the selection without Alt(Opt) can take forever.

Tip

> **Positioning a selection while making a selection**   At any point while creating a
> selection (without lifting your finger off the mouse), you can press the spacebar to repo-
> sition the selection marquee by dragging it around with your mouse. Release the space-
> bar, and continue to create the marquee selection.

The Marquee tool modifier keys are unique in that the action they perform is relative
depending whether they are pressed before or after the mouse button is clicked. If the
modifier key is pressed *before* the mouse button, the action changes.

The Marquee Tool Options Bar

If this is the first time you've worked with Photoshop, you may think the Marquee tools
are quite limited. After all, how often will you need to select a square, rectangle, ellipse,
or circle? The truth is that you can create just about any shape imaginable using these
tools if you learn how to use some of the features found on the Options bar shown in
Figure 5.9.

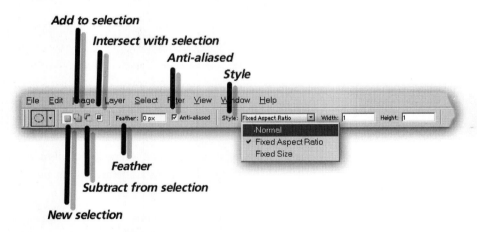

Figure 5.9   The Options bar adds more capability to the Marquee tools.

Here is a brief breakdown of what the items on the Options bar will do. You can refer to
Figure 5.9 as the items are explained:

- **New Selection**—When you select this option, a new selection is created. If there
  is an existing selection, this option cancels out the existing selection and replaces
  it with the new one you create. Some modifier keys will override this option
  (they will be covered shortly).

- **Add to Selection**—This option adds to an existing selection. If you have made a selection and would like to add to the selection without using the icons on the Options bar, you can press Shift to get the same result.

- **Subtract from Selection**—If you have an active selection and would like to subtract from that selection, you can select this option or use the modifier Alt(Opt) key.

- **Intersect with Selection**—If you choose this option when a selection is active, the result will be the intersecting areas of two selections. The key combination that can produce the same result is Alt(Opt)+Shift.

Note

> **About Boole**   These modifications to existing selections are sometimes called *Boolean* operations, named after George Boole (1815–1864), a British mathematician who invented a simple way to describe algebraic operations using the terms *and*, *but not*, and others. Unfortunately, a digital device was needed to carry out the Boolean operations, and that was not to happen for more than 100 years! Nonetheless, Boole was named a fellow of the Royal Society in 1857.

- **Feather**—This option allows you to give the selection a soft edge by blurring edges and building a transition boundary between the selection and surrounding pixels. This also gives the selection corners a rounded appearance because the greater you set the Feather number, the more you blur (or soften) the hard-edge results of the selection.

- **Anti-aliased**—This option smooths the jagged edges of a selection by creating transition pixels between the edge and background.

- **Style**—You can choose from these three styles:

  - **Normal**—This option enables you to determine the size of your selection as you drag.

  - **Fixed Aspect Ratio**—This option enables you to fix a ratio for your selection. For example, if you want the selection to be twice as high as it is wide, you would enter a **2** in the Height field and **1** in the Width field.

  - **Fixed Size**—This option enables you to enter values for Height and Width to create a precise selection (when the dimensions are known).

The Marquee tools interact with existing selections in four different ways. The default setting for the Marquee tools is *New Selection*. The ones you will use most often to interact with existing selections are the *Add to* and *Subtract from* settings. By using the Marquee tools in combination with these settings, you can make almost any irregular shape imaginable. The last setting, *Intersect with selection*, is a little unusual in that when you drag it over an existing selection, only the part of the selection that the two selections have in common will remain. Don't worry about this setting for now; you won't need it in too many situations, but that doesn't mean you shouldn't experiment. Once you understand what this setting can do, you might discover a time when this option fits perfectly with what you want to accomplish. That one time will make you glad that it is there.

Feathering the Selections

Until now, we have been considering selections that have a hard and defined edge. The circle mask used in the previous exercise had an Anti-aliased option. Anti-aliasing gives an edge a smooth look as opposed to a jagged, bitmapped look. But don't confuse the smooth look of Anti-aliasing with Feathering. Feathering builds a transition along the edges, in effect blurring the edges.

Often you may want to make a selection that has a soft edge. When you are moving someone or something from one photograph into another, for example, using a feathered selection helps the subject being moved blend into the picture more smoothly. You need to be careful with the amount of feathering you apply to the mask. Usually, just a few pixels are sufficient. If you put in a large amount of feathering, the object looks like it has a glow or is furry.

While you can do many things with the Marquee selection tools, they represent a really basic tool. When you need to create an irregular-shaped selection, it is time to consider the Lasso tools.

Rounding Up the Lasso Tools

Located under the Marquee tools on the toolbox, the Lasso tools are a collection of three different tools that you can use to draw both straight-edged and freehand edges when making an irregularly shaped selection. The three tools are

- Lasso tool
- Polygonal Lasso tool
- Magnetic Lasso tool

Unlike the Marquee tools, which produce closed shapes, the Lasso tools let you draw a meandering path around a subject and return to the beginning point to finish the selection. Note that if you release the mouse button or double-click it (depending on which tool you are using), Photoshop will make a straight line back to the starting point to complete the selection. So, unless this result is your intention, make sure you return to the starting point when using the Lasso tools.

The Lasso and Polygon Lasso Tools

All the Lasso tools act in a similar fashion. In the grand scheme of things, the Lasso tool is designed to draw freehand selections, and the Polygonal Lasso tool creates a selection made up of a series of straight lines. If you want to create a selection that combines both straight edges and rounded ones, you can toggle between these two tools by pressing the Alt(Opt) key while keeping your mouse button pressed. You might want to practice switching between these two tools since mastering this trick can come in pretty handy sometimes.

If you start by making a freehand selection with the Lasso tool, keep the mouse button pressed as you drag. When you want to switch to making straight edges in the middle of the selection process, stop dragging (but keep the mouse button pressed) and press down the Alt(Opt) key. As long as you keep holding down the Alt(Opt) key, you are free to release the mouse button and just click on corners to make up the straight line. If you want to return to the freehand Lasso tool, stop and press the mouse button; then release the Alt(Opt) key and continue dragging. Whew! Trust me—it's a lot easier to perform than to describe on paper! You'll get some practice in the "Let's Lasso Somebody" section later in the chapter.

Note

Polygon definition   According to the dictionary, the noun *polygon* is defined as any multi-sided figure. Polygon is not a dead parrot ("polly gone"—ya gotta work with me here). Therefore, the Polygonal Lasso tool is appropriately named.

The Magnetic Lasso Tool

The Magnetic Lasso tool will automatically detect the edge of an object for you—on one condition—if there is a high contrast between the color of the object (you are selecting) and the background color surrounding the object. When the colors are similar, this tool might not work as anticipated; otherwise, it can save you a lot of work. Oh—and if this condition applies to a part of the object but not the entire object, you can hold down the Alt(Opt) key to toggle between the Magnetic Lasso tool and the Lasso tool to finish the selection freehanded.

The Magnetic Lasso tool can be a great time-saver when you need to make selections. Essentially, you move the tool along an edge of the area you want to select (a high-contrast, well-defined edge works best). On edges that are poorly defined—when the colors inside and outside the edge are close to the same color—the tool needs a little help from you.

Using the tool is quite simple. Click once on the point where you want to begin the selection. This point is called a *fastening point*. Now move the tool (slowly and without holding down the mouse button) along the edge. Fastening points will appear along the edge of the selection as the computer tries to determine where the edge is. At some point, the computer will guess wrong. When it does make a wrong guess, stop and press the Backspace key. Each time you press the key, Photoshop removes the last point on the selection. Continue to do this until you get to a point on the selection back on the actual edge. You can try adding fastening points again, but usually, when the Magnetic tool guesses wrong, there is either a low-contrast edge, or something nearby (not on the edge) is pulling the tool away from the edge.

At this point you have several choices. You can change the settings in the Options bar and attempt to click your way through it—but this is not the best alternative. Instead, try clicking to create fastening points where you would like them to go, or press the Alt(Opt) key to switch temporarily to the Lasso tool; and while pressing the mouse button, drag the mouse along the edge. If the edge (confusing the Magnetic Lasso) is basically straight lines, you can switch to the Polygonal tool by holding down the Ctrl(⌘) key and then click from point to point.

Don't become intimidated over making a complicated selection. You might be thinking to yourself, "Man, I couldn't sign my name with a mouse to save my life." You're not alone. Very few of us can. That's why Photoshop has made so many ways available to create a selection. In addition, all the available methods can be combined to make selecting something as easy as possible. So switch selection tools, switch selection *methods*—whatever works. And there's a ton of ways to make it work.

Now, if it is still important to you to sign your name digitally, you might want to consider a graphics tablet instead of a mouse. The industry standard for graphics tablets is

Wacom Technology (www.wacom.com) if you want to look into these handy devices as an alternative. Does this mean you absolutely need a graphics tablet to make a Lasso selection? Of course not! It is completely possible to make selections with a mouse. Not only is it possible—we do it *all* the time.

Let's Lasso Somebody

Enough theory. Take a soda break if you need one, and when you return refreshed, we'll put some of this theory into practice and make some selections. The next exercise involves a groomsman named Jon in a cluttered church office wearing a ridiculously overpriced rental tuxedo. If his mother is going to frame this photograph, the background must be replaced with something a little less cluttered.

Combining Selection Methods

1. Open the TuxedoJon.psd file from the Examples/Chap05 folder on the companion CD.

2. Choose the Magnetic Lasso tool, and pick an area of high contrast between Jon and the background. Click at the edge of Jon and the background (his tuxedo is a good starting place). After you click, release the mouse button and simply drag a line around him. When you reach Jon's hair, or another area of low contrast, you might find it easier to define this area if you hold down the Alt(Opt) key to toggle to the Lasso tool and click and drag to make a selection near this area (of low contrast). Release the Alt(Opt) key when you're back to high contrast areas. Don't worry if your selection has mistakes (see Figure 5.10). You will fix that later.

Insider

If you would like to do this exercise without all the work of making a selection, you can use a ready-made selection. Step 3 explains how to use this selection. Otherwise, skip step 3, and continue on to step 4 to refine the selection.

3. Optional: Click on the Channels tab to view the Channels palette, and Ctrl(⌘)+click on the Tight Jon Outline channel. A selection of Jon will load. If the marching ant selection appears around the edges of the document instead of around Jon, the selection is inverted (this has to do with selection preferences; see Chapter 2, "The Critically Important Color and Gamma Calibration

Chapter"). If the preceding statement is the case, press Shift+F7 to invert the selection. Click on the Layers tab to move back to the Layers palette. Skip to step 6.

Figure 5.10   Using the Magnetic Lasso tool, you can quickly make an initial selection of Jon from the background.

4. Press **D** (default colors). Click on the Quick Mask mode icon on the bottom of the toolbox (or press **Q**). If the red tint color is not on Jon (but on the background instead), Alt(Opt)+click on the Edit in Quick Mask Mode icon below the color boxes on the toolbox to switch the tint to Jon.

5. Press **B** to switch to the Brush tool. On the Options bar, choose a soft round 5-pixel brush. Mode should be set at Normal, and Opacity and Flow should be at 100%. Press Ctrl(⌘)+plus sign to zoom in where you can get a good look at the edges where Jon meets the background. Hold the spacebar to toggle to the Hand tool when you need to maneuver around the image as you work. With

black as the foreground color, paint in areas of Jon that might have been missed. Press **X** to switch to white as the foreground color, and paint over mistakes or areas of the background that were included in the selection process. The goal is to cover Jon in red tint and to exclude the background (see Figure 5.11). Press **X** to switch back to black as needed. When you are satisfied with the selection (or red tint area), press **Q** to exit the Quick Mask mode and turn the red tint area back into a selection.

Insider

One of the ways to emphasize the subject is to blur the background using Gaussian blur. The problem with this approach is that the background is so cluttered, by the time you blur it enough to do the job, it looks sort of surreal. On top of that, Jon and the couch on his right are the same distance from the camera, so the perspective doesn't look right. For the best results, let's replace the background with a different one.

Figure 5.11   Use the Quick Mask mode to refine your selection.

6. Press Ctrl(⌘)+J to move Jon to his own layer. Click the Background layer to make it active. Open the Background.tif image from the Examples/Chap05 folder on the Companion CD. Position both documents so that you can see both (zoom out if necessary). Click the title bar of the Background.tif image to make it the active document. Choose the Move tool, hold down the Shift key, and drag the Background layer into the TuxedoJon.psd document window (see Figure 5.12). Holding down the Shift key will position the new background so that it is centered in the target document window. Close the Background.tif image without saving any changes.

7. Wow, the photograph has now replaced the previous cluttered one. Actually, the old background is still there, simply hidden by the new background. To prove the original photo is still there, click the eye icon on Layer 2 to toggle the layer's visibility to off so that the old background becomes visible. Click on the eye icon again (for Layer 2), and the new background returns. Wait, it gets even better! With the Move tool active and the new background layer active, you can move the background image around to position it.

Figure 5.12   Shift+drag the new background image into the TuxedoJon document.

8. Optional: If you see on Jon areas of the old background that need to be removed, click on Layer 1 (Jon's layer) to make it the active layer. Click the Add layer mask icon at the bottom of the Layers palette. The default colors (black and white) should still be your foreground and background colors. Press **B** for the Brush tool, and use black to paint away unwanted areas. Press **X** to switch to white, and paint away any mistakes you might make. When Jon appears perfect, right-click (Macintosh: hold Ctrl and click) on the layer mask thumbnail, and choose Apply Layer Mask to apply your changes (see Figure 5.13). Press Ctrl(⌘)+Shift+S if you would like to save this image to your hard disk.

As you can see, using a selection allows you to replace a background without losing the original background.

Figure 5.13   Use a layer mask if necessary to touch up any missed areas of old background on Jon.

Magic Wand Tool Magic

The Magic Wand tool is great for selecting areas containing similar colors. You should know a few things about this selection tool first to produce the best results. This section helps you figure out how the tool works and then do some cool stuff with it.

The first fact about the Magic Wand tool is that it's not magic (surprised?). Until now, all the selection tools we have used involved either closed shapes or lassos that surround the area to be selected. The Magic Wand tool acts a little like dropping a stone in a calm pool of water. The selection, like ripples of water, spreads outward from the starting point. It continues radiating outward, selecting similar (and adjacent) colored pixels until it reaches pixels whose color or shade is noticeably different from the starting point. These pixels are not included in the selection. The next exercise helps you understand how the Magic Wand tool works.

Handling the Magic Wand with Care

One of the first problems you may discover when working with the Magic Wand tool is that clicking in an area doesn't always produce a uniform selection. Instead, many little selection "islands" might pop up randomly within the initial selection. This happens because of a difference in color value from the starting point pixels and the pixels that make up these "islands."

You can resolve this issue in several ways. You could Shift+click on all the individual "islands" with the Magic Wand tool until they are all included in the selection. However, this is not the most efficient way to resolve the problem (although I'm embarrassed to admit that I am guilty of using this practice on occasion myself). Instead, try choosing Select, Similar; or try increasing the Tolerance setting and reselecting the same area again. The Contiguous option (when *un*checked) on the Options bar also acts in the same manner as Select, Similar. When Contiguous is checked, the selection will stop when it bumps up against pixels of different colors. When Contiguous is unchecked, the selection will include *all* similar colors within the image or within the layer (which brings us to another option to consider). When the Use All Layers option is checked, the selection is based on the entire image. When Use All Layers is unchecked, the selection is based on the image information of the *active layer only*.

Tip

> **Adding to selections**   Keep in mind that sometimes the selection "islands" are a result of areas that are vastly different in color. In this case (if you still want these "islands" to be included in the selection), choose a Marquee or Lasso tool and hold down the Shift key (Add to selection) while making a selection shape over the "islands." That should resolve the issue.

Something else worth mentioning: When you use Select, Similar to add to a selection, another problem could arise. If the selection goes too far into the part of the image that you *don't* want selected (especially at the edge of an object), there is another trick to consider. Did you know that when you use the Similar command, Photoshop uses the current Tolerance setting to determine which pixels can be included in the selection? This means that after you do an initial selection with the Magic Wand tool (at a Tolerance level of 32, for example), you can set the Tolerance option to a lower value (perhaps somewhere between 4 and 8) before going to the Select, Similar menu option. Then colors that are much closer to the original starting point will be the only ones added to the original selection.

Using the Magic Wand Tool to Create a Photo Composite

In this exercise, you will use the Magic Wand tool and a few other Photoshop features to create a photo composite from two photographs. In this case, I have an excellent exterior photo taken on a bright summer day in a rural Texas town, but I cannot see inside the building. I also have a great photo of a stairway in Ybor City, Florida. Our job will be to combine the two into a photo that can be used in a brochure for the purpose of increasing awareness of the problem of urban decay in the inner city.

An Exercise in Pane

1. Open the OldWindows.tif file from the Examples/Chap05 folder on the companion CD. From the toolbox, choose the Magic Wand tool.

2. On the Options bar, check the Contiguous option and set Tolerance to **30**. Click in the center of a windowpane, as shown in Figure 5.14. The selection instantly expands to select all the black pixels in the pane. Because the Contiguous check box was checked, the selection stopped at the edge of the windowpane.

3. To select the rest of the windowpanes, go to the Select menu and choose Similar. Now Photoshop selects all the pixels in the image that are within the Tolerance setting. Because there are no other black pixels in the image, all the pixels in the windowpanes are selected (see Figure 5.15).

4. Open the OldStairs.tif image from the Examples/Chap05 folder on the Companion CD. Press Ctrl(⌘)+A to select the entire image. Press Ctrl(⌘)+C to copy the image to the Clipboard. Close the file without saving any changes.

Figure 5.14   The Magic Wand tool quickly selects all the black pixels in the windowpane.

5

5. With the OldWindows.tif image as the active document, choose Edit, Paste Into, or press Ctrl(⌘)+Shift+V. The photograph of the stairs now appears to be the view through the windowpanes, as shown in Figure 5.16. The Paste Into command created a new layer containing the new background image of the stairs, along with a layer mask that reveals only the areas that initially were selected. With the Move tool, you can move the stairs photograph around. This is slightly different than the method used to move a new background into the TuxedoJon exercise. Hey, let's get even *more* creative.

Insider

You have one pane of glass left, and, even though it is dirty, it should be at least a little transparent. To accomplish this, you need to create another selection.

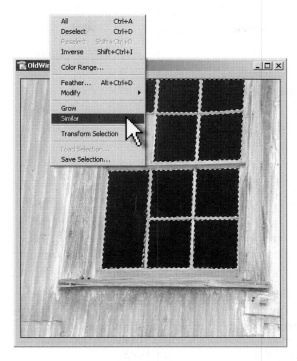

Figure 5.15   Use the Select, Similar command to add the remaining black windowpanes to the selection.

Figure 5.16   Using the Paste Into command, you can put stairs into the windows.

6. On the Layers palette, click on the Background layer to make it active. The Magic Wand tool should still be the active tool; if not, press **W** to make it active. Change the Tolerance setting to **15** so the selection will be limited to the pixels only in the dirty windowpane. Click in the center of the dirty windowpane.

7. To make the glass transparent, you'll modify the layer mask (on Layer 1). On the Layers palette, click on the thumbnail of the layer mask on Layer 1. Click on the Foreground color of the toolbox and change the color to a medium gray (R:129, G:129, B:129). Click OK. Press Alt(Opt)+Delete (Backspace) to fill the selection on the layer mask with this medium gray color.

8. Dirty windows are never uniformly dirty, so for a touch of realism, press **B** to switch to the Brush tool. On the Options bar, choose an irregular-shaped brush such as the Spatter 46-pixels brush. Set the Opacity to **35%**. Press **D** for the default colors, and make sure black is the foreground color (if it's not, press **X** to switch black to the foreground). Click once or twice in the windowpane to make it appear as though there are smudged areas that are dirtier than other areas (thus less transparent). Or maybe you would like to drag across the windowpane with the brush. Experiment and use the History palette to undo any brush strokes you don't like. When you are satisfied with your results, press Ctrl(⌘)+D to deselect. The resulting image is shown in Figure 5.17.

Figure 5.17   The dirty—but still transparent—window adds a realistic touch.

9. As a finishing touch, you should make some tonal adjustments so both photo-graphic images look like they belong together. On the Layers palette, click on the Background layer to make it active. Click on the Create new fill or adjustment layer icon at the bottom of the Layers palette and choose Levels. In the Levels dialog box, change the middle Input Level from 1.00 to **0.45** (as shown in Figure 5.18) and click OK. If you would like, you can save this file to your hard drive as a PSD file to maintain the layers, or flatten and save in a file format of your choice.

Note

> **A word about layer masks**   We have used a layer mask in two examples in this chapter, so we should talk a little about this marvelous feature. What *is* a layer mask? The layer mask shares a layer controlling the image on the layer it occupies, determining what is visible and what is not. Areas on the mask that are white are 100% opaque or visible, while areas of the mask that are black are completely transparent. So, it figures that if we were to paint a 50% gray brushstroke on the layer mask, the contents of the layer under the brushstroke would be 50% transparent. In the preceding exercise, we made the glass semi-transparent by using black and painting part of the layer mask under the glass with brush tools set at an opacity of 35% (creating a gray tone). That resulted in the layer containing the glass becoming 65% transparent (100% − 35% = 65%) Don't worry about the math. It isn't like I calculated the amount; I just tried several different settings (thanks to Undo) until I found one I liked. To learn the full scoop on this marvelous tool, see "Using the Layer Mask Feature," in Chapter 4, "Layers and Channels."

Getting the Best Selections (in the Least Amount of Time)

Whether doing art layout for work or for community projects (read: free), I have spent the past 10 years making selections. In that time, I have come up with a short list of Do's and Don'ts that I will share with you so you can benefit from my experience.

Make a First Rough Cut Selection

If the object you want to select is large and has a lot of meandering edges, make a ball-park selection first. You can take two routes with this possible solution:

- You can make a general selection just *outside* the object (precision is not necessary at this point). Then put the selection on a separate layer and use a layer mask to paint away what you don't need. Layer masks are very forgiving. What I mean by this is, when you are working in Layer Mask mode, you can easily fix mistakes. You paint with black to hide unwanted parts of the selection, and if you make a mistake, you paint with white to unhide the area.

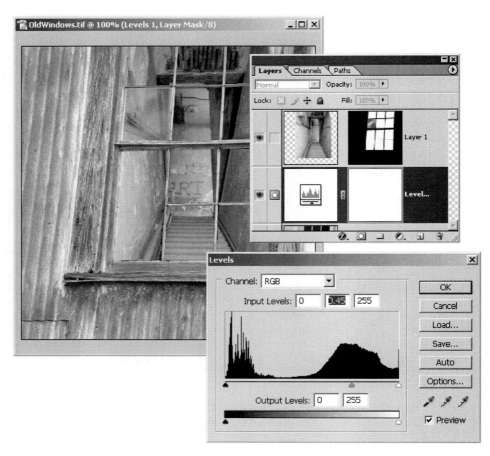

Figure 5.18   Use a Levels Adjustment Layer to make a tonal adjustment to the background image. If you use an Adjustment Layer, you have the flexibility of changing or tweaking the settings for the Levels command at any time.

- The other choice is to make a general selection just *inside* the object (again precision is not crucial) and then go into Quick Mask mode. Pressing **Q** toggles you in and out of Quick Mask mode. You create a selection by painting. You will see a tinted color (the default is red) appear wherever your selection is being made. Don't worry—you are not really painting tint on your object; the tint is just there to let you visualize where your selection will be. Similar to the way you use the layer mask, you paint with black to apply the tinted color and paint with white to remove tint. Your goal is to add the tinted paint to finish the selection you started.

Remember when I said to combine selection methods? This is a great combination of selection tools. When you press **Q** again (to toggle out of Quick Mask mode), you will see your tinted paint change to a selection (or marching ants).

Zoom and Move

You can set the Zoom to Actual Pixels to get an up-close-and-personal look at your image when doing the fine-point editing you need to do. Use either Ctrl(⌘)+ Alt(Opt)+0 (zero), or double-click the Zoom tool on the toolbox. Yeah, I know; if the image is large, it no longer fits on the screen. That doesn't matter. You can move around in several ways when you're in this close, but probably the best way I know of is to hold the spacebar to toggle the currently selected tool to the Hand tool (as long as you keep the spacebar pressed).

This suggestion is really a lifesaver. Imagine this scenario: You've magnified your view of an area to see it better. You are drawing a selection, and you have come to an edge of the document window. You need to move past the edge of the document window but don't want to lose the selection you've started (you're still in the middle of making this selection). No problem—you hold the spacebar, drag the image to expose more of the subject on the screen, and release the spacebar to pop back to your selection tool (finish where you left off).

Add Some and Take Away Some

Using the Add To Selection and Subtract From Selection modes, you can begin to shape the selection to fit the subject you are trying to isolate. Here is a trick that will save you time when doing this part: First, rather than clicking the buttons in the Options bar, use the key modifiers to change between modes. Pressing the Shift key changes to the Add To Selection mode, and pressing the Alt(Opt) key changes it to the Subtract From Selection mode. Just remember that you must press these modifier keys *before* you click the mouse.

If you use these modifier keys often, you will find that using them becomes intuitive. You'll be surprised at how quickly you can work with one hand on the keyboard and the other on the mouse. You'll soon know instinctively which key to press without even looking—kind of like touch-typing.

Another thought to consider: If you know you'll be using the Add To Selection and Subtract From Selection modes frequently, choose one of these options on the Options bar. This way, you need to use the modifier key only for the one that you didn't choose (on the Options bar).

Get in Close

On some areas you may need to zoom in at levels even greater than 100%. Photoshop enables you to zoom up to 1600%, which must be there for the purpose of selecting microbes and stray electrons. Try to remember two more shortcuts: Ctrl(⌘)+plus and Ctrl(⌘)+minus. These shortcuts enable you to zoom in and out of the document quickly. The only problem is that these shortcuts have become so instinctive with how I work—I've become *so* used to using them—that it never fails to disappoint and frustrate me when I press Ctrl(⌘)+plus while in Microsoft Word, and it *doesn't* zoom in on the document.

Now and again, return to Fit to Screen just to keep a perspective on the whole image. Speaking of keeping a perspective—when taking the time to refine your selection, keep in mind some questions to ask yourself (to gauge how much time to invest in this selection). Here are some examples of real situations that should adjust the degree of exactness you want to concern yourself with in making your selection:

- Are the edge colors of the object you are selecting almost identical to the background colors? If they are roughly the same colors, investing a lot of time producing a detailed selection doesn't make much sense since a feathered edge will work just fine.

- Will you be resizing the final image? If you are going to be making the current image larger, every detail will stick out like the proverbial sore thumb; so, any extra time you spend to make the selection (as exact as possible) will pay big benefits. If you are going to reduce the size of the subject, a lot of tiny detail will become lost when it is resized, so again you shouldn't invest a lot of time in the selection.

- Are you being paid for this job, or is it a freebee? Creating a complex selection is a time-consuming process. I once spent nearly half a day on a single selection.

Saving and Loading Selections

In the previous exercise, you had the opportunity to load a selection that I had made instead of creating it yourself. After making that particular selection (which took only about five minutes), I saved it as part of the Photoshop file. If a selection is not saved as a selection, it is lost as soon as the file is closed—even if the file is saved as a Photoshop PSD file.

The Alpha Channel

So, how do you save a selection? If you invest a lot of time making a selection, you should be able to save it. The process is simple: You use the alpha channel. Sounds like a science fiction channel on your local cable TV, doesn't it? The alpha channel actually is not a channel at all, but rather the name assigned for additional channels (in the Channels palette) used as general-purpose storage space in a graphics file. You can rename these channels, of course, but Photoshop will generate the alpha channels in numerical order. The new channel is still technically referred to as an alpha channel (or simply a channel) to differentiate it from the image mode channels (such as the Red, Green, and Blue channels found in an RGB document). How many alpha channels can fit into a Photoshop file? Good question. How big of a file can you live with? Adobe allows an image to have up to 24 channels (which includes color and alpha channels), but be warned that the more channels saved in a file, the higher the overall file size of the document.

Saving a Selection

So let's get back to the original question of saving a selection. You can get the same result a couple of different ways.

One method is to go to the Select menu and choose Save Selection. This opens the Save Selection dialog box, shown as item 1 in Figure 5.19. If the image already has an existing channel, you can add your new selection to the existing one, or you can save the selection to a new channel. Choose New and give the channel a descriptive name (as was done for the TuxedoJon image in the previous steps).

The second method is to view the Channels palette and click on the *Save selection as channel* icon at the bottom of the Channels palette (or Alt(Opt)+click on this icon to view a dialog box that will allow you to name the channel). An alpha channel with the selection information is generated (item 2 in Figure 5.19). Another way to rename an alpha channel is to double-click on the channel title to highlight the channel name and then type the new name (similar to renaming layers on the Layers palette).

You must save the image as a Photoshop (PSD) or a TIFF (TIF) file to save the channel information. If you don't save in one of these formats, Photoshop will do you the courtesy of giving you a single obscure warning message that some features will not be saved in the format that you have chosen before you save in that format and lose the channel forever.

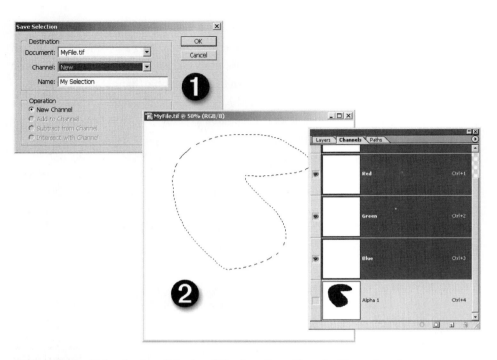

Figure 5.19   Using the Save Selection dialog box (item 1) or the Channels palette, you can save your selection as a channel.

5

Loading a Selection

When you open the file and want to access the saved selection from the channel, display the Channels palette and Ctrl(⌘)+click on the channel with your selection, or open the Select menu and choose Load Selection. Open and pick the name of the alpha channel that you or someone else tucked away into the image. This may surprise you, but many stock photography companies offer selections in their photos. One of these companies is Photospin (www.photospin.com), a great online photo subscription service, which offers large collections of photo objects on CDs (lots and lots of CDs).

Replacing an Overcast Sky

Taking photographs on an overcast day is always a mixed blessing. Because of the clouds, the illumination is diffused—and that's good. But these kinds of clouds also make the horizon of a landscape photograph uninteresting—which isn't so good. You can use the

Magic Wand tool in this type of situation to make an easy selection of the overcast sky. After you have selected the sky, you can replace it with an artificial one created in Photoshop or with another photograph of a sky with clouds that appear more interesting. Let's move on and see how this is done.

Adding a Cloudy Sky

1. Open the dscn0349.tif image from the Examples/Chap05 folder on the companion CD. Press **W** to switch to the Magic Wand tool. On the Options bar, set the Tolerance to **70** (this high setting ensures that all the areas around the branches will be tightly selected). Click in the upper-right area of sky. The selection marquee in Figure 5.20 shows the edges of the initial selection.

Figure 5.20   The Magic Wand tool is essential for replacing an overcast sky.

2. Choose Select, Similar. Wow! Now you have more selected than you wanted. That's easy to fix.

3. Choose the Rectangle Marquee tool from the toolbox. On the Options bar, click on the Subtract from selection icon. Click and drag a marquee over all the area

in the lower part of the photograph, where there's no sky, as shown in
Figure 5.21.

Insider

Dragging at the corner of your document window may help to give you some working
room when making this rectangular selection. Start the drag on the left edge (around the
tops of the monuments). Don't forget to include the highest monuments near the trees
in the marquee selection. If you need to reposition the selection as you create it, hold
the spacebar while you continue to keep the mouse button pressed. This enables you to
drag and reposition the marquee selection while you are creating it. When you have it in
the desired location (a tight fit above the monuments at the top edge), release the
spacebar and continue dragging down to the lower-right corner of the document.

Figure 5.21   Use the Rectangle Marquee tool and the Subtract from selection option to correct the unwanted areas of the selection.

4. Change the foreground color to a believable sky blue color (R:104, G:148, B:238)
   and leave the background color white.

5. From the Filter menu, choose Render, Clouds. The result of the Clouds filter is
   generated randomly. In other words, the result differs each time it is used.

Therefore, if you don't like the results on the first try, press Ctrl(⌘)+F to repeat the last filter used until you are pleased with the results. Another little-known trick is to hold down the Alt(Opt) key when you choose Filter, Render, Clouds; the result is a sharper, more severe rendering. When you have a result that pleases you, press Ctrl(⌘)+Shift+F to open the Fade dialog box (or choose Edit, Fade Clouds). In the Fade dialog box, change the Opacity to **50%** and set the mode to Hard Light (you can also try the Pin Light mode as an interesting alternative; see Figure 5.22). The replacement sky looks realistic enough to pass as the real thing. Press Ctrl(⌘)+D to deselect. Press Ctrl(⌘)+ Shift+S to save the file on your hard disk as WildFlowers.tif. Keep the file open for the next exercise.

Figure 5.22   This may be an artificial sky, but it looks better than the original slate gray one it replaced.

Making a Quick Panorama Using Selections

You also can use selections to move parts of images around quickly without using the Clipboard. In this exercise, you are going to use the WildFlowers.tif image from the preceding exercise and make a panorama image.

Creating a Panorama View

1. If the WildFlowers.tif image from the preceding exercise is not already open, open this file now.

2. Your first goal is to make the image a little wider. The background color should still be white. If it's not, press **D** for default colors (and press **X** if necessary to make white the background color). Right-click (Macintosh: hold Ctrl and click) on the title bar of the image and choose Canvas Size. In the Canvas Size dialog box, check the Relative check box, change the Width to **665** (pixels), and change the Anchor point to the button on the middle left (see Figure 5.23). Click OK. The photo now has a white rectangle on the right side.

Note

> **Coloring your new canvas size**   When the Canvas Size dialog box is used to enlarge the document dimensions, by default, Photoshop will automatically use the background color to fill in the added space. Some alternative choices are available in the dialog box to override the default background color, but still, the choices are limited. Keeping this fact in mind might be helpful if you intentionally want a specific color for the additional space added to the canvas size. Here's the exception to this rule: If there is no Background layer, the resulting expansion will then be transparent.

Figure 5.23   Use the Canvas Size dialog box to expand the width of your document by adding three more inches to the right side.

3. Choose the Rectangle Marquee tool from the toolbox. The Feather setting on the Options bar should be set to **0** px. Drag a selection beginning at the top of the original photograph to the right side of the farthest white monument and move down to the bottom-right edge where the image ends and the new canvas begins (see Figure 5.24). Don't forget that you can hold down the spacebar as you make the selection to reposition the marquee selection close to the monument (then release the spacebar and continue to drag to complete the selection). Now the fun begins.

dscn0349.tif @ 50% (RGB/8)

Figure 5.24 Make a selection with the Rectangular Marquee tool, similar to the one shown in the figure.

4. Hold down the Ctrl(⌘)+Alt(Opt) keys, and the cursor changes to a double arrow. Still holding these keys, click inside the selection and drag it over until it fills the new area you created. If you have the dexterity, press the Shift key as you drag to restrain the movement horizontally; otherwise, you can adjust the position using the up- and down-arrow keys. The selection should look like Figure 5.25.

Figure 5.25   Works great, but the seam prevents it from looking real at this point.

5. Press Ctrl(⌘)+D to deselect. On the Options bar, change the Feather setting to **3** pixels. The goal is to patch the seam area and to break up the repeating patterns. The most obvious repeated pattern appears where the two selections overlapped. Drag a selection from the line of trees to the left of the break, as item 1 points out in Figure 5.26. Using the same technique you used in step 3, Ctrl(⌘)+Alt(Opt)+click inside the selection and drag it over the break (as item 2 shows). When you're satisfied, press Ctrl(⌘)+D to deselect.

    Don't forget to set the Feather option back to the default of **0** for the next time you use the Rectangular Marquee tool.

6. Look at the image, and you will see more patterns that scream repair. To finish the job, choose the Clone Stamp tool from the toolbox. On the Options bar, choose the soft, round, 100-pixel brush. (The remaining options should be the default settings of mode set at Normal, Aligned checked, and 100% for Opacity and Flow.) Carefully pick areas that you want to use to patch the trouble areas, press Alt(Opt), and click on a sample area. Click in the trouble spots to repair the seams or any repetitious patterns that you want to minimize. Press Alt(Opt) to sample new areas frequently; and if you don't like a particular brush stroke, don't forget to use the History palette or press Ctrl(⌘)+Alt(Opt)+Z to undo as many steps as the History palette allows. Figure 5.27 shows the final results.

Figure 5.26   Use another selection (item 1) and move it over the seam (item 2) to help break up the repeating pattern near the seam. The goal is to make the image look like a single photograph.

Figure 5.27   A finished panorama in less than five minutes.

Summary

If you take away only one lesson from this chapter, I hope it's the understanding of how important selections are to working magic with your images. Photoshop isn't a mind reader; if you want to separate an object from a background, you have to select the object. Likewise, if you want to apply a filter to only a small section of an image, you must select the small section of the image to let Photoshop know what you want to change.

The second important concept I hope you grasped is the way you can combine all forms of selection tools to make a single selection. You are not limited to one tool for each job. Always think in terms of the best tool—or *combination* of tools—to make the job at hand as easy as possible. And don't forget to use Boolean functions when applicable (such as the Add To Selection or Subtract From Selection modes). The fact that Photoshop offers such a large variety of ways to create a selection makes it an extremely flexible and powerful program in which to work.

Chapter 6

Using the Pen Tools

You can use Quick Mask, a layer mask, or even the Eraser tool on occasion, and you still will not experience the precision with which you can select stuff using the Pen tools. The Pen tools produce and modify

In this chapter, you'll learn

- All about paths and the vector tools you use in them
- How to work with path anchors and segments
- How to use the Direct Selection, Convert Point, and Add and Delete Anchor tools
- How to create special effects with the Pen tool and Soft-Edge Brush Tip
- How to take paths to the max

6

paths; paths are vectors, and vectors can get right in there between the pixels and precisely sculpt the shape of your desires. This chapter is devoted to the Pen tools because, quite simply, once you get the hang of them, there's no return; you'll be hooked on these tools, and you'll want to teach all of your friends about using them to add power to paths and selections.

Paths, as in Those Things in Illustrator and CorelDRAW

In recent versions of Photoshop, Adobe Systems has beefed up the vector tool part because vector graphics and pixel-based images are two entirely different types of computer graphics. You will almost never confuse vector artwork with bitmaps, but through Photoshop, you can take the best properties of both kinds of graphics and meld them into *very* special bitmap images.

An Introduction to Vector Tools Before You Use Them

I found that with my own tutelage, it was better to know what a tool did by (gasp!) reading the manual instead of getting down to work and drowning in sludge—a result of driving before taking the car out of Park, as it were. Adobe documents the Photoshop tools very well in its owner's manual, but here we're going to show you the *relationship* between the tools. We explain how to best use the tools (including the shortcuts and the motions you'll use to design stuff). We also show you which tools are superflous most of the time. Illustrator users have an advantage here because Photoshop's Pen tool group is almost exactly like Illustrator's Pen set.

If you're completely new to these tools, not to worry. We're gonna knock on every door in the neighborhood, as follows.

In Figure 6.1, you can see what happens when you click and hold on the top-facing tool: You get a flyout palette on the toolbox. From here, you can select any of the path drawing tools and one modifying tool—the Convert Point tool. Most of the tools here are self-explanatory, except for the Convert Point and Freeform Pen tools.

- You use the Freeform Pen tool by simply dragging it around an image. When you stop dragging, path segments and anchor points will appear (a path can be open or closed). Anchor points are the square dots between path segments that can be manipulated using other tools to change directly neighboring path segments. Additionally, you can make the Freeform Pen tool magnetic (check this option on the Options palette), to automatically trace an edge where two colors meet. To do that, all you have to do is click on an edge where one color meets a different one in an image; then hover the cursor along the color edge, and the Freeform Pen does the rest by tracing the edge. If this is what you want from the tool, we recommend clicking at regular intervals with the tool to lay down anchor points. Why? Because the more anchors you create, the more accurate the finished path will be.

- You use the Convert Point tool to change the property of an anchor point. When a path passes through an anchor point, it does not have to do so smoothly. When you drag on an anchor point with this tool, if the path passing through the point is sharp, the tool will make the anchor point smooth. And if you tug on a direction point (covered shortly) that belongs to an anchor point, you'll make a smooth transition through the point a sharp transition. Finally, if you just click on an anchor point with this tool without dragging, you'll straighten out the path segments that meet at the anchor point.

As you can see in Figure 6.1, the Auto Add/Delete check box appears on the Options bar whenever you use the Pen tool. This option diminishes the need for the Add Anchor Point and Delete Anchor Point tools. With this check box checked:

- Whenever you click on an anchor using the Pen tool, the anchor is deleted (and the path changes shape).

- Whenever you click on a path segment, an anchor is created. And you can use the Convert Point tool to change the properties of the new anchor.

So there are two tools on the Pen tool flyout you really never need to access.

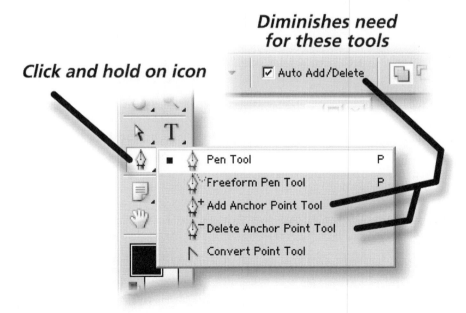

Figure 6.1   This flyout on the toolbox offers all the vector drawing tools in Photoshop.

6

Perhaps Adobe felt the Pen tool flyout was long enough and wanted to start yet another flyout for path-handling tools. In Figure 6.2, you can see the flyout for the path selection tools: the Path Selection and Direct Selection tools. We're going to describe what the Path Selection tool does first because you may not need to use it very often (getting its explanation out of the way to better concentrate on the more productive vector tools).

Figure 6.2   The Path Selection tool flyout.

Let's test drive the Path Selection tool, to provide good examples for the occasions that call for the tool.

Using the Path Component Selection Tool Two Ways

1. Open the Doodle.tif image from the Examples/Chap06 folder on the companion CD.

2. If you do not see any paths, press F7 to display the Layers/Channels/Paths grouped palette, and click on the Paths tab (to view the Paths palette). Click on the title called "Doodles" on the Paths list (it's the only path group in the image). Magically, the paths appear in the image window.

3. Choose the Path Selection tool from the flyout on the toolbox. Now click on the spiral doodle in the Doodles.tif image. All the anchor points will become filled, indicating that the entire shape has been chosen and can now be modified independently of the dot-shaped path (located next to the spiral-shaped path).

Insider

Note that Show Bounding Box is now an option on the Options bar. This is a good choice to click if you immediately want to rotate, distort, skew, or apply other Free Transform distortions to the selected path. But we're here to find stuff in the interface, and this is only one of two ways to send the selected path spinning.

4. Right-click (Macintosh: hold Ctrl and click), and then choose Free Transform Path from the context menu (or press Ctrl(⌘)+T). Immediately, control boxes for transformations appear on the Options bar, and you can type in a specific amount to change the orientation or shape of the path…but this is more boring than applying a transformation manually (and helps me show off another point with the tool).

5. Hover your cursor at a corner of the transform box, and then drag up and to the left. As you can see in Figure 6.3, I've rotated the spiral shape by −10 degrees (positive rotation is clockwise in Photoshop). Why don't you do this now, too?

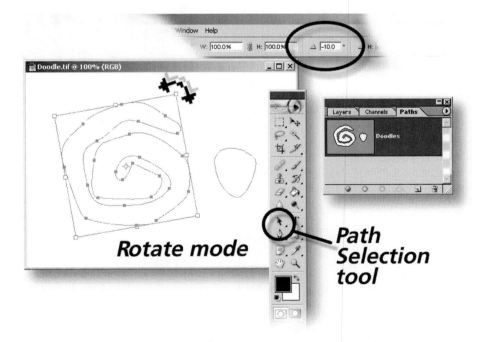

Figure 6.3 The Path Selection tool is really neat. (Do I have to have *all* good figure captions in this book?)

6

6. Heads up! To finalize the transformation, press Enter (Return). If you've goofed up the shape somehow and want another crack at rotating it, press Esc. This negates any proposed transformations you've made. You can also use the History palette to back your way out of an error (Window, Show History).

   Okey-dokey, you've seen one use for the Path Selection tool. Here's the other one:

7. With the Path Selection tool, marquee select both shapes (in other words, start dragging in the upper left of the image window and drag diagonally to the bottom right).

8. Now the Options bar looks entirely different, as you can see in Figure 6.4. You have the option of aligning the two paths vertically and horizontally. Tip: When you have more than two paths selected, you also have the choice of distributing the paths by position, which is a good way to evenly space the elements of a pattern.

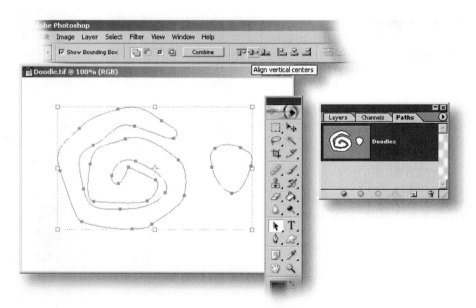

Figure 6.4   If you select two paths, your options for editing your work with the Path Selection tool are to align the paths vertically and/or horizontally.

9. That's it. That's "The Show" with the Path Selection tool. You can close Doodles.tif at any time and keep Photoshop open.

As I mentioned earlier, this chapter explores the manual use of path creation and editing tools. Photoshop shapes are also paths, but creating them is an automated routine, and instructions on working with shapes are included in Chapter 4.

The next section provides more than you would ever want to know about Photoshop paths. This is a "memorize everything you can" kind of section, but if you can come away with only three things about Photoshop path tools, you'll be working like a pro later in this chapter.

The Anatomy of a Path

A *path* in Photoshop consists of several components:

- First, a path has a *segment*; a path segment always has an anchor point at the beginning and end of it.

- These *anchor points* determine the course of a path as it passes through the point. When you click with the Pen tool, successive clicks create anchor points with straight path segments in between anchors.

- If you *drag* while you click, you create a *curved* path segment between where you are dragging and your previous click or drag. Also, when you drag while you're holding the mouse button, your finishing point is not an anchor point, but a different component of paths—the direction point.

- A *direction point* is at both ends of a curved segment, sprouting off the last anchor point you make. Direction points are connected to an anchor by direction handles, which determine the severity and direction of a curved path segment by the location at which you position the direction point.

Paths are wonderful for these reasons:

- They add virtually nothing to the saved file size. Alpha channels, in comparison, increase a file's saved size by about 25–33%.

- You can add to a saved path as long as it is visible onscreen, and new paths you create can be considered part of one saved path, even if the shapes don't touch one another (this is called a *discontinuous* path, in AdobeSpeak).

- Paths are invisible when you print an image, and they do not belong to any layer, which means that you can use the same path a number of times on a number of layers, as you will soon see.

Although paths do not print, things such as clipping paths have a visual effect on a layout. This means that those designs you make using the Pen tool do not print.

6

The Basic Path Tools

Before you do anything, click on the Pen tool on the toolbox. As you can see in Figure 6.5, the Options bar displays three different icons that will have an impact on the design you create. *Do not* click on the left icon; this icon will create a new (Shapes) layer, and many of the rules you will learn about hand-drawn paths will not apply (clipping paths are covered in Chapter 4, however).

Instead, click on the center icon, as shown in Figure 6.5. This is the normal work and save path mode for path creation.

Tip

Creating simple graphics   By the way, the right icon enables you to draw shapes that are immediately converted to pixels; no vector path or otherwise is involved. You might want to use this mode in combination with the Shapes tool (which calls up the Shapes palette on the Options bar) to make quick signs or flyers, when your graphics needs are undemanding.

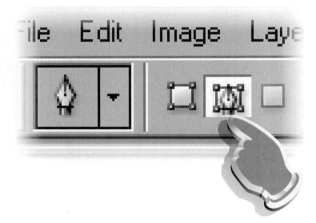

Figure 6.5   Create Work Paths using the Pen tool and other tools by first choosing the Path mode on the Options bar.

Now you know how to make a straight path segment and how to bend it as you progressively create a path. But how do you change the property of an anchor point, and how do you reposition it? Aha! Read on!

The Direct Selection Tool

You can access the Direct Selection tool by clicking it on the toolbox, but why change tools in the middle of an artistic effort? The smarter, easier way to access this important tool is to hold Ctrl(⌘) while the Pen tool is selected. You can then use the Direct Selection tool to bend a path segment (you click on an anchor to reveal the direction points used to steer the curve). The Direct Selection tool can also be used to click on an anchor and move it. This reshapes a segment of the path.

Figure 6.6 provides a review of anchor and segment techniques using the Pen and Direct Selection tools.

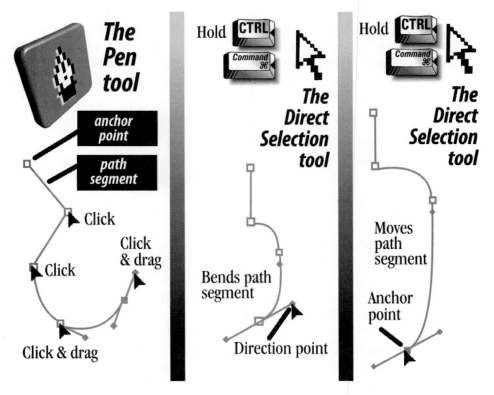

Figure 6.6   By using modifier keys, you can create paths and anchors, change the curve of a path, and reposition anchor points.

The more you work with Pen tools, the easier it becomes to make outlines of complex shapes in an image. You then can turn the path into the cleanest selection marquee you've ever seen by clicking on the Loads path as selection icon on the bottom of the Paths palette.

6

Note

> **Using tools without visiting the toolbox**   It is entirely possible—because I do it all the time—to use only the Pen tool and not to go fishing in the toolbox for other path tools. In the next section, you'll learn about the Convert Point tool. If you can access the Pen tool, the Direct Selection tool, and the Convert Point tool through modifier keys, why waste a visit to the toolbox and be taken away from your image work?
>
> Half the trick to using Photoshop is to learn ways (shortcuts) to keep your cursor close to your work. Who wants to run out to the paint store for varnish after spending hours sanding a chair? You want to continue, and not interrupt the creative process.

The Convert Point, Add Anchor, and Delete Anchor Tools

Like the Direct Selection tool, the Convert Point tool can be accessed without leaving the Pen tool. Hold Alt(Opt) to toggle from the Pen tool to the Convert Point tool. As described earlier in this chapter, the Convert Point tool determines whether a path segment is straight or curved (by clicking on an anchor point), and can change the direction of the path as it travels through an anchor point (by click+dragging with the tool to expose the direction points, and then dragging on a selection point).

Also, probably the least-used Pen tools you'll encounter are the Add Anchor and Delete Anchor tools, all shown in Figure 6.7. Why don't you need the "plus and minus" anchor tools? Because when you click on the Pen tool, the Options bar provides a check box called Auto Add/Delete. When you check this box and then click on a path segment, a new anchor appears. Conversely, clicking over an anchor with this option checked will delete the anchor point (and reshape the path).

We hope you've seen that six tools can be whittled down to two (the Path Selection tool and the Pen tool), if you know what the modifier keys are and understand the options. I hate to say this, but the *best* way to become proficient with the vector tools in Photoshop is to set aside 15 minutes a day with the tools and an image. Follow the contours in the image where colors meet, and refine the paths you draw. Within a week, you'll not only become an expert with the Pen tool, but you also will have accomplished the additional feat of lowering the learning curve (immensely) for programs such as Illustrator, Flash, LiveMotion, and InDesign (all of which make extensive use of Pen tool concepts)!

Okay, we've stressed paths enough without telling you what they're *good* for! In the next section, you'll deal with a real-world situation that calls for the use of the Pen tools. At least, the assignment is real in *my* world.

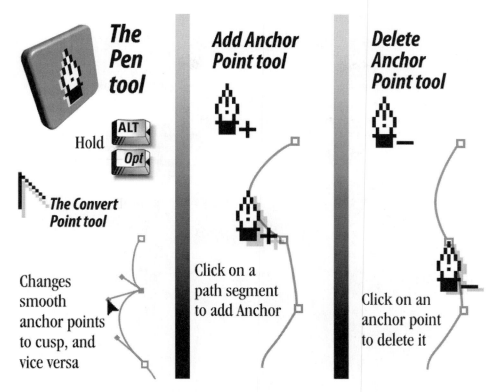

Figure 6.7   You can access the Convert Point tool by holding Alt(Opt) with the Pen tool chosen. And the plus and minus anchor tools are available automatically (when needed) if the Auto Add/Delete option is checked on the Options bar.

The Pen Tool and Special Effects

In the history of Photoshop, part of the "signature" of the program has been really life-like shadow and glow creation. There are a number of ways to create shadows and the inverse, glows, but the way you'll learn in the sections to follow involves using the path tool to accurately define the area that is to glow.

Easy Selections: Using Straight Paths

If you peek ahead to Figure 6.8, you'll see that the dice in the image are composed of nothing but straight lines—*path segments*, in the parlance of Photoshop's Pen tool.

To place a glow around either of the dice, you must define its outline first. This is where you'll use the Pen tool. Now the outline of a die is a closed one, so to learn something new in the steps to follow, you'll create a closed path. All set?

Creating a Closed Path

1. Open the Dice.tif image from the Examples/Chap06 folder on the companion CD.

2. Choose the Pen tool from the toolbox, as shown in Figure 6.8. Make sure you choose the Paths icon on the Options bar.

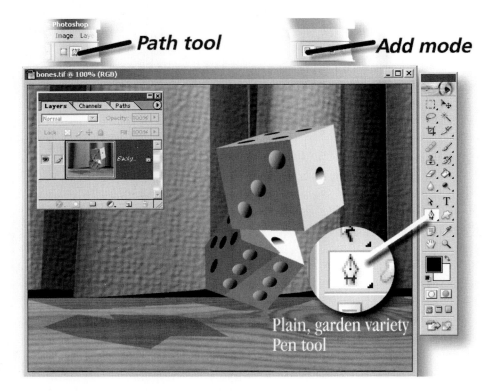

Figure 6.8   Choose the Pen tool, and use clicks—*not* clicks and drags—to create an outline around straight-edged shapes.

3. Hold Ctrl(⌘)+ the spacebar to toggle to the Zoom tool, and click over the top die until you are at 100% viewing resolution. If you are running a high resolution, such as 1,024 by 768 pixels on a large monitor, ignore this step because the image will probably load at 100% to begin with.

4. Follow the instructions on Figure 6.9. Click at the vertices of the die. If you cannot see all the die's vertices from your view through the image window, hold the spacebar to toggle to the Hand tool, and drag in your document window until the desired die area is in view.

When you reach the beginning anchor point, click on it to close the path. You can tell your cursor is positioned correctly when the cursor changes into a tiny pen point with a circle near the bottom right (see the enlarged view of the Close Path cursor in Figure 6.9).

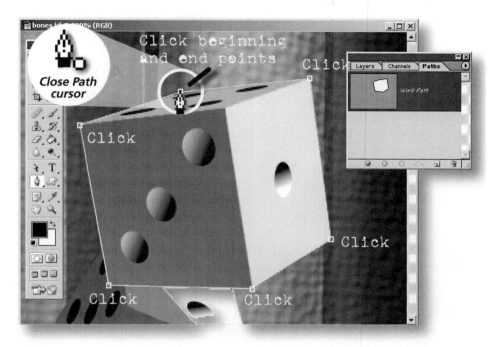

Figure 6.9   Click any place along the outline where there is a sharp turn in direction, and then click once over the beginning point to close the path.

Insider

> Whenever you create a path, it is called a *Work Path* on the Paths palette. What does this mean? Only one thing: A Work Path is overwritten as soon as you start creating a new path. And you don't *ever* want this to happen accidentally in your work, so you need to know how to turn a Work Path into a saved path that will remain indefinitely within the PSD, and various other file formats.

5. Click on the Paths tab on the grouped palette, and double-click on the Work Path title on the palette's list. A dialog box will appear.

6. Type **Bone** in the Name field, and then press Enter (Return) to make the Work Path into a saved path. Keep your work and Photoshop open.

Using a Path to Create a Selection

Now that you have created a path, here's the fun part: putting the path to some *use*! First, we need to copy the die shape and put it on a new layer. By doing this, we can put a glow *behind* the shape, so it *looks* like a glow.

C'mon. Let's (rock and) roll them bones:

Making a Selection Based on a Path

1. On the Paths palette, Ctrl(⌘)+click on the Bone title. This modifier key command loads the path as a selection and then hides the path from view so it cannot accidentally be deleted. You can use the Backspace and Delete keys to delete a selected path. Now, forget I said that—life is complicated enough—and check out Figure 6.10.

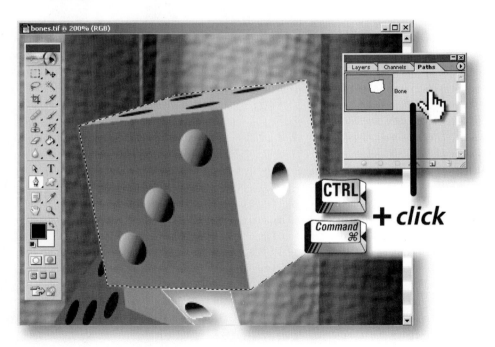

Figure 6.10   Ctrl(⌘)+click on the path title to both make a selection based on the path's outline and to hide the path from accidental editing.

2. Press Ctrl(⌘)+J to copy the selection to a new layer (Layer via copy). Figure 6.11 shows that you can also access this option by right-clicking (Macintosh: holding

Ctrl and clicking) and then choosing Layer via copy from the context menu, but a selection tool will need to be active for you to see this option on the context menu (one of the Lasso tools or the Rectangle Marquee tool will do).

Figure 6.11   Copy the selection of the die to a new layer.

Insider

By taking this shortcut instead of going to the main menu to create a layer and copy something to it, you have to pay the price of accepting the default name for the new layer; in this case, it's Layer 1. You can change the name of the layer at any time by double-clicking on the title and then typing in whatever you please, but in this simple, two-layer composition, labeling absolutely everything is really not necessary.

3. On the Layers palette, click on the Background layer title to make it the active layer. You will be working on the Background layer from this point on. Keep Photoshop and the image open.

Next, you will apply a glow to the die, using the Background layer as the target layer for the applied glow.

Using a Soft-Edge Brush Tip for Creating the Glow

As mentioned earlier, you can create a glow or shadow in more than one way in Photoshop. Many people design a shape that is larger than the object and then apply the Gaussian blur filter. However, we don't need to do this when we have a perfectly good path that can be stroked with a soft brush tip. Paths can be copied, stroked, used as the basis of a selection, filled—you name it.

Note

Copying a path   To move a path, hold Alt(Opt) while clicking on a path using the Direct Selection tool. Then drag the duplicate away from the original path. The duplicate and the original path are part of the same composite path because they belong to the same title on the Paths palette.

To copy a path to its own space in Photoshop, select the path, press Ctrl(⌘)+X (to cut the path from the current path layer title), and then deselect the path title by clicking on the blank area of the Paths palette (below the title list). Press Ctrl(⌘)+V and the path will be pasted onto a new Work Path title. (Don't forget to rename the Work Path title if you want to permanently save the path.)

Here's how to finish the piece:

Stroking a Path

1. Choose the Brush tool from the toolbox, right-click (Macintosh: hold Ctrl and click) to access the Brushes palette, select the 100 (pixels) soft tip, and then press Enter (Return) to make the palette go away. You should be working on the Background layer now.

2. Your new foreground color should contrast with the rest of a dim scene. Click on the foreground color, and if these are to be lucky dice, choose a pale lemon-yellow from the Color Picker as the color that will be stroked across the path. Click on OK.

3. On the Paths palette, click on the Bones title to view the path. Click the Stroke path with the brush icon at the bottom of the Paths palette, as shown in Figure 6.12.

4. If you want to remove the path from the creation (you no longer need it), drag the path title into the trash icon on the Paths palette.

5. To make this image one that can be saved to all different kinds of file types—including the proprietary Windows BMP and Macintosh PICT formats—you must flatten the image now. On the Layers palette, click on Layer 1 to make this the active layer, and press Ctrl(⌘)+E. This command is the shortcut for Merge down and does the trick here.

Figure 6.12   Unless you specifically choose the Brush tool for stroking the path, Photoshop will use the Pencil tool at its current size setting.

6. Choose File, Save As, and then save the file to a format that doesn't have to discard visual information. TIFF is my personal favorite, but there are enhanced TIFFs and plain TIFFs. You need to uncheck the Layers check box in the Save As dialog box to make a "normal" TIFF image that everyone with an image viewer can see. You can close the image at any time. Keep Photoshop open.

Tip

> **Saving your image**   Later, you might want to send your work to a friend using an email attachment. In this case, you would want to open the TIFF image in ImageReady and visually tune the piece so that image details that are lost through compression don't really show. In many cases, the File, Save for Web option in Photoshop might be just the ticket to help you save a copy of the file that will be low in file size (for sending friends via the Internet). For this image, the JPEG option would be the preferred file format.

Okay, enough of the simple stuff. If you're really willing to grow as an artist, you must overcome an annoying challenge we place before you. We're kidding about the annoying part. In the next section, you'll design a flower shape using paths; you'll duplicate and twist the paths and then fill them using a special fill mode to transform a blue ball into a *decorated* blue ball.

Taking Paths to the Max

Hey, you've glommed onto all these fun facts about paths and Pen tools, and so far, you've used only one of the tools. You start simple, you get simple results. What say you design a flower shape using two of the Pen tools, with curves and everything we discussed? After the following lesson, you can consider yourself Master (or Mistress, or Mattress) of Photoshop Paths.

To Make a Flower, You Start with a Single Petal

In Figure 6.13, you can see the image stickem.tif. It's darker here in the figure than it is on the companion CD; we want you to see clearly what it is you're going to create. No doubts about it—the outline is a complex path, but with instructions, you can create it with plenty of time left over to watch *The Sopranos*.

Silhouette of those stupid vinyl stickers
people put in the tub to hide cracks in tile work

Figure 6.13   The assignment? Trace around the outline of the flower in this file using the Pen tools.

Let's get down to business. Now, for once, we figured that the first seven steps in this assignment could also be called out in a figure. So if you get lost, look ahead to Figure 6.14. Even *I* got lost twice doing this, so this figure saved my neck.

Creating a Flower Petal by Tracing

1. Open the Stickem.tif image from the Examples/Chap06 folder on the companion CD, and zoom in on a petal to about 300% viewing resolution. You need this close-up view to see exactly where the anchors should be placed. With the Pen tool, click a point at the vertex that comes before the beginning of a petal. See item 1 in Figure 6.14 for this location.

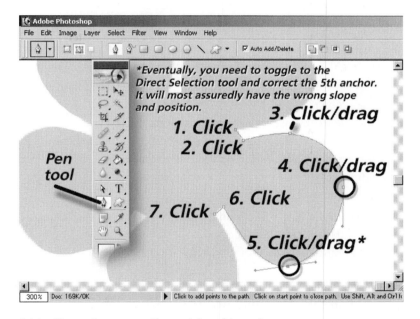

Figure 6.14   You can't go wrong if you stick to this road map.

2. Click at the beginning of the petal. Click again at the spot shown as item 2 in Figure 6.14. We're working clockwise in this example.

3. Click and drag at the next location, shown at item 3 in the figure. As mentioned earlier, when you do this maneuver, you wind up with a curve, and your cursor is hanging onto a direction point, and not the anchor it created. Weave the cursor a little until you see the curve conform to the template of the petal.

4. Click and drag at about the center of the petal, as shown in item 4. Generally, when you are creating a path, you need an anchor approximately every 90 degrees. Figure 6.14 shows that the middle of the petal is about 90 degrees away from the third anchor point. When you do it this way, editing an anchor point is easy. You can control the curve precisely, and the direction handles aren't so long that you have to go scrolling all over the screen to edit a curve.

6

5. Click and drag on the point shown in item 5. You need to fix a slight problem due to the fact that you've been drawing curves, and you're going into an anchor point that sharply bends the path as the path travels through it. Don't try to make this path segment conform precisely to the outline of the petal. Instead, make the curve fit the petal in this area as closely as possible, and you'll edit the anchor point later.

6. Click but don't drag the anchor at the location shown by item 6.

7. Click again as shown by item 7 in the figure.

8. Hold Ctrl(⌘) to toggle to the Direct Selection tool and then click on the fifth anchor. Drag the anchor or the direction points that are now visible (because you clicked on the anchor). Make the curve conform to the outline you are tracing.

9. Repeat steps 3–8 to close the path and complete the flower design. You can pick up where you left off by clicking again on the last anchor point with the Pen tool and then clicking and dragging a starting curve once more. When you come back to the first anchor, hover the cursor over the anchor until you see a tiny circle in the bottom right of your Pen tool cursor. This is the indication that your cursor is in the correct position to close the path.

10. Save the path by double-clicking on the Work Path title on the Paths palette, and name the path **Flower** in the dialog box that pops up. Click on OK, and keep this piece and Photoshop open.

In case this set of steps is too lengthy for you, and you want to proceed, you can open the Stickem.psd file from the Examples/Chap06 folder on the companion CD. There you'll find the completed path with nothing surrounding it. You can copy it to the ball image by holding down the Shift key while you drag the stickem path title from the Stickem.psd file into the Stickem.tif image window. (When you hold down the Shift key, the path will center perfectly into the image window.)

Uh-oh. The clock says it's time for a fun break now. This means you will copy the path to an image of a ball and duplicate and scale the pattern to make multiple flower designs on the ball.

Creating Many Flowers from a Single Path

Copying and making the flowers different sizes on the ball will make the ball look more lifelike. So let's get to it, using the Path Selection tool and the Free Transform mode.

Mapping Out a Decoration for the Ball

1. Make sure the flower pattern in Stickem.tif is visible. Then press Ctrl(⌘)+C. You don't have to select a path before copying it; however, you do have to make sure no marquee selection exists, or Photoshop will copy the image area instead of the path.

Um, you can also toss the Path title into a different image window to copy it there.

2. Close the Stickem.tif image (you can choose whether you want to save it; it's sort of served its purpose). Open the Ball.tif image from the Examples/Chap06 folder on the Companion CD. Zoom in or out until you can see the whole image in the workspace.

3. Press Ctrl(⌘)+V to paste the path into the picture. Now, in case you accidentally deselect the path, choose the Path Selection tool from the toolbox, shown as item 1 in Figure 6.15.

4. Click on the path and press Ctrl(⌘)+T to enter the Transform tool. Right-click (Macintosh: hold Ctrl and click) and choose Scale from the context menu, shown as item 2 in Figure 6.15.

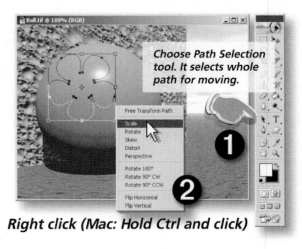

Figure 6.15   Choose the Scale command to make it possible for the path to be scaled up or down.

5. The flower path looks nice, but it's too large if you want several designs on the ball. Click and hold on a corner of the Scale bounding box, and then hold Shift and drag toward the center of the selection, as shown in Figure 6.16. Stop when the flower pattern is about 1/3 of its original size.

6

Insider

The Shift modifier key keeps the path in proportion as you scale it. You can also press the link button on the Options bar in the Scale section (it's the only link icon on the Options bar); this way, you don't have to hold the Shift key while you proportionately scale.

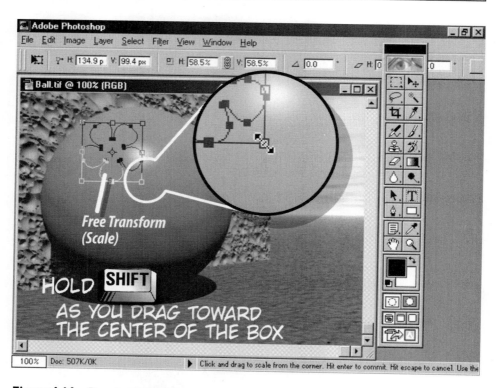

Figure 6.16   Drag toward the center to make a smaller flower; drag away from the path center to make a larger flower design.

6. Now's your chance to reposition the flower. Click inside the bounding box and drag the flower. To finalize your Transform edits, press Enter (Return).

7. Let's try a different tool to make a bunch of flowers of different sizes. Choose the Direct Selection tool. Hold down the Alt(Opt) key while you click on the flower path, and then drag away from the flower. Yeah! You've cloned the pattern!

Insider

If you want to, say, rotate, the duplicate path, release the Alt(Opt) key, right-click (Macintosh: hold Ctrl and click), choose Free Transform Path, and then hover your cursor slightly away from a corner of the bounding box until it turns into a bent arrow. Drag up or down, and the duplicate pattern will rotate. You also should make the duplicate a different size (you already know how to do this) and move it to a new location on the ball.

8. Create about five flowers. It doesn't matter whether a flower path goes outside the ball. You'll be painting and then cleaning up your painting work soon, so it's only natural—as with an actual ball—that parts of the pattern are obscured from your viewpoint. Figure 6.17 shows the work done in steps 7 and 8.

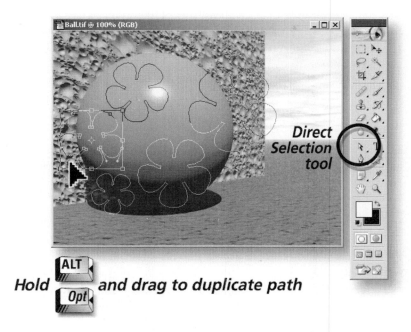

Figure 6.17   Use the Direct Selection tool to duplicate paths, and drag on a path segment while the whole path is selected to move the path.

9. Save your work to hard disk. Keep the design and Photoshop open.

It's time now to apply foreground color to the path areas and put the painted flowers in a special mixing mode for combining with the ball image. Plus, we'll do a little layer mask editing to perfect the design (you can review this technique in Chapter 4).

Here's how to finalize the piece:

Overlaying a Flower Pattern

1. With the Direct Selection tool, click on an empty area of the design so that no path has its anchors highlighted (indicating that it's selected). When *no* path is selected but all are visible, you can apply color using *all* the paths that are present without selecting every one of them.

2. Click on the Loads Path as a selection icon at the bottom of the Paths palette. This is a different way to load a selection and hide the paths, as explained earlier in this chapter. You can do almost anything two or more different ways in Photoshop.

3. Click on the Layers tab to view this palette, and then click on the Create a new layer icon on the bottom of the palette. Choose a bright orange color from the Color Picker by clicking on the foreground color selection box on the toolbox. Click on OK to exit the Color Picker after selecting your color.

4. Press Alt(Opt)+Delete (Backspace), and then press Ctrl(⌘)+D to deselect the selection marquees. Now you have your bunch of flowers, but something smells fake here.

Insider

When you cover an area with solid paint on a layer to work on top of the Background layer, valuable image info is hidden, such as shading and highlights. To make the flowers look like they were painted on plastic, you need to choose a different mixing mode than Normal, the default.

5. Choose Overlay mode from the modes drop-down list on the Layers palette. Overlay is a mixing mode in which highlights and shadows show through from layers underneath, and the objects (on the layer) mix with the underlying color so that the two colors combine and the brightness of the color on the Background layer is preserved. So now you have sort of a dirty orange pattern of flowers on the ball. I'm not knocking it; the image looks nice! Besides, this is the same effect as when a ball manufacturer silk-screens a bright pattern on a cool, neutral-colored plastic toy. Figure 6.18 shows where we are now in the steps.

6. If you did as recommended earlier, one or two of the flowers go outside the silhouette of the ball. No problem. Here, you'll find that the layer mask technique we worked with in Chapter 4 comes in handy once again. Click on the Add Layer Mask icon at the bottom of the Layers palette, and make sure that black is the current foreground color (press **D**).

7. Zoom in to about 300% viewing resolution, and hold the spacebar to scroll your view in the window so you can see one of the offending, overlapping flower designs. Choose the Brush tool, right-click (Macintosh: hold Ctrl and click), and choose the 13-pixel hard diameter tip.

8. Stroke over the outside edge of the ball until you've removed all the paint outside the ball (see Figure 6.19). Then do the same thing to any other overlapping flower shapes.

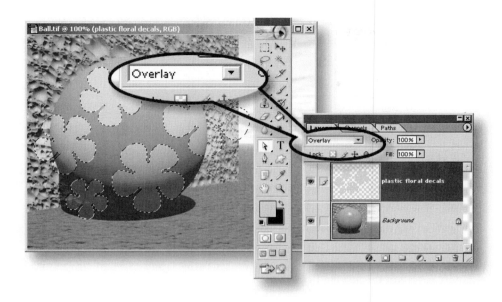

Figure 6.18   Use Overlay mode to better blend the flower patterns "into" the ball shape.

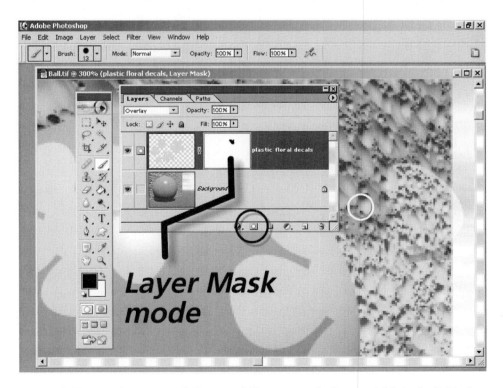

Figure 6.19   Use the Layer Mask feature to hide areas you don't want visible in the finished design, and then apply the mask to trash the unwanted pixels to finish the image.

6

9. When you think the flowers look all right in the image, right-click (Macintosh: hold Ctrl and click) on the Layer 1 mask thumbnail on the Layers palette (*not* the image thumbnail), and then choose Apply Layer Mask from the context menu. (If you don't see this choice in the context menu, you are on the wrong thumbnail.) Those pixels that lay outside the ball are now gone forever.

10. If you would like to change the color of the flowers or further experiment with the image, save it now in Photoshop's native file format—PSD. This file format ensures that you retain the Photoshop layers. If you think you're done and want to pack away your masterpiece as a single-layer work, choose Flatten Image (from the Layer menu), and then press Ctrl(⌘)+S to save it as the TIF it began its life as.

11. Take a well-deserved break. I think there's a Diet Dr. Pepper toward the back of the fridge, behind the Chinese take-out.

In Figure 6.20, you can see the finished piece in black and white (trust me, it's a mind-blower in color). There's nothing in the image to suggest that this is a retouched image because you chose the right blending mode for the flower designs and trimmed away the excess that was outside the ball's silhouette.

Figure 6.20   One of the outstanding characteristics of Photoshop is that with the right information, you can turn a nice picture into a *better* picture.

You've done it. You've worked your way through perhaps one of the hardest chapters in this book.

Well, I'm going to draw a path around *myself* right now, convert it to a selection, and then cut out of here. Or move to a different layer. Or something. What's important is the Summary, as follows.

Summary

You could spend a year learning all the undocumented or vaguely documented features in Photoshop, and I'm glad my publisher gave me the space to concentrate on stuff that's really important to your growth as an artist. Paths are core components of Photoshop, they are much overlooked in light of all the Web stuff packed into the program now, and by understanding the basic elements, you bring yourself one step closer to becoming a professional artist wielding a *verrry* powerful tool.

In the next chapter, we'll look at fantastic features in Photoshop that make the creation of your dreams a semi-automated process. Let's see what Photoshop filters combined with your own ingenuity can produce.

Chapter 7

Filters

After almost 10 years of plug-in filters being available for Photoshop, there really isn't much more to say, except for the hilarious and pointed motto of Alien Skin, makers of several suites of plug-ins, "We take the drudgery out of creativity."

In this chapter, you'll learn

- How to make the most of Photoshop's native filters
- How to use third-party filter packages

What do plug-in filters mean to the creative individual? Essentially, they do at least one of two things:

- They enable us to do things that would be very hard to do manually.
- The enable us to do things that would be impossible to do manually.

This chapter explores the "next step" in the use of plug-in filters: What happens when you use a versatile filter *in combination with* your own technical skills? The answer is, "something unbelievably wonderful," and the steps are in this chapter.

Photoshop's Native Filters

Basically, Photoshop CS's filters can be broken down into two categories: Gallery Effects filters (artistically bent filters that are a legacy of Aldus Gallery Effects plug-ins) and filters that are more "practical" in their use, such as removing noise, sharpening an image, offsetting a picture, and so on.

Note

Filter Gallery filters   The Filter Gallery contains filters that apply their effect uniformly pixel by pixel. Other filters do their magic by taking into account surrounding pixels. And that typically means that antialiasing is not used with these filters.

We'll dwell just a little on the new layout of the Gallery Effects filters and a novel use or two for them, but for the most part, you can discover the product of the Gallery type filters independently and you don't need a book to tell you how to use them.

The Filter Gallery

To facilitate the use of more than one filter or to preview many different filters in one fell swoop, Adobe has created the Filter Gallery. This section of the book doesn't contain any elaborate tutorials, so instead let's simply explore how the Filter Gallery works.

Open any image in Photoshop (a picture of a person might work well), and then choose Filter, Filter Gallery. As you can see in Figure 7.1, the Filter Gallery interface has three main areas: the image preview (larger than filter preview windows in the past), the actual controls for tweaking a filter's effects, and a thumbnail visual indicator showing what the available filters look like when applied to a tiny sailboat (sorry, the thumbnail images cannot be customized). Let's walk through the application of more than one filter in the Filter Gallery:

7

Using the Filter Gallery

1. Click on the triangle to the left of the Artistic folder in the middle of the interface. You'll see a lot of thumbnail previews appear. Click on, let's say, Paint Daubs. Two things happen: The image preview shows what the effect looks like on your target image, and the name of the filter appears on a title bar at the lower right of the interface. See item 1 in Figure 7.1 for the location of the flyout button (the triangle) for the folders, see item 2 for the location of the effect thumbnail, and see item 3 for the location of the effect title.

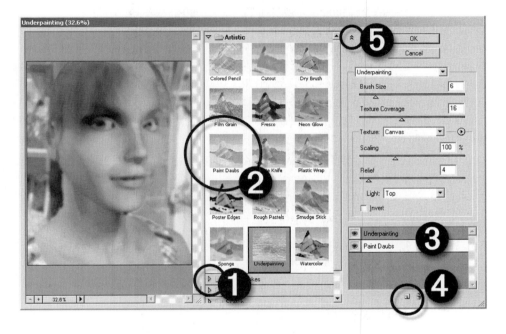

Figure 7.1   The Filter Gallery interface.

2. Feel free to do whatever you like in the right side of the Filter Gallery. The controls here are basically the same ones you might have used in previous versions of any specific filter.

3. Let's pile an effect on top of an effect. Click on the New filter (layer) icon (item 4 in Figure 7.1). Now click on a different filter thumbnail; I've chosen Underpainting. Realize that what you are doing is adding a filter to an already filtered image. You are *not* applying two filters to two different images and viewing a blend of the two.

4. Let's suppose you don't like adding Underpainting. You can click on a different filter thumbnail or remove the filter. To remove it, click on its title at the bottom right of the interface and then click on the trash icon (do not try to drag the title into the trash icon).

5. Let's further suppose that you feel that the filter thumbnails are a waste of space. Click on the double-chevron icon (item 5 in Figure 7.1) to hide the thumbnails. You can still choose effects from the drop-down list.

6. To conclude our exploration, let's say that you want the interface to take up the screen: Click on the percentage field at the bottom left of the interface, and choose Fit On Screen. There's no option to toggle back to normal view, so you have to drag the tread at the bottom-right corner of the interface up and to the left.

7. Click on OK or Cancel to leave the Filter Gallery.

You really can't escape the Filter Gallery, because even if you choose a specific effect from the Filter menu, the Filter Gallery is displayed. Now, though, you know its ins and outs.

In the section to follow, you'll see how to increase the size of a file while using a filter so that it still looks crisp and pleasing to the eye.

Using a Dry Brush Layer While Resizing

Images you create and edit are made up of *picture elements*, pixels. And an image is in this respect like a slice of cake you are given: You can *subtract* from the cake by eating a piece, but you cannot *add* to the slice you were given. You can subtract pixels from an image to make it smaller, and with minor sharpening, the image still looks fine. But how do you *upscale* an image? The answer is clumsily and not easily, because you're asking Photoshop to *create* pixels based on information neither you nor Photoshop possesses. The result of upscaling usually looks hard and ugly because Photoshop is forced to glean the color information added with new pixels upon existing image information.

One strategy for making an upscaled image look better is sharpening the edges in the image and smoothing out the areas where a solid color should exist. Let's look at Figure 7.2 for a moment. This image was taken with a disposable film camera, and the negatives were digitized at Wal-Mart and saved to a picture CD.

The problem with this image is evident upon opening it: The image is not very large. The FujiColor CD or Kodak Picture CD–based disks that fotofinishers create from your pictures are rendered to about 5MB, and after the inevitable cropping (because the viewfinder system on a disposable is pathetic), the image is perfect to email as a JPEG image, but not so swift if you want to make an inkjet print out of it. The Julian.tif image

7

is only 2MB or so. Typically, an inkjet needs 1/3 the true resolution of an image to render it to paper. Here's the math: My inkjet printer's true resolution is 720 dots per inch. That means the image needs to have a resolution of 1/3, or 240 pixels/inch. The image can therefore be rendered to about 3/34 by 3 inches at this resolution (open Julian.tif from the Examples\Chap07 folder and choose Image, Image Size to ascertain this). Of course, I can't find a frame for an image this small, and even if I could, it would look more like an insect on a wall than a framed picture. Nope, a 4 by 6 or 5 by 7 would be nicer, but how do we do that?

Let's take a trip through the digital kitchen that is Photoshop and see whether we can cook up something.

Figure 7.2 The image is only 2MB in saved file size.

Blending Dry Brush into a Photograph

1. With Julian.tif open, drag the Background layer title on the Layers palette onto the Create a new layer icon to duplicate the layer. The Background copy layer should now be the active layer. Right-click (Macintosh: hold Ctrl and click) on the title bar, and choose Image Size from the context menu. Leave the resolution at 256; a little extra resolution over the target of 240 won't hurt.

2. In the Image Size dialog box, check Resample Image, choose Bicubic Smoother from the drop-down list, and then type **6** in the Height field (see Figure 7.3). Click on OK to upscale the image.

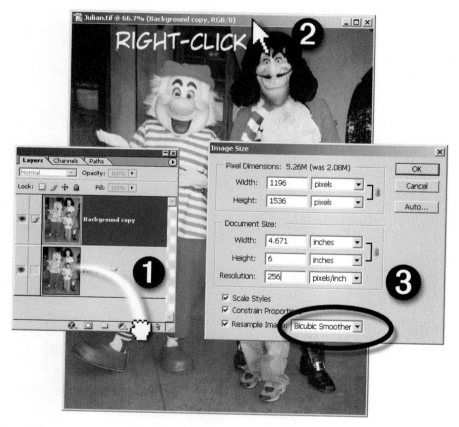

Figure 7.3   Upscale the image using the Bicubic Smoother interpolation method.

3. Choose Filter, Sharpen, and then choose Unsharp Mask. Use Amount: 39%, Radius: .9, and Threshold: 1 level. Through trial and error, I've found that these settings work well, with little or no artifacting (unwanted image noise or ghosting) in a number of situations. Click on OK.

4. Choose Filter, Artistic, and then choose Dry Brush.

5. Choose 0 as the Brush Size, 10 as the Brush Detail, and 1 for Texture, as shown in Figure 7.4. As you can see, the image is stylized but still legible, and it has smoother tones. But we're not done yet.

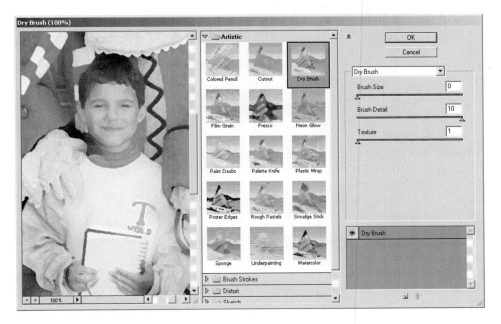

Figure 7.4   Use the Dry Brush filter to smooth out the tones and sharpen the edges of the copy on a layer.

6. Click on OK. Lower the opacity gradually for this filtered layer, and watch the image window. Stop lowering the opacity when the picture becomes more photographic than painterly. About 50% opacity should do the trick.

7. Choose the Eraser tool, choose a medium-sized soft tip, and set the Opacity for the tool to around 40% on the Options bar. Stroke once or twice over the face of the small boy, as shown in Figure 7.5. As for Captain Hook and his mate, really no erasing is necessary to reveal the unfiltered background image; these are stylized cartoons of people and can visually withstand a little Artistic Effects filtering.

8. Press Ctrl(⌘)+S, or you can close the file without saving.

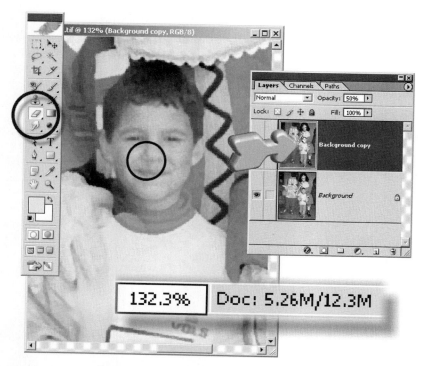

Figure 7.5   You've successfully increased the document size to about twice the original, with very little unpleasant noise, pixellation, or distortion added.

The method I just described is not perfect, for sure, but it's a better solution than leaving the file alone after upscaling it. The other alternative is to use a product called Genuine Fractals. This Photoshop plug-in examines an image to be upscaled for visual patterns and then substitutes fractal patterns for the actual image information. Fractal math can be scaled smoothly up or down, and although fractal math is "dumb" (it cannot add real information about the photograph at the time the photo was taken—to date, nothing can do this), it makes an interesting re-creation of an image when you want to dramatically scale up an image to 40 or 100 times its original size. The results? Well, honestly, they aren't a lot better than the results the preceding mini-tutorial provided; the resulting image looks a little "painterly." But if you really want to try the product, go to http://www.genuinefractals.com, the home of LizardTech Software, for a working demo.

Coming up next: Photoshop's Warp Type feature is great for making swooping, elegantly moving text, as you saw in Chapter 1, "Producing Awesome Images from the Start." But what if you need to warp not only text, but an entire graphics design? You use the Displace command. Follow me!

Displacing an Image Using Another Image

The Displace command in Photoshop is not the easiest thing to grasp intellectually. You create a grayscale image and then apply the image's brightness values to move pixels from side to side in a different image. For example, black pixels in the displacement map can move pixels downward in the target image, while lighter pixels can move the pixels upward in the target image.

Because this is a book on graphics, it would be better to show you a graphic example of how an elegantly created displacement map can curve an image so that it looks like the label of a soup can.

Here's how to create your own can label:

Displacing a Can Label

1. Open the can.psd image, and then open the label.psd image from the Examples\Chap07 folder on the companion CD. As you can see in Figure 7.6, the label is just about the right size to fit on the can, but it is flat, not curved.

Figure 7.6   The label can fit the can only if it's arced downward.

2. Minimize the can image for a while. Right-click (Macintosh: hold Ctrl and click) on the title bar of the label.psd design, and choose Duplicate. We might as well name it right now: Label Displacement.psd.

3. Press **D** for the default colors. Choose the Gradient tool. On the Options bar, set the gradient for Foreground to Background with the Linear Gradient icon selected. Hold down the Shift key (to constrain the gradient to a straight horizontal drag), and drag a linear gradient across the label, white to black, starting at the left edge and ending at the right, as shown in Figure 7.7. This is the grayscale image I mentioned earlier. Because the displacement map is the same size as the can label, the displacement pixels correspond one to one with the target image pixels.

Figure 7.7   Hold Shift if necessary to constrain the left-to-right gradient fill to absolute vertical orientation.

4. Now comes the tricky part. Did you know that you can adjust this simple gradient into a very precise, elegant displacement map by using the Curves command? Choose Image, Adjustments, Curves, or press Ctrl(⌘)+M.

5. Drag the black point and the white point straight up to about the place where you can see them in Figure 7.8. Then click an additional point about 2/5 of the way along the line and another 4/5 of the way across the line. Then click to make a new midpoint, and drag the middle point down until the curve looks like a semi-circle. The displacement map will create a dip in the target image that looks exactly like the curve, so the rounder it looks, the smoother the dip will look on the label.

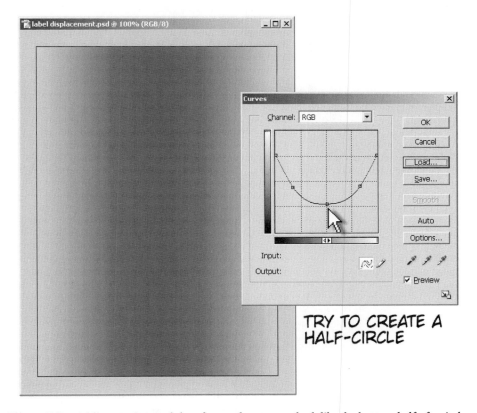

Figure 7.8   Add new points and then finesse the curve to look like the bottom half of a circle. Hold Alt(Opt) and click on Cancel to reset the curve if you mess up.

6. Click on OK, and then save this file in Photoshop's PSD format to your hard drive. You can keep the file open if you want, but there's really no point to it.

7. With the label.psd image in the foreground in the workspace, choose Filter, Distort, and then choose Displace.

8. In the Displace dialog box, specify **0** for Horizontal Scale (we want to move the vertical aspect of the label). Then type **35** in the Vertical Scale box, which means that the greatest amount of stretching the label downwards is limited to 35 pixels

(which is plenty). Choose Stretch to Fit and Repeat Edge Pixels; then click on OK, as shown in Figure 7.9. You will then see another dialog box in which you can choose a displacement map. Navigate to the Label Displacement.psd file created earlier, select the file, and click Open.

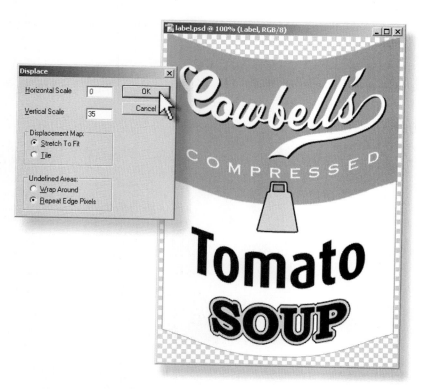

Figure 7.9   Choose to push (displace) the pixels in the label image so that they are located near darker and black pixels in the displacement map image.

9. Terrific! The rest is simple: Hold down the Shift key, and drag the label layer into the can.psd image to copy the layer to this document. Make the label layer partially transparent (lower the Opacity to around 47%) so you can see both the label and the edges of the can. Press Ctrl(⌘)+K, choose Bicubic Sharper from the Preferences menu, and then click on OK. Press Ctrl(⌘)+T to use Free Transform. Hold down the Shift key (to constrain proportions), and drag on the upper or lower corners to scale the label down so that the top and bottom of the label line up with the top and bottom of the can. Then drag on the middle handles (on the right and left sides) to match closely to the side of the can. Don't worry if the sides fall slightly outside the can (see Figure 7.10).

Figure 7.10   Scale the label down so that it fits on the can. Use Bicubic Sharper by pressing Ctrl(⌘)+K and choosing it from Preferences before scaling the label.

10. Double-click inside the label to finalize your Free Transformation edit, and then click on the Add Layer Mask icon at the bottom of the Layers palette. Use black and a hard-edged brush to erase everything that falls outside the edges of the can (if you erase too much, switch to white to correct any errors).

11. Press Ctrl(⌘)+S, stare in amazement at your newfound Photoshop skills, and then close the image at any time.

As you can see in Figure 7.11, the can looks pretty okay. Oh, yes, you'll probably want to lower the opacity of the label so the white of the label doesn't blind you, and I've included a shadow that you can activate and put on top of the label to better visually integrate it with the can.

Figure 7.11   The finished can.

It should not go without saying that if you want to create a waving flag, the Curves command should feature a wavy line, and if you want an image to tilt upward, the curves line should be in an inverted "U" shape. All the preceding displace information works because you know how to design a curve using the Curves command. More on curves in future chapters.

Working with the Lighting Effects Filter

If you've played with the Lighting Effects filter before hitting this chapter, you might be a little disappointed because it can't actually turn an overcast day into a sunny day. Instead, it treats the image as two-dimensional and flat; it merely adds a gradient of light to an already lit scene. Bummer? Not exactly. The Texture Channel of the Lighting Effects filter is a *very* handy resource for adding bumps and embossing to images.

Like the Displace command, the Texture Channel of the Lighting Effects filter "moves" pixels according to a map—a texture map. Lighter grayscale areas of the Texture Channel map appear to bump outward, and darker areas in the map make the target image's corresponding areas look like they're receding.

Here's a good, practical example showing how to make a Texture Channel in an image and create the appearance of a brick wall:

Creating a Bump Map

1. Open the Brick Wall.tif image from the Examples\Chap07 folder on the companion CD.

2. Double-click on the Quick Mask mode icon on the toolbox. In the Quick Mask Options box, choose Color Indicates Selected Areas, and then click on OK. Your image is in Quick Mask mode now.

3. Choose a small, hard brush, and then paint all the mortar in the image, as shown in Figure 7.12. Neatness does not count; reality often looks sloppy.

Figure 7.12   Paint Quick Mask over the mortar areas in the image. You will save this area where you paint on the mask as a selection to use later.

4. After you've done all the mortar work, click on the Standard Editing mode button (or press **Q** to exit Quick Mask mode), and then click on the Channels tab on the Layers palette. Click on the Save selection as channel icon, as shown in Figure 7.13.

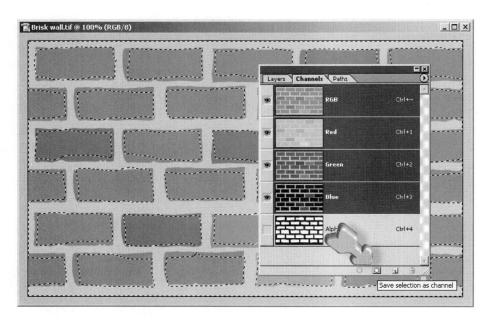

Figure 7.13   Save the selection you described using Quick Mask tint overlay.

5. Click on the Layers tab, press Ctrl(⌘)+D to deselect the current selection, and then click on the Create a new layer icon.

6. Choose a medium-sized brush for the Brush tool. Choose Dissolve mode on the Options bar, and set the Opacity to 20% for the brush. The Dissolve painting mode will create a fine spray of individual pixels.

7. Using black as the foreground color, paint an area about 1/4 the overall size of the image, brushing briskly, not lingering on an image area. Your image should look like that shown in Figure 7.14.

8. The grains on the layer aren't large enough to make the bricks look coarse. We want clumps, and to that end, you'll increase the size of the layer's contents. Press Ctrl(⌘)+K, change the Interpolation method to Bicubic Smoother, and click on OK. Press Ctrl(⌘)+T, and grasping a corner bounding box handle, drag away from the center of the image until almost all the image is covered with digital grit.

9. Double-click in the center of the Free Transform box to finalize your edit. Use the Eraser tool in combination with a soft tip and partial opacity to remove parts of the grit. Let your imagination guide you; see Figure 7.15.

7

Figure 7.14   Create a sand-like effect using the Brush on a new layer in Dissolve mode.

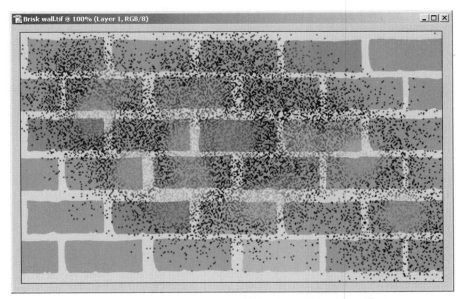

Figure 7.15   Erase some of the grit texture to give it an uneven look.

10. Choose the Brush tool again, and from the default set of brushes, choose the Rough Round Bristle artistic 100-pixel tip, as shown in Figure 7.16. Click and drag in various places to add character to the grit.

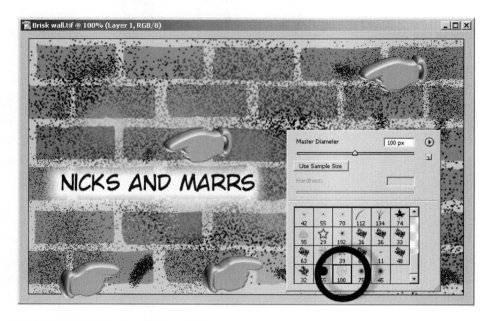

Figure 7.16   Make the roughness look uneven by adding an artistic stroke or two.

11. Ctrl(⌘)+click on the Layer 1 title to load the grit as a selection. Then click on the Alpha 1 channel title on the Channels palette, and press Alt(Opt)+Delete(Backspace) to fill the channel with black wherever a selection marquee appears. See Figure 7.17.

12. Press Ctrl(⌘)+D to deselect the selection marquees. Press Ctrl(⌘)+S; keep the file open.

Now, here's how to apply your work saved in the channel to the picture of the bricks:

7

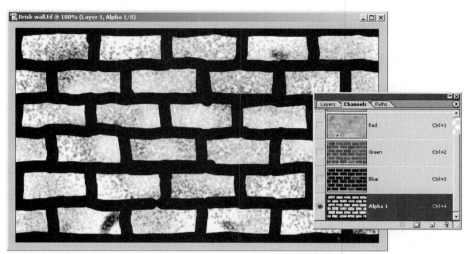

❶ Ctrl (⌘)+click on layer title to load selection

❷ Alt+Delete (Opt+Backspace) to fill selection in alpha channel

Figure 7.17   Fill the layer in the selected areas with black.

Mapping Bumps to the Bricks Image

1. Click on the Layers tab, and then drag the top layer (only) into the trash icon.
2. Choose Filter, Render, Lighting Effects.
3. Choose Directional as the Light Type, and then drag the light source dot toward or away from the image thumbnail until the overall exposure looks good for the thumbnail (the goal here is to achieve a similar color in the thumbnail view that matches the original image coloring). It will help accentuate the effect by leaving the light source dot at about an 11 o'clock position in the dialog box.
4. For Gloss, choose a matte finish. For Material, put the slider in the center (neither metal nor plastic). For the Texture Channel, choose Alpha 1 from the drop-down list, and then drag the height slider to about 39, as shown in Figure 7.18.
5. Click on OK. You should now have textured bricks.
6. Press Ctrl(⌘)+S. You can close the image now at any time.

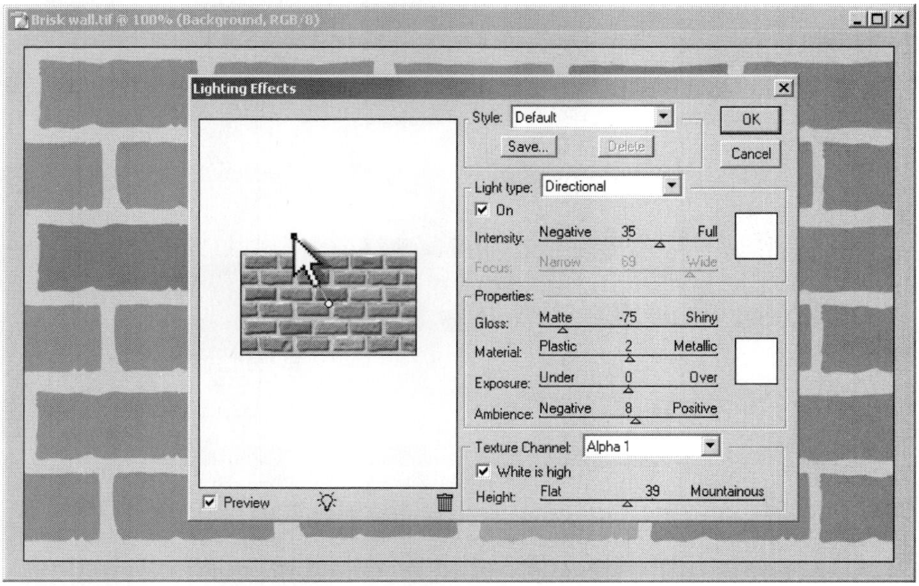

Figure 7.18   Use these settings to make the bricks appear to have texture.

The preceding example was sort of an "instant thrills" assignment; you now know the *basics* of how to make a textured image. But how do you make it more refined, more real in appearance? It's simple; you work more on the alpha channel details. Remember, in its default setting, dark pixels in the Texture Channel create the appearance of a recess, and light pixels create the appearance of a bulge. To reverse this scheme, you uncheck the White is high check box in the Lighting Effects dialog box.

In Figure 7.19, you can see at left the finished image, and at right, the corresponding Texture Channel image. You can also load them into Photoshop from the Examples\Chap07 folder on the companion CD to get a firsthand look. A little blurring, a little use of gray instead of black, and just some massaging got the Texture Channel file looking good. The more time you spend making a Texture Channel grayscale image visually interesting, the greater your reward will be.

Let's look now at some serious plastic surgery tools that you may think are gooey toys when you first open them.

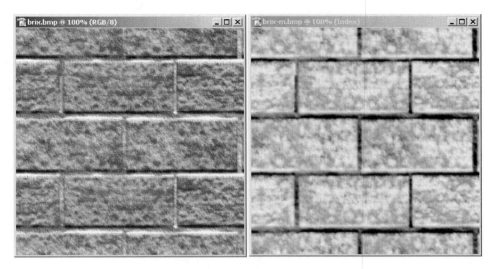

Figure 7.19   The more visually complex and tonally rich the Texture Channel, the more interesting the resulting textured image will look.

Exploring the Liquify Filter

The Liquify filter at first glance looks like a toy for disfiguring pictures of your boss or something. But it actually can be used for good instead of evil! Here's an assignment-based, taxi-driver's tour of the Liquify filter:

Changing a Nose Using the Liquify Command

1. Open the Safari Guy.tif image from the Examples\Chap07 folder on the companion CD. As you can see in Figure 7.20, Safari Guy's nose veers off-center, and it's a little twisted at the nostrils.

2. Choose Filter, Liquify. Click on the Forward Warp tool on the toolbox, set the Brush size to 100, set the brush Density to 50, and then set the Brush Pressure to 100. Naturally, in your own assignments, you'll want to fiddle with these settings, especially the pressure, that, when reduced, might give you more freedom to poke and prod the underlying image.

3. Click and drag briskly to the left, at the spots highlighted with an arrow in Figure 7.21.

Tip

> **Undoing your edit**   To undo your last editing move, press Ctrl(⌘)+Z. To undo an entire area and more than one move with the tool, hold Alt(Opt) and then brush over the affected area. The Reconstruct tool also will remove editing done by any tool; it's the tool located directly beneath the Forward Warp tool.

NOSE IS CROOKED
END OF NOSE IS TWISTED CLOCKWISE

Figure 7.20   No one's face is perfect, but you can *make* it perfect using the Liquify command.

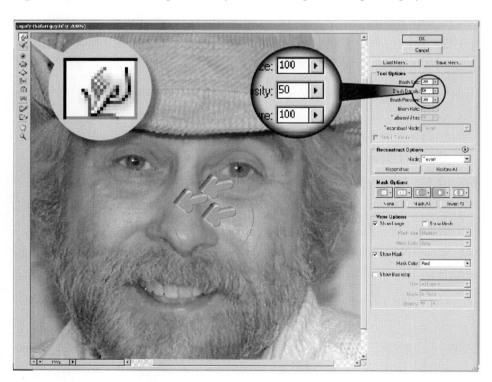

Figure 7.21   Drag ever so slightly using the Forward Warp tool.

4. Click on the Twirl Clockwise tool. Now we want to twirl Safari Guy's nose counterclockwise, so hold Alt(Opt) and then click, *do not* drag, over the nose once or
twice. See Figure 7.22.

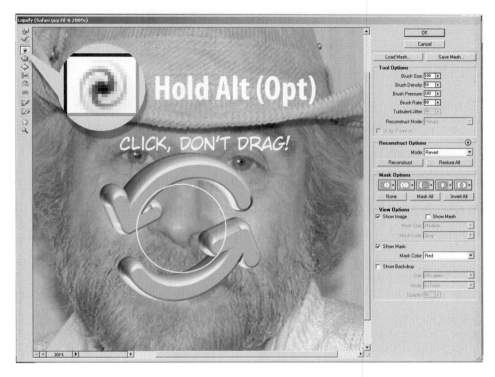

Figure 7.22   Hold Alt(Opt) to rotate image areas counterclockwise.

5. Switch back to the Forward Warp tool, and click+drag ever so slightly on the
area between the Safari Guy's nostrils to move it to the left. Massage the nostril
area ever so slightly with this tool to perfect the bottom of the nose.

6. Click on OK. Press Ctrl(⌘)+S; you can save or close the image at any time.
Close Photoshop for a moment now.

Pretty exciting work, eh? Like other edits you might make in Photoshop, the best work
should go unnoticed. In Figure 7.23, you can see "before" and "after" shots of Safari Guy.
He looks happier, and you just learned the basic controls for morphing an imperfect face
into a perfect one.

Next up, a filter you can manually load into Photoshop that will assist you in wonderful
3D creation.

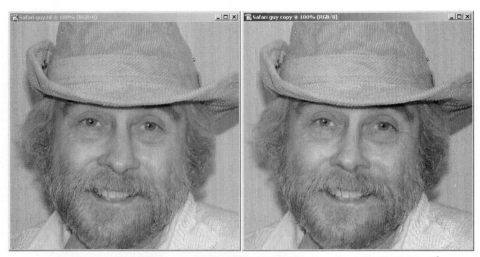

Figure 7.23   The Liquify filter can actually be used to create subtle changes in an image.

The 3D Transform Filter

Photoshop does not install several filters when you set it up. Among them is 3D Transform, a wonderful little utility that enables you to rotate and stretch anything in 3D space. We'll confine our adventures with this filter to warping text because you simply can't manipulate text any other way using Photoshop, and by learning the steps to follow, you can basically manipulate any image or text.

First things first, though. Here's how to install the 3D Transform filter:

Loading the 3D Transform Filter

1. After Photoshop is closed, load the installation CD, and then open the drive window for the CD player on your system.

2. Find 3D Transform.8bf on the installation CD, and then click on it and copy this filter file. Close the window, and then put the Inside Photoshop CS companion CD back into the CD drive (you'll need it for the upcoming exercise).

3. In the open window, go to the drive into which you installed Photoshop. Then navigate to the following program path: (*Your Drive letter*):\Photoshop CS\Plug-Ins\Adobe Photoshop Only\Filters.

4. Paste the 3D Transform filter into this folder. See Figure 7.24.

5. Launch Photoshop and get ready for an exciting tutorial.

X:\Photoshop CS\Plug-Ins\Adobe Photoshop Only\Filters

Figure 7.24   Paste a copy of the 3D Transform filter into this folder.

Now let's see what this filter can do:

Using the 3D Transform Filter

1. Launch Photoshop.

2. Create a new file—5 inches wide by 7 inches high, grayscale mode at 72 pixels/inch is fine.

3. With the Type tool, type the word **Rectangle** using a bold condensed font such as Impact, Helvetica Bold Condensed, Futura Bold Condensed, or Compacta—you get the idea. See Figure 7.25. If you don't have a typeface that's remotely similar, open the 3D Transform Type.psd file from the companion CD.

4. Choose Filter, Render, 3D Transform. Click on OK when prompted to decide whether you want the type rasterized (converted to no editable text—pixels).

5. Choose the Cube tool, and then drag starting from the far upper left (above the Rectangle letters) and continue to drag to the far right within the preview window to surround the text in a cube, as shown in Figure 7.26.

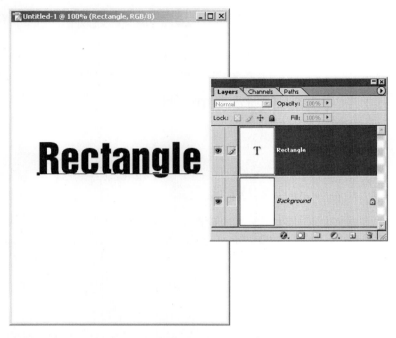

Figure 7.25   Type the word Rectangle to fit within the image window.

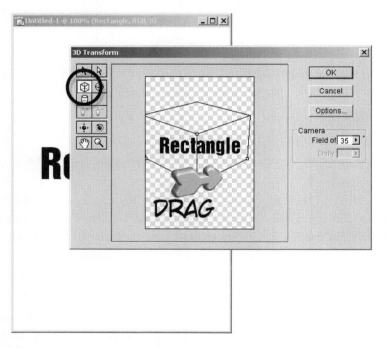

Figure 7.26   Drag a rectangle around the word *rectangle*.

6. Use the Selection tool if necessary to make the word encompass the bottom part of the box, as shown in Figure 7.26.

7. Click on the Trackball tool, and then drag upward in the proxy window until the text looks like that shown in Figure 7.27. If any of the original undistorted word can be seen, use the dolly controls to expand your view, but don't let the word run outside the proxy window. Click on OK to apply the effect.

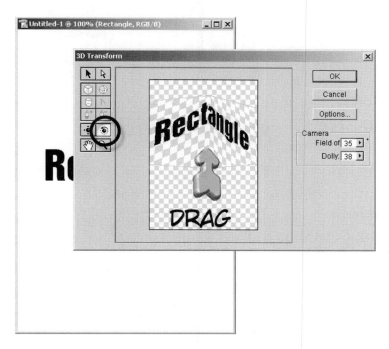

Figure 7.27   Create an upward "crease" in the text by dragging upward using the Trackball tool.

8. Let's try a different transformation. Type **Soft Drink**, centered, on two rows with tight leading. To access the typographic controls, click on the Toggle the Character and Paragraph palettes icon on the Options bar. Then set the justification to Centered, and use the same value for the leading as you do the character height. For example, if you've specified 72 points as the character size, specify 72 for the leading amount.

9. Press Ctrl(⌘)+Alt(Opt)+F to summon the last-used filter without applying it. Answer OK to rasterizing the type.

10. Choose the Cylinder tool, and then drag a cylinder around the Soft Drink text.

11. Choose the Trackball tool, and drag up and to the right so that the text is almost

running off the cylinder projection at the right, and you begin to see a gray stripe at left. Dolly in, as shown in Figure 7.28.

Figure 7.28   Warp the text so that it looks as though it is printed on the side of an actual soda can.

12. Click on OK.

13. Press Ctrl(⌘)+S; keep the file open.

Because these transformations are on layers, you can now put anything you like behind them. Personally, I think the Soft Drink transformation looks like a good logo just the way it is. You need to select and delete the gray "artifact" to the left of the type, but hey, it's a visually exciting piece the way it swoops and curves. However, you cannot achieve this effect using the Warp Type feature in Photoshop.

In Figure 7.29, I've added a box behind the **Rectangle** type and a slight drop shadow. See how visually interesting the text looks? Remember this trick the next time you have a package design you want to present. You can warp the entire package design, just as you did with the text.

It's time now to devote a little space to the filters that *don't* come with Photoshop: third-party plug-ins.

Figure 7.29   You can warp text, or an entire design, in 3D space using the 3D Transform filter.

Exploring the World of Third-Party Filters

Before we begin, I need to state that I have loaded and regularly use all the third-party filters you are going to see. I recommend them for what they can do and can mean to your work; however, I use some filters that I will not show off in this section, specifically KPT 3, 5, and 6, and XAOStools.

Having said this, let's look at some of the exciting offerings that third-party vendors have brought to the creative table.

Digital Element's Aurora

At the time of this writing, Digital Element has just released version 2 of Aurora, a background-generating program. It is not simply a cloud-making program: Aurora can write clouds of many different types (including the much-sought-after cumulus) "between" layers, injecting both clouds and oceanscapes "into" a scene. Additionally, these clouds look so real, that for many assignments, you can simply have the program write clouds into a file and you're done.

Using the filter can be as easy or as hard as you like. *Everything* is modifiable and customizable. But let's simply walk through ways to get a background into a visually boring image. Here's how you would do it if you had the filter:

Adding Aurora Clouds to an Image

1. Open an image that has a monotonous background—one with very few unique colors in the sky, such as that of an overcast day.

2. With the Magic Wand tool, click on the background, as shown in Figure 7.30. Increase or decrease the Magic Wand tolerance on the Options bar to make a clean selection of the drab background only.

Figure 7.30   Select the boring background out of the image.

3. In the Aurora interface, choose Presets, and then choose a sky that will visually integrate with the picture. As you can see in Figure 7.31, the interface contains controls to affect every parameter of the preset: placement of sun, cloud height, literally dozens of customization features.

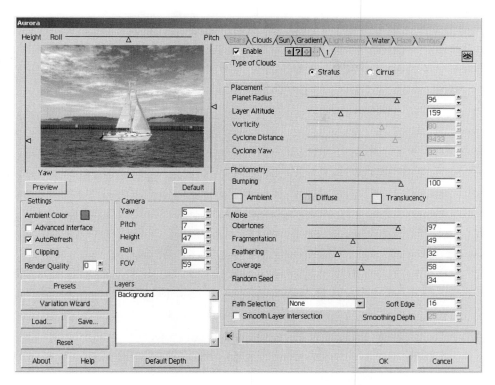

Figure 7.31   Aurora is a totally customizable cloud- and water-making machine!

4. Click on OK, and in a moment, the selection marquee you made is filled with a new sky, replete with realistic clouds.

As you can see in Figure 7.32, Aurora makes background enhancements a snap. If you do photo-retouching for a living, this filter is a must.

Note

Aurora and Verdant   Go to http://www.digi-element.com/index.shtml to download a free Windows or Macintosh trial of Aurora. Verdant (a tree-making filter) and Aurora can also be found on the companion CD.

Figure 7.32   The finished image.

Flaming Pear's Offerings

Flaming Pear offers very reasonably priced filters that do a wide variety of things. Stocastic printing is covered later in this book, but let me explain why Flaming Pear's India Ink filter is so cool.

Did you ever print a high-resolution black-and-white image from your laser printer? Doesn't it look dull and lifeless? The reason is that simply too much information is being reproduced; midtones in an image tend to muddy up the clarity of a black-and-white image, even though, ironically, the bulk of the visual information lies within the midtones. A solution to this muddiness problem is to remove information from the photo and to stylize it with a screen. And that's what India Ink does. Suppose you want to create a road-side sign selling pears. Naturally, the sign should contain a large image of a pear. Using Flaming Pear's India Ink filter, you can set the coarseness or fineness of the screen and choose the screen type. In Figure 7.33, I've chosen the BasketWeave filter at 4x magnification. As you can see, the image is as sharp and crisp as a fresh-fallen pear.

Another filter, which is just plain fun combined with amazing, is the Flood filter. This filter does only one thing: It reflects the top half of an image into what appears to be moving water. You can control the height of the water, the amount of distortion, and other parameters. Check out Figure 7.34.

Figure 7.33 The India Ink filter screens the image to a patterned fill that adds crispness and visual excitement to the image.

Figure 7.34 Flaming Pear's Flood filter makes instant art out of the most hum-drum image. Just add water!

Note

Flaming Pear You can download the trial versions of Flaming Pear products from http://www.flamingpear.com.

Power Retouche

Power Retouche is a suite of photographic correction and enhancement filters. It would be pointless to feature too many screenshots of this tool in a black-and-white book because most of the tools are for color correction. In addition to Lens Corrector (barrel correction), Color, and Brightness controls that go beyond Photoshop's native corrections, Power Retouche also has one of the sweetest duotone filters I've ever seen. "Wait," you say, "Can't I make duotones in Photoshop?" Yes, but Photoshop's duotones are for printing; they consist of two PostScript channels of ink specifications. Plus, you really can't print duotones to an inkjet printer because the preview merely shows what the inks will look like; there are no color channels.

Not so with Power Retouche's Toned Print filters. You can specify Sepia tone, Silver Gelatin—you name it—and the color channels remain color channels in the image file, and you can print the resulting file to an inkjet printer, and the results look spectacular, and life is *good*! See Figure 7.35 for an example of Power Retouche's interface.

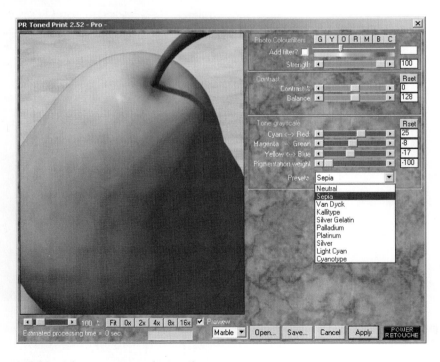

Figure 7.35   The Power Retouche interface.

Note

Power Retouche   A demo of Power Retouche is included on the companion CD.

If you're serious about color correction work, you owe it to yourself to try out this affordable suite.

Wild and Wacky Alien Skin Plug-Ins

Every once in a while, you'll have an off-the-wall fantasy composition in mind for an assignment. At these times, you'll want to check into Alien Skin filters. The Alien Skin plug-ins are eminently affordable, and they do stuff that other filters don't, such as creating an image out of tiny reproductions of the same image, burning the edges of an image and crumpling it, and creating other just-fun effects. Alien Skin produces Splat!, a border and fill utility in the spirit of Painter's nozzle set; Image Doctor, a very serious suite that helps remove JPEG noise from an image; Eye Candy 4000, a mending filter that goes beyond Photoshop's Healing Brush to provide your one-stop shop for embossing, producing water drops on an image, and more; and Xenofex, which is the logical extension of Eye Candy, complete with Lightning Effects and a really good Mosaic function.

In Figure 7.36, you can see what the Television filter can do to a piece. Note not only the scan lines, but the ghosting effect as well. And Television is only one of 14 filters, each of them capable of creating astounding effects with only a click or two.

Figure 7.36   Alien Skin's Xenofex filters include the Television plug-in. Sorry, but pay-per-view channels aren't included.

Note

> **Other demo software**   Demo versions of Alien Skin's Xenofex, Image Doctor, Splat!
> and Eye Candy 4000 can be downloaded from http://www.alienskin.com.

Auto F/X Filters

Auto F/X filters produce effects way beyond most people's expectations. The Mystical
Lighting filter, for example, is a user-applicable lighting effect you can use with a paintbrush to accent areas in an image. It's the closest thing to actually being able to change
the lighting in an image. The company's Mystical Tint, Tone, and Color filter produces
one of the best-aged sepia photographs I've ever seen. But perhaps the most useful day-
to-day filter is DreamSuite, which features chrome and gel filters. Want to produce gel
text that looks just like it fell off Apple's home page? Or perhaps you want the look of
metal so real you could touch it? Check out the DreamSuite filters.

Figure 7.37 shows two different applications of the DreamSuite filters to text in
Photoshop.

Figure 7.37   Auto F/X's DreamSuite re-creates the authentic look of chrome and gel.

Note

> **Auto F/X**   Demos of Auto F/X products are included on the companion CD.

Andromeda's 3Deluxe Filter

If you want to create 3D cylinders and cubes but don't know how to use a 3D modeling
program (or simply don't have the cash), Andromeda makes an affordable substitute in
the form of a plug-in filter for Photoshop. 3Deluxe can create textured, lit 3D primitives

(spheres, planes, cylinders) or can warp an image of your own onto any shape. 3Deluxe has a steeper learning curve than some filters, but the rewards are worth the additional effort. In Figure 7.38, you can see how the girl's face appears to be inside a sphere, and the other shapes are pure Andromeda synthesis.

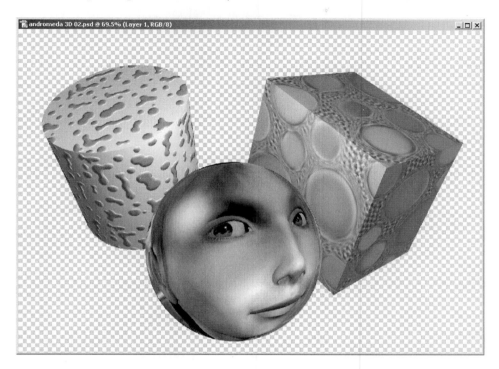

Figure 7.38   The Andromeda 3Deluxe filter can produce awesome objects with only a few mouse clicks.

Andromeda makes more than just the 3Deluxe filter, and it would be unfair to move on without a passing nod. Andromeda makes one of the best red-eye reduction filters out there at a very reasonable price, as well as a series of screens that offer a *lot* of user-customizable controls. If you're printing in black and white, Andromeda has you covered.

Note

Andromeda filter   Demos of Andromeda filter are included on the companion CD.

Shinycore's Path Styler

Have you ever wanted to emboss an outline, but you're unhappy with the sparse options in Photoshop? Well, if you can draw or import a path, Path Styler can turn your work into pure inspiration. Path Styler will add a bevel edge to your path in any of 49 odd patterns. And it can add a texture fill as well as lighting to the rendered path. Think of how quickly you could build a Web site with this power! In Figure 7.39, you can see how an elegant path can be made into a much more elegant painted object.

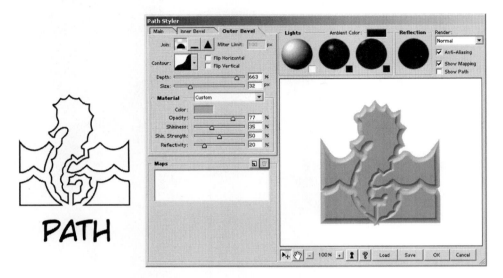

Figure 7.39   Path Styler is your single resource for magnificent objects that it draws from your own paths.

Note

Path Styler   The Path Styler demo can be found at `http://www.shinycore.com/`.

VisCheck: An Important Resource for Checking Color-Blindness

As we draw this third-party filter roundup to a close, we'd like to introduce you to a very serious, important filter for medical reasons. VisCheck (`http://www.vischeck.com/downloads/`) offers a free Windows download of a plug-in filter that can check for and compensate for the three most common types of color blindness. In the same sense that you want to oblige your Web audience with readable text and image tags for visually impaired individuals who use a reading machine, you will want to download and install this plug-in to see what color-blind people are seeing on your site.

In Figure 7.40, you can see how easy it is to interpret your designs to the color space of a color-blind person.

7

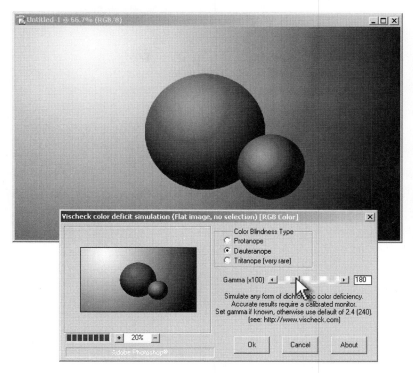

Figure 7.40   VisCheck's plug-in can help you detect flaws in a design when designing for the color-blind.

Be accommodating and be kind. If you're aware that some members of your audience are color-impaired, check out and use this free plug-in.

Summary

We hope you've learned several new things to do with Photoshop's native filters that you didn't know before. I particularly like the upscaling trick and the Displace filter steps, but you be the judge; when you need these techniques, the knowledge you've gained in this chapter will help you use them.

And admittedly, I didn't have a chance to cover all the third-party plug-ins on earth, simply because of the sheer volume of them! An estimated 300+ filters were available in 1995, and Heaven knows how many there are now. I've tried to pick the coolest, least-known filters, and I hope that you find something that an assignment is just itching for!

In the following chapter, you'll see how to use various methods to bring real-world photos and objects into Photoshop. Got a scanner? Got a minute? We'll show you how to make the most of your resources, how to measure images you want to acquire, and more.

Part III

Image Acquisition Basics

Chapter 8

Loading Digital Images into Photoshop CS from Digital Cameras, Photo CDs, Scanners, and More

Photoshop is a marvelous tool for manipulating, organizing, and storing digital images. With the availability of inexpensive digital cameras and scanners, you now can

In this chapter, you'll learn

- How to transfer images between a digital camera and your computer
- How to work with Picture and Photo CDs
- How to transfer images from non-camera sources
- How to convert non-digital images with a scanner
- How to prepare images to be scanned
- How to scan images into Photoshop
- How to scan negatives and slides

create and preserve these images. But to use the power of Photoshop to *edit* digital images, you first must get those images *into* the computer. You learn all about that process in this chapter.

But you probably have some non-digital images you'd also like to work with in Photoshop CS. Our lives and the lives of those who lived before us have been chronicled in albums and boxes full of photos, color slides, and negatives, many of which are in need of touch-up or repair. In this chapter, you learn simple techniques for converting non-digital images into digital images that can be opened and edited in Photoshop. This chapter also teaches you how to scan non-digital images. These images are forever preserved and immune to further effects of aging.

Bringing Images from a Digital Camera to a Computer

Understanding how your digital camera transfers images to your computer requires that you understand a little about your camera's basic anatomy. Your camera contains a sensor that captures the image, an internal computer that controls the images captured by the sensor, and a removable memory card on which the picture is stored (this memory card goes by many names including *media card* or *digital film*). To print or edit the image in Photoshop, you first must transfer the stored images from the memory card to a computer.

Memory Cards

Each camera is designed to use a particular type of card, with the exception of Olympus, which enables you to read two different types of media on a few models. Seven different types of memory cards are used by digital cameras:

- **CompactFlash (CF).** This is currently the most popular memory device for digital cameras, but MMC/SD cards are quickly becoming as popular. CF cards offer capacities up to 4GB, which can store a whole lot of pictures.

- **MultiMedia Card (MMC).** Smaller than the CF, the MMC is about the size of a postage stamp. This memory card is gaining in popularity because it can also be used in PDAs and MP3 players. The MMC can use the same reader as the SD card. A camera that can use MMC can also read an SD card, which is why the cameras and card readers usually list them together (MMC/SD).

- **SecureDigital (SD).** This card is a variation of the MMC, offering similar capacities and connectivity. The SecureDigital card, however, also has security features that PDAs and similar devices can use to protect sensitive information. Although the digital camera that uses MMC cards can usually use an SD card, it cannot use the secure features. Unless you're a secret agent needing to keep others from seeing the photos you have taken, this shouldn't be a major limitation.

- **MemoryStick (MS).** Invented and primarily seen on Sony equipment, the MemoryStick is about the size of a stick of gum and supports up to 128MB. The newer MemoryStick Pro supports capacities beyond 128MB but can be used only on cameras designed to support the Pro version.

- **SmartMedia (SM).** I call this the betamax of memory devices. When consumer digital cameras first appeared, the camera manufacturers offered either CompactFlash or SmartMedia. Today, no new cameras support SmartMedia. Even though this type of device is becoming obsolete, if your camera uses SM cards, you can find bargains galore online.

- **xD Picture card.** This proprietary card is used by Olympus and Fuji cameras. It is a little smaller than the MMC/SD card and has yet to see any popular support from other camera or memory manufacturers.

- **Microdrive.** This hard drive is encased in a CF card. A microdrive fits into the CompactFlash slot of a digital camera if the camera supports it; not all cameras that have a CF slot support microdrives. Microdrives come in capacities up to 4GB. They are noticeably slower than CompactFlash memory, but on very high capacities they offer a much more cost-effective storage solution.

Tip

Card Speeds   Many memory cards advertise that they offer accelerated speed. Several may claim to be 40 times faster than the average time needed to transfer an image from the camera sensor to the memory card. But remember that your camera's processor has to be capable of those lightning speeds, too. Be cautious about paying extra for memory cards with premium speed your camera can't support.

Connecting Interfaces and Card Readers

To transfer digital images from your digital camera's memory card to your computer, you simply attach your camera to the computer using a physical wire (usually a USB cable) or through an optional cradle or wireless connection. The computer's software recognizes the camera when it is attached and launches the appropriate application to move the photos from the camera's memory card into a folder you have designated in the computer. The transfer speed is controlled by the camera's computer.

Regardless of which make and model of camera or which computer platform you use, you transfer photos between the camera and the computer by using either the software that came with your camera or built into your operating system or by using manual file transfers. The transfer method you use is determined, in part, by the way your camera is attached to the computer.

You can access the contents of your digital camera through a computer in these two physical ways:

- You can attach the camera's processor to the computer through a cradle, wire, or wireless connection.
- You can connect the camera's memory card to the computer's processor using a *card reader.*

The following sections of this chapter discuss these methods.

Transferring Images Through a Wired or Wireless Connection

The first digital cameras used serial connections to transfer photos from the camera into the computer. Setting up such transfers was complicated and unbelievably slow. To put the transfer speed into perspective, transferring the contents of a 16MB memory card took 20 minutes. Today, nearly every digital camera offers a USB connection to transfer the photos.

> **Tip**
>
> **Serial connections are obsolete for transferring digital images**   If your camera's only connection is a serial interface, you should definitely consider replacing the camera with a newer one. Or, at the very least, you should consider the purchase of a *card reader,* which reads the images off the camera's memory card and enables you to copy them to your computer. (You'll read about these tools later in this chapter.)

Various interfaces are used for transferring digital images from camera to computer through a wired or wireless connection. Each method offers its own advantages and disadvantages, including convenience of setup and speed of transfer. These methods include

- **USB 1.0/1.1.** This is the most common interface found on digital cameras today. The original USB connection, it is usually described in the literature as simply *USB.* There are two versions of USB, but because 1.0 and 1.1 are essentially the same, they are both called *USB.*
- **FireWire (IEEE 1394).** Most commonly found on video cameras and professional digital cameras, FireWire/1394 offers speeds that are 40 times faster than USB. This interface has several different names. The name *FireWire* was coined by the Apple Corporation, which restricts its use to only Apple-related products. *IEEE 1394* is the name of the FireWire specification approved by the Institute of Electrical and Electronic Engineers (IEEE) and can be used by any manufacturer. To top it off, Sony named its version of the same interface *iLink.* The important thing to know is that no matter what name is used, the interfaces are identical.

8

- **USB 2.0.** This is the newest version of USB, which offers speeds slightly faster than FireWire. To take advantage of the higher speed requires a computer with a USB 2.0 connection. If a USB 2.0 device is plugged into the older USB connection, it will still operate but at the slower speed of USB 1.0/1.1.

- **Wireless.** A few cameras offer wireless connectivity. The advantage is being able to connect to the computer without the need to physically attach it to the computer. The disadvantage is that the data transfer speed is noticeably slower and subject to interference from both microwaves and some wireless phones.

Accessing Images Through a Card Reader

As mentioned earlier, when the camera is connected to the computer, the camera's built-in processor controls the transfer of images to the computer. Although plugging your camera into the computer is convenient, this approach presents a few disadvantages. First, the camera must be turned on during the transfer, which, unless you have an AC adapter, reduces the charge on the camera's batteries. Next, the processor in your camera is specifically designed to process images and store them on the media card; so, although the camera's processor does transfer the images, it usually can't transfer them as fast as the receiving computer can accept them. To get around this speed bump, you can use an external hardware device called a *card reader* that allows the computer interface to directly read the camera's removable media.

Card readers come in various configurations, each defined by the type of interface used to connect to the computer and type of memory card the card readers can read. Here are the most common card reader connection interfaces:

- **USB/USB 2.0.** The majority of card readers use this interface.

- **PCMCIA (PC Card).** The PC card is usually the preferred reader for people owning Notebooks. A newer version of the PC card interface offers 32-bit transfer, making it the fastest reader available today (even faster than USB 2.0 and FireWire).

- **FireWire (IEEE 1394).** Although this interface offers great speed, it hasn't been very popular. The reason is that a FireWire/1394 reader requires a 6-pin connector to draw the power the reader requires from the host computer. Unfortunately, almost all Notebooks offer only 4-pin connections, greatly limiting the reader's usability.

Note

> **A few other interface options**   For the record, a few other interfaces have been used to connect card readers. They are the small computer system interface (SCSI), parallel, and even a card reader that could be inserted into a floppy disk drive. An older digital camera that remains very popular is the Sony camera, which saves its images to a floppy disk. All these devices are obsolete or soon to be. With the newer readers costing less than $25, you won't save any money by buying one of the more antique readers, so avoid them!

Some card readers are dedicated devices, meaning that they can read only one type of memory card. For example, a MemoryStick reader can read only…a MemoryStick. Most of the card readers available today are designed to read CompactFlash (CF) cards, but some can be used to read other types of cards using optional adapters. The media fast replacing CF in new camera designs are the MultiMedia Card (MMC) and its near identical counterpart, the SecureDigital Card (SD). I expect MMC/SD to be offered on most readers in the near future. The alternative to the dedicated reader is the six-way card reader, which costs about the same as the dedicated reader except that it can read all different types of camera media.

Depending on the platform (Mac or PC) and the version of operating system you use, the card reader is usually identified automatically when you insert it, without the need to install any additional software. If you are using an older OS (such as Windows 98SE), you may need to install additional drivers. In such cases, you need to read the instructions that came with the card reader to see what, if any, additional software is required for the OS to recognize the reader.

After the card reader and media are connected to the computer, your camera's memory card appears as a new hard drive. I should point out that if you attach a six-way card reader to your computer, it appears as six new and different hard drives—one drive for each type of card connector in the reader. Being faced with six new drive icons on your screen for the first time can be a little disconcerting.

Tip

> **Transferring images**   Even though your camera's memory card appears as a disk drive to the operating system, you should always transfer the photos from the memory card to your computer before editing them in Photoshop. The memory card is many times slower than your disk drive and may not have the additional storage capacity required to make edits. Therefore, trying to edit a photo directly from the memory card is not a good idea because it will make any photo editing an extremely slow process at best—an impossible task at worst.

Transferring the Photos to the Computer

Regardless of how your camera is connected to the computer, moving images from the memory card of the camera into the computer is similar to moving files from a CD or other media source. It's always a good practice to be well organized, so first create a folder on your computer in which to place the photos. Maybe you want to title the folder with a date that applies to when the pictures were taken, or maybe a descriptive name such as **Hawaiian Vacation**. After the folder is created, you're ready to transfer the photographs from the memory card of the camera into the newly created folder.

Three methods are commonly used to transfer images from your camera's memory card to your computer. You can transfer the files manually, through third-party software, or, if you work in Windows, through the Windows Image Acquisition (WIA) program. The following sections discuss these methods.

Manual Transfer

Manual transfer is the simplest method of the three. When a card reader or camera is plugged into the computer, it appears to the computer as a hard drive. The transfer itself is a piece of cake:

Simple Steps for Manual Image Transfer

1. Use an OS utility such as Windows Explorer or the Mac Finder to view your computer. Create a new folder for the images on the computer's hard drive.

2. Locate the hard drive icon that represents the memory card/camera, and select all the files you want to transfer.

3. Move the files from the card into the folder on the computer's hard drive. You can do this either by dragging the files, copying and pasting the files, or choosing the File, Save menu option.

Automated Transfer

Automated transfer involves plugging the camera into your computer and following the instructions of the third-party software that launches when the camera is recognized. The appearance and operation of the software depend on the camera being used. Figure 8.1 shows the NikonView 6 that ships with Nikon digital cameras. Some of these applications offer sophisticated image management features, such as the ability to modify filenames, add keywords, change file formats, and more. But fear not if your software doesn't contain such features. Photoshop's File Browser has a myriad of features up its sleeve to serve all your needs.

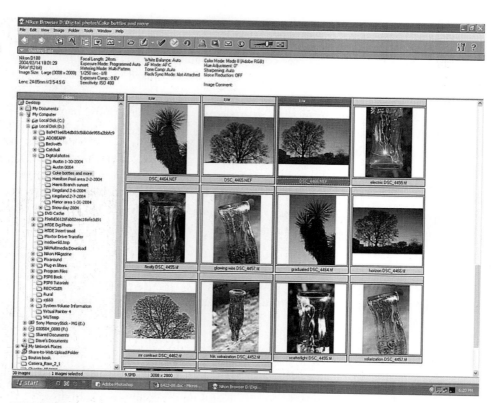

Figure 8.1   This is an example of the kind of software that ships with digital cameras to transfer and view the images.

Tip

> **Resetting image file numbering**   You should make sure that your digital camera doesn't reset its image file numbering when the memory card is removed and replaced. If the file numbering is reset, the result is that many images will have the same filenames. Depending on the third-party software you're using to transfer the images and the way it is configured, duplicate filenames may result in newer images overwriting older ones. Check your camera's menus for a resetting command, and disable it to avoid this problem.

Transferring Images with WIA Wizard

True to its name, WIA is available only for use with Windows. If your digital camera supports WIA, the software allows you to import files from the camera directly into Photoshop CS using the File, Import menu.

Of the three transfer methods described here, WIA is the only one that allows you to import the images directly into Photoshop without first transferring them to your camera's hard drive. There is no advantage to transferring the images from the camera to the computer from within Photoshop.

To use this method, open the File menu and choose Import, WIA Support. Depending on your camera and operating system, the resulting dialog box will vary in the features it offers. Generally, the options are relatively straightforward. You select the images and click the Get Pictures button. Follow the software's prompts to complete the process.

Tip

Is your camera supported?   Early in the transfer process, WIA may ask you to choose the digital camera from which to import the images. If your camera doesn't appear as a choice, the problem could be

- Your camera isn't turned on.
- Your camera doesn't support WIA (most newer cameras do, however).
- The physical cable connecting your camera to the computer isn't properly seated.

Rotating Transferred Images

After you've transferred the images, you can use Photoshop to open the folder with the images in it and rotate the images that require rotation to put them in the correct perspective. To rotate images, follow these steps:

Straightening Up Transferred Images

1. Select the images in the File Browser that you want to rotate. You can select multiple images by holding down the Ctrl(⌘) key as you click on the images you want to select, or hold down the Shift key and select a continuous group of images by clicking on the first and last image for the group.

2. Right-click (Macintosh: hold Ctrl and click) on one of the selected images, and choose the appropriate rotation option from the context menu. Photoshop will display a warning dialog message to explain that the rotation applies only to the thumbnail in the File Browser and the image isn't officially rotated until the image is actually opened and then saved with the rotation changes.

3. Right-click (Macintosh: hold Ctrl and click) again on one of the selected images in the File Browser, and choose Apply Rotation from the context menu; the rotation will be applied to the image without the need to open the image and resave it. Once you are aware of this fact, go ahead and click the Don't Show Again option on the pesky warning dialog box that pops up when images are rotated.

This is also a good time to throw away the really bad photos (flash didn't fire, finger over lens, out of focus, and so on).

Combining the Power of Film and Digital with Photo CDs

According to Kodak, by the year 2006 less than 20% of all photos will be taken using film. Most industry analysts think the figure will be much smaller. Does this mean that you must convert to a digital camera to experience all the features of Photoshop CS? Not at all. If you're comfortable using a film camera and don't want to change, you certainly can enjoy the benefits Photoshop CS has to offer regardless of the source for those images.

Picture CDs

With many consumers making the change to digital cameras, the film developers are keeping pace. Most one-hour developers now offer picture CDs in addition to or in place of standard prints from your film when it is developed. When this type of service was first offered, it was very expensive and required a waiting period because the developer had to send the images to another location to create the CD. Today's newest film developers can process the film and create the CD all on the same machine.

Many developers offer two types of photos on CD. There is the generic type and the Kodak Picture CD. The house brand or generic CD contains photos scanned from your color negatives and saved in JPEG format on a CD. Typically, these CDs cost about $4–5 extra, but if you don't get any prints made, you are still ahead financially. Kodak-affiliated developers offer the Kodak Picture CD, which costs a few dollars more than the generic house-brand CD.

Getting the images from the CD to Photoshop is really brain-free. All the images are on the CD in either TIFF or JPEG format. Use either the Open or File Browser feature to select the image you want to work on in Photoshop. Just remember that you cannot save the images back on the CD, and you must use the Save As feature to save the image on a hard drive.

With the Kodak Picture CD option, you get your film negatives and your photos on a CD in JPEG format. The CD also contains a collection of software tools that allow you to perform basic cropping, red-eye removal, and several other options for sharing the prints on the Internet and printing them. The features provided in the free software are not intended to replace the professional results possible with Photoshop. But for quick and dirty work, they're a simple option.

Kodak PhotoCDs (PCDs)

Another available CD option is called a Kodak PhotoCD. This service uses Eastman Kodak's proprietary PhotoCD (PCD) writer to scan your negatives and write the images to a CD-ROM. PCD writers are a combination film scanner and file writer. After each

8

negative is scanned, the PCD writer (a very expensive piece of hardware) writes a single PhotoCD file for that image. The PhotoCD file format is a proprietary compressed format that Photoshop and many other graphics applications can read.

As mentioned earlier, the PCD hardware is extremely expensive, so don't expect a "mom and pop" photo-finisher or even a big retailer such as Target or Wal-Mart to have this machine at its store. Usually, when a local photo-finisher offers PhotoCD service, the film you give it is shipped to a large custom-processing plant that has a PCD writer. Because the processing probably won't be done locally, you might have to wait at least two days to get your finished PhotoCD back from your local photo-finisher.

Opening PhotoCD Images in Photoshop

When you get your PhotoCD from the photo-finisher, all you need to do is plop the CD into your CD-ROM drive and launch Photoshop. Because the PhotoCD is a read-only device, you need to transfer the photos to your computer before you can work on them with Photoshop.

There is nothing special about a PhotoCD; physically, it is the same as any other CD you might load. What makes a PhotoCD special is the file format in which the images are stored and the compression format, which is part of the file format.

Each image on a Kodak PhotoCD is stored in a single file called an *image pac*. The following five sizes (resolutions) of the image can be opened from a single image pac:

- 72KB (128 by 192 pixels)
- 288KB (256 by 384 pixels)
- 1.13MB (512 by 768 pixels)
- 4.5 MB (1,024 by 1,536 pixels)
- 18MB (2,048 by 3,072 pixels)

The image pac file itself actually contains the file at 4.5MB only. An application's PhotoCD import filter uses a proprietary method of interpolation (resizing), along with special hinting information found in the image pac, to produce the other sizes from the 4.5MB file. *Interpolation,* or resampling, is the method of resizing an image by adding pixels to make the image larger or subtracting pixels to make it smaller.

Because the five different sizes of the image are not actually stored in a PCD file, a combination of compression/decompression and interpolation must take place when you choose to open the image in Photoshop at the 72KB, 2.88KB, 1.13MB, or 18MB size. I recommend that you choose to work with the 4.5MB size image whenever practical because it will have the sharpest focus. The reason? Even the best interpolation reduces the focus of an image as pixels are added or removed to create a new image size.

Creating a Contact Sheet

The PCD writer prints an index print to go along with every PhotoCD. The *index print* (tiny, numbered thumbnails of all the images stored on the PhotoCD) is something you *don't* want to lose because, from the outside, every PhotoCD looks identical. The numbers next to the thumbnails on the index print correspond to each image file on the PhotoCD: The first image on a PhotoCD is Img0001.pcd, the second is Img0002.pcd, and so on. Because the thumbnails are so tiny (and as added insurance in case you lose the index print), you might want to take advantage of Photoshop's Contact Sheet feature to create your own, more legible digital contact sheet. You can find the Contact Sheet feature by opening the File menu and choosing Automate, Contact Sheet II.

So, the inevitable question looms, "How does this compare to other image acquisition methods?" Today, I must say that a digital camera produces the best images you can work with in Photoshop, and PhotoCDs prove to be approximately the same or a little less quality than image-negative scanner images. Why? Because you treat your own images with kid gloves, whereas a PhotoCD plant handles your images like a business. Film scanners, which once were popular only with professionals, are now finding their way to a larger consumer base. Although the technology is still officially available, PhotoCDs aren't used as much these days because, for a reasonable amount, you can buy a very high quality film scanner. You'll read more on this subject later in this chapter.

Converting Non-Digital Images: Scanner Basics

Up until now we have been considering the transfer of images from digital cameras or pictures on a CD into the computer. The odds are, however, that you have many photos, slides, and negatives that you would like to convert to digital images. You can do that by scanning the images using a flatbed or film scanner. You then can work on the scanned images in Photoshop. The scanner is a marvelous tool that can turn almost any photograph, printed image, or even 3D object into a graphic image file that can be brought into Photoshop for enhancement, correction, or restoration. And, scanned image files are impervious to the wear and tear of time, unlike printed images or film negatives.

The following sections give you a scanner quick-start by explaining how flatbed and film scanners work and by defining some basic scanner lingo. In the remainder of the chapter, you will learn how to get the best possible scans of photos, slides, and negatives.

Flatbed Scanners

Flatbed scanners are simple devices, and their operation is not unlike the copy machine at your office:

1. You place a photo face down on the scanner glass. Beneath the glass is a light source and a scanning mechanism called a *scan head.*

8

2. The scanner uses a small motor to move the scan head under the image that is placed on the copy glass. As light bounces off the page from the scan head, it captures the light. The head can read very small portions of the page—less than 1/120,000th of a square inch.

3. A recording device (called a *CCD sensor*) captures the reflected light and converts it into electrical signals. These signals are converted into computer bits (called *pixels*) and sent to your computer.

That's all there is to a flatbed scanner. It is the best choice for scanning photos and just about anything flat—and some things that are not so flat. I have successfully captured 3D objects up to 4 inches thick (which is about the focusing limit of most flatbed scanners).

Most flatbed scanners now offer templates and settings to scan film negatives and color slides. For general-purpose work, scanning film and slides on a flatbed produces acceptable output, but for critical work with slides and negatives, you need a film scanner (discussed in the next section of this chapter).

When buying a flatbed scanner, you always see the advertised specs boasting some high scanning-resolution capability. Although some of these specs might be important to the quality of the image the scanner is capable of producing, you will rarely find the need to scan at the highest setting when using a flatbed scanner. I personally almost never need to scan above 300 dpi. How do you know what you need? Simple. Consider what you plan to do with the image.

For example, if you just want a quick copy of an image to send in an email message to your aunt, you want to scan at a low resolution (around 72 dpi) to keep the file small. If you're scanning an image that will be sent to a professional printer or you want to edit the image after you scan it, scan at the higher resolution of 300 dpi.

When you're dealing with a professional service, ask how many lines per inch (lpi) the service needs to output. The service rep might typically give you a number of 133. A good rule of thumb is to double this number for your scanning (input) dpi. In this case, 266 will yield a sufficient resolution to output your image. So, if you round up (for good measure) to 300 dpi, you can see that you're back to my original premise that you will rarely need to scan images higher than 300 dpi.

By the way, it is this setting of lines per inch (or line screens) in professional printing that causes what is known as *moiré pattern*. When you scan a printed image, such as a picture from a magazine article or newspaper, it usually develops a checkered pattern or something that looks like a plaid on it. When the patterns of the tiny dots used to print the picture (called *screens*) are scanned, they develop their own pattern. You can reduce (not eliminate) these patterns in two different ways:

- You may be able to use your scanning software to minimize the moiré effect with the Descreen option. Some scanning software has a preset for this. For example, your software might have a setting for *newspaper and magazines*, which means the descreening is accomplished automatically for those items.

- The second possible way around this pattern is to use Photoshop filters. Open the Filter menu, and choose Noise, Despeckle.

Note

A word on descreening   Be aware that regardless of how an image is descreened, the result is a softer picture, meaning it loses some of its sharpness. This result may be a small price to pay for the reduction of those annoying moiré patterns. Using the Unsharp Mask filter can help alleviate this problem.

Scanning and Copyrights

A word to the wise: Just because you *can* scan it doesn't mean you *should* scan it. Sounds sort of Zen, doesn't it? I'm sure most of you are aware that nearly everything in print is copyrighted in one form or another. Most of these cases are obvious. For example, you wouldn't think of scanning a photograph from an issue of *National Geographic* and selling it as wallpaper for your desktop. (You wouldn't…right?) Although that would be an obvious copyright infringement, others are more subtle. For example, it is illegal to make copies of any photograph that was made by a professional photographer or studio. Examples are school photos and wedding pictures taken by a pro—not the cheesy ones taken with the disposable camera during the reception. It is a fact of law that even though you may have paid this person or organization to take the picture of you or your loved ones and paid for the materials, the image still belongs to that person, and duplicating it is a violation of U.S. Copyright law. So be careful what you scan.

Film Scanners

As good as flatbed scanners have become in recent years, if you need to make high-quality scans of negatives and color slides, you should use a dedicated film scanner. Because most negatives and slides are very small, film scanners have a scan head that can resolve at a very high resolution. In addition to the higher resolution, most quality film scanners have extra features that remove and correct defects in ways that are not possible with flatbed scanners. The price of a quality film scanner, like all scanners, has dropped considerably in the past three years.

Here are some tips to keep in mind that will help you get the best possible scans from your film scanner:

- **Handle with care.** Make sure that your negatives are dust, hair, and fingerprint free; this is extremely important. If any foreign substance is on either side of the negative, the scanner will see it and add it to your image. And although some film scanners have a built-in technology to account and adjust for dust, dirt, and scratches, you should make sure you keep possible distortions to a minimum. Cleanliness goes a long way in acquiring a great image when you're using a film scanner.

- **Invest in some film-handling equipment.** For best results, use a pair of cloth film-handling gloves before you even think about taking your negatives out of their sleeves. If you don't have film-handling gloves available, always handle photos and negatives by their edges. Also, resist the urge to blow the dust off a negative. Do you really want that stubborn shred of celery (that had been caught in your teeth) projected at your film? Instead, dust both sides of the film with a compressed-gas duster such as Dust-Off by Falcon. You can find the gloves and compressed gas in most photo stores and online.

- **Keep the negatives safe when you're finished with them.** Put the negatives back in their original carriers or plastic sleeves. Negatives scratch easily, so handle with care.

- **Film grain.** Although people who work with film on a regular basis might intuitively know this one (and think to themselves, "Yeah—duh!"), it might not be as obvious to the rest of us: The film speed of your negatives affects the clarity of the scan. A high ISO (formerly called *ASA*) film will produce an extremely grainy scan.

You'll learn more about all these tips and the scanning process in "Scanning Negatives and Slides," later in this chapter.

Talking about some scanning terms now might be useful. Some of these terms, however, aren't merely limited to scanning; they also apply to images in general.

Scanner Terms and Concepts

Whether you are talking about car engines or makeup, every area of interest has its own terminology. Scanners have their own buzzwords as well, and it is helpful to understand them and the way they apply to your scanner and your images.

Pixels

As you gotta know by now, all bitmap images are made of the building blocks called *pixels*, a term used to describe the smallest part of a raster (bitmap) image. Pixels have two characteristics you need to remember: They are rectangular, and they can be only one color. This means that a digital picture is like a mosaic composed of hundreds, thousands, if not millions, of colored tiles or pixels (see Figure 8.2). If you own or have looked at ads for digital cameras, you have already been exposed to the term. The first topic discussed when talking about a digital camera is how many millions of pixels (megapixels) the camera can capture.

Figure 8.2   Like this Greek tile mosaic, digital images are made up of tiny parts called pixels.

The answer to the sometimes-asked and often-misunderstood question "Hey, how big is a pixel?" is both simple and complex. The fact is that a pixel has no fixed dimensions unless spoken about in relation to a unit of measurement. For example, *30 pixels* is meaningless in size. It's like saying, "This car gets 50 miles." Fine. Per what? A pixel's relative size becomes meaningful when it gets a denominator, and the resolution is described as a fraction, such as 35 pixels/inch—which is a *really* low resolution!

Resolution

Resolution is easily the most misused term in computer graphics. It defines the density of pixels—or said another way, how many pixels must fit into an inch or other unit of measure. Let's do a brief exercise to try to understand the relationship between pixels and resolution:

How Do Pixels and Resolution Interact?

1. Press Ctrl(⌘)+N to create a new document. In the New dialog box, set Width to 4 inches, Height to 2 inches, Resolution to 72 pixels/inch, Mode to RGB Color, and Background Contents to White (see Figure 8.3). Click on OK.

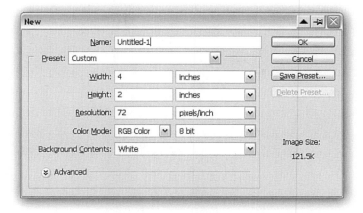

Figure 8.3   Create a new image that is 4×2 inches with a resolution of 72 ppi.

Insider

> You aren't actually going to use this file to create an image, only to understand a point. Just pretend for now that this file contains a really dynamic image. What do you know about this file? Well, you know that, when viewed at actual pixel size (screen resolution or 100% zoom level), this image is not very large on the monitor. You also know that if you print this masterpiece (just play along, okay?), this lovely image will print 4 inches wide and 2 inches tall—but at a really crummy printing resolution because most inkjets require at least 200 pixels per inch rendering resolution. You know the dimensions as sent to the printer because you set those dimensions when creating the file. Let's move on.

2. Right-click (Macintosh: hold Ctrl and click) the title bar of the image, and choose Image Size. You then see that the Document Size is 4"×2" as expected. The Pixel Dimension (the screen representation) is 288×144. This dimension also is expected because you know the resolution is 72 ppi. So, if you do the math and multiply 72×4, you get 288 (and similarly 72×2=144). So the size of each pixel square is large enough to pack 72 of these pixel squares into each inch. With me so far?

3. Now we'll cheat a little. Instead of opening another new document, let's play with the numbers in this Image Size dialog box to see what happens if the image had been created at a different resolution (more pretending on your part). In the Image Size dialog box, make sure Resample Image is checked, and change the Resolution to 600 pixels/inch. Wow! Figure 8.4 shows a comparison of the Image Size information of the same images if they were created at different resolutions.

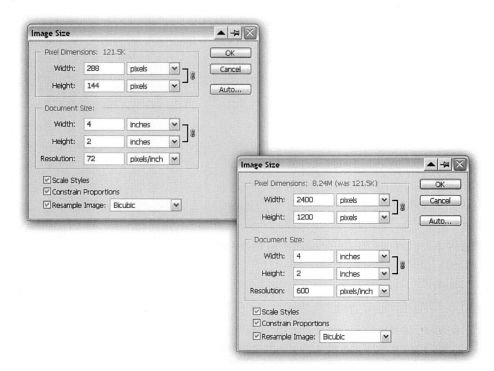

Figure 8.4   A comparison of Image Size information dialog boxes shows the difference resolution makes.

4. Just for fun now, click on OK to apply the changes to the Image Size dialog box, and watch the document window become too big to view entirely in your workspace when the zoom level is set to 100%.

So what did you learn here? At first glance, you may have noticed only the obvious. When you increase the resolution of the file, it becomes really huge on the screen. But that's only part of the story. Did you notice that the printable size (or Document Size dimensions) remained the same? The image still prints at dimensions of 4"×2". This means that more pixels will be packed into the same size image, offering more detail and clarity than the image that was printed at 72 ppi. There's more clarity because the size of each pixel is smaller to allow for squeezing 600 of these pixel squares into 1 inch as opposed to the original image that had to have only 72 of these squares in each inch. Now, if we go back to our original question—"How big is a pixel?"—is it more apparent that the size of the pixel is related to the resolution? By the way, did you also notice that the 72 ppi file had an estimated file size of 121.5KB, and the 600 ppi file would take up 8.24MB of hard disk space?

Scanner Color-Depth

The second most advertised technical feature of a scanner is the color depth. Most scanners capture three primary colors: Red, Green, and Blue (RGB). The number of different shades of each color the scanner can capture determines how many colors the scanner can scan. For example, the output of most scanners used to be 24-bit color. That means the color for each of the three colors (called *channels*) is limited to the number of different shades that can be expressed by 24 bits, which is roughly 16.7 million colors. Most scanners offer color depths greater than 24 bits.

Although it seems reasonable that a greater color depth would produce superior color, the quality difference between a scan produced with a 24-bit versus a 48-bit scanner can rarely be seen with the naked eye, but in this case the visual evidence can be misleading. Just because the details aren't visually obvious doesn't mean they aren't available. When an image is scanned at 16 bits per channel (48-bit), and tonal adjustment tools are later applied to it in Photoshop, the image suffers almost no degradation and there is a much greater chance that detail lost in the shadows of the image can suddenly be recovered or pulled out of the image, making these details more obvious.

Scanner Color Modes

Also called *color models* or *color space*, the *scanner color mode* setting determines the way your scanner and computer see the colors in your scan. Although more than a dozen different names are used for color modes, the following are the most common:

- **Line Art.** This mode is also known as *black-and-white*, which is descriptive because the image has only two colors—black and white. A classic example is a standard business card or a sheet of text printed with a laser printer. Be aware that when the term *black-and-white* is used to describe a movie or television show "way back when," the mode actually being identified is grayscale, which is the next color mode.

- **Grayscale.** Like line art, grayscale mode has only one color (black), but it can display 256 different shades or tints of black—hence, the term *grayscale*. A "black-and-white" photograph is an example of a grayscale image because it contains many brightness values, from 100% black, to say, 50% black to 0% black (white).

- **256 Color.** This color space also has several names. A favorite color space on the Internet, it is also called *8-bit color* or *indexed color*. An image in 8-bit color is composed of up to 256 different colors. Depending on the number of colors in the original image, an image with a palette of 256 colors can look as simple as the Sunday comics (because this kind of image contains fewer than 256 colors) or can look as complex as a photograph as long as the color *range* (also known as gamut) is still within the 256-color limitation.

Tip

Don't scan at 256 colors Even if an image is to be used on the Web, you should never scan it at 256 colors if you plan to edit it afterward. Always scan it as 24-bit RGB color.

- **RGB Color.** RGB color space wins the prize for most names. It is also called *24-bit color, 16.7 million, Millions of color* (by Apple), *true color*, and many more. This is the color mode of choice for all color scanning. It will give your scanned color images a large enough palette of colors to faithfully represent the image when scanning.

- **Web Color Graphics.** This setting might appear in lieu of the 256 color model. Even though the image you are scanning may eventually be converted to 256 color, it is still wise to scan the image using the RGB color setting. It's best to edit the image in full RGB color mode and use Photoshop's Save For Web feature to preview how the image will look when reduced to 256 colors.

- **48-bit Color.** This mode provides greater detail in the captured scan but also creates an extremely large file size. Use this mode with caution if you don't have a critical need to capture the detail at the highest setting.

Preparing an Image to Be Scanned

Scanners today are fantastic. They can scan at higher resolutions and capture a greater range of colors than scanners made only a few years ago. Regardless of how good they are, many scanned images don't look as good as they should simply because the image or the scanner wasn't properly prepared before scanning. In the sections to follow, you will discover the simple but necessary steps to prepare an image to be scanned and also ways to evaluate the completed scan.

Proper Scanning Tools

The procedures for preparing the scanner and the images to be scanned are simple and require common household items. Keep these tools near your scanner, so you won't be tempted to skip the "prep work" before scanning:

- **Glass cleaner.** Necessary to clean the scanner glass; I recommend using a small spray bottle.

- **Lint-free cloth.** Many expensive paper and cloth products are labeled lint free. Paper towels work as good as most, but I get the best results using old undershirts. They have been through the dryer so many times that they are soft and functionally lint free.

8

- **Soft brush.** Most photo stores have several excellent brushes designed specifically for photos. Some are anti-static; others are very wide to make brushing the entire photo easier. Although these brushes are good, I have found the brush that comes with blush makeup works just as well—with the understanding that it is a stiff brush and must be applied lightly. Never use one of these brushes that has actually been used to apply makeup, though!

- **Plastic drafting triangle.** This tool can be used to help align photos to avoid crooked scans. I use two different sizes, but just about any small one will do.

- **Pad of quadrille paper.** This paper is used for aligning photos on scanner glass. Get a cheap pad of quadrille paper, not the expensive paper made for draftsmen.

- **Restickable adhesive glue stick.** This is the same adhesive used for those little sticky notes stuck all over our lives. It can also be useful when aligning photos.

Again, these tools should be conveniently located for use before you scan; I keep all of mine in a small plastic basket next to my scanner.

Now that you're properly armed, let's see how to prepare an image for scanning.

Tip

> **Don't rotate too often**   Whenever you rotate an image in Photoshop, the image suffers from mild distortion, which reduces its overall sharpness. The exception to this rule occurs when images are rotated in increments of 90°; these rotations do not produce any loss of sharpness because the angles of rotation keep the pixels aligned perfectly in both the horizontal and vertical axes (no resampling is necessary). In contrast, the image rotated at angles other than 90° increments causes Photoshop to re-create or resample every pixel in the image to adjust for the rotation. The most common result of resampling is a noticeable loss of detail and an overall softening of the photo. Again, you can see why aligning the image properly in the scanner is the best way to go.

Three Steps of Scanning Preparation

As you read through this section, you might think that preparing an image for scanning is a laborious ritual. But when you know what to do, preparing for the first scan takes less than a minute, and prepping subsequent scans takes less than 15 seconds.

Although you can remove unwanted debris in the computer, doing it that way takes time. I did three timing runs with three different photographs with varying amounts of dust, dirt, and dog hair on them. On the average, I was able to remove the debris using Photoshop with the Healing Brush tool in about 8 minutes. I then cleaned all three images and the scanners before scanning them in again. Cleaning the scanner glass and each photo took about 20 seconds. Hence, it is true that while we never seem to have enough time to do the job right, we always find time to correct the mistakes.

I recommend these three steps to prepare a scanner and the image to be scanned: Clean the scanner glass, remove dust and surface dirt from the photo, and align the photo carefully to produce an image that's straight and in proper perspective. The following sections discuss each of these processes in detail.

Clean the Scanner Glass

Make sure the scanner glass is clean before starting a scanning session, unless you're scanning in 3D objects like fudge brownies or soup. Just kidding about the soup. Don't scan soup. Apply the glass cleaner to a soft cloth; do not spray or pour it directly on the scanner's glass surface.

All scanner manufacturers have their own set of preferences for glass cleaners. For example, HP recommends glass cleaners that don't contain ammonia, and Microtek recommends using alcohol. If your scanner recommends alcohol for scanner glass cleaning, use isopropyl rather than rubbing alcohol. The latter contains oils such as lanolin and will leave a film on your scanner glass.

The important point is to clean the glass and remove any streaks on the surface. The best way to check whether the glass surface is clean is to lift the lid of the scanner; you should be able to spot any streaking easily if the scanning light is on.

Tip

> **Foggy glass**   When you're checking your glass for cleanliness, you may notice a faint fogging on the bottom side of the copy glass. This occurs sometimes and, as a rule, has little to no effect on the scanned image. Do not attempt to remove the glass unless the manufacturer has provided instructions on how to do so safely.

Warning

> **Don't scratch the glass surface**   Most cheap paper towels have a coarse texture because they are meant to be used to clean countertops. This coarse texture can create fine scratches on the scanner glass. If you cannot find an old T-shirt or its equivalent, a roll of high-quality paper towels will do the trick.

Remove Dust and Debris from the Photo

Evicting dust and debris from the photo, slide, or negative can be challenge. Gently brush the dust off a photo, taking care not to scratch the photo surface. One of my brushes has a little squeeze bulb on it to blow the dust away while brushing. If the dust is clinging to the photo, the humidity in the room is probably pretty low, and the photo may have a static charge, which serves to turn the photo into a dust magnet. Be patient and the dust will come off.

You might want to avoid the temptation to remove dust and debris with a blast from canned air. Although there is nothing inherently wrong with using these pneumatic blasters, you should be aware of some drawbacks. First, blowing air across a photo can produce a static charge on the photo, which tends to attract more dust. Second, giving the scanner a blast to remove debris scatters the dust or particles on anything in close proximity to the scanner. Third, canned air is a far more expensive solution than the traditional ones discussed in this chapter. I keep a can of air handy to blow out my keyboard on occasion and for precious little else.

Align the Image Properly

Don't be tempted to place the image on the scanner using the edge of the scanner glass as a guide, flop down the lid, and hope for the best. If you spend a few moments to properly align the photo on the scanner, you won't need to correct the alignment later with Photoshop. This will result in a better scan because the process of rotation can degrade image quality.

So, how do you align a photo in the middle of the scanner glass? The answer depends on what you're scanning. If it is a photograph whose edge is parallel with the border edge, use this simple technique:

Getting the Alignment Right

1. Place a plastic right triangle on the scanner glass with one side against the edge, and then align the photo against the adjacent edge of the triangle, as shown in Figure 8.5.

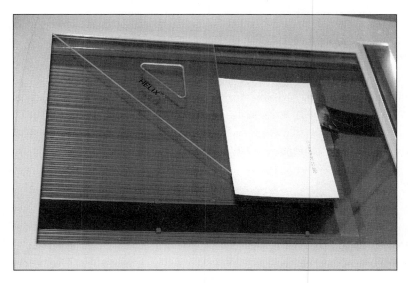

Figure 8.5 A plastic triangle offers the best way to physically align photos on a scanner glass.

2. After the photo is aligned, leave the plastic triangle and the photo in place, and slowly close the lid on the scanner. If the image being scanned is very thin and lightweight, be aware that the air flow produced when replacing the lid too fast can cause the photo to move easily.

3. Make a preview scan. Use the cropping ability of the scanner software to define the selection area that includes the photo but excludes the clear plastic triangle from the final scan.

Tip

Resize while scanning   If you resize an image in Photoshop, a process called *resampling* occurs. No matter how good Photoshop is at resampling, the image still suffers a loss in sharpness and detail. However, if you use the scanner software options to resize the image before scanning, the scanner can rescale the image without the associated loss of detail. A good use of this feature is when you might need to scan a photo for a publication or newsletter, and you need the image to fit a specific size for its final placement. After you have cropped the photo with the selection, you can tell the scanner what size the output needs to be, and it will do all the math and produce a scanned image at the desired size. (You also can indicate the output size as a percentage of the original size.)

Scanning Near the Edge

Most flatbed scanners today produce excellent quality scans. The typical scanner operates by moving the scanning head along the length of the scanner during the scan. Because of the way the scanning mechanism operates, the quality of the scan will be better near the middle of the scanning surface than it will be near the edges of the glass surface. Keep in mind this is all relative, so this is not to say that photos placed near the edge of the scanner glass will be terrible. It is just a fact that scans made with the photo positioned away from the edge of the glass will have a slightly better quality. How much better is determined by the quality of the scanner. Less expensive scanners do a poorer job of scanning the edge than do higher quality scanners.

Scanning an Image into Photoshop

Now that you are ready to scan, launch Photoshop and choose File, Import. Select the scanner from the menu that appears. Some scanners might have a button that you can press to launch the scanning software.

8

Tip

Avoid the WIA   When you start a scanner from within Photoshop on the Windows XP platform, avoid using the WIA interface if you can. This primitive tool does not use many of the scanner features and therefore will not produce the best possible scanning results.

Regardless of which method you use, the actual scanning process is pretty much universal. The following sections describe the basic steps of any scanning process.

Previewing the Image

Most scanning software provides a preview button that produces a preview of everything on the scanning surface. Depending on your scanner, the preview scan might occur automatically after the scanner warms up. A preview scan is a low-resolution representation of the scanned image. Even though the preview is a low-quality image, it can still be useful to help select the area to be scanned and to help verify that the color mode setting appears correct.

Selecting (Cropping) the Image

After you've previewed the image, most scanning software allows you to select (crop) the surface area to scan just the necessary image area you're targeting. Some scanners may attempt to automatically select the image area for you, and most of the time they will do a good job. In two situations, automatic cropping might not work well: when the border color of the image is similar to the color of the scanner lid and when you want to scan only part of the image. Here are some quick steps for selecting the image area:

Refining Your Selection with Zooming

1. On the preview, click and drag a rectangle of the area that you want to scan, as shown next. After you have made a rough selection, you can move the selection bars by clicking and dragging them to the desired position.

2. Verify that the vertical edges of the photo being scanned align with the vertical selection lines. If they don't, cancel, reposition the photo, and try again.

3. After you've made the first selection, locate the button or command that zooms in the selected area. On the Epson dialog box, for example, it is the button with the magnifying glass in the Preview section. On HP scanners, it is usually a magnifying glass icon. When this feature is enabled, the scanner will scan the image again, and the selected area will fill the preview window. At this point, you can make any final adjustment to the selection bars.

When you have the selection the way you want it, you need to make only a few more checks.

Choosing Color Mode Settings

Most scanning software can do a sufficient job of automatically determining the best settings. If you have several photographs to scan and don't want to invest the time to manually choose settings, or the quality of the resulting scans isn't critical, the automatic settings might fit your needs just fine. Because of the way the automatic features are designed to work in adjusting exposure and color controls, you will get a good scan most of the time. But you might want to take a few minutes to adjust the settings manually for photos that have specific concerns such as color fading, overexposures, or backlighting.

Scanning the Image

At this point, go ahead and scan the image. If you launched the scanning software from within Photoshop, the image will appear in the Photoshop workspace after the scan is complete. You may need to close the scanning software interface to access the image. If you initiated the scanning software using a button on the scanner, you might be offered the option of sending the image to a photo-editing program, printing the image, or saving the image as a file.

Reviewing and (If Necessary) Rescanning

The last step is to evaluate the scanned image. The preview image was a low-quality view, so now is your chance to truly evaluate the results.

Even the best of us occasionally discover that the scanned image we just made is crooked, or dust and particles weren't properly removed, or maybe we forgot to adjust the proper resolution and zoom settings. If you are unhappy with your scan and the problems are due to errors in the scanning process, you can simply rescan the image. If, however, the scan has only a few small dirty defects and appears to be in good shape otherwise, using the Healing brush or the Clone Stamp tool to remove them in Photoshop may take less time.

Note

> **Is the image over- or underexposed?**   The scanner sets its exposure based on the average values of the entire image being scanned. So if, for example, one part of a photo is really overexposed (also called *blown out*), it will affect the scanner's overall exposure settings and produce a darker than desired scan.

Tip

> **Zoom level affects what you see**   When you're viewing an image within Photoshop, be aware that the image may appear to have distortion. Check the zoom level. When you view at a zoom level other than 100% (Actual Size), you are viewing an approximation of what the image would look like. The most common forms of distortion are diagonal lines, moiré patterns, or jagged lines. The type of image can also affect how much distortion you might notice. For example, a color photo may suffer little to no distortion, whereas a black-and-white (line art) image may appear badly corrupted. The zoom percentage is displayed in the title bar of the image window, so make sure you are viewing at 100% to get an accurate idea of how the image truly appears.

8

Scanning Multiple Images with Crop and Straighten

A fast way to align more than one photo is the new Crop and Straighten command. Use this command to scan multiple images, which Photoshop then automatically straightens and saves to individual files. Before this command was available, scanning multiple photographs with a flatbed scanner typically resulted in a huge image consisting of the individual photographs with lots of whitespace in between.

To use this marvelous feature, lay the photos you want to scan on the scanner glass (make sure they are not touching) and close the lid. Choose File, Automate, Crop and Straighten, and Photoshop CS takes control by automatically detecting each photograph on the scanner glass, rotating it, and cropping away any white borders. When the scan is finished, each photo on the scanner appears in a separate window. Crop and Straighten is a totally automatic feature with no user adjustments or intervention required. The very best part is that it works perfectly almost every time.

Scanning Currency? Photoshop CS Has a Surprise

Adobe has incorporated anti-copying technology in Photoshop CS, which prevents you from opening image files of U.S. or European currency. Photoshop CS cannot prevent the scanning of currency (because scanning is done by third-party software), but if you scan paper currency and attempt to open this image in Photoshop, the program will not display it. Photoshop contains additional built-in programs that can recognize an image that is U.S., European, or Far Eastern currency. When you attempt to open such an image, a warning appears.

Scanning Negatives and Slides

Scanning film produces superior results that can be achieved from scanning a print of the same image. There are several advantages to scanning negatives and slides:

- Film (a negative or slide) is the original image, whereas a print is a second-generation copy.
- Film provides a greater dynamic range (contrast) than is provided by prints.
- When the photograph is printed, some tonal range and color information are lost or modified. The original information can't be recovered from a print. However, the original film will still contain the information and yield more detail in a film scan.

This doesn't mean that you shouldn't scan color photograph prints—just that scanning film produces noticeably better output than is possible from the prints. This is especially true if you plan on enlarging the image to any degree. In the following sections, you learn more about the process of scanning negatives and slides.

Cleaning Negatives and Slides

Before scanning negatives or slides, you must clean them. To both clean and scan images correctly, you should learn how to recognize the emulsion side of film from the base side. Hold the film up to the light and rotate it slightly. The emulsion side of the film is dull; the base side is shiny. If the two sides don't seem noticeably different, look at the direction of the film's *curl*. Typically, film curls down slightly along its length; the emulsion side of the film will be inside or under this curl. Though all film requires delicate handling, the emulsion side requires much more care, so as not to scratch away or damage the actual image information embedded on the film base.

You may be familiar with the expression "Cleanliness is next to godliness." When it comes to slides and negatives, it is fair to say that cleanliness is next to impossible. Whereas cleaning is important with scanning photographic prints, its importance when it comes to slide and negative scanning cannot be overstated. The reason is that the small size of the original, when combined with the great degree of enlargement produced by the scanner, results in even the smallest dust specks becoming the size of small boulders.

Cleaning slides and negatives can be tricky. I say this because they appear to be natural magnets for dust and fingerprints—much as an expensive silk tie attracts soup stains. As mentioned earlier, don't blow on film or negatives to remove dust; use a soft brush or, if necessary, canned or compressed air.

Tip

If you do use canned air   Always blow air across a mounted slide, not at it. There is sufficient force in even canned compressed air to blow a slide right out of its mounting.

As you learned earlier in the chapter, there are several inherent problems with canned air: It costs too much, it can spit propellant onto the negative or slide, and it isn't all that powerful when the can is half-empty (or half-full if you're an optimist). If you're scanning negatives and slides a lot, I recommend going to your local hobby or craft store and purchasing an air compressor that's used for air-brushing.

Scanning the Film or Negative

Scanning either color slides or negatives with a dedicated film scanner is reasonably simple. The software that came with the film scanner must be installed for you to be able to scan color negatives. Then you can follow these simple steps:

Using the Film Scanner

1. Clean the film and note the manufacturer (Kodak, Fuji), the kind of film (Royal, Kodak Gold, Fujicolor Superia), and the ISO by reading the edge of the film negative. For most color slides, the type is usually printed on the slide mounting.

(You'll learn about the special challenges of converting color negatives in the next section of this chapter.)

2. Place the film or slide holder in the scanner as directed by the manufacturer. In most cases, you place the film emulsion side down.

3. Perform a preview scan. Make sure the software is set for either negative or positive. Also, ensure that the settings are correct for the film manufacturer, type, and ISO setting.

4. Set the output size, and scan the negative or slide.

Working with Color Negatives

Scanning color negatives is a whole lot different than scanning positive slides or prints. As you may have noticed, color negatives have an overall orange mask, designed to aid photo printing of negatives onto regular photographic paper. The orange mask makes scanning color negatives difficult without special software.

Printing positive images from color negatives requires that the image be inverted—just as with black-and-white negatives. But to print a color negative, you also have to remove the orange mask color by balancing it out (this color is a strong greenish blue when inverted to positive). The software that comes with your film scanner has a Negative mode to perform this function. Because the shade of orange varies among film brands, and even in different films from the same manufacturer, it is important to make sure that the film negative settings on the scanner software are set to the correct manufacturer and type.

Digital ICE: Almost Too Good to Be True

If a scanner category is ever added to the Nobel Prize, Digital ICE™ would win hands down. This marvelous invention from Kodak is a combination of special hardware and software built into the scanner that actually removes (not covers up) defects found in scanned slides and negatives. Figure 8.6 shows two versions of an actual negative, scanned once without Digital ICE and again with Digital ICE applied.

Digital ICE technology automatically enables the film scanner to correct for some of the defects of dust, scratches, and dirt without degrading the image quality or slowing the scanning process.

While Nikon film scanners were the first to introduce Digital ICE, several companies now offer Digital ICE with their slide scanners. Although the defect removal technology works best on film scanners, some companies now offer the same automatic defect removal on their flatbed scanners.

Figure 8.6   The original negative (top) without Digital ICE and the improved image (bottom) after Digital ICE was applied.

8

Summary

Scanning, obviously, is composed of a little art and a little science. If you obey the rules—keeping the source material free from dust and lint, and scanning the image at a right angle to the scanner's platen—the "hard stuff" has been addressed, and you can spend more time on your personal creativity. Keep in mind the color modes, too. Evaluate a source image according to its color "needs," and you can't go wrong. Although digital cameras are wildly popular these days, there's still a place in your artist's bag of tricks for a scanner. How else can you acquire flat artwork and take direct samples of flat stuff such as a waffle or some blades of grass?

Chapter 9

Digital Photography and Photoshop: A Checklist for Better Imaging

A few years ago digital cameras were expensive toys that cost nearly as much as a used car and produced images that were acceptable but could not compare with those produced with film cameras. That was then and times have changed. When Kodak announced that by 2006 more than 70% of the photography in the U.S. would be digital, most analysts agreed they had underestimated the market. So when it comes to digital photography, it really isn't a matter of *if* you'll get a digital camera, but *when* you'll get a digital camera.

In this chapter, we're going to examine what makes digital photography different from the film experience and—more importantly—how to use the new features that Adobe included in this latest version of Photoshop just for digital photographers.

Moving from Film to Digital Photography

With the exception of the size and the LCD screen on the back, most digital cameras sold today look a lot like their film counterparts. With the increased acceptance of digital photography by film processors, you don't even need a computer to use a digital camera. You can shoot the family holiday photos, take your digital film (memory card) down to the same place that used to develop your film, and get back photos. Although digital photos may appear similar to film photos, there are several major differences in the ways the two types of images are captured. Knowing these differences is important if you want to consistently take good digital photos.

Capturing Images

A film camera works on a principle that is more than 150 years old. When specific combinations of chemicals (film) are exposed to light, their chemical composition changes, and these changes make up a continuous tone negative. The amount of light that strikes the film determines the exposure of the film. Exposure in a modern film camera is controlled by the size of the opening in the camera lens, called *aperture*, and the length of time the light is allowed to enter the camera, called *shutter speed*.

Note

> **Photography wasn't always easy!**   Matthew Brady, famous U.S. Civil War photographer, really had to work hard to take his photos. Because there was no film, in a darkened wagon he first had to mix and pour the chemicals on a glass plate (which was usually 8×10 inches), transfer the glass plate to the large camera, hold the shutter open for several seconds (all the time hoping his subjects didn't move), and then transfer the plates back into the wagon to develop them before the chemicals dried. Photography is much easier today.

Exposure in a digital camera works in a similar fashion, except that a light sensor is located behind the lens instead of film. The sensor is the same type that is found in a scanner. Through a process that is too complicated to imagine, the sensor and the rest of the associated electronics in your camera produce a digital image and store it on the

9

camera's removable storage media—sometimes called *digital film*. Like a film camera, a digital camera uses the aperture of the lens to control the size of the opening that lets in the light, but it doesn't need to use a shutter to control how long the light strikes the sensor. It just turns the sensor on and off, which explains why your digital camera doesn't sound like a film camera when you take a picture—no shutter sound. (The exceptions are professional digital cameras, which have a real shutter, and some digital camera models that play a cute little sound byte sounding like a real shutter.)

Beyond this basic difference in how exposures are controlled, there are three major differences between film and digital cameras. They involve the way color balance is controlled, the way film and digital respond to overexposure, and the aspect ratio of film versus digital image format. This last difference has to do with the size and ratio of the captured image, which affects how you compose your photographs.

Controlling Color Balance

With the exception of professional film, almost every roll of film sold in stores is designed to be exposed outdoors in bright daylight. Every light source has a *color temperature* that affects how colors appear under that lighting. Table 9.1 gives a brief summary of light temperatures, sources that fall within those temperatures, and the temperatures' respective effect on subjects illuminated by these sources.

Table 9.1   Color Temperature and Color Casting

Temperature in °Kelvin (K)	Source	Color Cast
1,000°K	Candles; oil lamps	Red
2,000°K	Very early sunrise	Red
2,500°K	Household light bulbs	Orange
3,500 to 4,100°K	Fluorescent bulbs	Cool
5,000°K	Typical daylight; electronic flash	Bluish—cool
5,500°K	Sun at high noon	Bluish—cool
6,000°K	Bright sunshine on a clear day	Blue
7,000°K	Slightly overcast sky	Blue
8,000°K	Hazy sky	Heavy blue color cast
9,000°K	Shade on a clear day	Blue
10,000°K	Heavy overcast	Blue

Your digital camera has a feature called Automatic White Balance (AWB) that attempts to automatically adjust the color balance settings for the color temperature of the scene being photographed. Often AWB doesn't correctly read the color in the scene. Each digital camera manufacturer offers an assortment of white balance presets such as cloudy, incandescent, fluorescent, and so on. Although using presets doesn't guarantee the colors in your photo will be accurate, it usually reduces the amount of color cast.

Two other possible solutions to achieve correct color balance may or may not be supported by your camera: RAW format and White Balance (WB) calibration. RAW format applies no white balance settings when the image is saved so that you can adjust it later. We'll learn more about using a RAW format later in this chapter. WB calibration enables you to calibrate your camera's white balance for the light source being used. You probably want to check the documentation that came with your camera for calibration specifics.

Controlling Exposure

When you take photos with a digital camera, it won't be long before you discover some photos have areas that have turned pure white, called *specular highlights*. When you take

Figure 9.1   Detail in the overexposed part of an image is lost forever.

photographs using film, bright areas of a scene may be overexposed, but detail is usually preserved even in the brightest areas. The reason for these bright spots is that film has greater latitude than the sensor in your digital camera. Unlike underexposed areas in photos where part of an image blows out like the white portion of the tomb of the unknown soldier at Arlington (refer to Figure 9.1), there is no way to restore it. With a digital camera, you can prevent blowouts when taking photos of subjects that have bright spots by selecting a metering system setting (like center-weighted or spot) to take a reading on the brightest part of the scene. Using your camera's shutter-lock (usually accomplished by pressing the shutter button down halfway) to hold the setting, recompose the photo and press the shutter the rest of the way. In Figure 9.1, the reading was taken on the soldier, and as a result, the tomb was overexposed (unlike Figure 9.2 in which a reading was made on the bright spot of the tomb).

Figure 9.2   Using a light reading from the brightest area of the scene allows the details to be preserved.

Composing Pictures Using Digital Aspect Ratios

Aspect ratio is a proportion expressing the width to the height of a photo. For example, a 3:2 aspect ratio means that the photo is 3 units wide for every 2 units of height. It is a little known fact that the default aspect ratio of most digital cameras produces images with a slightly different aspect ratio than film cameras. When you print your photos, you'll discover that photo paper conforms to the aspect ratio of film rather than digital format. This difference in ratios means that you must crop your digital photo to fit the standard photo sizes; as a result, you lose parts of the image near the edges. To prevent this from causing problems with your image composition, I suggest you frame your shots with a little extra headroom to allow for cropping later.

Choosing Image Compression and Quality Settings

The number of photos a film camera can take is dictated by the number of exposures on the roll of film you use. With digital cameras, the number of exposures that will fit on a memory card is controlled by the following factors:

- **Sensor size of the camera.** Larger sensors produce bigger images and fewer photos per memory card.

- **Resolution.** Some digital cameras allow you to change the physical dimensions of the images created by the sensor.

- **Type of image.** In addition to JPEG, some cameras can save images as TIFF and RAW images; some of these formats save files in larger sizes than do others, so the format you choose determines how many images you can save to a single card.

- **Quality levels.** On most consumer cameras, the quality setting determines how much the image is compressed when it is stored on the media.

Although all these factors affect the number of photos that your memory card can hold, the file format in which you save images and your camera's quality levels setting are the factors that you will change most often. The quality settings are usually controlled through one of the many menus on your digital camera's LCD screen. The names used to describe the amount of compression vary between camera manufacturers; check your camera's user manual for details.

Fast Facts About File Format Compression

The color photographs that are created by 3–4 megapixel digital cameras result in very large files. Until recently, removable memory cards for digital cameras were expensive and came in relatively small capacities. As a result, digital images were stored in a compressed file format known as JPEG. Today, more memory card options are available, and digital cameras are being used by a wider number of people for a broad variety of purposes. As a result, you can choose a file format that works best for your images and photography needs.

Using JPEG compression lets you squeeze the maximum number of exposures into the memory card, but the compressed images suffer a slight loss of quality. At the lowest compression levels, the quality loss is small. At higher levels of compression, the deterioration becomes apparent in the form of tiny random pixels, called *artifacts*, that appear near high-contrast edges.

Today's digital cameras can also store photos as uncompressed TIFF files, which provide a somewhat better image quality than that of JPEG. The advantage of the TIFF format is that it uses *lossless* compression, meaning that there is no loss of pixel information and therefore no degradation in the image quality (when saving with this format). On the surface, that sounds great, and you would assume that for the best photographs, you would only need to save the images in TIFF format and everything would be just dandy; however, this format does have some drawbacks. First, TIFF files are huge; therefore, the number of images you can store on the memory card is significantly reduced—to one third of what could be stored as JPEG images. Decreased storage capacity isn't the only disadvantage of using TIFF; these files take a long time to write to the memory card, and while the camera is saving an image, it cannot be used for anything else. So TIFF isn't a "fast and convenient" choice.

Storing images as RAW files is an even better solution. RAW images are stored with just the image data itself—no white balance, exposure, sharpening, or other processing information. In images stored in JPEG and TIFF files, this processing data adds measurably to each pixel stored in the image. As a result, RAW files are dramatically smaller than JPEG or TIFF files without losing any of the actual image detail. Later, working with Photoshop CS, you add the processing information before printing the image, which also means you have more hands-on control of your final images. And the RAW format enables 16-bit image editing. You'll learn more about the RAW file format and working with it in Photoshop CS in later sections of this chapter.

Higher Compression Means Lower Image Quality

You can increase the number of images you can store on your memory card by increasing file compression, but there is a catch to this choice: As the compression increases, the quality of the resulting photo decreases. A coworker of mine took a family vacation to Hawaii, and for the first time he took a digital camera. When he got back, he was very disappointed with his photographs. Assuming that there was something wrong with the camera, he brought the CF card with the images still on it for me to look at. I immediately noticed it was the 16MB card that came with the camera, and it had almost 100 images on it! Figure 9.3 shows a photo of his grandson; the insert zooms in on the face to show the effects caused by heavy compression settings.

The "after the fact" solution is to pack a larger memory card and use higher quality settings.

Figure 9.3   The effects of low-quality level settings aren't very pretty.

Tip

> **Don't down the memory!**   If you are almost out of exposures on your media card and don't have a spare, you can lower the quality settings and get additional exposures. Just remember, though, that you also will lower the quality of the images you capture when you make this change. Only you can make the decision as to whether it's more important to capture additional images or capture only the highest quality images. And next time, be prepared by investing in a media card (or two) that will allow for more storage space for your images.

Determining Which Quality Level Setting Is Best for You

I have discovered that many users assume that they must set their camera to the maximum quality JPEG setting to get good photos. Although there is nothing wrong with doing that, it isn't necessarily the answer for every digital photographer. Here are some questions you can ask yourself that will help you determine which setting to use:

9

- Are the pictures for print or the Web? If you plan on shooting photos only for attaching to emails or posting on a Web site, you can, in most cases, use the lowest quality setting possible to get the maximum number of exposures; lower-resolution images load faster and are therefore preferable for Web use.

- What photo size do you typically use?

- How big is the sensor in your camera?

Note

> **Shoot high, save small**   Keep in mind that even if you take pictures at the highest setting, you can still use Photoshop to save a separate version of the file at a lower resolution for the Web. If, however, you choose to shoot your images at the lowest resolution, you cannot reverse this idea (of altering the file to a higher resolution quality) if you later decide you want high-quality prints.

Tip

> **About compression artifacting**   When shooting photos with a lot of detail or high-contrast edges in them (like the Eiffel Tower, a lace tablecloth, or whatever), you should always change the settings to maximum quality for those shots because the effects of compression are most noticeable on these types of photos.

If most or all of your printed photos are the standard 4×6 size, a moderate or average (not the best) setting is more than sufficient.

If you have a camera with a large sensor (4 megapixels or larger), you can still use a moderate or average setting without noticeable loss of picture quality.

Review your camera options and set the image quality to the highest setting that seems appropriate for the type of photography you're doing and the importance of the images you're capturing. A picture is equivalent to capturing a moment in time, and you can't go back and retrieve that moment again. While not all images are winners, you might consider one or two to be definite "keepers." It would be a shame if those images were captured on the lowest setting and resulted in low-quality prints.

In addition, if you decide to use the photo for image editing work, you'll soon learn there are many benefits to working with a high-quality image over a low-quality image (that contains less pixel information). Every pixel you can capture is valuable information. The trade-off is that you may not be able to fit as many images on the media card, but this is a small price to pay to get better images from your camera.

Advantages of 16-bit Image Editing

In addition to the advantage of white balance and other tonal corrections for the original image, the main advantage of working with a 16-bit image is that it contains more information in each channel. This means that when you start to apply tonal corrections or effects to a 16-bit image, noticeably less deterioration will be caused by the process because the image has more color and detail information. You will find that when 16-bit images are made larger using Resample, the resulting enlargement looks better than if it was done using the same amount of resampling on an 8-bit image. Now that Photoshop CS offers full editing capabilities on 16-bit images, you can produce some photographs that would even make a *National Geographic* photographer envious.

RAW Versus JPEG Images

A photo taken and saved as a RAW file and then converted to a 16-bit TIFF image produces a superior photo when compared to the same photo taken and saved as a JPEG at its highest quality setting. So, if this is true, should you take all your photos in RAW format if your camera supports it? The answer depends on you. What do you consider to be important? For all the advantages offered by using the RAW format, the fact is RAW files still use up more space on the memory card than the JPEG format, and RAW takes more time and effort to process. The rewards can be well worth the effort when the resulting image turns out great. But you need to weigh the advantages and disadvantages and ask yourself what is more important. Are you seeking a long-term final result or a short-term quick solution for your image needs?

For example, the JPEG option will yield lower file sizes, it will write to a memory card quicker, and you can open the JPEG image in Photoshop and begin editing immediately. But the trade-off is that you lose the creative flexibility in making decisions on how the image is processed, and you are stuck with the processing choices that your camera made for you. Sure, you can still apply adjustments (such as Levels, Curves, and so on) within Photoshop, but you are altering pixels and changing original pixel information that could yield some undesirable results. In contrast, the RAW plug-in allows you to make those adjustments as *part* of the processing choices, not as a *post*-processing adjustment. See the difference?

So, is the RAW format really worth all this extra hassle and work? Again, the answer depends on you. RAW is vastly superior to a JPEG file on many levels, but how important is it to you to invest the time to ensure you capture this quality into your images? If you simply intend to snap a few shots that you want to email to a friend and don't have the time to invest, then by all means, opt for the JPEG settings. But if you're on vacation and want to have keepsake images to remember those moments in time forever, shooting in RAW mode might be worth the time and effort.

9

Another solution is to use both formats (if your camera supports JPEG and RAW). Set the camera to JPEG (highest resolution) to shoot ordinary photos, like historical signs on buildings, or to document damage to a vehicle after an accident. When you're shooting photographs that are critical or include timely events (such as wedding photography, photos for publication, and the like), shoot in RAW mode.

Tip

> **Digital camera formats**   The best part of working with a digital camera is that you can change its format any time you want. You can even save files in several formats on the same card. The reason is that, regardless of the format you choose, to the memory card, they're all bits. So, if you prefer a JPEG setting but want to shoot a few critical shots in RAW, don't forget to change the setting back to JPEG when you're done, or else you might be surprised later when your memory card tells you it's full.

The RAW File Format

Earlier in this chapter, you read about the advantages and disadvantages of working with the TIFF and JPEG file formats. You also learned a bit about the RAW format. Although this format originally was available only on high-end digital cameras, even some mid-range cameras now offer a RAW format setting. It is definitely a worthwhile feature to look for when considering a new camera purchase. To understand the advantage of the RAW file format, you first need to understand a little more about how a digital camera processes an image before saving it to the memory card.

When the image is captured by the camera sensor in any mode other than RAW, the computer in the camera processes the sensor data before saving it to the memory card. White balance, exposure, tonal corrections, sharpening, and other adjustments are applied to the image before it is saved. If the camera saves images in RAW format, the unprocessed data from the camera sensor is saved on the memory card. You can then edit the white balance, exposure, and other image factors later in Photoshop CS.

This *unprocessed* Charged Coupled Device (CCD) or Complementary Metal Oxide Semiconductor (CMOS) sensor data is saved using a proprietary format that is specific to the camera's make and model, such as Nikon's NEF file, Canon's CRW file, Kodak's DCR file, and so on. The benefits of these formats are similar to those of the TIFF format; there's no compression, so RAW images are high quality. But wait, there's more! The resulting image file size is smaller than a TIFF, and because the file is unprocessed, it will have a faster write time to the memory card than a TIFF image. Even better, because the information is unprocessed, the creative control is in *your* hands for determining white balance, exposure, and sharpening. You aren't forced to accept the camera's choices for these items.

Adobe's Camera RAW Plug-In

Before Adobe added support for RAW format, these files could be opened only by using proprietary software that came bundled with the camera. This software was often slow and limited in the features it offered. Adobe recognized the importance and potential of this file format and made the first version of its Camera RAW plug-in available at an extra add-in cost for Photoshop version 7. Now, the Camera RAW plug-in is bundled with Photoshop CS.

Using Photoshop's Camera RAW plug-in, you can do the processing that is normally done by the camera (at the time of the shooting). You can change the white balance setting, exposure, and many more settings in Photoshop, just as if you were back at the scene, adjusting the camera settings to capture the photo as you want it to look. The only two factors of a photo saved in RAW format that you cannot correct are focus and shutter speed.

The Camera RAW plug-in also enables you to work with 16-bit images in Photoshop. Bit depth measures how much color information is available to display or print for each pixel in an image. Greater bit depth (more bits of information per pixel) means more available colors and more accurate color representation in the digital image. Traditional RGB files in Photoshop are made of three 8-bit channels (24-bit color). Using the Camera RAW plug-in, you can save the image as either an 8-bit or a 16-bit file.

Note

> **Higher depth, bigger file size**   Keep in mind that along with a higher bit depth, the file size will increase significantly as well. Another consideration in deciding on bit depth is the intended destination for the file. If outputting to another application, you may want to stick with the more accepted 8-bit file.

Before Photoshop CS, precious little editing could be done on 16-bit files. They could be opened, but there was little support for applying filters or using layers and brush tools. But with Photoshop CS, you can do a lot of your editing in 16-bit files. Not all the filters are currently available, but you now have access to the more commonly used filters. You can also use layers, brush tools, and many other features that weren't available to 16-bit images in previous versions of Photoshop.

Working with the Camera RAW Plug-In Interface

Adobe's Camera RAW plug-in is fast, extremely versatile and flexible, and a joy to use. Simply open a RAW file in Photoshop, and the plug-in will automatically launch, opening the main Camera RAW screen, as shown in Figure 9.4. This window displays the RAW file's image, along with a control panel, tools, and sliders for making processing choices.

9

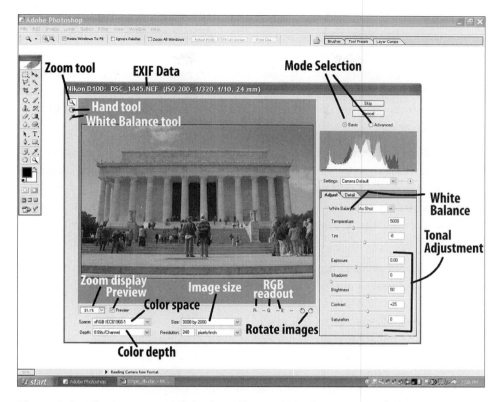

Figure 9.4   The Camera RAW dialog box offers a wealth of correction tools for converting RAW images.

The Camera RAW plug-in has two modes of operation, Basic and Advanced, which are controlled by the radio buttons in the upper-right corner of the window. By default, the plug-in opens in Basic mode.

The EXIF data (camera name, image filename, ISO, shutter speed, aperture, and lens information) are read from the file and displayed in the title bar of the dialog box.

A few familiar tools are included on the upper-left side of the dialog box. The Zoom and Hand tool control the display in the preview window. Double-clicking the Zoom tool changes the display to 100%, which is necessary for evaluating settings used to make finely detailed edits, such as sharpening. Double-clicking the Hand tool returns the image to the Fit to Screen preview size.

The one familiar icon that isn't what it appears to be is the eyedropper-like tool. This tool does not select colors but instead is a White Balance tool. Click on this tool, and then click on any part of the preview image that should be white or a pale neutral gray; the Temperature and Tint (indicated by the sliders on the Adjust tab, which you learn more about later) will automatically change to neutralize the color you selected. If your image has specular highlights (blowouts caused by light reflections), do not use those areas as a white reference. Instead, aim for a color that you know should be off-white (rather than a pure white). Sometimes when you click on the color you think should be white or neutral gray, the image will make a horrific shift toward unwanted colors. Double-clicking this tool restores (or resets) the white balance to the original settings so you can start from scratch again.

Directly below the preview window are options that allow you to change the zoom level and toggle the Preview option on or off to display between the original and current settings. An RGB readout reflects the RGB values of pixels in the preview window underneath the current position of the cursor. Rotation icons allow you to adjust (or rotate) the image orientation in the preview window. You must still rotate the image using Photoshop before saving it.

Below these options are controls that allow you to make choices about the color space, bit-depth, resolution, and size of the image.

Using the Adjust and Detail Tab Tools

In addition to the eyedropper White Balance tool, you can change the white balance manually by adjusting the White Balance, Temperature, and Tint settings in the Adjust tab to the right of the preview window.

The initial WB settings reflect the settings of the camera at the time the photo was taken. The White Balance drop-down list reflects the Camera Default setting along with options for other preset settings that could help to adjust white balance based on certain lighting conditions (such as a cloudy day or Tungsten lighting). You can use one of these presets from the drop-down list, or you can try your hand at adjusting the WB by moving the color Temperature and Tint sliders. These two sliders work together to help adjust WB. Moving the Temperature slider to the right decreases the color temperature, making the colors in the image appear warmer; moving it to the left increases the temperature, thereby making all the colors appear cooler.

The readout of the Temperature slider is an approximation of the color temperature in degrees Kelvin (which is how color temperature is measured). After you have used the Temperature slider to get the color temperature as close as you can, use the Tint slider to fine-tune the color, removing any remaining color cast.

To change the overall exposure of the image, use the Exposure slider. Moving the slider to the left darkens the image; conversely, moving the slider to the right brightens the image. Because this slider is designed to mimic Exposure settings on a camera, the Exposure slider settings are displayed as f-stops. For example, a +2.0 setting is the equivalent of increasing the aperture by two stops. Although the f-stop listing may be helpful, the best way to select the best exposure is to hold down the Alt(Opt) key while moving the Exposure slider. This method gives you a view of any highlights that may blow out (go completely white) while making adjustments with this slider. The rest of the sliders on the Adjust tab are standard tonal adjustments with the exception of the Shadows slider, which operates like the Black Point slider of the Levels command.

On the Detail tab, you can use the Luminance Smoothing slider to lower grayscale noise. The Color Noise Reduction slider lowers chroma noise. Moving either of these sliders to zero turns off their respective noise reduction. Be cautious when using either of these noise reduction settings because they can produce an undesired softening of image detail. You should always set the preview to 100% or higher when viewing the effect of either of these two controls.

> **Note**
>
> **No more floating histogram**   If you used the original Photoshop Camera RAW plug-in, you will notice a few changes. The histogram is no longer a floating display (hooray!).

Using Advanced Mode Settings

If you select the Advanced Mode, two additional tabs appear in the Camera RAW plug-in dialog box: Lens and Calibrate (see Figure 9.5).

The three slider options on the Lens tab allow you to compensate for the effects of using a wide-angle lens. The only difficulty you may experience with these controls is that they assume that the light falloff is uniform and symmetrical, which is not always the case. See the online help for a detailed technical explanation of how these sliders work.

The Calibrate tab in the Advanced Mode has Hue and Saturation sliders to help adjust or fine-tune color casts in the image. Sometimes colors rendered by the Photoshop Camera RAW plug-in may not look as expected. This could be due to the differences between the camera's profiles and the RAW plug-in's built-in profile for your digital camera model. Other reasons might include pictures taken in non-standard lighting conditions (especially if the conditions extend outside the compensating range of the RAW plug-in).

In most cases you won't need to fiddle with these settings, but if you consistently see an unwanted color shift in the RAW images that you're processing, try using these sliders to adjust or remove any excess Red, Green, or Blue color cast in the image to help achieve more neutral colors. Adjust the Hue first, and then adjust its Saturation while watching the preview image until it appears correct to you. After you've done this, you can save the settings from inside the dialog box, and these saved settings can then be used to modify the built-in settings for other RAW files.

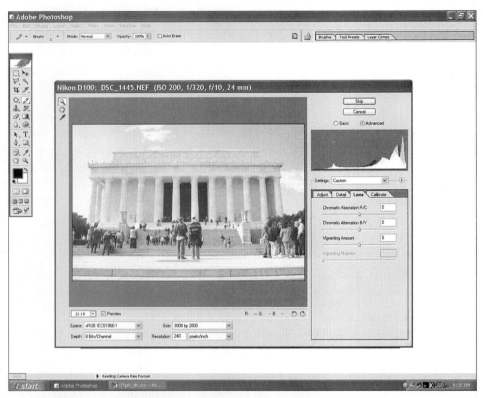

Figure 9.5   The Advanced Mode for the Camera RAW plug-in dialog box provides two more tabs with additional options.

Editing a RAW Image

Although there are no hard and fast rules about using the Camera RAW plug-in, use these basic steps to produce good images in most cases:

Working with a RAW Image

1. Open a RAW image using File, Open, or navigate to a file using the File Browser. The Camera RAW dialog box opens.

2. The first step is to correct the white balance. You can use the White Balance, Temperature, and Tint sliders to adjust the white balance. Another way to correct the white balance is to use the White Balance tool (the one that looks like an eye-dropper). Remember, if you make a mistake with the White Balance tool, double-click the tool icon to return the image to its original settings.

3. Change the overall exposure of the image using the Exposure slider.

Insider

> I recommend holding down the Alt(Opt) key and moving the slider to the right until your highlights begin to blow out and appear in the preview; then you can back it off a little.

4. Adjust the Shadows, Brightness, Contrast, and Saturation sliders as necessary; remember to keep the preview window zoom level at 100% and to check the preview window often to be sure the adjustments are having the right effect.

5. Click the Detail tab, and use the Luminance Smoothing slider to reduce grayscale noise. Use the Color Noise slider to reduce chroma noise.

6. After you adjust all the settings for the desired effect, click on OK to process the image and open it in Photoshop.

7. From the Photoshop window, you can save a copy of the image in any file format you choose, such as a TIFF or JPEG. The original RAW file is not altered, but the plug-in will remember the settings applied to this RAW file so they are available the next time the file is opened.

Note

> **Raw files**   Photoshop can open a RAW file, but neither the Camera RAW plug-in nor Photoshop can save a file as a RAW file. A RAW file is your digital version of a negative, with all the original information off the camera's sensors. The Camera RAW plug-in is merely a tool for processing that information from this digital equivalent of a negative—in this case, the RAW file.

Summary

Digital cameras are here to stay. And the more you know about their inner workings, the more personally satisfying your imaging experiences will be. Keep in mind color balance, use image compression to your advantage, and you can't go wrong. Oh, yes, and keep the RAW format in mind when you want to edit at the highest quality.

We move into another part of the book now and start combining color correction with Photoshop's power of selections. Come along!

Part IV

Correcting, Restoring, and Retouching Images

Chapter 10

Color Correction and Selections: Creating Beautiful Hands

For ages, the human body has been the subject of paintings and sculptures, for a couple of important reasons:

- The human body is beautiful.
- The human body is expressive.

In this chapter, you'll learn

- How to select image areas for color correction
- How to correct color
- How to correct the background in an image
- How to create a reflection within an image
- How to add the effect of falling snow within an image
- How to add image highlights

You'll find a lot of busts in museums because the human head is an expressive study. Through the ages, sculptors have shown us emotional expression by carving the human face with flared nostrils, wide eyes, sallow cheeks, pursed lips—you get the idea.

Well, the human hand takes a back seat to none of this in its ability to express emotion. Posed, hands can convey hate, fear, love, anguish, shyness, regret, mysticism—a full range of human emotions.

This chapter takes you through the process of working with an average pair of hands and transforming them into a beautiful, magical pair of hands. You learn to select image areas for correction, correct the image color, create new objects within the image, and add highlights to make image areas "pop." You'll be amazed by what Photoshop and your own talent can do!

Photoshop, Selections, and Color Correction

Photoshop provides us with many ways to correct color and make selections. In fact, Photoshop's power lies in the fact that the program is so multi-layered—allowing us to constantly discover new methods and new ways to perform a task.

Making a selection is no exception. Whether you're trying to select an easily distinguishable object in a photograph, a not-so-easily-distinguishable item (like wispy strands of hair or a transparent glass), or a completely abstract shape, Photoshop provides the tools you need to make these selections. This versatility might be the single source of the program's greatest power.

It should come as no surprise that the same can be said for color correction. Photoshop's smorgasbord of color correction choices could leave you feeling lost. You could easily become overwhelmed, asking yourself, "Which method do I choose?" The answer is quite simple: Choose the method that can achieve the best result *efficiently*!

There is no one single *best* method for color correction. If there were, Photoshop would have given us a magical universal tool, and this book would be two pages long! My personal advice would be to dedicate yourself to becoming a sponge when it comes to learning how to edit images in Photoshop. As a sponge, absorb as much information about Photoshop tools and techniques as you possibly can, so that you understand the many options available for correcting an image. That way, you'll be able to quickly assess an image to determine what can (and needs to be) corrected and can reach for the tools that will get the job done efficiently. This ability is what separates the professionals from the amateurs.

Levels, Curves, Color Balance, Channel mixer, Hue/Saturation, Calculations, and so on are among the myriad of choices. Why so many choices? Because no two images have the same needs or require the same correction technique. A solution that works effectively in one image can turn totally wrong in another. There's no one correct technique for solving image problems. The same can be said of using filters to enhance images. Filters must not be a sort of camouflage for bad retouching, nor should they cover a lack of skill or imagination. Filters are there to support what we are "saying" in our work, like music can enhance the atmosphere of a movie. When it comes to image retouching and repair, some pros may turn up their noses if you don't use a specific technique. But we aren't into snootiness in this book; we simply point our noses at the monitor and experiment with what works!

Selection for Color Correction

As hinted at the beginning of the chapter, we'll be using a photo of a pair of hands for our selection and color correction work. It'll be easy and educational! For our first exercise, open the Hands Start file from the Examples/Chap10 folder on the companion CD.

This picture was taken in the late afternoon in the woods, which explains the "cold" colors. Your eyes are extraordinarily able to compensate and to adapt to color casting. When you take a picture of someone in a forest, the color of that person's skin might look completely natural to *you*, but your camera will catch the green cast caused by the sunlight filtering through the leaves. The camera will see cold colors and skin with a green cast, and that's what it captures onto film or memory chip.

We'll correct that color problem in a moment. But first, look at the background of this image. It's not very exciting in itself, but the way light is playing there holds some interest.

With these two items in mind—cold colors and light shape of the background—we're ready to start working on the image.

Setting Up an Image for Color Correction

1. Open the Hands Start.psd image from the Examples/Chap10 folder on the companion CD. On the Layers palette, right-click (Macintosh: hold Ctrl and click) on the Background layer title and choose Duplicate Layer. Name the duplicate layer **Extraction**. Maybe you can guess what's next! The Extract tool will be used to make a selection. Choose Filter, Extract or press Alt(Opt)+Ctrl(⌘)+X.

2. The goal is to select the hands and the bubble. In the Extract dialog box, choose the Edge Highlighter tool, and keep the brush size at 31 pixels. Most of the background color in the image is green (which happens to be the default Highlight color under Tool Options for the Edge Highlighter tool). Changing the Highlight color to Red may help to make the selection process easier to view (see Figure 10.1). Leave the Fill color at Blue.

3. Before making the selection, perform a test run. The Edge Highlighter tool marks the edge between the areas you want to keep and the areas you want to discard. Just follow the line of the bubble a little (the goal is to have some of the edge highlight tint fall inside the bubble and some of the color fall outside the edge). Stop. Now at the right of the Extract dialog box, check the Smart Highlighting option, and then continue to drag your brush. Do you see the difference? Your line has become much smaller and more accurate. Leave this box checked to make a selection because you need to keep the highlights of the nails and bubble in the selection.

4. Hold down the Alt(Opt) key, and click the Reset button. (This tip applies to most of Photoshop's dialog boxes; when the Alt(Opt) key is held down, the Cancel button toggles to a Reset button, which allows you to start from scratch.) Be warned, however, that when you reset the dialog box, you may also have to adjust your Tool Options again (Brush size and Highlight color). Okay? Now start at the left side of the bubble, and draw your line just a little *out* of the area you want to select. Your selection *line* should look like the one in Figure 10.1.

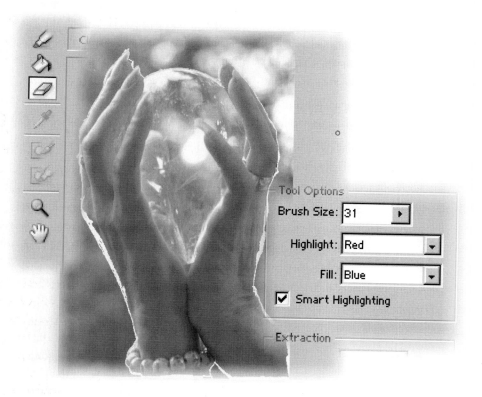

Figure 10.1   Trace around the hands using a 31-pixel diameter brush tip.

Insider

If you need to zoom in on your subject, remember that all the keyboard shortcuts will work within the Extract dialog box. Press Ctrl(⌘)+plus key to zoom in (or the minus key to zoom out). Also, pressing the spacebar will toggle to the Hand tool, which allows you to scroll around the document as you make your edge selection. Don't forget to make a continuous selection around the bottom edge of the document (where the hands meet the bottom window edge).

5. Now you have to let Photoshop know which part of the selection area you want to keep—the area outside the edge that was just created or the area inside the newly created edge. To do this, you will need to fill the area you want to keep. Choose the Fill tool—the paint bucket—and click inside your selection. See Figure 10.2.

Figure 10.2 Click inside the edge created to designate the hands and bubble as the selection fill (or the area you want to keep).

6. Before clicking on OK, you can preview the selection and refine it, if necessary. Click Preview, and then in the Preview section of the dialog box, click the drop-down menu next to the Show option and choose Original. You can refine your selection by using either the Edge Highlighter tool or the Eraser tool. Don't forget to fill your selection area each time! When you're finished, click on OK to exit the Extract dialog box. Your selection should look like Figure 10.3.

10

Insider

If your selection shown in the Preview window isn't perfect but looks close enough, avoid wasting a lot of time in the Extract dialog box trying to perfect it. Instead, click on OK to accept the selection. Now that you're back in the Photoshop interface, you have a wealth of tools at your disposal for perfecting the extraction selection. For example, you can use the Eraser tool or a layer mask to delete unwanted areas—or make use of the History Brush tool to paint missing areas back into the image. But since the emphasis for *this* chapter is to teach selection tool techniques, read on for even another method of refining this Extraction layer.

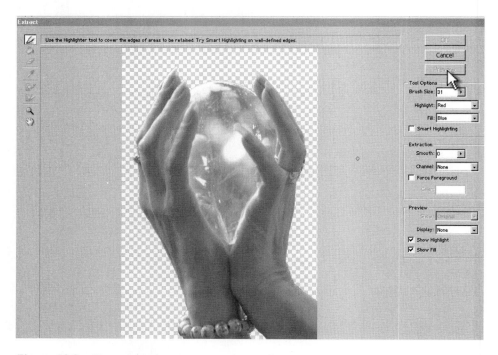

Figure 10.3   You can preview your extracting work.

7. Turn off the visibility for the Background layer by clicking on the eye icon to the left of the Background layer (on the Layers palette). After taking a closer look at the selection results, you'll understand why it's best to work on a copy of the Background layer instead of the original.

8. Click on the eye icon to the left of the Background layer to turn on the visibility again. Click on the Background layer to make it the active layer. Ctrl(⌘)+click the Extraction layer to load the information from this layer as a selection. On the toolbox, click the Edit in Quick Mask Mode icon, or press **Q**. Be sure black is the

foreground color. Zoom in to your picture, and choose the Brush tool. Choose a 13-pixel hard round brush—hard, because you need sharp edges. Make sure the Options bar has the Brush mode on Normal and 100% Opacity and 100% Flow. You should see a red tint color fill the areas of the extraction results; therefore, you should also be able to see areas that weren't included (but should have red tint). Conversely, you're likely to see red tint in areas that spilled into other areas that shouldn't have been included. Paint with black to add red tint to the areas you want to keep, and paint with white to remove red tint from the areas you don't want. When you're satisfied with the results, click the Edit in Standard Mode icon (or press **Q** again) to exit the Quick Mask mode.

Tip

Putting a layer behind a layer To get an even better view of the selection layer, try this trick. Ctrl(⌘)+click on the Create a new layer icon at the bottom of the Layers palette. When you hold down the Ctrl(⌘) key, the new layer will be created below the active layer (instead of above the active layer). Choose a bright color that provides a contrast from the colors in the image, and press Alt(Opt)+Delete(Backspace) to fill the new layer with this contrasting color. This technique allows you to easily see any empty spaces or spilling that can occur at the edges (which may not always be apparent without the contrasting color behind the target layer). Delete the contrasting color-filled layer after viewing the results (or at least turn off the visibility to this layer before performing the next set of steps).

Insider

When you're entering Quick Mask mode, you may see red tint filling the background areas instead of the hand and bubble areas. If this is the case, hold down the Alt(Opt) key and click on the Edit in Quick Mask Mode icon again to toggle the settings from *masked areas* (tint color on the background) to *selected areas* (tint color on the hands and bubble).

9. A new refined selection will now be apparent when you exit the Quick Mask mode. With the Background layer still active, press Ctrl(⌘)+J to copy the new selection to a separate layer. Name this layer **Cool Hand**. Drag the Extraction layer to the trash icon at the bottom of the Layers palette. Right-click (Macintosh: hold Ctrl and click) on the Cool Hand layer title, and choose Duplicate Layer. Name this duplicate layer **Warm Hand**.

10. Press Ctrl(⌘)+Shift+S to save this file to your hard drive. Name the file and keep it open.

10

Color Correction

Now that the hands have been selected from the Background layer and there are separate copies of the selection, it's time to get down to some basic color correction techniques:

Variations

1. Make sure the Warm Hand layer is the active layer. Then choose Image, Adjustments, Variations.

2. Follow the guide and mind your steps! Check the Midtones option; then click once on More Yellow, once on Lighter, once on More Red, and once on Lighter.

3. Now check the Highlights option, and click once on Darker. Finally, check the Shadows option, and click once on More Cyan (see Figure 10.4). Click on OK. On the Layers palette, set the blending mode for the Warm Hand layer to Color.

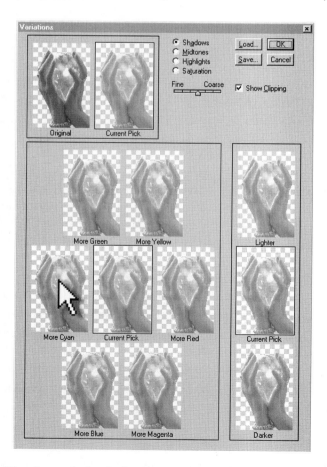

Figure 10.4   Warming up the hands also attenuates some of the harsh shadows.

By the way, did you notice that not only were we able to correct color for the tones in the hands and bubble, but we were also able to reduce the effect of some harsh shadows on the hands at the same time?

Before going further, let me add just another remark about the Extract filter. It's totally *destructive* of everything that isn't within the selection. Keep this fact in mind! And if you need to work on another part of the image, *duplicate* it first, as we did in the preceding exercise.

Working on the Background

Enhancing the background of the composite image will help draw out the hands and will both integrate them with the background and make them the "star" of the composition.

Enhancing the Background

1. Ctrl(⌘)+click on the Warm Hand layer to load the selection. Press Shift+F7 to invert the selection.

2. Click on the Background layer to make this the active layer. Press Ctrl(⌘)+J to move the selection of the background onto a new layer. Rename this layer **Normal**. Right-click (Macintosh: hold Ctrl and click) on the Normal layer, and choose Duplicate layer. Name the duplicate layer **Filter Effects**.

Insider

You're creating a duplicate layer here because I think it's always better to leave the Background layer alone.

3. Click on the Filter Effects layer to make it the active layer (if it's not already). Filter Effects should be above the Normal layer.

4. Choose Filter, Sketch, Water Paper and choose **15** for Fiber Length, **60** for Brightness, and **80** for Contrast (see Figure 10.5). Click on OK. Press Ctrl(⌘)+F twice to apply the same filter (with the same values) two more times. These settings are arbitrary and made by trial and error. In your own assignments, you will most assuredly choose slightly different values.

5. With the Filter Effects layer still active, choose Filter, Brush Strokes, Sumi-e. Enter **10** for the Stroke Width, **2** for Stroke Pressure, and **16** for Contrast (see Figure 10.6). Click on OK. *Immediately* choose Edit, Fade Sumi-e. The Fade option is like an "undo" on a slider and is available only to "undo" or "fade" the last action performed. After you perform another action or step, you gain the ability to fade that next step, but you lose the ability to fade the last filter effect. In the Fade dialog box, lower the Opacity to 80% and click on OK. On the Layers

10

palette, change the blending mode for the Filter Effects layer from Normal to Difference. Better, hmm? The image now is more stylized and showcases the hands.

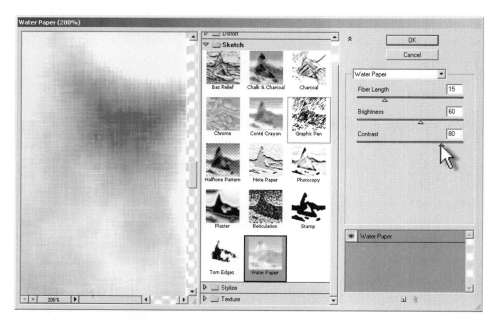

Figure 10.5   Apply the Water Paper filter to the background of the image.

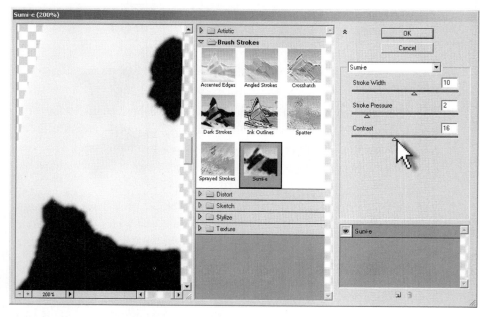

Figure 10.6   Use the Sumi-e filter after applying the Water Paper filter.

6. Let's save the selection of the hands to use later. Ctrl(⌘)+click one of the Warm Hand layers to load the selection we will save. Choose Select, Save Selection and name the selection **Hands**. Click on OK and press Ctrl(⌘)+D to deselect. You can save your image, and if you prefer to continue work on a flattened version, create a *duplicate* of your image (choose Image, Duplicate and give another name to the duplicate version of the file). Even if you flattened your image, any selection you saved will remain in your file when the Alpha Channels option is checked in the Duplicate dialog box (see Figure 10.7).

Warning

On flattening files   Occasionally, you will see the instruction to flatten a file (and save as a separate version). This stems from the concept that the file size can be reduced by flattening, thus saving hard drive space and resources (while work is performed on the file). But be warned that while you may be saving on disk space, there is a trade-off: You *lose flexibility*. If you choose to flatten a file, you should do so for a very good reason— and saving disk space may not be a good enough reason when 200GB hard drives are becoming the norm.

As you work with Photoshop, you learn that every single layer offers a possible time-saving value when you need to return to the file later for editing. Trust me when I tell you that in my own early work with Photoshop, I felt like kicking myself many times for flattening a file, thus eliminating the flexibility to make use of valuable layer information.

So, you may want to consider avoiding this practice in your own work and flatten a "copy" of the file only for purposes of sending to friends via the Internet (so they can "Oooh" and "Aaaah" over your work).

7. Press Ctrl(⌘)+S; keep the file open.

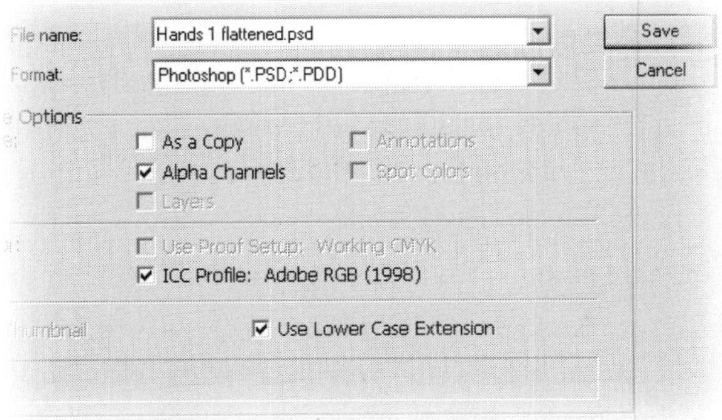

Figure 10.7   Save the selection to the file.

Creating Reflected Hands

The bubble in the image (you can find strange things in the woods, even a giant soap bubble) presents some disturbing highlights and nasty spots. Now you'll remove them all and, in the process, create a mirror image of the hands in the bubble:

Creating a Reflection

1. Right-click (Macintosh: hold Ctrl and click) on the Background layer, and choose Duplicate layer. Name this duplicate layer **Lower Background**, and click on OK. It's always wise to leave the original Background layer intact and perform any work on a duplicate copy.

2. The Lower Background layer should now be the active layer. Choose the Lasso tool or the Magnetic Lasso tool from the toolbox to make a selection inside the bubble. (Be careful not to include the foreground fingers in this selection, but do include the fingers *behind* the bubble.) Avoid coming too close to the upper edge of the bubble; leave a kind of crown. Don't worry if the selection isn't perfect because we'll correct that in the next step.

3. Press **D** for the default colors. Press **Q** to enter Quick Mask mode to polish the selection (as we did earlier in this chapter). Choose the 19-pixel hard round brush (or smaller if needed for the tight spots), and with black as the foreground color, add to your selection where needed. If necessary, press **X** to switch to white and paint away areas where you have selected too much; then press **X** and continue to paint with black as necessary (see the selection marquee in Figure 10.8). When you're satisfied with the selection, press **Q** to exit Quick Mask mode. Choose Select, Save Selection, name the selection **Inside Bubble**, and click on OK. You will need this selection later.

4. Press Shift+F7 to invert the selection, and then press Ctrl(⌘)+J to copy the selection to a new layer. If you turn off the visibility to the Background and Lower Background layers, your new layer should look similar to Figure 10.9. Remember to turn the visibility back on for the other layers after you finish checking out the new layer. Rename this new layer **Upper Background**.

   Now that you have emptied the bubble, you will fill it—with the hands!

5. Click on the Lower Background layer to make this the active layer. Choose Select, Load Selection, choose Hands (the previously saved selection) from the drop-down list for the Channel option, and click on OK. Press Ctrl(⌘)+J to copy this selection onto a new layer. Rename this new layer **Long Hands**.

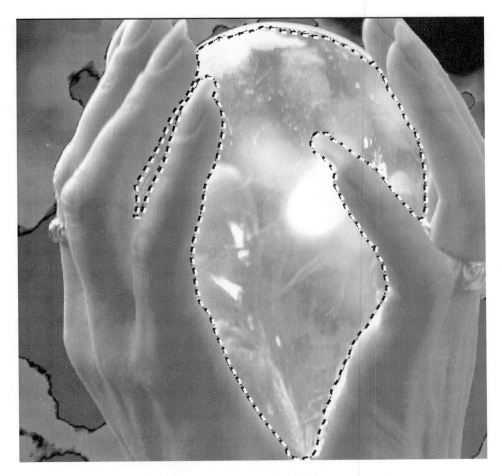

Figure 10.8   Create a selection that encompasses the bubble.

6. Press Ctrl(⌘)+T to enter the Free Transform tool. Now enter the following values on the Option bar: X: **755.6**, Y: **793.9**, W: **30.6**, and H: **48.7** (as shown in Figure 10.10). Right-click (Macintosh: hold Ctrl and click) and choose Flip Horizontal. Right-click (Macintosh: hold Ctrl and click) again and choose Flip Vertical. Press Enter (Return) twice, or double-click inside the bounding box to exit the Free Transform tool and commit the changes.

7. The long hand is a touch too dark; let's make it warmer and brighter. The Long Hands layer should still be active. Click the Create new fill or adjustment layer icon at the bottom of the Layers palette, and choose Hue/Saturation. In the Hue/Saturation dialog box, enter **20** for Saturation and **25** for Lightness (see Figure 10.11). Click on OK.

Figure 10.9   Create a layer with no bubble.

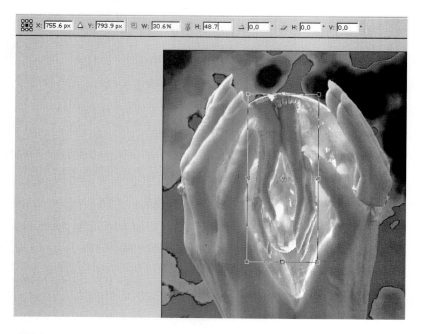

Figure 10.10   Squish the reversed hands selection a little.

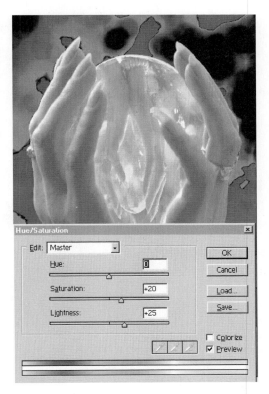

Figure 10.11 Use the Hue/Saturation command on the Adjustment Layer to lighten the hands reflection.

8. Press Ctrl(⌘)+G to group the Adjustment Layer to the Long Hands layer below (which will apply the effect to the Long Hands layer only). On the Layers palette, lower the Opacity for Long Hands layer to 85%. With the Long Hands layer as the active layer, check the box to the left of the Hue/Saturation layer to link these two layers together. Click on the arrow at the upper-right corner of the Layers palette, and choose New Set From Linked. Name the set **Long Hand**, and click on OK.

Insider

If you feel as though you've performed enough image editing for the moment, and want to take a shortcut to placing the hands copy inside the globe, we have the solution waiting for you on the CD. Open the Long Hand file from the Example/Chap10 folder on the companion CD. Just choose the Move tool on the toolbox, press Shift (to center the copy), and drag into your image (between the Upper Background and the Lower Background layers). The image will fall into place with the right colors. But you need to lower the opacity of the Long Hands layer to 85% and also erase what covers the fingers and nails. See Figure 10.12.

10

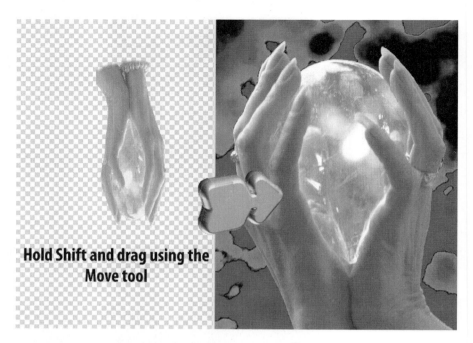

Hold Shift and drag using the Move tool

Figure 10.12   Drag a copy of the premade hands into your image.

> **9.** Press Ctrl(⌘)+S; keep the file open.

Adding a Snow Globe Effect to the Composition

Do you like snow globes? You know, those orb-shaped knickknacks with snowmen in which snow appears to fall when you shake them? No? You *hate* them? My wife is *crazy* about them. And I (almost) always do whatever my wife likes. So, let's add some snowflakes in the bubble:

The Forecast Calls for Snow

> **1.** Click on the Upper Background layer to make this the active layer. Alt(Opt)+click on the Create a new layer icon at the bottom of the Layers palette. Name the new layer **Snowflakes**, and click on OK. Choose Select, Load Selection, choose Inside Bubble from the Channels drop-down list, and click on OK.
>
> **2.** Click on the foreground color of the toolbox, and choose a pale whitish-blue color from the Color Picker (R: 245, G: 255, B: 253). Click on OK. Press Alt(Opt)+Delete(Backspace) to fill the selection with foreground color. Do not deselect yet.

3. Choose Filter, Distort, Polar Coordinates, check the Polar to Rectangular option, and click on OK. You should then see a shape similar to the one in Figure 10.13. Press Ctrl(⌘)+D to deselect. On the Layers palette, set the blending mode of the Snowflakes layer to Dissolve, and set the Opacity at 5%.

Figure 10.13   Use the Polar Coordinates command to create a distortion for the snowflakes that'll make them look as though they are swirling around in the globe.

4. Click on the Add layer mask icon at the bottom of the Layers palette. Press **D** for the default colors, and with black as the foreground color, use the Brush tool (and maybe a large 65-pixel, soft-edge brush) to paint away just a little of the snowflake effect on the left side to give the snowflakes a narrower shape, as shown in Figure 10.14.

5. If you prefer to have a better view of the Snowflakes layer, Ctrl(⌘)+click on the Create a new layer icon (to create the layer below the Snowflakes layer). Fill this new layer with a dark color (black will do nicely), and you will be able to see the effect very clearly.

6. When using the Dissolve blending mode, especially at a low opacity, be aware that what you see is not what you will get. Flattening the image will change the appearance of the pixels in the effect. To see what this means, flatten the image, and look at the difference in the snowflake effect. Now press Ctrl(⌘)+Z to undo the flattened image step.

Figure 10.14   Create a narrow region of falling snow.

7. Fortunately, you can save your effect. How? Layer 1 (the layer with the black fill) should still be active. Ctrl(⌘)+click on the Create a new layer icon (to make another new layer under Layer 1). Click on the column to the left of Layer 1 and to the left of the Snowflakes layer to link these layers together (the top three layers should now be linked—with Layer 2 as the active layer). Now watch carefully, and you'll discover a trick that not many people know about. You will learn how to merge layers (or in this case, make a composite layer) without actually merging the original layers (keeping the original layers intact—look ma, no merging). Hold down the Alt(Opt) key, click on the arrow in the upper-right corner of the Layers palette, and choose Merge Linked. When you hold down the Alt(Opt) key, the command will be performed on the empty layer without merging the layers above it. Press Ctrl(⌘)+plus key to zoom in to the document at about 600–800% (see Figure 10.15).

8. Layer 2 should still be the active layer. Choose the Magic Wand tool from the toolbox. On the Options bar, make sure the Contiguous and Use All Layers options are *un*checked. Click once in one of the white pixel areas. Press Ctrl(⌘)+minus key to zoom back out and return to a normal view. Choose Select, Save Selection, and name the selection **Snow**. Figure 10.16 shows the new selection of Snow. You can delete Layer 1 and Layer 2 now (drag them to the trash icon). You no longer need them. Do not deselect yet.

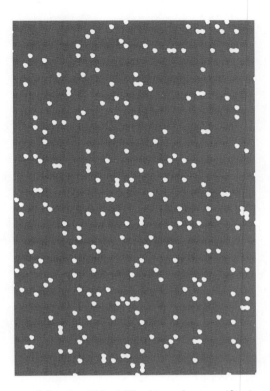

Figure 10.15   Your snowflakes should look like this under magnification.

9. Press **D** for the default colors, and press **X** to make white the foreground color. Click on the Create a new layer icon and, with the selection still active, press Alt(Opt)+Delete(Backspace) to fill the selection with white. Do not deselect yet! Click on the Paths tab to view the Paths palette. Click the Make work path from a selection icon at the bottom of the Paths palette (the fourth icon from the left), and you will see a Work Path title appear (on the palette).

10. Make sure white is still your foreground color. Choose the Brush tool and, on the Options bar, choose a 5-pixel, soft-edge round brush. You won't actually need to use the Brush tool, but the type of brush and the size of brush selected here will affect the next step (when you stroke a path). Now click on the Stroke path with brush icon at the bottom of the Paths palette (the second icon from the left). Deactivate the Work Path by clicking on an empty space on the Paths palette (under the Work Path title name). Go back to the Layers palette, and you will see *splendid* snowflakes that will not change their shape if you flatten your image.

11. Press Ctrl(⌘)+S; keep the file open.

10

Figure 10.16   Create a selection from the snowflakes.

Adding a Glowing Burst to the Bubble

Ready for the final touch? Now we'll add some glow at the top of the bubble:

Creating a Highlight

1. Alt(Opt)+click on the Create a new layer icon at the bottom of the Layers palette. Name the new layer **Glow**, and drag this layer to the top of the Layers palette (so it is above the other layers).

2. Choose the Elliptical Marquee tool from the toolbox. Hold down the Shift key to constrain the Ellipse to a perfect circle, and make a very small circle at the top of the bubble (see Figure 10.17 for the size and exact location). Hold down the spacebar, and drag (while creating the circle) if you need to reposition the circle to the correct position.

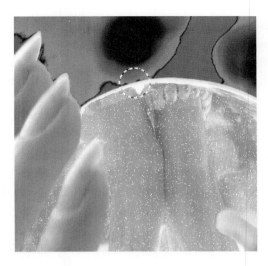

Figure 10.17 Create a small elliptical selection.

3. Feather the selection to 3 pixels. With black as the foreground color, press Alt(Opt)Alt+Delete(Backspace) to fill the selection with black. Press Ctrl(⌘)+D to deselect. Click on the Create new fill or adjustment layer icon at the bottom of the Layers palette, and choose Hue/Saturation. In the Hue/Saturation dialog box, enter **180** for Hue, **100** for Saturation, and **100** for Lightness (see Figure 10.18).

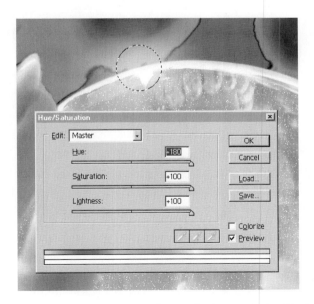

Figure 10.18 Use the Hue/Saturation controls to make the area in the elliptical selection look bright.

4. Press Ctrl(⌘)+G to group the Hue/Saturation layer with the Glow layer below. With the Glow layer active, click on the column to the left of the Hue/Saturation layer to link these two layers. Click the arrow at the upper-right corner of the Layers palette, and choose New Set From linked. Name the new set **Glow 1**, and click on OK.

5. Right-click (Macintosh: hold Ctrl and click) the Glow 1 layer set, and choose Duplicate Layer Set. Name the duplicate set **Glow 2**. Open the Glow 2 set, and click on the Glow layer to make it the active layer. Ctrl(⌘)+click on the Glow layer to make the selection active. On the toolbox, click the foreground color, and in the Color Picker, enter the values R: **245**, G: **237**, B: **8** and click on OK (see Figure 10.19 for the values).

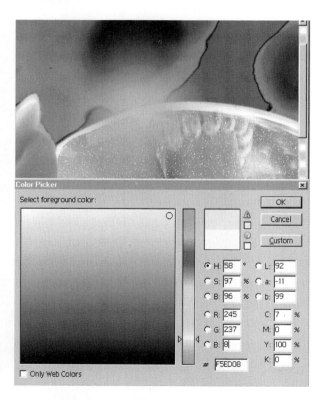

Figure 10.19   Add a golden touch to the burst.

6. Press Alt(Opt)+Delete(Backspace) to fill the selection. Press Ctrl(⌘)+D to deselect. Finally, double-click the thumbnail on the Hue/Saturation layer, and check the colorize option. Then enter the following values **58** for Hue, **50** for Saturation, and **90** for Lightness (see Figure 10.20).

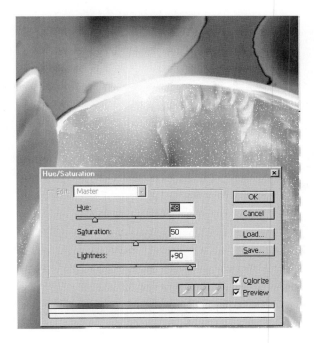

Figure 10.20 Brighten up the glow.

7. Press Ctrl(⌘)+S; you can close the image at any time now.

I'll bet that you didn't think a picture—a poor picture at that—could become a stunning display of beautiful hands and a mystical bubble after a little massaging in Photoshop!

Summary

We hope, through the course of this chapter, you've seen that great art doesn't just happen; it has to be *made*. And as with the example of the beautiful hands, you had some heavy-duty *helping* hands to lead you to your goal. Did you see how selections depend on color correction to get the job done, and vice versa? You also learned here that the Extract command is invaluable when you need to make a quick, precise selection. All in all, you've once again used Photoshop's features to transform an image into a piece of expressive art.

Chapter 11

Working with Picture CD Pictures

Anyone familiar with the previous editions

of the *Inside Photoshop* series might notice

that this particular edition delves much

more into digital photography. The reason

In this chapter, you'll learn

- What Picture CD is and isn't, and what you can do with it

- How to prepare Picture CD images for email

- How to print Picture CD images

- How to catalog Picture CD images

is that the consumers' transition from using film to using digital is stronger and at a faster pace now more than ever before.

If you're young, you are familiar with 35mm film. If you are older, you remember the 110 and Disc film. And if you're as old as I am, you remember the daguerreotype, er, I mean, the 126 format. But practically all these film formats, even the most popular—35mm— are on the waiting list for extinction.

Meanwhile, manufacturers are scrambling to create services and products that bridge the gap between silver-halide–based imaging and digital imaging. One such product, which just happens to be the topic of this chapter, is Kodak's Picture CD.

Picture CD is a relatively inexpensive and quick way to digitize your 35mm film. Best of all, Picture CD is available nearly everywhere that film is processed. Even in my small town of Westminster, Maryland, nine businesses offer the Picture CD service. So, if you're still using 35mm film and want to digitize your photos, this chapter will give you the lowdown on what to expect, what not to expect, and how to make the best images possible from your Picture CD photos.

What Picture CD Is and Isn't

Before we talk about what Picture CD is, let's talk about what Picture CD isn't. Picture CD isn't for high-quality professional and commercial use. Nor is Picture CD for the non-professional who demands more than just average quality in his or her imaging.

Now that we know what Picture CD isn't, let's talk about "What it is, man!"

Before Picture CD, if you wanted to digitize your 35mm masterpieces, you had basically three choices: scan the photograph that was made from the film, scan the actual film (film scanners are expensive!), or have the negatives transferred to Photo CD (time-consuming and somewhat expensive). The most popular and the lowest long-term cost is the flat-bed scanner for scanning the prints. But here's the rub: The print is a second generation from the film, and the photographic paper cannot replicate a very large percentage of the subtle tones and colors contained in the film. These options left an opening for the development department at Kodak to come up with a product that helps bridge the gap between traditional and digital photography within the non-professional consumer market.

The image resolution and JPEG compression in Picture CD may leave some consumers disappointed. But what Picture CD does have going for it is that the images are from direct scans of the film—a very good thing; you'll read more about this later in the chapter.

At the time of this writing, only digital cameras in the five-figure price range can yield images close to 35mm film. Scans that come directly from the film can give you far more subtle tones and colors than if you were to scan a photograph printed from that negative. Photographic paper just isn't capable of replicating all the information contained in the film.

The Issue of Resolution and Quality

I have to admit that before researching Picture CD to write this chapter, I had the impression that this product not only had very little potential, but also near zero quality. I figured that the largest, best image that you could print from a Picture CD was a wallet size. So, although I was a skeptic at the beginning, I have revised my impressions and now see a lot of potential in this product.

When you bring in a roll of film for Picture CD, you can get up to 40 images on the CD. It's not that those images take up a lot of disk space; on the contrary, the average Picture CD image is between only 500KB and 700KB. So, what's all the extra CD space used for? Except for the Kodak programs (a slideshow and a bare-bones editing program), all but about 15MB on the disc is left unused.

So, with each image averaging only 500–700KB, you would think the quality for a Photoshop pro like yourself would be unacceptable. Right? Well, let's take a look.

Each image is saved in the JPEG format at a quality of around 66%. The image is not saved at the highest quality (100%), but the opened image file is around 8.4MB. Not bad. Most importantly, as mentioned previously, the image was scanned directly from the negative; this is where Picture CD images shine.

The film contains millions more shades, tones, and colors than a print that's made from a negative. Plus, a scan from the film is far sharper than a scan from the print. These two advantages—a sharper image with millions more shades and colors—make the Picture CD images very appealing for those photographers who want to digitize their film at a reasonable cost.

Picture CD is a cousin of Kodak's Photo CD (or would that be "parent" because Photo CD was first?). In Photoshop, I opened two similar images, one from a Picture CD and the other from a Photo CD, and set them side by side. Both were fairly similar in quality (both photos were taken with the same camera and same lens). I must point out that the Photo CD was burned way back in 1995, and today's equipment might be, should be, higher quality and yield sharper images.

A negative, er, downside to Picture CD is that the images are saved in the sRGB color space. The lowercase s signifies "small." The sRGB format tosses out lots of colors to yield a smaller file size.

Before each photo is burned onto the CD, the operator can rotate the image so that its orientation is correct when you view the thumbnails in Photoshop's File Browser, for example. The operator can also make color and density adjustments as needed to improve the image's quality before burning.

So, if you are taking that bridge from traditional photography to digital, I recommend that you give Picture CD a try to see whether it meets your needs. Later in this chapter, you will work with a couple of actual Picture CD images, and that should give you a better idea of what this product can do for you.

What About Cost and Time?

Kodak's higher-priced alternate choice to Picture CD is Photo CD. But, not only is the Photo CD more expensive, the turnaround time is usually one to two weeks. Compare that to Picture CD's one-hour turnaround time, and you might find Picture CD more appealing.

The cost is a reasonable $7.99 to have up to 40 images burned (all at the same time) onto the Picture CD when you bring in a roll of film to be developed. That's the actual cost of burning to the CD. Expect to pay around $2.15 to have the film developed and more if you want prints included.

You do have another choice that could cost a lot more money—burning a lot of negatives. And I mean a lot, as in 200–300. But, as with any time you order a Picture CD, after each order is completed, the CD is closed. Therefore, if you need to have a bunch of photos on one CD, they must be burned at the same time.

What Formats Can Be Burned onto a Picture CD?

Believe it or not, the Picture CD equipment is designed to accept and burn images that are already digital. "Why would a consumer pay to put digital images onto a CD?" I asked Mike and Candace at the local Target. The most common reason is that these consumers want to get the images off their digital camera's card and onto a CD because they do not have a CD burner. The Picture CD equipment is capable of accepting virtually all media cards that digital cameras use. Additionally, you can even burn images from a standard CD to a Picture CD.

But, in terms of traditional photography, both 35mm and APS films can be used for Picture CD. You can bring in undeveloped film or film that has already been developed.

Working with Picture CD Images

The average consumer will have two main uses for the Picture CD product: emailing and printing. Well, okay, there is one more use—editing your images in Photoshop with the knowledge and skills that you learn from this book!

We'll let the rest of the book take you on the journey into creativity. Here, we'll talk about emailing and printing your Picture CD images. Then we'll move on to using the File Browser to catalog your Picture CD images.

Preparing a Picture CD Image for Email

If you want to email your Picture CD pictures to friends and relatives, sending the full-size image straight off the CD might not be the best idea. The file sizes average around 500KB—a bit large for those with dial-up service. And unless the recipient's screen resolution is set higher than 2,100×1,400, only part of the image will be visible on the screen at one time.

So, to speed up the download time and enable the viewer to see your entire photo without having to use the scrollbars, you need to apply some edits to the image. The dimensions need to be reduced; then the image needs to be sharpened and saved with a JPEG quality setting that does not compromise image quality. Most of these edits can be programmed as an Action so that Photoshop does all the work. Mmm, sounds like a good tutorial!

In the following set of steps, you will assign a function key to the new Action so that preparing a horizontal image for emailing is as easy as pressing F3. You will create this new Action to set the image's width to 800 pixels and then apply the Unsharp Mask with a specific setting. Finally, you'll take a quick trip to the Save For Web feature to preview your JPEG settings before saving the image.

Creating an Action for Email Images

1. Open the 017_9.jpg image from the Examples\Chap11 folder on the companion CD.

Insider

An explanation of how each file's name is determined might be useful here. The first number, the number before the underscore, is the image's sequential number on the CD. The number after the underscore is the number of the photo on the filmstrip.

2. If the Actions palette is not visible in your workspace, choose Window, Actions.
3. Click the Create new action icon at the bottom of the Actions palette (second icon from the right). The New Action dialog box appears.
4. In the Name field, type **Email prep for horizontal**, and then choose F3 for the Function Key (see Figure 11.1). Click Record.

Note

> **If Photoshop has F3 reserved**   A check might appear in either or both of the Shift (Enter) or Control boxes. If so, this indicates that Photoshop has F3 reserved for something else. Just be sure to remember what keystrokes are needed to run this action!

Warning

> **Be careful when recording actions!**   Be very careful in everything you do in Photoshop while you're recording an Action! All inadvertent edits will also be recorded. Although you can go back and edit the completed Action, you'll save a lot of headaches if you avoid mistakes while recording.

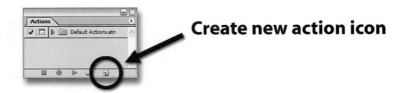

Create new action icon

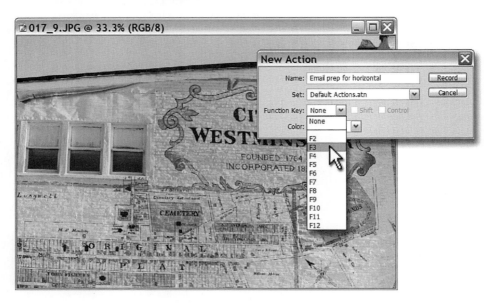

Figure 11.1   Name the new action Email prep for horizontal.

5. Right-click (Macintosh: hold Ctrl and click) on the image's title bar, and choose Image Size from the menu. In the Image Size dialog box, be sure Constrain Proportions is checked, and then type **800** in the top-most Width field, as shown in Figure 11.2. Click on OK.

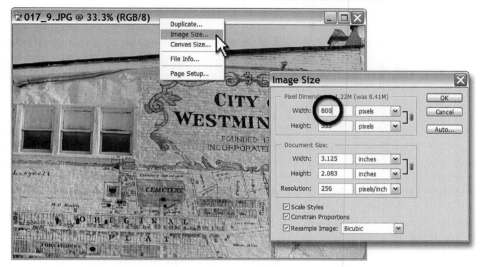

Figure 11.2   An 800 pixel-wide horizontal Picture CD image fits nicely (meaning, completely) on most monitors.

6. Choose Filter, Sharpen, Unsharp Mask, and use the following values: Amount: **68**, Radius: **1.5**, and Threshold: **0** (see Figure 11.3).

Insider

The values in step 6 are not universally perfect for all 800-pixel wide images, but these values are acceptable for email-quality images that were burned onto a Picture CD.

7. Click the Stop playing/recording icon at the bottom of the Actions palette (the left-most icon). Your new action to prepare horizontal Picture CD images for email is now ready. (Come to think of it, this action can be used on any image, Picture CD or not!)

8. Time to save the image for the smallest file size that contains the best quality. From the main menu, choose File, Save For Web.

9. Click the 2-Up tab (in the upper–left area of the dialog box) so that you can see the original image (left window) and a preview of the image with the current Quality setting (right window). Click the right-facing arrow at the Quality field, and drag the slider to about 42, as shown in Figure 11.4.

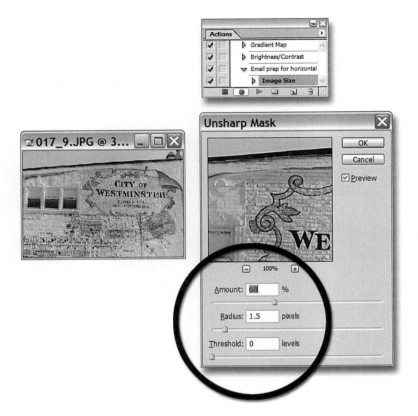

Figure 11.3   All resampled images need sharpening, and the Unsharp Mask is the best tool for the job.

Insider

> This quality setting of 42 maintains most of the image's original detail. If you drag the Quality slider to 0 (zero) and look at the area of the image where the roof and sky meet, you can see JPEG artifacts (image degradation due to using too low a quality setting)—not a good thing!

10. Click Save. In the Save dialog box that appears, be sure that Images Only (*.jpg) is chosen in the Save as Type field and that Default Settings appears in the Settings field (see Figure 11.5). Type a custom name in the File Name field, and click Save.

Now that you've created this action, the next time you have a horizontal Picture CD image that you want to email, just press F3 (or whatever key combination you assigned to this action), and Photoshop will do all the work!

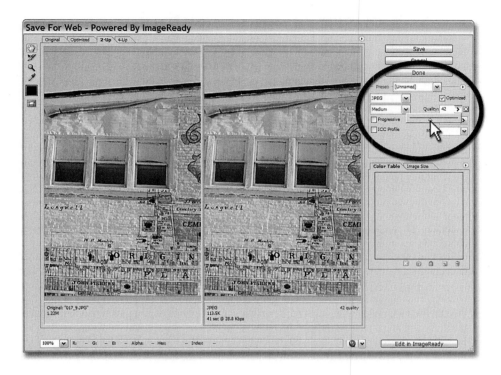

Figure 11.4   The Save For Web dialog box is handy when you want to compare your original image to a particular Quality setting.

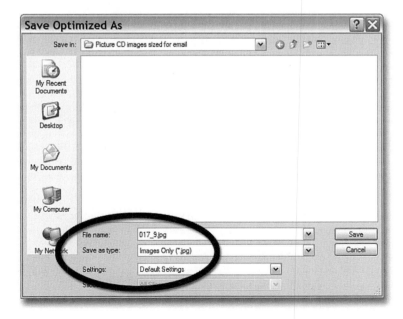

Figure 11.5   Make sure you are saving the image as a .jpg only and with the default settings.

You can follow the preceding steps to create an action for sizing vertical images to your specifications. You need only to enter a specific value for the Height field in the Image Size box, instead of a value for the Width. Because most people have their monitor resolution set at 800×600 pixels, you might want to use 600 for the Height value when creating a similar action for vertical images.

We've covered preparing a Picture CD for emailing, but what about printing? Yes, you probably ordered prints with your film processing and Picture CD, but maybe you'd like to print the image at a different size, or maybe print out a copy after you've done some creative Photoshop editing. So, let's look at printing your Picture CD photos.

Printing Picture CD Images

With color printers hitting rock-bottom prices, chances are that you have a printer and are interested in printing your Picture CD photos. After all, with Photoshop, you can improve and add some creativity to your photographs.

So, what's the best size and resolution to print your Picture CD images? Well, the answer depends on what the meaning of "best" is.

If you have a low-quality printer, you can print your Picture CD images at any size. The quality of the images probably exceeds the quality of your printer. On the other hand, if you have a medium- to high-quality printer, you will notice a reduction in the image's quality the larger you print your image. So, it's really your call.

Run some tests with a Picture CD image on your printer. Print your image at different sizes, closely examine the prints, and then determine how large you can print your Picture CD photos before the reduction in quality is obvious. Come to think of it, a set of steps to help you get started on your testing would be helpful!

In the following set of steps, you will prepare a Picture CD image for printing in three different sizes. First, you will prepare to print the image with its actual dimensions. Then you will change the image size to print a larger image. And finally, you will prepare the image for Photoshop's Picture Package, where you can place multiple copies of the same image on a single sheet of printer paper. Oh, speaking of printer paper, be sure you are using "photo quality" paper in your printer for your Picture CD photos; using regular paper is the surest way to get terrible quality prints from your photographs!

Preparing a Picture CD Picture for Printing

1. Open the 009_17.jpg image from the Examples\Chap11 folder on the companion CD.

Alternatively, you can open one of your own images on your Picture CD. Just be sure to choose a vertical image, not horizontal; these steps are written for a vertical image.

2. Right-click (Macintosh: hold Ctrl and click) on the image's title bar, and choose Image Size from the menu. (We're just checking the dimensions of the image as it was burned onto the CD.)

   As shown in Figure 11.6, the image is approximately 5 1/2×8 inches—large enough to print on an 8 1/2×11-inch sheet of photo paper and still leave a white border that nicely frames the image.

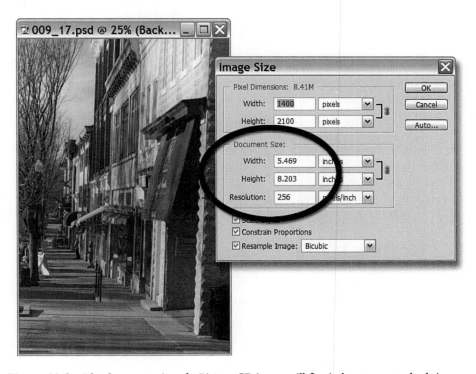

Figure 11.6   The document size of a Picture CD image will fit nicely onto a standard size sheet of printer photo paper.

3. Click on OK to close the Image Size dialog box. The most critical step before printing a Picture CD image is sharpening. From the main menu, choose Filter, Sharpen, Unsharp Mask.

   Click and drag in the preview window so that you can see the roofline shown in Figure 11.7. Usually, the best places to help you determine the Unsharp Mask settings are areas that contain a strong contrast. You want to sharpen the image as much as possible but not so much to create a halo effect (which appears first at high-contrast areas).

Enter the following settings: Amount: **106**, Radius: **2.5**, and Threshold: **0** (see Figure 11.7). You can click and hold over the preview window to see the original image before sharpening and then say, "Wow, what a difference!"

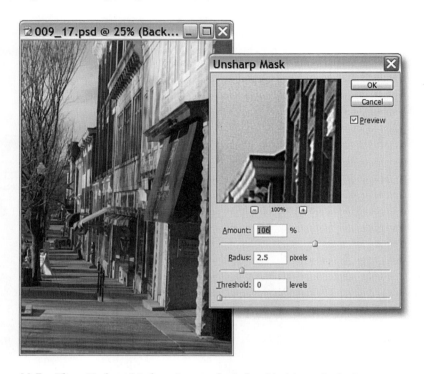

Figure 11.7   These Unsharp Mask settings work nicely with this particular image.

4. Click on OK. Now, at this point, you can choose File, Print to print this image. Again, what you will print is an image from a Picture CD at its original dimensions, but it will be much sharper and therefore look quite good!

5. Now that this Picture CD image is sharper, let's print it at a larger size. Right-click (Macintosh: hold Ctrl and click) on the image's title bar, and choose Image Size from the menu. Uncheck Resample Image. Uncheck Resample Image. (Yes, that sentence was repeated on purpose!) Change the Height to 10 inches (see Figure 11.8). Notice that the Resolution (pixels/inch) went down, from 256 to 210. Click on OK.

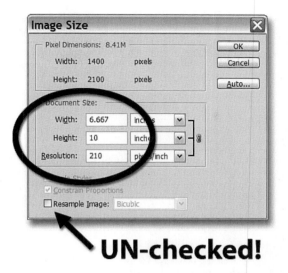

UN-checked!

Figure 11.8   With Resample unchecked, any changes in the dimensions of the image will force changes in the image's resolution.

Warning

Resampling reduces quality   Resampling an image forces Photoshop to do some guesswork on what pixels to either create or toss away. This process reduces the quality and sharpness of your image. When the Resample Image option is turned off (unchecked), you'll notice the ability to adjust the pixels (at the top of the dialog box) becomes unavailable. The reason is that Photoshop is not going to make any changes to the actual number of pixels when Resample Image is unchecked. Photoshop is just looking at the image in a different way—adjusting the pixels per inch to get the desired printable size without adding or removing pixels. Avoid resampling whenever possible, especially with Picture CD pictures!

6. At this point, you can print this larger image. Again, what you will print is an image from a Picture CD at a larger dimension, but because the resolution (actual number of pixels contained within the image) was not altered, it will still look sharp.

7. For the final change in image size, let's crop the photo just a little bit to proportionately fit into the 3 1/2×5 Picture Package format and then reduce the dimensions. Choose the Rectangular Marquee tool from the toolbox. On the Options bar, choose Fixed Aspect Ratio from the Style drop-down menu, and then type **3.5** for Width and **5** for Height (see Figure 11.9).

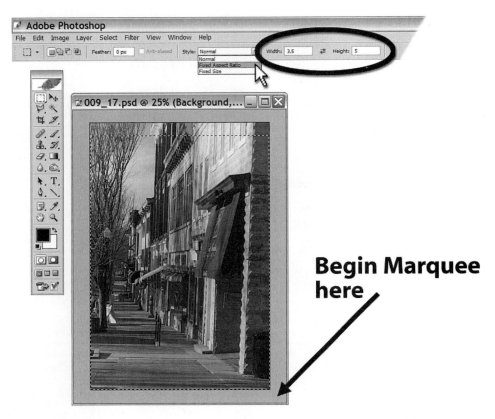

Figure 11.9   Create a rectangular marquee selection that has the aspect ratio of the target Picture Package size.

8. Drag the bottom-right corner of the image window slightly away from the image to create some space between the image and the window. Starting just outside the lower-right corner of the image, click and drag up and to the left until the marquee reaches the left edge of the image. Release the mouse button (refer to Figure 11.9).

9. From the main menu, choose Image, Crop. The image is now ready to fit into the 3 1/2×5 Picture Package frame. Press Ctrl(⌘)+D to deselect the marquee.

10. One last time, right-click (Macintosh: hold Ctrl and click) on the image's title bar, and choose Image Size from the menu. With Resample Image unchecked, change the Document Size Width to 3.5 inches. Notice and remember that the resolution (pixels/inch) increased to 400. Click on OK.

11. Choose File, Automate, Picture Package. Within the Document field, choose 8.0 × 10.0 in for the Paper Size, (4)3.5×5 for the Layout, and type **400**—the same as the image—for the Resolution (see Figure 11.10).

Figure 11.10   After cropping your image to fit the aspect ratio of your target Picture Package size, enter the image's current resolution, and then let Photoshop do all the remaining work.

12. Click on OK and watch Photoshop do its magic. Voila! Now you can print four copies of this 3 1/2×5-inch image on one sheet of photo paper—with each image at a high-quality resolution (see Figure 11.11).

13. You can close the files at this time, with or without saving changes to either of these images.

Let's review the three main edits you applied in the preceding set of steps:

- First, before printing the image at its actual dimensions, you used Unsharp Mask to sharpen the image. (If you need to be convinced how important that step is, print an unsharpened image and then a sharpened image, and compare them side by side!)

- Second, with the image already sharpened, you increased its dimensions without resampling the image. Although the resolution dropped slightly, the print would remain fairly sharp.

Figure 11.11   For those special photos on your Picture CD, you can easily print multiple copies for framing and snail-mailing to relatives.

- Third, you cropped the image to a specific aspect ratio so that the image would fit perfectly into the intended Picture Package format.

Tip

Saving in JPG loses image information   Any time you edit a Picture CD photo and want to save that image, do not save it in the JPG format! The JPG format tosses away image information, and the more often you save the image, the more information is tossed out; as a result, image quality suffers over time with each new save. Save the file in Photoshop's native format (PSD) or TIFF to preserve the current quality.

Now that you know more details about how to prepare a Picture CD image for email and printing, let's move on to our final what-can-I-do-with-Picture CD images topic: cataloging your images using Photoshop's File Browser.

Cataloging Picture CD Images

The title of this section could actually be "Cataloging Your Digital Images." We're going to take a short trip to Photoshop's File Browser, and everything that is explained here can apply to a group of digital images from any source, not just a Picture CD.

If you start accumulating many digital images, at some point you may want to catalog all or most of your images. After all, say you have more than 300 images and you need to find a photo of a fire hydrant. Rather than get all burned up from the frustration of sifting through all those images, you can apply a keyword, *fire hydrant*, for any of your images and then have Photoshop do the searching for you.

Let's look at how the File Browser can work for you.

Designing the Structure of a Collection of Images

The most important step to cataloging a lot of images is to create an understandable and efficient structure for your collection. Most people can grab a spoon in the silverware drawer when all the utensils are grouped by classification rather than when everything has been tossed into one big pile. The same is true of your many images: Neat, tidy groups make for happy eaters, er, Photoshoppers.

Here's a suggestion for how to design the structure of your collection of images. First, make a new folder on a hard disk that has a lot of unused space. Name that folder something like **Picture CD Images** or **Digital Camera Images**. Then create sub-folders, naming them with the date the images are downloaded to your computer. If you use the date, you'll never run into the problem of naming a folder with an existing folder name. Besides, you don't need to create folders according to subject matter; the File Browser can sort the images for you. Also, if you try to add Picture CD images to a folder that already contains the images from another Picture CD, you'll have a big filename problem: The new batch of images is named exactly the same as the existing batch!

After you stuff a few folders full of images, you'll want to give them some kind of identifiable notation so that you can easily sort through all those images. You can apply information to an image file in three ways that that will help the sorting procedure: using flags, using keywords, and entering metadata.

Assigning Flags and Keywords

Assigning a flag might be your step to cataloging a large group of image files. For example, you can flag the images in a folder you want to keep. Then, using the Show, Unflagged Files sorting feature, you can view only the unflagged images, which you can then easily select and delete.

To flag an image, right-click (Macintosh: hold Ctrl and click) on the image's thumbnail, and choose Flag from the context-sensitive menu, as shown in Figure 11.12. Notice that a small flag appears at the bottom-right corner of the thumbnail.

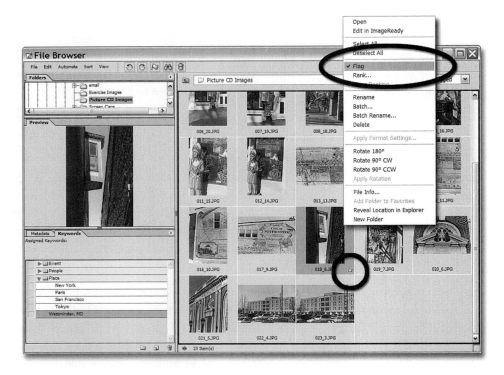

Figure 11.12   You can flag an image's thumbnail by choosing Flag from the context-sensitive menu.

Assigning a keyword to an image can be as quick and easy as two mouse clicks: Click the thumbnail, and then click the existing keyword that you want to assign to that image.

In Figure 11.13, you can see that a new keyword named *Westminster, MD* was created and the selected thumbnail in the far-right column (also showing in the Preview window) was assigned that same keyword as indicated by the check mark in the left column.

You assign a keyword by either clicking once in the check box or double-clicking on the keyword. You create a new keyword by clicking the New Keyword icon to the immediate left of the trash icon in the Keyword window.

If you need more powerful tags for your searching capabilities, consider using metadata.

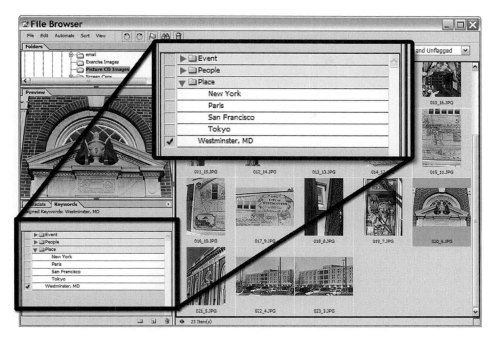

Figure 11.13   You can assign a keyword to an image simply by placing a check mark in the column to the left of the keyword.

Working with Metadata

You can actually insert information directly in the image's file by working with the Metadata feature in the File Browser. (You can also add some metadata information using the File, File Info dialog box.)

Metadata is increasingly important in many types of professional graphics work, especially where images are involved in publishing workflows.

You can take advantage of custom metadata even if you view your images only on your own monitor. In Figure 11.14, you can see the Metadata window at the lower left of the File Browser. Some metadata was already written into the file when the image was burned to the Picture CD, but you can add further information as shown under the heading IPTC (which stands for International Press Telecommunications Council). Just click in a blank area to the right of the pencil icon and the name of the metadata, and then type your custom information.

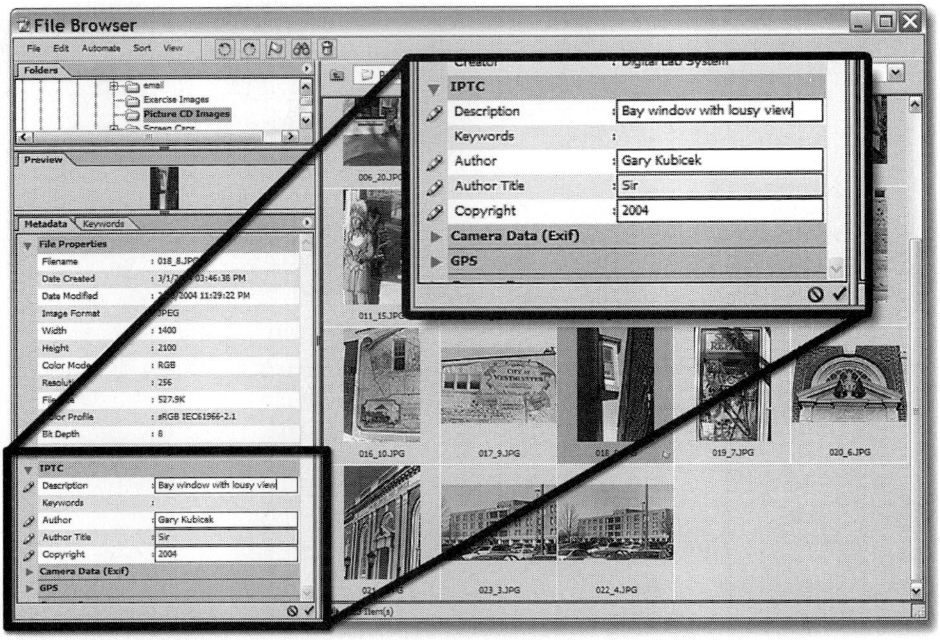

Figure 11.14   To enter custom metadata information, click in a blank field and begin typing.

Performing a Search

You can tell Photoshop to search for images by sorting for flags, keywords, or specific information in the image's metadata.

To search for images with or without flags, choose your preference from the Show drop-down that is located at the upper-right corner of the File Browser, as shown in Figure 11.15.

To search by keyword or metadata, click on the respective menu button (right-facing arrow) that is located to the right of the Metadata or Keywords tab, and choose Search from the menu (see Figure 11.16). The Search box that appears is identical for keyword or metadata searching.

You can perform a search for specific keywords and metadata within a particular folder or within an entire network. The time you spend cataloging your images quickly pays off when you need to find one specific image among hundreds, or thousands, of images.

Figure 11.15 Sorting by flagged and/or unflagged files is as simple as choosing your preference from the Show drop-down.

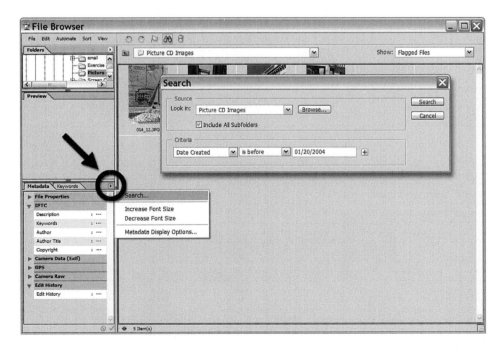

Figure 11.16 Enter your search criteria to find specific images using keywords or metadata.

Note that the preview window in the File Browser can be resized. You can customize the File Browser to fit a certain configuration for the way you prefer to work; then you can choose Window, Workspace, Save Workspace and give the File Browser configuration a title. For example, maybe you like to resize the preview windows so they're huge, and you like separate configurations for *wide* images as opposed to *tall* images. You could conceivably flag all the wide images in a folder to view under the "wide" configuration, and when using the "tall" configuration, choose to show the unflagged files.

Summary

If you were already familiar with Kodak's Picture CD, I hope this chapter has helped you take fuller advantage of this product. If you knew nothing about the Picture CD, maybe now you'll give it a try and use some of the techniques in this chapter. Come to think of it, some of the techniques in this chapter can apply to any image—not just those on a Picture CD!

Chapter 12

Curves and Adjustment Layers

It is a cold, hard fact that when you're working with digitized photographs, you will need to apply some amount of color adjustment. Chances are, you'll win the lottery before you bring a photograph into

In this chapter, you'll learn

- The fundamentals of applying Curves
- All about Curves—what it is and does
- How to use Curves with Adjustment Layers
- How to apply minor corrections using Curves
- How to find and remove a dominant color's influence
- How to apply corrections in each color channel
- How to create contrast in a color channel
- How to apply Curves to selected areas
- How to create special effects using Curves

Photoshop and find that the colors are perfect. Color correction ranks as the third inevitability in digital life, right after system halts and a monthly AOL CD in your mailbox.

Curves is Photoshop's most powerful color correcting tool. There is virtually no photograph that the proper Curves settings cannot improve. Curves gives you unparalleled precision for making color adjustments. Here's an excellent analogy: Curves is to color correcting as a scalpel is to cutting, whereas all other color correcting tools in Photoshop are like a butter knife.

The second topic in this chapter's title is Adjustment Layers. Although we discuss only a couple of the available Adjustment Layers, they all work on the same principle: By using Adjustment Layers to edit images, you can change the settings you enter indefinitely without applying any changes to the original image. This is cool, very cool!

So, with the following pages containing the practical applications of Curves and Adjustment Layers, let's continue our journey into this chapter.

Laying the Groundwork for Applying Curves

In this chapter, we introduce you to Curves and provide you with a solid foundation on which you can build your expertise through practice with color correcting. Before you start working with the examples, though, take a moment to read through some of the groundwork upon which this chapter is built, so you'll have a better idea of where you're going and what you'll learn from the exercises. Here's a list of some of the basic principles and guidelines you should keep in mind when working through the exercises in this chapter:

- The discussion and sample images are limited to the RGB color space (most of our readers use RGB). Although the basic principles of using Curves apply to all color spaces, the characteristics of each color space deserve a study beyond the scope of one chapter. The RGB color space is big enough for all-purpose work and is ideal for digital images. If you plan to output your images (film, print, and so on), you might find the need to develop a different approach to correcting color than what is suggested here.

- The goal of color correcting is to improve the image's tonal range and color, not to reproduce the actual colors at the scene or of the scanned photograph. We don't always know or remember the actual colors in the scene. Say, for example, I shot a picture of a spectacular sunset with my royal blue yacht in the foreground, and you offer to color correct the scan of the image. You know that the boat is royal blue; therefore, you make it royal blue. But I disagree with the red in the sky; it's not the hue of red that I saw. Because you have no way of knowing the true colors in the scene, you correct for the known color(s) and move the rest into an *acceptable* range.

- You'll use two methods to determine the Curves adjustments: numerical values of specific areas in the image (using the Eyedropper and the Info palette) and what the colors look like on your monitor. Each method is acceptable, depending on the intended use of your photo. For example, if you will view a particular image only on your monitor, correct the colors as you see them on your monitor.

- Each of the six stepped procedures in this chapter uses a different image, and each image contains its own unique problems. The solutions to those problems progress from a basic correction to more advanced techniques.

- Making numerous trips to the Curves command to correct numerous images is the best way to learn how to use Curves. As the story goes, a tourist in New York City asked a native how to get to Carnegie Hall. The response was, "Practice, practice, practice."

- Using Photoshop's Adjustment Layers is the preferred method for making image corrections. An Adjustment Layer works like a filter on a camera lens, and the corrections are placed *into* this layer, leaving the original pixels unchanged. Each change you make to the original pixels degrades the quality. Adjustment Layers also allow you to modify your settings indefinitely, without harming innocent pixels.

- The Adobe 1998 profile is the preferred default color space for all-around, general-purpose imaging work. When you're working with the files in the Examples/Chap12 folder, if you receive a Mismatching Profile message box, press Ctrl(⌘)+Shift+K, and change the RGB Working Space to Adobe RGB 1998. Then, in the Color Management Policies section, make sure Preserve Embedded Profiles is the choice in all drop-down boxes. Also, make sure all the Ask When Opening check boxes are unchecked. See Chapter 2, "The Critically Important Color and Gamma Calibration Chapter," for more information on the Adobe 1998 profile.

Warning

> **Producing histograms** If you want to produce accurate histograms, we strongly recommended that you uncheck the Use Cache for Histograms option in the Memory & Image Cache section of Photoshop's Preferences. Using the cache to calculate histograms (used in commands such as Variations, Levels, and Curves) is a quick but much less precise method of producing histograms. Unchecking this preference setting makes histograms more accurate!

- Perception of color can be very subjective. All of us are influenced by personal preferences and our own ability to perceive colors, so you might not agree with some of the color settings given in the exercises. You might see a particular yellow that you would describe as a traffic-light yellow, whereas someone else might see it as a lemon yellow. You might prefer the colors in a photograph to have a pastel quality, whereas the guy next to you might prefer bold, fully saturated colors. We address the issue of individual color perception and how Photoshop CS evaluates color in "Using the Color Sampler Tool," later in this chapter.

- An image tends to look complete if it has a full range of tones from black to white. Without a black point and white point, the photo will look *flat*—lacking contrast. There can be exceptions to this rule, but this is the philosophy we'll adopt when correcting most of the photos in this chapter. To achieve that "complete" look in our photos, we'll take these steps:

  - Correct for the known colors.

  - Adjust the remaining colors to fit into an acceptable range.

  - Create a full range of tones.

Okay, now that you have a better understanding of what to expect from this chapter, let's take a spin into the Curves.

Using Curves and Adjustment Layers

Curves is Photoshop's most powerful color adjusting tool. In fact, the Curves tool is not exclusive to Photoshop. Most scanning software includes Curves as one of the optional color adjusting commands. So, what you learn here you can take to your favorite scanner's interface.

Curves and Adjustment Layers are a powerful duo in your color-correcting adventures. Curves provides unmatched precision for color correcting. And Adjustment Layers enable you to change your settings anytime and forever without affecting the image's original pixels.

Working with the Curves Dialog Box

Let's look at the Curves dialog box. At the left in Figure 12.1, you can see its default setup. The default grid within this dialog box has four horizontal and vertical divisions and, also by default, the entire dialog box is set at its smallest view size. You can press Alt(Opt)+click to toggle the grid to the finer setting, as shown to the right of the figure. The more detailed grid makes it easier to describe where you need to place the control points. You can also click the grow box (bottom-right corner) to toggle between large and default sizes of the Curves dialog box.

Also in the figure, you can see the black-to-white gradients at the left and bottom of the grid. The gradient indicates the direction of the curve—in other words, which control point on the curve is associated with the image's highlights, and which control point is associated with the image's darkest areas. You can reverse the gradient (direction of the curve) by clicking the double-arrow at the center of the horizontal gradient.

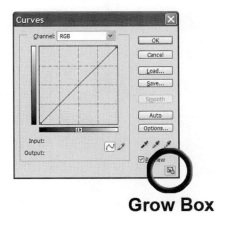

Figure 12.1   The default Curves dialog box, on the left, can be toggled to the larger size, and the grid can be made finer, as shown in the box on the right.

Also, notice the Channel drop-down. You will use this menu to select the different color channels and enter adjustments where needed.

The curve has two control points, one on each end. You can add up to 14 more control points, giving you a total of 16 (unlike the Levels command, which gives you only three adjustments: white point, black point, and gamma). With 16 control points on your curve, you can make your adjustments as specific as changing only 1/16 of the image's entire tonal range.

The following list contains the most important stuff to remember about Curves. Moving the curve causes one of several things to happen in your image:

- In the RGB channel, moving the curve toward the upper-left corner of the graph lightens your image; moving the curve down toward the lower-right corner darkens your image (see Figure 12.2).

12

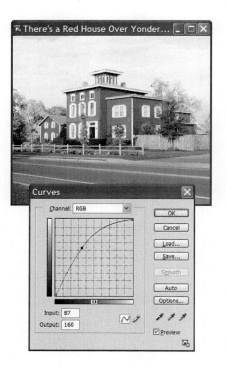

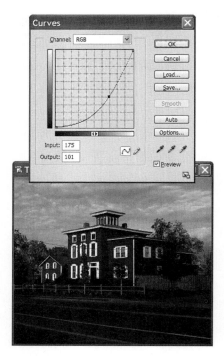

Figure 12.2 You can lighten or darken the tones in an image by moving the curve upward or downward.

- In any of the color channels (Red, Green, or Blue), moving the curve toward the upper-left corner of the graph increases that channel's color (increasing blue in the Blue channel, for example). Any movement of the curve toward the bottom-right corner increases that channel's opposite color (increasing yellow in the Blue channel, for example), as diagrammed in Figure 12.3.

- Moving a corner point of the curve (to make the curve line more vertical) increases the contrast in the image; any flattening of the curve line (making it more horizontal) reduces the contrast (see Figure 12.4).

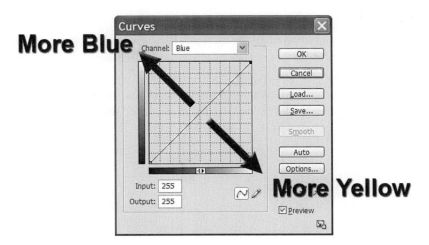

Figure 12.3   Increase a channel's color by moving the curve upward or decrease the color by moving the curve downward.

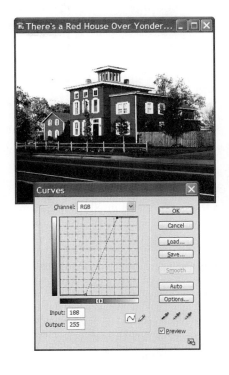

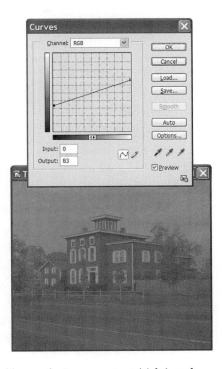

Figure 12.4   Making the curve line more horizontal lowers the image contrast (right); making the curve line more vertical increases the contrast (left).

Using the Color Sampler Tool

The Color Sampler tool (located on the toolbox within the Eyedropper nested toolset) is an invaluable aid for color correction in Photoshop CS. When you select the Color Sampler tool and then click within your image, Photoshop places a Color Sampler where you've clicked. The Color Sampler reads the colors of the pixels in that area of your image. The numerical values of the colors at the location of the sampler are continually displayed in the bottom section of the Info palette.

The Color Sampler tool works just like the Eyedropper in that both read the color values of pixels. And, like the Eyedropper, the Color Sampler enables you to define the area that it reads; you do that in the Sample Size drop-down menu on the Options bar (Point Sample, 3 by 3 Average, and 5 by 5 Average). The difference between the two tools is that when you click a Color Sampler in your image, the sampler stays put (until you remove it or move it, of course!).

Both the Color Sampler tool and Eyedropper read color values far better than your eyes and your perception are able to. Although your eyes can deceive you when evaluating color, the Eyedropper tool reads a color perfectly every time. A line from a song written back in the '60s sums it up quite well: "Believe none of what you hear and half of what you see."

Four factors are worth mentioning here to help you understand why you can't always trust your eyes (and why the Color Sampler tool is such a valuable aid in color correction):

- First, you might describe a particular yellow as banana yellow, and the guy on the corner might describe it as lemon yellow.

- Second, and quite inescapably, your eyes change (read *worsen*) as you age. If you take the industry standard color perception test called the Munsell test today and then again 20 years from now, your score *will* be lower.

- Third, your eyes are subject to a phenomenon referred to as *chromatic adaptation*, which occurs when your eyes adapt to a particular color problem and make it "better" the longer you stare at it. You can easily prove the concept by opening any sample file on the companion CD from this chapter and staring at it for a few minutes. The image will look better and better, almost to the point where you'll think, "The colors look fine." But think again! After you color correct the file and compare the before and after images, you'll fully appreciate the power of chromatic adaptation.

- Finally, your perception of a color is influenced by the surrounding colors. This phenomenon is called *simultaneous contrast.* You can experience this phenomenon by opening the Simultaneous Contrast.psd image from the Examples/

Chap12 folder on the companion CD. The green square at the left is surrounded by a dark blue square and appears brighter and lighter than the green square at the right, which is surrounded by a pale yellow square.

Working Through the Color Correction Examples in This Chapter

The remaining sections of this chapter describe six different stepped procedures for correcting color using Curves and Adjustment Layers. The procedures for correcting the colors in most of the sample images are to remove any color cast in the white and in the black areas, enter any other needed color changes, and then adjust the tonal range. At the end of each procedure, you will view the before and after versions of the image to see the dramatic improvement that you've created.

If you read books like I do, you like to skip around. In this case, if you are not familiar with Curves, I strongly recommend that you read the next section of this chapter and complete the steps within it. That section contains a lot of specific information on how to use Curves and the Info palette and lays a foundation for the remaining examples. In other words, as the chapter progresses, the complexity of the color adjustments increases and the explanations on how to complete certain tasks decrease.

Applying Minor Corrections with a Curves Adjustment Layer

Okay, enough scientific stuff, let's have some fun with Photoshop.

In the following exercise, you will place two Color Samplers in the image, one for the highlight and the other for the shadow. Then you will create a Curves Adjustment Layer and correct the colors in the image using the numbers in the Info palette as your guide. Your goal in this exercise is to remove any color cast in the whites and shadows, thereby correcting the colors within the entire tonal range.

Applying Minor Curves Corrections

1. Open the Crew.psd image from the Examples/Chap12 folder on the companion CD. (Before your eyes are influenced by chromatic adaptation, can you see what colors need adjusting in this image?)

2. Press the **F** key one time for the Full Screen Mode with Menu Bar. Hold down the Ctrl(⌘)+spacebar to toggle to the Zoom (in) tool, and click four times on the fourth guy from the left. This view is ideal for easy placement of the two Color Samplers. From the main menu, choose Window, Info to show the Info palette (you might need to drag the palette's tab into your workspace if it's currently in the docking well).

3. From the toolbox, choose the Color Sampler tool (click and hold on the Eyedropper to show the set of nested tools, and choose the Color Sampler from the flyout). In the Options bar, be sure that 3 by 3 Average is selected for the Sample Size.

4. Click once on the white area of the crew member's upper back. To place the second Color Sampler, click once on the posterior of the guy to the immediate left of guy you placed the first Color Sampler on. See Figure 12.5 for these locations. At the bottom of the Info palette, notice that each of the Color Sampler readings is listed.

12

Figure 12.5   Click the first Color Sampler in the white area on the guy's back, and click the second Color Sampler on the seat of the guy to the immediate left. Be sure that 3 by 3 Average is chosen for the Sample Size in the Options bar.

5. Press Ctrl(⌘)+0 (zero) to zoom the image to fit on your screen. You should view the entire image when adjusting the colors.

6. At the bottom of the Layers palette (Window, Layers), click the Create new fill or adjustment layer icon (third from the right), and choose Curves from the menu. The Curves dialog box appears. If needed, drag the box to a corner of your screen so that you can see most of the image and the Info palette.

7. Look at the #1 RGB numbers at the bottom left of the Info palette. Your numbers should be close to R:251, G:255, B:238. Although red and green are fairly close in value, the blues are way down, meaning that in the highlights of Color Sampler #1, yellow (the opposite of blue) is too high.

8. Click on the Channel drop-down, and choose Blue from the menu. Because the highlights are what you're correcting here, click on the top control point on the curve (at the upper right), and drag the point directly left until the B: value in the Info palette is closer in value (within 2 or 3) to the R: and G: values (see Figure 12.6).

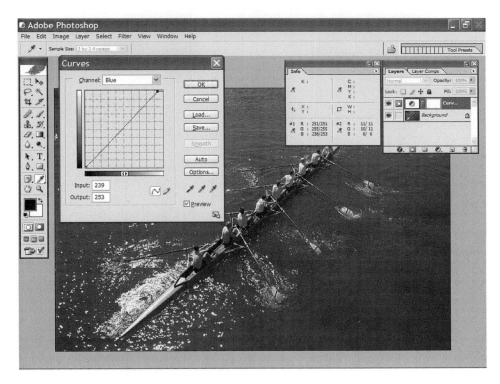

Figure 12.6   Move the top-right control point (white value) to the left until the B: value in the Info palette for the #1 Color Sampler is closer in value to the other two colors.

Insider

Giving you exact numbers to aim for in the Info palette would be misleading. The exact location where you place your Color Samplers might not be exactly where I placed my Color Samplers. Therefore, guidelines such as "Bring the values of the numbers closer together" serve you well in color adjusting.

Also, a value spread of only 1 or 2 between the three colors is not critical for the sample images.

9. While you're in the Blue channel, look at the #2 Sampler readout in the Info
    palette (at the bottom right). Your blue value is most likely lower than the red
    and green values. In the Curves graph, click on the bottom-left control point
    (black value), and drag the point directly upward until the B: value in the Info
    palette is close to the other two values, as shown in Figure 12.7.

Insider

You can also use the arrow keys to move a control point. For a small Curves movement
such as described in step 9, you might find using the arrow keys easier.

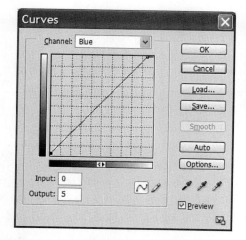
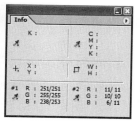

Figure 12.7   Move the black control point for the Blue channel upward to remove the slight
amount of yellow in this tonal range.

10. If the R: value for your #1 Sampler is 2 or more points lower than the other col-
    ors, click the Channel drop-down in the Curves dialog box, and choose Red.
    Then click the white control point (top right) on the graph, and press the left-
    arrow key once or twice.

11. Now that you have removed the color cast in the highlights and shadows, the
    final correction for this image is to adjust the entire tonal range using the RGB
    channel. Click on the Channel drop-down, and choose RGB from the menu.

12. The #2 readout in the Info palette is for the black areas in the image, and those
    numbers should be closer to 0 (zero). Click the bottom-left control point in the
    Curves graph, and drag the point directly to the right until the #2 values are 3 or
    lower.

13. Now make one last adjustment for the tonal range. Click on the curve at the cen-
    ter of the graph. This point affects the midtones. Drag the middle point upward

and to the left approximately one half of a grid box to lighten the midtones (see Figure 12.8). Click on OK.

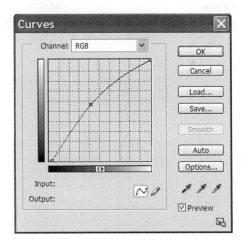

Figure 12.8   Lighten the image by moving the center of the curve upward and to the left.

14. With the Color Sampler as the active tool, hold down the Alt(Opt) key, and click on each of the two Color Samplers to remove them from the image. Hold down the spacebar, and click and drag in the image to move its view so that most of the image is unobstructed by palettes and the toolbox.

15. On the Layers palette, click the Curves 1 visibility icon (the eye icon) off and on to see the before and after versions of the image after making your Curves adjustments (see Figure 12.9). Your final image should be lighter, bluer, and contain more contrast than the original. In fact, more dimensional is another accurate description. Good work!

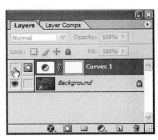

16. Close the image without saving (unless you want to save it)!

Figure 12.9   Turn off and on the Adjustment Layer's visibility to see the significant changes you made using Curves.

You just corrected the colors in an image that many would say looked fine with its original colors. But, after entering a few adjustments, you can clearly see a significant improvement.

Coming up around the next curve is an explanation of how to correct the colors in an image in which every pixel is biased by a strong, dominant color.

Finding and Removing the Dominant Color's Influence

Photoshop users who are familiar with the selection tools might be tempted to select the areas that are affected by the color cast and then remove the cast only in those selected areas. But that technique is counter-productive because a color cast affects the entire image, and the entire image benefits from removing the offending color. Yes, certain situations or specific effects require the selecting and correcting of certain areas of the image (as you will see later in this chapter). But for most images with a color cast, you should resist the temptation to color correct specific areas.

The sample image in the following set of steps is a photo of a very, very red sunset with trees and buildings silhouetted in the foreground. The trees and buildings are biased toward the overwhelming color of the red sky and need to be made black.

Removing a Color Cast

1. Open the Sunset.psd image from the Examples/Chap12 folder on the companion CD. (Before your eyes are influenced by chromatic adaptation, can you see what colors need adjusting in this image?)

Insider

A blazing sunset (or sunrise!) always makes an eye-catching photograph. But often the extensive reddish hues throughout the image actually tint areas that should not contain any reds, as you can see in the shadow and black areas.

2. From the toolbox, choose the Color Sampler tool. Check to be sure that 3 by 3 Average is currently selected for Sample Size in the Options bar.

3. Click once on the almost-black area at the bottom-right corner of the image to place a Color Sampler there. The Info palette appears, and the color values for the Color Sampler you just placed are shown at the bottom left of the palette (see Figure 12.10).

Insider

If your Info palette opened from within the Options bar, drag the palette by the tab into your workspace. You need this palette to be continually visible.

4. The RGB values in your Info palette for #1 should be 41, 6, and 6, respectively (give or take 1 or 2 for each color). These numbers indicate that green and blue are equal, but that red is way too high. This area of the image is supposed to be black, and all color values should be equal and near 0 (zero). Drag the image by the title bar to the bottom-right area of your workspace to make room for the Curves dialog box.

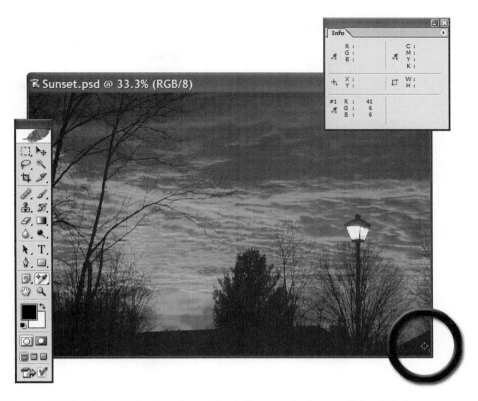

Figure 12.10   Place a Color Sampler on the dark area at the bottom right of the image.

5. At the bottom of the Layers palette, click the Create new fill or adjustment layer icon (third from the right), and choose Curves from the menu. Drag the Curves dialog box to the upper left of your workspace. Again, you want to see most of the image while color correcting.

6. You need to adjust red, so from the Channel drop-down, choose Red.

7. The Color Sampler is in an area that should be black, so on the curve, click the bottom-left control point (the black control point) to make it active. You need to reduce red, and to accomplish that, you need to move the control point to the right. Click and drag the point directly to the right until the R: value in the Info palette is equal to the G: and B: values (see Figure 12.11).

8. Now that you've removed the offending color cast from the image, it's time to adjust the tonal range of the image. In the Curves dialog box, choose RGB from the Channel drop-down.

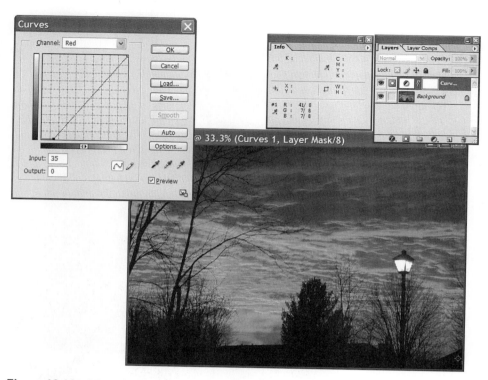

Figure 12.11   Move the black control point in the Red channel to the right until the R: value equals those of the G: and B: values for the #1 Color Sampler in the Info palette.

9. The details in the clouds near the top of the image can be better revealed if the midtones are made slightly lighter. Click on the curve nearest the center of the grid, and drag the point upward and to the left about one half of a grid box, as shown in Figure 12.12.

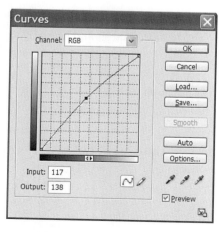

Figure 12.12   Lighten the midtones by moving the middle of the curve upward and to the left.

10. Now make one more movement of the curve. The RGB values for the Color Sampler, as shown in the Info palette, are a bit high for black. Click and drag the black point (bottom-left point) directly to the right until the RGB values are anywhere between 0 and 3. Click on OK (see Figure 12.13).

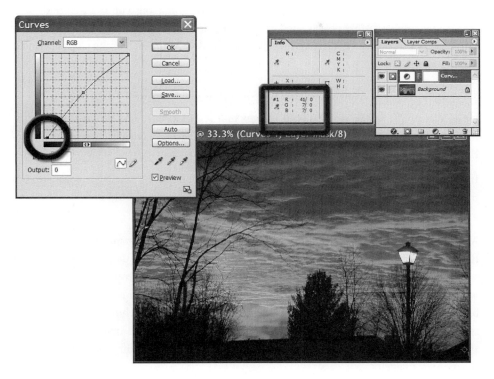

Figure 12.13   The current RGB values in the Info palette for the Color Sampler are too high for black and need to be reduced to around 0 to 3.

11. With the Color Sampler tool still active, hold down the Alt(Opt) key, and click on the Color Sampler in the image to remove it.

12. It's time to compare the before and after versions of your color correcting. In the Layers palette, click the visibility icon off and on for the Curves 1 Adjustment Layer.

   The areas that are supposed to be black are now black. And the sky contains more cyan (the opposite of red) in the shadows, as it would naturally.

13. After you're finished admiring your work, close the image. **Tip:** Save this image to your hard drive for future reference.

You just removed a color cast that affected the entire image. The method you used to find the offending color and the intensity of that color was to sample an area of the image that should show equal values for all three of the RGB colors—which, for the Sunset image, is the area that should be black.

So far, you have applied minor Curves corrections (for a big color difference!) and removed a color cast that was created by a strong, dominant color. Let's advance further into Curves and work with an image that needs adjustments in each of the color channels.

Applying Corrections in Each of the Color Channels

Up to this point, you've worked with images that required only one or two adjustments in the color channels. More often than not, though, images require corrections in all three of the color channels.

In the following set of steps, you'll learn a technique for quickly identifying the areas of the image that should be black and the areas of the image that should be white by using a Threshold Adjustment Layer.

Also, you will apply a finishing touch to the image by using the Unsharp Mask (yes, that title and the filter's purpose are kinda oxymoronic!). In fact, you'll use the Unsharp Mask on all the remaining sample images. Every photograph that is brought into the digital world benefits from a sharpening filter. We will use the Unsharp Mask because it's the best of Photoshop's four sharpening filters and the professional's choice. The sharpening is applied after the color correcting because, in many cases, the image actually looks sharper after the colors have been adjusted, and the last thing you want to do is over-sharpen an image!

Adjusting Curves in Every Channel

1. Open the Boats.psd image from the Examples/Chap12 folder on the companion CD. (As in the previous sets of steps, before your eyes are influenced by chromatic adaptation, can you see what colors need adjusting in this image?)

2. At the bottom of the Layers palette, click the Create new fill or adjustment layer icon, and choose Threshold from the menu. The Boats.psd image immediately becomes black and white with no gray tones.

Insider

You're going to use the Threshold command to quickly find the area in the image that should be adjusted to be black and the area that should be adjusted to be white.

3. Drag the Threshold slider to the right so that the Threshold level reads 225 (see Figure 12.14). The deck closest to the camera (starboard deck, for those boaters among you) of the boat in the foreground appears to be the best location for the white value (see Figure 12.14). This is the place where you will place one Color Sampler.

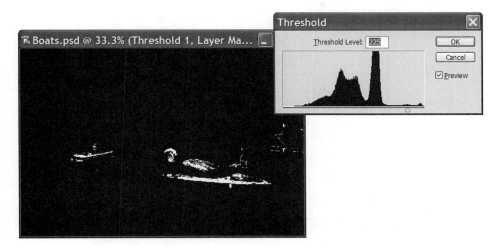

Figure 12.14   The deck of the boat in the foreground is the ideal location to place the Color Sampler to measure and adjust for the white value in the image.

4. Now drag the slider at the bottom of the Threshold histogram to the left until the image has at least one credible black area (around 60 in the Threshold Level field). The best area to adjust to black is at the bottom-right corner, under the dock (see Figure 12.15). (You can uncheck Preview to see the original image and identify this location.) Click on OK.

Insider

"Credible black area" means any area that should actually be black in the image. This area is often a medium to large dark shadow or a black object, and should not be tiny specks of black.

You are leaving this Threshold Adjustment Layer in the Layers palette to help you locate exactly where to place the first Color Sampler, and then you will delete that Adjustment Layer.

5. From the toolbox, choose the Color Sampler tool, and click once at the center of the triangular-shaped black area under the dock (shown in Figure 12.14) to place the #1 Color Sampler.

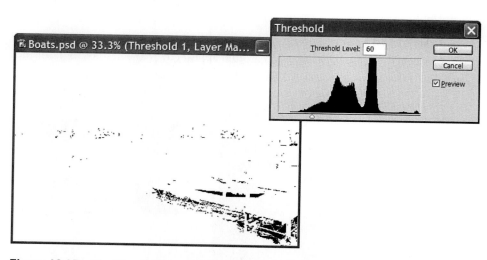

Figure 12.15   The Threshold command can quickly reveal the darkest area(s) in the image that should be black.

Note

> **Placing Color Samplers**   Be sure to place all Color Samplers in areas larger than the Sample Size that you've specified in the Options bar. Here, use 3 by 3 Average.

6. In the Layers palette, drag the Threshold 1 Adjustment Layer to the trash icon at the bottom right of the palette. Hold down the Ctrl(⌘)+spacebar to toggle to the Zoom (in) tool, and click three times over the boat in the foreground. With this zoomed-in view, you can more accurately place the next Color Sampler. Click once in the center of the white edge of the boat's deck, as shown in Figure 12.16. Be careful not to click on the strip of red.

7. Press Ctrl(⌘)+0 (zero) to zoom the image to fit on your screen. Drag the image by the title bar to the lower-right corner of your workspace to make room for the Curves dialog box.

   Now that you have one Color Sampler located on an area for the black tone and one on an area for the white tone, click the Create new fill or adjustment layer icon, and choose Curves from the menu. Drag the Curves dialog box to an area of your workspace that allows you to see most of the image.

8. Start by looking at the #1 readout in the Info palette (the black area in the photo). Although the spread is actually quite close (my numbers are R:40, G:42, B:39), a very slight adjustment in the green channel will tighten the spread. Choose Green from the Channel drop-down. Click once on the black control point (bottom-left corner), and nudge the point directly right by using the right-arrow key until the G: value is identical to either of the other colors.

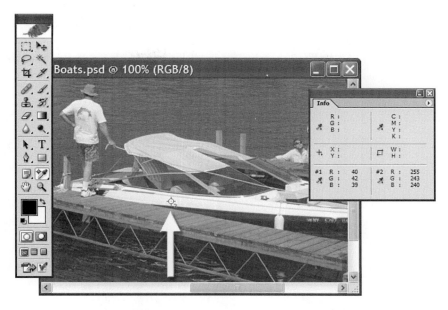

Figure 12.16   Click the Color Sampler tool on the (almost) white area of the boat.

While you're in the Green channel, check the #2 readout in the Info palette to see whether any adjustments are needed. If your numbers are like mine (and most likely they are!), the green value falls in the middle of the spread, so no green adjustment is needed for the highlight.

9. Choose Red from the Channel drop-down. The #2 readout in the Info palette shows that red is substantially higher than the other colors. The #2 readout represents the highlight in the image, so click the top-right control point in the Curves graph, and drag it straight downward until the R: value equals the G: value.

10. Choose Blue from the Channel drop-down. Click the top-right control point to make it active, and then use the left-arrow key to nudge the point until the B: value is equal to either of the other colors in the #2 readout.

11. Now it's time to adjust the tonal range of the entire image. Choose RGB from the Channel drop-down in the Curves dialog box. Click the black control point (bottom-left point), and drag it directly right until the values for the #1 readout are 5 or less.

Now click the white control point (top-right point), and drag it directly left until the values for the #2 readout are 255.

12 (margin)

12. The image needs to be slightly lightened. Click a control point on the curve at the center of the grid, and drag it upward and to the left about one fourth of a grid. Figure 12.17 shows what the Curves dialog box and Info palette should look like after you complete this step.

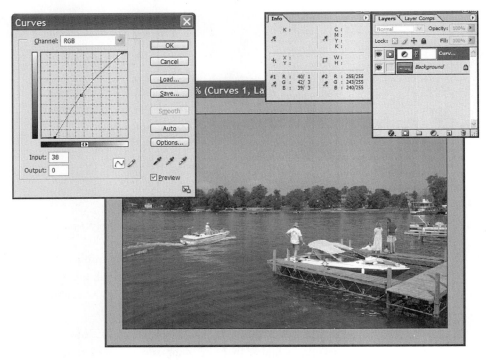

Figure 12.17   Adjust the tonal range of the image by moving the curve in the RGB channel.

13. You're ready for a final check on the color adjustments you've applied so far. You have adjusted the curves for the white and black points and for the tonal range in the composite (RGB) channel, but you have not looked at the midtones. Can you find a midtone area in the image that gives clues as to whether any adjustments are needed?

    The wood for the dock is not as neutral in color as it should be. Drag your cursor (which is now an eyedropper) to the widest area of the dock. The upper-left section of the Info palette displays the RGB values for the place where your cursor is in the image. For the wood, the green value is much lower than the other two colors (see Figure 12.18). In other words, this image has way too much magenta in its midtones.

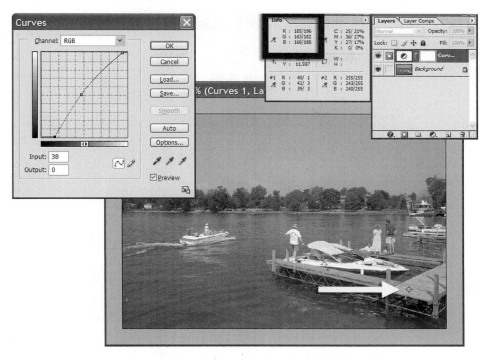

Figure 12.18 While the Curves dialog box is still open, you can rest the eyedropper cursor over an area in the image and see the RGB values in the Info palette.

14. Choose Green from the Channel drop-down in the Curves dialog box. Click on the curve at the center of the grid to place a control point there. Using the left- and up-arrow keys, nudge the control point upward and to the left until the color of the wood is more neutral (about two presses of each key should do the trick).

15. After you complete step 14, notice what has happened to the G: value for the #1 readout in the Info palette: The value has increased. Let's reduce the value and finish this color correction.

    Click on the black control point (bottom left) in the Green channel, and using the right-arrow key, nudge the point until the G: value is equal to either of the other colors. Click on OK.

16. Time to apply the finishing touch: the Unsharp Mask. Click on the Background layer in the Layers palette (you want to sharpen the image, not the Adjustment Layer!). From the main menu choose, Filter, Sharpen, Unsharp Mask. Enter the following numbers: Amount: **74%**, Radius: **1.3** pixels, and Threshold: **0** levels (see Figure 12.19). Click on OK.

12

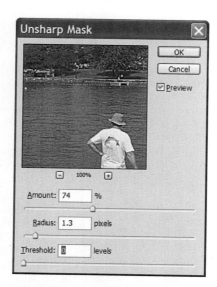

Figure 12.19   These settings for the Unsharp Mask work well to sharpen the boat's image.

17. Now check out your work. In the Layers palette, click the visibility icon off and on for the Curves 1 Adjustment Layer to see the before and after versions of this image. The after image turned a flat, magenta day at the lake into a bright, blue day—a perfect day for boating!

When you're finished admiring your work, close the image with or without saving.

As a reminder, the sequence for correcting the colors in most images is to remove any color cast in the white and in the black areas, enter any other needed color changes, and then adjust the tonal range.

Let's take another curve in the road and look at a valuable technique: adding detail to a specific color by increasing that color's contrast.

Creating Contrast in a Color Channel

As stated near the beginning of this chapter, any movement of the curve toward a vertical angle adds contrast. Normally, we think of adding contrast to the entire image, the RGB channel.

When contrast is created in a color channel, however, the most obvious effect is an increase in detail in the object(s) of that particular color. This increased detail is especially helpful when the object contains many shades of red, green, or blue, as in the following sample image.

Creating Contrast in a Color Channel

1. Open the Tree in Autumn.psd image from the Examples/Chap12 folder on the companion CD. As in the previous sets of steps, before your eyes are influenced by chromatic adaptation, check to see what color adjustments this image is screaming for.

2. Let's find the areas in the image that should be white and black. From the main menu, choose Image, Adjustments, Threshold. Drag the slider to the left to about 34 in the Threshold Level field. For an area to adjust for black, the shadow from the half-barrel appears to be the best location (see Figure 12.20).

   Now, to find the area for white, drag the Threshold slider to the right to about 230. Okay, so the white picket fence was a give-away; we could have figured that out on our own. Click on Cancel, and remember these two areas!

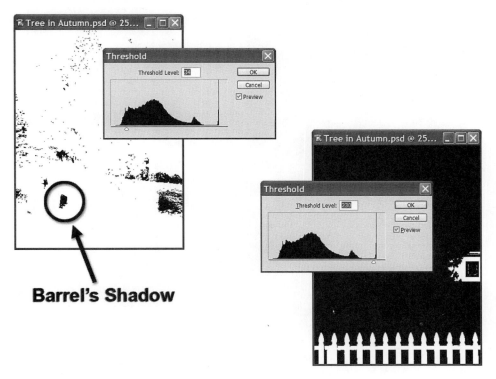

Barrel's Shadow

Figure 12.20   The barrel's shadow and the picket fence are ideal locations to adjust to black and to white, respectively.

3. Choose the Color Sampler tool from the toolbox, and click once in the center of the shadow that the barrel casts and once in the center of a white area on the picket fence.

4. At the bottom of the Layers palette, click the Create new fill or adjustment layer icon, and choose Curves.

5. In the Info palette, the #1 readout shows that blue is too low. So, in the Curves dialog box, choose Blue from the Channel drop-down; then click and drag the lower-left control point directly upward until the spread between all three numbers is only 1 or 2.

   While you're in the Blue channel, look at the #2 readout (for the white area in the image) in the Info palette. You need to adjust blue here also. Click the control point for white (upper-right point), and drag it directly left until its value equals the other two colors. Your Curves dialog box and Info palette should look like the ones in Figure 12.21.

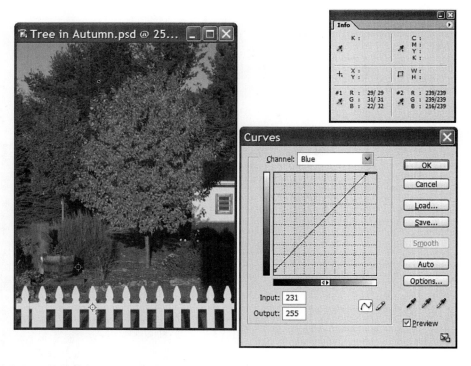

Figure 12.21   After you adjust the black and white points in the Blue channel, the yellow color cast is removed from the image.

6. You're now going to add contrast to the Red channel in the midtone range. Remember, moving the curve to a more vertical angle increases contrast, so to add contrast to only the midtones, you will create a slight S-shaped curve. Choose the Red channel. Click two points on the curve, one point being three vertical gridlines from the left edge of the grid and one point being three vertical gridlines from the right edge (see Figure 12.22).

Insider

Adding contrast within a color channel brings out detail in that color range within an image. We want to add contrast to the reds in our sample image because the leaves in the main subject (the tree) contain mostly red, and we like bold, saturated colors—in this example anyway!

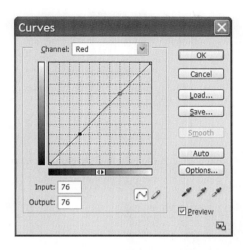

Figure 12.22   Place two control points on the curve at the locations shown here.

7. One at a time, click on each control point, and move them to create a gentle S-shape.

   Notice the red values for the #1 and #2 readouts in the Info palette shift after you create the S-curve. Click on the bottom-left control point, and move it straight upward until the R: value is within 1 or 2 of the other color values. Then click the upper-right control point in the Curves graph, and move it straight downward until the R: value is equal to the other two colors. Your Curves dialog box and Info palette should look like the ones in Figure 12.23.

8. Now that you've corrected the colors, adjusting the tonal range is next. Choose RGB from the Channel drop-down. Click the black control point (lower-left point), and drag it directly to the right until the values in the #1 readout in the Info palette are around 5 or less. Next, click the white control point (upper-right point), and drag it directly to the left until the values read 255 (see Figure 12.24).

9. You should notice that the image darkened substantially in the midtones. To correct this problem, click on the curve at the center of the grid, and move the control point upward and to the left about one half of a grid box. Click on OK to close the Curves dialog box.

12

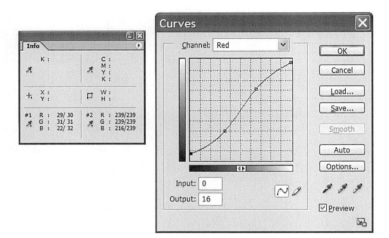

Figure 12.23   Create a slight S-curve to the line, and then re-adjust the black and white values in the Red channel.

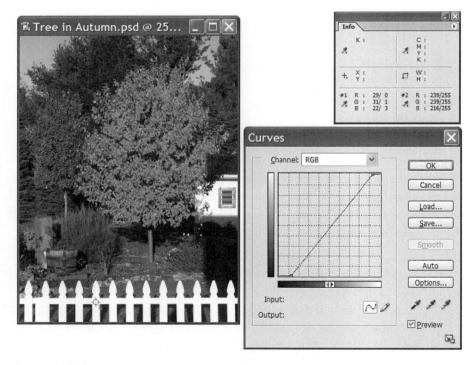

Figure 12.24   Move the image's darkest and lightest tones to black and white values.

10. With the Color Sampler tool still active, hold down the Alt(Opt) key, and click on each of the Color Samplers in the image to remove them.

11. You'll now apply sharpening to add the finishing touch to this image. On the Layers palette, click the Background layer so that the filter is applied to the image, not the Curves 1 layer. From the main menu, choose Filter, Sharpen, Unsharp Mask.

    Notice in the preview window that the colors of the tree are the original colors; the preview window does not include the Curves Adjustment Layer, only the active layer. And because color correcting visually sharpens the image, you need to watch the effects of your settings in the image itself. So, hold down the Ctrl(⌘)+spacebar keys to toggle to the Zoom (in) tool, and click two times in the image over the tree. At this view, you are better able to see the preview of the effects of your settings.

12. Although the amount of sharpening is a matter of personal choice, here are the settings and the reasons for the numbers I recommend in this step. First, move the Threshold to 0. Generally, you use a high Threshold setting for images that contain very little detail—the opposite of the Tree in Autumn image. Next, move the Radius setting to 1.3. Most images, except low-resolution images, benefit from a Radius setting between 1 and 2. Finally, move the Amount setting to about 147. The Amount determines the power of the Unsharp Mask, and 147 seems to work well for this image. When your Unsharp Mask dialog box looks like the one shown in Figure 12.25, click on OK.

Figure 12.25 These settings for the Unsharp Mask reveal the detail in the trees.

13. Press Ctrl(⌘)+0 (zero) to zoom the image to fit on your screen.

14. Now take a look at your work. In the Layers palette, click the visibility icon off and on for the Curves 1 Adjustment Layer to see the before and after versions of this image. The after version shows much more accurate colors and contrast.

15. When you're finished admiring your work, close the image with or without saving.

There's quite a difference in your before and after versions, isn't there? The white fence is white, the image has a full range of tones, and the red tree shows a lot more detail. In fact, the treetop no longer looks like a large clump of out-of-focus leaves; the differentiation between each leaf is much more obvious.

The topic around the next curve solves the problem of how to color correct an image that needs two individual color corrections in each of two areas of the image. Sometimes applying the same Curve adjustment to the entire image does not bring out the best in the image and a separate color adjustment is needed for each area.

Applying Curves to Selected Areas

Color correcting purists shun the thought of selecting areas in an image and applying local corrections. Their reasoning is sound, though: What's wrong in one part of the image affects the entire image even though it might not be obvious. However, paradigms are being broken almost daily in this age of ever-improving digital imaging software. My approach is this: Use whatever tools you have to improve the image as much as possible.

The sample image for the next set of steps contains two areas that have distinctly different color and tonality problems. Applying the same Curves correction to the entire image would not yield the best possible image. Therefore, you will select each area, one at a time, and then apply a color correction for that area only.

Adjusting the Color in Selected Areas

1. Open the Subway.psd image from the Examples/Chap12 folder on the companion CD. This time-lapse photo was taken just as a subway train was entering a Washington, D.C., station. As in the previous sets of steps, take a moment to decide what's wrong with the colors and tonal range of this image.

Insider

Here's a hint: The contrast is way too low, the concrete walls should be neutral in color, and the floor should be red.

2. Press the **F** key once for the Full Screen Mode with Menu Bar. Hold down the Ctrl(⌘) key; then press the + (plus) key one time to zoom in one step. You will use the Polygon Lasso tool to select areas outside the image, so you'll need this extra space around the image.

3. Choose the Polygon Lasso tool from the toolbox (if needed, click and hold on the Lasso tool to open the nested set). Use the Polygon Lasso tool to select the tile floor. To accomplish this, first click outside the left edge of the image where the tile floor meets that edge of the image; then, in a clockwise direction, click at each corner to follow the shape of the floor (see Figure 12.26). Although you should do your best to follow the edge of the tile floor, precision is not critical here.

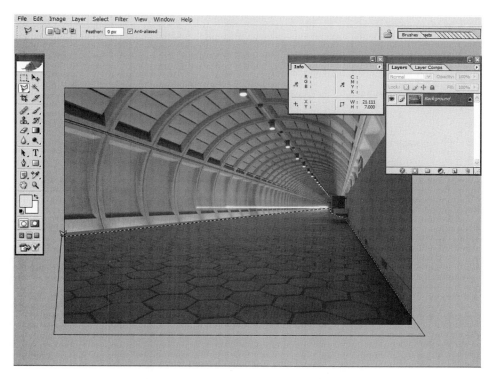

Figure 12.26   Start your selection outside the image, follow all the edges of the tile floor, and then select outside the image again to return to your first click location.

4. At the bottom of the Layers palette, click the Create new fill or adjustment layer icon, and choose Curves from the list. Move the Curves dialog box so that you can see the entire tile floor.

5. The floor is way too green, so choose Green from the Channel drop-down. Click two control points on the curve so that the curve contains three somewhat equal sections.

You need to move both control points downward to remove the green in the floor. Because most of the tonal range is dark, pull the left control point that you added down a little further than the other point. Be sure to use Figure 12.27 as a guide!

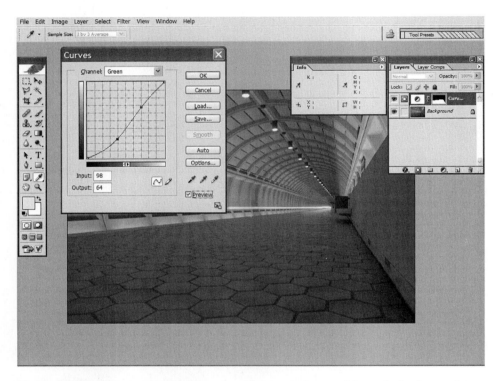

Figure 12.27   This curve in the Green channel removes the greenish cast in the floor and especially in the darker tones.

6. Now the floor needs a little extra red and then an overall tonal adjustment. Choose Red from the Channel drop-down. Click one control point on the curve at the center of the grid, and move it up and to the left about one fourth of a grid box.

7. Next, choose RGB from the Channel drop-down, and add some contrast and lighten the midtones. To accomplish this, click on the top-right point (the white point), and move it directly left about one half of a grid box. Now click the black point (bottom-left corner), and move it directly to the right to the next vertical gridline. Then click on the curve at the center of the graph, and move the point up and to the left about one half of a grid box. Be sure to use the curve shown in Figure 12.28 as a guide for your curve. Then click on OK.

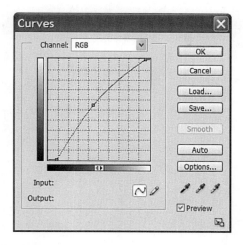

Figure 12.28   This curve setting adds contrast and lightens the midtones in the floor area.

8. For most of the remaining steps, you will correct the colors for the wall areas. The quickest method for making a selection of the wall is to Ctrl(⌘)+ click on the Curves 1 layer mask in the Layers palette (to load the mask of the floor as a selection). Then press Ctrl(⌘)+Shift+I to inverse the selection (or from the main menu, choose Select, Inverse).

Warning

> **Working with artificial light**   A fair warning is due here: Any scene lit by artificial light will show a color cast when photographed. In this sample image, the color cast is green and yellow and is difficult to correct. So, because concrete is naturally a neutral color and we would attempt to keep the color spread as small as possible, due to the extreme color cast, we can accept a spread as high as 8 or 10.

9. Choose the Color Sampler from the toolbox. You need to place all four Color Samplers in the image and at various tonal ranges. Rather than describe the exact location for each of the Samplers, I refer you to Figure 12.29. Be sure that the order of your clicks matches those in the figure (for example, your first click should be where the #1 Sampler is in the figure).

10. Create a new Curves Adjustment Layer, and then move the dialog box so that you can easily see the wall area.

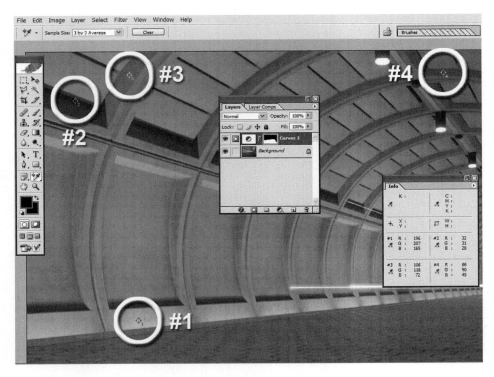

Figure 12.29 Click to add Color Samplers in the locations and the order shown here (the view of the image was zoomed in to help show the locations).

11. For each of the Color Samplers you placed in the image, you need a control point on the color channels in the Curves dialog box. So, hold down the Ctrl(⌘)+Shift keys, and click one time on each of the Color Samplers in your image. (The control points will not show in the RGB channel, only in each of the color channels.)

12. The procedure for adjusting the colors is to reduce the color value spread for one Color Sampler readout in the Info palette at a time and then move to another Sampler readout. Begin with the #1 Color Sampler.

The #1 readout in the Info palette shows that green needs to be reduced. So, in the Curves dialog box, choose the Green channel. To find which control point represents the #1 readout, click in the image directly over the #1 Color Sampler, and note where on the curve a circle appears. Now, on the Curves graph, drag that control point associated with the #1 readout downward and to the right until the G: value in the Info palette is within 8 or so of the R: value.

13. Next, notice that the B: value (in the #1 readout) is much lower than the other colors. In the Curves dialog box, choose the Blue channel. Notice that the control

point representing the #1 readout (it's a black dot) was selected when you adjusted the corresponding control point in the Green channel. Click and drag that control point upward and to the left until the B: value is close to the other two colors. Figure 12.30 shows what the Green and Blue curves and the Info palette look like after you complete this step.

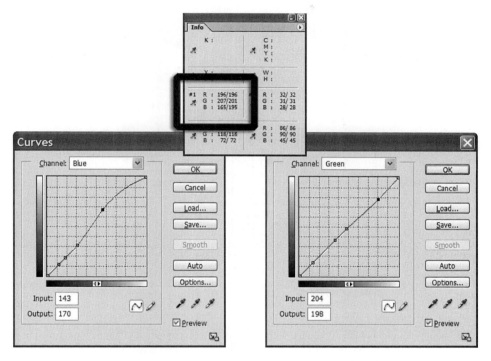

Figure 12.30   After you complete step 13, the Green and Blue curves and #1 readout in the Info palette should look similar to those shown here.

14. The values in the #2 readout are close enough already and do not need any adjustments. So, work with the values in the #3 readout, and use the same procedure described in the preceding step to reduce the color spread. Continue this procedure for the #4 readout in the Info palette. After you complete this step, your Info palette and the Blue and Green curves should look very similar to those shown in Figure 12.31.

Note

> **Moving control points**   You might find making small adjustments to the location of the control points is easier when you use the arrow keys. Also, after you move one control point, the readout in the Info palette for a color you have already adjusted might change. If this happens, move that control point again as needed.

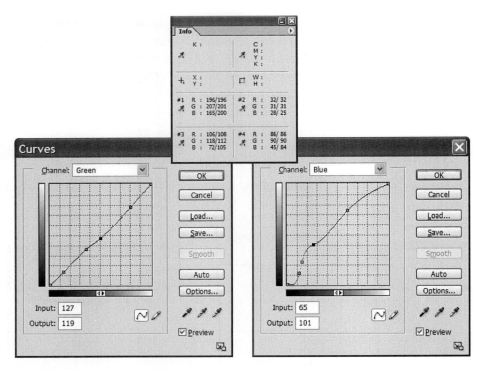

Figure 12.31   The color cast created by the artificial lighting as rendered on film requires a lot of finagling of the curves—something not possible with any of Photoshop's other color adjusting commands.

15. It's time to adjust the tonal range in the wall area. Contrast needs to be added, and the midtones need to be slightly lightened. Choose the RGB channel in the Curves dialog box. To add contrast, lighten the lightest values by dragging the white control point (upper-right point) directly to the left to the first vertical gridline.

16. Next, darken the darkest tones by dragging the black control point (lower-left point) directly to the right about one half of a grid box. Then click on the curve at the center of the graph, and drag it upward and to the left about one fourth of a grid box. Refer to Figure 12.32 for the locations of these control points. Click on OK. Whew, that completes the color correcting for those dingy green walls!

17. Hold down the Alt(Opt) key, and click on each of the four Color Samplers to delete them. On the Layers palette, click the Background layer to make it active for editing. From the main menu, choose Filter, Sharpen, Unsharp Mask. For the Amount, enter **102**; for the Radius, enter **2.0**; and for the Threshold, enter **0**. Click on OK.

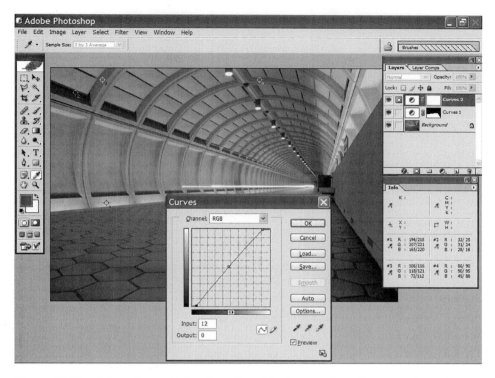

Figure 12.32   After color correcting the walls and in the RGB channel, increase the contrast and lighten the midtones.

18. Let's set up the Layers palette so that viewing the before and after color corrections requires only one mouse click. Click on the Curves 2 layer, and then link this layer with the Curves 1 layer (click in the empty box in the column second from the left on the Curves 1 layer). From the Layers palette menu (opened by clicking the triangle located at the upper-right corner of the palette), choose New Set From Linked (see Figure 12.33), and click on OK.

19. Now check your work. In the Layers palette, click the visibility icon off and on for Set 1. The after version shows much more accurate colors and contrast. The Curves corrections you created required advanced skills. Good work!

20. You can close your image at any time, but I highly recommend that you save this image with your color corrections to your hard drive for future reference!

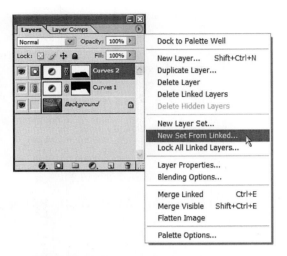

Figure 12.33   Placing the two Adjustment Layers into one Layer Set enables you to toggle on and off only one visibility icon to view before and after versions.

You just completed the most difficult Curves color correction in this chapter and the assignment that contains the most significant difference between the before and after versions. Good work!

Now let's take the last curve in the road and cover one more topic: using Curves to create *in*correct colors!

Using Curves for Special Effects

You can do more with Curves than correct the colors and the tonal range in photographs. You can take the color correction in the opposite direction and make the colors very incorrect! In fact, you can distort colors in ways that only the Curves command can create; no other Photoshop command or filter can create the whacked-out colors that Curves can!

In the following short set of steps, you will apply a curve setting that greatly distorts the colors in a photograph of the front of an antique car. Afterwards, you are encouraged to experiment on your own.

Creating Special Effects with Curves

1. Open the Ford Greyhound.psd image from the Examples/Chap12 folder on the companion CD.

2. Click the Create new fill or adjustment layer icon at the bottom of the Layers palette, and choose Curves from the menu.

3. In the Curves dialog box, drag the black control point (bottom-left point) straight up to the top-left corner of the graph. Next, click a control point at the middle of the curve, halfway between the white and black control points. Do not move this point; it is needed to anchor the curve at that location.

4. One at a time, click on the curve halfway between two of the current control points, and drag straight down to the bottom of the graph. The shape of the curve should look like the letter *W* (see Figure 12.34).

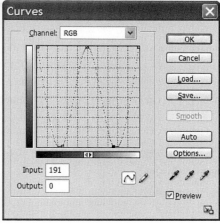

Figure 12.34   Although the effect is hard to see in this black-and-white figure, unconventional curve shapes can distort colors like no other Photoshop command.

5. Continue experimenting with the shape of the curve in the RGB channel as well as in each of the color channels.

6. Close the image.

Before the advent of digital imaging, achieving the kind of color special effects you just created required hand-painting and a lot of time! Now, in a matter of minutes, you can create wonderful effects and change the settings for those effects anytime you want!

We now come to the end of this chapter and using Curves and Adjustment Layers. Actually, you don't need to bring your time in Curves to an end. While the techniques discussed here are still fresh in your memory, I strongly recommend that you take a more critical look at some of those photos that you thought contained perfect color and apply some curves!

Summary

In this chapter, you started by working with an image that needed only minor Curves adjustments, yet the result of those corrections produced a significantly better image. Then you progressed through more difficult color problems and successfully corrected each one.

Now that you understand the fundamental concepts of using Curves to adjust colors in an image, you are well on your way to correcting your own images. Seeing the before and after versions of the sample images gave you a more critical eye for correct and incorrect color in your own photographs. Now it's time to make your own curves!

12

Chapter 13

Keeping Up Appearances: Techniques for Retouching Images

I call this project "Keeping Up Appearances"…after all, it's often said that appearances are everything!

In this chapter, you'll learn

- How to assess an image for retouching
- How to improve overall color
- How to remove unwanted image elements
- How to use color to enhance image elements
- How to add new elements to the image
- How to finish the image makeover using some final touches

In this particular project, we will take a ho-hum, rather dreary-looking photograph of a beautiful old house and give it a Photoshop makeover.

Why? Well, just think of the possibilities. Perhaps a real estate agent has engaged your services to create images for sales brochures. Or maybe you are thinking of doing some home improvements of your own, and you are wondering what your house would look like with a new coat of paint. Or how about those new shutters or windows you have been admiring? Or maybe you have been thinking of doing some landscaping, and before investing in a major project such as this, you want to see how it would look. Whether you are doing work for a home renovator, a landscape artist, a real estate agent, or just for yourself, there are many reasons that you might want to go through an exercise such as this one.

13

Thanks to the power of Photoshop CS, all that you can imagine is possible! By following along with me, as we proceed through this makeover, you will gain the knowledge, skills, and confidence to tackle your own photo makeover project.

This particular assignment is written to a beginner's level so that anyone who is new to Photoshop CS can just *jump right in*. As we start out, I will explain, in some detail, the various tools that we will be using and how they work. If you want to join in but have more than beginner skills, just skip over these explanations and move right to the numbered steps. And, for more advanced users, do not hesitate to use your own ideas, techniques, and tools. In fact, I encourage you to think outside the box and create your *own* unique house makeover!

Making First Assessments for the Project

We are going to take the "before" image shown in Figure 13.1...

Figure 13.1   The original, before image.

...and transform it into the image you see in Figure 13.2!

Figure 13.2   The finished, virtual mansion!

Specifically, in this exercise, we will cover the following topics:

- Straightening the photo
- Improving overall color
- Removing unwanted elements (and fixing some existing ones)
- Enhancing the sky
- Coloring the shrubs and vines
- Adding new elements (and fixing a few others)
- Adding some final finishing touches

Breaking our project down, taking it one step at a time, makes for a less daunting job, and that's what we do in the sections that follow.

If you are a new user to Photoshop, this project might, at first glance, look difficult and complicated. Well, I can assure you that it really is not! Don't be intimidated; just jump in and do it and, along the way, don't be afraid to make some mistakes. Trial-and-error is still my preferred method to learn new skills in Photoshop!

Rotating the Image!

The best way to begin is at the beginning, and in this case, that means rotating the image to a vertical view and saving a copy of that view as our master image—the one we'll work on in the retouching exercises in this chapter. So let's let 'er rip!

Saving a Vertical View of the Image

1. Open 219Burnet.jpg from the Examples\Chap13 folder on the companion CD.

2. Oops! The first thing that we need to do is rotate the photograph to a vertical view. Choose Image, Rotate Canvas, 90° CW (Clockwise). There, that's better!

3. Make sure that your Layers palette is open (press F7). Now double-click on the Background layer in your Layers palette to unlock it. When the new layer dialog box pops up, rename the layer **Original.** Click on OK to apply the changes. Press Ctrl(⌘)+J to duplicate the layer, and now the Layers palette will show two layers: the Original layer and the copy that is automatically named Original copy.

4. Hide the Original layer by clicking the eye icon to toggle off the view for this layer on the Layers palette. Now save the image to your hard drive as **219Burnet.psd** (Photoshop's primary and native file format) by clicking File, Save As and choosing Photoshop (*.psd) from the Format drop-down list.

This is our master image, and I will refer to it as such throughout the exercises. Keep the master image open. We're going to study it and start working on it.

Studying the master image, with the goal in mind as to what you want to accomplish, is by far the most important aspect of any project.

Studying the Master Image for Improvements

The house itself is a beautiful structure. Its rooftop could use a new paint job and perhaps an awning repair is in order, but other than these minor areas, we will not be tampering at all with the basic structure. It's the *setting* that really requires the major work or photo enhancement.

You might be thinking that it would have made sense to take this photograph on a beautiful spring day. And you would be absolutely right. It would have! Sure, taking the photo then would have saved us a lot of work, but where is the fun in that? The fact of the matter is, circumstances don't always allow for the optimum situation in photographs. Let's imagine that in this particular case, the client (a fictional real estate agent) provided you with the photograph. His or her instructions are simple and precise, "Turn it into a spring setting, and generally just improve the property for salability purposes." If it's winter and the house is going to sell in the spring (when most houses do), photographing the property during the spring, when it's at its best, would be physically impossible. Now you can imagine that this is often the case in real life. But, for us, this is not a problem…Photoshop CS to the rescue!

Having studied the image, with a goal in mind, I had a general idea as to how I wanted to "enhance" it, or rather how my imaginary client wanted me to enhance it. As you can see in my finished version, my "vision" was that of a near perfect spring day setting. I imagined a green lawn, a bluer sky, flowering window boxes to dress up the house, a few shrubs and mature trees, a new walkway, and even a "story book, picture perfect" white picket fence. Just the kind of house that anyone would want to immediately buy and move into!

As the vision unfolded in my mind's eye, I decided that I wanted to get rid of many parts of the photograph and then, apart from the house, I wanted to retain or simply enhance others. Studying a photograph like this, as you can see, is very important. My study armed me with a general "plan of attack," which is so necessary before embarking on any photo restoration or enhancement project.

Straightening the Image Perspective

Before doing anything at all to the picture, let's "straighten it out." You can clearly see that the house in this image seems to be slanted slightly to the left. The perspective of the house, as photographed from ground level, needs to be adjusted. That's what we'll do in this exercise.

Straightening It Out

1. To see this picture in its entirety, first fit the image to your screen by choosing View, Fit on Screen or pressing Ctrl(⌘)+0. Make sure that your rulers are showing. If they aren't, press Ctrl(⌘)+R or choose View, Rulers.

2. Now let's drag out some vertical and horizontal guidelines from the rulers to help us straighten things out. To do this, click and hold down the mouse button anywhere on either of the horizontal or vertical rulers, and drag to position a guideline. The guideline will appear when you release the mouse button. After you have dragged out your guidelines, you can quickly reposition them using the Move tool (V) along distinct vertical and horizontal lines for the house. Set up at least three vertical and three horizontal guidelines along the edges and approximate center of the house, as shown in Figure 13.3.

Figure 13.3   Use this figure as a reference for placing guidelines.

Note

Using View, Snap   If you have the View, Snap option enabled, your center guidelines will "snap" to the center of your image.

Insider

> The next step will make use of the Transform tool to straighten the house. It might help to press Ctrl(⌘)+ the minus key to lower the zoom level of the image document. Then drag a corner of the document window out to expand the working area, and give yourself room for adjusting the handles on the Transform tool for the next few steps.

3. The Original copy layer should still be the active layer on the Layers palette. To line up (or square up) the house to your guidelines, press Ctrl(⌘)+T, or choose Edit, Transform, Distort. If you use the shortcut, position the mouse pointer anywhere within the bounding box, right-click (Macintosh: hold Ctrl and click), and choose Distort from the context menu.

4. Drag the top right and left guide handles (indicated by an open square box at the corners) so that the horizontal and vertical lines of the house line up with the guidelines, as shown in Figure 13.4. Before committing your change, you can always drag out some more guidelines to see how your alignment is progressing. When you're satisfied, press Enter(Return) on your keyboard to accept the transformation, or click the check mark at the upper-right side of the Options bar to accept the changes. Figure 13.4 shows what the before (dotted line) and after (solid line) distortion will look like when making adjustments.

Insider

> If you find the guides distracting, you can toggle them on and off by pressing Ctrl(⌘)+H. This command gives you the freedom to turn the guides back on if needed again later. If you want to permanently clear away the guides, choose View, Clear Guides, or use the Move tool to drag them back onto the rulers.

5. The photograph will now be *askew*, meaning that there will be an empty canvas area where you realigned it. So let's crop the image. Use the Rectangular Marquee tool (M), and positioning it in the lower-right corner, drag a selection up and out to the left until the top corners of your selection meet the blank canvas area. Release your mouse, and you will see what are often referred to as "marching ants." They indicate an active selection. If you don't select it right the first time, just start your selection over again. When you're satisfied, choose Image, Crop to resize your master image to your selection. Press Ctrl(⌘)+D to deselect.

6. On the Layers palette, double-click on the layer title name (Original copy), and type **Aligned** to rename this layer. Press Enter(Return) to commit the changes to the layer name.

13

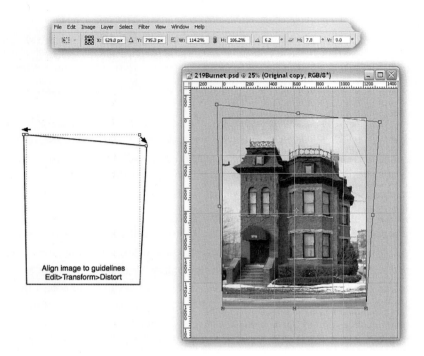

Figure 13.4   Use the Distort option for the Transform tool to adjust the image perspective. The settings shown on the Option bar (in this figure) may vary in your own work, but these settings can still be a useful aid in determining whether you're on the right track in the Transformation process.

Insider

Naming your layers is a good habit to get into. It helps you to keep track and quickly identify a layer when you need to go back to it. Believe me, when you have a project that involves 20–50 or even a 100+ layers, you can imagine how much time would be wasted searching for the layer that you need to edit!

7. Press Ctrl(⌘)+S to save your master document. Doing this will overwrite your first saved version. Get into the habit of saving in this manner after every major change that you make to your master file just in case you need to revert back to it.

Keep the file open for the next exercise.

Improving Overall Color

The next task to tackle in this image is to improve its overall color, brightness, and contrast. It appears to lack some richness and depth, but we can quickly improve this by applying a Curves Adjustment Layer.

As you learned in Chapter 12, "Curves and Adjustment Layers," using an Adjustment Layer allows you to make a visual change to the image, without touching the original photograph itself. This is commonly referred to as a *non-destructive* editing process. Not only does using this technique leave the original photograph intact, but it also allows you to go back at any stage during the editing process and adjust the initial settings.

Using Adjustment Layers to Improve Color

1. At the bottom of the Layers palette, click the Create new fill or adjustment layer icon, and choose Curves. The Curves dialog box will open, and a new Curves 1 layer will be added to the Layers palette. The default channel, RGB, is the one that you'll work on.

Insider

> If you Alt(Opt)+click anywhere in the grid area of the Curves dialog box, you can toggle between large or small grid squares. If necessary, Alt(Opt)+click to toggle to the larger grid squares.

2. In the Curves dialog box, a diagonal line runs from the lower left (black) to the upper right (white), as shown in Figure 13.5. Click to add two points on the line: a point where the first corner grid squares intersect near the lower-left and upper-right corners. Drag the lower-left point down a little, and observe the change to your image. Drag the upper-right point up and to the right slightly. You may want to experiment with the Curves option to find a setting that suits your eye, but Figure 13.5 shows the settings described here.

Insider

> If you feel you've made a mistake in adjusting the curve line, hold down the Alt(Opt) key to toggle the Cancel button to a Reset button and start from scratch again. If you would like to delve deeper into understanding the power behind a Curve adjustment, you won't want to miss out on Chapter 12.

13

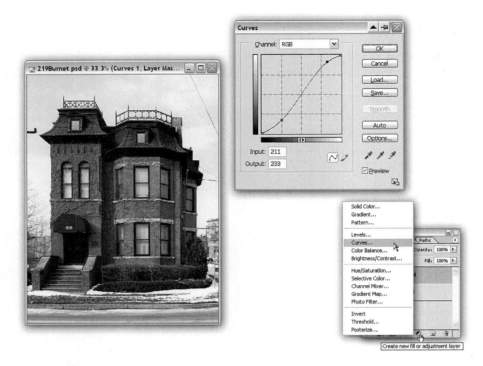

Figure 13.5   Duplicate a curve similar to the one shown here to increase the contrast and improve the overall color.

3. When you're satisfied with the preview that you see, click on OK to apply the adjustment. Don't worry too much at this point if you're not 100% satisfied with what you see. Remember, this is only an Adjustment Layer, and you can always go back and change its settings at any time just by double-clicking on the thumbnail on the Layers palette.

4. Important: Press Ctrl(⌘)+S to save your work again and keep the file open!

What we've done up 'til this point has been pretty basic and simple, yet effective in its own way. To appreciate these minor adjustments, click the eye icon beside your Original layer to turn its visibility back on. Click its layer thumbnail, and while holding down your mouse button, drag it up to the top of the Layers palette stack. Release your mouse button to reposition the layer, and then toggle its eye icon off and on to see the changes that you have made. Don't forget to drag the Original layer back down to the bottom of the stack before continuing with the rest of the assignment.

In Chapter 13, "**Keeping Up Appearances: Techniques for Retouching Images**," you'll see how to cyber-spruce up a charming but run-down manor and even change the climate to make the whole scene sunny. Don't call your realtor before you check out this chapter!

In Chapter 24, "**Ten Photoshop Tricks**," you'll learn how to turn a bunch of text into a photograph. Whether it's Lincoln and the Gettysburg address, or your own picture made out of your resume, you'll get a kick out of this provocative and fun trick.

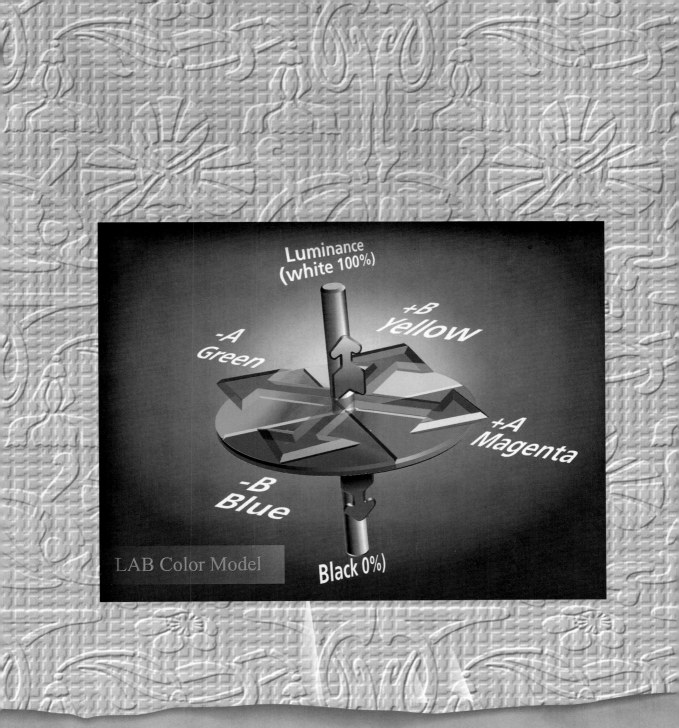

The LAB color model is composed of a Lightness channel and two channels of chromacity. The LAB color space is so large that it can be compared to that of human vision, and Photoshop uses this space when it converts images between color modes. Get the low-down on color spaces in Chapter 2, "**The Critically Important Color and Gamma Calibration Chapter**."

In Chapter 16, **"Color Balancing and Adjustment Layers: Creating a Cover Girl Image from an Average Picture,"** a pretty but flawed picture of a girl is transformed into a glamorous cover girl image. Really hunker down and learn some of the best image-editing tricks out there, all in this chapter.

In Chapter 7, "**Filters**," you'll learn, among other things, how to warp and wrap a label around a cylindrical shape in an image. The Displace filter is only one of many you'll want to try out under the user-friendly guidance of this chapter.

Does this guy own two guitars? No, but Photoshop sure helps make it *look* that way. Come explore how to replace a main element in an image in Chapter 18, **"Replacing the Main Elements in an Image."**

Human hands can be as beautiful and as expressive as the human form or the human face. Take a look at how to get the most out of a picture of hands in Chapter 10, "**Color Correction and Selections: Creating Beautiful Hands.**"

In Chapter 20, **"Typography and Page Layout in Photoshop,"** you'll get the insider's scoop on creative ways to use text, suggestions on fonts to choose, and hands-on experience using Photoshop's Type tool.

In Chapter 24, **"Ten Photoshop Tricks,"** you'll see how to create a painting out of some simple images. Watch out, Painter—Photoshop's got some aces up its sleeve!

Chapter 24, **"Ten Photoshop Tricks,"** will also guide you through the delicate process of replacing a ho-hum sky with a dynamic one. Sorry, but we have no clue as to how you add a frog to an image, though. :)

Replacing grayscale tones in an image with color can be a snap when you check into Chapter 24, "**Ten Photoshop Tricks**." Learn the tricks to sampling colors from an image and applying them to a different one.

"Surrealistic Photoshop" is the name of Chapter 17, and in it, you'll see how to hang a gallery on thin air! Learn the tricks to impossible but believable image retouching when you read this chapter.

This is an impossible picture! Imagine getting all these kids to sit still! Great pictures are sometimes not taken, but instead manufactured with the help of a few digital photos and Photoshop. Take a gander at the secrets to image composition in Chapter 14, **"Retouching a Group Scene by Creating a Composite Image."**

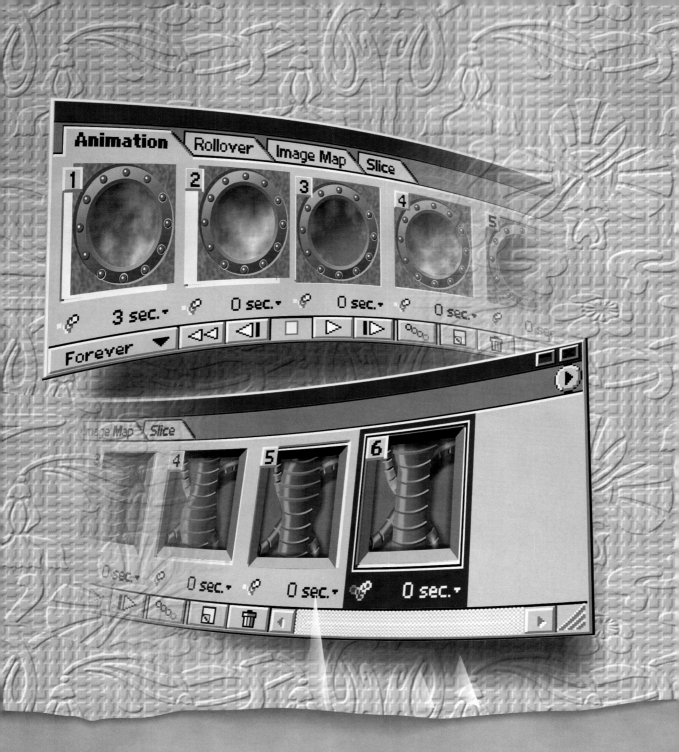

Chapter 22, "**Animations and Rollovers**," takes Photoshop's sister program, ImageReady, out for a spin and shows you just how easily you can create effective and eye-catching animations.

Chapter 24, **"Ten Photoshop Tricks,"** shows you how to take a blurry, flat, "too-ugly-to-put-in-a-wallet" photo and stylize it, restoring some of the focus and adding attractive detail. The secret's all in knowing which filters to use. Get out your bookmark!

For the Birds!

Just for the fun of it, check out Chapter 1, **"Producing Awesome Images from the Start."** Nothing is required of you except a sense of whimsy and an eagerness to play with Photoshop's features as part of an out-of-the-box experience.

Note

> **Repositioning layers**   A few useful observations may help when using a dragging method to reposition a layer on the Layers palette. First, you can quickly identify exactly what layer is active (the layer that you're working on) by its color. The active layer is highlighted a deeper shade than the non-active layers. Also, you may notice a thin white line between layers. When you click and drag a layer to reposition it, notice that the image thumbnail reverses to a negative, and the layer itself turns black. When you position the active layer between any of the remaining layers on the Layers palette, a dotted line appears around the layer button as you move it, and a black line appears where the thin white line used to be. If you're dragging from the bottom to the top, the black line appears above the top layer to indicate that, when you release your mouse button, the layer will be repositioned above the black line (a black line will appear below the bottom layer when dragging a layer to the bottom of the stack). Go ahead and try moving your layers back and forth to get comfortable with this method.
>
> Keep in mind, if dragging isn't your cup of tea, you can use a keyboard shortcut to reposition the layers. Ctrl(⌘)+] (right bracket key) moves the active layer up the stack, and Ctrl(⌘)+[(left bracket key) moves the active layer down the stack.

Now comes the real work, so get ready!

Removing Unwanted Elements

After studying the original photograph and deciding on a plan of attack, I've identified some elements that need to be removed from the photograph.

The next exercise will concentrate on removing the hydro wires, which are an unattractive distraction. Additionally, there is some ice on the house that would realistically be out of place in the spring setting we've chosen for this scene. The street sign, nearby buildings, and any other evidence of winter (such as the snow and leafless shrubbery) will eventually be replaced with new elements to make the spring version more convincing (we'll worry about these items later in the chapter).

As always, it is a good idea to get in the habit of working on a duplicate layer when undertaking major changes. This gives you the freedom to delete the layer and start fresh if things do not go as planned. Let's begin the next phase of repair.

Cloning and Patching Away Unwanted Elements

1. Click on the Aligned layer to make it the active layer. Press Ctrl(⌘)+J to duplicate this layer. Rename the Aligned copy layer by double-clicking on the layer title and typing **Elements Removed**. Press Enter(Return) to accept the name change to the layer.

2. Next, you'll remove the hydro wires. Hold down Ctrl(⌘)+spacebar to toggle to the Zoom tool (Z), and drag a marquee around the hydro wire in the upper-right corner of the document window to zoom in on this area of the image. If necessary, hold down the spacebar to toggle to the Hand tool, and reposition your view to ensure a clear view of the hydro wire in the upper-right corner (see Figure 13.6).

Figure 13.6   Zoom in to get a clear view of the hydro wire before removing it. The figure also shows how your Layers palette should look at this point.

Note

> **Clearing up palette clutter**   If, at any time, you find your workspace area becoming cluttered with palettes, you can quickly toggle these palettes off and on by pressing the Tab key. You can also reposition any palette by clicking on its title bar and dragging it around the workspace, or you can double-click on its title bar to toggle between a collapsed and expanded view.

Insider

> The Patch tool is the perfect tool for getting rid of this wire, but first you need to make a selection around the wire. You can use the Patch tool itself to make a selection, but this tool operates in the same way as the Lasso tool: You must make a freehanded selection. Because the object in this instance is straight and narrow, and because you can use any of Photoshop's selection tools before using the Patch tool, it will be easier to use the Polygonal Lasso tool to make a selection around this object. After making the selection, you can use the Patch tool to repair the area.

3. Choose the Polygonal Lasso tool (L) from the toolbox (click and hold on the Lasso tool until it appears from the fly-out menu). Click once at the top edge of the document and near one side of the wire. Because this wire goes to the edge of the document, you can actually make the remaining clicks in the title bar or scrollbar areas of the document to ensure that the selection goes to the edges of the document. Click again outside the edge of the bottom area of the wire. If necessary, hold down the spacebar to toggle to the Hand tool, and scroll to the bottom area of the wire for a better view. Click again outside the bottom area on the other side of the wire, and make a fourth click on the title bar area of this side to surround this wire area. When you have made enough clicks to surround the wire, double-click to close and complete the selection. Marching ants should now appear around the wire area, as shown in Figure 13.7.

Polygonal Lasso Tool

Figure 13.7   Make a tight selection around the wire to ensure the selection extends all the way to the edge of the document.

4. Choose the Patch tool (J) from the toolbox (it's grouped with the Healing Brush tool). On the Options bar, make sure that the Source option is selected (the remaining options should be unselected). The Elements Removed layer should still be the active layer on the Layers palette.

5. With the Patch tool, simply click inside the selection area around the wire, and drag this selection down and to the left slightly, as shown in Figure 13.8. You can see the sample area change in the selection you are dragging, and this sample

area will be mirrored in the original selection space, where the wire was located. When the area in the wire selection space looks good, release your mouse, and the Patch tool will repair this area and remove the wire. Press Ctrl(⌘)+D to deselect.

Patch Tool

Figure 13.8   Use the Patch tool, and move the selection to rid the area of this unattractive wire. The Patch tool makes use of the Source pixels (the location area that you drag the selection to) to average with the original selection area for a flawless result.

6. Press the spacebar to toggle to the Hand tool, and scroll the document view over to the upper-left edge. There, you will find a protruding pipe, which you can remove from the image by using the Patch tool again. Use the Patch tool to make a loose selection around the pipe area, as shown in step 1 of Figure 13.9. Click inside the selection, and drag the selection up and to the right slightly to sample a new area of the sky. When you're satisfied with the sampled area, release the mouse button, and Photoshop will repair the original selected area with information from the new sampled area (see step 2 in Figure 13.9). Press Ctrl(⌘)+D to deselect.

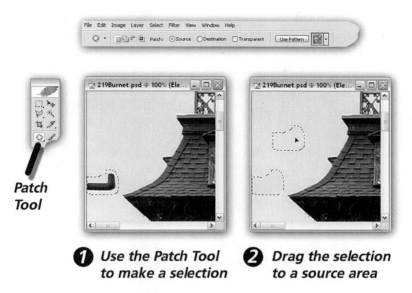

❶ Use the Patch Tool to make a selection

❷ Drag the selection to a source area

Figure 13.9   Use the Patch tool again to make a selection around the protruding bar, and move the selection to an appropriate sampling area.

Insider

> The Patch tool and Healing Brush tool operate by averaging the texture of the selected area with the texture from the Source area. As you can see, this averaging method works quite well for many situations. However, if you scroll back over to the upper-right side of this image, you'll notice some ice and a few more wires. These items intersect areas of the house in which it is important to retain the well-defined edges and details. Therefore, for these areas, the Clone Stamp tool will perform better.

7. Press the spacebar to toggle to the Hand tool, and scroll back over to the upper-right side of the document until the ice and nearby wires are in view. Choose the Clone Stamp tool (S) from the toolbox. On the Options bar, choose a soft round 35-pixel brush, and refer to Figure 13.10 for the remaining settings. Here, you want to sample an edge close to the top portion of the ice particle (near the roof edge) and line the brush up perfectly over the ice (to clone in this edge area). So pay attention to the following trick to accomplish this feat. When you hold down the Alt(Opt) key, the cursor will change to a circle containing a bull's-eye–like cross-hair. Hold down the Alt(Opt) key, and use the cross-hair to align the brush with the edge area to the right of the ice; click once to sample the appropriate area, but do not release the Alt(Opt) key just yet. Continue holding the Alt(Opt) key as you slide the brush over the top area of the ice, and use the cross-hair to approximate where the edge of the roof should fall. When you're satisfied with the position of your brush, release the Alt(Opt) key, and then click once or twice to clone in the sampled edge to this area (see Figure 13.10).

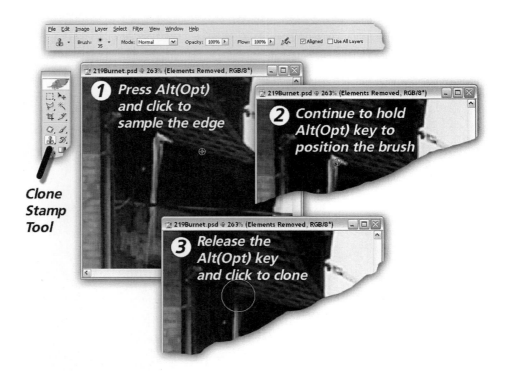

Figure 13.10   Use the Clone Stamp tool and the sampling Alt(Opt) key bull's-eye cursor to help position the cloning brush properly.

8. Step 7 helped to clone the horizontal edge of the roof, but if you feel you need to clone in the vertical edge as well, repeat the same technique to fine-tune the vertical edge.

9. Lower the brush size to a soft round 21-pixel brush, and continue to use this technique to clone away the remainder of the ice and wires. Sample frequently and sample appropriate areas. Be sure to use the previous technique when cloning away wires that intersect the edges of the house. And remember to use the History palette (or Ctrl(⌘)+Alt(Opt)+Z) to undo any brush strokes you are unhappy with. Another useful hint to keep in mind is that after you've cloned away enough wires from the edge of the house, you can switch to the Patch tool again to patch the remaining wires in the sky area.

10. Choose an appropriate brush size, and use this cloning technique to clear away some of the snow from the bottom step of the house, as shown in Figure 13.11. Sample from appropriate areas. For example, look for a bottom edge of bricks without snow (to sample from), and clone this information in areas where snow

obscures the bottom edge. Again, use the History palette if you don't like a particular brush stroke. Plus, keep in mind that most of the snow areas will be replaced with different elements later, so remove just enough to give an edge to the bottom of the brick steps (without worrying about the rest of the snow areas).

Tip

> **Sampling with the right tool**   You can also use the Rectangular Marquee tool or Polygonal Lasso tool to make a selection to define a working area that will include the bottom edge area of the brick steps. Then you can use the Clone Stamp tool to clone in sampled bricks along this bottom edge (within the selection area). This extra step can help to define a clearer edge at the bottom and give you the freedom to sample from bricks that are the right color, without limiting you to sample an area that contains an edge.

Before   *After*

Figure 13.11   Carefully find sample points to clone away the snow from the bottom step area in the image.

11. When you're satisfied with the results, press Ctrl(⌘)+S to save your work. Keep the document and Photoshop open for the next exercise.

Okay, take a break and congratulate yourself! A break is important at this point, not only because you've worked hard, but also it's always a good idea to step back and admire how far you've come. Press Ctrl(⌘)+ the minus key to zoom out and admire all the changes made to the entire document at this point.

Changing the Season: Enhancing Image Elements

The preliminary spring-cleaning work (so to speak) has been completed. You've straightened out the image *and* the house. You've improved the overall contrast and coloring of the image and made further improvements by removing unsightly items. The prep work is done, so now it's time for a change of season. Spring is around the corner.

Enhancing the Sky

So what is one of the obvious qualities of spring? Bluer skies, right? Certainly, spring isn't a time for dingy, light-colored, or overcast skies. Therefore, the next exercise will concentrate on finding an easy and workable method to isolate the sky to enhance this part of the image.

The Magic Wand tool works in this particular case because there is not a lot of detail in the sky, and there is a good amount of contrast between the sky and the other elements in the photo.

Making Over the Sky

1. Choose the Magic Wand tool (W) from the toolbox. On the Options bar, set the Tolerance to 50, and make sure the Anti-aliased option is checked (uncheck the remaining items, as shown in Figure 13.12). Click on a blue area of the sky. Most of the sky will be selected, but not all of it. To fix this by adding to this selection, hold down the Shift key, and click on a white cloud area of the sky. Your selection should look similar to Figure 13.12. The selection will include areas that you don't want to include, but don't worry; you'll fix that in the next step.

2. To fine-tune this selection, choose the Rectangular Marquee tool (M) from the toolbox. On the Options bar, click on the Subtract from selection icon, or use the keyboard modifier by holding down the Alt(Opt) key. Drag a rectangle selection at the bottom of the image to subtract any unwanted selection areas. Use this method to continue to subtract any unwanted selection areas that appear on the house (for example, remove any selections around the window areas). When you're satisfied that the sky is the only area selected, move on to the next step.

3. On the Layers palette, click on the Curves 1 layer to make it the active layer. Press Ctrl(⌘)+Shift+N to create a new layer, and name this layer **Sky Color**. Click on OK.

4. Click on the foreground color swatch, and choose a rich blue color (R:82, G:44, B:205). Click on OK. Press Alt(Opt)+Delete (Backspace) to fill the sky selection with the blue foreground color. Press Ctrl(⌘)+D to deselect. On the Layers palette, change the layer mode to Color Burn, and lower the Opacity to 50% (see Figure 13.13).

Figure 13.12   Use the Magic Wand tool and the settings you see here to make a selection of the sky area.

Figure 13.13   Create a new layer and fill the sky selection with a rich blue color. Adjust the layer Mode and Opacity to give the new color a more realistic effect.

5. Press Ctrl(⌘)+S to save your work. Keep the document and Photoshop open. There's still more work to be done.

Coloring the Shrubs and Vines

Okay, the sky color is definitely a richer spring-like hue now, but something has to be done about those brown leafless shrubs and vines. At this point, the image can't quite convince us that spring has arrived. So let's do some colorizing to lay the foundation for greener shrubs and vines.

Making Over the Shrubs and Vines

1. On the Layers palette, the Sky Color layer should be the active layer. Press Ctrl(⌘)+Shift+N to create a new layer above the Sky Color layer. In the New Layer dialog box, type **Painted Shrubs** for the Name, change the layer Mode to Color, and lower the Opacity to 60% (see Figure 13.14). Then click on OK.

Figure 13.14   Create a new layer, and adjust the layer mode and opacity within the New Layer dialog box.

2. Click the foreground color on the toolbox, choose a rich green color from the Color Picker dialog box (R:71, G:118, B:46), and click on OK.

3. Choose the Brush tool from the toolbox. On the Options bar, choose a soft round brush (a 35-pixel brush might be about the right size). Start painting over the shrubs to the right of the steps (see Figure 13.15).

4. Press Ctrl(⌘)+Shift+N to create a new layer above the Painted Shrubs layer. In the New Layer dialog box, type **Painted Vines** for the name, change the layer Mode to Color, and lower the Opacity to 60% before clicking on OK.

5. Click the foreground color on the toolbox, and choose a slightly darker green from the Color Picker dialog box (R:56, G:89, B:27). Click on OK.

Figure 13.15   Use the settings shown here for the Brush tool, foreground color, and Layers palette options. Then paint some spring into the shrubs.

6. The Brush tool should still be the active tool. On the Options bar, choose a hard round 3-pixel brush (Brush Mode should still be set at Normal with 100% for Opacity and Flow). Press Ctrl(⌘)+ the plus key to zoom in close enough to see the vines that wrap around the house bricks (around 200–300% zoom level will work well). Use the small hard brush to paint over the vines on the house. Hold down the spacebar to toggle to the Hand tool when you need to scroll to a different area as you work. This job may seem rather tedious, and the effect won't be obvious at first, but be assured that completing this step is worth taking the time and the trouble. It lays a good foundation for the vines and prepares the image for the elements you will be adding later.

7. Press Ctrl(⌘)+S to save your work. Keep the image and Photoshop open.

When you're finished with this painting part of the project, grab some refreshment. After all, hand painting all those vines was hard work, and you deserve a break.

Now that the basic foundation of the image is complete, the next steps will involve adding the various spring elements. Oh, what fun it is to play *virtual landscaper!*

Insider

> If you prefer not to take the time to paint in all the vines, a file has been provided for your convenience with all the hard work already done for you. Open vines.psd from the Examples\Chap13 folder on the companion CD. On the Layers palette, the Painted Vines layer is the one you will concentrate on. Don't worry about the Vines layer at this point (which is why it is hidden). Position both documents so that you can easily see each image window in the workspace. If necessary, press Ctrl(⌘)+ the minus key to lower the zoom level for both documents. Click the title bar of the vines.psd document so that this is the active document. Hold down the Shift key, and drag the Painted Vines layer from the Layers palette into the 219Burnet.psd document window. When you hold down the Shift key, the layer will center itself perfectly within the document window. If necessary, press **V** to switch to the Move tool, and use the arrow keys to fine-tune the positioning of this Painted Vines layer.

Adding New Elements

This part of our project is commonly referred to as *photo compositing*—basically, creating a new image using the elements from other images. We've included a large variety of image files on the companion CD for the photo compositing part of this assignment. All the elements have been included in the Examples\Chap13 folder. The necessary files have already been prepared for your immediate use. However, if you prefer to find and use your own elements, by all means, have fun and experiment.

Adding Leaves to the Vines

You're probably ready to start the real work. The Examples\Chap13 folder on the companion CD provides eight different vine files to choose from. Basically, you will be placing, scaling, and rotating these elements to fit along the major vines painted earlier in the chapter. Let's get started.

Adding Some Spring to the Vines

1. The 219Burnet.psd document should still be active in your workspace. On the Layers palette, click the arrow in the upper-right corner, and choose New Layer Set from the context menu. In the New Layer Set dialog box, type **Vines** for the name and click on OK (see Figure 13.16).

Insider

> Notice that a folder appears in your Layers palette. Use this folder to hold all the vine layers until you're satisfied with the results. Then you can merge all the layers in this set or folder so that the vines are contained on a single layer, which reduces overall file size.

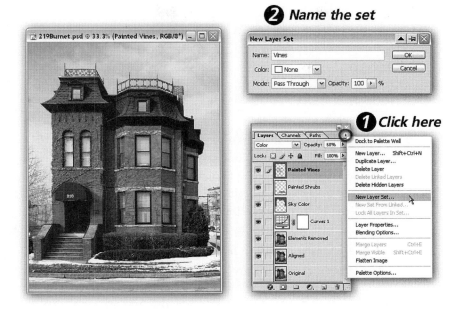

Figure 13.16   Create a New Layer Set to help keep all the future vine layers organized into one folder on the Layers palette.

2. Let's open one of the vine images. Open vine01.psd from the Examples\Chap13 folder on the companion CD. Press **V** to switch to the Move tool. Position both the vine01.psd and 219Burnet.psd files so that you can easily see both windows in your workspace. Click in the vine01.psd file, and drag the vine into the 219Burnet.psd document window. Notice that this new layer is automatically placed in the Vines folder.

3. On the Layers palette, double-click on the layer title, and rename this layer **vine01**. Press Enter(Return) to commit the new name to the layer. Repeat this step with the remaining seven vine images (on the companion CD), renaming each respective layer to coincide with the filename. You will now have a copy of all eight vine images contained in the Vines layer set, and you can close the original vine files without saving any changes. It will now be easier to duplicate these layers, as needed.

4. To avoid confusion, let's turn off the visibility for all vine layers other than the one we're currently working on. On the Layers palette, click on the eye icon to the left of each vine layer title until you reach the vine01 layer (leave the eye icon or visibility turned on for this layer). Click on the vine01 layer to make it the active layer.

Insider

Here's a part in the assignment that will require some initiative and imagination as you place leaves on the vines. Look at the vines that intertwine all along the front of this house, and then look at the shape of the leaves on the vine01 layer. Decide where in this image the vine leaves would fit best. The transformation process in the next step will rely on your artistic sensibilities, so try to visualize the best placement for each vine element and work toward this goal until you are satisfied with the result. Let's start.

5. If necessary, press Ctrl(⌘)+ the plus or minus key until you are at a comfortable zoom level for working with the vines. Press Ctrl(⌘)+T to access the Transform tool for the vine01 layer. You will see a bounding box appear around the leaves. Hold down the Shift key while dragging on one of the corner control handles to constrain the proportions as you resize the object.

6. If you need to rotate the object, hover your mouse cursor near the outside of the bounding box until the cursor looks like a bent double arrow; then click and drag to rotate (see Figure 13.17). If you need to reposition the object, click inside the bounding box when the cursor looks like an arrow head, and drag to reposition the item to line up the leaves with your intended spot on one of the vines. You can also use the arrow keys to reposition the object.

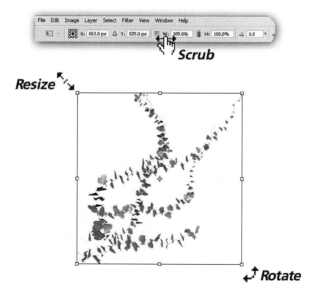

Figure 13.17   Press Ctrl(⌘)+T to enter the Transform mode, and then resize, rotate, and reposition the vine01 layer into the desired location.

7. You can fine-tune any transformation by entering numerical data into the appropriate Options bar area. For instance, if you've rotated an object using the click-and-drag method, but you know that you need to fine-tune and adjust the rotation by one degree, you can enter the appropriate number in the rotate box on the Options bar and then press Enter(Return) to make the adjustment stick. Something new to Photoshop CS is the ability to "scrub" data into the box. To use this new feature, try this while the Transform tool is activated: On the Options bar, hover your cursor near the W (for Width or Horizontal Scaling). You will see the cursor change to a double-arrow. Now click and drag to the right or left, and you will see the numerical values for that item go up or down depending on which direction you drag the cursor. So, if you don't want to type a number into the boxes, scrub the number in—as if there was an invisible slider. By the way, this scrub ability is not limited to the Transform tool; it is available for *any* of the dialog boxes that require numerical data. When you're satisfied with the transformation, press Enter(Return), or click on the check mark at the upper-right of the Options bar to accept the changes.

Note

> **Using the cursor to gauge repositioning**   When you place a cursor inside a Transform bounding box to reposition the object, the cursor is a good indicator of what is going to happen. When you hover the cursor inside the bounding box, it will appear as an arrow head to indicate that you are about to move the object within the bounding box area. If you move too close to the center reference point, the cursor will display a circular reference point icon next to the arrow head cursor. This change tells you that you will be moving the reference point rather than the bounding box itself. Keep in mind that transformations happen relative to this reference point. So, for example, if you move the reference point outside the bounding box and rotate the box, it will rotate around this new reference point location (outside the box) rather than around the center of the object (which is the default location for the reference point).

8. Repeat steps 5–7 for the remaining vine layers. Simply click on the layer to make it the active layer, and turn on its visibility. Press Ctrl(⌘)+T to make the necessary transformations. Press Enter(Return) when you're satisfied with the results. If you want to duplicate any of the vine layers, click on the layer to make it active, and press Ctrl(⌘)+J.

9. Press Ctrl(⌘)+S to save your work. Keep the document and Photoshop open for the next exercise. If you have the vines.psd file open, you may close that file without saving changes.

Insider

> Once again, a file has been provided if you prefer to have this part of the project com-
> pleted for you. Open the vines.psd file from the Examples\Chap13 folder on the com-
> panion CD (if you don't have it still open). Click on the Vines layer to make it the active
> layer and to toggle the visibility on as well. With the Move tool active, hold down the
> Shift key, and drag this layer into the 219Burnet.psd document window. If necessary, use
> the arrow keys to fine-tune the position of the vines (check Figure 13.2 to see the posi-
> tion of vines in the finished product). If you decide to use this layer, you can delete any
> vine layers that you don't want by dragging them to the trash icon at the bottom-right
> corner of the Layers palette.

If you chose to use the vine layer provided in the vines.psd file, you can delete any of the
remaining vine layers that are not needed. However, if you took the time to create your
own vines for the house, you might have quite a long list of vine layers inside the Vines
layer set. If you want to hide the long list of layers from view, click on the arrow next to
the Vines layer set title to collapse the folder and hide the layers that are inside this folder.
Clicking again on the arrow will toggle the folder open again.

Whether you keep all the vine objects on separate layers or merge them all into one layer
is a matter of personal preference. While merging these layers will help keep file size
down, by doing so you lose the option of later tweaking the position or size of only one
of these vine objects. Personally, I think it's always better to choose flexibility over a
smaller file size. But if you decide you *would* like to merge them, the simplest way is to
make the bottom vine layer active and link this layer to the remaining vine layers. Then
click on the arrow in the upper-right corner of the Layers palette, and choose Merge
Linked (see Figure 13.18).

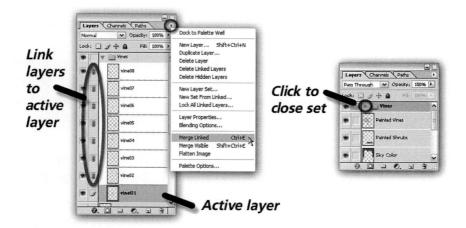

Figure 13.18   Link the layers and choose the Merge Linked option from the Layers palette
menu if you want to merge the vine layers into one layer. Otherwise, keep the layers, and simply
close the set folder to keep the confusion level low when you don't need to view these layers.

Adding New Landscaping Elements

The next exercise will add some more elements to spruce up the walkway. After you've worked so hard on the climbing vines, the next exercise should seem like a snap. So let's get started.

Improving the Landscape

1. On the Layers palette, click on the Vines layer set title to make it the active layer. Open the walkway.psd file from the Examples\Chap13 folder on the companion CD. You might know the routine by now. Position both documents so that you can easily view them in your workspace. Use the Move tool to drag the walkway from the walkway.psd window into the 219Burnet.psd document window. Position the walkway in front of the steps. That was pretty easy, wasn't it? Close the walkway.psd file without saving any changes. The walkway layer should now appear above the Vines layer set title in the Layers palette. If it doesn't, drag it to the top of the stack, or press Ctrl(⌘)+] (right bracket key) until it's at the top of the list.

2. Let's just fine-tune this new walkway a touch. Click on Add layer mask icon at the bottom of the Layers palette. Click on the eye icon to the left of the walkway layer title to temporarily turn the visibility off for this layer so that you can easily view the bottom step area. Choose the Polygonal Lasso tool, and click along the bottom edges of the steps and brick area to make a selection of the bottom step area similar to the one shown in Figure 13.19. You're simply trying to include a section of the bottom step outline, so it isn't important how far up the selection goes (in height).

3. Click on the eye icon to the left of the walkway layer to turn the visibility back on. The layer mask thumbnail should be active (see Figure 13.20). Black should be the foreground color; if not, press **D** for the default colors. Press Alt(Opt)+Delete (Backspace) to fill the selection with black on the layer mask to reveal the base of the steps on the walkway.

4. Open the picket_planter.psd file from the Examples\Chap13 folder on the companion CD. Drag the picket fence element into the 219Burnet.psd document window. Close the picket_planter.psd file without saving changes.

5. The Picket-fence layer should be the active layer in your 219Burnet.psd document. Press Ctrl(⌘)+T to access the Transform tool. On the Options bar, click the Maintain aspect ratio icon (it looks like a chain link, as shown in Figure 13.21). Then, on the Options bar, type **35**% for the Width and press Enter(Return). The Height should automatically adjust to 35% as well. Press Enter(Return) again to commit the changes and exit the Transform tool.

13

Figure 13.19 Add a layer mask to the walkway layer, turn off the visibility to the walkway layer, and make a selection of the bottom step and brick area.

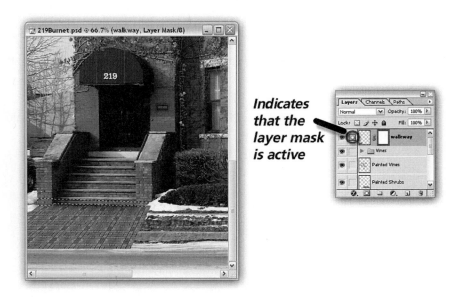

Figure 13.20 Use a layer mask to fine-tune the place where the edges of the steps meet with the edge of the walkway.

Figure 13.21 Shrink the picket fence element down to size. The fence should be large enough to cover snow areas near the shrubs.

6. Press **V** to switch to the Move tool. Position the Picket-fence layer so that it is below the shrubs and close to the walkway area (it is acceptable to leave a slight space between the fence and walkway because we will be adding a shrub later to this area to hide the snow in this corner area). Press Ctrl(⌘)+J to duplicate the layer. Hold down the Shift key, and move the fence copy toward the right horizontally until it lines up near the end of the first Picket-fence layer (it works well to overlap the fence ends slightly; you can use the wood slabs as a guide to piece them together when overlapping). Holding the Shift key constrains any movement perfectly horizontal in this particular situation. Repeat this process until you have six copies of this layer, making the fence long enough to place below the shrubs in the front yard, as shown in Figure 13.22.

7. On the Layers palette, click on the column to the left of the Picket-fence layer titles to link the layers to the top active layer, as shown in Figure 13.22. Press Ctrl(⌘)+E to merge linked layers. Double-click on the layer title, and rename this layer **Picket-fence flowers**. Press Enter(Return) to commit the new name to the layer.

Figure 13.22   Duplicate the fence layer as needed to create a longer fence—as one of the new components for the front yard landscaping makeover.

13

8. Open the grass.psd file from the Examples\Chap13 folder on the companion CD. Drag the Grass layer from the grass.psd document into the 219Burnet.psd document window. Use the Move tool to position the Grass layer below the picket fence. The goal is to have the grass overlap the bottom area of the picket fence and also meet up to the walkway edge as well.

Insider

Don't be concerned if some of the elements, such as the walkway and grass, do not extend all the way to the bottom edge of the document. You will fix this problem later in the chapter with some appropriate cropping.

9. Press Ctrl(⌘)+S to save your work. Keep the 219Burnet.psd file and Photoshop open for the next exercise.

Adding Ready-Made Elements

You're almost there; you just need some window boxes, a couple of shrubs, trees, and a few finishing touches to finish the transformation. Before you know it, you'll be done. This might be a good time to take another break to allow some time to sit back and admire the work so far. You've worked hard.

Before you continue with your landscaping work in this image, let me take some time to explain the logic behind the next exercise and what you will find on the companion CD. The previous exercises provided some insight into ways to transform and adjust composite elements to fit within the master image. So, in the interest of time, the next exercise will provide ready-to-go files that require a simple drag-and-drop-into-place process. However, if you would like to take the initiative of resizing each element on your own, you will find the necessary files available to do so. Keep in mind that, for this chapter exercise, you will find a plural version and a singular version of the filenames on the companion CD. The plural version, such as trees.psd, is simply the resized, ready-to-go composite version made up of the singular file versions—in this case, the tree01, tree02, tree03, and tree04 files.

These ready-to-go files were made simply by working with the original files provided on the CD. In some situations, we duplicated the element layers, such as for the window box and shrub elements. And from there, we used the Transform tool to resize, rotate, distort, and in some cases flip the images. In the case of the shrubs, we also needed to adjust the color to achieve a richer green.

We would like to encourage you to experiment on your own with these images. There are many methods for tweaking a nicer green color for the shrubs. A variety of Adjustment Layers might do the trick, such as Hue/Saturation or Color Balance. Or you can try creating a new layer, painting on the layer with a deep green color. (Hint: Ctrl(⌘)+click on the shrub layer to load as a selection, and fill the selection on the new layer with the green color.) Then experiment with layer Mode settings and Opacity to obtain the desired green needed in the shrubs. The Multiply or Color mode might work well with a low Opacity. Simply adjust and play with the settings until you find something visually pleasing.

You should also note that, in the case of the window boxes, some flowers were cloned to different places to help break up any patterns that could be a dead giveaway that the same element was used multiple times within the image (a tell-tale sign of compositing as well). With all that said, let's start working on the condensed version for the remaining elements.

Adding the Ready-To-Go Landscaping Versions

1. Open the window_boxes.psd file from the Examples\Chap13 folder on the companion CD. If necessary, press **V** to switch to the Move tool. Drag the Window Boxes layer into the 219Burnet.psd document window. Use the Move tool to position the window boxes perfectly near the base of the windows, above the shrubs. If necessary, use the arrow keys to nudge these elements into place. You can close the window_boxes.psd file without saving changes.

2. Now, let's add some shrubs to this image. Open the shrubs.psd file from the Examples\Chap13 folder on the companion CD. Drag the shrubs into the master document window. Close the shrubs.psd file without saving changes. Position the shrubs so that they fall nicely into place, with one on each side of the walkway and one at the far right end of the existing hedge. That will hide any remaining

snow areas near the bricks and at the left edge area of the picket fence. If necessary, use the arrow keys to nudge the new shrubs into place.

Insider

Again, if you feel adventuresome, you can use the original single shrub file, which is also provided on the companion CD (shrub.psd, not to be confused with the shrubs.psd file). The original file was resized to fit into the image. Then the layer was duplicated and flipped horizontally to use for the two shrubs at the far right and far left.

3. Open the trees.psd file from the Examples\Chap13 folder on the companion CD. Drag the tree layer into the master document window. Close the trees.psd file without saving changes. Position the trees so that they help to cover up the unwanted information near the right and left sides of the house image. If necessary, use the arrow keys to nudge the trees into place. Place the left edge of the trees up against the left edge of the document window (don't be too concerned about the right edge; you will use cropping in the next step to rid the image of any unwanted space). Refer to Figure 13.2 as a guide for placing these elements appropriately.

4. Now it's time to crop away some of the unwanted space. Switch to the Crop tool from the toolbox. Start in the upper-left corner, and drag down and to the right. The goal is to exclude the unwanted areas at the right and at the bottom of the image (see Figure 13.23). Use the handles on the bounding box area to fine-tune the crop. When you're satisfied, press Enter(Return) to commit the crop changes.

Insider

When you're using the Crop tool, sometimes you might experience difficulty in fine-tuning the border areas of the bounding box. If you ever run across this difficulty, suspect a Snap feature as being the culprit. When the Snap feature is turned on, the Crop tool will attempt to snap to the edges or to specific grid intervals within the image. Go to the View menu, and make sure there is no check mark next to the Snap item (on this menu). If this item is checked, click on it to toggle off this feature. After that, your Crop tool should be a lot more agreeable to the desired adjustments.

5. Press Ctrl(⌘)+S to save your work. Keep the image and Photoshop open for the next exercise.

Note

Want a rock?   The companion CD also includes a rock element (rock.psd). It is purely an optional decorative item included in case you would like to add it for visual interest or maybe to disguise an unsightly area in the master image. If you're satisfied with the composition at this point, leave it out; otherwise, take some time to add and experiment with the rock file on your own.

Figure 13.23   On the left, you see a crop in progress as the unwanted space is removed from the master image; the results are shown on the right.

Adding Some Finishing Touches

You've come a long way. The image could certainly pass for a spring-time setting. However, there are still a few details that might help to improve the overall look even further. We're done adding elements, but let's fine-tune the image.

Many of the elements that we added were resized to fit into the master image. Because the scaling process tends to soften the added elements (due to lost pixels), the first question to ask yourself is whether any of these elements could benefit from some sharpening. Next, consider the lighting. Try to imagine where the lighting source is coming from, and add some appropriate shadows, maybe even some additional lighting itself. The next exercise will show you how to take care of all these fine details, to put the finishing touches on your revamped mansion.

Taking Care of the Small Details

1. The ready-to-go drag-and-drop elements were already sharpened for you. But if you took the time to add the elements from scratch, you'll also want to apply some sharpening to the necessary layers. For now, the Picket-fence flowers could benefit from sharpening. On the Layers palette, click on the Picket-fence flowers layer to make it the active layer. Choose Filter, Sharpen, Unsharp Mask. In the

Unsharp Mask dialog box, type **50%** for Amount, **0.5** (pixels) for Radius, and **0** for Threshold (see Figure 13.24). Then click on OK.

Figure 13.24   Use the settings shown here to sharpen any layers as needed.

Insider

If you feel other element layers could benefit from some sharpening, simply click on the appropriate layer title to make it the active layer; then press Ctrl(⌘)+F to apply the last filter and settings to that layer. Next, let's add some shadows.

2. Imagine the light is coming from high up and from the left. You'll need a shadow of the left tree that falls at a steep angle. On the Layers palette, click on the tree's left layer to make it the active layer, and press Ctrl(⌘)+J to duplicate it. Press Ctrl(⌘)+[(left bracket key) to move the copy below the trees left layer, and double-click on the layer title to rename this layer **Tree Shadow**. Press Enter(Return) to commit the new name to the layer.

3. Press **D** for the default colors. Black should be the foreground color. Press Alt(Opt)+Shift+Delete (Backspace) to fill the content of this layer with the black foreground color. Press **V** to switch to the Move tool. If you move this layer slightly, you'll be able to see the effects because this layer is currently hiding

behind the tree's left layer. On the Layers palette, change the layer Mode to Multiply and lower the Opacity to 50% (see Figure 13.25).

4. You will use the Transform tool next and will need some working room to see the bounding box handles. Press Ctrl(⌘)+ the minus key to zoom out to about 25%. Drag out the bottom corner of the document window to give some working room area. Press Ctrl(⌘)+T to bring up the Transform tool. Right-click (Macintosh: hold Ctrl and click), and choose Distort from the menu. Now drag on the handles until you produce a tree shadow that falls on the side of the house near the steps and on the walkway below the tree, similar to Figure 13.25. When you're satisfied with the results, press Enter(Return) to commit the transformation changes.

Figure 13.25   Distort the Tree Shadow layer to achieve a shadow that falls at a realistic angle onto the house and walkway. The settings shown here in the Options bar might help to aid in adjusting the Transform tool for your own project.

5. Choose Filter, Blur, Gaussian Blur, and enter **2** (pixels). Click on OK.

6. Click on the shrubs layer to make this layer active. Press Ctrl(⌘)+J to duplicate it. Press Ctrl(⌘)+[(left bracket key) to move the layer below the shrubs layer. Rename this layer **Shrub Shadow**, and change the layer Mode to Multiply and the Opacity to 70%. The foreground color should still be black. Press Alt(Opt)+Shift+Delete (Backspace) to fill the shrubs on this layer with black.

Press Ctrl(⌘)+F to apply the last Gaussian Blur settings to this layer. Press **V** to switch to the Move tool, and move the Shrub Shadow layer slightly down and to the right until you can see the shadow peek out slightly from behind the shrubs.

7. Repeat this same process for the Window Boxes layer. Start by clicking on the Window Boxes layer to make it the active layer, make a duplicate layer, and so on. Rename the duplicate layer **Window Box Shadow**.

8. Click on the top layer (trees right), and press Ctrl(⌘)+Shift+N to create a new layer. In the New Layer dialog box, name the layer **Light Layer**. Also, while you have this dialog box open, change the layer Mode to Overlay and the Opacity to 70%. Click on OK.

Insider

As you work through the next step, imagine light beaming across the house, starting from the upper-left side of the image and streaming toward the lower-right area. Figure 13.26 shows a black-and-white representation of the places to apply white color in the next step. Don't worry about confining your brush strokes to the house only. Go ahead and make bold, broad diagonal strokes across the entire image, and we'll explain how to clean up the unwanted areas later. So if you don't paint exactly as shown here, or if you paint into any unwanted areas, don't worry. Just watch the image, and concentrate on using your judgment to achieve a natural look.

Figure 13.26   This black-and-white image indicates where you will be applying white color to simulate light streaming across the house.

9. Press **D** for the default colors, and then press **X** to switch white to the foreground color. Choose the Brush tool (B) from the toolbox. On the Options bar, set the Flow to 50%; the Opacity should remain at 100%, and the brush Mode should be set to Normal. Choose a large, soft round brush; start with a 300-pixel brush and change the Master Diameter setting from 300 to 500 to temporarily create a 500-pixel soft round brush (see Figure 13.27 for the correct settings). Press Enter(Return) to dismiss the Brush palette.

Figure 13.27 Use a large, soft round brush with the settings shown here. The brush is huge, so give your document window some working room to make space for those broad strokes.

10. Again, it might help to press Ctrl(⌘)+ the minus key to zoom out and then drag a corner of the document window to give some working room around the image border area. Start at the upper-left area of the document, and make a broad diagonal stroke down toward the lower-right area. Repeat with another stroke below that one and so on until you cover down to the lower-left corner area. Click once near the slanted rooftop areas. Don't forget to use the History palette to undo any strokes you're not happy with.

11. Now, let's clean up any unwanted paint, beginning with any areas that spilled over into the sky. This area is actually easy to fix because you already have a layer

that can provide you with a perfect selection of the sky. Ctrl(⌘)+click on the Sky Color layer to load a selection of the sky. Make sure, however, that the Light Layer title is the active layer; if necessary, click on the Light Layer title to ensure that it is the active layer. Press the Delete (Backspace) key to remove the paint from any sky areas. Press Ctrl(⌘)+D to deselect.

12. Next, we want to remove the paint from areas where there should be deep shadows (areas where light is blocked). Choose the Eraser tool from the toolbox, and choose a soft round 65-pixel brush with the settings shown in Figure 13.28. Press Ctrl(⌘)+ the plus key to zoom in. Hold down the spacebar to toggle to the Hand tool, and drag until you have a view of the rooftops. The Light layer should still be the active layer. Start near the rooftops, and brush to erase any dark shadowy areas (refer to Figure 13.26 as a guide for areas that might need to be removed). Press the spacebar as needed to adjust your view of the image as you work.

Figure 13.28   Use the Eraser tool settings shown here to erase away any remaining unwanted areas.

13. Now we should give the walkway a bit of wear, to make it look more authentic. Click on the Walkway layer to make it the active layer. Press Ctrl(⌘)+ Shift+N to create a new layer. In the New Layer dialog box, name the layer

Walkway Wear, and change the layer Mode to Overlay and the Opacity to 60% before clicking on OK.

14. White should still be the foreground color. Choose the Brush tool from the toolbox. On the Options bar, you can leave the previous Flow setting of 50%, but change the brush to the Spatter 59-pixel brush (see Figure 13.29). Now simply click in the center areas of the walkway to add a little wear and fading.

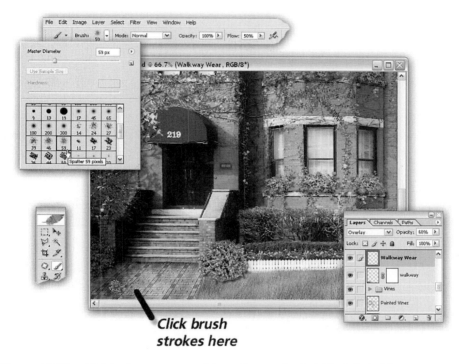

**Click brush
strokes here**

Figure 13.29   Click in the center area of the walkway to begin "aging" the bricks. Use your judgment, and don't forget to use the History palette to undo any strokes you aren't happy with.

   15. Press Ctrl(⌘)+S to save your work.

You have been given the skills to make repairs on this image, so if you would like, we can suggest one more item that could give you the opportunity for a little more practice. Click on the Elements Removed layer to make it the active layer, and press Ctrl(⌘)+J to duplicate it. Remember, by working on a copy, you can always delete the layer if you don't like the results. Now, on your own, do some repair work on the peeling paint areas around the rooftop, on the eaves, and along the attic windows. Use whatever tool you feel will do the job appropriately. Some areas can benefit from the Patch tool, Healing Brush tool, or the Clone Stamp tool. Other areas might require you to use the Brush tool and an appropriately sized brush. Remember, when you're using the Brush tool, you can press the Alt(Opt) key to toggle to the Eyedropper tool and sample nearby colors. Also, don't forget that your Flow setting is at 50% from the last exercise, but this setting may work well. If not, adjust it back to 100%.

Your finished image should now look very close to the one shown in Figure 13.2. Now, wouldn't this make our fictional real estate agent happy and help to speed up the sale of this property?

Summary

In this chapter, you learned to use a number of tools to retouch a photographic image. You learned how to rotate the image and change its perspective and how to evaluate an image to determine what kinds of changes you want to make to it. You used Curves Adjustment Layers to change the overall color and the Clone and Patch tools to remove unwanted image elements. You used color to enhance individual image elements, and you learned how to add new image elements—both "raw" and "ready-made." Finally, you learned a number of techniques for fine-tuning your composited and edited image. Be proud of yourself for having accomplished this assignment! We hope that you found it to be not only educational, but also rewarding, and we hope that you will use your new skills and confidence to tackle your own makeover projects.

Part V

Ambitious Image Editing

Retouching a Group Scene by Creating a Composite Image

In this chapter, you'll learn

- How to select components for a composite image

- How to determine which image elements must be replaced

- How to select, add, resize, and retouch image areas

- How to add decorative elements and text to the composite image

If there isn't a Murphy's Corollary for photography, there should be at least a dozen of them, and at the top of the list should be, "The larger the number of people in a scene, the greater the chance that at least one of them will have their eyes closed, their finger in their ear, or adopting some other pose that is an embarrassment."

And this corollary, taken to the max, applies to a kid's birthday party. Take a dozen kids, all charged on sugar from the cake and soft drinks, and try to get them to sit still for 1/200th of a second!

No problems, but only solutions here. Part of the trick to arriving at a perfect picture is to take as many pictures as you can once the gang is assembled. With digital cameras, you have to forget about how many exposures you have left…the media is completely recyclable. By overshooting—taking multiple pictures of a particular moment or event—you can later cut and paste together the optimal scene.

Maybe you're asking yourself at this point, "Why?" Well, here's the premise behind my initial idea. If anyone reading this chapter has ever thrown a birthday party, you will certainly understand how important it is to send Thank You cards to the guests. My idea was to personalize those Thank You notes with a picture documenting the fun that all the children had at the party. With this in mind, my goal was to get a group shot showing all the happy faces. It would not only make a nice picture for the Thank You card, but also serve as a nice memento of the event for everyone involved.

Now, "perfect" has traditionally *not* meant "natural." "Perfect" has always sort of suggested "contrived." But then again, Photoshop is not a traditional tool, so if you follow the steps in this chapter, you can indeed get a group setting that looks both perfect *and* natural.

In Figure 14.0, you can see the unretouched qaggle of kids; we've labeled them all for reference as you work your way through the exercises in this chapter.

Figure 14.0   The original photo. About as well choreographed as a Chinese fire drill.

Choosing Image Material

Before you dive into a composite piece, it's important to survey the material. While looking over all the images captured for a birthday party assignment such as this—or any similar project for that matter—you need to keep in mind concerns such as these:

- Which image will be the starting point? Try to choose an image that will have most of the components already contained within that image. The benefits, of course, will be fewer edits. The less you need to repair or edit, the fewer clues there will be that you made any edits.

- Based on the starting point image, which components will need to be edited or added (or in this case, which party participants are needed from other image sources)? This question leads us into the next concern.

- Which potential replacement images show happy facial expressions for participants? Typically, one or two subjects will always be captured giving a neutral expression, no matter how many pictures were taken. In those situations, just go with the best possible choice.

- And finally, after you narrow down the images that show the subjects with happy expressions, which of these images come closest to the same camera angle as the starting image? This might not be an intuitive point to consider, but it's an important point to try to train yourself to take into consideration. Finding images at a similar angle will help to provide similar lighting and convincing body and facial angles. When you take the time to think about it, you'll realize what an important consideration this can be.

With these thoughts in mind, we chose a starting image along with some alternative images to borrow from. All these images are on the companion CD, so you can use them to play along in the exercises for this chapter.

Basic Editing Investigative Work

Now that we've chosen the images we'll use to create the composite group image, the decision processes are just beginning. When you work on an assignment such as this, you first have to examine the starting image and decide what will go and what will stay. If any items in the starting image need to go, you next need to decide whether you will you be able to mask (or hide) those items with the subjects that will be added later or will need to perform preliminary edits to hide the unwanted parts.

I have the responsibility—or maybe the advantage—of working out the logistics of this assignment before presenting it to you. Here's what I've discovered.

Deciding What Goes, What Stays

Look at the starting image shown in Figure 14.1. It may be necessary at this point to inform you that there are a total of nine characters to assemble for this group shot. On the plus side, five bodies in this image are good to go. This image has a clear view of the four characters in the front row and a good view of an overtly happy fellow in the second row (to the right). More than half the characters for this group shot are accounted for.

Out of the remaining four characters; one fellow's face is obstructed, the other has his eyes closed for the shot, and—due to this camera angle—the other two characters are out of view behind the young man at the far left. On the negative side, to make sure everyone is included in this group photo, you will need to add four of the nine characters into a more advantageous position to help their participation in the event become more obvious.

Figure 14.1   The starting image has many desired components already in place, but there's still much to be done to achieve the final goal.

Deleting Image Areas and Tackling Other Prep Work

I also have the advantage of knowing a few other details that you'll need to pay attention to in order to make this group composite work. When you swap out a different version of the boy in the far back (I'll call him Tim because I think that might be his actual name), you'll find out that there will be a very small space where Tim's leg might come in handy for filling that small space later. See, the image you will use for his face is from another shot that doesn't show the rest of his body. So we'll need to preserve the bottom half from this starting image to fill in that gap. Therefore, in preparing the starting image, you'll make a selection of Tim's leg area and set it aside on a separate layer for later.

The other prep work needed involves the boy we'll refer to as Craig. As you can see in the figure, Craig's head is obstructed by one of the front-row participants. You will ultimately replace this image of Craig with an alternative that has him naturally peeking out from behind the person in a manner that shows more of his face and body. But to avoid a two-headed Craig, you will need to do some preliminary work to disguise the area where his head currently resides in the starting image.

How do we do all this? Well, c'mon, let's get started on tackling the first set of problems described.…

Starting Image Prep Work

1. Open StartingImage.tif from the Examples\Chap14 folder on the companion CD. Press the Ctrl(⌘)+plus key a few times until the zoom level is at around 200%. Hold down the spacebar to toggle to the Hand tool, and scroll the image until you have Tim's leg and clothes in view.

2. Choose the Polygonal Lasso tool from the toolbox. Starting at the inside left edge of Tim's green shirt, click as close to the inside edge as you can, and continue to make clicks in a counterclockwise direction around the bottom clothes and leg area. The goal is to capture as much of this part of Tim's body area as possible, but you don't need to concern yourself with making a perfect edge selection. Make a selection that gives some breathing room above Tim's leg as well, similar to the selection shown in Figure 14.2.

Note

Selections?   If you need to brush up on the use of the Polygonal Lasso tool, see "Rounding Up the Lasso Tools," in Chapter 5, "Harnessing the Power of Selections."

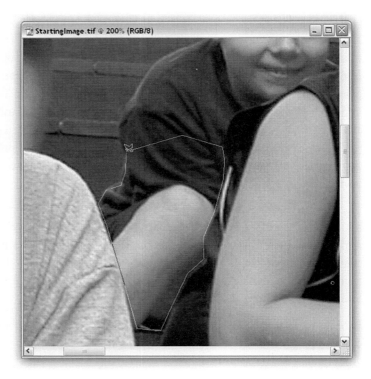

*Polygonal
Lasso
Tool*

14

Figure 14.2   Make repeated clicks with the Polygonal Lasso tool to grab Tim's lower body area within a selection.

3. Press Ctrl(⌘)+J to put the selected area onto a new layer. On the Layers palette, double-click on the Layer 1 title, and rename the layer **Tim's Leg**. Press Enter (Return) to commit the name change.

4. Click the arrow at the upper-right corner of the Layers palette, and choose New Layer Set. Name the new set **Tim**, and click on OK. Drag the Tim's Leg layer into the Tim layer set. Click the arrow next to the layer set title to close the layer set, and then click the eye icon to the left of the layer set title to toggle the visibility off for the Tim layer set. Put this set aside for now. You'll return to it later in the chapter.

5. Next, you'll clone a section of the house over Craig's head to hide the head from view. Click the Background layer title to make it the active layer. Press Ctrl(⌘)+Shift+N to create a new layer. In the New Layer dialog box, name the layer **House Repair**, and click on OK.

6. Choose the Clone Stamp tool from the toolbox. On the Options bar, choose a 35-pixel soft round brush. Mode should be set to Normal. Set Opacity and Flow to 100%, and check both options for Aligned and Use All Layers. Make sure you are zoomed in to about 200% to get a good view of the area you need to concentrate on.

Insider

The next several steps give specific guidelines for getting an accurate cloning effect. If you pay close attention to the instructions on how to do this, you can clone a fairly flawless section of the house over Craig's head with relative ease.

7. You can see a vertical pipe just to the right of Craig's head. Use the edge of this pipe to take a Clone Stamp *sample*. Hold down the Alt(Opt) key, and don't release it until we tell you to later in these instructions. When the Alt(Opt) key is pressed, the cursor has crosshair lines that can be helpful in lining up the center of the cursor with the edge of the pipe and at a position that is halfway between the horizontal slats on the wall. Pick a spot just above Craig's head in a clear area of wall space. When you're confident that the cursor is correctly positioned, click once to sample, but still continue to hold down the Alt(Opt) key to use the crosshair guide lines.

8. Now move the cursor to line up the crosshair in a similar manner, but this time over a pipe edge near Craig's head (and again, at the halfway point between the horizontal slats you would see if Craig's head weren't in the way). When you're confident that you have the cursor lined up correctly, release the Alt(Opt) key, and then click and drag over the top portion of Craig's head, sweeping across the top and working your way down. When you start to see more of Craig's head appear while cloning, stop and release the mouse button. Figure 14.3 shows a sample point and the starting brush stroke below the sampled area.

9. Because the Aligned option is checked, you don't need to resample; the original sample point is your starting point again. Simply hold down the Alt(Opt) key to see the crosshair cursor again, and position the cursor over a new area of Craig's remaining head, where the edge of the pipe should be—and again halfway between horizontal slats. Don't click yet, but release the Alt(Opt) key. You may need to press the Alt(Opt) key once more to toggle back to the Clone Stamp brush again. Once you're back into the brush mode, do another sweep across more of Craig's head area. Repeat this process until most of his head is sufficiently covered with wall area. If you don't like a brush stroke or the sample point, press Ctrl(⌘)+Z to undo, and simply try again until you're satisfied.

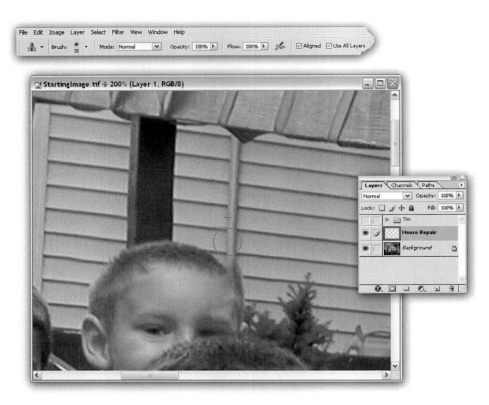

Figure 14.3   Use the settings shown here for the Clone Stamp tool. Paint on a new layer. Take your time positioning the Clone Stamp tool when sampling and again before painting in cloned areas.

10. A small shrub is also visible to the right of where Craig's head was. If necessary, lower the brush size, sample, and then clone in a small area of tree if you feel the shrub needs to be extended slightly over Craig's ear. Pay attention to the positions of the horizontal slats when you sample the shrub, and position the brush appropriately for cloning. Don't worry about hiding the lower portion of Craig's face because later additions will cover this area. Figure 14.4 shows an example of the finished area after cloning.

11. Press Ctrl(⌘)+Shift+S, and save this file to your hard drive in native Photoshop format (PSD). Keep the file and Photoshop open for the next exercise.

Whew! Basic prep work accomplished. You are now ready to assemble the rest of the characters and start positioning them into the main image.

Figure 14.4 Clone in enough wall area to conceal most of Craig's face. Use proper brush alignment to get an effective clone quickly.

The Composite Process Recipe: Select, Add, Retouch

Adding the extra people to the scene involves a process that will remain relatively consistent for each individual. Once an alternative image has been found to borrow the subjects from, the first step is to make a selection of the subject. After a selection has been made, the next step is to move the subject into the main target image. From there, decisions are made about whether any additional alterations are needed, such as resizing the subject to fit the scene.

Advanced Photoshop Magic: Select, Add, Retouch

Photoshop has a wealth of selection tools to help us tackle the first item on the agenda: making a selection. And in many instances, combining several selection tools can be an efficient method to use when making a selection. Like everything else in Photoshop, there is no right or wrong way of accomplishing this task, and as you become more familiar with the program, you will develop your own methods that are comfortable to the way you work.

Choosing a Selection Tool

I tend to favor using Quick Mask to make a selection for this type of assignment. Chapter 5 discusses the basics of how to use Quick Mask, but for those of you who need a refresher (or who haven't read through some of the previous chapters), I'll briefly explain that Quick Mask mode is a method that allows you to paint a tint color over an area to visualize what will be included in a selection. The reason I feel comfortable with Quick Mask as my method of choice for an assignment such as this has to do with the nature of the subjects. The subjects are people. Therefore, their shapes are complex, and simple geometry selection tools such as the Rectangular or Elliptical Marquee tools would feel rather awkward. Furthermore, the colors in the image vary, which makes using the Magic Wand tool an equally awkward selection method.

Another consideration has to do with the fact that we're working with a photograph, which means the edges for the subjects are anti-aliased, soft edges. So it seems very natural in this case to turn to Quick Mask as a selection method. What better match than to paint a Quick Mask tint using a soft-edge round brush to define the soft edges of the subjects in a photograph?

And don't forget, because you need to be particular only about the edges in this instance, you can still speed up this selection process by combining tools, as mentioned earlier. Start with a Lasso tool to make an initial selection of the center area for the target subject, and then fine-tune the rest with the soft-edge brush.

Selecting, Adding, and Resizing an Image Component

Our first subject is Craig. You will apply the information just described in selecting him out of an alternative image and placing him into the main image. From there, you will need to resize and find an appropriate position, and if any further adjustments are needed to make him fit, you'll learn about those as well. Let's get started:

Replacing Craig

1. The StartingImage.psd file should still be open. On the Layers palette, click on the Tim layer set title to make it the active set. Then click the arrow in the upper-right corner of the Layers palette, and choose New Layer Set. In the New Layer Set dialog box, name the set **Craig**, and click on OK.

2. Open Craig.tif from the Examples\Chap14 folder on the companion CD. Press Ctrl(⌘)+plus key until zoomed in to about 200%. Hold down the

spacebar to toggle to the Hand tool, and scroll the image until you have a clear view of Craig.

3. Choose the Polygonal Lasso tool from the toolbox. The goal is to make a preliminary selection that includes most of Craig's face and body. Click once starting near an inside edge area of Craig, and continue to click at regular intervals working around the inside edges to select the majority of Craig, as shown in Figure 14.5. Hold down the spacebar whenever necessary to move more of Craig into view as you work.

Figure 14.5 Make a selection that encompasses the bulk of the subject.

4. After you make a selection, press **Q** to enter Quick Mask mode, or click the Edit in Quick Mask Mode icon below the color swatches on the toolbar. Now, I explained where this icon is located for a reason. You should see a red tint fill the selection area inside Craig. If, instead, you see the red tint filling the area *outside* Craig, hold down the Alt(Opt) key, and click the Edit in Quick Mask Mode icon to toggle the settings to Selected Areas rather than Masked Areas. The icon should appear as a clear square with a tinted circle in the center, not the other

way around. You can also double-click on this icon to see a dialog box with the settings for Quick Mask.

5. Press the Ctrl(⌘)+plus key until the zoom level is about 300%. Hold down the spacebar to toggle to the Hand tool, and scroll the image until you have a clear view of an edge area for Craig. Choose the Brush tool from the toolbox. On the Options bar, Mode should be Normal, and Opacity and Flow should be 100%. Choose a 9-pixel soft-edge round brush. Black should be the current foreground color; if not, press **D** for the default colors.

6. Start painting to fill in the edge areas of Craig's face and body to add these areas to the initial red tint selection area. If you make a mistake, press **X** to switch white to the foreground, and paint away the mistakes. Press **X** to switch to black again, and continue painting until a red tint selection area covers Craig, similar to the one shown in Figure 14.6.

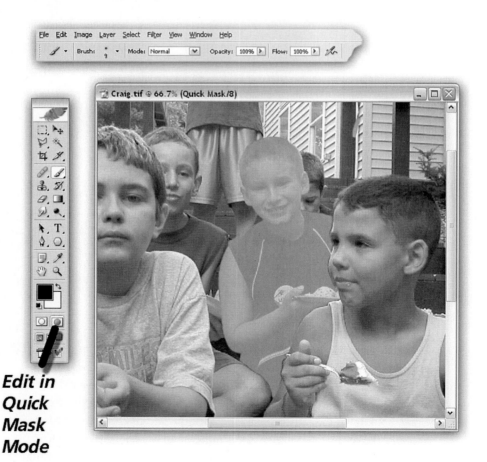

Edit in Quick Mask Mode

Figure 14.6   Use Quick Mask Mode to fine-tune the selection process for a particular subject.

7. When you're satisfied with the selection area, press **Q** to exit Quick Mask, and a selection marquee should surround Craig. Press Ctrl(⌘)+C to copy Craig.

8. Now click the title bar of the StartingImage.psd document to make this the active image again. If necessary, press the Ctrl(⌘)+minus key until the zoom level is 33.3% so that you can view the whole image. On the Layers palette, the Craig layer set should still be active. Press Ctrl(⌘)+V to paste Craig into the image. You should now see a new Layer 1 appear in the Craig layer set. Double-click the Layer 1 title, and rename the layer **Craig**. Press Enter (Return) to apply the name change.

9. Craig is a little small for this image, so you'll need to resize him. Press Ctrl(⌘)+T to enter the Transform tool. On the Options bar, click the Maintain aspect ratio icon that looks like a chain link. Type in **111.2%** for Width, and press Enter (Return). The Height will automatically adjust to the same amount. Press Enter (Return) to exit the Transform tool (see Figure 14.7).

Figure 14.7   The settings shown here will resize Craig to a comparable size consistent with the perspective of the second-row participants.

Insider

> I determined the Width amount in step 9 by watching the image as I manually resized by
> dragging on a corner handle (with the Maintain aspect ratio icon toggled on). This
> seemed to be the size that made Craig's face appear similar in size to the other boy in
> the second row (the one wearing a yellow shirt).

10. Press **V** to switch to the Move tool, and position Craig similar to the position
    shown in Figure 14.7. The goal is to make the seat of his pants sit realistically on
    the step that's showing behind the first-row group. When you're satisfied with his
    position, you will use a layer mask to hide the areas that overlap the boy in front.

11. Click the Add layer mask icon at the bottom of the Layers palette. Press **D** to
    make sure the default colors are used (black should be the foreground color). If
    needed, press the Ctrl($\mathcal{H}$)+plus key until the zoom level is about 200% to make
    it easier to see the details. Hold down the spacebar to toggle to the Hand tool,
    and scroll to an area where Craig overlaps the front-row boy.

12. Choose the Brush tool from the toolbox, and start with a 21-pixel soft-edge
    round brush. Start painting away the parts of Craig that fall on top of the front-
    row boy (see Figure 14.8). If you paint too far, press **X** to switch to white as the
    foreground color, and correct any needed areas or mistakes. Also, lower the brush
    size if necessary to get into the finer areas. Press **X** to switch to black again to
    resume the masking work. Don't forget to pay attention to the part of Craig's
    arm that might overlap the shirt of the other front-row boy. If any blue fringing
    appears near Craig's head or ear (leftover colors from the previous image), use
    black and a 9-pixel soft-edge brush to remove (or mask) those small details as
    well.

13. Sharpening Craig up a little might help because resizing him earlier resulted in a
    softer look when pixels were adjusted. On the Layers palette, click the thumbnail
    next to the masking thumbnail for the Craig layer to make the layer active for
    editing. Choose Filter, Sharpen, Unsharp Mask. Use the settings shown in Figure
    14.9 for the Unsharp Mask, and click on OK.

14. Figure 14.10 shows how the finished result should look. Press Ctrl($\mathcal{H}$)+S to save
    your work. Keep the StartingImage.psd file and Photoshop open for the next
    exercise. You can close the Craig.tif file without saving changes.

If you've masked correctly, Craig should look like he fits right in with the crowd. In fact,
a small area of plate with cake and ice cream sticks out the other side of the front-row
boy. This was leftover image material from the original Craig, but if the positioning is
just right on the new Craig, it seems to fit into place quite well.

Figure 14.8 Use black foreground color and the Brush tool to mask away unwanted areas; switch to a white color to unhide hidden (masked) areas.

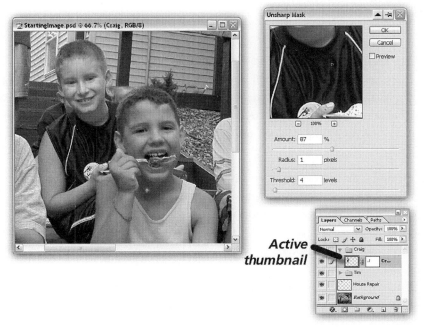

Figure 14.9 Make sure the correct thumbnail is active, as shown here. The settings shown in this figure for the Unsharp Mask filter should give a nice sharpening effect.

14

Figure 14.10   Use a layer mask to mask away the necessary areas to make Craig fit more naturally into the new environment.

Adding Drew and Josh: More Practice in Resizing and Positioning

The Drew and Josh characters will be selected from the same alternative image; therefore, you'll take care of these two participants within the same exercise. The idea is essentially the same as the preceding exercise. Make a selection of each character, and move them into the main image. Then take care of any resizing, positioning, and masking needs.

The method I chose to select Drew and Josh is identical to the method used for selecting Craig. But to avoid redundancy as much as possible for those of you reading through the assignment, I've already performed the hard work in advance for you. I saved the selections made using Quick Mask in an alpha channel, and I will show you how to access that selection information. But if you prefer to get more practice in this technique, feel free to make the selections on your own, and skip the steps using the alpha channels. By the way, an alpha channel is also available for the Craig.tif file, but I neglected to mention it earlier because I felt it was important to understand how the selection was created.

With that little curve-ball tidbit of information, let's start adding more party participants to the scene:

Drew and Josh Replacements

1. Open Drew&Josh.tif from the Examples\Chap14 folder on the companion CD. Click on the Channels tab to view the Channels palette, or choose Window, Channels. Ctrl(⌘)+click on the Drew channel to load the selection. You should now see a selection surround Drew in the image window (see Figure 14.11). Press Ctrl(⌘)+C to copy this selection.

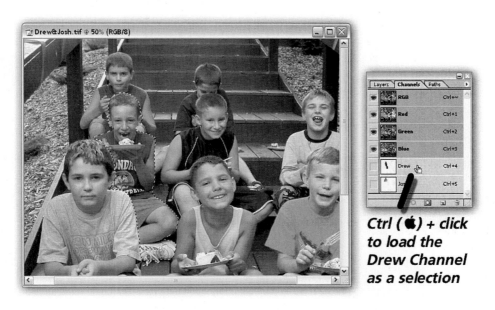

Ctrl (⌘) + click
to load the
Drew Channel
as a selection

Figure 14.11   Use the Drew alpha channel to load a selection of Drew.

2. Click on the StartingImage.psd title bar to make this the active document in the working space. Click the Layers tab to return to the Layers palette, and click the Craig layer set title to make it active. Click the arrow next to the set title to close the set. Now click the arrow in the upper-right corner of the Layers palette, and choose New Layer Set. In the New Layer Set dialog box, rename the set **Drew and Josh**, and click on OK. Press Ctrl(⌘)+V to paste Drew into the image. Double-click on the Layer 1 title, and rename the layer **Drew**. Press Enter (Return) to commit the new layer title.

3. Click on the Drew&Josh.tif title bar to make this image the active document again. Return to the Channels palette once more, and Ctrl(⌘)+click on the Josh

alpha channel title. Press Ctrl(⌘)+C to copy Josh, and close the Drew&Josh.tif image without saving changes.

4. The StartingImage.psd document should be the active document again. Press Ctrl(⌘)+V. Return to the Layers palette, and double-click on the Layer 1 title to rename the new layer **Josh**. Press Enter (Return) to commit the new layer title. You'll need Drew and Josh to be behind Craig, so on the Layers palette, drag the Drew and Josh layer set below the Craig layer set title.

5. You'll work on Josh first. Click the eye icon to the left of Drew to toggle the visibility off for this layer. Next, click on the Josh layer to make this the active layer. Press Ctrl(⌘)+T to use the Transform tool. On the Options bar, click the Maintain aspect ratio icon, and type **128.5%** for the Width. Press Enter (Return), and the Height will automatically adjust to the same amount. Click inside the bounding box, and position Josh as shown in Figure 14.12. Press Enter (Return) to commit the changes.

Figure 14.12   Use the Options bar settings shown here to transform the size of Josh. You can also use the X and Y values to position Josh within the document window to the same location. Also, pay attention to layer set order; the Layers palette stacking order should be as it appears here.

6. Click the Add layer mask icon at the bottom of the Layers palette, and choose the Brush tool from the toolbox. Perform the same masking steps that were explained for Craig in steps 3 through 7 of the preceding exercise. Use black as the foreground color to mask away unwanted areas, and use white to correct any mistakes. A 21-pixel soft-edge brush might work well for the job, but adjust the size as needed for smaller areas. And don't forget to mask the areas that fall between where Craig and the boy in the front row intersect. Use the Ctrl(⌘)+plus and minus key to zoom in or out as needed while you work. Press the spacebar to toggle to the Hand tool to scroll the document view when needed as well.

7. Click the Drew layer to turn on the visibility, and make it the active layer. Press Ctrl(⌘)+T to enter the Transform tool. Click the Maintain aspect ratio icon on the Options bar, and type in **110**% for Width. Figure 14.13 shows the remaining values for the Options bar to help position Drew. Don't forget the rotation value of 2.9 also shown in the figure. When you're satisfied, press Enter (Return) to commit the changes, or click on the check mark icon at the right side of the Options bar.

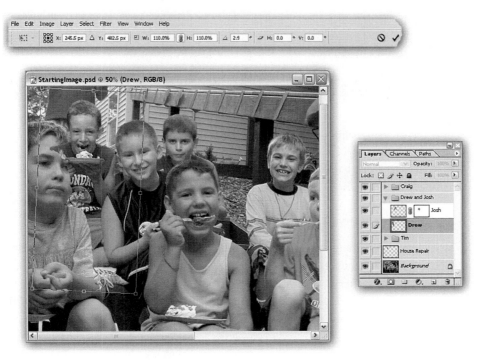

Figure 14.13   Use the Options bar settings shown here to transform the size and position of Drew. This character may benefit from a slight rotation as well.

8. Click the Add a layer mask icon at the bottom of the Layers palette, and on your own, mask away the appropriate areas so that Drew fits into the scene. Again, zoom in as needed, and use the spacebar to toggle to the Hand tool to maneuver the view as you work. Inspect all the areas, especially Drew's shoe that may overlap into Craig's pants. Figure 14.14 shows how the image should look after you've finished this section of the exercise.

Figure 14.14   You're almost there. The party's starting to look good!

9. Close the Drew and Josh layer set. Press Ctrl(⌘)+S to save your work, and keep the image and Photoshop open for the next exercise.

Take a break. You deserve it. Have a piece of cake.

Even though you were instructed to resize Drew and Josh, I didn't suggest applying a sharpening filter for these two characters because, in reality, the image should lose some focus and become softer as you move further back in the distance within the image. It's acceptable if these two appear softer. In fact, for some reason, Drew may look slightly sharper than Josh and perhaps too sharp despite the resizing effort. If you find this to be the case, you might prefer to make the Drew layer active; then choose Filter, Blur, Gaussian Blur; and experiment with an amount that softens him up a tad (a Radius of .5 pixels might work).

Adding Tim: Retouching Around an Added Element

Only one more character needs to be added to the party scene. If you recall, we selected Tim's leg early in the assignment and set it aside on a separate layer. If you look at the space between Craig's head and Drew's arm, you'll see a portion of the old Tim remaining. We want the new Tim to peek out from behind Craig and use the leg segment that was set aside to fill this space where the old Tim is currently visible. Let's add a new Tim to the picture:

Adjusting Tim's New Position

1. Open Tim.tif from the Examples\Chap14 folder on the companion CD. Go to the Channels palette, and Ctrl(⌘)+click on the Tim channel to load the selection of Tim. Press Ctrl(⌘)+C to copy, and close the Tim.tif file without saving changes.

2. The StartingImage.psd file should now be the active document in the working space. Go to the Layers palette, and open the Tim layer set. Click the Tim's Leg layer to make it the active layer. Press Ctrl(⌘)+V to paste the new Tim into the image. Double-click on the Layer 1 title, and rename the new layer **Tim**. Press Enter (Return) to commit the new title name.

3. Press **V** to switch to the Move tool, and move Tim so that he is positioned perfectly behind Craig's head, as shown in Figure 14.15. Tim is about the correct size for this image, and if you position him just right, you don't need to use masking this time around.

4. Now press Ctrl(⌘)+plus key until the zoom level is about 200%. Hold down the spacebar to toggle to the Hand tool, and scroll until you have a clear view of the space below Tim's upper half (between Craig's head and Drew's arm). Click on Tim's Leg layer to make this the active layer on the Layers palette. With the Move tool still active, move the leg until you see it pop into view, and position it as shown in Figure 14.16.

5. Click on the Tim layer to make it the active layer, and press Ctrl(⌘)+ Shift+N to create a new layer. In the New Layer dialog box, type **Gap Repair** for the layer name, and click on OK. On the Layers palette, click the eye icons to turn the visibility off for all the layer sets and layers except for the ones pertaining to Tim (peek ahead to Figure 14.17).

Figure 14.15   You only need to worry about positioning Tim correctly into the scene.

Figure 14.16   Position Tim's leg as shown in this figure. You can still see a small gap, but you'll fix that in the next few steps.

6. Choose the Clone Stamp tool from the toolbox. On the Options bar, choose a 17-pixel soft-round brush. Make sure the Use All Layers option is checked and the remaining settings are as shown in Figure 14.17. Hold down the Alt(Opt) key to click once to sample an area of material folds in the pants. Then position the brush to clone in the fold at the appropriate spot to fill in the gap area. If you're unsatisfied with a brush stroke, press Ctrl(⌘)+Z, or use the History palette to undo the stroke and try again. Extend the clothing into the gap area by sampling often, and then clone the material folds properly into the gap section, as shown in Figure 14.17.

Figure 14.17   Clone enough material to cover the gap area that will be visible between the remaining characters when the visibility for their layers is turned back on.

7. When you're satisfied with the cloning work, click the eye icons to the left of the remaining layer sets and layers to turn the visibility back on. Close the Tim layer set, and press Ctrl(⌘)+S to save your work. Keep the image and Photoshop open for the next exercise.

This new image is looking good, wouldn't you agree? This might be a good time to inspect all the newly added characters for any fringing. For those of you not familiar with the term, *fringing* occurs when the subjects still have a few pixels of unwanted color surrounding the outside edge boundaries. Perhaps during the original selection process, you selected slightly more than was needed, and bits of the old background remain. If you detect any traces of fringing or unwanted colors surrounding the subjects, simply click on the layer mask for the appropriate character, and paint it away with black foreground color and a small soft-edge brush.

Adding Decorative Elements and Text to Create a Greeting Card

You can add a few more items to this image to finish it off. To help that festive party mood, a few balloons couldn't hurt. And if you keep in mind the original goal of sending this image to the participants as a keepsake and a Thank You note, you'll need text with a catchy headline to pull it all together.

Finding Third-Party Text and Objects

Balloons and text are provided in separate files on the companion CD to help finish the project. The file containing balloons has several layers to choose from. You'll add only two of them in the next exercise, but if you want to experiment with creating your own arrangement, please don't hesitate.

The 3D text provided in another file was created using Xara 3D. For anyone not familiar with this wonderful little program, it makes creating 3D effects for text and objects extremely easy. It's also incredibly easy to learn. If you would like to know more about this program, you can find information at the following URL address:

```
http://www.xara.com/products/xara3d
```

While you're at it, you might want to check out the other products this company offers; they're all wonderful.

Note

> **About Xara 3D**   Xara 3D is a Windows product, but it runs on the Mac very well under emulation. Also check out Ulead's Cool 3D for "instant" 3D text.

After creating the text in Xara 3D, I exported the text as a JPEG file. Then I opened it in Photoshop and removed the background color—a simple process using the Magic Wand tool. However, when doing similar projects, you don't need to possess a 3D program. Experiment with fonts and effects that can be achieved within Photoshop. This powerful program can create anything you can imagine. And if you lack ideas of your own, you can find a wealth of tutorials and downloads for Photoshop on the Internet. The Adobe Web site is a great starting point. You can download a ton of Styles and Actions to help create a wide range of effects.

Adding the Elements and Using Layer Styles
Enough talk. Let's add the finishing pieces:

Throwing Balloons and Text into the Mix

1. The StartingImage.psd file should still be open. On the Layers palette, click the House Repair layer to make it the active layer. Open balloons.psd from the Examples\Chap14 folder on the companion CD.

2. Position the balloons.psd document so that you can easily see both document windows within your workspace. The balloons.psd image should be the active document. On the Layers palette, click on the Balloon Pairs layer, and drag it into the StartingImage.psd window. Close the balloons.psd image without saving changes.

3. Press **V** to switch to the Move tool, and position the balloons as shown in Figure 14.18. Click the Add layer mask icon at the bottom of the Layers palette. Press the Ctrl(⌘)+plus key to zoom in close, and hold down the spacebar to scroll the balloons into view. Choose the Brush tool and a 9-pixel soft-edge brush. With black as the foreground color, mask away any areas that overlap the boys in the image. Also, remove any balloon strings that fall in front of the boys (see Figure 14.18). Remember to press **X** to switch to white foreground color to paint back in any mistakes; then press **X** to switch to black again and resume the masking work.

Figure 14.18   Position the balloons so that the strings fall behind the boys, and use a layer mask to remove the overlapping string area as well as any other areas where the balloons overlap the image characters.

4. Open Thanks.psd from the Examples\Chap14 folder on the companion CD. Position the Thanks document so that you can see both document windows within the workspace. With Thanks.psd as the active document, hold down the Shift key, and drag the Thanks To The Gang layer into the StartingImage.psd window. Holding down the Shift key helps to center the text in the new document window. Close the Thanks.psd file without saving changes.

5. Drag the text layer to the top of the Layers palette stack, or press Ctrl(⌘)+] (right bracket key) until the layer moves to the top of the stack. Press **V** to switch to the Move tool. Hold down the Shift key to constrain the vertical movement, and drag to position the text in the lower portion of the image (peek ahead to Figure 14.19).

6. Click the Add a layer style icon at the bottom of the Layers palette (it looks like an *f* at the far bottom left), and choose Outer Glow. In the Layer Style dialog box, the Outer Glow options should now be showing. Click the color swatch, change the color to a rich gold (R:205, G:169, B:46), and click on OK. Opacity should be at 75%, Noise at 15%, Spread at 10%, Size at 43 (px), and the remaining settings at the default, as shown in Figure 14.19. Don't click on OK just yet.

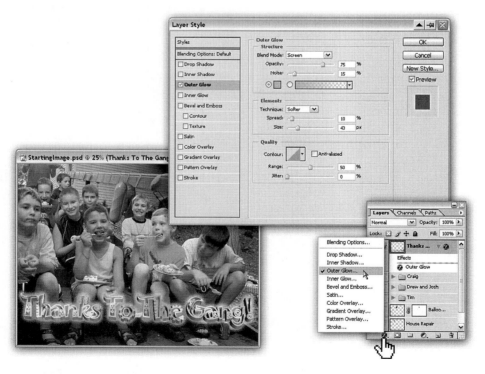

Figure 14.19   Use the settings shown here to add an interesting outer glow effect to the text layer.

7. On the list at the left side of the Layer Style dialog box, click on Drop Shadow to select that option, and view the settings. In the Drop Shadow options, click on the color swatch, choose a soft muted blue (R:120, G:151, B:221), and click on OK. Uncheck the Use Global Light option, and apply the following settings: Opacity: 75%, Angle: 92°, Distance: 27 (px), Spread: 0%, and Size: 66 (px). Next, click on the arrow to view the drop-down list next to the Contour option, and select the bottom-left Half Round option (see Figure 14.20). When you're satisfied, click on OK.

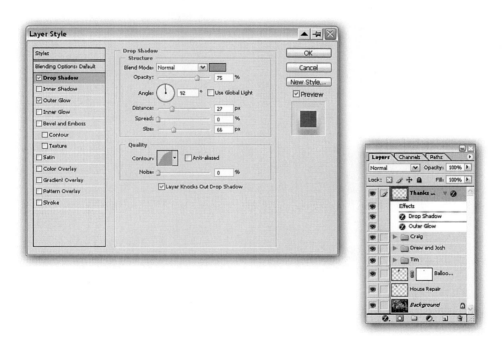

Figure 14.20   Use the settings shown here to throw an interesting drop shadow into the mix. Pay close attention to the Contour setting.

8. You're finished. Press Ctrl(⌘)+S to save your work.

Figure 14.21 shows the final image. In the last part of the preceding exercise, you applied a combination of layer styles to the text to add a little more visual appeal. I tried to use options that most people don't consider exploring, such as the Contour or Noise options. In your own work, don't forget to explore the Layer Style dialog box; using it is half the fun. The effects—or combination of effects—are endless.

14

Figure 14.21   The full party gang assembled for the final image results.

Summary

It's a print. Send off the card, and reap the rewards in the form of compliments. Well, maybe not *this* card, but a similar card from a party with people you *actually know*. And it's always my wish that a by-product or side effect of working through such a project will solidify skills that you can take with you to future projects or endeavors.

This chapter concentrated on assembling parts from various images into one main image. Typically, when you need to do something of this nature, you should always be aware of lighting. Do your best to pay attention to the lighting in the target image, and choose images with similar lighting conditions to borrow from. This helps to keep the giveaway signs of editing to a minimum. Lighting may not have been emphasized enough in this assignment because all the images were taken the same day under the same lighting conditions, so the hard part was already taken care of for us. But never neglect this concept; it's an important one.

The next important concern was position and angle. Which available photos yielded the most comparable angles to provide a convincing conclusion?

Once the actual assembling of image parts was underway, you were able to get some practice working in Quick Mask mode to make selections and using layer masks to refine your work. When working with layer masks, you may have noticed that I gave no instructions to *apply* the layer masks once the masking work was completed. The reason behind this is to provide flexibility. As long as the layer masks remain intact, none of the pixels are permanently removed (merely masked or hidden). So if you ever decide you want to come back to this file sometime in the future and move a character into a different position, all you need to do is repaint the layer mask to reveal or mask the necessary pixel information needed for the adjustment. Pretty cool, huh?

I hope this assignment also taught you a few tricks on how the Clone Stamp tool cursors can play an active role in helping you clone with more precision. And last but not least, you learned how to organize the layers in your Layers palette for easy and quick identification. May these skills serve you well and the force be with you. (Sorry! Guess I was having a Star Wars flashback.)

Chapter 15

Creating a Dream Image from a Hopeless Snapshot

You know the scenario. You decide to get out the camera and take some pictures. You may or may not have talent as a photographer, but if you're like most of us, the latter is closer to the truth. You want a magical

In this chapter, you'll learn

- How to decide what you can (and should) correct in an image
- How to correct color, crop images, and eliminate blemishes
- How to remove red-eye
- How to paint over areas in a photograph and add texture to painted areas
- How to make the most of some image flaws
- How to work with the Camera RAW plug-in in Photoshop

camera that can take a perfect picture *every time* to compensate for your lack of skills. You're hoping against hope that the Auto feature on your new digital camera will be just the ticket to accomplish this magic.

Well, if it makes you feel any better, I definitely fall into the category of untalented photographers. Proof of that fact will be evident in the images you'll be working on for this chapter. But there's hope for the flawed pictures that I take; this hope comes packaged within the richness and depth of Photoshop. If you have hopeless images of your own, don't give up on them so quickly. If they have any hint of potential, you can use Photoshop to pull out the best and minimize (or even eliminate) the worst.

This chapter will cover retouching and repair techniques that can be useful for most photographs. The exercises will touch on basics such as removing red-eye, removing skin blemishes, correcting color, sharpening, performing a hint of digital plastic surgery (to give the skin a more youthful appearance), and using simple cropping as an effective tool for improving images. The chapter will also touch on the RAW format and Adobe's RAW plug-in because this file format, combined with the plug-in (that ships with Photoshop CS), can be a great way to improve color and quality for the photos you'll want to take in the future.

Deciding What's Important to Correct

When you are preparing to correct a photographic image with Photoshop, your first task is to decide what you think needs to be corrected. Then you have to decide what things you *can* correct in the image. Examine the photo closely, and make a mental list of what you like about the photo and what you dislike. Just about every indoor image I take needs some sort of color correction, and that's not unusual; lots of people use Photoshop to correct color in photographic images. So this will be the first item addressed in the exercises to follow. What are some of the other issues? Well, the young man in the first image you'll be working on (see Figure 15.1) is going through that awkward pimply-faced-teenager stage. Underneath all that skin-rebellion can be some very attractive features. So let's pull them out.

And from time to time, you might even run into a photo that is a compositional disaster. In this case, there are too many distractions in the background, but you might be able to fix it simply by cropping; you'll see how this will become effective for the image you'll be working on in the next few exercises. But this chapter also shows you how to make the best of a "bad" image, by using a good sense of humor. Go with the flaws and play them up. You learn more about this concept later in the chapter.

Correcting Color, Cropping, and Touching Up Blemishes

There are more kinds of blemishes than just the pimply-faced kind described in the preceding paragraph. The photo shown in Figure 15.1 contains plenty of those kinds of blemishes, but it also demonstrates many other problems that are a result of poor photography skills.

Figure 15.1   We need to make the main subject the focal point and minimize all the distracting problems plaguing this image.

Here's the setting: my son's graduation day from high school. He has agreed to pose for some pictures. I start out like most people, taking many shots of him standing up straight and posing right into the camera, and at some point our pet cat strolls by wanting to grab some of the attention. As my son bends over to pet the cat, I steady the camera on the stairway railing to shoot one more picture. Later, when I look over the images, it turns out that this pose (or lack of posing) is the image I like best. But the image has many blemishes. The railing that I used to steady the camera is a huge blemish at the bottom part of the image. And the angle of the shot shows a reflection of the photographer (me) in the mirror on the background wall and a glaring flash off the camera as the picture was taken.

The image also suffers from the improper indoor lighting conditions that can be a common mistake. But fear not! These problems also can be easily corrected and compensated for.

I didn't want these kinds of flaws to ruin the potential I saw in this photo. What potential? Well, remember I said to examine the photo and make a mental list of what you *do* like about a particular image? For this image, I liked that the subject seemed relaxed for this particular shot. It shows in his face, which brings me to the second item I liked most about this photo. Under all those blemishes is a handsome face; I want that to shine through.

The first item on the agenda is to color correct the image. We can accomplish that through a two-phase process using an Adjustment Layer and Photoshop's new Shadow/Highlight command.

After we've corrected the color in this image, we can use a simple fix for many of the problems surrounding the main subject: cropping. Many people neglect this effective tool, but simple cropping can often remove distracting items, forcing the viewer to focus on the main subject. So never underestimate this easy and effective solution. After cropping the image, we'll use the Healing Brush to touch up this young man's skin and make use of another Adjustment Layer to brighten his teeth. Let's get started.

Correcting Color with an Adjustment Layer

Photoshop lists a variety of color correction commands under the Image, Adjustments menu. Many of these commands are also available under the Layer, New Adjustment Layer menu, which is also available as an icon at the bottom of the Layers palette. Whenever possible, use an Adjustment Layer when correcting color.

Here's why: If you access a color correction command from the Image, Adjustment menu, the correction is applied directly to the image layer. No going back, except through the History palette. After the image is saved and closed, the results are permanent. But by using an Adjustment Layer, you gain an infinite amount of flexibility. The adjustment is a separate layer that sits above the image layer, and that fact gives you a wealth of options for editing the image. You can come back months later and change the adjustment settings; or, because the adjustment is a layer, you can lower opacity, change layer modes, and apply a layer mask. If you do a lot of work in Photoshop, you will quickly learn to appreciate the benefits of Adjustment Layers.

Color Correction, Phase One

1. Open GradStudent.tif from the Examples\Chap15 folder on the companion CD. Press Ctrl(⌘)+plus key a few times until the zoom level is about 200%. Hold down the spacebar to toggle to the Hand tool, and scroll the image so that you

can see the white color of the subject's shirt. You will need a good clear view because you will be using this shirt area to set the white point in the next step.

Note

> **No rule of thumb**   Photoshop offers a wealth of color correction tools. There is no panacea to cover every situation. Color correction can be completely subjective—in other words, a matter of personal taste. The same holds true for the tools that you choose to use.

2. Click the Create new fill or adjustment layer icon at the bottom of the Layers palette, and choose Curves. In the Curves dialog box, click on the White Point eyedropper; then, in the document window, click the area that should be the whitest. In this case, an area along the top edge of the shirt appears to be the closest to a pure white (peek ahead to Figure 15.2). Keep the Curves dialog box open.

3. Next, use the Curves dialog box to lighten up the overall image tones. To accomplish this, click on the center of the diagonal line (across the grid that is located within this dialog box). Drag this center point slightly up and to the left until the Input field reads somewhere around 110 and the Output field is approximately 140, as shown in Figure 15.2.

Figure 15.2   Click on the area that should be the whitest point in the image. Next, lighten up the overall image tones.

Insider

Once you click to make a point on the diagonal line, you can also type the numbers (provided in these steps) into the Input and Output fields if you prefer this method over dragging.

4. Our next goal is to deepen the darker tones slightly. In the same grid, click on the point of the line at the bottom-left corner, and drag it slightly to the right (perfectly horizontal with the bottom edge of the grid), until the Input number reads approximately 13 (see Figure 15.3). Output should read 0 (and again, you can also select the point on the line and type these numbers into the Input and Output fields). Click on OK. Press Ctrl(⌘)+minus key to zoom out to view more of the image. Keep the image and Photoshop open for the next exercise.

Figure 15.3   Drag the lower-left corner point of the gridline to the right to deepen the darker tones slightly.

In these steps, we've completed only the foundational work for color correcting this image. The more you experiment with these tools, the more you will find which tools are your own favorites. I always like to start with Curves and then combine other tools to achieve the desired results. You might be asking how I arrived at the numbers for the Curves dialog box? The truth is simply a matter of experimenting and eyeballing the results. If we're playing true confessions again, I don't intuitively know what numbers to plug in. But I know enough to be dangerous. The image still needs correcting. Let's use a new feature to bring out the highlights and shadows.

Adjusting Color and Brightness with the Shadow/Highlight Command

The Shadow/Highlight command is new to Photoshop CS and a pretty powerful adjustment tool. This adjustment command does not simply lighten or darken the entire image; it lightens or darkens based on the surrounding pixels (the local neighborhood) within the shadows or highlights. For this reason, the Shadow/Highlight command is perfect for fixing photos with serious backlighting problems (a person silhouetted against a well-lit background, for example), and this is also what the default settings are aimed at.

When the Show More Options box is turned on, more controls are available for the Shadow and Highlight. They include controls for Amount, Tonal Width, and Radius. Larger values for the Amount slider provide greater lightening of shadows or greater darkening of highlights. Tonal Width controls the range of tones that will be modified. Smaller values restrict the adjustments to only the darker regions for Shadow and only the lighter regions for Highlight correction. Larger values include more tonal regions (such as adding the midtones) that are being adjusted. And Radius controls the size of the local neighborhood around each pixel to determine whether a pixel is in the shadows or highlights.

The slider options available in the Adjustment section of the Shadow/Highlight dialog box differ when you are working on a color image versus a grayscale image. For example, Color Correction is available when you're working on a color image, and it allows you to fine-tune the colors in regions of the image that have changed. In general, increasing values tend to produce more saturated colors, and decreasing values produce less saturated colors. And because the Color Correction slider affects only the *changed* portions of the image, the amount of variation this slider will provide depends on the amount of change made in the Shadow and Highlight sections of the dialog box.

No Adjustment Layer option is available for this tool, so we'll work on a copy of the Background layer for our color correction work.

Color Correction, Phase Two

1. On the Layers palette, drag the Background layer to the Create a new layer icon at the bottom of the palette (to make a duplicate copy of this layer). Choose Image, Adjustments, Shadow/Highlight. In the Shadow/Highlight dialog box, check the Show More Options box. Whoa! Didn't know all those options were there, did ya? Type in the values shown in Figure 15.4, and click on OK.

Figure 15.4   Again, there was no scientific formula for the numbers chosen in this figure. The goal was to bring out more details in the image, so finding the right numbers was merely a matter of playing with the sliders until we accomplished the goal.

Tip

> **Fine-tuning the Radius control**   If the Radius is too large, the adjustment tends to brighten (or darken) the whole image rather than brighten the subject only. Experiment with different Radius settings to obtain the best balance between subject contrast and differential brightening (or darkening) of the subject compared to the background.

2. Our next goal is to remove some of the hues that lean toward red tones. Click the Create new fill or adjustment layer icon at the bottom of the Layers palette, and choose Color Balance. In the Color Balance dialog box, click the Midtones option. In the three fields for Color Levels, type the following numbers: **–3, 7, 20**. Click the Highlights option, and in the three Color Levels fields, type **0, 5, 10**, as shown in Figure 15.5. Then click on OK.

Figure 15.5   More experimenting led to the numbers shown here. The goal was to move the sliders away from the tones that yield orange or reddish tints.

3. Let's apply one more adjustment to desaturate the color slightly to neutralize the skin tones. Click the Create new fill or adjustment layer icon at the bottom of the Layers palette, and choose Hue/Saturation. In the dialog box, drag the Saturation slider to the left until it reads **–20**, as shown in Figure 15.6; enter **3** for Lightness. Click on OK. Keep the image and Photoshop open for the next exercise.

Figure 15.6   Use the Saturation slider to help make the skin tones more neutral, and brighten the overall image slightly with the Lightness slider.

Cropping the Image

As mentioned earlier, never underestimate the power of cropping. In many instances, cropping can be used to effectively cut away the bad parts of an image. Learning how to recognize when and what to crop can often make the difference between producing a bad photo and a great one. By removing the outer clutter with an effective crop, you force the viewer to focus on what is important in the image.

There are a couple of ways to crop an image. The first is to crop what you see in the camera's viewfinder when taking the photo. Zoom in or out until you have the image framed the way you want it in the viewfinder before taking the shot. As you can see from the image you're working on, not everyone has a trained eye for this yet. In this case, the alternative method is to use Photoshop's Crop tool to achieve the desired results.

What are some ideas to keep in mind when cropping? Whether you crop by using the camera's viewfinder or Photoshop's Crop tool, you should crop for interest. Focus on what really matters, and crop with that goal in mind. But you might have other concerns. Maybe you need to crop to fit a specific print size. In this situation, you can find an option on the Options bar to type in a width and height amount for a specific crop range. Sometimes cropping can be used to help make a crooked image appear straight. Even though you can rotate and straighten an image in Photoshop, sometimes cropping for a straightening effect might yield a more interesting result. These are just a few points to consider when you're cropping for your own projects.

Cropping Out Unwanted Elements

1. Choose the Crop tool from the toolbox, and drag a selection around the cat and main subject. Then use the handles on the bounding box to adjust the crop further. The goal is to crop out the distractions at the bottom of the image. You might want to drag the handle on the middle-right side of the box so that you remove the electrical sockets on the wall. Drag the top-middle handle to just below the mirror, and keep the cat tail in the image when dragging the left-middle handle (see Figure 15.7). When you're satisfied, press Enter (Return) to commit the crop.

Figure 15.7   Use the Crop tool to make a crop similar to the one shown here to eliminate all the distractions in the image. What a difference a well-orchestrated crop can make, huh?

Insider

> If the crop handles don't respond to the place where you want to go (when dragging the handles)—in other words, the borders of the bounding box keep snapping to a point that you don't want—the fix is to turn off the snap options. Go to the View menu, and if a check mark appears next to Snap, choose Snap to toggle off the check mark. Then go to the View menu again and choose Snap To, None.

2. Press Ctrl(⌘)+Shift+S to save the document. Choose the native Photoshop PSD file format, and keep the image and Photoshop open for the next exercise.

Touching Up with the Healing Brush

We've come a long way in cleaning up this image. All that's left is to clean up some minor problems for this young man. Most of the blemishes on the skin can easily be corrected with the Healing Brush tool. In this case, using this tool is the digital equivalent of going to the dermatologist. And while we're at it, we'll give this young man the digital equivalent of a trip to the dentist's office for some teeth-whitening.

Skin Correction with the Healing Brush

1. With the GradStudent.psd file still open, press Ctrl(⌘)+plus key to zoom in until you're at 300%. Hold down the spacebar to toggle to the Hand tool, and scroll the document until the face is in view. Click on the Background copy layer to make it the active layer.

2. Choose the Healing Brush tool from the toolbox. Right-click (Macintosh: hold Ctrl and click) to access the Brush palette. Change the diameter to 6 (px), and make sure Hardness is set to 100%. Press Enter (Return) to dismiss the Brush dialog box. Hold down the Alt(Opt) key to sample a good skin area near the upper-right area of the forehead, as shown in Figure 15.8. Now simply click (don't drag) over the blemishes in the skin. Remove any blemishes you can find by simply clicking over them.

3. Optional: The Healing Brush tool functions by averaging out the texture and color of the sampled area with the target area. This averaging may cause a slight blue color to appear in the skin tones when you click near areas that approach the edge of the blue hat. If this occurs, switch to the Clone Stamp tool. On the Options bar, uncheck the Use All Layers option, and switch to a 9-pixel soft round brush. Alt(Opt)+click to sample a good skin area near the offending blue skin tones, and click (don't drag) over the blue tones to eliminate them (see Figure 15.9). Be careful not to click into the hat and sample areas close in color to the target area. The Clone Stamp tool uses exact information from the sampled area (rather than averaging the areas as the Healing Brush does).

Insider

> On the Options bar for the Healing Brush tool and Clone Stamp tool, you'll find Aligned and Use All Layers options available. These options play an important role in making the tool perform a specific way.
>
> The Aligned option determines whether your sample point remains fixed or moves relative to your brush strokes. When Aligned is selected, the sample point travels relative to your brush strokes. When you release the mouse after making a brush stroke, the next sample point will start where the last sample point ended (unless you resample). When the Aligned option is deselected, the sample point will still travel relative to your brush stroke, but when you release the mouse and start a new brush stroke, the sample point will revert to the original starting point once again.
>
> The Use All Layers option will allow you to sample from all visible layers. This feature is useful if you want to do your brush strokes on an empty layer using information from the layer below. When this option is deselected, only the information from the active layer is being used.

Figure 15.8   Alt(Opt)+click to define a source spot for correcting the texture of the blemished areas.

**Clone
Stamp
Tool**

Figure 15.9   Use the Clone Stamp tool to compensate for any weaknesses in the Healing Brush tool, such as blue-tint color spilling into the skin tones near the hat edge.

4. Press Ctrl(⌘)+plus key to zoom in to about 400%. Hold down the spacebar, and scroll so that the mouth and teeth are in clear view. Double-click on the Quick Mask mode icon (below the color swatches on the toolbar). Make sure the Selected Areas option is chosen in the preferences (the default color of red and Opacity of 50% will be fine for our needs). Click on OK. The default colors of black and white should now appear on the toolbox color swatches. If not, press **D** for the default colors.

5. Choose the Brush tool from the toolbox. On the Options bar, pick a 5-pixel soft round brush. The mode should be set at Normal, and Opacity and Flow should be set at 100%. If you haven't read any of the previous chapters that made use of Quick Mask mode, let me briefly explain that the goal is to paint the teeth. When you paint in Quick Mask mode, a color tint appears to indicate the areas that will eventually become a selection. In this case, we want to select the teeth. With black as the foreground color, start painting in the teeth (the default tint color of red will appear wherever the brush strokes are made). If you make a mistake, press **X**

15

to switch the foreground color to white, and paint away the mistake areas. Press **X** again (to switch to black) and continue painting until the teeth are selected, as shown in Figure 15.10. If necessary, lower the diameter of the brush size to paint the smaller teeth. When you're satisfied, press **Q** to exit Quick Mask mode, and a selection marquee of the painted area will appear.

Figure 15.10   Use Quick Mask mode to paint the teeth, and then turn the painted area into a selection when you're done.

Insider

> We will use a Levels Adjustment layer to whiten the teeth. Because we made a selection of the teeth area before going to an Adjustment Layer, the Adjustment Layer will automatically mask the areas that are outside the teeth selection (this is evident by the black fill color on the mask thumbnail for the Levels Adjustment layer). In other words, the Levels command you are about to use will make adjustments only to the selected area and will not affect the remaining areas of the image.

6. Click the Create new fill or adjustment layer icon at the bottom of the Layers palette, and choose Levels. In the dialog box, we want to brighten the white tones and minimize the black tones. First, slide the white Input slider to around 225 (or you can type the number into the appropriate Input Levels field). Next, slide the black Output slider to around 31 (or type the number in the appropriate Output Levels field). Figure 15.11 shows the values you want to set in the Levels dialog box. Click on OK.

Figure 15.11   Keep your eye on the teeth (in the image) while dragging the white Input slider and black Output slider, and you will see how to visually determine an appealing result when whitening teeth in future projects.

7. Press Ctrl(⌘)+minus key to zoom out a little. Remember that because the Levels adjustment is on a separate layer, you have the freedom to tweak this adjustment further for more natural results. If the teeth look unnaturally white, lower the Opacity on the Layers palette for the Levels Adjustment layer until it appears more natural. Somewhere around **55%** might do the trick.

8. Let's sharpen up the image a tad before finishing. Click on the Background copy layer to make it the active layer. Choose Filter, Sharpen, Unsharp Mask. In the dialog box, enter **87** for Amount, **1.4** for Radius, and **7** for Threshold (see

Figure 15.12). Click on OK. Choose Edit, Fade Unsharp Mask. Lower the Opacity to **60**% and click on OK. (As you learned in Chapter 12, "Curves and Adjustment Layers," it's always best to save the sharpening step for last, as other corrections can make the image appear sharper. By sharpening last, you avoid over-sharpening.)

Figure 15.12   The values used in the Unsharp Mask Filter are again values that were obtained through experimentation. I tend to over-sharpen and then use the Fade command to partially undo and fine-tune the effect.

9. Press Ctrl(⌘)+S to save the document. Close the file now, but keep Photoshop open.

Figure 15.13 shows the original image and the finished image side by side. Granted, the book contains grayscale images, but I believe you can still appreciate the differences even with this limitation.

Original Image   *Final Image*

Figure 15.13   When comparing the before and after images, you can clearly see that many of the distractions are no longer present. The focus is now on the handsome young man in the final image.

The Dreaded Red-Eye

We've all seen it. You snap a photo of a friend or relative, and the results look like something out of a horror movie. What causes red-eye? The basic fact is that the pupils naturally respond to light exposure by expanding in low-light levels and contracting in high-light levels. If you're in a low-light environment, the pupils expand to a large size, and when a flash goes off, the light travels through the dilated pupil and reflects off the blood vessels behind the retina. This reflection is translated back to the camera in the form of a distracting red spot.

You can use certain photographic techniques and equipment to reduce the possibility of red-eye in an image. Some of these measures are as follows:

- Turn on the lights to reduce the need for a flash or, at the very least, to allow your subjects' pupils to contract, which will leave less area for light to reflect.

- Take advantage of "red-eye reduction" features on your camera. When you use these features, the camera fires a pre-flash to help reduce the size of your subjects' pupils before firing off the actual flash when the picture is ultimately snapped.

- Have the subjects look away from the lens. Some cameras further help this measure by designing a flash that pops up or away from the camera as opposed to one that is located closer to the lens.

- Some cameras provide an option to add an external flash. This option completely removes the flash from the lens area; it can be a costly but effective solution if you shoot a considerable number of photos that result in red-eye.

The fact remains that, despite understanding the causes and solutions, red-eye still happens on occasion. Fortunately, Photoshop can help repair this common problem as well.

The next exercise introduces another image from the Examples folder on the companion CD. This image has a number of problems that we'll address in subsequent exercises. First, let's concentrate on color correction (using the new Shadow/Highlight command) and, of course, red-eye.

Color Replacement Tool and Shadow/Highlight Command

1. Open JustSittingAround.tif from the Examples\Chap15 folder on the companion CD.

Insider

The image looks dark, and I'm rather fond of tweaking this kind of problem by experimenting with the Shadow/Highlight command (that is new to Photoshop CS). So I'll deviate from my general rule of going to Curves first and go directly to the Shadow/Highlight command instead. However, keep in mind that this adjustment command is not available as an Adjustment Layer. For this reason, we will duplicate the Background layer and make the adjustment to a Background *copy* layer.

2. On the Layers palette, drag the Background layer to the Create a new layer icon at the bottom of the palette (to duplicate this layer).

3. Choose Image, Adjustments, Shadow/Highlight. In the dialog box, make sure the Show More Options box is checked. Use the settings shown in Figure 15.14, and click on OK.

4. Taking care of red-eye is next on the list. Adobe has decided to equip Photoshop CS with a new tool that's perfect for this situation: the Color Replacement tool. Press Ctrl(⌘)+plus key until you are zoomed in to about 400%. Hold down the spacebar to toggle to the Hand tool, and scroll until the eyes are in view. Press **D** for the default colors so that black is the foreground color.

Figure 15.14 The values used here in the Shadow/Highlight dialog box were obtained through pure experimentation, playing with different numbers until the image had an overall brighter quality without losing detail in the shadows.

5. Choose the Color Replacement tool from the toolbox (this tool is grouped with the Healing Brush and Patch tools). Figure 15.15 shows the (recipe) options used for fixing red-eye. Make sure the following choices are set as follows on the Option bar: Mode: Color; Sampling: Once; Limits: Discontiguous; Tolerance: 30%. Anti-aliased should be checked. Right-click (Macintosh: hold Ctrl and click) in the image window to access the brush size palette, and choose a brush size that is slightly smaller than the area you will be correcting. In this case, lowering the diameter to around 4 pixels should do the trick. Press Enter (Return) to dismiss the palette.

Insider

> We'll use a hard-edge brush for the Color Replacement tool, but on some images you might find a softer-edge brush works best. If this is the case, simply lower the Hardness level (to obtain a softer edge) when fine-tuning the brush palette options.

6. Notice that the cursor for this tool contains a crosshair in the center of the brush. Use this crosshair to click over the offending red pixels, and continue to click over offending pixels until all evidence of red-eye is removed (see Figure 15.15).

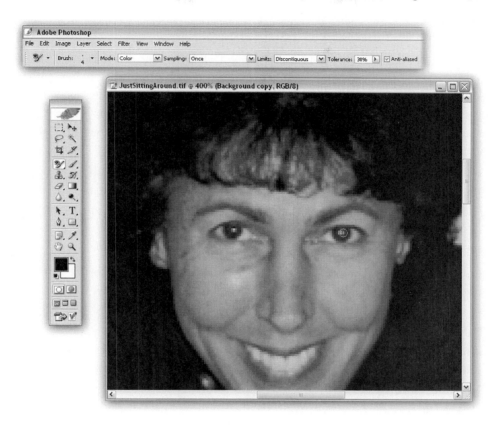

Figure 15.15   Click over the offending red-colored pixels to rid this woman of red-eye.

7. Press Ctrl(⌘)+Shift+S and save this image to your hard disk in the native Photoshop PSD file format. Keep the file and Photoshop open for the next exercise.

The image is looking better, but we still have more work to do to give a youthful glow to this face.

Digitally Reversing the Aging Process

The next exercise will concentrate mostly on the woman's face. You'll use a new layer to paint over some age spots and dark circle areas under the eyes. You will paint with colors sampled from the actual image to accomplish this and use a low Flow brush setting to give a more natural result.

There's something else you need to keep in mind when painting new areas onto a photograph. Just about every photographic image has some level of noise throughout the image. *Noise* is that grainy quality that becomes especially noticeable when you zoom in at a high magnification on a particular area. In a normal view, a color may appear to be a continuous, smooth color; when viewed at a higher zoom level, the same area appears to contain a pattern of colored pixels. We refer to that effect as *grain*.

When you apply color using a Brush tool, the color applied will be smooth and lack this kind of noise or graininess. To compensate for this, you will apply a Noise filter to the layer when the painting is completed (in an attempt to match the same quality of noise seen within the photograph). Next, you'll make a composite layer that will be used to apply a blur filter effect to further reduce uneven skin tones and wrinkles.

And last, you will use a technique to restore texture that was eliminated by the blur filter effect of the composite layer. We have our work cut out for us, so let's get started.

Painting and Adding Grain

15

If you are concerned that you do not have painting skills, don't worry, and have faith in yourself. The low Flow setting used in this next exercise has the added advantage of making subtle changes. Combine this with the benefits of the History palette, and this kind of painting repair work suddenly becomes very easy. Also, by painting on a separate layer, you have the additional benefit of trashing the layer if you need to start from scratch again.

As mentioned before, doing this type of painting will be less obvious if you remember to add grain (by applying a Noise filter) after you've completed the painting portion of your work. The next exercise will show you how; it's an easy process as well.

Painting Over Irregular Skin Tones

1. The JustSittingAround.psd image should still be open. If necessary, press Ctrl(⌘)+plus key until zoomed in to about 400%. Hold down the spacebar to toggle to the Hand tool, and scroll the image until the woman's face is clearly in view. You will concentrate mostly on the area under the eyes and near the cheeks.

2. Click the Create a new layer icon at the bottom of the Layers palette. The new
   layer should now be the active layer and at the top of the Layer palette stack
   (drag this new Layer 1 to the top if it's not already there). Choose the Brush tool
   from the toolbox, and on the Options bar, choose a soft round brush that's small
   enough to paint areas under the eyes (but not so small that it will slow down the
   work). A 9-pixel soft round brush seems to be the appropriate size for the work
   in *this* image. The brush size will vary in your own projects when you're working
   with other images. On the Options bar, make sure the Mode is set to Normal,
   Opacity is 100%, and Flow is set to 20% (see Figure 15.16).

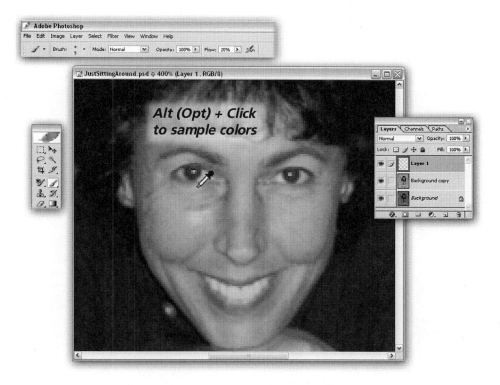

Figure 15.16   Hold down the Alt(Opt) key to sample a color. Use the Options settings shown
here to do the painting repair work.

3. Hold down the Alt(Opt) key to toggle to the Eyedropper tool, and sample a light
   patch of skin color just below the left eye, as shown in Figure 15.16.

4. The goal is to camouflage the circle and wrinkled areas below the eyes along
   with the age spots that look like a streak of darker color below the left eye. With
   the current sampled color, start painting just under the eyes near the nose, as

shown in Figure 15.17. When necessary, hold down the Alt(Opt) key to sample a skin tone color that will match more closely to the area you're trying to repair. For example, sample a rosy color from the cheek to paint over the age spots.

Insider

> Experiment and drag the brush to apply color in small sections at a time. If you're unhappy with a particular brush stroke, press Ctrl(⌘)+Z to undo, or use the History palette to undo more than one stroke at a time. Then repaint the area until you're happy with the results. The goal is to cover just enough to make the skin tones under the eyes more appealing. You don't need to cover the area too heavily to accomplish this. And don't forget to constantly resample to get colors that will be natural to the area you're working on. When you're satisfied, move on to the next step to apply a noise filter to the newly painted layer.

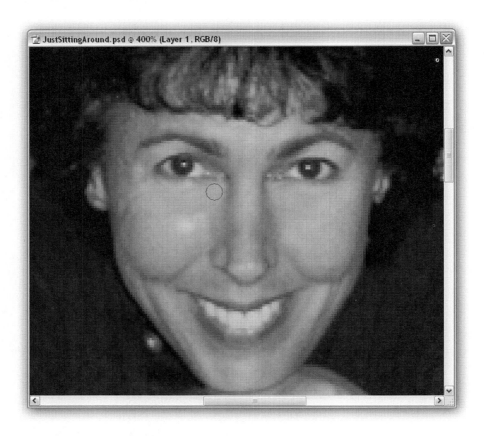

Figure 15.17 Start strokes close to the nose and brush outward, away from the nose. Sample colors frequently to give a smoother appearance under the eyes.

5. Now let's use the Add Noise filter to match the grain of the painted areas to that of the surrounding image area. Zoom in on the image to a high magnification level before using this filter, and adjust the view in the document window so you can easily see the areas that were painted on the new layer. Now compare the grain of the painted-on areas to the grain that exists in the original image (surrounding this area).

Insider

Under the Distribution section of the Add Noise dialog box, I prefer using the Gaussian rather than the Uniform option because the Uniform option will randomly generate noise, whereas the Gaussian option will distribute noise color values in a more consistent manner. The Monochromatic option within the filter's dialog box should also be checked because this will limit the noise to the tonal elements within the image without introducing or adding new colors to the mixture. To determine the Amount setting, watch the document window, and find an Amount level for the newly painted areas that will closely match the surrounding grain in the original image. This is the same method I used to arrive at the settings for the next step.

6. Choose Filter, Noise, Add Noise. In the Add Noise dialog box, make sure that the Gaussian and Monochromatic options are checked. Type **1.2** for the Amount (see Figure 15.18) and click on OK. This setting determines the amount of noise you'll add to the selected area.

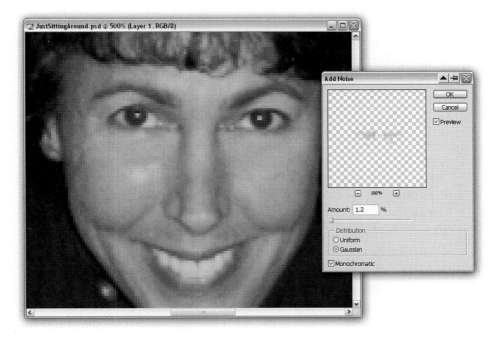

Figure 15.18   Use the settings shown here to give the newly painted layer a grain quality that matches the original image.

7. Observing the next change from a lower zoom level might be helpful. Press Ctrl(⌘)+minus key until you're zoomed out to about 300%. On the Layers palette, lower the Opacity to about 75% to further enhance the naturalness of the painted layer. Press Ctrl(⌘)+S to save the work, and keep the file open for the next exercise.

Insider

No one is perfect, so with this fact in mind, it's a good idea to allow some of the original layer to peek through to prevent the retouching from looking faked. The Opacity amount is an objective decision, and the amount might vary for your image or for similar future projects, but somewhere between 70–80% might do the trick.

Creating a Blur Filter Effect

Next, we will make a composite layer that combines the Background copy layer with Layer 1. This composite layer will be used to apply a blur filter effect and to take the "more youthful look" we're giving our subject to the next level.

Here, you want to create another blank layer below the top two layers and use this blank layer to create a composite layer from the top two layers. You will then move the composite layer to the top of the layer stack and apply a Gaussian Blur filter to this composite layer. Use a layer mask to hide the blurred layer. Then, by painting on the mask, you will control the areas and the *amount* of blur to specific skin areas in the image. This procedure may sound complicated, but the process won't be intimidating after you dive into the next exercise. Let's get started.

Making a Composite Layer

1. Click on the Background layer to make it the active layer. Hold down the Alt(Opt) key, and click the Create a new layer icon at the bottom of the Layers palette. Name the new layer **Composite Blur**, and click on OK. The new Composite Blur layer should be positioned in the correct stacking order (below the Background copy layer). Click in the column to the left of the Background copy layer and Layer 1 to link the Composite Blur layer to the two layers above it (peek ahead at Figure 15.19).

2. Hold down the Alt(Opt) key, click on the right-facing arrow in the upper-right corner of the Layers palette, and choose Merge Linked from the context menu (see Figure 15.19).

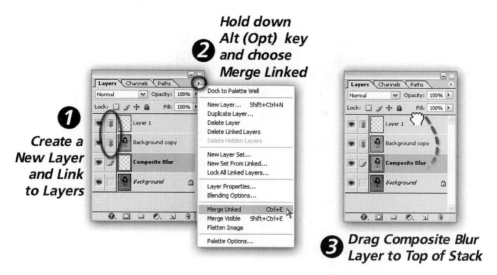

Figure 15.19   By holding down the Alt(Opt) key when choosing the Merge Linked option, you can create a merged layer without actually merging the original layers. The merged information appears on the target layer, which in this case was an empty layer created in the previous steps.

3. Drag the Composite Blur layer to the top of the stack on the Layers palette. Choose Filter, Blur, Gaussian Blur, and apply a Radius of 1 pixel. Click on OK (see Figure 15.20).

4. Hold down the Alt(Opt) key, and click the Add layer mask icon at the bottom of the Layers palette (peek ahead to Figure 15.21).

Insider

When you hold down the Alt(Opt) key, the layer mask will be created with a black-colored fill, which will completely mask (or hide) the Composite Blur layer. In other words, it will appear as if the blurred effect we just applied no longer exists. But trust me, the blurred information is still sitting on the layer waiting for you to selectively use the blurred effect as needed in the next few steps.

5. The layer mask should now be the active thumbnail, and the default colors should be showing on the color swatches on the toolbox. If necessary, press **X** to switch white to the foreground. Choose the Brush tool from the toolbox. On the Options bar, the last settings you used should work fine (Mode: Normal; Opacity: 100%; and Flow: 20%). Choose a 17-pixel soft round brush, and paint to blur the skin areas (see Figure 15.21).

Figure 15.20   Use the Gaussian Blur filter to apply enough blur to help smooth out all the skin impurities. Find the lowest Radius amount that can accomplish this goal (and avoid excessive over-blurring).

15

Insider

Choose a brush size large enough to paint the face and still fit into some of the smaller spaces—like the one between the nose and lips. Using a brush size that is too small will slow down the work, and you run the risk of making your work appear less natural. Using a brush that is too large doesn't allow you to control the smaller areas on the face (to maneuver around the eyes and mouth); plus, it might also spill over into areas outside the face. So try to determine a brush size in your own work to fit that happy medium.

6. With white as the foreground color, start painting all the skin areas (don't forget the skin area on the hand). Avoid painting the eyes and mouth if possible, but don't worry if your painting spills into these areas. You'll touch this up later. Watch carefully as you paint, to avoid over-painting. Watch the image and paint just enough blur onto the face and hand to give a smoother skin appearance, but not too much so that it appears unnatural.

Figure 15.21   Use white paint and a layer mask on a blurred layer to apply enough blur to skin areas for a youthful appearance.

7. When satisfied with the results, you can correct any areas where clarity and details are crucial. Press **X** to switch black to the foreground color. On the Options palette, change the Flow to 100%, and lower the brush size diameter to around 9 pixels so that you can fit into the smaller areas of the eyes and mouth. Paint a steady stroke over each eyebrow, and also paint the eyes, mouth, and teeth. By doing so, you remove any spillage into these areas and restore the details. A click or two at the base of the nose, near the nostrils, might help also. If you see any spillage blurring on the shirt or hair, paint in these areas as well to restore the detail. If you feel you blurred any areas of the face too much, lower the Flow setting back to 20%, increase the diameter of the brush size again, and make a swift sweep using black foreground color in areas that might appear over-blurred.

8. The overall image needs a little sharpening. Right-click (Macintosh: hold Ctrl and click) on the Background copy layer, and choose Duplicate Layer. Name this layer **Sharpened Version**, and click on OK. Choose Filter, Sharpen, Unsharp Mask. In the dialog box, apply my favorite settings: Amount: **87**, Radius: **1.7**,

Threshold: **4.** Then click on OK. Next, choose Edit, Fade Unsharp Mask, lower the Opacity to **70%**, and click on OK.

9. Press Ctrl(⌘)+S to save your work. Keep the image and Photoshop open for the next exercise.

Because you applied the Unsharp Mask filter to a separate layer copy of the image layer, you now have the flexibility of controlling the sharpening effect even further. You can choose to reduce the sharpening effect even further by lowering the Opacity on the layer or toggling the visibility off for this layer if you decide you don't want *any* sharpened effect at all (maybe you prefer a softer look to the image). Check the fixed areas to be sure they are not too obvious in an unsharpened state. I think the sharpened layer looks just fine as is, but this might be an idea to keep in mind for future projects.

We're almost done. We just need to address one more small detail before we finish.

Restoring Texture

Earlier, we painted away the circles and wrinkles under the eyes and then added noise to the painted layer to make the retouched work blend more naturally into the rest of the image. We did this because all photos have a certain amount of grain or noise. In duplicating that noise, we essentially made our retouch work less detectable.

Well, guess what? When we applied a blur filter to parts of the skin, the blur smoothed away some of that grain (or texture) in the image. I have a trick up my sleeve for fixing this problem. But first, let me explain how it works, so you'll understand the process.

You have a layer mask associated with a layer that has a blur filter applied. Where there is black color sitting on the layer mask, the blurred effect is hidden. Conversely, where there is white color (on the mask), the blur is exposed. But don't forget that you used a low Flow setting when painting on the mask, so the white areas aren't pure white. Therefore, when you restore the grain or texture, you want to restore with the same intensity that matches the amount of blur exposed. With me so far?

The next exercise will restore grain to only those areas where a blur effect was painted. You'll do this by creating a layer and filling it with 50% gray, thus covering the entire image with gray. You'll then use a layer mode that hides any tones that fall into the 50% gray tonal range. Why are we creating a gray layer and then hiding the gray? Well, before you hide the gray, you will apply the same Add Noise filter you used earlier onto the layer that contains a solid 50% gray fill. Then, when the layer mode is changed, the 50% gray tones will drop out, but the grain or texture from the Add Noise filter will remain visible.

The next step will be to add a layer mask to this grain layer—one that is identical to the mask used on the blur layer—so that the grain layer is visible only in the areas required, which corresponds to the areas visible through the blur layer mask.

I hope my explanation hasn't confused you too much. Maybe it'll all make sense when you see this process in action.

Adding Texture and a Copied Layer Mask

1. The JustSittingAround.psd image should still be open. Click on the Composite Blur layer to make it the active layer. Hold down the Alt(Opt) key, and click the Create a new layer icon at the bottom of the Layers palette. Name this layer **Grain**, and click on OK.

2. Choose Edit, Fill. In the Contents section of the Fill dialog box, choose 50% Gray for the Use field, and click on OK (see Figure 15.22).

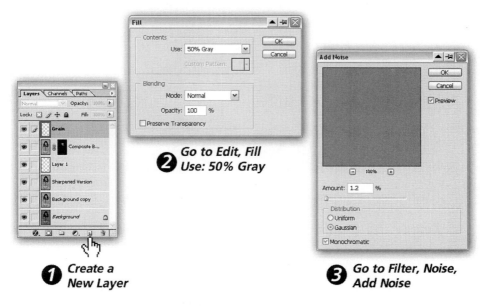

Figure 15.22 Fill the new layer with 50% gray. Don't be alarmed if this layer hides the image entirely; this effect is only temporary and will be fixed in the next few steps.

3. Choose Filter, Noise, Add Noise. In the Add Noise dialog box, duplicate the same settings used previously (see step 6 and Figure 15.18 in "Painting and Adding Grain"): Make sure the Gaussian and Monochromatic options are checked, and enter **1.2** for Amount, as shown in Figure 15.22. Then click on OK.

4. On the Layers palette, change the layer mode from Normal to Hard Light (see Figure 15.23).

Insider

In this exercise, I've chosen the Hard Light mode, but the Overlay mode might be an alternative layer mode to consider because it works in a similar manner for this kind of situation. Right about now, notice that the grain is filling the entire image, which ultimately means that there is *extra* grain in the image, especially in areas where it's not needed. This makes the image too *harsh*. The next step will correct this problem. You will duplicate the layer mask from the Composite Blur layer onto the Grain layer. Now pay attention; it's very important that you have the correct layer active when doing this next trick to duplicate the layer mask.

5. Make sure the Grain layer is the active layer (if not, click on the Grain layer to make it active). Now drag the layer mask thumbnail located on the Composite Blur layer to the Add layer mask icon at the bottom of the Layers palette (see Figure 15.23). By doing so, you create an exact duplicate layer mask on the target layer (in this case, the Grain layer).

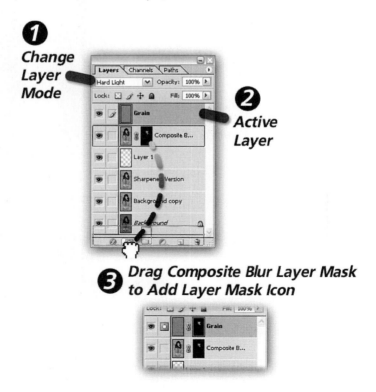

Figure 15.23   Change the layer mode to Hard Light for the Grain layer. Then, making sure to keep the Grain layer as the active target layer, drag the Composite Blur layer mask to the Add layer mask icon.

Now, a subtle grain effect should be restored to the skin areas. Zoom in on the face, and toggle the visibility for the Grain layer off and then back on to see the difference.

6. If you want, crop some of the background area away using the Crop tool. (This action is optional, and you can peek ahead to the final image in Figure 15.24 to see the crop I chose to apply.) Press Ctrl(⌘)+S to save the file. You can close the file at any time. Keep Photoshop open for the next exercise.

That's it. Your subject should have a youthful glow. Figure 15.24 shows the before and after images.

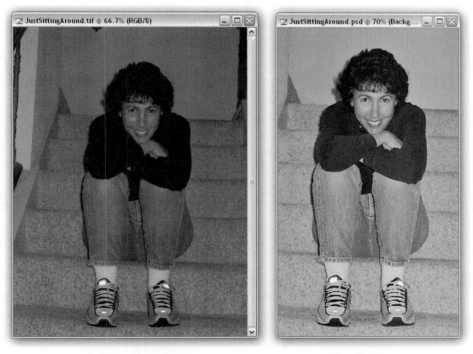

Original Image   **Final Image**

Figure 15.24   A side-by-side comparison makes you appreciate the differences. The final image on the right is of an attractive young woman, wouldn't you agree? Bet you never would have thought the original image on the left could have so much potential.

Always remember that it is a good practice to duplicate your image layer when you need to make changes to the original image layer. This practice gives you the freedom to make changes and still have a backup copy of the original source image if something should go wrong and you want to start from scratch. Always think in a way that makes use of layers. Layers provide a built-in flexibility for all projects. For example, in the preceding exercise, we used a gray filled layer as a means to apply grain and texture to the image. Because this grain is applied to a separate layer and not directly to the image itself, you have the flexibility of transforming the layer to help match the grain more precisely (should this benefit ever become a needed feature for future projects). Plus, you have the added flexibility to make use of layer masks, opacity, and layer modes. The possibilities are endless when you tap into layers.

Also, keep in mind that the painting method used in the preceding exercise to remove the dark areas under the eyes is also an ideal method for removing flaws and wrinkles around a jawline or neck. A double-chin is a perfect example, but you might discover many other uses in your own projects or photos.

If you ever find yourself in a situation in which you want to remove a double-chin, just use the same brush settings (the low Flow setting) and be observant. Pay attention to which tones on the skin to sample and which tones will look the most natural to simulate the lighting and shadows that might fall on the neck below the jawline, and change brush sizes when necessary to use the appropriate brush for the job at hand. For example, if you need to redraw a line to redefine a jawline, sample the current colors in this area. You might need a small brush here, but you might need to switch to a larger brush when painting *under* the jawline on the neck area. And don't be afraid of painting either. I hope you saw how easy it was to paint with a low Flow setting. You were able to control how much paint to add, and it was kind of cool to watch the flaws slowly disappear. Just remember to fix up all the flaws in the face first before applying a blur effect to a composite layer. After all, you don't want to have all the flaws come back to haunt you on the blurred layer.

Image Problem? Use It, Don't Lose It

Now we're ready for the kind of image correcting I enjoy the most—*no correcting at all!* Let me describe the setting for the image you're about to see. For one week out of the year, my daughter's school celebrates school spirit by allowing the students to dress in a different theme for each day. One day is Pajama Day, another is School-Colors Day, and well, you get the idea. One day in particular was known as Wacky Tacky Day, and I thought my daughter looked rather cute in the wacky fabrics she pulled together as an outfit for that day. I wanted to take pictures, but she wasn't too enthusiastic about the idea and not in the mood to model and show off for the camera. So I strolled by her room and quickly snapped a few shots. As you'll soon discover for yourself, her room isn't the best setting for a picture.

When I glanced at the downloaded images, my first impression was "Oh, these photos aren't useful for anything. Look at all the clutter. It would take hours to edit this stuff out, and I'm not so convinced the final result would be worth the effort."

After I filed the images away, a funny thing happened: The images kept cycling through my mind. I kept thinking about them and thinking of funny captions to go with them—captions such as "She may not be neat, but she has a talent for camouflage," or along the same lines, "Her chameleon-like skills enable her to blend into her environment."

Technically, this next exercise may not fall into the category of photo retouching, but it is a quick and easy exercise that is pertinent to the topic of how to make the best of a hopeless snapshot. I included a postcard template file that was designed to give a creative setting and to help show off this disastrous image in a way that plays up the flaws in a humorous manner.

Making a Postcard

1. Open ResponsibleTeen.tif from the Examples\Chap15 folder on the companion CD. Suddenly, everything I've been saying makes sense, huh? Your eye doesn't know where to focus first—too many distractions.

2. Open PostcardTemplate.psd from the Examples\Chap15 folder on the companion CD. If you look at the Layers palette for this file, the Pic Placeholder layer should be the active layer (within the open Placeholders set). If this layer is not the active layer, open the Placeholders set, if necessary, and click on the Pic Placeholder layer title to make it active.

Insider

> When you drag one image into another image, Photoshop automatically places the new image layer from the source file above the current active layer for the target file. Ultimately, we want the ResponsibleTeen image, which will be the source image, to rest on a layer above the Pic Placeholder layer in the target PostcardTemplate file. So by making Pic Placeholder the active layer beforehand, you ensure that the new image will automatically fall above this layer when placed into the file.

3. Arrange the images so that you can easily see them both. If necessary, press Ctrl(⌘)+minus key to zoom out until the images are small enough to see both in the workspace. Click on the title bar of the ResponsibleTeen.tif image to make it the active document. Drag the Background layer title from the Layers palette into the PostcardTemplate.psd image window (see Figure 15.25). Once placed in the Postcard file, the teen image might look funky, but don't worry, the next steps will fix this. You can close the ResponsibleTeen.tif image without saving changes.

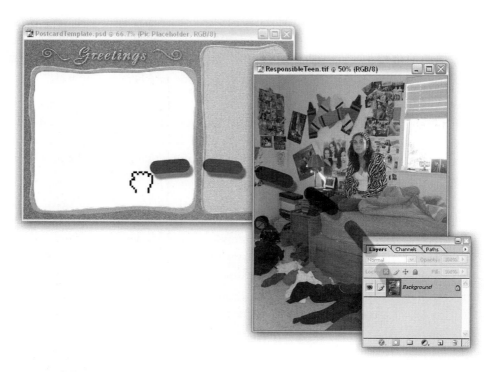

Figure 15.25   Drag the Background layer title from the ResponsibleTeen image into the PostcardTemplate image.

4. On the Layers palette for the Postcard file, a new Layer 1 should be sitting above the Pic Placeholder layer. Layer 1 should also be the active layer. Press Ctrl(⌘)+G to group this image Layer 1 with the Pic Placeholder layer.

5. The image is still too big for the Pic Placeholder area, so let's resize it. With Layer 1 as the active layer still, press Ctrl(⌘)+T to activate the Transform tool. On the Options bar, click the Maintain aspect ratio icon (it looks like a chain link between the Width and Height fields). In the Width field, type **65**%, and the Height field should automatically adjust to the same value. If necessary, click inside the bounding box area to move and reposition the image (see Figure 15.26). The goal is to make the teenager and as much of the clutter as possible visible within the Pic Placeholder window. But be careful that you don't move the image too far, or else it might fall outside the boundaries of the Pic Placeholder window, which will cause the white border area of the Placeholder layer to show through. When you're satisfied with the position and size, press Enter (Return) to commit the transform.

Maintain Aspect Ratio

Figure 15.26   Use the Options bar values shown here to transform the size and position of the image. If you want to duplicate the exact positioning, simply use the same X and Y values shown here as well.

6. Because the image was resized, it lost some of its focus. Let's apply an Unsharp Mask filter to restore some of the sharpness again. With Layer 1 still active, choose Filter, Sharpen, Unsharp Mask. Yup, you guessed it; use my favorite recipe settings: Amount: **87**, Radius: **1.7**, Threshold: **4**. Then click on OK. Next, choose Edit, Fade Unsharp Mask, lower the Opacity to **50%**, and click on OK.

7. On your own, choose the Text tool, along with a font and font color. To the right of the Pic Placeholder window is a Text Placeholder window. Simply click over this area with the Text tool, and type a clever caption. After typing the text, you can play with different fonts or different values for the other fields in the Character palette. This is a great way to become familiar with the options for the Character and Paragraph palettes.

Insider

If you like, borrow one of my previous captions, or click the eye icon to the left of the Text layer set on the Layers palette to see the caption I already provided for the image. See Figure 15.27 for a look at the finished product.

Figure 15.27   Toggle on the visibility for the hidden Text layer set to complete the finished product shown here.

8. Press Ctrl(⌘)+S if you want to save this file to your hard drive. You can close the file at any time. Keep Photoshop open for the next exercise.

I bet you have a ton of images that you can make into equally amusing postcards to send to friends and family. For example, at some time in your life, you probably took a photo (for insurance purposes) of damage done to a car that was involved in an accident. You probably never thought of using this photo for anything beyond documenting the damage. But what if you were to use this type of image with a caption like "Breaking up is hard to do." Greeting card companies better watch out! If you take the time to think about it, you could come up with a bazillion ideas for all those hopeless photos.

Everything You Wanted to Know About RAW—But Were Afraid to Ask!

Before finishing this chapter, you need to be aware of an important plug-in built into the new Photoshop CS interface. It's known as the Camera RAW plug-in. Adobe first announced this plug-in around February 2003. It was originally sold as a separate product to install for version 7 of Photoshop. But, thankfully, Adobe decided to bundle the plug-in within the Photoshop CS interface—and if you haven't had the opportunity to use this plug-in yet, you're in for a real treat.

What Is RAW?

RAW format, by definition, is the raw data information. This means it is a high-quality lossless file format that contains all the information (in its entirety) that comes off a digital camera's sensors before it is worked over by the camera's interpretations for white balance, sharpening, compression, and so on. What does this mean to you? Well, it's the equivalent of a digital negative. All the information is preserved within the RAW format, and the best part is that the RAW format takes up less file space on a memory card than the TIFF format (which is the next best possible format for saving high-quality images on a memory card). Many digital cameras support the RAW format, and if you're thinking about buying a digital camera sometime soon, make sure that the camera *does* indeed support RAW.

If your camera supports RAW, find out how to change your settings, and start taking all your digital images in this format. You may not be able to fit as many images on a memory card compared to a JPEG setting, but the advantages of this file format far outweigh the disadvantages. If you happen to take the perfect shot, you're guaranteed to have a high-quality version of the file for printing purposes. If, for example, you choose to capture your photos in a JPEG format (to save space), the images may look fine for viewing on a monitor but won't be as sharp when printing, compared to a higher quality file format.

How Do You Access the RAW Files?

Many cameras that support the RAW format may also provide their own software for downloading and converting RAW files into JPEGs or TIFFs. The only problem with most of this software is that it's excruciatingly slow and limiting. You don't always have choices or the flexibility to determine how to interpret the RAW data on your camera.

Now, here comes Adobe, the company known for its innovative software that makes the graphics world a much better place to be in. The Camera RAW plug-in is no exception. It is extremely responsive and flexible. If you have access to Photoshop CS, just toss all the other software that came with your camera to convert RAW images. Adobe's Camera RAW plug-in will give you all the power you need for handling those RAW files. Enough superlatives. Before I show you how the plug-in works, let me briefly explain how to move the RAW files onto your hard drive.

The easiest method is to use Windows Explorer (or the Mac equivalent, Finder). After the camera is turned on and properly plugged into the computer (usually via a USB cable), the computer will automatically recognize the camera in some manner. For example, when I plug in my camera and turn it on, it shows up in Windows Explorer listed with my drives. (Explorer displays a camera icon, but in many cases, the camera might be listed as a Removable Drive, with a drive letter assigned to it.) When I double-click on the camera icon (or the appropriate drive), Windows Explorer reveals all the files currently on my camera's memory card. If the files are in RAW format, they appear with an extension that varies depending on your camera. Canon uses a .CRW file extension, Nikon uses .NEF, and Kodak uses a .DCR extension, to name a few.

At this point, you can simply select all the files by pressing Ctrl(⌘)+A and then choosing Edit, Cut or pressing Ctrl(⌘)+X to remove the files from the memory card. Navigate to a location on the hard drive to store the images, and choose Edit, Paste or press Ctrl(⌘)+V to paste the files in the new location. I find it helpful to create a folder with the current date for the images and paste them into the dated folder. In one sweep, this method clears the memory card to allow room for more pictures and moves the image files to the hard drive.

If the Cut option isn't available (after you select the files on the camera's memory card), another method is to choose File, Save and navigate to a desired folder on the hard drive (within the Save dialog box). Then you can delete the files from the memory card after you complete this task.

How Do You Use the Camera RAW Plug-In?

Using Camera RAW is fun and easy. Simply open any RAW file (such as file with a .CRW extension), and the plug-in will automatically launch. You can do this either by choosing File, Open and then navigating to a RAW image file or, better still, choosing Window, File Browser and navigating to the folder that contains your RAW files. The File Browser is sophisticated enough to display thumbnails of your RAW files. Double-click on one of the images from the File Browser, and again, the RAW plug-in will automatically launch.

Figure 15.28 shows a sample of what the plug-in dialog box offers when you open any RAW image file. Refer to the callouts in Figure 15.28 as you read the following descriptions:

- **Item 1**—In the upper-left corner of the dialog box, you'll find the Zoom tool, Hand tool, and a White Balance tool. The same keyboard shortcuts that work in Photoshop will work within the RAW dialog box as well. You can essentially use the Ctrl(⌘) key combined with the plus or minus keys to zoom in or out. You can also hold down the spacebar to toggle to the Hand tool. There's no real urgency to click on these two icons if you're accustomed to using keyboard shortcuts, but you might find the White Balance tool useful because it adjusts the white balance to compensate for poor lighting conditions in the image. To use the White Balance tool effectively, you need to click on an off-white (not a pure white) color within the image. If you're not sure which color to click on, don't fret; Adobe has provided several other means or methods for determining white balance.

- **Item 2**—The White Balance section of this dialog box offers two ways to correct poor lighting conditions. You can click on the drop-down menu and choose from the preset white balance options that come closest to mimicking the same lighting conditions under which the image was taken. Or you can leave the option to the default As Shot and try to obtain the proper white balance adjustments by tampering with the Temperature and Tint sliders.

- **Item 3**—The bottom section of the dialog box provides many options that allow you to control items such as zoom level, color space profile, bit depth (8-bit or 16-bit), size, and resolution of the image.

- **Item 4**—This area of the dialog box provides a visual reference to RGB values when you hover your cursor over various spots in the image. Icons are also provided here to enable you to rotate the image within the dialog box interface.

- **Item 5**—When the Advanced option is checked, the Lens and Calibrate tabs appear, offering more slider choices to tweak the image. The Basic option displays the Adjust and Detail tabs only.

- **Item 6**—The Histogram provides a visual reference to tonal range as adjustments are applied to the image.

- **Item 7**—The right-facing arrow reveals the Camera Raw plug-in context menu, which offers options to save or load settings. These options come in handy if you have more than one image shot under the same conditions. You can make the adjustments once and save the settings. Then, when you open other images, you can simply load the previously saved settings to apply the same adjustments to other images.

If you would like more information about Camera RAW, Adobe has a slew of wonderful tutorials for a variety of issues on its Web site. You can also go directly to the following Adobe Web page to view a QuickTime movie on Camera RAW basics:

`http://www.adobe.com/digitalimag/tips/phs7rbrawbasics/main.html`

Just click on the Click to view the movie link.

Well, enough theory. I included a RAW file in the Examples\Chap15 folder on the companion CD to take this plug-in for a test drive.

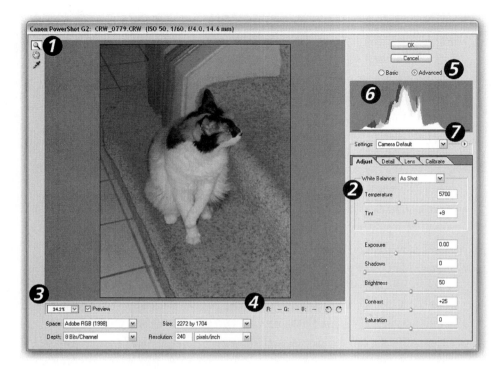

Figure 15.28   This Camera RAW plug-in dialog box is packed with features to control and fine-tune the way you want your image to look.

Note

> **Remember to experiment**   All the values I have chosen for this exercise were obtained purely through experimentation. I adjusted the sliders until I was pleased with the results in the preview window. You don't need to understand complicated photography concepts, but the more experimentation you do with color settings, the better you'll become at using them.

Camera RAW

1. Open CRW_0770.CRW from the Examples\Chap15 folder on the companion CD. When the Camera Raw dialog box appears, you can see the image in the preview window.

2. At the bottom of the box, make sure the color space is set to Adobe RGB (1998). The other settings should default to the ones shown in Figure 15.28.

Insider

In the steps to follow, you can use the Histogram as a visual reference to understand when changes are moving the image in a positive direction or a negative one. As mentioned before, the Histogram gives a visual for the tonal range, and a healthy Histogram will be more evenly spread out with a gradual peak near the center (rather than crunched up to a limited area within the Histogram box). If the Histogram tonal range starts to bump up against the sides of the box, this could be an indication that colors are being clipped out. In other words, the pure white or pure black tones are being eliminated from the image (which also limits the total number of color values within the image).

3. The Temperature for this image is currently set at 5200. Keep your eye on the difference in color tones when you move the Temperature slider so that it reads **5950** (or type the amount in the Temperature field). Also, note an improvement in the Histogram. Adjust the Tint slider until it reads **20**. Again, you can see an improvement in both the image tones and Histogram. To prove it, toggle the Preview option off and on to observe the difference between the original values and the new values that were just entered. When you're done comparing, make sure the Preview option is selected (on) for the next steps.

4. You will apply an adjustment on the Exposure slider, and again, try to pay attention to both the changes in the image and the changes in the Histogram. The default setting is 0, but type **1.4** for the Exposure value. Also, change the Shadows slider from 0 to a value of **1** instead. If you want to experiment, try to type a higher value in the Shadows field and watch the Histogram slide up the lower-left side of the box (an indication that colors are becoming clipped). Return the value back to **1** after you've finished experimenting. The remaining sliders seemed to work best when left on the default settings (see Figure 15.29).

5. Before exiting this dialog box, play with the other sliders to get a feeling for what they do. Don't forget to click on the other tabs (Detail, Lens, and Calibrate) to explore the options available there as well. If you get too far off and want to return to the original settings, simply hold down the Alt(Opt) key to toggle the Cancel button to a Reset button. Click on the Reset button and start from scratch.

6. When you're done experimenting, return the values to the ones described in this exercise, and click on OK. The dialog box will close, and the image will be displayed in Photoshop. You have your choice of saving the file in any file format typically available or closing the file without saving changes. You can close the image and Photoshop when you're done.

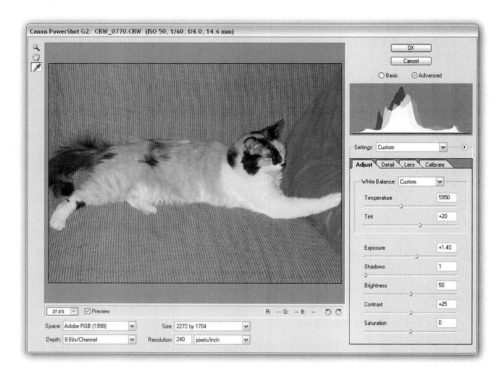

Figure 15.29   Use the settings shown here for this image.

Remember that the RAW format is the equivalent of a digital negative. You can open the same RAW image file again and again—each time tweaking the settings to achieve a different effect. The original information from the camera's sensors will forever be preserved within the RAW file, and you can save the results achieved (through the plug-in) as any file format appropriate for your work (PSD, TIFF, JPEG, or whatever you prefer).

Summary

We covered a lot of territory in this chapter, which included an introduction to a few new tools, such as the Shadow/Highlight command and the Color Replacement tool. We also covered useful ways to make the best of older features such as Adjustment Layers, the Healing Brush tool, the Clone Stamp tool, and the Cropping tool. You've learned how to take a poor image and make it great through cropping, color correction, and by using various image correction techniques to remove flaws. You've also seen examples of how useful creativity and humor can be in image retouching and correction.

15

As always, it is my hope that the information here will be useful material to apply to your own projects at home or work. Try to think outside the box. Imagine how many of these photo-retouching tricks and techniques can be applied to areas that are beyond the scope of the way they were used in this chapter. For example, remember the method used to paint a mild blur onto the skin (to simulate a youthful appearance)? You could use a similar method to control a blurred background (to simulate depth of field) or to remove beard stubble from a man's face that shows signs of a five o'clock shadow. And most important, don't be afraid to experiment; experimentation is the key to how many of these tricks and techniques are born.

Chapter 16

Color Balancing and Adjustment Layers: Creating a Cover Girl Image from an Average Picture

When my friend Monica looked at the CoverGirlStart.tif image (on the companion CD and in Figure 16.1), she exclaimed, "How beautiful! She looks like a golden angel. And *look,* the light at her

In this chapter, you'll learn

- How to assess an image for lighting and composition flaws
- How to edit unnecessary clutter from the image background
- How to use blending modes and gradients to add background interest
- How to use the Clone Stamp tool to edit eye highlights
- How to eliminate harsh shadows and blemishes
- How to eliminate bright, distracting colors
- How to touch up details and eliminate dust, scratches, and minor image flaws
- How to adjust image focus
- How to size and lay out an image with text for a magazine cover

left—it could be her *aura*." Monica, bless her soul, is an expert and teacher in *shakra* and vital forces. "But," I just had to point out, "did you see those finger spots on the left panel side? They're really ugly, aren't they?" "I don't see it like that," she answered. "It seems to me it's something like heavenly light bubbles."

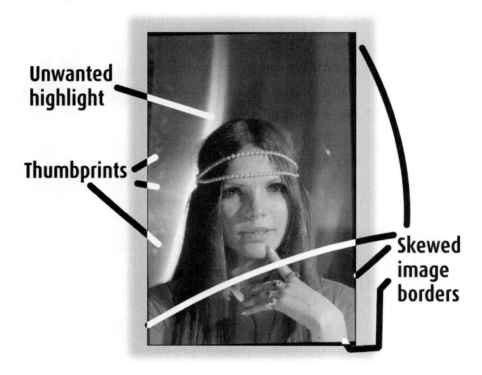

Unwanted highlight

Thumbprints

Skewed image borders

Figure 16.1   It's better to get creative with Photoshop to fix the image problems than to get creative with your imagination, excusing flaws!

Hope springs eternal, doesn't it? :)

Let's do a reality check here. We are facing a picture with severe overcast problems, hideous shadows, a dreadful background, and an out-of-focus character. This chapter has the answers for the problems in the cover girl image. The chapter also offers techniques for creating ideal images from so-so ones that you might have lying around.

Examining the Flaws in the Image

The man who took the picture shown in Figure 16.1 may have been thinking to himself that he was a great professional photographer. He used a lot of studio goodies: spots, reflecting plates, and so on. But unfortunately, he forgot the principles of lighting and portrait photography.

The photographer of this image neglected to correctly capture the lighting, and that's a basic flaw. What is a picture if it is not a play between light and shadow? With that "interplay," we express our artistic intent and create atmosphere.

In portrait photography, the basic rule is that, to achieve the most flattering images of folks, you should light men from the side and light women and children from the front. Though this rule has a few exceptions, in general light used this way *paints* women and *sculpts* men.

Capturing the Right Light

Although Photoshop can work miracles, it's best if you "get it right in the can"—in other words, get that snapshot looking as good as it can in the lens, and leave Photoshop work for the finishing touches.

Light is the essence of a picture. The way you use it will affect the general atmosphere—from romantic to dramatic, or completely flat. Before you click the shutter, always take a few seconds to look from the position where the light is coming from and see how it interacts with the main subject. How many people are disappointed when looking at the "beautiful" picture they took of a loved one in the sunset and the face is nothing more than a "black hole"? Always shooting away from the sun is just common sense, or if you need to shoot into the sun, use a flash fill. Again, Photoshop is there to *help* to correct or to transform a poor photograph, but it can't *replace* a badly taken picture. Pay some attention before shooting, and avoid a lot of trouble trying to repair bad lighting and poor color balance.

Removing Unwanted Border and Making Basic Color Correction

Obviously, the subject of this image is the girl. Did the photographer succeed in making this point obvious? Not really. The background and the girl's blouse overwhelm the subject in this portrait. In a "conventional" portrait, the key elements are the subject's eyes and lips. Okay, let's concede that the jewelry in this particular context also has a part to play, but only as a secondary role.

In this exercise, you're going to make some basic corrections to the color in the CoverGirlStart image. This exercise begins, however, with some adjustments to straighten the image by eliminating the black line at the bottom and right side of the picture.

In the following steps, you'll bring back the right color information:

Making Basic Corrections

1. Open CoverGirlStart.psd from the Examples/Chap16 folder on the companion CD. Press Ctrl(⌘)+the minus key to reduce the view of the image to less than the workspace. Drag on the bottom corner of the document window (to stretch it out for more breathing room) until gray background is visible in the document window.

2. Press Ctrl(⌘)+A to select the entire image. Press Ctrl(⌘)+T to activate the Transform tool. Right-click (Macintosh: hold Ctrl and click) and choose Perspective from the context menu. Take the bottom-right handle, and move it down beyond the document border and into gray area until the black edge area is no longer visible within the document. Then take the upper-right handle, and move it to the right until the image looks like that shown in Figure 16.2. The goal here is to remove the black edges from the document window. When you're satisfied, press Enter (Return), or click on the check mark on the Options bar to apply the transformation, or double-click inside the image (any of these commands can be used to finalize the Perspective edit).

Figure 16.2   Use the Perspective mode of the Free Transform feature to eliminate the black areas on the bottom edges of the image.

3. Now, we need to deal with the horrendous orange color cast. Right-click (Macintosh: hold Ctrl and click) on the Background layer, and choose Duplicate Layer to make a copy of your Background layer. Name this layer **Work in progress** in the Duplicate Layer dialog box. Click on OK. The duplicate layer is now the current editing layer.

Tip

Working on the Background layer   Make it a rule to always work on a copy of the Background layer and never on the Background layer itself. You can also copy layers by dragging them onto the Create a new layer icon at the bottom of the Layers palette. Holding down the Alt(Opt) key while dragging the layer to the Create a new layer icon opens the Duplicate Layer dialog box, where you can change the name of the duplicate layer.

4. Click the Create a new fill or adjustment layer icon (at the bottom of the Layers palette). Choose Selective Color. Orange is composed of red and yellow, so your first correction will deal with these two colors. At the bottom of the Select Color Options dialog box, select the Absolute option. Colors should be set at Reds. Add 1% to Yellow and −10% for Black. In the Colors drop-down menu, select Yellows. Add 1% to the Cyan value, −100% for Magenta, −100% for Yellow, and increase Black to 14%. See Figure 16.3 for these new values. Leave all the other color values unchanged and click on OK.

Insider

Although step 4 is scripted with values I used, you could arrive at these values yourself by looking at the target image and making changes with the Selective Color sliders. You'll naturally do this in your own work. Just make sure you understand what the color problem is, and then alleviate it by choosing negative values for unwanted colors and positive values for colors that are not predominant enough in the image. See Figure 16.4 for a color wheel that describes color opposites. For example, if an image contains too much orange, look at the *neighboring* colors for the components—the colors that border the target color. And look across from a color to find its color opposite.

5. Click on the Create a new fill or adjustment layer icon at the bottom of the Layers palette, and choose Levels. We will treat each color channel separately. In the Channel drop-down list, choose the Red channel. Enter the following Input Levels values: **14**, **0.95**, and **255**. For the Green channel, enter these values: **4**, **1.08**, and **255**; and for the Blue channel, enter these values: **0**, **1.13**, and **255**. Click on OK. Figure 16.5 shows all these values: The Red channel information is labeled 1; the Green channel is labeled 2; and the Blue channel values are shown in the example labeled 3.

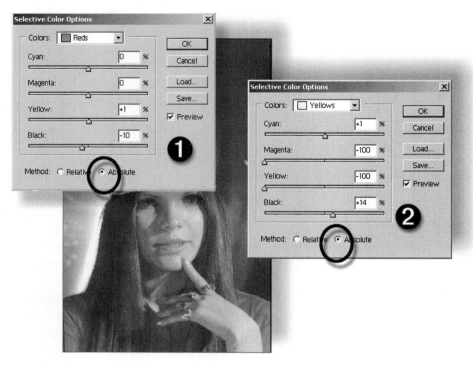

Figure 16.3   Use the Selective Color feature to add a basic color balance to the image.

16

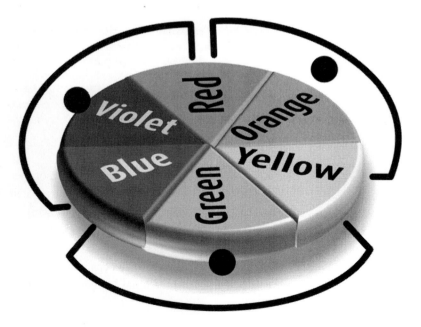

Figure 16.4   Color opposites lie directly across from each other in the color wheel.

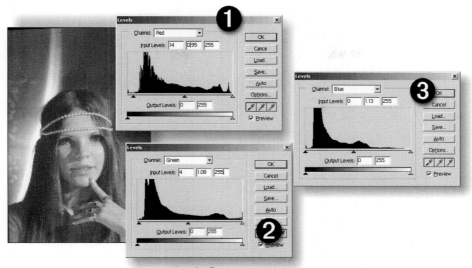

Figure 16.5   Use the Levels command on each color channel to remove color casting.

6. Again, click on the Create a new fill or adjustment layer icon at the bottom of the Layers palette, and then choose Color Balance. Look at Figure 16.6 for the values to enter for the Midtones, Highlights, and Shadows: Red: 14, .95, and 255; Green: 4, 1.08, 255; and Blue: 0, 1.13, 255. Be sure that the Preserve Luminosity option is checked before you click on OK.

7. The image still has a light yellow overcast that will disappear in one click. Click on the Levels 1 Adjustment Layer to make this layer active, and change the blending mode from Normal to Saturation.

   The girl now has a nice, smooth, and soft skin tone.

8. Press Ctrl(⌘)+S; keep the file open.

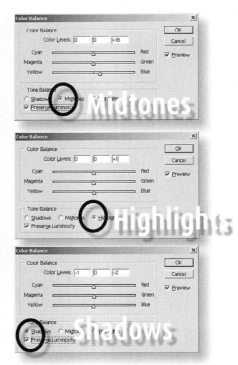

Figure 16.6   The Color Balance command is yet another feature for neutralizing color casting.

Cleaning Up the Image Background

The background is a real cacophony and distracts from the main subject. We will elimi-nate the distractions from it. At the same time, we will perform some hairdressing to clear away all the stray hair:

Smoothing Out the Image Background

1. Choose the Magnetic Lasso tool from the toolbox, and follow the edge of the hair *on* the head, but not the chunky strands that are sticking out around the model's head. Start from the middle upper-left side of the head hovering the tool (don't drag the Magnetic Lasso tool) to the right toward the shoulder, down and follow-ing the frame, and then up to the left shoulder, back to your starting point (see Figure 16.7). A little circle will appear at the right of the Magnetic Lasso tool indicating that your selection is complete. Single-click to accept the selection, and the typical "marching ants" will appear to display the selection. You will refine this selection with the Quick Mask feature, but first press Shift+F7 to *invert* the selection—the image background.

Figure 16.7   Here's the selection you've made with the Magnetic Lasso tool.

2. Type **Q** to enter Quick Mask mode. Your selection area now should have a red color overlay.

Insider

> You can change the red for another color (the author used a bright green to differenti-ate the Quick Mask from the shirt) by double-clicking the Quick Mask icon on the tool-box and picking a color of your choice. The Quick Mask icon is the circle-in-a-rectangle icon on the right, toward the bottom of the toolbox (see Figure 16.8). You can also hold down the Alt(Opt) key and click on the Quick Mask icon to toggle between selected areas and masked areas. In other words, you can toggle to determine whether you pre-fer your selection to contain the Quick Mask fill color or the areas that are masked (*not* selected) to contain the fill color.

3. Press **D** for the default colors of black (foreground) and white (background). Use black to add to your selection and white to subtract. On the toolbox, choose the Brush tool, and start with a 13-pixel *hard* brush. Vary the size of your brush for more precision, and refine the selection in the image. Make sure the Option bar has the brush Mode set to Normal and Opacity and Fill set to 100%. The hard brush is okay here because your new background will be neutral, and the edges of the girl's image will melt into it. When you're satisfied with the results, press **Q** to exit Quick Mask mode and turn the colored paint into a selection.

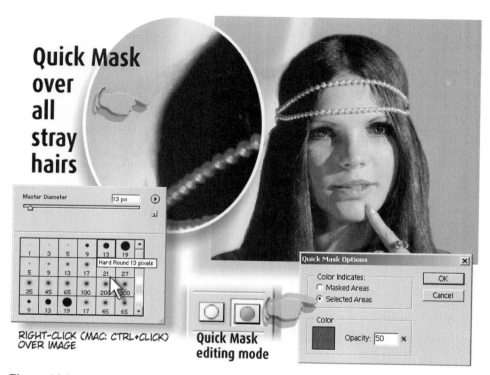

Figure 16.8   Use Quick Mask instead of a selection tool to "paint" an overlay that will become a selection marquee.

Tip

> **Softening selection edges**   If you are creating a background selection and then adding a background that is very different from the original in tone and values, you should soften the selection's edges even more than in these steps so that the fringe will be less apparent. Use a soft brush tip, and lower the opacity of the brush while masking. Figure 16.9 shows the settings for the Brushes palette.
>
> But you also must be careful using a soft brush; too smooth a selection edge can give a "muddy" effect. Photoshop allows you to have complete control over the brush qualities. At the right of your screen, click in the folder called Brushes. Click the Brush Tip Shape option to the left of the dialog box. There, you can define the hardness of your brush and the spacing. The adjustments made there also help to maintain film grain or noise in the photo. See Chapter 3, "Setting Preferences, Customizing, and Optimizing Photoshop CS," for detailed information on how to modify and create brush tips.

4. With the Work in progress layer active, press the Backspace (Delete) key to remove the background.

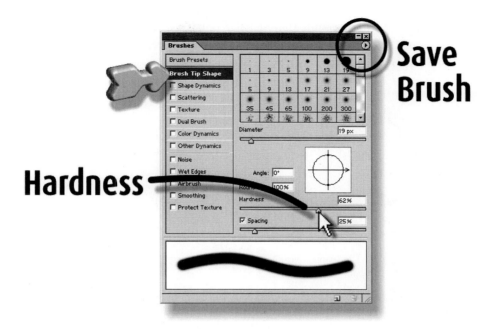

Figure 16.9   You use the Brushes palette to control the angle, hardness, and other features of a brush tip.

5. Let's test to see whether the selection of the girl is really all set for editing. Hold down the Ctrl(⌘) key, and click on the Create a new layer icon at the bottom of the Layers palette. (When you hold down the Ctrl(⌘) key, the new layer will be created *below* the active layer instead of above the active layer, which is the usual default position for a new layer.) Go to the toolbox, click the foreground color, and from the Color Picker, choose a color contrasting with the hair and clothes, such as a fluorescent green. Click on OK. Press Alt(Opt)+Delete(Backspace).

6. Zoom in to the picture, and look carefully to see whether it contains unwanted fringing along the selection edges. If so, click on the Work in progress layer to make it the active layer. Click on the Add Layer Mask icon at the bottom of the Layers palette (second from the left), and using black as the foreground color and a small brush, refine the selection edges (switch colors and paint with white to correct any unwanted brush strokes). When you're satisfied with the results, right-click on the mask thumbnail, and choose Apply Layer Mask to permanently apply the changes. Drag the colored layer into the trash at the bottom-right corner of the Layers palette; this layer is no longer needed.

7. On the Layers palette, right-click (Macintosh: hold Ctrl and click) on the original Background layer, and choose Duplicate Layer from the context menu. Name this

layer **Base new background**. Choose Filter, Blur, Gaussian Blur, and select a radius of 250 pixels (see Figure 16.10). Click on OK. Press Ctrl(⌘)+F to run the filter a second time. You now have a quasi-neutral base.

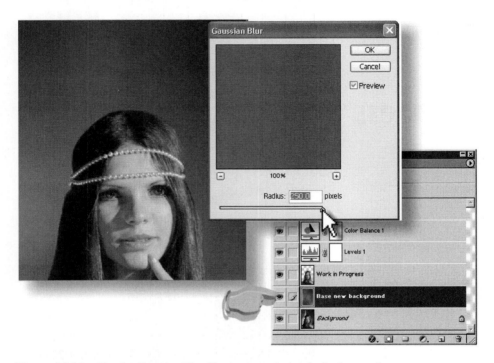

Figure 16.10   Use the Gaussian Blur filter to smooth out the background areas.

8. The Body Girl selection will be needed later. Ctrl(⌘)+click on the Body Girl layer to activate the selection. Choose Select, Save Selection, and name the selection **Body Girl**. Click on OK. Press Ctrl(⌘)+S; keep the file open.

Adding a Diamond to the Image Background

A cover girl necessarily has to be on the cover of a specific magazine, right? Because our future cover girl is decked out in precious stones and the like, let's pretend that the magazine is about gems. Therefore, a stylized diamond in the background can only enhance the beauty of the overall picture without distracting from the main focal points of the composition.

You will add a shiny diamond just above the girl's head by creating three gradients to be doubled:

Adding a Diamond Highlight to the Background

1. Let's make our first set of three layers. Click on the Base new background layer to make it the active layer. Click on the Create a new layer icon at the bottom of the Layers palette. Make sure that white is the foreground color and black the background color. If they are not, press **D** for the default colors of black and white. Press **X** to swap white as the foreground color.

2. Choose the Gradient tool from the toolbox. On the Options bar, choose the first gradient style from the drop-down menu (Foreground to Background), and click on the Diamond Gradient icon (last one on the right). Start to drag about 1/4 inch from the top middle of the head (see Figure 16.11). Name this layer **Black Gradient**.

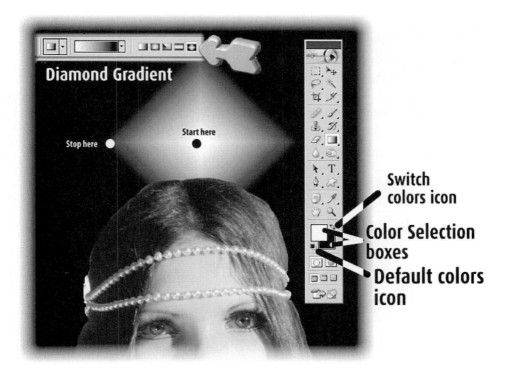

Figure 16.11   Create a diamond shape using the Diamond gradient.

3. Click on the Create a new layer icon again, and click the background color on the toolbox. In the Color Picker, choose a soft peach color by entering the following values: R:**172**, G:**108**, B:**89**. Black should still be the foreground color. Begin to drag your gradient about 1/4 inch above the middle top of the girl's head. See Figure 16.12 for shape and values. Name this layer **Peach Gradient**.

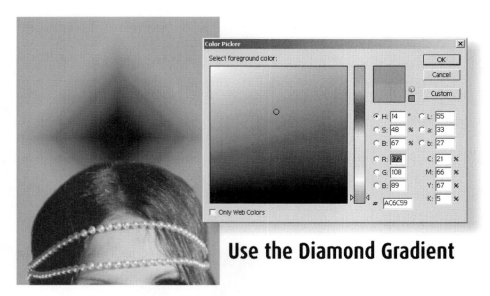

Use the Diamond Gradient

Figure 16.12   Add a second color gradient to enhance the first.

4. Now, make a third and final layer. Click the Create a new layer icon. Click the background color, and enter the following values: R:**101**, G:**89**, B:**172**. The foreground is now a purple color, and the foreground color is still black. Again, start a few pixels higher than the middle top of the girl's head—a little more than for the Peach Gradient—and drag up about 1/4 inch. See Figure 16.13 for shape and values. Name your last layer **Purple Gradient**. Click on the top of the three Gradient layers, change the blending mode to Difference, and lower the Opacity to 50%.

5. Click on the Black Gradient layer, and change the blending mode to Difference and the Opacity to 80%.

6. The Peach Gradient remains on Normal for the blending mode with an Opacity of 100%. Activate this layer by clicking on its title on the Layers palette. Check the box at the left of the Black Gradient layer and also the Purple Gradient layer to *link* these layers together. Click the right-facing arrow at the top-right corner of the Layers palette, and choose New Set From Linked on the flyout menu. Name this set **Diamond 1**. Right-click the Layer Set, and from the context menu, choose Duplicate Set. Name this set **Diamond 2**. Click on OK.

    The final magic touch is to change the blending mode and opacity of the set. By default, the blending mode is Pass Through.

7. Change the blending mode of the Diamond 2 set to Luminosity, and bring the Opacity to 80%.

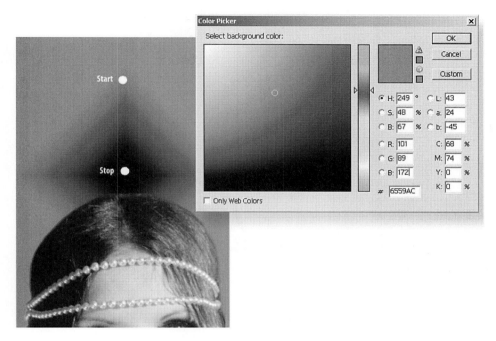

Figure 16.13 Add a third diamond gradient to finish the effect.

8. Change the blending mode of the Diamond 1 set to Difference, and reduce the Opacity to 20%. Change the name of the Work in progress layer to **Body Girl**. Press Ctrl(⌘)+S to save your work. Keep the image open.

   Figure 16.14 shows the final result.

For those who tried to make the diamond but did not succeed in creating the same shape, we have a small present on the companion CD. Click on the Base new background layer to make it the active layer. Open the file Diamond.psd. You will find the set already made. Choose the Move tool, and while holding down the Shift key, drag the Layer Set into the Cover Girl document. The new diamond set should land above the Base new background layer since we made it the active layer.

Flatten your image, or if you prefer to keep a file with all the layers you just made, duplicate your image and then flatten the duplicate.

This is a good time to take a break, get up and stretch, and review your voicemail messages. In the following section, you'll work on lighting and the shadows in the cover girl image.

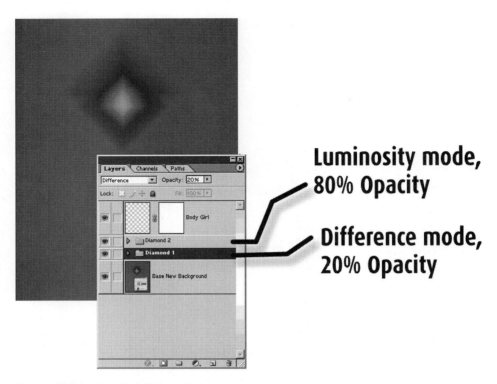

Figure 16.14   The final diamond effect.

Editing Eye Highlights

Okay, return the last of your telephone messages, and take a long, deep breath because this journey into retouching and embellishment, although not tremendously difficult, will require patience and some concentration. But each little step will carry its own reward—promise!

To begin with, if you zoom at 200% on the eyes, you will see that the girl's eyes are a little unfocused; apparently, she doesn't know where to look. Each eye has two catch lights, which is one too many per eye and is partially responsible for that "distant gaze." But which is the good catch light, and which needs to be edited away?

A basic optics principle tells us that the catch light must be in the opposite area of the lightened part of the eye—the bottom part of the eye, usually, that receives indirect lighting. In this case, the upper catch light is the good one we have to keep.

If you take a closer look—don't lean forward, but rather zoom in to the eyes—you'll notice that the "bad" catch light is also spreading out into the pupil. See Figure 16.15 for reference.

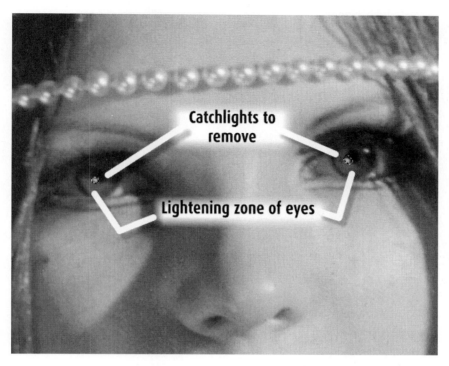

Figure 16.15   There are two catch lights per eye, and that is one too many!

Let's tackle adjusting the highlights (catch lights) now:

Fixing the Catch Lights in the Eyes

1. Click the Create a new layer icon on the Layers palette, and name it **Catch Lights**. On the toolbox, choose the Clone Stamp tool. On the Options bar, choose a 3-pixel hard-round brush. Check the Use All Layers option. Set the brush Mode to Lighten and the Opacity to 80% on the Options bar.

2. The bad catch lights cover both the iris and the pupil of each eye. Alt(Opt)+click to sample just under the catch light. And to maintain consistent image noise, click—do *not* drag—a few times into the iris zone to cover the white dot in the iris area. If you accidentally clone in the pupil, just erase it with the Erase tool, or press Ctrl($\mathcal{H}$)+Z to undo the misplaced edit.

3. To cover the white in the pupil area, use the same brush tip, but set the blending mode on Darken and sample a black area of the pupil just above the catch light. Do not *overdo* your cloning to maintain the transparency in the eye.

4. Comparing the two eyes, you'll notice a white spot at the bottom right of each iris (see Figure 16.16). The one on the left is okay, but the one on the right is partially covered by an undesirable shadow. We will give it the same shape as the white spot in the left eye area.

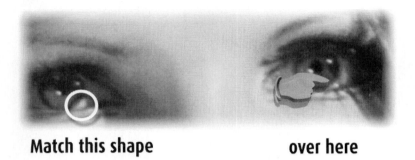

Match this shape   **over here**

Figure 16.16   The lower part of the right eye needs to be fixed.

5. Click the Create a new layer icon on the Layers palette, and name it **Right eye lower right spot**. Go back to the Clone Stamp tool, put the brush Mode on Lighten, and set the Opacity at 60%. Check the Use All Layers option on the Options palette, and sample in the white spot under the left eye. Click, do *not* drag, over the target area. Try to match the shape of the lower white spot in the left eye.

6. You put this minor retouch on its own layer because you need to blur your cloning a little without blurring the catch light cloning. Choose Filter, Blur, Gaussian Blur, and then choose 0.5 pixels as Radius. Click on OK.

7. Click on the Catch Lights layer to make this layer active, and click the box at the left of the Right eye lower right spot layer to link the two layers together. On the Layers palette, click on the right-facing arrow, and from the flyout menu, choose New Set From Linked. Name the Layer Set **First correction eyes**; you will return to it later.

   Be patient! The cover girl assignment is a gradual buildup!

8. Press Ctrl(⌘)+S; keep the file open.

Editing the Shadows

The inaccurate lightening created particularly ugly shadows on the girl's face. You will not remove them entirely; instead, you will reduce the shadows enough to give the girl's face a nice, smooth appearance:

Fixing Dark Shadows on the Cheeks

1. Begin with the banana-shaped shadow on the right cheek. From the toolbox, choose the Lasso tool (the Magnetic Lasso tool is okay, too) and a feather of 3 pixels on the Options bar (use a higher feathering value when working with higher resolution images). Look at Figure 16.17 to see the selection.

Insider

When you are using the Magnetic Lasso tool, keep in mind that it locks onto the areas where it senses a high contrast between pixels; thus, the tool works best in a high-contrast situation. In most high-contrast situations, you make the tool function simply by gliding the mouse near the selection area. However, if you decide to use the Magnetic Lasso tool for this selection and find the tool has difficulty in the lower-contrast areas (such as where the shadow meets with the hair line), you can click frequently in these spots to help the Magnetic Lasso tool stay on target. By clicking frequently along this area, you can keep the Magnetic Lasso tool on track and prevent it from straying too far off course.

Figure 16.17   Create a selection marquee around the banana-shaped shadow.

2. Move this selection by dragging it just outside the shadow zone. Click on the Background layer to make it the active layer. Press Ctrl(⌘)+J to copy this selection to a new layer. Name this layer **Right check repair**. With the Move tool, move the contents of this layer until it covers the shadow area.

3. Momentarily lower the opacity of this layer to 30% to be able to see beneath the contour of the cheek. A little of the "new skin" falls out of the line of the cheek. To erase it, add a layer mask by clicking on the Add Layer Mask icon on the Layers palette. Be sure that the foreground color on the toolbox is set to black and the background color to white.

4. Choose a small hard brush of 3 or 5 pixels, and using black to erase, redefine the cheek's contour. If you erase too much, simply switch to white to restore what you've hidden using black.

5. Reset the Opacity to 100%. A black spot that still remains at the bottom of the new cheek can be covered with the Clone Stamp tool. Alt(Opt)+click the Create a new layer icon at the bottom of the Layers palette, and name it **Black spot right cheek**. Zoom in to 200%, choose the Clone Stamp tool, choose a 5-pixel round brush, and set the brush Mode to Lighten and the Opacity to 80% for the tool. Sample some good information just to the left of the black spot, and then click a few times over the spot to cover it. This is an optional step; in your own editing work, you may not discover any black spots.

6. Your repair appears to be a little too bright. First, lower the Opacity of this Black Spot layer to 45%. Then, choose Filter, Blur, Gaussian Blur, and enter **1.2** pixels for the Radius.

7. The left edge of the Right cheek repair layer is also too apparent. Return to the Gaussian Blur filter, but this time choose a Radius of 2.2 pixels. Finally, bring the Opacity of the layer to 75% to let the original shadow show through a little.

8. Now, put the right cheek retouching in its own set. With the Right cheek repair layer active, check the box at the left of the Black Spot Right Cheek layer, click the right-facing arrow at the top-right corner of the Layers palette, choose New Set From Linked on the flyout menu, and name the set **Right cheek retouch**. Figure 16.18 shows the right cheek before and after retouching.

9. Press Ctrl(⌘)+S; keep the file open.

16

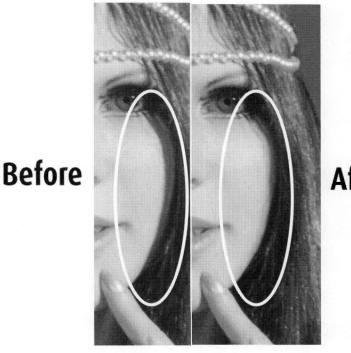

Figure 16.18   The shadow area is softened by copying and filtering the area.

It's time now to work on the left cheek shadow:

Retouching the Opposing Cheek

1. Click on the Background layer to make this layer active. Choose the Lasso tool, and lasso a large selection of the shadow on the left cheek, as shown in Figure 16.19. With this selection active, choose Select, Color Range. Set the Fuzziness to 12. With the Eyedropper tool, click first in the red color in the shadow area. Click on the middle Eyedropper+ tool, and add to the selection by sampling more of the red values. Try to match the Figure 16.20.

2. Click on OK. This selection has to be refined to include almost all the shadow.

3. Press **D** for the default colors of black and white. Press **Q** to enter Quick Mask mode. Choose a soft-round brush with an Opacity of 60–80%, and paint with black to add more shadow areas, as shown in Figure 16.21. Press **X** to switch to white, and paint away any mistakes at 100% Opacity.

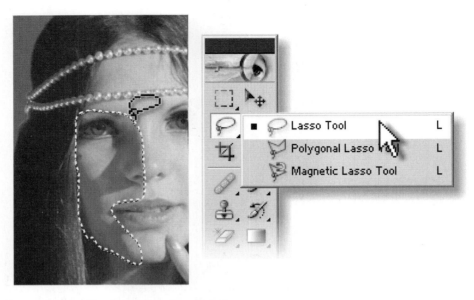

Figure 16.19   Use the Lasso tool to select the area.

16

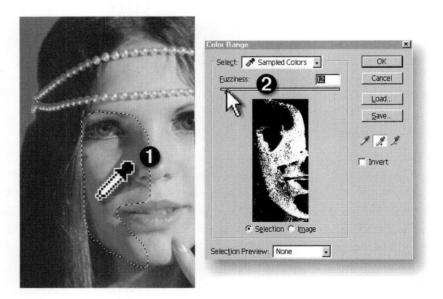

Figure 16.20   Use the Color Range command in combination with the Add to selection function to select the harsh shadow areas.

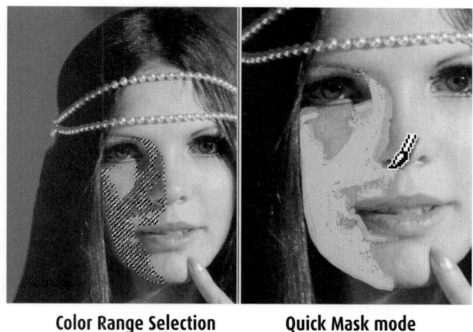

Color Range Selection   **Quick Mask mode**

Figure 16.21   Use the Quick Mask mode to add to the selection.

4. Press **Q** to exit Quick Mask mode and return to Standard Editing mode. Press Ctrl(⌘)+J to copy the selection to a new layer. Name the layer **Lightening Left cheek**. You will put some light color on the shadow. Ctrl(⌘)+click on the Lightening Left cheek layer title to load the selection and make it active for the next step.

5. From the toolbox, choose the Eyedropper tool, or press I, and sample a light skin tone value near the lips. (You can also click on the foreground color to open the Color Picker and enter the following values: R:**197**, G:**181**, B:**141**, as shown in Figure 16.22.) With this color as the foreground color, choose the Gradient tool from the toolbox. On the Options bar, choose Foreground to Transparent from the gradient edit box, and click on the Reverse option to reverse the transparency. Also, click on the Reflected Gradient option. See Figure 16.23.

6. Start your gradient under the cheek at the edge of the hairline, and drag diagonally upward to about 1/4 inch, as shown in Figure 16.23. Keep the selection active, and lower the Opacity of the layer to 35%. Choose Filter, Blur, Gaussian Blur, and then enter **30.7** pixels for the Radius. Click on OK. Press Ctrl(⌘)+D to deselect the selection.

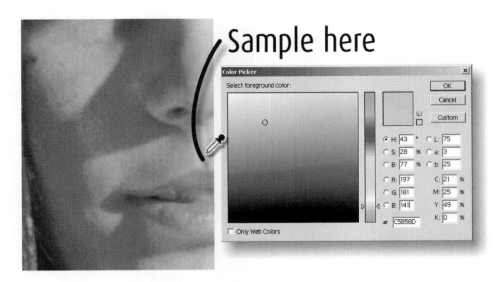

Figure 16.22   Sample an area that represents a medium skin tone with which you'll paint over the harsh skin areas.

16

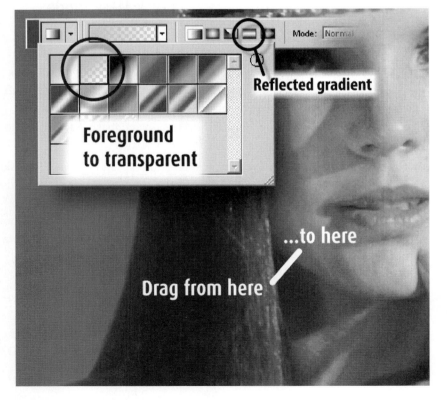

Figure 16.23   Use a reflected linear gradient to smooth out the skin tones.

7. You are not finished yet with this shadow area. Ctrl(⌘)+click the Lightening Left
    cheek layer title on the Layers palette to load the non-transparent pixels on the
    layer. Press Ctrl(⌘)+J to copy this selection onto a new layer. Name the new
    layer **3 shadows**. Choose the Lasso tool from the toolbox, and marquee the
    shadow at the left of the mouth. Hold down the Shift key to add to the selection
    with a marquee of the shadow at the contour of the cheek and the shadow to the
    left of the eye. Figure 16.24 shows you the three selections.

Figure 16.24   Select these areas using the Lasso tool. You'll address these harsh areas next.

8. Choose Filter, Blur, Gaussian Blur, and then enter **30** pixels for the Radius. Click
    on OK. Press Ctrl(⌘)+D to deselect. Click the Add Layer Mask icon on the
    Layers palette. Then, with black as the foreground color, take a soft-round 9-
    pixel brush (when zooming at 100% on the image), reduce the Opacity to 55%,
    and erase the blur effect along the contour of the cheek and chin (see Figure
    16.24). Also, reduce the Opacity of this layer to 35%. With the Lightening Left
    cheek layer still active, click on the Add Layer Mask icon at the bottom of the
    Layers palette. Black should be the foreground color (if not, press **D** for the
    default colors). Choose the Brush tool and a 27-pixel soft-round brush. Set
    Opacity and Flow to 100%. Using black, paint away any blurred color that

spilled over beyond the jaw line or into the hair, as shown in Figure 16.25. Press **X** to switch to white if you need to correct any painting mistakes while touching up these areas. When you're satisfied, right-click (Macintosh: hold Ctrl and click) on the layer mask thumbnail, and choose Apply Layer Mask from the context menu.

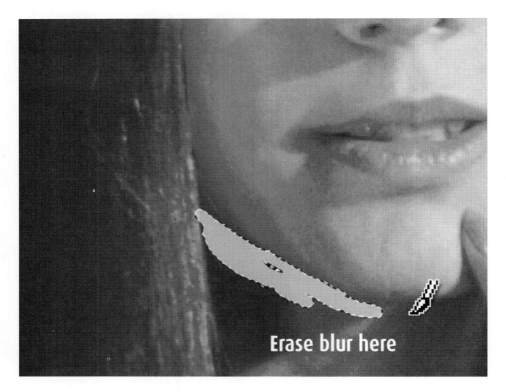

Figure 16.25   Sharpen the cheek line by erasing some of the blur here.

9. Our last work on the left cheek is to eliminate the blemish. Click the Create a new layer icon, and name it **Blemish**. Choose the Clone Stamp tool from the toolbox. On the Options bar, check the Use All Layers option, set the brush Mode to Lighten, select a soft-round brush that is a little larger than the blemish, and set Opacity to 60%. Alt(Opt)+click to sample under and at the right of the blemish; click once or twice on the blemish to cover it (see Figure 16.26).

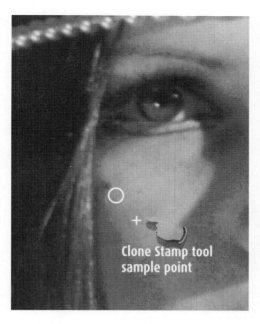

Figure 16.26   Clone over the blemish.

10. Let's create a new set to keep order in what could be a ponderously large number of layers. Click on the Lightening Left cheek layer title, and click the box at the left of the 3 shadows layer and Blemish layer to link them together. Click the right-facing arrow at the top-right corner of the Layers palette, and choose New Set From Linked on the flyout menu. Name the set **Left cheek retouch.**

11. Let's now turn our attention to the neck and fingers. With the Lasso tool and a 3-pixel Feather, make a rough selection of the shadows in the neck and on the fingers, as shown in Figure 16.27. (Hold down the Shift key to add to the selection areas, or hold down the Alt(Opt) key to subtract any mistakes from the selection.) Click on the Background layer to make it active, and press Ctrl(⌘)+J to copy the selection to a new layer. Name the new layer **Neck and fingers.** Drag this layer to the top of the Layers palette. Ctrl(⌘)+click the layer to make the selection active, and choose Select, Color Range. From the Select menu at the top of the dialog box, choose Shadows and click on OK.

12. Press **Q** to enter Quick Mask mode, and with a 9-pixel soft-round brush at 80% Opacity (Mode set to Normal), refine the edges of your selection (use black to add to the selection or white to undo Quick Mask selection areas that are unwanted). Press **Q** to exit Quick Mask mode and make the selection active.

Figure 16.27 Select the neck and finger shadows area as the next area to lighten.

13. As for the left cheek shadow, you will cover the shadow on the neck and fingers with a gradient. Click the foreground color, and in the Color Picker, enter the following values: R:**188**, G:**172**, B:**165** (see Figure 16.28). Go to the Gradient tool. Foreground to Transparent, Reflected Gradient, and Reverse should still be the active options on the Options bar. Drag your gradient from outside the bottom of the selection—near the collar—up toward the nail of the middle finger. Press Ctrl(⌘)+D to deselect. Set the Opacity of the layer to 25%. Choose Filter, Blur, Gaussian Blur, and enter a Radius of **30** pixels. Click the Add Layer Mask icon at the bottom of the Layers palette, and use black and a soft-round brush (set at 100% Opacity) to erase the overflow of blurring that goes into the line of the neck, the collar, the hair, and the rings (switch to white to correct any mistakes made during the layer mask process). When you're satisfied, right-click (Macintosh: hold Ctrl and click) on the layer mask thumbnail, and choose Apply Layer Mask.

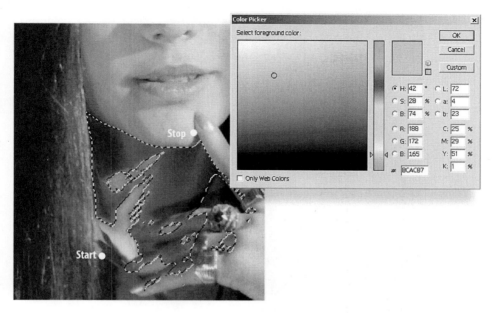

Figure 16.28   Choose the appropriate color to use to paint over the shadow areas.

14. The new shadow is too soft. Let's add a little grain to match the picture. Choose Noise, Add Noise. Enter **4.44** for the Amount, and check the Uniform and Monochromatic options. You want only "gray noise," so you don't choose Gaussian.

15. Press Ctrl(⌘)+S; keep the file open.

Toning Down Distracting Colors

Remember that our goal is to *highlight* the girl's face, to make it the point of attraction in the image. However, we are still distracted by the (too) red sweater, which is visually springing into the foreground. Let's find a more neutral and harmonious color:

Toning Down the Sweater

1. Select the sweater with the Lasso tool. Be sure to select all the parts of the sweater (hold down the Shift key or use the Add to selection icon on the Options bar). Don't worry about the sweater appearing "under" the hair; you'll correct this problem using a unique method later.

2. Click on the Background layer to make it the active layer, and press Ctrl(⌘)+J to copy the selection to a new layer. Name the new layer **New Sweater**.

Ctrl(⌘)+click to make the selection active again. Click the foreground color on the toolbox, and in the Color Picker, choose R:**69**, G:**66**, B:**64** (see Figure 16.29). Press Alt(Opt)+Delete(Backspace) to fill the selection with the foreground color, and set the blending mode for the layer to Color. Press Ctrl(⌘)+D to deselect.

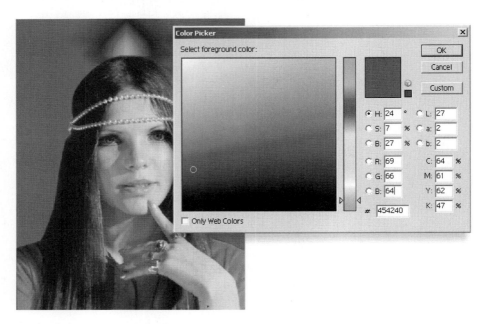

Figure 16.29   Use the Color blending mode to slightly change the color of the sweater.

3. With the Lasso tool, select the sweater partially covered by the hair near the collar. Choose Select, Modify, Expand, and then choose 1 pixel value. Move the marquee upward in the hair out of any red area. Click on the Background layer to make this layer active, and press Ctrl(⌘)+J to move the selection to a new layer. Name it **Middle hair**. With the Move tool, drag the Middle hair downward to cover the red sweater and hair area with "new" hair. Clever, eh?

4. Repeat the same steps for the remaining red sweater areas in the right hair areas. Select with the Lasso tool; choose Select, Modify, Expand; and then choose 1 pixel. Move the marquee to an appropriate area of the hair out of any red area. Click on the Background layer, and put this selection on its own layer. Rename the layer **Right hair**. With the Move tool, drag to cover the red sweater hair with "new" hair. See Figure 16.30 for the selections.

16

Figure 16.30   Add new hair on its own layer to cover the original hair on the sweater.

5. On your own, make a new Layer Set that contains the New sweater layer, Middle hair layer, and Right hair layer. Name the set **New sweater**.

Wow! That's quite an improvement. *Now* the girl is really—and at last—in focus.

6. Press Ctrl(⌘)+S; keep the file open.

Okay, take a break and run to the nearest drugstore to buy a big bottle of sparkling water to celebrate the event. I'm waiting here for you!

Refining and Touching Up Image Details

Our conquest for beauty brings us further in targeting the remaining red cast, spots, dust, and scratches; refining the hair; cleaning the teeth; and enhancing the lips and eyes. Our journey is not finished yet!

Clearing the Hand of Red Spots

You will first get rid of the remaining red spots on the fingers and hand:

Cleaning Up the Hand

1. Take the Lasso tool, and using the Add to selection mode (found as an icon on the Options bar), select the spots of red one by one, as you can see in Figure 16.31. When you're finished, right-click (Macintosh: hold Ctrl and click) on the Background layer title, choose Layer via Copy from the context menu, and name the new layer **Hand red correction**.

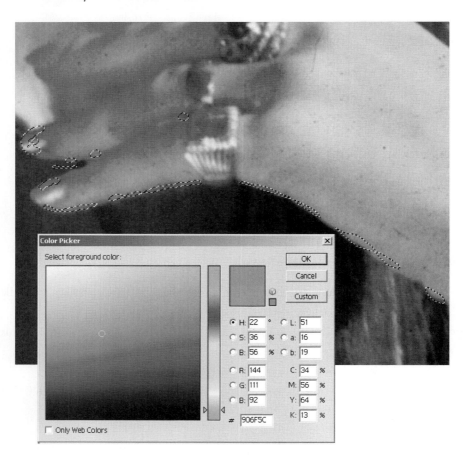

Figure 16.31   Select the red spots that you want to paint over.

2. Check the Lock transparent pixels icon on the Layers palette for the current active layer. On the toolbox, click the foreground color, and enter the following values in the Color Picker: R:**144**, G:**111**, B:**92**. Press Alt(Opt)+Delete(Backspace) to fill with foreground color. Choose Filter, Blur, Gaussian Blur, and then enter **4** pixels for Radius. Choose Filter, Add Noise. Enter **4** for the Amount; then check the Uniform and Monochromatic options. Click on OK.

3. It's high time to do something about the dust and scratches on the hand and forearm. With the Lasso tool, select the hand and forearm. Right-click on the Background layer title, and choose Layer via Copy from the context menu. Name this layer **Hand scratches**.

4. For the *small* scratches, choose Filter, Noise, Dust & Scratches; then enter **2** for the Radius and **6** for the Threshold (see Figure 16.32).

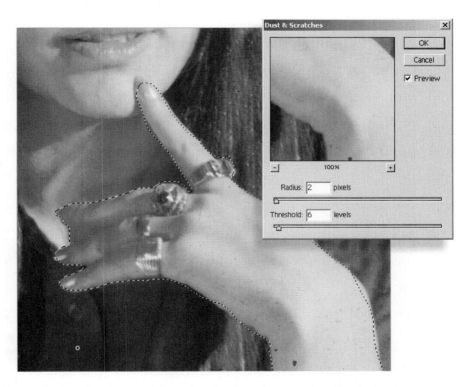

Figure 16.32   Use the Dust & Scratches filter for minor scratches over the hand area.

5. On the History palette (F9), click the Create new snapshot icon (the middle icon at the bottom of the palette). Immediately choose Edit, Undo Dust & Scratches. At the top of the History palette, check the box at the left of the new snapshot to make it the History source.

6. Choose the History brush (press **Y**) from the toolbox. Zoom in at 100%, choose a 19-pixel soft brush, reduce the Opacity to 80%, and "paint" over the lighter scratches. To cover the larger and darker scratches, use the Clone Stamp tool with a 16-pixel brush, and reduce the Opacity to 70% (with brush Mode at Normal). After cloning, link the two layers together and make a new set. Name it **Hand repair**.

7. Open the Right cheek retouch set. Click on the Right cheek repair layer to make it the active layer. Click the Create a new layer icon, and name this layer **Dust cheek and forehead**. Choose the Clone Stamp tool, and be sure the Use All Layers option is checked. Using a small 7- to 9-pixel brush, cover all the dust spots on the right cheek, forehead, nose, and lips (don't forget to sample frequently in appropriate areas), as shown in Figure 16.33. When you're finished, close the set.

Figure 16.33   Clone over all the motes of dust you see on the face.

8. Press Ctrl(⌘)+S; keep the file open.

Finessing the Hair and Forehead Shadows

In your first selection of the girl, you were asked to "neglect" all the stray hair, remember? Well, looking closer at the picture, you can still see stray hairs and a few unwanted wisps on the girl's forehead. Figure 16.34 shows what you need to clean up and how the image should look after. But how do you do that?

Figure 16.34   On some areas of the forehead, there are still unwanted strands of hair.

Removing the Stray Hairs

1. It's time to make a new layer and name it **Hair cloning**. Choose the Clone Stamp tool and an appropriate size round brush. On the Options bar, set the brush Mode to Lighten and the Opacity to 70%. Next, take a sample very near an area of hair, clone, then resample in a different area near another hair spot, and clone again. Sample as many times as needed to cover the hair (see Figure 16.35). You *absolutely* must do this to keep the skin values in balance. And for the very same reason, click, *don't* drag, when you clone over the hair.

2. On the forehead (see Figure 16.36), there is an area of hair where the skin is visible. You've guessed it: You need to make a new layer and name it **New hair locks**. Choose the Clone Stamp tool, and cover this area with new hair (sampled just to the left of this area). This time on the Options bar, set the brush Mode on Darken, and sample several times to create a natural shape in the hair. Link these two layers to make a new set, and name the set **Hair Removal**.

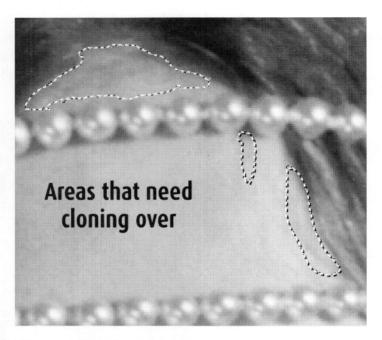

Figure 16.35   Clone, don't paint, over these areas.

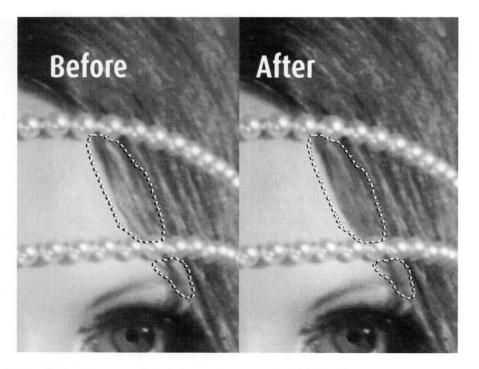

Figure 16.36   Clone over these hair areas to remove the "highlights."

There's one last editing move for the forehead zone—the shadow zone on the left, as shown in Figure 16.37.

Figure 16.37   This area is in shadow and needs correction.

3. Alt(Opt)+click the Create a new layer icon on the Layers palette. In the New Layer dialog box, name the layer **Left forehead shadow**, choose Overlay for the Mode, and then check the Fill with Overlay-neutral color (50% gray) option. Click on OK. Drag this new layer to the top of the Layers palette list. Make sure white is the foreground color (if necessary, press **D** for the default colors, and press **X** to switch white to the foreground). Choose a 17-pixel soft-round brush. On the Options bar, set the brush Mode to Lighten and the Flow to 2%. Paint into the shadow area until a pink shadow color starts to appear; stop when you see this happen.

4. Make a new layer, and name it **Forehead clean and noise**. Change the blending Mode to Lighten. Be sure you clone good information, sampling several times at

the edges of the to-be-cloned area. And use a very low opacity for the brush. And remember to click over the area, don't drag, to maintain the grain structure of the image.

5. To blend your cloning smoothly into the girl's forehead area, choose Filter, Blur, Gaussian Blur, and then enter **1** pixel for the Radius.

6. Choose Filter, Noise, Add Noise, and enter **1** for the Amount. Click on the Gaussian and Monochromatic options. Choose the Blur tool from the toolbox. On the Options bar, set the brush Mode to Lighten and the Strength to 8% to blend the hairline and shadow area. When you're finished, lower the Opacity of this layer to 60%.

7. To maintain "order" in the layers, put these last two layers in a new set. Name the set **Left forehead shadow**.

8. Press Ctrl(⌘)+S; keep the file open.

Cleaning Up a Cover Girl's Smile

How about a little virtual trip to the dental hygienist next? As you can see, the girl's teeth are nice, but the photography is hiding this fact. Here's how to make a whiter, brighter smile:

Performing a Little Virtual Dentistry

1. Zoom to 400% in the teeth area. You need to clean up the girl's teeth by diminishing the shadows. First, with the Lasso tool, select the teeth area. Right-click (Macintosh: hold Ctrl and click) on the Background layer title, and choose Layer via Copy from the context menu. Name the new layer **Teeth** (see Figure 16.38).

2. Choose the Dodge tool from the toolbox. On the Options bar, choose Shadows, and set the Exposure to 30%. Choose a soft-round 27-pixel brush. Drag a few times over the shadow area of the teeth.

3. Let's polish further by creating a new layer fill with overlay gray. Alt(Opt)+click the Create a new layer icon. For blending mode, choose Overlay and check the Fill with neutral gray 50% box on the Layers palette. Name this layer **Teeth repair 2**. With the same brush size, paint over the entire shadow area to lighten these areas.

4. Some black spots will still remain, even after the Desaturate step. Create a new empty layer, and name it **Black spots**. Choose the Clone Stamp tool, and check the Use All Layers box. Next, sample several good areas around the black spots with a 9-pixel brush, and click, *don't drag*, to cover.

Look at the left of the upper teeth row. You can see a "black hole" in Figure 16.39.

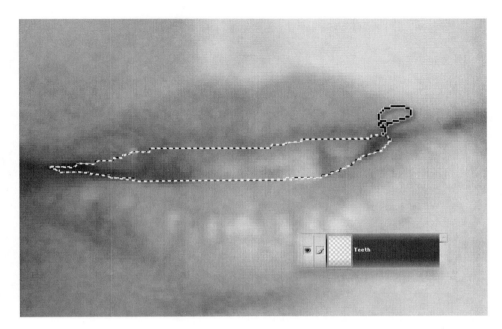

Figure 16.38   Select the teeth area using the Lasso tool.

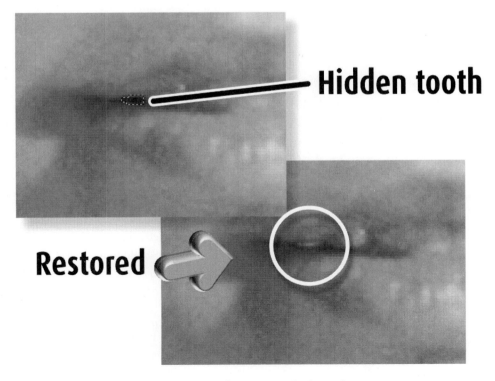

Figure 16.39   The lighting creates an unfortunate gap in the teeth.

5. You will fill the visual gap with a new tooth. First, make a new empty layer, and again choose the Clone Stamp tool. Sample several times using different values to make a natural-looking tooth. Name this layer **Teeth**. Choose Filter, Blur, Gaussian Blur, and then enter **1** pixel for Radius. Finally, choose Filter, Noise, Add Noise; choose 6% for the amount; and then check the Uniform and Monochromatic boxes. Reduce the Opacity of this layer to 35%, to fade it away a little.

6. The last thing to do is to link all your teeth repair layers and bring them into a new set you can name **Teeth cleaning**.

7. Press Ctrl(⌘)+S; keep the file open.

Adding Some Lip Gloss

The color of the lips needs to be a little more saturated, and some highlights need to be turned off:

Color and Tone Correcting the Lipstick

1. Click on the Background layer to make it the active editing layer, and with the Lasso tool, make a selection around the model's lips. Don't worry about including the teeth in your selection because you will work only on the red values in this selection. Right-click (Macintosh: hold Ctrl and click) the Background layer title, and choose Layer via Copy from the context menu. Name the new layer **Color Lips**.

2. With this layer active, click the Create a new layer icon, and name the new layer **Filling Highlights**. Press Ctrl(⌘)+G to group it with the previous layer.

3. You have to partially cover the highlights on the lower lip. Choose the Clone Stamp tool, set the brush Mode to Darken, and lower the Opacity to about 25–30%. Set your viewing resolution to 200%, and choose a 5-pixel soft brush. Sample several times above and below the highlights; then click, *don't* drag, to maintain the "grain" of the image over the highlights.

4. When you're satisfied with the results, reduce the Opacity of the Filling Highlights layer to 40% to let through just a few of the highlights. Click the Create a new fill or adjustment layer icon at the bottom of the Layers palette, and choose Selective Colors. The Colors option at the top of the dialog box should be set on Reds. Enter the following values: Magenta: **+15**, Yellow: **+25**, Black: **–15**. Check the Absolute option and click on OK. Press Ctrl(⌘)+G to group the Adjustment Layer to the previous lips' layers (see Figure 16.40).

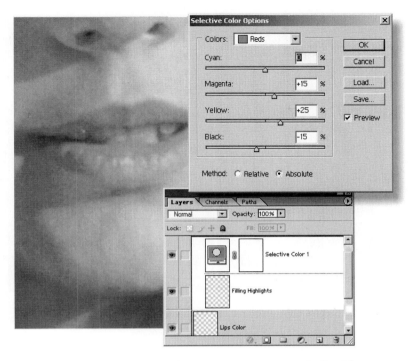

Figure 16.40   Use a Selective Color Adjustment Layer to correct the lipstick.

5. The last procedure in this area is to diminish the shadow under the lower lip, as shown in Figure 16.41. Alt(Opt)+click the Create a new layer icon at the bottom of the Layers palette. In the New Layer dialog box, choose Overlay for the Mode, and check the Fill with Overlay-neutral color (50% gray) option. Name this layer **Lower Lip shadow**, and click on OK. Drag this layer beneath the Color Lips layer. Choose a 9-pixel soft-round brush, set the Opacity to 5% (Flow at 100%), and set brush Mode to Lighten. With white as the foreground color, paint to fade the shadow.

6. When you're finished, make a new Layer Set from these four lip corrections layers, and name it **Lips Selective color**.

7. Press Ctrl(⌘)+S; keep the file open.

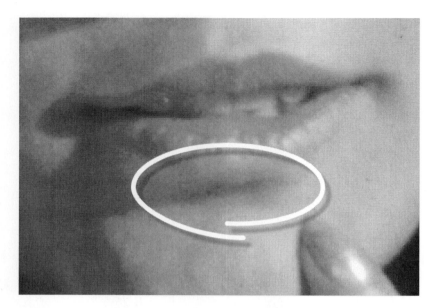

Figure 16.41   Use an Overlay layer to remove the harsh shadow beneath the chin.

Creating Some Eye Enhancements

Now that you've cleared up the surrounding areas of this image, it's clear that the model's face could use some more work. To finish retouching the model's face, you will "enhance" the eyes:

16

Cleaning Up the Tear Ducts Around the Eyes

1. Zoom in the eyes at 200%. Your first goal is to create three natural tear conduits (the tear ducts plus the conduits at the opposing side of the eye) using the left tear duct of the right eye as a reference point.

2. First, create a new layer and name it **Tear Ducts**. Set the blending Mode of the layer to Soft Light, and lower the Opacity to 35%.

3. Click on the foreground color, and enter these values (which were obtained by sampling a color in the right side of the tear conduit): R:**196**, G:**156**, B:**123**. Click on OK. See Figure 16.42 for the three tear conduits to construct and the values to use.

4. Take a 19-pixel soft-round brush. On the Options bar, set the brush Mode to Lighten, and set Opacity and Flow to 100%. Paint in the shadow areas shown in Figure 16.43, trying to match a natural shape. Erase any excess color with the Eraser tool.

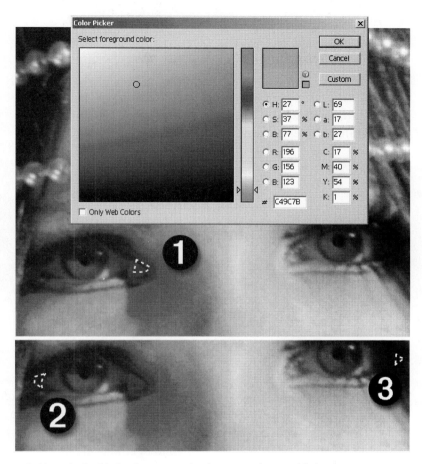

Figure 16.42 The highlighted areas are the duct areas that need lightening.

5. Create a new layer, in Soft Light mode, and name it **Eyes White**. Set white as the foreground color on the toolbox. On the Options bar, click the Airbrush icon, set the Flow to 10%, and click once with a 35-pixel soft-round brush over the white areas of each eye. Again, clean the overspill with the Eraser tool.

6. Select the eyebrows using the Lasso tool. Right-click (Macintosh: hold Ctrl and click) on the Background layer title, and choose Layer via Copy from the context menu. Choose the Burn tool from the toolbox. On the Options bar, choose Midtones for the Range, and set the Exposure to 10%. Stroke slightly over the eyebrows.

7. Press Ctrl(⌘)+S; keep the file open.

To enhance the attraction of the eyes a little more in this cover girl image, you will refine the makeup:

Adding Makeup to the Model

1. With the Lasso tool, make a marquee as shown in Figure 16.43 (remember to hold down the Shift key to add to your selection). Create a new layer, name it **Beige Makeup**, and set the blending mode to Color.

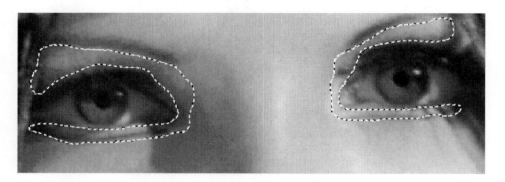

Figure 16.43   Beige makeup will enhance the eye areas.

2. Click the foreground color, and in the Color Picker, enter the following values, which will lend a little contrast to the eye area: R:**224**, G:**202**, B:**144**. Click on OK. Press Alt(Opt)+Delete(Backspace) to fill the selection with the foreground color. Click on OK. On the Layers palette, lower the Fill to 30%. *Do not deselect yet!*

3. With the same selection active, create a new layer, and name it **Gray Makeup**. Again, set the blending mode to Color (this layer should be above the Beige Makeup layer). Click the foreground color, and enter the following values: R:**83**, G:**80**, B:**78** (see Figure 16.44). Click on OK. Press Alt(Opt)+Delete(Backspace) to fill the selection with the foreground color. Click on OK. On the Layers palette, lower the Fill value for the layer to 10%. Now, press Ctrl(⌘)+D to deselect the marquee.

4. Press Ctrl(⌘)+S; keep the file open.

Figure 16.44   Neutral, gray makeup has to be added to the eye areas, as well.

Adding Color to the Irises

The *crème de la crème* of your retouching work on the model is a touch of new color in the irises of her eyes:

Adding Vibrancy to the Eyes

1. Choose the Elliptical Marquee tool, hold down the Shift key to constrain the selection to a perfect circle, and select the iris in the left eye. Use the Add to selection icon on the Options bar, and again hold down the Shift key to make another selection of the iris for the right eye. When you're making an elliptical selection, it helps to imagine starting the selection at around 10 o'clock (for the desired selection area) and dragging toward 4 o'clock (also, holding down the spacebar while dragging allows you to reposition the selection marquee if needed). Right-click (Macintosh: hold Ctrl and click) on the Background layer title, and choose Layer via Copy from the context menu to make a new layer of the selection. Name the layer **Only the eyes**.

2. Ctrl(⌘)+click on the Only the eyes layer to activate the selection again. Click the Add a new fill or adjustment layer icon at the bottom of the Layers palette, and choose Hue/Saturation. Check the Colorize option. Bring the Hue slider to 90

and the Saturation slider to 10. Click on OK. Figure 16.45 shows the selection and the Hue/Saturation values to enter. Click on OK. The layer mask for this Adjustment Layer will be active. If you notice any spilling of color into the pupils or the rim of the eyes, choose white as the foreground color, and paint away these areas with the appropriate size soft-round brush (make sure the Options bar for the Brush tool shows the Mode at Normal and Opacity and Fill set to 100%).

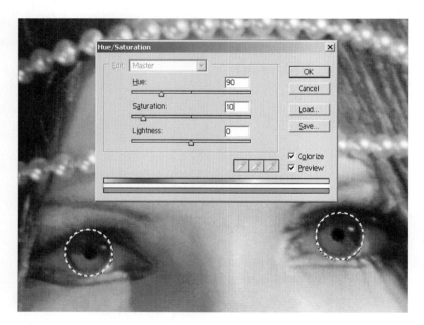

Figure 16.45   Adding color to the eyes themselves helps make them the main visual attraction.

3. Put all these last retouch layers in their own Layer Set. Name the set **Eye retouch**, as shown in Figure 16.46, and press Ctrl(⌘)+S to save the file!

4. Flatten your image. If you want to keep the layers, choose File, Save As and save the flattened image under a new name.

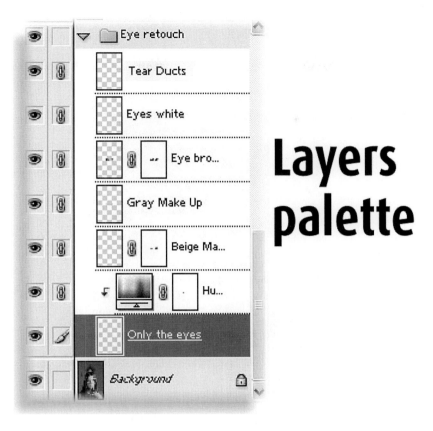

Figure 16.46   Here are the contents of the Eye Retouch Layer Set.

Softening the Image Focus

Before constructing the magazine cover, we will first make a false focus effect by blurring the background and, partially, the girl. No, no, I'm not joking. Remember the prime focal areas: eyes and lips:

Adjusting the Image Focus

1. If you have flattened your image, first duplicate your Background layer by dragging it to the Create a new layer icon at the bottom of the Layers palette. Even though the image is flattened, all the selections saved earlier are available. Choose Select, Load Selection, and then choose Body girl from the Channel drop-down list. Invert the selection (Shift+F7), right-click (Macintosh: hold Ctrl and click)

on the Background copy layer title, and choose Layer via Cut from the context menu.

2. Choose Filter, Blur, Gaussian Blur, and then enter **10** pixels for the Radius (see Figure 16.47). Click on OK.

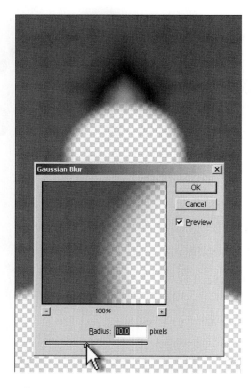

Figure 16.47   Blur the background even further, this time blurring the edges, too.

3. Click on the Background copy layer (to make the layer with the girl's body active). Go to the History palette and make a snapshot. Check the box at the left of this new snapshot to make it the History source. Choose Filter, Blur, Gaussian Blur, and enter **2** pixels for the Radius (see Figure 16.48). Click on OK.

4. View the document at 50%. Choose the History brush (at 80% Opacity) from the toolbox. On the Options bar, set the brush Mode to Lighten. Then, using a 35-pixel soft-round brush, bring the pearls, eyebrows, eyes, makeup, lips, teeth (one or two strokes), nose (one stroke), some hair locks *near* the face, jewels, and painted nails back into sharpness.

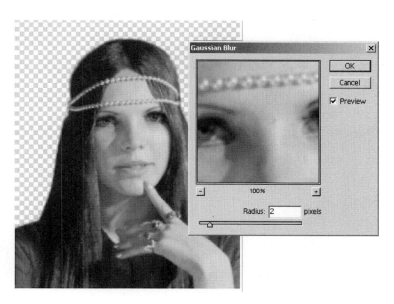

Figure 16.48   Soften the cover girl just a little. You'll selectively restore focus shortly.

5. With the layer containing the girl's body still active, click the Add a new fill or adjustment layer icon at the bottom of the Layers palette, and then choose Brightness and Contrast. Enter +**10** for the Contrast. Click on OK.

6. Press Ctrl(⌘)+G to group your effect to the girl's layer only. On the Layers palette, the layer mask thumbnail for the Adjustment Layer should be active. With black as the foreground color, remove all the contrast by pressing Alt(Opt)+Delete(Backspace) to fill the Adjustment Layer mask completely with black foreground color. Choose the Brush tool and an appropriate size soft-round brush. On the Options bar, set Opacity to 50%, Flow to 100%, and brush Mode to Normal. With white as the foreground color, bring back some contrast, randomly, in the hair and on the face. Figure 16.49 shows you where to maintain the contrast and where to paint.

7. Finally, click on Layer 1 to make it the active layer. Make a selection of the Diamond above the head (with the Polygonal Lasso tool). Press Ctrl(⌘)+J to copy the selection onto a new layer. On the Layers palette, click the Create a new fill or adjustment layer icon, and choose Color Balance. Enter the values as shown in Figure 16.50: Shadows: **0**, **2**, and **2**; Highlights: **5**, **5**, and **5**.

8. Put these last layers in their own set, and name it **Blur and Contrast**. Save your file and keep it open.

We will end the journey by making a magazine cover with our young model.

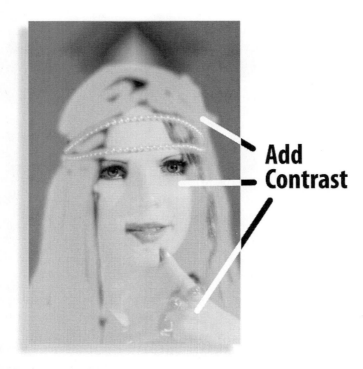

Figure 16.49   Add contrast in the areas shown with masking.

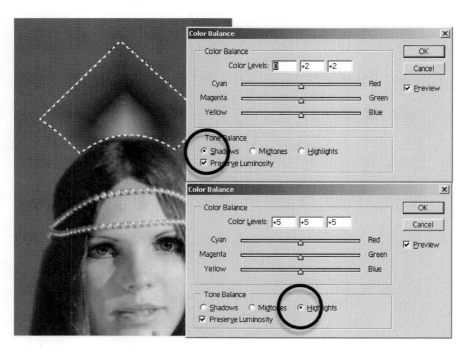

Figure 16.50   Add a final Color Balance adjustment.

Turning the Cover Girl into a Magazine Cover

Creating magazine cover artwork is a discipline in and of itself, and beyond the scope of this chapter. However, you will indeed finish the cover girl design using text. The purpose of this section is to run you through some steps to finish the cover, but also to serve as a mini-sampler on good layout and text use. For more extensive information on Photoshop text handling, check out Chapter 20, "Typography and Page Layout in Photoshop."

Creating a Magazine Aspect Ratio and Size

First things first: The cover girl image is not the proper aspect ratio for a magazine cover. This problem could be fixed in two ways:

- Oversizing the image's horizontal aspect, making the image wider and then filling in the new space with background color (which you will find is not always easy with all images)

- Cropping the image, thereby allowing the author to sneak in another Photoshop feature to this chapter!

Let's quickly (and accurately) crop the image so it becomes standard magazine aspect—8 1/2" by 11". Then, we can move on to a mini-discussion about typography and type placement:

Cropping an Image by Aspect Ratio

1. Double-click on the Hand tool to zoom out of the cover girl so you can see the edges of the image. It might be a good idea, too, to drag the edges of the image window away from the image so you can see extra gray background (the border area).

2. Choose the Rectangular Marquee tool from the toolbox, and then on the Options bar, choose Style: Fixed Aspect Ration. Type **8.5** in the Width field and **11** in the Height field.

3. Drag from the upper-left edge of the window to the lower-right edge. Then, drag inside the resulting selection marquee so that the image is cropped in an eye-pleasing area. See Figure 16.51 for the author's idea of "eye-pleasing."

4. Choose Image, Crop. Press Ctrl(⌘)+D to deselect.

5. Choose Image, Image Size, or you can right-click (Macintosh: hold Ctrl and click) on the image's title bar to access this command.

Figure 16.51   Create a marquee in an aesthetically correct area of the image, maximizing the horizontal measurement of the image from left to right. You don't want to crop out too much!

6. Uncheck the Resample image check box, and then type **8.5** in the Width field (the Height field should automatically adjust to around 11 inches if the Constrain Proportions option is active). You'll notice that the resolution changes. This change is okay; actually, it's very good because Photoshop is telling you that not one pixel in the image is being changed (resolution is inversely proportional to image size as measured in inches). Click on OK.

7. The image, once you've added type, can now be printed to an accurate magazine size. Heck, if you own an 11" by 14" printer, by the end of this chapter, you can print the cover girl, trim your printout, and paste it onto a magazine!

8. Press Ctrl(⌘)+S; keep the file open.

16

The next step is the much-promised mini-tutorial on type. Then, after you understand the hows and whys of the template you'll apply to the Cover Girl image, you'll have worked a modern miracle from start to finish.

A Page Layout Primer

Let's suppose for the purposes of our example that the name of the magazine is *Gem Trends*. Let's further suppose that only three main text elements appear on the cover:

- The magazine name
- The title of the issue and date
- A cover story headline

Forget the price, skip the UPC code; we're going for a "comp" of a cover, mercifully unlittered by all the prerequisite text that usually appears.

Now, check out Figure 16.52. You're going to refer back to this figure in this section. At left, you'll notice a stylized drawing of the cover girl image, with whitespaces titled "negative space" in five areas.

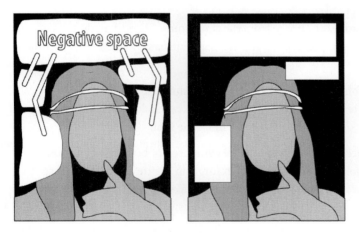

Figure 16.52   Refer to this illustration for type placement and choice of font.

Rule number one in good design is

- Asymmetrical is always better than symmetrical.

Nature is asymmetrical, my college roommate's head was asymmetrical, and good design flows and moves when it is asymmetrical. For this reason, it's a good idea not to use all five slots called "negative space" in Figure 16.53, but instead to use the top for the magazine name, a space to the right and underneath the magazine name for the date and title, and then an oblong shape at the bottom left for a "teaser" concerning the contents of the magazine.

The sketch to the right in Figure 16.53 shows, blocked in, the locations of the text. Believe it or not, areas on the cover now balance out without being symmetrical: The magazine name is wide and squat in contrast to the tall, slim model's image, and the block of copy to the left balances the model's hand at right.

> **Tip**
>
> **Looking for an adventure?**   As a little adventure/exercise in good layout, why not pick up a copy of a magazine with a cover layout you like. See how the elements fit together harmoniously and asymmetrically? Then look at an awfully laid-out magazine cover, and enumerate the mistakes the artist made.

Contrast and Typography

When you open the GemText.tif image from the companion CD, you might notice familiar font choices. I used Apple Garamond for the magazine name and date and Futura for the "teaser" text.

Okay, why were these fonts used? The reasons are both simple and open-ended. Basically, two pairs of styles are readily recognizable with typefaces: Gothic and Roman, and serif and sans serif. Let's tackle the definition of the first style first:

- A **Roman** typeface has characters that are composed of both thick and thin strokes. If you look at the Peignot Bold example in Figure 16.53, you can see that the vertical strokes are heavier than the horizontal strokes that make up each letter.

- A **Gothic** typeface has characters that are made up of strokes of the same width. Futura, Benguiat Gothic, Courier, Avant Garde, and Century Gothic are all Gothic fonts.

- A **serif** is a ligature at the end of a character stroke that caps the ends of the stroke. As you can see in Figure 16.53, Garamond is both a Roman typeface and a serif one. Notice the little stubs at the ends of the strokes that make up each character.

- A **sans serif** font has no serif (*sans* from the French *without*). Helvetica characters have no cap at the bottom or top of each character, but instead end in a miter tip. Other sans serif fonts are Arial, Antique Olive, and Futura.

16

It is simply a good typography rule to mix contrasting fonts. For example, if you use a serif font such as Times Roman in a headline, the layout is begging for a sans serif font such as Helvetica for the body copy. Also, a Roman, serif font tends to work well with a Gothic, sans serif font. And this is why I chose Garamond for the magazine name and then Futura for the "teaser" text.

Tip

> **Using condensed typefaces**   Condensed typefaces work effectively as headlines because you can get more characters per inch than a regular font. Apple Garamond is a condensed font, and as such, a short headline such as *Gem Trends* can be used at a higher point size, thus taking up more space and garnering more attention. To make a condensed font out of a regular one in Photoshop (also known as "faking it"!), type your text, press Ctrl(⌘)+T to place the Free Transform box around it, and then drag a side anchor point toward the center of the text.

Enough Discussion! How to Add Text to the Image!

I created an image file called GemText.tif that contains rasterized (rendered, non-editable) text spaced and arranged perfectly for quick addition to your cover girl work. In the steps to follow, you'll copy the image to a channel, load it as a selection, and add an element of professionalism and dimension to your magnificent retouching work!

Loading and Painting in a Text Selection

1. Open the GemText.tif image from the Chap16/Examples folder on the companion CD.

2. Arrange the cover girl and GemText image windows so that you can see both. With GemText as the active window in the workspace, click on the Channels tab of the Layers/Channels/Yadada grouped palette. Hold Shift (to keep the channel image centered as it is copied), and drag the Gray channel title into the cover girl image, as shown in Figure 16.53. Surprise! The cover girl image has a new channel!

3. Close the GemText image, and then Ctrl(⌘)+click on the Alpha 1 channel title on the Channels palette. Doing this loads the information in the file as selections.

Insider

> If, by chance, the black areas load instead of white, press Shift+F7 now.

Figure 16.53   Copy the GemText grayscale channel into the cover girl image.

4. Click on the top layer to make it active. Click on the Create a new layer icon on the Layers palette, and with white as the foreground color, press Alt(Opt)+Delete(Backspace) to fill the selection with white, creating text.

5. Choose the Brush tool, and choose a 9-pixel hard-round brush tip (on the Options bar, set Mode to Normal and Opacity and Flow to 100%). Click on the foreground color selection box on the toolbox, and in the Color Picker, choose a light blue: R:**134**, G:**121**, B:**255** is fine.

6. Using the hard brush, stroke over the words *Diamond* and *guys*, as shown in Figure 16.54. Now, a casual passerby will immediately be impressed with these two key words on the cover.

7. Press Ctrl(⌘)+D to deselect. Press Ctrl(⌘)+S to save; keep the file open.

   Your file should now look like that shown in Figure 16.55.

16

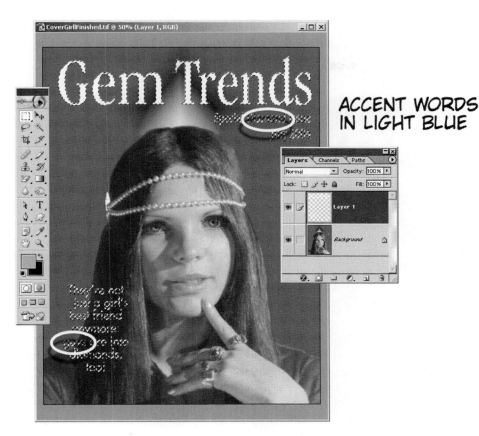

Figure 16.54 Use color in text to your advantage! Highlight words that you want to pop out at the reader.

Here's a short list of steps to finalize the image. Very simply, you will want to slightly sharpen the eyes and lips. To do this, begin by choosing the Background layer, not the layer with the text on it:

Selective Sharpening

1. Click on the Background copy layer, and choose Filter, Unsharp Mask. Enter **50%** for Amount, **3** pixels for the Radius, and **0** for the Threshold (see Figure 16.56). Click on OK.

2. Go to the History palette and make a snapshot. Choose Edit, Undo Unsharp Mask. On the History palette, check the box at the left of the snapshot you just made. On the toolbox, choose the History brush; then set the Mode to Normal

and the Opacity to 75%. Next, choose a 9-pixel soft brush to paint over the lips and teeth and a 17-pixel soft brush for the eyes, eyebrows, and makeup.

3. Press Ctrl(⌘)+S. You can close the image at any time.

Figure 16.55   The finished cover girl!

Figure 16.56   Apply a moderate amount of sharpening.

If you want to be able to change the text later, leave the image as is. However, if you want to print it or make a smaller copy for the Web, flatten the image (or a duplicate). Saving to the TIFF file format ensures that a wide audience can open, print, and appreciate your work!

Summary

Granted, the assignment in this chapter was not short, but it was indeed straightforward. And the next time you choose to retouch a cover girl, the steps will be simple, too, because you now have a feel for Adjustment Layers and the power of color correction. Again, the values you used in this chapter were unique to the image, and in your own imaging work, you'll want to let your eyes be the judge of how much red, for example, to add or subtract from an image area.

That's it! Our model can begin her paper career, and we can go on to the next chapter!

Chapter 17

Surrealistic Photoshop

The word *surreal* is used to describe something as having a dream-like quality. Since we all dream, we all have a personal connection to those illogical and strange

In this chapter, you'll learn

- How to composite photographs to create surrealistic images in Photoshop
- How to remove image areas with a layer mask
- How to refine layer masks
- How to insert a layer into a Layer Set
- How to use Adjustment Layers
- How to flip and transform a layer
- How to employ quick methods to create layer masks
- How to replace masked-out image areas
- How to touch up the final image
- How to create and use Layer comps

images that are surrealistic. There is something eye-catching and intriguing about a sur-realistic image. Hang an image of a train charging out of a fireplace among paintings of landscapes and portraits, and the surrealistic image will draw more interest and curios-ity from the viewers. Surreal images prick our sense of logic as we stop to study them. Logic is safe and makes us comfortable because it is understandable and familiar. The surreal is illogical and gives us little to guide us through our normal daily lives. One of the most famous surrealistic painters, Salvador Dali, once said, "The only difference between myself and a madman is that I am not mad!"

With more and more personal computer users having access to image-editing programs, the number of surrealistic images is growing exponentially. The joy of creating a "Gee whiz! How'd you do that and what the heck *is* it?" kind of image is being discovered by more people every day. After all, programs such as Photoshop give you unrestrained power to create any image you can imagine. In the world of digital imaging, your imag-ination is your only limitation.

This chapter shows you how to masterfully composite two photographs in Photoshop to create the surrealistic image titled Sky Gallery. This chapter, in fact, could have been titled "Combining Images in Photoshop." But because it has the title "Surrealistic Photoshop," I would be remiss if I did not sprinkle throughout this chapter some concepts and ideas of surrealistic art to help you get your own surrealistic juices flowing.

Tip

> **About surrealism**   Surrealism often presents familiar objects in unfamiliar ways. One concept seen in many surrealistic images, for example, is the use of a dramatic change in scale of one object within its normal environment. For example, imagine a giant apple that completely fills a room.

So, be prepared to learn compositing techniques and ways to think like a madman—without being mad.

17

Removing Large Image Areas with Layer Mask

Layers are one of Photoshop's most consistently valuable features. Had Adobe never added layers, Photoshop would have gone the way of Pong (a very old computer game). I always tell my students, "If there is only one thing you need to know about Photoshop, know layers!"

If you are new to Photoshop or are not familiar with layers, point your learning compass backward for a moment. Here's a real-life example that reveals the value of layers. In 1994, using Photoshop version 2.5 (no layers), I composited sections of 12 images into

1 image. The process took 40 hours! Two years later, using version 3.0 (the first version with layers), I re-created that same image in less than 1 hour.

As previously mentioned, Sky Gallery is a composite of two photographs. Since every set of steps in this chapter involves working with layers, by the time you've completed the image, you will have gained a lot of skill and knowledge about this most valuable feature.

The first areas you will work on are the gallery walls; they need to be removed to provide the area for the sky. You can remove areas of layer contents by using one of two methods: applying a layer mask or erasing/deleting the pixels. Applying a layer mask should be your choice 95% of the time. The layer mask enables you to remove (hide) areas of the layer as well as return (unhide) those areas later; there are no permanent changes to your image. In contrast, erasing/deleting layer contents completely and permanently removes the pixels. (Note: Erased pixels can be restored only if that edit is listed in the History palette.) Erasing pixels is recommended only if you are completely certain that those pixels will not be needed in the future.

In the following steps, you will use the Magic Wand tool to select the walls and then apply a layer mask to hide the walls:

Removing the Walls with a Layer Mask

1. Open the Gallery.psd image from the Examples/Chap17 folder on the companion CD.

Note

> **35mm film flaws**   The Gallery image was acquired from an old 35mm film scanner. The vertical scratches on the walls should normally be repaired, but since we are removing the walls, the repair would be a waste of time.

2. From the main menu, choose File, Save As and save the image as **Sky Gallery.psd** on your hard disk.

3. In the Layers palette, double-click on the Layer 0 title, and rename the layer **Original Gallery**. Press Enter (Return) to commit the new layer name. Customizing layer titles is highly recommended if you are interested in quickly identifying layer contents.

4. Right-click (Macintosh: hold Ctrl and click) on the Original Gallery layer in the Layers palette, and choose Duplicate Layer from the context menu. Name this duplicate layer **Gallery**, and click on OK, as shown in Figure 17.1. You will make numerous changes to the Gallery image, so it's always a good idea to work on a duplicate just in case you need the original image later.

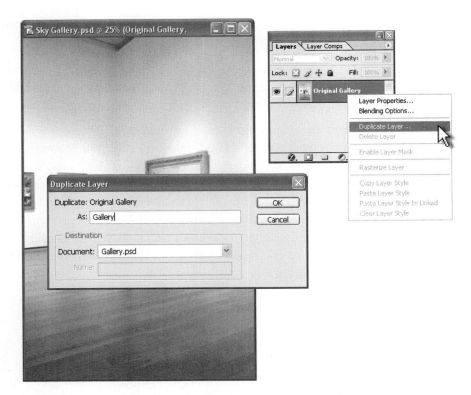

Figure 17.1   Duplicate the Original Gallery layer, and rename the duplicate Gallery.

5. To finish setting up the Layers palette, click on the eye icon to turn off the visibility for the Original Gallery layer, hiding the layer. The Gallery layer should still be the active layer. Click the Add layer mask icon at the bottom of the palette to add a mask to the Gallery layer (see Figure 17.2).

6. Press **W** for the Magic Wand tool. On the Options bar, enter **55** for the Tolerance and check Anti-aliased and Contiguous (be sure Use All Layers is not checked), as shown in Figure 17.3.

7. Position your cursor slightly above the lady's head and click (see Figure 17.4). Hold down the Shift key (so that subsequent mouse clicks add to the current selection), and click on the wall and ceiling areas above the current selection, as shown in Figure 17.4. Do not Shift+click near the paintings; the current Tolerance setting is too high and will select areas of the paintings. You will remove these wall areas in the next set of steps.

Figure 17.2   Turn off the Original Gallery layer's visibility. Then click the icon at the bottom of the Layers palette (second from the left) to add a layer mask to the Gallery layer.

17

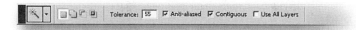

Figure 17.3   Through trial and error, we determined these settings in the Options bar for the Magic Wand to make selecting the wall area quick and easy.

Figure 17.4   Click once just above the lady's head, then Shift+click on the non-selected areas above the current selection, but don't worry about the area near the paintings.

8. On the Layers palette, click on the layer mask thumbnail (the Gallery layer) to make it the active thumbnail. Press **D** for the default colors, and with black as the foreground color, press Alt(Opt)+Delete(Backspace) to fill the selection with black on the layer mask (see Figure 17.5).

9. Press Ctrl(⌘)+D to deselect. Press Ctrl(⌘)+S to save your image. Leave the image and Photoshop open for the next exercise.

Good work! You now have a nice, open gallery that is ready—well, *almost* ready—for the sky to be inserted.

But Sky Gallery isn't quite ready for the sky image because we need to touch up the layer mask. A close inspection reveals jagged edges and areas that the Magic Wand missed. So let's perfect these areas next.

Figure 17.5   Fill the selected area with black to mask and hide the wall area.

Refining an Imperfect Layer Mask

Creating art using computers is really cool, especially for the artistically challenged, like myself. Give me a medium in which each application of paint or chisel or whatever is a total commitment (no undo's), and I'll make a mess worthy of the trash can every time.

But fortunately, Photoshop allows us nearly unlimited latitude for finessing our work.

In the following steps, you will remove the remaining wall areas and polish the layer mask edges to perfection:

Applying Finishing Touches to the Layer Mask

1. Press **B** for the Brush tool (if the Pencil tool is active, click and hold on the Pencil icon in the toolbox, and choose the Brush tool from the flyout menu).

2. Press **F** one time to change the screen mode to Full Screen mode with menu bar. Hold down the Ctrl(⌘)+spacebar keys to toggle to the Zoom (in) tool, and click three times over the large painting.

3. On the Options bar, click on the Brush Preset Picker, and set the Master Diameter to 10 px and the Hardness to 50%. Flow and Opacity should be set to 100%, and Mode should be set to Normal on the Options bar. Click once on the wall area just below the bottom-left corner of the large painting. Then hold down the Shift key, and click on the wall area just below the bottom-right corner of the painting (see Figure 17.6). Holding down the Shift key forces the Brush tool to draw a line from the previous click point to the next click point.

Figure 17.6 Drawing a straight line on the layer mask below the painting is quick and easy with a click and Shift+click technique.

4. Use the same technique for the wall area near the right edge of the painting. Then freehand paint to mask away any remaining wall areas near the painting.

5. Hold down the spacebar to toggle to the Hand tool. Drag in the image to move the view so that you can see the entire baseboard on the wall on the right. Use the click, Shift+click technique described in step 3 to apply a layer mask on the near-black area of the baseboard (see Figure 17.7). Move the view (spacebar+drag) so that you can see the baseboard on the left wall, and remove the near-black area there as well.

Figure 17.7   Remove the near-black area of the baseboard on both walls.

6. Again, using black foreground color and the same Brush technique (on the layer mask), paint away any wall area at the bottom of the painting of the child to the left of the woman.

7. It's time to check the layer mask to be certain that the entire wall is hidden. Press Ctrl(⌘)+0 to zoom out so that the image fits on your screen. Hold down the Ctrl(⌘) key, and in the Layers palette, click on the Gallery layer mask thumbnail to load the mask as a selection.

   You should see a selection only around the two paintings, the lady, and the floor. If you see a marquee in the wall area, as shown in Figure 17.8, this indicates the location of opaque pixels that need to be masked. Press Ctrl(⌘)+D to deselect and paint with the Brush tool over any of these areas.

8. Make certain the entire wall is masked. To do so, Ctrl(⌘)+click on the layer mask thumbnail again to check, or press Ctrl(⌘)+D to deselect.

17

CTRL (CMD)+CLICK

Figure 17.8   The area of a layer mask is easily revealed by loading the mask as a selection.

    9. Press the **F** key two times to return to the Standard Screen mode.

  10. Press Ctrl(⌘)+S to save your image. Leave the image and Photoshop open for the next set of steps.

You just learned a few neat tricks for perfecting a layer mask and quickly checking your work.

Tip

> **Another concept of surrealistic art**   Contort familiar items into unrealistic shapes—for example, melting metal clocks on a desolate beach. (Sound familiar?) Hint: Experimenting with Photoshop's Liquify command to contort images is worth the effort.

Now that the walls are neatly hidden, we can insert the sky into the image. Compositing two images first requires dropping one image into the other image. And Photoshop's layers make this process as easy as a click and drag!

Inserting a Layer into a Layer Set

Photoshop's success as the world's leading image-editing program can be attributed to Adobe's willingness to listen to consumer feedback. Versatility and an organized work environment seem to be high on many users' lists of requests. Layers provide versatility and Layer Sets provide organization.

We've already worked with layers, so let me introduce Layer Sets. Say you have 30 layers for one image. To view most of those layers, you need to extend the palette to the full height of your screen, and yet you still need to scroll to view the entire Layers palette. Layer Sets are folders where you can drop any number of layers. The sets can be open to show all the layers inside or closed so that all you see is the set layer. For example, instead of scrolling through 30 layers on the Layers palette, you can place 10 layers inside each of three Layer Sets, enabling you to view only 10 layers at once. Layer Sets are cool, especially for neat-freaks.

In the following steps, you will create a new Layer Set in your Sky Gallery.psd image. You will then insert and transform a layer containing an image of the sky and clouds from another image.

Adding and Positioning the Sky

1. With your Sky Gallery.psd image open, click the Create a new set icon (third from the left) at the bottom of the Layers palette.

2. Double-click on the Set 1 title, and type **Sky** to rename the Layer Set. Press Enter (Return) to commit the new name. On the Layers palette, drag or press Ctrl(⌘)+[(left bracket) to move the Sky Layer Set below the Gallery layer (see Figure 17.9).

3. Open the Sky.psd image from the Examples/Chap17 folder on the companion CD.

4. Be sure you can see part of your Sky Gallery.psd image (move the Sky.psd image if needed). Click on the title bar of the Sky.psd document to make sure it is the active document in the workspace. On the Layers palette, drag the Sky layer into the image window of the Sky Gallery.psd document.

Note

The Sky layer   In the Layers palette, notice that the Sky layer drops directly into the Sky Layer Set.

5. Close the Sky.psd image without saving changes.

17

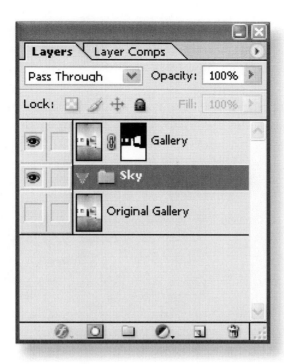

Figure 17.9 After you rename and move the Sky Layer Set, your Layers palette should look like this.

6. Press **V** to switch to the Move tool. Be sure that Auto Select Layer is unchecked in the Options bar, and then drag in the image to move the Sky layer to the top center of the image.

Tip

The Auto Select feature When the Auto Select Layer feature is toggled on, your cursor will determine the active layer every time you click in the image document. Whenever you click in an image document, the layer that contains the object (beneath your cursor) will automatically become the active layer in the Layers palette.

While this might sound like a real time-saver if you have a ton of layers accumulated in one document, sometimes this feature can become a pain in the neck if it is toggled on in the Options bar. So here's a killer tip: *Never* check the Auto Select Layer option on the Options bar. Instead, while the Move tool is active, hold down the Ctrl(⌘) key, and click on an object in the document when you want to access this feature. This keyboard shortcut allows you the flexibility to use this feature on demand (only when you need it).

7. Press the **F** key once to move to Full Screen mode with menu bar view. Press the Tab key once to hide all the interface elements. You're going to extend the Transform box away from the image because you need this additional screen space.

8. Press Ctrl(⌘)+T to activate the Transform command. Hold down the Shift key, and drag the bottom-left corner anchor of the bounding box downward and to the left until the sky area is scaled, as shown in Figure 17.10.

Figure 17.10   Drag the bottom-left corner of the bounding box down and to the left until the lady's head is surrounded mostly by sky rather than clouds.

9. When satisfied, press Enter (Return) or double-click inside the Transform box to apply the scale change.

Note

> **Transforming**   Applying the Transform command reduces the image quality of the area being transformed. Additionally, the more times you transform an image area, the more the quality deteriorates.
>
> Keep in mind the subject matter of the image area you are transforming. The Sky layer is fuzzy and without areas of detail and can be transformed numerous times before image deterioration is apparent. Conversely, the quality of an image of a person's face might handle only one, slight transformation before the details are compromised.

10. Press the **F** key two times to return to the Standard Screen mode. Press the Tab key once to unhide the interface elements.

11. Press Ctrl(⌘)+S to save your changes. Leave the image and Photoshop open.

Okay, all the components for the final Sky Gallery are assembled and ready for your expert Photoshop skills to complete the final image.

Let's give our attention next to increasing the visual appeal of this new Sky layer by adding contrast and adjusting the saturation of the colors.

Using Adjustment Layers

Adjustment Layers, like layer masks, enable you to enter temporary or permanent adjustments to your image without altering the original pixels. This is a very cool capability. Say, for example, you add contrast to the original pixels but then a month later decide that you added too much contrast, so you want to go back to your original image. Well, guess what? You can't; the tones you removed when you changed those original pixels are gone and can never be recovered. Had you applied the contrast using an Adjustment Layer, the original tones would still be intact, and you could change your mind—and the contrast—every day, forever!

Now that you have an idea of the value and principles of Adjustment Layers, let's create a few and add some visual punch to the Sky layer.

In the following example, you will use Adjustment Layers to add contrast to the sky using the Curves command. Then, you'll remove any color from the clouds and make the sky more blue.

Making a Grayish Sky Blue

1. With your Sky Gallery.psd image open, the Sky layer (not the Layer Set) should be the active layer in the Layers palette. If not, click on the Sky layer to make it the active layer.

2. At the bottom of the Layers palette, click the Create new fill or adjustment layer icon (third from the right), and choose Curves from the menu. The Curves dialog box will appear.

3. If the graph in the Curves dialog box shows only four horizontal and vertical grid divisions, position the cursor on the graph area, hold down the Alt(Opt) key, and click once. Your graph should now have 10 horizontal and vertical divisions, as shown in Figure 17.11.

4. Time to add two points to the curve. Starting at the top-right corner of the grid and going down and to the left, count where the curve (now a straight line) meets the third vertical gridline from the right. Click to add a point on the line at this location. Now, starting from the bottom-left corner, click where the curve intersects the third vertical gridline from the left. The location of these two points is shown in Figure 17.11.

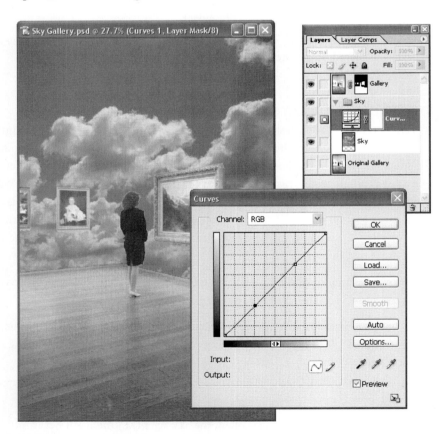

Figure 17.11   Click two points on the curve, each point located three gridlines from the side of the graph.

17

5. Drag the lower point down and to the right one half of a grid square so that the point is located in the center of the grid square. Move the upper point upward and to the left, also one half of a grid box so that the point is located in the center of the box. Your Curves graph should now look like the one shown in Figure 17.12.

Insider

> This s-shaped curve adds a slight amount of contrast to the image. (A more pronounced s-shape would add more contrast.) Of course, you could add contrast with the Brightness/Contrast command, but that results in a rather coarse adjustment. The Curves command gives you more control and can yield a more natural and gentle contrast.

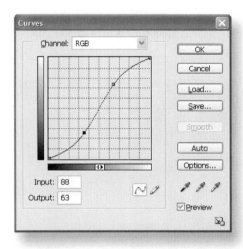

Figure 17.12   Dragging the two points to create a slight s-curve adds a little contrast to the image.

6. Click on OK. Notice the Curves Adjustment Layer in the Layers palette. With any Adjustment Layer, you can double-click the left-most thumbnail to open the dialog box and make changes to your settings.

7. Now that there is a greater contrast between the clouds and sky areas, selecting the sky will be easier. Click the eye icon to turn off the visibility for the Gallery layer. (This step is important because the Color Range command will select from all the visible layers, and we want only the sky layer!) Another preparatory step needed before using the Color Range command is to ensure the correct setting for Quick Mask. On the toolbox (below the color swatches) are two icons (one to enter and one to exit Quick Mask mode). Look at the one toward the right (to

enter Quick Mask). If this icon appears to be a white square with a shaded circle in the middle, hold down the Alt(Opt) key, and click on the icon once to toggle it to a shaded square with a white circle in the center.

Insider

> There are two major settings for Quick Mask: One is Masked Areas, and the other is Selected Areas. When the Selected Areas setting is active, the areas that are tinted with Quick Mask will become the selected marquee areas. When the Masked Areas setting is active, the opposite occurs: Areas that are *not* tinted with Quick Mask will become the selected marquee areas. For the steps to follow, the setting for Quick Mask needs to be toggled to Masked Areas.

8. Choose Select, Color Range. At the bottom of the Color Range dialog box, click on the flyout menu for Selection Preview, and choose Quick Mask. Drag the Fuzziness slider to 40, and click in any area of the blue sky. All the areas that are not selected at this point are overlaid with Quick Mask (see Figure 17.13).

Figure 17.13   For the sky area, choosing Quick Mask for the Selection Preview best indicates what areas are selected.

9. Click the Eyedropper+ tool (the center eyedropper under the Save button), and click in any other sky areas that show Quick Mask to add them to the selection. Click on OK to the Color Range command.

10. Check your image for small imperfections in the Color Range selection; they appear as small marqueed areas, like those you can see in the sky and clouds of the image in Figure 17.14. To remove those areas, press **Q** for the Quick Mask mode, press **B** for the Brush tool, and then press **D** for the default colors. With black as the foreground color and a brush size of 80 pixels, paint in any cloud areas (the goal is to have Quick Mask tint color fill the cloud areas). Be careful not to paint at the edge of a cloud; the edges are nearly perfect already.

Figure 17.14   Any small marqueed areas in the sky or in the clouds indicate an imperfect mask.

11. After you have painted Quick Mask in the cloud areas, press **X** to switch white to the foreground color. Paint in the sky area wherever you see Quick Mask tint (to remove the tint from the blue sky areas).

12. Press **Q** to exit the Quick Mask mode. Click the Create new fill or adjustment layer icon at the bottom of the Layers palette, and choose Hue/Saturation from the menu. Drag the Saturation slider to +25.

This increase in saturation darkens the sky area somewhat, so now drag the Lightness slider to +6 (see Figure 17.15). Click on OK.

Figure 17.15   To make a blue sky bluer using traditional photography, you need to attach a costly (polarizing) filter to your camera lens. Today, all you need is a Photoshop technique!

Insider

In a photograph, light, colorless objects are often tinted by the influence of large, same-colored areas. In our image, the clouds are influenced by the blue sky and contain too much yellow. And rather than adjust for the yellow, we can desaturate the cloud areas to completely remove any color in the clouds. That will give them the nice, clean look that we expect from clouds—especially surrealistic clouds!

13. Let's desaturate the clouds. On the Layers palette, Ctrl(⌘)+click on the Hue/Saturation 1 layer mask thumbnail (right-most thumbnail) to load the mask as a selection in the image. Because we want the clouds to be selected, press Ctrl(⌘)+Shift+I to invert the selection.

Now, click the Create new fill or adjustment layer icon at the bottom of the Layers palette, and choose Hue/Saturation from the menu. Drag the Saturation slider all the way to the left until it reads −100. Drag the Lightness slider to +10 to give a little more punch to the desaturated clouds (see Figure 17.16). Click on OK.

Figure 17.16   Load the layer mask from the first Hue/Saturation Adjustment Layer as a selection. Invert the selection so that only the clouds are affected by the second Hue/Saturation Adjustment Layer.

14. Click the eye icon (the empty box in the far-left column) to toggle on the visibility for the Gallery layer. Press Ctrl(⌘)+S to save your changes. Leave the image and Photoshop open.

> **Tip**
>
> **Homegrown surrealism**   Here's another concept of surrealism that could help you develop your own ideas: Meld two or more objects into one object. For example, create a waterfall that, at the bottom, melds into a tree trunk.

Okay, on to the next step in completing your Sky Gallery image: creating a reflection of the sky in the gallery's floor.

Flipping and Transforming a Layer

The counterpart to Photoshop layers in the old cartoon-making industry is the acetate on which the scenes and characters were painted. And like acetate, layers can be flipped and rotated. But unlike acetate, layers can be stretched, squished, and have their opacity reduced.

In the following steps, you will create a reflection of the sky in the floor. To achieve that effect, you will copy the Sky Layer Set, merge the layers in that set into one layer, flip it vertically, and then transform the set to create the illusion that the sky is reflected in the floor. Whew! Here we go:

Flipping, Reflecting, and Transforming the Sky Layer

1. The Sky Gallery.psd image should still be open. On the Layers palette, right-click (Macintosh: hold Ctrl and click) on the Sky Layer Set, and choose Duplicate Layer Set from the context menu (see Figure 17.17). Click on OK.

2. All the layers in the Sky copy set need to be merged into one layer. Click on the Sky layer within this set, and click on the columns to the left of the Curves 1, Hue/Saturation 1, and Hue/Saturation 2 Adjustment Layers to link these layers to the active Sky layer (within the Sky copy Layer Set). Press Ctrl(⌘)+E to merge these layers down onto the Sky layer.

3. Drag this Sky layer to the top of the layer stack in the Layers palette. Since we no longer need the Sky copy Layer Set, drag this set to the trash can at the bottom right of the Layers palette. Click on the Sky layer at the top of the layer stack to make it active for editing. Your Layers palette should look like Figure 17.18.

4. Press **F** one time for the Full Screen mode with menu bar.

5. From the main menu, choose Edit, Transform, Flip Vertical to flip the Sky layer upside down.

6. Press **V** to switch to the Move tool. Press **4** to reduce the opacity for this layer to 40%.

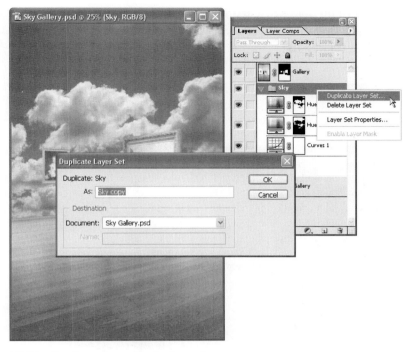

Figure 17.17 Duplicate the entire Sky Layer Set.

Figure 17.18 The current setup for the Layers palette should appear as it does here before transforming the Sky layer.

7. Hold down the Shift key, and drag the sky downward in the image until the top of this Sky layer is located at or near the top-right corner of the large painting, as shown in Figure 17.19.

Tip

Using the Shift modifier   By holding down the Shift key while you drag, you constrain the movement to maintain a perfectly vertical placement.

Figure 17.19   Position the Sky layer so that the top of the layer touches the top-right corner of the large painting.

8. Hold down the Ctrl(⌘) key, and press the minus key two times to zoom out twice. You'll need a lot of screen space for the next step.

9. Press Ctrl(⌘)+T for the Transform command. Right-click (Macintosh: hold Ctrl and click) inside the Transform box, and choose Distort from the context menu.

10. Drag the bottom-right and bottom-left anchors downward and outward, as shown in Figure 17.20. (Note: To re-create this transformation shape, you can alternatively enter into your Options bar the same numbers shown in the figure.) Then double-click inside the Transform box to apply the transformation.

Figure 17.20   Drag on the anchors to create a realistic-looking reflection off the floor.

11. Press Ctrl(⌘)+S to save your changes. Leave the image and Photoshop open for the next exercise.

Good job! As you can see, your image is coming together very nicely!

Now, we need to perfect this reflection because the sky on this layer should not be visible anywhere outside the floor area. So, let's move on and remove this extra sky area.

Using Quick Methods for Creating a Layer Mask

Applying a layer mask over the unwanted areas of the reflected sky can either be tedious and time-consuming, or simple and fast. I think we all would prefer the simple-and-fast method, right?

Although the area where we need to apply the layer mask appears complex (it's not simply a circle, for example), we can define the area in just a couple of quick steps. Then, with the ideal brush tip, we can trace along the lady's legs and then finish creating the mask.

In the following steps, you will apply a layer mask on the areas that are outside the floor area. C'mon—

Creating a Layer Mask Outside the Floor Area

1. On the Layers palette, Ctrl(⌘)+click on the Gallery layer mask thumbnail to load the mask as a selection. Click the Add layer mask icon at the bottom of the Layers palette (second from the left).

2. Press **D** for default colors so that black is the foreground color (if necessary, press **X** to switch black to the foreground). From the toolbox, choose the Polygon Lasso tool.

3. Press the Tab key to toggle off the palettes. Hold down the Ctrl(⌘)+spacebar keys to toggle to the Zoom (in) tool, and click two times over the hem of the lady's skirt.

4. Position your cursor to the right of her legs, and click once on the edge of the baseboard. Click again on the baseboard to the left side of her legs. Now, click around the two paintings and above her head, as shown in Figure 17.21. If necessary, hold down the spacebar to toggle to the Hand tool to maneuver around in the document view.

5. With the Sky layer mask still active, press Alt(Opt)+Delete(Backspace) to fill the selection with black foreground color. Press Ctrl(⌘)+D to deselect. That was quick work for everywhere except the lady's legs.

6. Hold down the Ctrl(⌘)+spacebar keys, and click three times over the lower part of the lady's legs. Press **B** for the Brush tool. Press the Tab key to toggle on the palettes. From the Brush Preset Picker, create a 10-pixel Master Diameter tip with a Hardness setting of 0%.

Figure 17.21   Use the Polygon Lasso tool to create a selection along the baseboard and around the paintings.

7. Paint along the edges of the lower part of the lady's legs and shoes, as shown in Figure 17.22. (Note: A selection marquee was created for the figure to help define this area because a lot of color detail can be lost in a black-and-white figure! No pun intended!)

Insider

> If you make a mistake, press **X** to switch to white as the foreground color, and paint to undo any errors. Then press **X** to switch to black again, and continue painting the legs.

8. Continue painting to apply black to the layer mask on the lower leg areas. Then press Ctrl($\mathcal{H}$)+0 to fit the entire image on your screen.

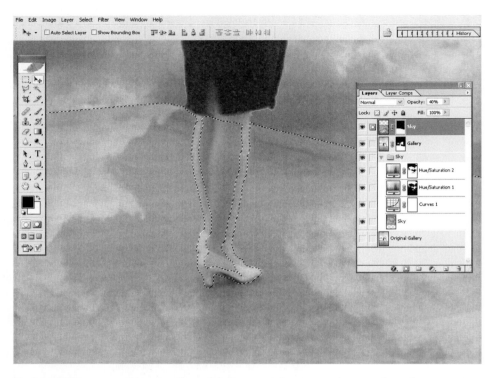

Figure 17.22   Paint along the edges of the legs, and then paint a layer mask on the remaining areas that show the Sky layer. (Note: The marquee on this image is for illustration purposes only!)

   9. Press **2** to reduce the opacity to 20%—a bit more realistic opacity for a reflection off a wood floor. Now, your image should look like Figure 17.23.

   10. Press Ctrl(⌘)+S to save your changes. Leave the image and Photoshop open.

Great! Your surrealistic image is coming together quite nicely! You've replaced the walls with a photo of the sky and reflected that sky off the floor.

> **Tip**
>
> **A surrealistic example**   Before we move ahead, here's another concept used in surrealistic art: Place an object in an illogical surrounding. For an example of this concept, well, let's try this chapter's image!

Now, let's take the surrealistic idea in Sky Gallery one step further and remove the painting on the left.

Figure 17.23   The Sky Gallery image in progress—almost near completion!

Unpainting a Painting: Removing and Replacing Image Areas

Gone are days when you had to accept everything—including mistakes—that showed in the photograph you shot using film. For example, that telephone pole extending out of Uncle Fred's head is no longer a permanent growth but can now be digitally removed. Any element that you just don't want in the photo is subject to your Photoshop skills. And this leads us to the next phase of creating the Sky Gallery image: removing a painting to leave only an empty frame.

In the following steps, you will mask the painting in the left frame and reflect the frame off the floor.

Unpainting a Painting and Reflecting the Frame

1. Open your Sky Gallery.psd image if it's not already open. On the Layers palette, click on the Layer Mask thumbnail on the Gallery layer to make it active for painting.

2. You should still be in Full Screen mode; if not, press the **F** key one time for the Full Screen mode with menu bar. Press Ctrl(⌘)+spacebar, and click four times over the left-most painting to zoom in to a view that is close enough for detailed work.

3. Press **D** for default colors so that black is the foreground color. The Brush tool should still be active; if not, press **B** to switch to the Brush tool. On the Options bar, open the Brush Preset Picker, and set the Master Diameter to 3 px and Hardness to 0%. Hold down the Shift key, and in a clockwise direction, click on each of the four corners of the painting near the inside edges of the frame (see Figure 17.24).

Figure 17.24   Using a 3-pixel brush tip, Shift+click on each of the painting's four corners.

4. From the toolbox, choose the Polygon Lasso tool. Click at each of the four corners inside the masked line, and then press Alt(Opt)+Backspace(Delete) to fill the marquee selection with black foreground color on the layer mask, as shown in Figure 17.25.

Figure 17.25   Fill the marquee with black color to hide the painting on the Gallery layer mask.

5. Press Ctrl(⌘)+D to deselect the marquee. Notice that the inside edges of the frame that you just created are much smoother than the outside edges. Not good! Consistent edges are a sign of a good digital artist. Let's fix those raggedy edges. Press **X** to switch white to the foreground color (black). The same Brush tool settings from step 3 should still be active.

6. Using the Shift+click technique (see step 3), pick one ragged edge and click on one outside corner; then Shift+click on the opposite corner of that edge to restore a smoother edge to the frame (no more ragged edges). You might need to repeat this technique more than once for each edge. Figure 17.26 shows smooth edges on all sides of the frame except the top for comparison purposes. (Be sure to smooth all sides before continuing!)

Figure 17.26   Use the layer mask to remove jagged areas along the edges of the frame.

7. Press Ctrl(⌘)+0 (zero) to fit the image on your screen. On the Layers palette, right-click (Macintosh: hold Ctrl and click) on the Gallery layer, and choose Duplicate Layer from the menu. In the As field, rename the layer **Frame**, and click on OK.

8. Right-click (Macintosh: hold Ctrl and click) on the Frame layer mask thumbnail, and choose Apply Layer Mask. Choose the Rectangular Marquee tool from the toolbox, and drag a selection around the empty frame. Press Ctrl(⌘)+Shift+I to invert the selection. Press the Delete (Backspace) key to delete all the layer's contents except the frame. You won't see any changes in the image, but the Frame thumbnail will now look empty except for the frame. Press Ctrl(⌘)+D to deselect.

9. Choose Edit, Transform, Flip Vertical to flip the frame upside down. Press **V** to switch to the Move tool. Hold down the Shift key, and drag the frame straight down so that it is about the same distance from the baseboard as the original frame.

17

10. Press Ctrl(⌘)+T for the Transform command. Right-click (Macintosh: hold Ctrl and click) inside the Transform box, and choose Distort from the menu. Drag each of the corner anchors to conform the shape, as shown in Figure 17.27. When satisfied, double-click inside the box to apply the transformation.

Figure 17.27   Transform the frame so that it appears to reflect off the floor.

11. Press **8** to reduce the Opacity of the Frame layer to 80%.

12. Press Ctrl(⌘)+S to save your changes. Leave the image and Photoshop open.

Your Sky Gallery image looks finished now, doesn't it? "No!" I hope you said! That is correct; even at full image view, you can see that the edges of the lady are lighter than they should be. The Magic Wand (from the first exercise) did a quick and decent selection, but obviously not a perfect one. In the next section, you'll get edgy with the Clone Stamp tool and complete your Sky Gallery image.

Examining the Image and Applying the Final Touches

To finish up the Sky Gallery image, you will look for any imperfections in the sky area. You will also use the Clone Stamp tool along the edges of the lady's image. As you can see, a halo effect along her clothing and hair is screaming, "This is sloppy edgework!"

In the following steps, you will examine the Sky Gallery image and remove the halo effect that surrounds the lady's clothing and hair.

Inspecting the Image and Applying the Finishing Touches

1. The Sky Gallery.psd image should still be open (and the Full Screen mode with menu bar view should still be active). Press the Ctrl(⌘)+spacebar keys to toggle to the Zoom (in) tool, and click two times over the upper-left quadrant of the image.

2. Most likely, you will see a few white specks in the sky area (the blue area, not the clouds) in your image. If so, click on the Gallery layer mask thumbnail, and then press **B** for the Brush tool. Using a Master Diameter (brush tip size) of around 70 px and black as the foreground color, paint (on the layer mask) over the white specks (see Figure 17.28).

Figure 17.28   You can quickly remove any white specks in the blue sky area by painting on the layer mask for the Gallery layer.

3. Toggle to the Zoom (in) tool (Ctrl(⌘)+spacebar), and click two times on the image of the lady. Hold down the spacebar to toggle to the Hand tool, and drag in the image to move the view so that you can see from the top of her head to her knees. At this view, you can clearly see a light border on the edges of her clothing and hair.

4. Click on the Gallery layer thumbnail (left-most thumbnail), and then press **S** for the Clone Stamp tool. From the Brush Preset Picker in the Options bar, define a brush tip having a Master Diameter of 9 px and a Hardness of 0%.

5. Let's remove the light edge on her right shoulder. Position your cursor about one half of the Brush tip's diameter away from the light edge and near where her shoulder meets her hair. Alt(Opt)+click at this location, and then paint along the edge of her shoulder to paint the darker color over the light border (see Figure 17.29).

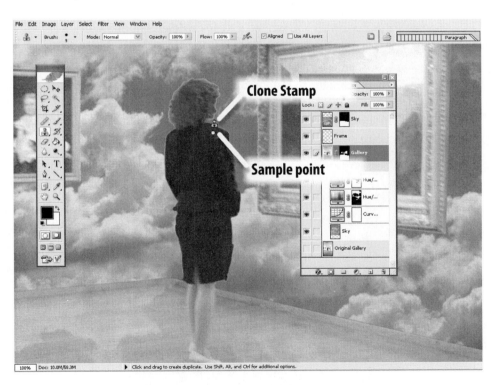

Figure 17.29   Using the Clone Stamp tool, Alt(Opt)+click near the light border edge, and then paint over the edge of the lady's shoulder with the darker sampled color.

6. Repeat the technique described in step 5 for the remaining light border areas, including around the lady's hair. Be sure to Alt(Opt)+click frequently to create a new sample area that is just inside the edge.

7. Notice that the edges of the lady's image are much sharper than the edges of the baseboard and the bottom edge of the large painting's frame. Consistent edges should be a priority, so let's fix this detail. On the Layers palette, click on the Gallery layer mask thumbnail (the sharp edges are located in this mask), and then choose the Blur tool from the toolbox (press **R**). In the Options bar, define a 10-pixel diameter tip with Hardness at 0%, Strength at 40%, and uncheck the Use All Layers option.

8. Using a slow, smooth, and careful motion, apply the Blur tool along all the sharp edges. Glance at the floorboard or bottom edge of the frame occasionally as a reference for how much to blur. Be careful to keep the tool moving—the longer the tool is in one location, the more that location is blurred. You want to create a consistent blur along the entire border.

9. While we're working in this area of the image, notice the raggedy left edge of the large painting's frame. Hold down the spacebar to toggle to the Hand tool, and drag in the image so that you can see the entire left edge of the painting.

10. Use the Brush tool with a diameter of 6 px, and with white as the foreground color (if needed, press **X** to switch to white as the foreground color), use the click and Shift+click technique to restore some of the frame's edge and eliminate the sharp, jagged edge. If the top edge of your frame needs perfecting, do that now. Figure 17.30 shows what the edges of the lady's image and the frame should look like at this point.

Figure 17.30   Attention to detail and consistent edges are qualities to always strive for.

17

11. Press Ctrl(⌘)+S to save your changes. To see and admire your entire image, press Ctrl(⌘)+0 (zero) to fit the image on your screen. Figure 17.31 shows the completed image at this point of the chapter. Leave the image and Photoshop open for the next exercise.

Figure 17.31 The completed Sky Gallery image.

Okay, good work! For all intents and purposes, you have completed your Sky Gallery image. In doing so, you've used layers, layer masks, Layer Sets, and Adjustment Layers. There is one more feature of layers that you should know about, and it's new to this version of Photoshop. This feature is called Layer comps.

Tip

More surrealism hints Now that we're nearing the end of the chapter, allow me to add one more concept used in surrealistic art: Take an object that changes with time, and place it in an illogical environment. Here are two examples: an egg "sitting" in a bird-cage and a landscape at night, yet with a daytime sky.

Let's apply one more change to the Sky Gallery image just so that we can take Layer comps out for a spin.

Creating and Using Layer Comps

Layer comps enable you to create different layer visibility scenarios and quickly toggle through each setup. For example, you created an image that contains dozens of layers for a client. Your client wants to see three different versions, each showing or hiding a variety of different layers. So, rather than searching through the Layers palette and turning the visibility off or on for specific layers, you can predefine each of the three setups so that your client doesn't become frustrated and farm his work to someone else (someone else who knows how to use Layer comps!).

The image we've created in this chapter has potential for more than one version. Using the Layer Comps palette, we can quickly change the view from one version to another.

In the following exercise, you will create a slightly different version of your Sky Gallery image and then create two scenarios (document states) in the Layer Comps palette.

Creating Layer Comps

1. With your Sky Gallery.psd image open, right-click (Macintosh: hold Ctrl and click) on the Original Gallery layer at the bottom of the layer stack on the Layers palette. Choose Duplicate, and in the As field, rename the duplicate layer **Small Gallery**. Click on OK.

2. While still working in the Layers palette, drag the Small Gallery layer up, immediately above the Sky layer set. Press **F** for Full Screen mode with menu bar (if that is not the current view).

3. Press Ctrl(⌘)+T for the Transform command. Hold down the Shift key, and drag any one of the four corners inward until the Transform box is about the size of the small frame. Now, click inside the box, and drag the image inside the empty frame (see Figure 17.32).

4. Hold down the Ctrl(⌘)+spacebar keys to toggle to the Zoom (in) tool, and click five times over the Transform box. This view gives you plenty of room and detail to make small adjustments to the transformation. Continue to scale the image (Shift+drag on any corner anchor) so that the image's left and right sides slightly overlap the frame's left and right inside edges, as shown in Figure 17.33.

Figure 17.32   Scale the image proportionately (Shift+drag), and position the image inside the frame.

5. Right-click (Macintosh: hold Ctrl and click) inside the box, and choose Distort. Drag the top-right corner anchor down slightly so that the top edge of the box is parallel with the top edge of the frame. Now, drag the bottom-right corner anchor upward until the bottom edge of the box is parallel with the bottom of the frame (see Figure 17.34).

6. When satisfied, double-click inside the box to apply the transformation. Click the Add layer mask icon at the bottom of the Layers palette (second from the left). Press **B** for the Brush tool. Set the diameter to 20 px. With black as the foreground color (press **D**), paint over the areas of the Small Gallery layer that extend beyond the outside edges of the frame.

7. The image inside the frame looks too much like a photograph to be "hanging" in a gallery with paintings. Let's apply a painterly filter. First, click on the Small Gallery layer thumbnail (left-most thumbnail) so that you don't apply the filter to the layer mask! Next, choose Filter, Filter Gallery.

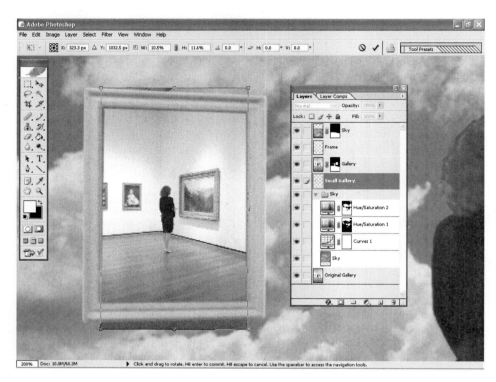

Figure 17.33   Scale the image so that the left and right edges slightly overlap the frame's inside edges.

Insider

> The Filter Gallery is a new Photoshop feature that enables you to quickly preview any or all of the filters. Even though I used the word *quickly*, using this feature is very processor intensive—but still much faster than going through each of the filters one at a time.

17

8. Click and drag in the preview window to move the view so that you can see the entire Small Gallery image. Click the right-facing arrow at the Artistic folder to open the list of filters in this category.

(If this is your first time using the Filter Gallery, take a few moments to explore and preview some of the listed filters.)

Click on the Dry Brush thumbnail, and then drag the sliders so that Brush Size is 0, Brush Detail is 10, and Texture is 3 (see Figure 17.35). This filter and these settings closely replicate the style of the large painting. Click on OK to apply the filter.

Figure 17.34 Use the angles of the top and bottom sides of the frame as guides for the correct perspective.

Okay, the Small Gallery image looks pretty bad, eh? Let's fix it. Press Ctrl(⌘)+0 (zero) to fit the entire image on your screen. The Small Gallery image doesn't look so bad now, but it needs to look more like a painting. Press Ctrl(⌘)+F to re-apply the last-used filter.

9. Okay, it's time to set up the Layer comps. But before you do that, let's get rid of that painting over to the left of this image. Press the] (right bracket key) seven times to increase the brush size to 80 px, and paint over the entire left-most painting to remove it completely. Now click the Layer Comps palette tab, or choose Window, Layer Comps. Click the Create New Layer Comp icon at the bottom of the palette (second from the right). Name the Layer comp **Small Painting** (see Figure 17.36), and click on OK.

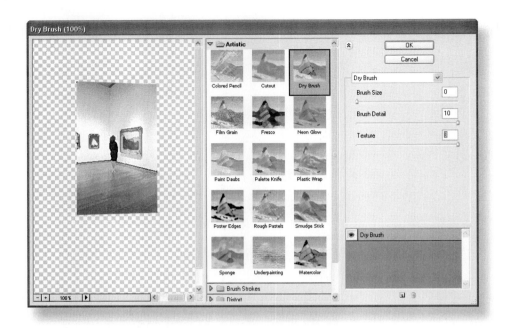

Figure 17.35   The Filter Gallery enables you to quickly preview each of the filters from just one dialog box.

10. Let's create a different version of the Sky Gallery image. On the Layers palette, click the eye icon to turn off the visibility for the Small Gallery layer and the Frame layer.

11. Return to the Layer Comps palette. Click again on the Create New Layer Comp icon at the bottom of the palette and name it **No Small Painting**. Click on OK.

12. On the Layer Comps palette, click in the far-left column for the Small Painting Layer comp. You should see the small painting and the reflection of the small, empty frame in the floor.

Click in the far-left column of the No Small Painting Layer comp. You should now see the small frame only and no reflection in the floor (see Figure 17.37).

17

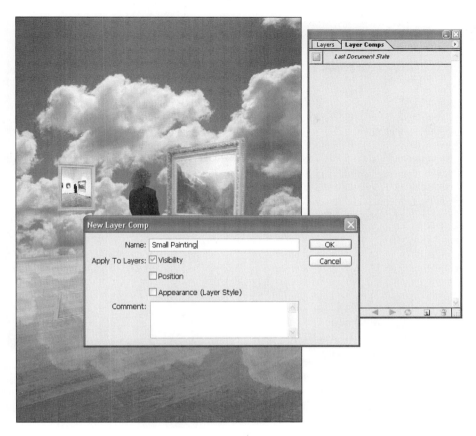

Figure 17.36   Layer comps enable you to view different versions of your image—a wonderful feature especially when you're working with a client.

13. Press Ctrl(⌘)+S to save your changes. Close your image any time.

Again, Layer comps are invaluable, especially when you have a demanding client or simply want to quickly toggle through different versions of your image to help you decide which version you like best.

We now come to the end of this chapter and our creation of the dream-like Sky Gallery image. But we hope you've come to the beginning of *your* journey in creating your own surrealistic images.

Figure 17.37   The Layer Comps palette is very helpful when you can't decide which version you like best!

Summary

In this chapter, you worked with precision and attention to detail using layers, layer masks, Layer Sets, Adjustment Layers, and Layer comps. Take full advantage of these powerful Photoshop features when creating a composite image.

Equally important to creating an eye-catching image is the concept or idea of your image. The concepts of dream—like images (surrealism) that are sprinkled throughout the chapter were used by masters of the style and are excellent launchpads for developing your own style. Happy dreams!

Chapter 18

Replacing the Main Elements in an Image

Magicians and military strategists alike can agree that "the best place to hide something is in plain sight." And so it goes with digital retouching; with the right lighting and

In this chapter, you'll learn

- How to isolate an image from its background

- How to use resizing and the Free Transform feature to add an object to an image

- How to use transparency to align image elements

- How to use Quick Mask mode to select and copy image elements

- How to use the Clone Stamp tool to touch up the image

- How to add shadows to blend in imported image elements

camera angle, you often can replace a sizeable section of a photo and make it look perfectly natural. Let's see how this can be done.

Gare Gets a New Guitar

Gary Eden used to play in a rock group with me, but that was eons ago, and he's since traded in his blazing Gibson electric for a modest Tama acoustic guitar. However, after receiving a phone call a short time ago, I don't think he's given up his rambunctious rock-and-roll spirit. He had sent me a photo of him with his tame guitar, and I decided to gift him with a version that featured him playing a legendary Les Paul guitar. There are plenty of potential pitfalls when trying to retouch an object this large into a picture, not to mention where to procure a photo of a vintage guitar.

> **Note**
>
> **Tama is good**   This chapter is riddled with lines such as "removing the Tama guitar." I have nothing against Tama guitars, and nothing negative should be inferred. I'm showing how to replace one image area with another; that's all.

Last things first: I wrote to the Gibson Company, and the folks there happily gave me permission to download and share with you readers a high-resolution image of a Les Paul from their pressroom (see Figure 18.1).

Figure 18.1   The two images that you'll use in this chapter.

Now to the hard stuff…

Creating a Selection Around the Guitar

The first thing you need to do is to isolate the Les Paul guitar from its background. For
this task, I recommend using the Pen tools because it provides a crisp, clean separation
of the guitar from its background. If you didn't read Chapter 6, "Using the Pen Tools,"
right now would be a good time to do so. Alternatively, the path has already been created (see Figure 18.2), so you can get down to work in only a few steps if you feel you
don't need the practice.

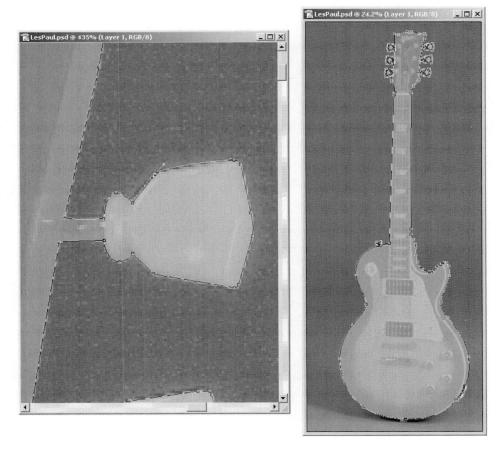

Figure 18.2   Create a path along the edge of the guitar.

Adding the Guitar to the Guitarist Image

If you look carefully at Figure 18.1, you'll see that the guitar is viewed at 16.7%, while the picture of Gary is viewed at 25%. This means that the guitar is almost twice as large as it needs to be for the "guitar transplant." This is okay, however; you really don't need to resize the guitar now because you will need to dynamically resize and rotate it later, as you fit the guitar into place in the Gary image.

Note

> **The Resize Windows to Fit option**   By default, the Resize Windows to Fit option is turned off, and that is the desirable setting for the purposes of the exercise in this section of the chapter. But for future use, you may want to go back and toggle this feature on.

Here's how to use Photoshop's window resizing option along with the Free Transform feature to put the Les Paul in Gary's lap:

Copying, Resizing, and Rotating the Guitar

1. Load the GaryTama.tif image from the Examples/Chap18 folder on the companion CD. Then load the LesPaul.tif image from the same folder.

2. Click on the Zoom tool, and then on the Options bar, *un*check the Resize Windows to Fit box if it's checked.

Insider

> When the Resize Windows to Fit option is turned on, the window enlarges to fit within the workspace whenever a Zoom tool function is used (which includes when you toggle to the Zoom tool through the Ctrl(⌘)+spacebar keyboard shortcut). You can view a similar option in the General Preferences by pressing Ctrl(⌘)+K. Check the Zoom Resizes Windows option in this dialog box to resize the window to fit your workspace whenever the document zoom view is altered using the keyboard shortcut of Ctrl(⌘) and the plus or minus keys (or the menu equivalent). If you like the idea of having the window resize to fit when zooming in or out of the image—regardless of the method used to do so—you'll want to check these options in both places. The General Preference option will resize the window only when you're using the Ctrl(⌘) key with the plus or minus keys to zoom. It will not resize the window when you access the Zoom tool (to zoom in or out). Only by selecting this option for the Zoom tool do you get the best of both worlds.

3. Press **V** to choose the Move tool, and click on the title bar to the LesPaul image to make this image the active document in the workspace.

4. Click on the Paths tab to view the Paths palette. Click on the Guitar title to reveal the path surrounding the guitar, and then click on the Load path as a selection icon at the bottom of the Paths palette.

18

5. In one deft move, drag the guitar selection into the GaryTama image. Close the LesPaul.tif image without saving changes.

6. Press Ctrl(⌘)+the minus key two or three times—whatever it takes to make the viewing resolution for the GaryTama image about 16.7%. Drag on the corner of the document window to expose plenty of gray window background around the image.

7. Press Ctrl(⌘)+T to display the Free Transform box. Hold down the Shift key to constrain proportions, and drag on a corner of the Transform bounding box toward the center of the guitar until the body appears to be about the same size as the body of the acoustic guitar in the image (see Figure 18.3).

Figure 18.3   Zoom out of your current view so you can see the entire *selection* of the guitar when in Free Transform mode.

8. Hover the cursor outside a corner of the bounding box, and when the cursor changes to a bent arrow, rotate the guitar until the neck is aligned with the neck of the Tama guitar. Then resize the guitar, again using the Shift key, if necessary (see Figure 18.4).

Tip

> **Placing the center reference anchor**   When rotating the guitar, place the center reference anchor within the Free Transform box at the center of the guitar body. Just click and drag that icon to the body.
>
> Also, you can zoom in for a more precise view by pressing Ctrl($\mathcal{H}$)+the plus key.

Figure 18.4   Rotate the guitar so that the necks line up in degree of rotation.

9. When the guitar is the correct size and rotation, double-click inside the bounding box to finalize the edits (or press Enter).

10. Press Ctrl($\mathcal{H}$)+Shift+S, save the image in Photoshop's native file format as **GaryLesPaul.psd**, and keep the file open.

Actually, the hard part of this assignment is finished! What lies before you is some fancy image retouching.

Performing Some Precision Alignment

A fellow guitarist might note now that Gary isn't actually playing a chord; the neck of the Tama and the Les Paul aren't in perfect alignment. But you're going to *make* it perfect!

Using Transparency to Align the Guitar Necks

1. Zoom in to about a 1:1 viewing resolution (100%) of the GaryLesPaul image.

2. The guitar layer (Layer 1) should be the active layer. Press 5 on the keyboard to send the guitar to 50% opacity.

3. Carefully, with the Move tool, drag the guitar neck back and forth until Gary's fingers appear to be placed between the frets, and the last fret appears to be aligned with the last fret on the Tama guitar (see Figure 18.5).

Figure 18.5   Align the neck so that it appears that Gary's left hand is fretting the neck.

4. Press 0 to return the guitar to 100% opacity.

5. Press Ctrl(⌘)+S; keep the file open.

Obviously, the image doesn't look right at the moment; Gary's fingers are behind the new Les Paul addition, and most pop stars don't play this way. That's why we have a section coming up to address this gross oversight.

Playing with Fingers That Are Playing

Making these changes is easy stuff; in the steps to follow, you'll copy Gary's left fingers to a new layer. And in the process, you'll be able to sustain the illusion that he's fretting on a new guitar.

Here's how to use the Quick Mask mode to copy the fingers:

Quick Mask Selecting the Fretting Fingers

1. Zoom in to a 200% viewing resolution of Gary's left hand. I know, I know, the image is a little pixelated because the photographer saved it using a high-compression JPEG setting. Click on the eye icon of the guitar layer to toggle off the visibility and to hide the guitar from view.

2. Click on the Background layer to make it the active layer on the Layers palette. Choose the Brush tool on the toolbox. Click on the Quick Mask icon (or press **Q**).

Insider

> Look at your Quick Mask icon on the toolbox. If it is a shaded square (with a *white* circle in the center), hold down the Alt(Opt) key and click on the Quick Mask icon again to toggle the settings so that the icon appears as a white square (with a *shaded* circle inside). What does this do? Well, Quick Mask will respond to Quick Mask color tint in two ways. One setting will *exclude* all the image areas you paint with Quick Mask color tint, while the other setting will select *only* the image areas you paint with Quick Mask color tint. The latter setting is preferred for our work.

3. Right-click (Macintosh: hold Ctrl and click) over the image to display the Brushes palette. Choose a hard-tip round brush, and then drag the Master Diameter slider to about 27 (px). Press Enter (Return) to dismiss the Brushes palette.

4. Black should be the foreground color (if not, press **D**). The Options bar should display a Normal Mode and 100% setting for Opacity and Flow. Paint over the fingers from top to bottom, and then stop where the fingers cross over the bottom of the guitar neck.

Insider

> If you make a mistake, press **X** to switch to white as the foreground color and paint away any mistakes. Press **X** to switch black to the foreground color again, and continue to paint as before.

5. When satisfied, press **Q** to exit Quick Mask mode, and then click on the guitar layer on the Layers palette.

18

6. Press Ctrl(⌘)+J to move the selected fingers to a new layer. Alternatively, you can choose a selection tool such as the Rectangular Marquee tool, right-click (Macintosh: hold Ctrl and click) over the selection marquee, and choose Layer via Copy, as shown in Figure 18.6.

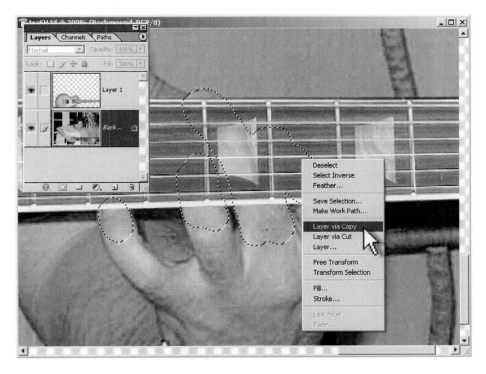

Figure 18.6   Copy the area you created using the Quick Mask feature.

7. Click on the eye column for the guitar layer (Layer 1) to make it visible again. Then drag the fingers layer (Layer 2) above the guitar layer. Your image should look like that shown in Figure 18.7. Congratulations! The deception is well underway.

8. Right now is a good time to rename the layers. Double-click on their current title names to rename each layer, and type in some evocative labels such as **Fretting Fingers** and **Les Paul guitar**. Whatever.

9. Press Ctrl(⌘)+S; keep the file open.

What's good for the left hand is equally good for the right. In the section to follow, you'll select the picking hand and arm for copying.

Figure 18.7   With a copy of the fingers on top of the stack of layers now, it really looks as though Gary is fretting the guitar.

Quick Masking and Copying the Strumming Arm

Now, more of Gary's right appendage needs copying than his fretting hand because more of his right appendage is covering the guitar. You already have experience selecting the fingers, but how do you select Gary's slightly hairy arm? You use a hard brush tip for the fingers, select only the arm, and then paint a few strokes with a small, angled brush to pick up some of the shadow/hair to the right of the arm.

Let's get to it!

Selecting the Strumming Arm

1. Hide the guitar layer again, and click the Background layer as the editing layer (also called the *target* layer).

2. Zoom in to a 300% viewing resolution. Choose the Brush tool, and then click on the Quick Mask icon (or press **Q**).

3. Black should be the foreground color. Right-click (Macintosh: hold Ctrl and click), choose 15 pixels for the Master Diameter of the tip, and choose 100% hardness. Press Enter (Return) to dismiss the Brushes palette. Brush over the fingers in Gary's right hand, as shown in Figure 18.8. If you make a mistake, press **X** to switch to white and paint to correct the mistakes. Press **X** to switch to black and resume work.

Figure 18.8   Cover the finger areas with Quick Mask.

4. Continue upward masking the inside edge of Gary's arm. Don't bother with the arm hair at the moment (see Figure 18.9).

5. Continue masking the inside edge of the arm until you meet the area where the guitar body ends (the top edge). Work your way down, along the inside edge of the other side of the arm. When you're done painting the edges, switch to the Polygonal Lasso tool. Click inside the Quick Mask paint areas (along the middle of the tint areas) at the edges of the arm to create a selection that will include some of the Quick Mask tint and also surround the middle of the arm (that hasn't yet been filled with Quick Mask tint). With black as the foreground color, press Alt(Opt)+Delete(Backspace) to fill the remaining interior of the arm with Quick Mask tint color. Press Ctrl(⌘)+D to deselect the selection.

6. Switch to the Brush tool once again, and make a custom brush tip. Scroll down, choose the Watercolor Small Round Tip from the Brushes palette, and reduce the Master Diameter size to 7 pixels. Press Enter (Return) to dismiss the Brushes palette. Stroke along some individual arm hairs, as shown in Figure 18.10.

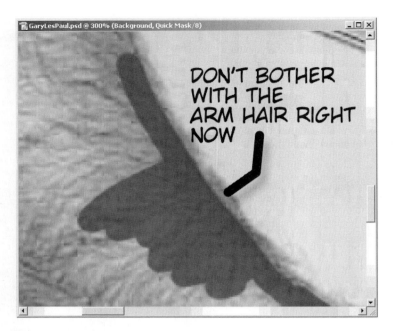

Figure 18.9   Mask only the inside edge of the arm.

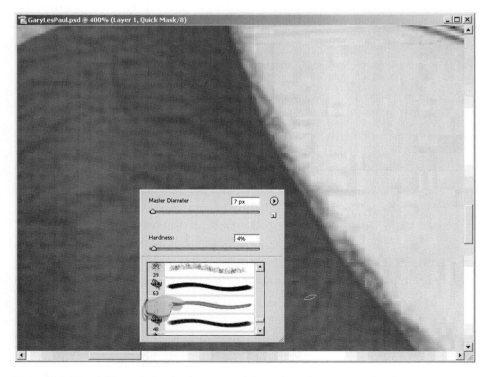

Figure 18.10   Add arm hair selections at partial opacity using a custom brush.

7. Press **Q** to exit Quick Mask mode and switch back to Standard Editing mode. Press Ctrl(⌘)+J to put the selection onto a new layer.

8. Click the eye column to toggle the visibility on for the guitar layer. Drag the fingers-and-arm layer to the top of the layers stack on the Layers palette, and then sit back, zoom out, and take a look at your handiwork! Check out Figure 18.11 to see where you should be right now.

Figure 18.11 It's a strange-looking guitar, but Gary certainly looks as though he's playing it!

9. Press Ctrl(⌘)+S; keep the file open.

You guessed it! The remaining steps will show you how to clone away the Tama guitar.

Clone Stamp Tool Techniques

Using the Clone Stamp tool by itself isn't hard. What *might* be a challenge, however, is knowing *when* and *where* to use the tool. Not to worry; this book contains solutions, not problems. In the steps to follow, we'll go from the "easy" cloning to the "difficult" cloning.

Cleaning Up the Bottom Edge of the Guitar

Now it's time to clean up a bit. We'll start at the bottom of the Tama guitar:

Cloning Away the Bottom of the Guitar

1. Zoom in to a 300% viewing resolution of the bottom of the guitar.

2. On the Layers palette, click the Background layer to make it the active (editing) layer.

3. Choose the Clone Stamp tool, choose a hard brush tip, and adjust the Master Diameter to about 30 pixels.

4. Alt(Opt)+click at the far left of the mullion edge on the window, as shown in Figure 18.12, and then stroke with the Clone Stamp tool on the mullion edge and into the guitar. Continue stroking until the bottom of the guitar disappears. If necessary, repeat this process if some of the old guitar is peeking out of the bottom-left edge of the image (also near the window area). If necessary, reduce the size of the brush to fit into smaller areas when Alt(Opt)+clicking to determine the target area for the cloning work.

5. Press Ctrl(⌘)+S; keep the file open.

Removing the Tama Guitar: Part II

The second area within which we'll work is Gary's armpit. The top half of the body of the guitar has to go, and although a little more talent is required than in the preceding set of steps, navigating this course is still fairly easy. Let's go!

Cloning Away the Top of the Guitar

1. Zoom to about 200% viewing resolution at the top left of the Tama guitar.

2. Alt(Opt)+click with the Clone Stamp tool over a crease in Gary's shirt using about a 30-pixel brush tip.

3. Clone over an area where a crease is truncated by the Tama guitar, as shown in Figure 18.13.

18

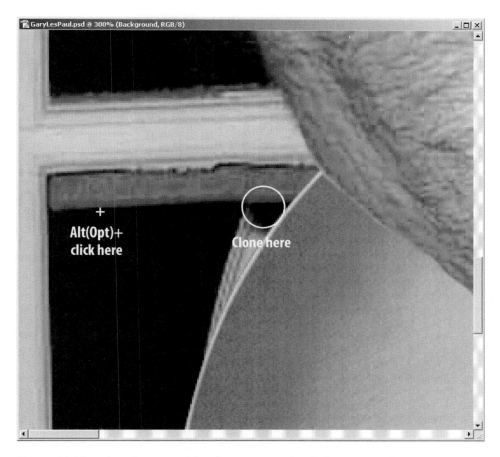

Figure 18.12   Align the target of the Clone Stamp tool with the source, and then stroke away.

Tip

Extending creased areas   Here's a useful tip to help align a crease area that you intend to extend using cloned information (sampled off the same crease). Hold down the Alt(Opt) key and click to sample your crease, but don't release the Alt(Opt) key right away. When this key is pressed, your cursor takes on a kind of bull's-eye shape, which can be very useful to help in aligning your cursor with the intended cloning area. With this in mind, continue to hold down the Alt(Opt) key as you move your cursor to the proper position. Make use of the bull's-eye to line up in the proper spot. Then, holding the cursor steady, release the Alt(Opt) key and start clicking to clone with more precision. When using this trick, you should not click until after you release the Alt(Opt) key; otherwise, you will in effect only be sampling a new area instead of actually cloning to that area.

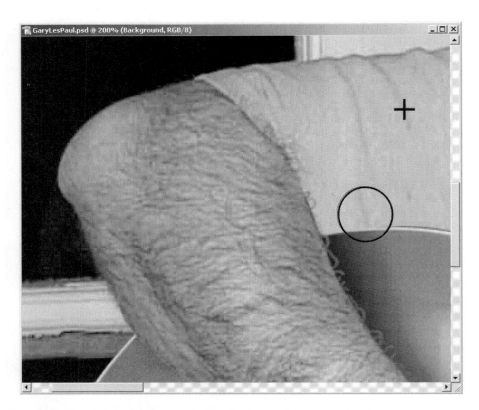

Figure 18.13   Continue the creases in the shirt by sampling creases in other areas.

4. Clone over plain areas with sampled plain areas and other shirt creases with samples of creases until the top left of the Tama guitar body is gone. If areas of colors don't seem to transition smoothly (with the Clone Stamp tool), switch to the Healing Brush tool. Alt(Opt)+click to sample a color for the transition area, and then click a few times over the areas that need to transition more smoothly (where a shift of color may occur in the shadows of the shirt). In other words, use the Clone Stamp tool for most of the dirty work, and then use the Healing Brush tool to refine it.

5. Press Ctrl(⌘)+S; keep the file open.

Let's carry this cloning stuff further in the image now.

Cloning Away the Top Right of the Tama

You don't need special instructions to clone away the Tama guitar area closest to Gary's neck, but some advice might help. Again, you are going to have to clone over folds of cloth in the shirt, and there's no reason you can't occasionally use a sample of the shirt area you reconstructed in the preceding set of steps.

Let's get to work:

Continuing the Cloning Work

1. Press the spacebar to toggle to the Hand tool, and drag the image within the window so you can see the top right of the Tama guitar body.

2. Use about a 30-pixel brush tip, and clone over guitar areas that are adjacent to smooth shirt areas with a sample of a smooth shirt area, as shown in Figure 18.14.

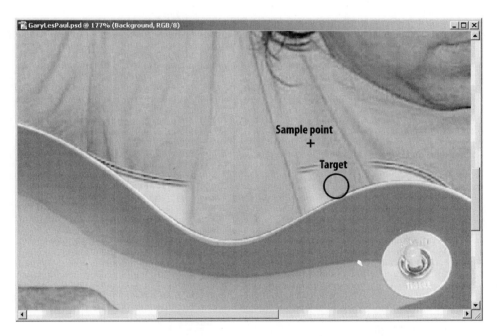

Figure 18.14   Clone visually corresponding areas into areas hidden by the guitar body.

3. When you come to an area that needs a clothing fold, sample an area directly near it, or a fold in the shirt that you reconstructed earlier where the top left of the Tama guitar used to be.

4. Press Ctrl(⌘)+S; keep the file open.

To finalize the removal of the Tama guitar body, you must work on its remaining bottom right. But there's not very much "non-guitar" area from which to sample!

Finishing Removing the Tama Guitar

You'll notice that as you cloned over the bottom left, top left, and top right of the guitar body, you now have more "non-guitar" shirt area from which to clone. However, because there are slight tone differences across the shirt, you might want to squeak away as much original shirt area as you can in the bottom right—the only remaining area of the acoustic guitar.

Here's how to finish the cloning work:

Cloning: The Final Chapter

1. Using the Hand tool, pan down the window until you can see the last remaining vestiges of the Tama guitar body.

2. With the Clone Stamp tool and a tip of about 30 pixels, Alt(Opt)+click over the large fold in the shirt, and then drag over the body of the guitar where it meets a different fold in the cloth. You will need to resample frequently because there isn't very much original area from which to sample.

3. Work from right to left, slowly and deliberately, as shown in Figure 18.15.

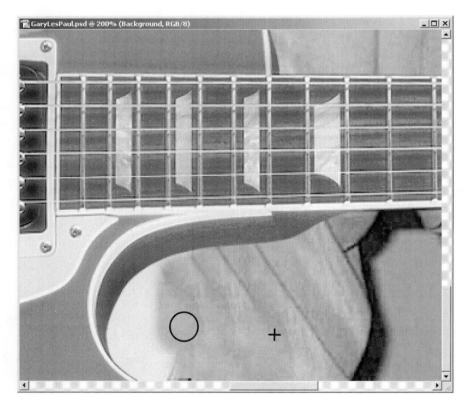

Figure 18.15   Work from right to left, sampling frequently.

4. If you feel it's necessary, open a new window (Window, Arrange, New Window); then sample from the upper-left shirt area, and clone into the lower-right area. There's a lot more cloth from which to sample, but it's not exactly the same tone.

5. Press Ctrl(⌘)+S; keep the file open.

You're done! If you look at the piece while zoomed out, you can see that you've done magnificent retouching work. But one thing is missing still. Gary's Tama guitar cast a slight shadow on his shirt, and his hands and arm cast a slight shadow on the guitar. Let's see how to add these details to the new shirt areas and the Les Paul guitar.

Adding Shadows to the Scene

Now, here's the deal: Because this scene is a gross fabrication, we want to do as little as possible to tip our Photoshop hand and add something that screams "*retouched*!!!" Therefore, we won't add a ton of shadow to the new image, but instead a whisper or two.

Here's how to add a realistic hint of shading to the composition:

Adding Shadows to the Scene

1. Zoom out to 100% viewing resolution.

2. Click on the Create a new layer icon on the Layers palette. A new layer will appear between the Les Paul guitar and the Background layer. Rename this layer **Guitar Shadow** if you like.

3. Ctrl(⌘)+click on the Les Paul layer thumbnail on the Layers palette to load the guitar as a selection.

4. Press Alt(Opt)+Ctrl(⌘)+D to open the Feather dialog box, or if you have a selection tool active, the feather option is available on a context menu when you right-click (Macintosh: hold Ctrl and click); see Figure 18.16. Choose about 9 pixels, and click on OK.

5. Press **D** for default colors. With black as the foreground color on the toolbox, press Alt(Opt)+Delete(Backspace) to fill the selection with black foreground color. Press Ctrl(⌘)+D to deselect the marquee selection.

6. With the Move tool, drag the shadow down and to the right slightly because this is the way the light is naturally casting shadows in the image.

7. On the Layers palette, adjust the Opacity for the shadow layer down to about 90% by dragging on the Opacity slider.

Figure 18.16   Feather the selection into which you'll create a shadow.

8. With the Lasso tool, create a selection similar to that shown in Figure 18.17. The goal is to remove the Guitar Shadow areas where a shadow already exists from the old guitar. With the Guitar Shadow layer as the active layer, press Delete (Backspace) to remove the shadow from the selection area. Press Ctrl(⌘)+D to deselect.

9. Next, we need to merge the strumming arm and the fretting hand layers together. Click on the strumming arm layer to make it active. This layer should be at the top of the list with the fretting hand layer just below it. Press Ctrl(⌘)+E to merge the top (strumming hand) layer down onto the (fretting hand) layer below.

10. Load and create a shadow for the arm and hands as you did with the guitar. Repeat steps 2–7 to guide you through the process. Make sure to position the new layer for the shadow below the arm and hands layer (on the Layers palette).

Figure 18.17   Remove the shadow that isn't being cast by anything!

11. Erase the shadow area that is falling on Gary's shirt, as shown in Figure 18.18. Also, remove any shadows that fall below the guitar fretting bar (near the fretting hand). Either use the Eraser tool to delete the necessary areas, or select the offending areas and press Delete (Backspace) to remove the shadow from the appropriate layer.

12. Press Ctrl(⌘)+S; keep the file open.

You've done it! You've virtually landed a $2,500 guitar in the lap of one verrrrry appreciative guitarist! Zoom out and take a look at your work, as shown in Figure 18.19.

Figure 18.18   Erase the inappropriate areas of shadow.

Figure 18.19   Now, can you retouch in a bass player, a drummer, and a stack of Marshalls?

Summary

As mentioned at the beginning of the chapter, sometimes the best place to hide something is in plain view. The idea of retouching in a whole guitar is so outrageous that the viewing audience isn't going to be looking for such changes. And for this job, we needed just three things: accurate rotating and scaling of a replacement guitar, some adroit cloning moves, and a little shadow play. Set your sites high from now on; don't be intimidated by a seemingly impossible challenge. Pull the tricks you've learned out of your hat…and go for it!

Chapter 19, "Restoring a Historic Poster," kicks off a new part in this book, designed to appeal to illustrators and folks who just need a bit of clever typography once in a while. On deck, the restoration of an antique poster. Get your Pen tools and fonts ready!

Part VI

Illustration, Page Layout, and Photoshop

Restoring a Historic Poster

In this chapter, you'll learn

- How to assess image colors for restoration

- How to plan an image restoration project

- How to align image elements by rotating a template

- How to vectorize image elements

- How to convert a selection to a path

- How to replace typography

- How to add a border to restored text

- How to rescale and reconstruct an image

- How to add foreground elements to the restored image

Let's face it, ever since Indiana Jones (or Lara Kroft, for the younger generation), archaeology has become sexy. And what greater reward for any would-be archaeologist than the chance to restore an important relic? Well, this chapter offers the chance in the form of a scan of a WPA poster.

> **Note**
>
> **About the WPA**   In 1935, Franklin Delano Roosevelt established the Works Progress Administration (WPA), as part of his New Deal program to put millions of unemployed Americans back to work. In July 1935, Federal One was established within the WPA as a central administration for the arts-related projects. The WPA lasted from 1935–1943.

Now, first of all, this poster is part of the Works Progress Administration Poster collection, held by the Library of Congress, and is available for viewing through the LOC's Historical Collections for the National Digital Library. You can find many, many WPA posters at high resolution online, specifically at `http://memory.loc.gov/ammem/wpaposters/highlights.html`.

The poster we'll use in this chapter is from this site; it's public domain and royalty free, originally created by M. Weitzman. In your own work, if you choose to use the techniques described in this chapter, make certain that you're not infringing upon someone's copyright.

Let's begin our archaeological digs with the scan of the poster. What can we glean from the scan?

Checking Out the Colors in the Poster

First, let's not get our hopes too high of ever restoring the original colors in the poster. As you can see in Figure 19.1, the acquisition was made with a Kodak color reference strip next to it. Here's a brief history of the whats and whys of this scan of the poster:

The scan is of a silk screen on poster board image of the mountains of Montana, and it's a fairly striking illustration, dark and somewhat moody. Its simple posterized geometry and limited colors make it perfect source material for creating a vector version of the image. But did it always look this way? Are we seeing the original colors of the poster, the ones that were there when the ink first dried on the poster board? The answer is almost certainly no. What we see in the file is not what the silk screenist saw. Age, sunlight, and pollution changed the colors of pigments in the printed poster as the years went by. To complicate matters, the colors we see in the digital file also have a history that is separate from the original poster.

This much we *do* know about how the digital file came into being: The poster entered the Federal museum's collection in 1940. Sometime after 1940 and before the 1990s, the poster was photographed and a slide was made. We presume that the Library of Congress took good care of the poster and photographed it under the best possible conditions. Even so, the colors in the original poster may have changed, and the slide's capability to produce an accurate record of the original silk-screened colors is limited by the fact that the color space and the nature of the pigments are different. Then, as time went by, the colors in the slide film changed as the pigments aged and were exposed to light. How much change occurred, we don't know.

Figure 19.1   When this image was taken, a Kodak color reference strip was added for historical purposes.

In the early 1990s, an intermediate negative film of the slide was made, incorporating a copy of the Kodak Gray Scale strip and the Kodak Color Control Patches next to the slide. This was the first time we were given a base reference point to what the colors and tonality of the image were at the time the intermediate negative film was made. The high-resolution digital TIFF that the Library of Congress distributes on its Web site and the one you are working with were created by scanning the intermediate negative film with the strips.

You might have wondered about the purpose of the Kodak Color Control and Kodak Gray Scale strips on the side of the image. These targets are used as known tonal reference points by the scanner operators and others (including you) who work with the resulting digital file. Instead of guessing where the white, black, and midpoints in the image were located, the scanner operator can set the scanner software's tonal controls accurately by sampling the appropriate patches on the gray scale strips. However, it looks as though the decision was made to scan the image without in-scanner correction and give the file's end users the ability to make corrections on the file in Photoshop as they see fit. The inclusion of the color control and gray scale strips allow those who want to use them known color and gray scale reference points on which they can base their corrections.

You can use these strips as shown in Figure 19.2 in tandem with the Levels command to establish baseline black, white, and midpoint levels in the image. Figure 19.2 shows the results of using the Levels eyedroppers to set the black point, the midpoint, and the white point by clicking on patch B, patch M, and patch A, respectively, on the Kodak Gray Scale. As you can see in this figure, the image has become brighter and has more color. Depending on your goals, you may create a faithful reproduction of the image as best as your current resources allow and continue making adjustments using the Levels and Curves and other commands with the Color Control and Gray Scale strips as your guide. Or not. The "aged" period colors look pretty nifty to me, and they may provide just the period effect you're looking for.

Figure 19.2   Use the tones to gauge the brightness levels in the image.

19

The Game Plan

Okay, the poster is of sufficient resolution to print, but let's say that we want a copy that can be scaled smoothly to any size. This means we want to make a copy that consists of paths. Before we get out the Pen tools, though, we need to straighten out the poster within the image, as you can see. And paying attention to details here, it's obvious that we'll need to replace the text in the poster—tracing out the original text and correcting it would take far too long. Not to worry; you'll take care of everything step by step, under the tutelage of yours truly.

Rotating the Template

Because we will use 0% of the original poster in our re-creation, straightening out the poster is okay, thus losing a little of the original poster detail. Let's fix the poster now:

Straightening Out the Poster

1. Open the SeeAmerica.tif poster from the Examples/Chap19 folder on the companion CD.

2. Zoom out so you can see the poster from edge to edge.

3. With the Rectangular Marquee tool, select the poster out of the background, with about 1/4" around the edges to spare.

4. Right-click (Macintosh: hold Ctrl and click) and choose Layer Via Cut from the context menu. Delete the Background layer.

5. Press Ctrl(⌘)+R to display the rulers, and then drag guides, both horizontal and vertical, to frame the edges of the poster, as shown in Figure 19.3. You'll notice that the poster is indeed crooked, and this is what we're going to fix.

Figure 19.3   Match guides to the outside edges of the poster.

6. Press Ctrl(⌘)+T to enter Free Transform mode. Then right-click (Macintosh: hold Ctrl and click) and choose Distort from the context menu.

7. Line up the edges of the white line around the poster with the intersection points of the guides, as shown in Figure 19.4. (See inside the circles where the edges are aligned?) When you're satisfied, press Enter (Return) to finalize your edits, and save the poster to your hard disk as **SeeAmerica.psd**.

19

Figure 19.4   Use the Distort Free Transform mode to align the poster edges with the guides.

Now the fun begins!

Vectorizing the Mountains

As stated earlier, half this restoration process is to make a vector copy of the poster so that it can be scaled up or down without any information loss. And to begin to do this, we need the Pen tool. Take a look at the black of the mountains in the poster. You'll trace this color area and save it as a path.

Here's how to begin:

Tracing the Mountain Shadows

1. Zoom into 100% viewing resolution on the poster. Hold down the spacebar (to toggle to the Hand tool), and scroll until you can see the top left of the poster.

2. Choose the Pen tool from the toolbox. On the Options bar, make sure the Paths icon and the Add to path area icon are chosen. Click a point at the far left where the black part of the poster begins.

3. Keep clicking points at the edge of the black mountain area until you run out of visible area, as shown in Figure 19.5.

Figure 19.5   Click, don't drag, points along the black edge to create straight path segments.

4. When you can go no farther, hold the spacebar to toggle to the Hand tool, and scroll the window until you can see more of the black edge. Release the spacebar, and continue clicking points at the edge of the black shape.

19

5. Zoom out and click an anchor point at the bottom right of the black shape (on the vertex of the guides). Then click a point at the bottom left at the vertex of the guides, and finally, close the path by clicking at the start point.

6. Choose the Direct Selection tool from the toolbox, and choose View, Snap from the menu. Drag the last three points you clicked to the guides, to ensure that the edges of the poster re-creation have perfectly horizontal and vertical edges (see Figure 19.6).

Figure 19.6   Align the corner anchor points with (the intersection of) the guides.

7. On the Paths palette, double-click on the Work Path title and name it **Black**. You've saved the path you just created, so you can now add to it.

8. Scroll to the upper-right corner of the poster. With the Black path title active on the Paths palette, create an outline around the other mountain shadow using the Pen tool, as shown in Figure 19.7.

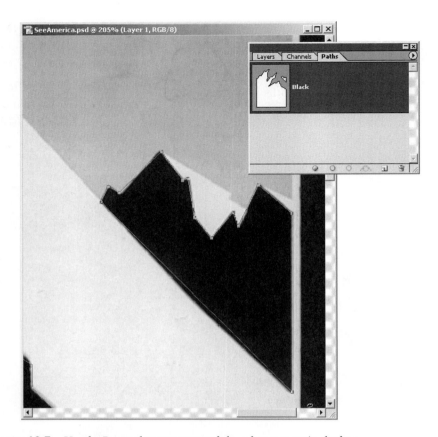

Figure 19.7   Use the Pen tool to trace around the other mountain shadow.

9. Now that you have traced all the black areas, you can work on the white areas. Zoom into the top of the poster, deselect the black paths by clicking on a blank space on the Paths palette (below the title list), and then with the Pen tool, trace out the white area of the mountains, as shown in Figure 19.8. Don't forget to double-click on the Work Path, and then name it something evocative, such as **White**.

10. As you did with the black areas, add all the white areas to the saved path. There are three mountain faces and two small peaks toward the middle of the poster.

11. Press Ctrl($\mathcal{H}$)+S; keep the file open.

Now that you've traced the major sections of the poster, it's time to concentrate on the figure of the guy on the horse. The poster shows this figure in silhouette, so we need a strategy here.

19

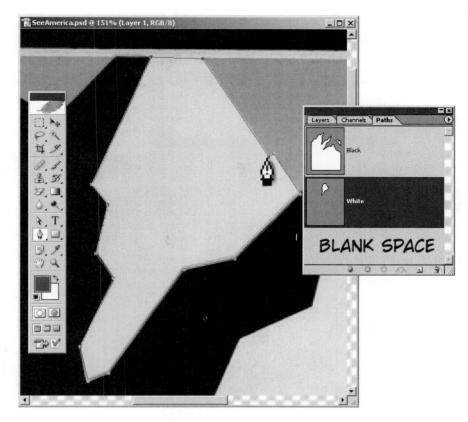

Figure 19.8   Trace the white areas of the mountain.

Converting a Selection to a Path

Using Photoshop's Convert Selection to Path feature fits right into our workflow here. But we must say that, with small selections, the accuracy of the feature isn't 100%. If you want to go off and do some independent study—and hand-trace the cowboy and his horse—more power to you, and that's what I would do. Study Chapter 6, "Using the Pen Tools," for valuable tips on doing this! But for now, we're going to work through a different technique for exploration's sake.

Here's how to vectorize the cowboy:

Creating a Path from Selection Information

1. Note that the highlights on the cowboy and horse were painted using an edged brush because the line width varies. We must do the same. Choose the Brush tool, and then choose Window, Brushes (F5 is the shortcut).

2. Choose a 3-pixel, hard-edge brush. Angle it by first clicking on the Brush Tip Shape title and then dragging on the top or bottom dot on the circle to determine the amount of distortion of the round shape.

3. Point the arrow associated with the brush shape to about 10 o'clock, as shown in Figure 19.9.

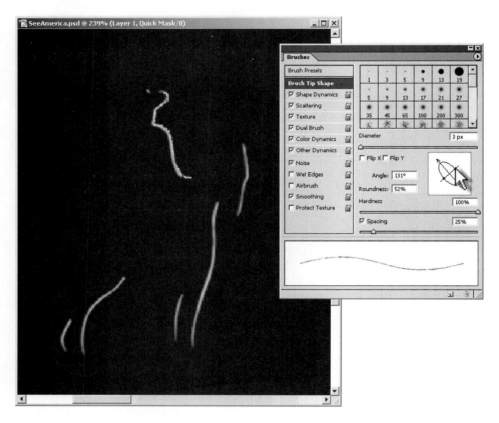

Figure 19.9   Create a brush tip that will vary in width as you paint.

4. Choose white as the foreground color on the toolbox. Click on the Create a new layer icon at the bottom of the Layers palette to create a new layer for the poster image.

5. Stroke over the highlight to the silhouette.

6. Ctrl(⌘)+click on the new layer thumbnail to load your strokes as selections.

7. Click on the Make work path from selection icon on the bottom of the Paths palette, and then name the path **cowboy**, as shown in Figure 19.10.

19

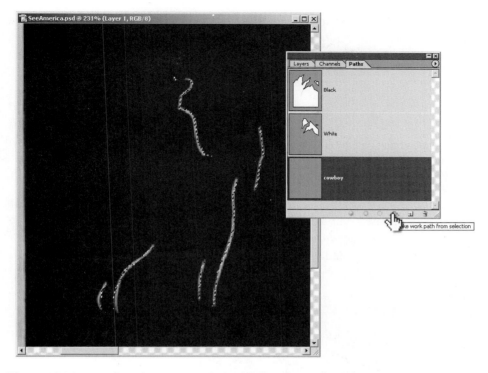

Figure 19.10   Let Photoshop create paths based on the current selection.

8. Press Ctrl(⌘)+D to deselect the selection, and then toss the current layer into the trash icon.

9. Press Ctrl(⌘)+S; keep the file open.

Do you see all that typography at the bottom of the poster? Well, believe it or not, the vectorizing of type is going to be the easy part of this assignment. Read on!

Replacing Text

Here's the deal: If you have a healthy supply of retro fonts loaded on your machine, keep reading. If not, close Photoshop for a moment, and load AirstreamNF and GothamRailCompanyNF, both typefaces in the Examples/Chap19 folder on the companion CD. I worked with Nick Curtis to provide these commercial fonts free of charge to you especially for this chapter's assignment, and I'll bet Nick would appreciate it if you checked out his advertisement in the back of this book!

It would be ridiculous to try to hand-trace or even auto-trace each character on the poster, so instead, we'll use aesthetics and good judgment to find fonts that would be good substitutions for the *existing* typefaces. We have and use artistic license.

Now, load the fonts on your system, and let's get cracking, replacing the existing text:

Adding New Text to the Poster

1. Choose the Type tool from the toolbox. On the Options bar, specify GothamRailCompanyNF as the font, specify 24 points for font size, left-align text, and click on the color swatch and choose white. We'll play with the scaling of the text in a moment.

2. Create an insertion point just above the "SEE AMERICA" text, and then in lower-case, type **see america**, as shown in Figure 19.11. The lowercase letters in this typeface have top and bottom brackets, a nice ornamental touch. Press Ctrl(⌘)+Enter(Return) to commit the text to a layer.

Figure 19.11   Create a new headline.

19

3. Press Ctrl(⌘)+T to put the headline into Free Transform mode.

4. Click inside the bounding box to drag the headline so that it aligns with the top left of the original headline. Take the top-right transform handle and drag it up, down, and/or to the right to make the headline fit the same area as the original headline (see Figure 19.12).

Figure 19.12   Stretch and reshape the headline while it's in Free Transform mode so that it precisely covers the original headline.

5. Press Enter (Return) to commit the changes you've created (or double-click within the Free Transform box).

6. Choose Layer, Type, Create Work Path. Congratulations! Your type is now a path on the Paths palette. Go to the Paths palette, and rename the Work Path title to save it as **See America**.

7. Press Ctrl(⌘)+S; keep the file open.

Now, it shouldn't be too hard to figure out how to do the subhead, "Welcome to Montana"! You use the same steps as those in the preceding exercise, except you change the font to AirstreamNF (see Figure 19.13). Before you do that, though, consider these two tips:

- Make sure that the See America path is deselected before you try to put the Welcome to Montana subheadline into Free Transform mode. Deselect the See America path by clicking on an empty area of the Paths palette. If you neglect to do this, the See America path will be put into Free Transform instead of the new text just created.

- To make life easier on yourself down the road, you might want to put all the text on the same path title (the text will eventually be the same color and so on, so why not?). To do this, click on the Welcome to... path title (on the Paths palette) to make this title active. Press Ctrl(⌘)+X (to cut the path from this title). Then click the See America path title (on the Paths palette) to make it the active title, and press Ctrl(⌘)+V. You will now see that the Montana paths fall neatly below the See America paths on the same paths title.

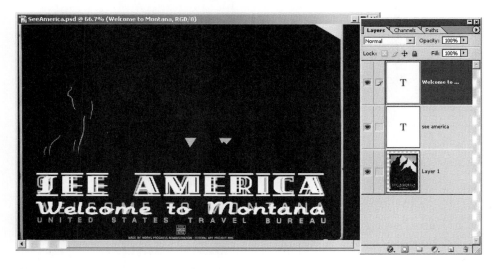

Figure 19.13   Use the AirstreamNF font for the subheadline.

Adding the Last of the Text

To finish up with the text, you'll notice that the United States Travel Bureau legend appears in orange at the bottom of the poster. Here's a good rule of typography: "Don't use fancy text when the point size is small and the message is long." Fair enough. In the original poster, Eurostile was used for the Travel Bureau text; good, clean, solid type. You don't have to own Eurostile, however, to finish vectorizing this poster; Arial will do nicely, and there are only three people on this planet who don't own Arial.

I'm going to let you do this last piece of text yourself, but I need to mention something first: The kerning—the spacing between letters—is wider than average with the Travel Bureau text. The solution? Use Photoshop's Character palette (Window, Character) to increase the inter-character spacing by 700% (see Figure 19.14).

Just follow the steps in the preceding example to position and reshape the text, and then create a Work Path from it. Here's the difference, though: Do not put the path with the rest of the text, because to re-create the poster, you have to make the Travel Bureau text a different color than the See America text. You'll save big-time headaches filling the path if you keep it as a unique path within the file.

Figure 19.14   Keep the kerning loose on the Travel Bureau text.

Adding a Border

Adding a border to the paths you've already created is a really simple procedure. But it's a necessary step, and if you haven't fooled with Photoshop's Shape tools yet, this will be good experience.

Here's how to add a rectangular border:

Montana: North of the Border

1. Press Ctrl(⌘)+minus key to zoom out of the poster until you can see the entire image. Double-clicking on the Hand tool on the toolbox will do this.

2. Click on an empty area of the Paths palette so that the shape you create is *not* added to existing paths.

3. Choose the Rectangle (shape) tool from the toolbox.

4. Click on the Paths icon on the Options bar.

5. Drag a rectangle over the border of the poster, as shown in Figure 19.15.

6. Rename the Work Path to save it (**Border** might be an appropriate name for the path title). Press Ctrl(⌘)+S; keep the file open.

Figure 19.15   Create a rectangular border for the poster.

The Payoff: Rescaling and Reconstruction

Okay, now comes the fun part. We're going to put into motion the reconstruction of the poster. And to add a little zest to the experiment, we're going to scale the poster, to prove to all that paths are resolution independent.

Let's start with the scaling:

Scaling the Poster and Beginning the Reconstruction

1. Right-click (Macintosh: hold Ctrl and click) over the document title bar, and choose Image Size.

2. In the Image Size box, check the Resample Image check box, type **800** (pixels) in the Height field, and click on OK.

3. On the Layers palette, drag the text layers to the trash icon at the bottom right of the palette to delete these layers. Click on the Create a new layer icon on the bottom of the Layers palette.

19

4. With the Eyedropper tool, sample an area of deep orange at the top of the poster.

5. Press **X** to swap foreground/background swatches, and then click to sample some of the deep yellow color just above the mountains.

6. Press **X** again to swap foreground and background colors so that deep orange is the foreground color.

7. Choose the Rectangular Marquee tool, and drag a rectangle that touches the white border of the poster.

8. Choose the Gradient tool from the toolbox. On the Options bar, choose the Foreground to Background gradient, and click on the Linear gradient icon. Drag a gradient starting at the top of the poster and ending a small distance below the starting point so that most of the poster is deep yellow, as shown in Figure 19.16. Hold down the Shift key as you drag to keep your gradient drag in a perfectly vertical line.

9. Press Ctrl(⌘)+D to deselect the marquee. Press Ctrl(⌘)+S to save your work. Keep the file open.

Figure 19.16   Drag a gradient to replace the one in the poster.

Moving Right Along

This poster restoration stuff is going to go more quickly than you can imagine, and it's all because you made the up-front effort to trace out all the graphic elements.

Let's keep going:

Adding Foreground Elements to the Poster

1. On the Paths palette, click on the Black path title to make it the active path.
2. Click on the default colors icon on the toolbox (or press **D** for the default colors).
3. Click on the Fill path with foreground color icon at the bottom of the Paths palette, as shown in Figure 19.17.

Figure 19.17   Fill the path you created using foreground color.

4. Click on the White path title. Press **X** to swap foreground and background colors, and click on the Fill path with foreground color icon on the bottom of the Paths palette.

5. Just to get artsy here, sample the pale lilac on the Kodak strip to the left of the poster (see Figure 19.18).

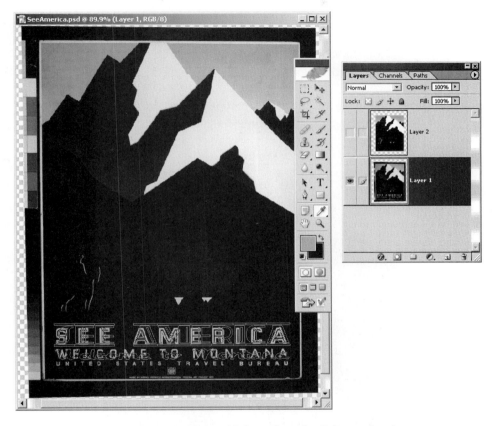

Figure 19.18   Choose the text, and then fill the paths with a light purple color.

6. Click on the See America path title, and then click on the Fill path with foreground color icon on the bottom of the Paths palette.

7. Sample a burnt orange color from the poster. Actually, you can take the sample from the top of the poster, without having to hide this layer and sample from the original poster.

8. Choose the US Travel Bureau path, and fill it with foreground color.

9. Choose white as the foreground color. Click on the Border path title, and then choose Edit, Stroke from the menu. Enter a 4-pixel width and click on OK.

10. Choose the cowboy path. Now, here's where filling techniques might vary, depending on how you created the cowboy path. If you carefully traced the cowboy by hand with the Pen tool, choose white as the foreground color, and click on the Fill path with foreground color icon. However, if you had Photoshop trace the cowboy, filling the path might not produce as pronounced an effect as you would like. If this is the case, choose the Cowboy path, and then load the path as a selection. Then choose Edit, Stroke, and stroke the selection from the center, using a 2-pixel width.

11. You're done. Unbelievable, right? You can now crop the poster if you choose. Save the file, and you can close it at any time.

In Figure 19.19, you can see the finished restoration/re-creation. Compare it to the original, and I think you'll agree that you did the designer a great artistic service with this revival.

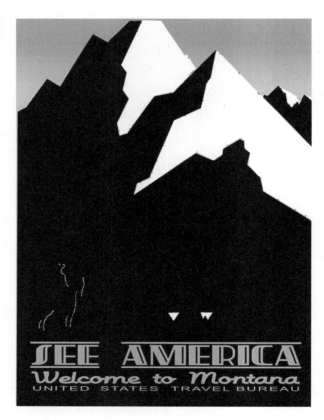

Figure 19.19   Photoshop is the ideal companion to graphics ideas, both old and new.

Perhaps one of the undiscovered perks of all this work is that you can go back and scale up this image as large as your computer's memory will allow and fill in the paths once again. When you do, you'll have a crisp, perfectly traced version of the same poster. Paths are vectors, vectors are scalable graphic elements, and these elements can be filled over and over again, regardless of size. Paths will never lose graphical detail.

Summary

Well, with a little effort, you've discovered how to resurrect a poster from more than half a century ago. But don't think that the techniques that are now yours can be used *only* on WPA posters! You can now quickly replace the text in an existing piece of work, and you can scale elements smoothly as paths.

> **Tip**
>
> **Scaling paths**   You can scale paths by using the Free Transform mode, just as you can with text. All you do is choose the path's title on the Paths palette, press Ctrl(⌘)+T, and off you go.

Just plan your piece; set aside the time you think it will take to trace each differently colored element, and know that the actual filling part is going to go like lightning.

If you had a little fun with typography in this chapter, get set to have a lot of fun in the following chapter! Learn the ins and outs of professional typesetting in less time than it takes to say "umlaut," remake a garage sale sign, and generally kick out all the jams in an exciting, informational, properly kerned adventure.

Chapter 20

Typography and Page Layout in Photoshop

Photoshop type tools are an exciting aspect of the world of typography in general. In this chapter, we examine both type and Photoshop's capabilities for using type.

In this chapter, you'll learn

- How to size, merge, lay out, and align text to create a sign
- How to use the Paragraph palette
- How to lay out and design documents using Photoshop type
- The basics of typography, typefaces, and type design
- Best practices for using type in Photoshop

20

Photoshop now has a Type tool that is equivalent in power to the Type tool in an illustration program (such as Adobe Illustrator). We also have at our finger-"taps" a Free Transform tool, with which we can rotate and stretch type that remains editable, and a spell checker. Photoshop has come of age, and its typographic controls are among the best found in many applications these days. And that's reason enough to devote some space to the *art* of text arrangement—layout. This chapter covers some conventional and some not-so-conventional layout types, a little of something for everyone, and a *lot* of information on how to use Photoshop's text-handling features.

Working with type, though, is not simply a matter of knowing how to use the Type tool. Anyone can add type to his or her image, but *understanding* and using good *design* are what sets the professional apart from the amateur. With design in mind, this chapter is divided into three major tasks. The first task takes you through a makeover of a sign. The second task explains how to use the Character and Paragraph palettes like the pros do. The remaining sections of the chapter explore typefaces and some basics of good design when using type, along with a career-saving dissertation on the "Swiss Grid System."

The Garage Sale Sign Makeover

I drove out the other day with my camera (I used a car—the camera was an add-on) and took about a half-dozen pictures of garage sale signs. The worst offender in the typographics/sales arena is featured in Figure 20.1. You'll notice I've added some numbered callouts to the sign; I'll explain them after you take a look at the figure.

Here are some important guidelines for making any kind of informational sign or posting. Their numbers correspond to specific problems I've called out on the sign in Figure 20.1:

1. **Placement of your ad is important.** You can see that I've pointed out two signs here, though only one sign faces the camera. Both of these signs carry the same information, but the one on the far side faces the traffic in the far right lane—too far away to be read).

2. **Choice of fonts is important.** The folks who are having this house sale apparently own only a worn-out felt-tip marker for creating signage. Only the first car in the lane facing the sign can read it.

3. **Poorly placed text is a bad reflection on the designer's sense of planning.** The folks having this sale apparently wanted to re-use the sign, so they put carton tape over the original date and hastily scrawled *today* on the sign. Fine. What day is *today*, folks?

Figure 20.1   You can't sell something if your audience can't read your sign! There are two signs on this post; the one directly behind the one you can see here faces the opposite direction.

4. **Revisions to the sign should be definitive.** Notice that you can still read *Sunday* on the sign, even after the folks taped over the word. This makes me feel as though the people don't know where to get more cardboard and create a new sign. I'm aware of at least three revisions on the sign, and all three "cover-ups" are done inexpertly.

5. **Direction markers should be correct and well thought-out.** I admit that I've tampered with this photo, disguising the *real* address so my neighbors don't drop by and kill me. But I *can* tell you right now that the arrow on the sign is pointing *away* from, not toward the address.

6. **Try to compose all the physical elements of your sign to withstand the weather.** These signs are taking more of a bruising than necessary from the wind and weather. Why? Because the paper is slightly larger than the cardboard backing. Folks, get a can of 3M Spray-Mount, a utility blade, and a metal ruler, and do the trimming on the garage floor. If you don't *have* these materials, perhaps *I'll* run a garage sale soon and offer them :)!

20

Okay, I've been negative far too long here. In the following section, you'll see how to use these guidelines and then set up and begin the document that will become a professional garage sale sign.

Page Setup and Importance of the Text Elements

It is unfortunate that Photoshop, unlike its sister program PageMaker, does not offer tiling when outputting to a personal printer (or any output device). Tiling divides a single large image into multiple pieces for output on a typical personal printer; the tiled pieces can be printed and laid out together to form the large image. So, for example, if a laid-out page is too large to fit on an 8 1/2" by 11" piece of paper, the application creates several pieces of the file output from a personal printer so that you can then paste together the pages to make a big sign. Without tiling, we need to tile the sign *manually*, which means we have to begin with calculations. Not a big deal.

First, a 16" by 20" sign with the appropriate font weight will definitely reach the reading audience from their cars. Coincidentally, four 8 1/2" by 11" pieces of paper collectively measure 17" by 22", so printers—none of which print right to the edge of the paper—will leave room for you to overlap the tiles on paper.

Conceptually, the most important thing your sign must communicate is what event is going on. Follow these steps to get on your way to professional sign creation:

Beginning a Garage Sale Sign

1. Press Ctrl(⌘)+N, and in the New dialog box, specify a size for the sign that is 16" high by 20" wide. Make the Resolution 72 pixels per inch, choose Grayscale color mode, and use a white background. Press Enter (Return) to create the new document. Press **D** for the default colors (black and white).

2. Alt(Opt)+click on the Create a new layer icon at the bottom of the Layers palette, and name the new layer **Garage Sale**. Click on OK. Use the Rectangular Marquee tool, and on the Options bar, choose Fixed Size for Style. Enter **19 in** for Width and **3 in** for Height. Click and drag in the document to create the fixed-size rectangle and to position it as shown in Figure 20.2. With black as the foreground color, press Alt(Opt)+Delete(Backspace) to fill the selection. Now, you can compose this sign the right way. You can move this headline box anywhere you like, um, *after* you've added the text and linked layers! Press Ctrl(⌘)+D to deselect.

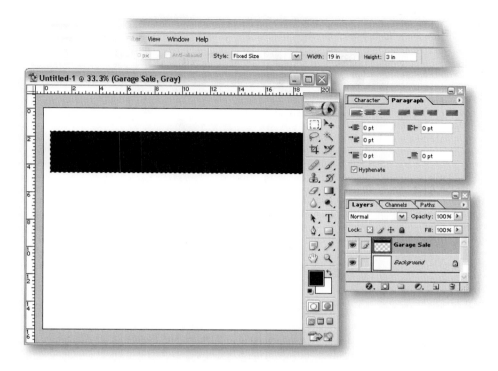

Figure 20.2   Create a black rectangle for which you'll add white type.

3. Press **X** to switch white to the foreground color. Click the Type tool in the image window. Choose a sans serif font for the headline by first clicking on the Character palette icon on the Options bar to display it. Why sans serif? Because serif fonts look stupid when you use all caps, and without serifs on a font, you can tighten the space between characters and not sacrifice legibility. In Figure 20.3, you can see that I've chosen Olive Antique. Futura, Arial, Helvetica, Compacta, and Balloon Bold are also good choices. Choose a size of about **211** points. As you know, 72 points equal 1 inch, so you're creating text that's a little less than 3" tall, and it will fit in the rectangle. With white as the color for the Type tool, type **Garage Sale!** Press Ctrl(⌘)+Enter(Return) when you're satisfied to commit the text onto a layer. If you look over at the Layers palette, you'll see that you have a new layer with only **Garage Sale!** as the layer's contents.

Insider

If you are using a font other than Olive Antique, as shown in this exercise, you might need to adjust any references to point size, tracking, and so on to accommodate the font you will be using. Experiment with the numbers to get the desired effect.

20

Figure 20.3   Reversed text—text that's light against a dark background—is attention-getting, but don't over-use it.

Note

> **Don't waste image resolution no one will ever see**   The document's resolution is only 72 pixels per inch because no one is going to stick his nose directly on the sign and critique its lack of image resolution. Seventy-two pixels per inch will print just fine to a 600 dpi laser printer, and your goal is to attract someone who will never see it closer than a car's length away.

4. With the Move tool, drag the white text, and visually center it within the black rectangle. Press Ctrl(⌘)+T to summon the Free Transform box, as shown in Figure 20.4, and stretch the text so that it fits nicely inside the black rectangle. Double-click inside the Free Transform box to apply the changes to the text.

5. Let's say that the sale is for the weekend—Saturday, August 25, and Sunday, August 26. These elements need to stand out but also be subordinate to the *Garage Sale* text. As they say in the ad biz, "something's gotta give," and the dates can be slightly subordinate and still be legible. Press **X** to switch to black as the foreground color. Choose the Type tool and click in the document window. Type **Saturday, August 25th,** and press Ctrl(⌘)+Enter(Return) to commit the text. In the Character palette, adjust the point size to **150 pt** (the point size might differ slightly depending on the font you're using). If necessary, hold down the Ctrl(⌘) key to toggle to the Move tool and reposition text.

Figure 20.4   Stretch the text so that it fills the rectangle.

Insider

The words in the date are not of equal importance. *August 25th* and *August 26th* will res-
onate with the viewers—especially if they have calendar wristwatch—more than the
actual days. Happily, you can mix fonts in the tool dialog box.

6. Highlight **August 25**, and use the Character palette to change the highlighted text
to a bold version of the font you're using. In typography, you have three
recourses for emphasizing text: using italic (naturally), using bold, and adjusting
the point size. Bolding the text accomplishes the goal beautifully (see Figure
20.5). Press Ctrl(⌘)+Enter(Return) to commit the text to a layer.

7. Drag the Saturday, August 25th text layer onto the Create a new layer icon at
the bottom of the Layers palette (to make a duplicate copy of this layer). With
the Move tool, drag the duplicate text layer so that it's positioned beneath the
original text. Choose the Text tool, and highlight the word *Saturday* and type
Sunday instead. Then highlight the *5* and type **6** instead, so the date reads
Sunday, August 26th. Pretty neat labor-saving trick, eh?

8. If necessary, use the Move tool to drag the dates beneath the *Garage Sale* lettering.

9. Choose File, Save As, and save your work as **Hey!Sale.psd** in Photoshop's native
file format to your hard disk. Keep the image open.

Let's think about the relative importance of the rest of the sign's text now.

20

Figure 20.5   You can make a font bold or change an entirely different font by highlighting it and using the Character palette.

Sizing Up the Rest of the Text

The following elements are missing from sign:

- The address of the garage sale. This an important selling point.
- The hours for the sale. This is a "throw-away" line in terms of selling importance; its type size can be small. People come to the sale any darned time they feel like it. It's America.
- If these signs are to be hung on phone poles and street lamps (which is technically illegal in most states, but one seems to care), you should create an equal number of signs with left-facing and right-facing arrows, and make the arrows BIG. Then your hired he (most likely your son, daughter, or the neighbor's kids) can choose which way a sign's arrow is to face when they get to a pole.

Additionally, and optionally, you might want to sprinkle one or two subtle prompts to attend the sale on the sign—but not at the expense of cluttering up the sign. My experience in sign-making has uncovered these two truths:

1. People will read the lettering inside the arrows. You can make a large arrow for the sign and put a "selling point," such as "All sane offers accepted," inside the

arrow in white text. This will make bargain hunters feel as though they're on easy turf.

2. Regardless of how small you print your sign, people can read the words *Free*, *New*, and *Save* with both eyes closed. So without messing up the various weights of text on the sign, you can run the message *Save $* about five or six times across the top of the sign at about 24 points, and it *will* be read.

I'm going to leave you alone while you create the arrows, text in the arrows, street address, hours, and Save $ elements. Because text is always rendered to a unique layer, you should have no problem (and actually a lot of fun) pushing the text around until it looks like a well-composed sign. We used to do this in the advertising trade with print layouts, but we used pieces of paper. You've got it easy. We would occasionally lose a headline or misplace a graphic!

If you would like to follow my layout (laying text on it to see whether it's a good size), Hey!Sale.tif is in the Examples/Chap20 folder on the Companion CD.

Also, you might want to use the arrow shapes that are available when the Custom Shape tool is selected. Create a new layer, and use the Paths option to drag and create the arrow.

Tip

> **Use the Direct Selection tool**   By using the Paths option, you can switch to the Direct Selection tool and click on the arrow to see the path points. Then move the points to fine-tune the arrow to fit your size needs. Hold down the Shift key to select more than one point at a time for moving.

When you're satisfied with the arrow's size and shape, press Ctrl(⌘)+ Enter(Return) to make the arrow a selection. Create a new layer, and fill the selection with black (press Ctrl(⌘)+D to deselect). Next, create the white text that sits on top of the arrow.

Merging and Aligning Text

Photoshop CS has a feature that you would normally expect to find in a vector drawing program such as Illustrator. You now have an Align command at your cursor-tips. And that means all the text you've laid out in the image window can be perfectly aligned—yet another touch that'll attract attention.

Also, it would place less of a stress on your computer's hard disk and memory if this sign were smaller in file size. So, in the steps to follow, you'll merge the layers to a single layer after everything has been laid out correctly. Keep in mind that you may want to save a separate version of the file (with all layers intact) so you can easily edit it for future garage sale sign needs.

Finalizing the Sign

1. Save two copies of the file, one with the necessary layers visible so that the arrow is facing right, and the other with the layers visible for the arrow to be facing left. Click on the Garage Sale! text layer's title on the Layers palette, and then press Ctrl(⌘)+E. This key combination activates the Merge Down command. Now, the Garage Sale text and the black rectangle are on one layer.

2. You will also want to make two versions of your sign with the arrow layer pointing in opposite directions. To do this, drag the arrow layer to the Create a new layer icon at the bottom of the Layers palette to make a duplicate of this layer. Turn off the visibility for the original arrow layer. With the duplicate arrow layer active, press Ctrl(⌘)+T, right-click (Macintosh: hold Ctrl and click) inside the Transform bounding box, and choose Flip Horizontal to flip the duplicate arrow in the opposite direction. Make a duplicate layer for the text that appears inside the arrow by dragging this layer to the Create a new layer icon. Position the duplicate text layer above the duplicate arrow layer. Turn off the visibility for the original text layer to get a clear view of the duplicate versions. Use the Move tool to adjust the position of the text for the flipped arrow and text. When satisfied, you can turn off the visibility to the necessary arrow and text layers to display the appropriate direction (depending on which direction to point when printing the sign).

3. Choose the text layer above the arrow, and then press Ctrl(⌘)+E to merge the arrow with the text. Turn off the visibility for this newly merged layer. Then turn on the visibility for the arrow and text layers (facing the opposite direction), and repeat the merge process.

4. Click on the Background layer to make it the active layer, and then click on the right column check boxes (on the Layers palette) for all the layers. All the layers are now linked.

5. Choose Layer, Align Linked, Horizontal Centers, or choose the Move tool and click on the Align horizontal centers icon from the Options bar—exactly as you see it in Figure 20.6. With the Background layer as the active layer, this aligns and centers all the elements in relation to the Background layer, and you're just about finished with the sign.

6. Choose Flatten Image from the Layers palette's flyout menu.

7. Save the file as **Hey!Sign.tif** in the TIFF file format to your hard drive. Here's a hint: In the History palette, go back to the step before you flattened the image. Turn on the layer with the arrow facing the opposite direction, and turn off the visibility for the other arrow. Flatten the image again, and save this file with a slightly different name (like **Hey!Sign2.tif**). Keep the image open in Photoshop.

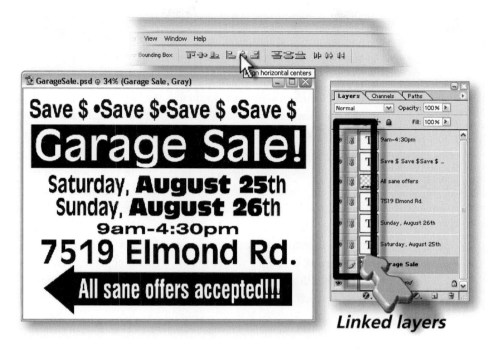

Figure 20.6 Linked layers can be aligned. Try saying that twice, fast.

We've now concluded the composition of the garage sale sign, but we aren't done by a country mile. You still need to chop the sign into four pieces that can be sent to a laser printer. And this procedure requires a little planning and still more of Photoshop's features.

Creating a Tiling Sign

Before we go any further, go to your nearest office supply store and get fluorescent laser paper. Hot lemon and hot pink are obnoxious colors, sure to attract attention as garage sale signs, and you can use the rest of the paper for wrapping presents. Before you leave, pester the clerk for some cardboard, ideally the cardboard that filing cabinets and knockdown furniture came in. The larger the cardboard, the less you compromise the signs' appearance.

The Rectangular Marquee tool can be set to select areas for cropping at almost any specified height and width. We know that the file size is 16" (in height) by 20" (for the width). Get ready to bring those lamps, the bike training wheels, and that velvet painting out of the basement and into the garage!

20

Cropping and Assembling the Signs

1. At 25% viewing resolution of the sign, drag the image window borders away from the sign so you can clearly see the file's background.

2. In case you would like to know how to make these calculations in pixels, Alt(Opt)+click on the document sizes area (located at the bottom-right area of the program's status bar). You can see that 20" at 72 ppi is 1440 pixels, and 16" at 72 ppi is actually 1,152 pixels.

3. Choose the Rectangular Marquee tool from the toolbox. On the Options bar, choose Fixed Size from the Style drop-down list. In the Width field, type **720 px**, or **10 in** if you prefer to do the math in inches. (You can use either measurement in Photoshop. Just signal which measurement method you are using by typing **px** for pixels or **in** for inches after the number.) In the Height field, type **576 px**, or **8 in** if you're doing this in inches. Why these amounts? Because you're going to bisect copies of this document so they will output to a personal printer. These measurements will dissect this file into four equal parts that will fit onto a normal letter-size sheet of paper.

4. Click in the upper left of the image window, outside the live area. The marquee will snap to the upper-left corner and create a perfect selection of one quarter of the sign. See Figure 20.7.

5. Press Ctrl(⌘)+C and then press Ctrl(⌘)+N, and accept the defaults options in the New dialog box by pressing Enter (Return).

6. Press Ctrl+V and then press Ctrl+E to make the image a single layer image.

7. Press **D** for default colors (white should be the background color), and then choose Image, Canvas Size from the main menu.

8. In the Canvas Size dialog box, type **11** (inches) in the Width field, and then type **8.5** (inches) in the Height field, as shown in Figure 20.8. Although the live area of each quarter of the sign is smaller than these dimensions, Photoshop will want to output to standard paper size—and besides, you will need to overlap the quarters to build the entire sign.

9. Repeat steps 5–8 on the other three quarters of the sign. In Figure 20.9, you can see the trim areas colored in. Naturally, you don't want to color in your own images; I illustrated it this way to show you how this jigsaw of a sign will all fit together.

Figure 20.7   You can crop an image by setting the Marquee tools' Options bar to Fixed Size.

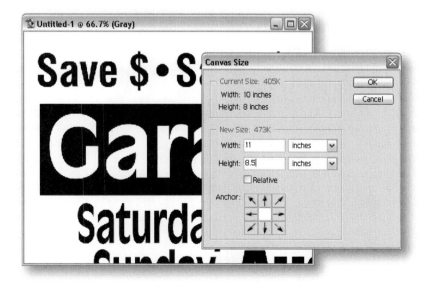

Figure 20.8   Create a border around the original pasted graphic by increasing the Canvas Size.

Inside areas should be
trimmed on one side…

and overlap the trim
area on the facing tile

Figure 20.9   When these page-size graphics are printed, there will be trim space around all four sides of each quarter-document.

10. Print several copies of each quarter of the sign (it also might be a good idea right now to save each piece as **1.tif**, **2.tif**, and so on). Every printer is different, but I recommend printing to 600 dpi, using non-PostScript rendering technology— only because Hewlett-Packard's Resolution Enhancement Technology delivers a decent print very quickly, and these prints do not need to be half-toned or experience any other process that PostScript technology affords.

11. Work in the garage with the doors open. Trim the inside edges of alternating pages (in other words, trim inside edges only on 1 and 3, or 2 and 4), match up the four pieces, glue them together and…what am I talking about? None of this stuff has *anything* to do with Photoshop! Lesson is completed!!! See Figure 20.10.

In the section to follow, we'll explore the Character and Paragraph palettes, which we haven't covered yet.

Figure 20.10   Ever wonder what the world would be like if we *all* communicated effectively? There would be fewer TV situation comedies, for starters....

Exploring the Character and Paragraph Palettes

Adobe has added some new icons to the Character palette that are worth explaining. Take a look at Figure 20.11, and follow along as we identify and explain how to create these effects using the new icons located near the bottom of the Character palette.

The effects of the new icons in the Photoshop CS Character palette are as follows:

1. This is the font with no effects applied.

2. **Faux Bold.** This option is helpful if the font you have chosen does not provide a bold font style option. The Faux (French for *false, fake*) Bold icon can aid in producing a bold effect.

3. **Faux Italic.** If there is no italic option for the particular font you have chosen, this icon, similar to the Faux Bold, can simulate an italic style in its place.

20

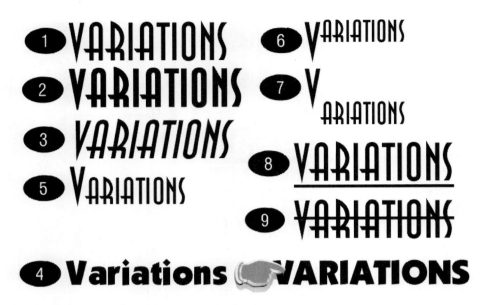

Figure 20.11   These are the effects of using Photoshop's new Character palette icons.

Note

> **Using Faux Bold**   As of this writing, characters with the Faux option applied to them will *not* export properly to PDF files, but this is not really Photoshop's problem. If you don't have a bold version of a font, then buy one, or choose a more complete character set.

4. **All Caps.** This icon is pretty much self-explanatory. When turned on, it formats the text in all uppercase characters, as though you had pressed your Caps Lock key.

5. **Small Caps.** This icon formats type in small caps but does not change characters that were originally typed in uppercase. If a small caps feature is designed into the font, Photoshop uses the font's small caps; otherwise, Photoshop generates faux small caps when you choose this option.

6. **Superscript.** This option reduces the text in size and shifts it above the type baseline of the normal text. If the font does not support superscript, Photoshop generates a faux superscript.

7. **Subscript.** This option reduces the text in size and shifts it below the type baseline of the normal text. If the font does not support subscript, Photoshop generates a faux subscript.

8. **Underline.** This option applies a line under horizontal type, or a line to the left or right of vertical type. Underline Left or Underline Right options are available only on the menu when vertical text is used.

9. **Strikethrough.** This option allows you to apply a horizontal line through horizontal type or a vertical line through vertical type.

Figure 20.12 shows the Character palette flyout, with the names of the new icons (the variations on the letter *T* that stretch across the bottom of the palette).

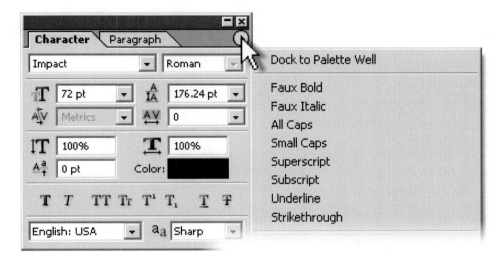

Figure 20.12 The flyout menu options from the Character palette spells out the icon options for you. The Underline option gives you a choice of Underline Right or Underline Left when you have vertical type active. You have only one Underline choice when horizontal text is used.

Using the Paragraph Palette

As you've probably guessed, paragraph text should contrast against headline (display) text. Paragraph text should be smaller, for example; 12 to 18 points defines paragraph text in most situations. Paragraph text also should probably be of a Roman type family because sans serif text (such as Arial) set in blocks can give you a headache. Photoshop offers alignment options for paragraph text that we will uncover right now.

Taking a Look at the Paragraph Palette

Figure 20.13 shows nine callouts on the Paragraph palette. We will explain what each one does before performing an assignment using paragraph text.

20

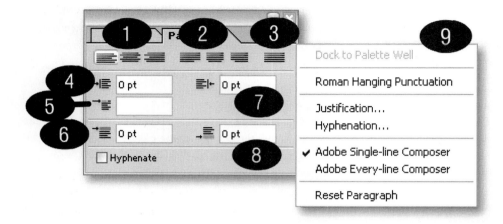

Figure 20.13   The Paragraph palette with the flyout menu extended.

Here are some guidelines for using the Paragraph palette options:

1. **Paragraph alignment.** As the icons clearly indicate, you have your choice of left, center, and right alignment for paragraph text. Suggestion? Stick to flush left in your paragraph work. Centered long lines of text and right justification are unfamiliar to readers, and yep, long lines can cause whiplash, confusion, and resentment on the readers' part!

2. **Last line justification.** Having two or three words at the end of a paragraph with excessive inter-character (kerning) spacing looks positively awful, so this option lines up the last line of a paragraph to left, center, or right. (Hint: Left alignment works best in 99% of your paragraph work.)

3. **Full Justification.** This option aligns both the left and right sides of a paragraph to the column margin. Although having smooth margins on both sides of the text looks very impressive, justification sometimes causes problems called *rivers* in paragraphs. Rivers are blank spaces between words that link visually to run down through the paragraph. An excessive amount of rivers can be distracting to the readers; we'll deal with rivers a little later.

4. **Indent Flush Left.** If you want to set off a paragraph from the rest of the column, you can indent the left of the highlighted text. When you indent the left side of a paragraph, you probably need to indent the right side, too, to keep the text looking balanced on the page (callout 7).

Note

Changing alignment   Sometimes you need to highlight text with the Type tool to create alignment changes, and other times when you make global changes, you merely click an icon on the Paragraph palette—no highlighting and any tool can be active.

5. **Indent First line in paragraph block.** Okay, here's a little typesetting rule. We're sure you've seen indented paragraphs. This area on the Paragraphs palette does exactly that; generally, two to three characters in width creates a nice paragraph indent. But you also have the option of putting a space between paragraphs (callout 8). Use one or the other but not both when you create multiple paragraphs.

6. **Put Space before paragraph.** This option adds a space at the top of each paragraph to separate it from the preceding paragraph. This is the same deal as callout 8, except here the space between paragraphs starts at the top, and not the bottom of a paragraph. The practical distinction between spaces before or spaces after paragraphs in a long document is largely lost here! Advice: If you put a space after paragraphs, there is little sense in putting a space before paragraphs, unless you are setting off a left and right indented paragraph (such as a quote).

7. **Indent Flush Right.** This option goes hand in hand with the Indent Flush Left option (callout 4). We can see no reason to use this without the other.

8. **Add Space after paragraph.** Use the same rules as we discussed in callout 6.

9. **Paragraph flyout menu.** Good stuff resides on the palette, and we'll discuss it blow by blow in the following sections.

An Étude in Page Layout

If you open Gryphon.psd from the Examples/Chap20 folder on the companion CD, you will see that we've laid out a page to account for a footer (the name of the publication and page number at the page bottom) and marked off columns. We've also given a bigger margin on the left because we're pretending that this is a right-facing page in a magazine, and you need that extra little measure to bind the page into the magazine.

I don't believe in composing a full page of text in Photoshop, any more than I would compose a page of text in Illustrator or XARA. Text should be composed in a word processor or text editor and then imported into Photoshop—and you can then decide to spell check it or not. The only disadvantage to doing this is that you can incur some "bad breaks" in the text because the imported Clipboard text might have hard returns that do not suit the width of your paragraph text column.

Note

> **Making your own breaks**   Bad breaks not only look dumb, but they can also distract the readers. Chances are, you will not get through your career without working with a copywriter. Nor will you survive without hearing some form of the term *breaks*, as in "this line is breaking well." In this chapter, you'll notice that we advise you to break lines to make "reading sense." For example, "Been there" is broken before the next line, "done that." Readers will mentally insert a pause at the end of each line, so always try to break a thought within a paragraph so that it reads well.

20

In the steps to follow, you will work with the Gryphon layout just to get your feet wet in the art of paragraph setting. To get a feel for the look and *color* of a typeset page, you will work with *greeking* (nonsense text, usually strings of Greek/Latin words, hence the term *greeking*).

Note

About page color   *Page color* refers to how dense a page looks from arm's length. This is totally a function of what font you use. Bold fonts will make the color of the page dense and oppressive, and no one will want to read your paragraphs. On the other hand, light or even condensed fonts are so spindly in their architecture that the page color is light and hard to read because the lettering is so fine and indistinct. We will use Times New Roman in the following steps because, although unimaginative when you have 3,000,002 fonts out there to use, Times has proven itself to have exactly the right color on a page, whether you use 8 point or 16 point.

Here goes! Just follow along; be observant. There is no particular goal to our experimenting—no grades or anything will be passed out—so let's get to it!

Experimenting with Paragraph Text

1. Open the Gryphon.psd file from the Examples/Chap20 folder on the companion CD. Also, open the Greeking.txt file (from the same folder on the companion CD) in a text editor program. Highlight and copy all the text, and close the Greeking.txt file. Then make your way back to Photoshop with the Clipboard loaded with text.

2. Press **D** to make black the foreground color. Click on the Type tool, and then click on the menu icon on the Options bar to open the Character and Paragraph grouped palettes. Click on the Paragraph tab. On the Options bar, choose Times New Roman and 12 points. (See? You can access both the Character and Paragraph attributes at the same time in Photoshop CS!)

3. Marquee drag the Type tool in the left column, starting at the left guideline and stopping when your cursor is about to thwack the sleeping gryphon at the page bottom. Press Ctrl(⌘)+V and BINGO!—type fills the type marquee box you created (see Figure 20.14). Press Ctrl(⌘)+Enter(Return) to commit the text box.

4. On the Paragraph palette, type **24 pt** on the Indent first line field on the Paragraph palette. Check out Figure 20.15. Cool, huh? By the way, the default alignment for imported text is flush left, but we'll change the imported paragraph's alignment shortly.

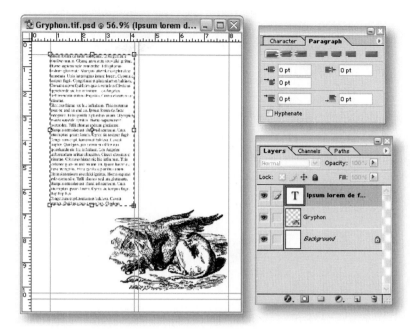

Figure 20.14   Type flows into the marquee box you created.

Insider

Now, remember when you're working with the Text tool, pressing the Enter (Return) key will *not* commit the creation of the type box. Instead, doing so will most certainly kick the cursor down to the next line to start a new paragraph of type (who would have thunk?). So to commit the text, remember to use the check mark icon on the upper right of the Options bar, or press Ctrl(⌘)+Enter(Return), or use the Enter key on the keypad section of the keyboard. You can press the Esc key, the keyboard shortcut, to cancel the creation of text, or you can click on the cancel "no" symbol icon on the Options bar.

5. With the Type tool active, click in the text box to view the text box and handles. Take a hold of one of the bottom corner handles (or the bottom center handle) of the text box, and drag straight down until all the text is visible (the text will run over part of the gryphon). Then highlight the text, as shown in Figure 20.16, starting at the point where it runs over the gryphon and down to the ending point, and press Ctrl(⌘)+X to cut it. Drag the bottom middle handle up to meet the end of the current text. Press Ctrl(⌘)+Enter(Return) to commit the changes.

20

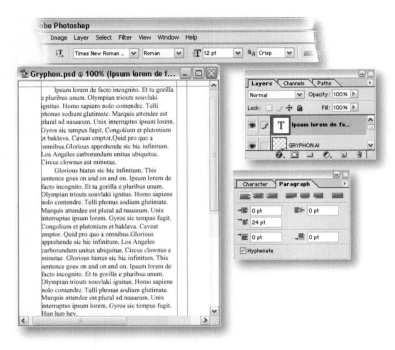

Figure 20.15   Only a click or two are required to add polish to imported text, such as paragraph indenting.

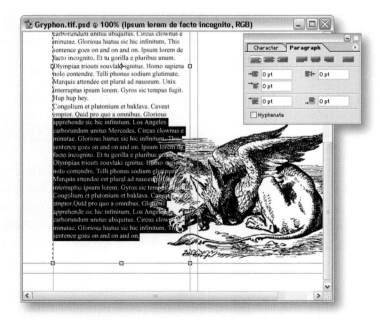

Figure 20.16   The column we set up for you in this layout doesn't cut it when you have an illustration in the way.

6. With the Type tool, marquee drag a narrower column to the bottom of the page, and then press Ctrl(⌘)+V to paste text into the second type box, as shown in Figure 20.17. Adjust the top middle handle to make the text appear as if it flows naturally with the text above it, and press Ctrl(⌘)+Enter(Return) to commit the text box. You may have to return the first indent to 0 pt on the Paragraph palette for this text layer.

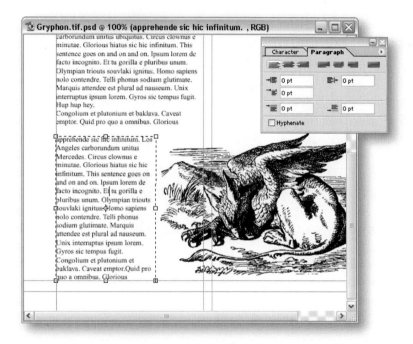

Figure 20.17   Creating a new, narrower column for the text is not too bad on the layout side of things.

7. On your own, copy some of the original text from the first text box, and create a third marquee box to flesh out the right column now. Don't forget to press Ctrl(⌘)+Enter(Return) to exit the text boxes, and adjust the paragraph formatting if necessary.

8. To be honest, trying to read flush left type, when it has so few words per line, may make you feel like you have whiplash again. Click on each text layer, and then click on the Justify All icon on the Paragraph palette; the paragraphs will look nice and neat, but the last lines in each paragraph will have funky spacing, as shown in Figure 20.18.

20

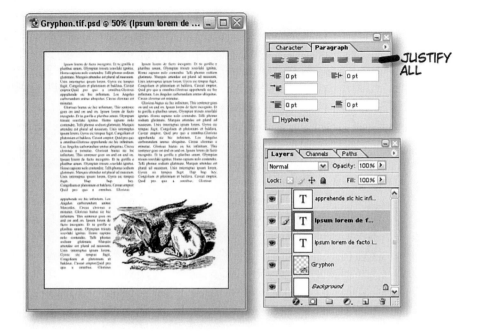

Figure 20.18   Professional, easy to read, clean. Lewis Carroll would have been proud of you!

9. One or more of the paragraphs are bound to have a last line that spans the column width. Yuck! Instead of choosing Justify all, click on each text layer, and use the Justify last left icon on the Paragraph palette, as shown in Figure 20.19.

10. It's time to fool around with some of the other features of the Paragraph palette. Center justification is okay, but it requires a larger than average point size (so there are fewer words per line and you avoid reader whiplash), and it's really good for only a paragraph or two. Delete the two large text blocks by dragging their title on the Layers palette into the trash icon.

11. Choose the Gryphon layer, and with the Move tool active, move the gryphon to the bottom center of the page. It's okay; he's sleeping.

12. Click on the layer containing the small text box to make this layer active. With the Move tool still active, drag this text box above the gryphon. Click on the Center text icon, and with the Text tool active, click on the font size box on the Options bar and choose 18 pt. Click on the text to activate the text box handles, and adjust the layout to look something like that shown in Figure 20.20. Click on the check mark on the Options bar to commit your text.

Figure 20.19   Add finesse to your layout by tucking the last line of a paragraph up to the left of the column.

Insider

> If you have been paying attention, you will notice that we have been able to apply changes such as paragraph alignment and even change font size to all the text within a text box simply by making the text layer active. If you need to make a change in font size to a specific portion of text within a text box, you need to highlight the text before making the change. However, you can make global changes simply by activating the text layer and adjusting the options.

13. Okay, we're into the home stretch of trying out neat stuff on the Paragraph palette. We need to examine one last justification type: right justification. Click on the Right align text icon on the Paragraph palette. With the Move tool, move the text to the left bottom of the page, and click on the Gryphon layer to move the gryphon to the right. The text should now be to the left of the gryphon, as you can see in Figure 20.21. Quite honestly, folks, the need for right justification may be rare. Trying to read it is a pain in the neck in most situations; however, short sections of text, such as captions, can work effectively—as you can imagine after seeing this figure.

14. Press Ctrl(⌘)+S if you want to save the file to your hard disk.

20

Figure 20.20   Sometimes simple and symmetrical works. You always need to try out your options.

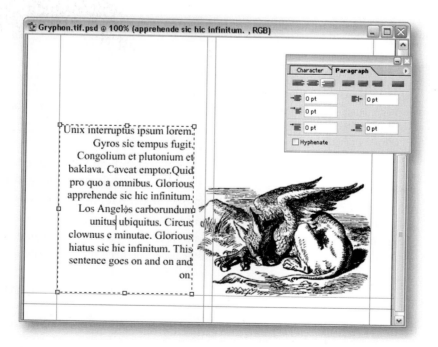

Figure 20.21   Right justification is sort of like a fire extinguisher; you may never need it, but it's nice to have around.

Working from the *general* to the *specific* is always a good artistic technique, so to conclude our tour of the Paragraph palette, let's look at strategies for combating *rivers* and *orphans*.

Fighting Rivers and Orphans

As mentioned earlier, a river is an unsightly, vertical lightning bolt sort of shape that is blank space running through several paragraphs. Your solutions are these:

- Carefully kick up one line any single words at the beginning of lines directly below a poorly letter-spaced line. In many cases, this trick will eliminate one line of the river. This mess is caused by imported text that can have hidden line breaks in it, and you import these breaks along with the text. And remember, I stand firmly against composing paragraphs in Photoshop: It's good, but it's just not a word processor or text editor.

- Do what the earlier Note recommended. If a word won't fit at the end of a line, and as a result, the spaces look extremely wide between characters, take the first word on the following line and condense it by 90 to 95% using the Character palette. No one is going to notice this ingenuity/trickery.

- As a last resort, turn on hyphenation. I detest hyphenation because it interrupts your reading. However, sometimes it's the only way to get rid of rivers in your paragraph blocks. Tip: Do NOT allow hyphenation to occur more than two lines in a row. If you do, this is simply called bad typesetting, and it's also a pain in the, um, neck to read.

All right, it's time for orphans and widows. An *orphan* is a single word (sometimes two) at the end of a paragraph. You've probably noticed such words in amateur newsletters and stuff. A *widow*, on the other hand, is the end of a paragraph—again, perhaps only a word or two—that does not belong at the top of a page or column; it looks bad and reads awkwardly.

Now, look back at Figure 20.21. Yup, there's an orphaned word, *on*, on its own line, lookin' really lonely. The solution to this problem is to kick two or three words down a line and then adjust the lines so that more words appear on the last line, as you can see in Figure 20.22. What happens with the justification is that the line from which you borrowed words will expand slightly. Then, you need to remove the space at the end of the line and use, if necessary, the Justify Last feature on the formerly orphaned line.

20

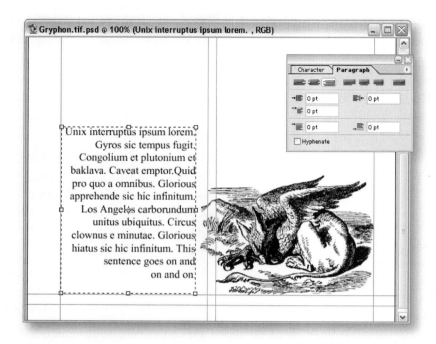

Figure 20.22   Hey, have a heart and take care of an orphan today!

Bouton, What About the Flyout Features?

Unless you're another William Randolph Hearst, you have puh-lenty to absorb in this chapter without taxing your mind further. But there are probably three things you need to be able to access that I'll explain now, to make even the fussiest typesetter out there happy.

Hanging Punctuation

Nothing except perhaps a Las Vegas dance costume looks worse than punctuation marks beginning a paragraph. For some reason, nice blocks of perfectly aligned text are highly legible, and the quotes should hang *outside* the column.

In Figure 20.23, I copied an interview (I knew it had quote marks in it) into a column in Photoshop and then checked the Roman Hanging Punctuation feature (off the Paragraph palette flyout menu).

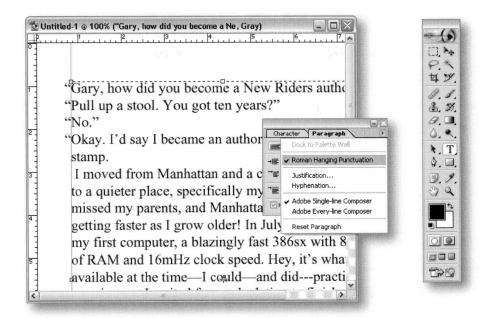

Figure 20.23   Hanging punctuation is much easier on the readers' eyes than an inset quote mark kicking off a paragraph.

If your text has a punctuation mark at the beginning or end of a line, by using the Hanging Punctuation feature, you can move that mark outside the bounding box so that all the letters line up vertically along the left and right edges of the box. Whether to use this feature is generally a designer's call—there are no hard-set rules stating when and when not to use hanging punctuation—but it *will* show a prospective employer that you know how to use this typographic element. By the way, as a common example, bulleted lists are supposed to have hanging indents.

Hyphenation and Justification Fine-Tuning Features

Here's where Adobe has decided to put a PageMaker feature or two into Photoshop. Although you may never need to use the Hyphenation and Justification features, they are located on the flyout menu. As you can see in Figure 20.24, you have total control over where a hyphenation breaks, compliments of the Hyphenation dialog box. Hyphenation is ultimately determined by the spell checker; the two have to work together to find the best hyphenation break, but again, you have the final say by typing values in this dialog box.

As far as justification goes, with paragraph (that is, small) text, you might want to leave the default options alone. If you work with HUGE font sizes, you can always decrease the

20

leading to 100% or below here (100% is called *dead leading*, because in theory, not a lot of space is left between lines, and you *want* that when setting headlines). Word spacing and letter spacing are also welcome if you inherit an unruly font that thinks a space character between words is way too wide (a space that the spacebar makes is actually a character embedded in a font). If you use a font like this all the time, here's where you can make corrections. As the obvious alternative, instead of making all these permanent, global changes to text handling, why not fine-tune your text using the up-front controls on the Paragraph and Character palettes, as the need arises?

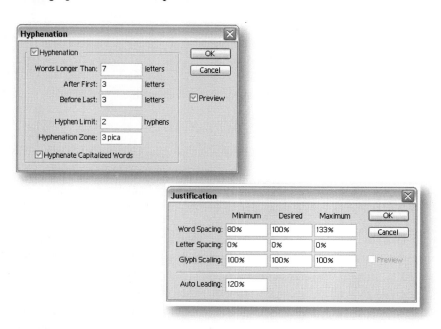

Figure 20.24   The Hyphenation and Justification features are only a click away. If your assignment is spacing-critical, and you're not getting the results you want, perhaps you can fine-tune your typography right here.

Note

Correcting fonts   What with all this talk about text, it wouldn't kill you to buy Macromedia Fontographer, or better yet, Pyrus Software's FontLab. You can then correct a font from the get-go, instead of coping with it while you work in Photoshop.

Whew! This is becoming a seminar on desktop publishing! Let's just weather out this next section (which might just change your style of designing!), and then we'll get to the standard "fun part" at the chapter's end.

Layout and Design Using Photoshop Type

As we've mentioned to the point of annoyance in this book, you always need to have a plan before you sit down and design anything—even a garage sale sign. There simply isn't the space in this book to write about good page layout, but we squeaked in a little of the most important concepts of good layout into this section. To begin with, there's something I learned in college (ever see a school ring made up of cave paintings on stone?) concerning layout that will not fail you if you follow along. It is here we introduce the "Swiss Grid System."

The Swiss Grid System

The Swiss Grid System is so ridiculously simple, it's sophisticated. Employing the Swiss Grid System in your work simply entails dividing the page into columns and rows. Revolutionary thought, huh? But still, designers will plunk items on a page nilly-willy and not think twice about it.

In Figure 20.25, you can see at left a layout for a magazine that uses the Swiss Grid System. The page is broken down into two columns and three rows, and all that is asked of the designer is, "What goes where?" It's a tight, readable layout. Meanwhile, fretting away on the right of Figure 20.25 is an inexpertly designed layout. Why? Because nothing lines up with anything; the eye has no page rules to follow. Don't let this happen to you! Go Swiss!

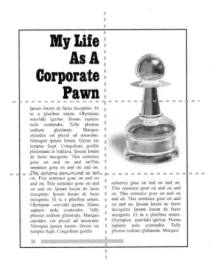

2 by 3 grid layout   No layout. And it shows.

Figure 20.25   The Swiss Grid System not only helps you sort out page elements, but also guides the readers in any direction *you* choose.

20

This Swiss Grid stuff is almost infinitely extensible. Figure 20.26, provides two more examples of using the Grid in your work. As you can see, this system is not a pair of handcuffs; in fact, it sets your ideas and your designs free (from misinterpretation, from criticism, and so on).

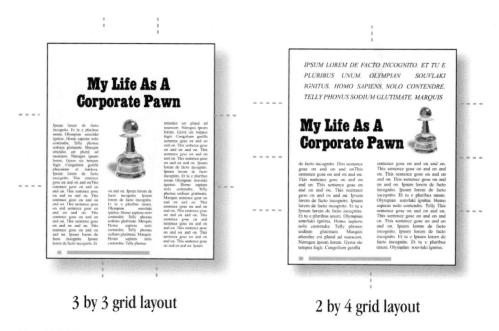

3 by 3 grid layout   2 by 4 grid layout

Figure 20.26   Step One to effective design: Make yourself a grid on your layout page.

We hope it goes without saying that, "First you thoroughly understand the rules, and it is only then that you can experiment and break a few of them." Obviously, not every illustration in this book follows the Swiss Grid Rule, but then again, we authors usually know what we are doing, and much of the material in this book is not *supposed* to be a page layout—you've got your callouts, your schematics, and all the rest!

Leading the Viewer's Eye

Our last piece of sound advice before getting down to some fun has to do with directing a reader's eye. It is not only well within your capability to force the reader to look at page elements in a certain order, but it's your *duty* as an effective communicator to do so.

Briefly, as shown in Figure 20.27, the left party flyer not only uses a 2×3 grid, but it also has elements arranged so that the dominance first falls on the little guy who simply sets the tone for the flyer. Second, the eye falls on the message "Let's Party!" and assuming that you want to party, third and last are the particulars: when, where, why, how, and so on.

Sadly, on the right of the figure is a flyer designed by Marvello the rollerskating chimp. There is no order. Size of elements is ignored. Are you beginning to see how "order" is possibly your biggest friend when it comes to new territory—such as typography—as your career blossoms?

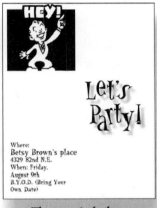

The eye is led to
resting places in the
right order.

The eye has no idea where to start.
The invitation goes into
the circular file.

Figure 20.27   Order, priority, manipulation of importance of elements all help you to simply say what it is you're getting *paid* to say!

Ahem. We shall now relax a little and get on with the discovery of fonts and Photoshop's Type tool. It's as important to leave this chapter knowing proper font choice and placement as it is knowing how to arrange garage sale signs and paragraphs.

Typography

Just as Geography is the study of the Earth, Mythology is the study of unicorns and fairy princesses and stuff, and Olliology is the study of Laurel and Hardy (sorry), Typography is the study of type—how it works (or doesn't) to convey a message. Typography also invites the examination of columns of text (how wide you should make a column using a specific font before the reader's head starts boinging like an old-fashioned carriage return) and how the placement of text along with pictures helps constitute a good page layout.

20

Understanding Typefaces and Type Design Basics

First, notice the last word in the heading: *Basics*. It is impossible to explain everything about typefaces and design in one chapter, much less *a third of* a chapter! The study, creation, design, and application of type is a profession, and many books have been written on the subject. As of this writing, if you enter **typography** in Google.com's search engine, you get—well—a google of *pages* of resources! If you find working with text fascinating, we highly recommend that you buy a few good books on the subject.

If you're as old as we are—most of the authors were around to witness the discovery of fire—you remember the good old days of the manual typewriter. Choosing a typeface (font) was simple: You used the typeface that came with the typewriter! Things started getting complicated—and interesting—when IBM introduced the Selectric typewriter in which the font element was a metal ball with all the characters on it, in the center of the typewriter well. You could swap the type balls to use exotic fonts such as Script, Delegate, and Orator (this is thinly veiled sarcasm, okay?). However, the variety of monospaced fonts was meager, the daisy-wheel element eventually replaced the (expensive!) IBM type balls, and the level of quality you, as a personal publisher, could attain was a step above all the publishing firms you might find along the Serengeti.

Then came the personal computer and the curse of having hundreds to thousands of typefaces from which to choose. For the novice, having this massive selection of fonts was like being in a candy store with someone else willing to pay the bill. Newsletters, brochures, letters, and anything else that required text suddenly looked like an all-you-can-eat buffet—a different typeface for each paragraph or article. Additionally, the layout of the text lacked the basic design principles that books and newspapers have used for decades. For example, fonts that are best used for headlines were used in paragraph text, which made reading very difficult.

The problem was the worst for the Windows platform, where CorelDRAW users were treated to more than 1,000 fonts (some of high quality, while others would cause a PostScript device to barf). It seemed every Corellian felt compelled to use as many fonts as possible, without realizing that entries for the fonts were being made in *Win.ini*, and if *Win.ini* grew over 64KB, the machine would not run properly. The Macintosh has a built-in limitation of 512 fonts loaded at the same time (or 16MB of font families—this is all based on OS X), and you know, professionally, that's about all you ever need on a daily basis. Wild fonts such as Renee Mackintosh (after the Scottish furniture designer) Arnold Boecklin, Shelley Allegro, and others really need to be loaded about once every year; you use this stuff only for weddings and the holidays.

Okay, enough complaining. Let's take a look at five basic classifications of typefaces.

Classifying and Choosing Typefaces

During the decision-making process of buying a new car, you have an idea of your needs and you've created a list, or classification, of the vehicles that best meet those needs. Then you decide which vehicle to buy. Why should choosing a font be any different? Sure, a font has less passenger-side leg room, but that's not the point.

The following classifications should help you get started with identifying and knowing where to use (and *not* use!) certain categories of fonts.

Serif

Serif is a Latin word that means *feet*—the "your socks go over them" type—not the measurement. The identifying characteristics of a serif font are the small extensions (the feet) at the ends of the lines that make up the letter. Figure 20.28 shows an example of a serif font and identifies the feet areas.

Figure 20.28   Serif typefaces have a finishing stroke on most letters.

The serifs help guide your eye along the line of text and make identifying letters and words easier and quicker. For these reasons, serif fonts are ideal for *body text* (paragraph text). As you can see, this book has the body text set in a serif font.

Sans Serif

The *sans serif* typeface is without (sans) feet (see Figure 20.29). The strokes, or lines, that make up each letter are simple and straightforward in design.

20

Antique Olive

Futura

Helvetica

Compacta

SANS SERIF FONTS

Figure 20.29   The less ornate sans serif font is strong for quick recognition of short lines of text.

The most frequently seen use of a sans serif font is in the headlines of a newspaper. Sans serif fonts also work well in subheads, captions, callouts—situations in which only one or two lines of text are used and the text must command attention.

Note

Subclasses of type families   Within families of typefaces, there are subclasses. You don't need to know many to become proficient at type selection. In fact, we're going to highlight only two here: the Roman and the Gothic classes. Roman fonts have thick and thin lines making up the stems (the strokes) that make a letterform. You can have Roman Serif (item 1 in Figure 20.30; the font is called Garamond), and Roman Sans Serif (item 2 in Figure 20.30; this font is called Optima).

On the other side of the family, you have your Gothic fonts. Gothic fonts are easy to detect because the strokes that make up the character are uniform in weight. Item 4 in Figure 20.30 is VagRounded, a Gothic sans serif font. And although you don't come across a lot of Gothic serif fonts, Lubalin Graph (named after Herb Lubalin, a designer and font creator in the 1960s–1970s), is a Gothic serif font, item 3 here.

❶ Roman Serif

❷ Roman Sans Serif

❸ Gothic Serif

❹ Gothic Sans Serif

Figure 20.30   Fonts can come in Roman or Gothic versions.

Script

Script typefaces are easily identified as having the characteristics of elegant handwriting. Script fonts are often very beautiful and can even evoke emotions. Set, for example, the words, "I love you" in Arial or Helvetica (a stoic sans serif font available on most computers). Then rewrite those words in a script font, like Deanna Script or Vivaldi, and notice which of the two typefaces best conveys the intended emotions (see Figure 20.31).

Figure 20.31   Script typefaces convey a personal and warm touch, whereas the sans serif font is cold and inflexible.

Although the script typeface seems more personal than most other fonts, you should avoid using a script font for body text or long lines of text. Similar in application to the sans serif font, the script font looks best in short lines of text, as in logos or invitations.

20

Decorative

Decorative fonts are designed for basically one reason: to attract attention. These fonts come in the widest range of designs (see Figure 20.32) and are sometimes referred to as *Display faces.*

Figure 20.32   You find the widest range of designs in the decorative style typeface.

Decorative fonts are not designed for readability in long lines of text; rather, they are good for dramatic emphasis. Decorative fonts work well, for example, in advertisement headlines, restaurant menus, logos, and posters.

The Pi Font

The Pi font, short for *Pic*ture, is not made up of an alphabet at all, but instead is made up of tiny symbols, cartoons, fingers pointing, and so on. Zapf Dingbats is perhaps the best known Pi font, but there are many others, sometimes called *ornaments* or *extras*. Adobe Minion, a Roman serif font, has an accompanying font called Minion Ornaments. Designers use these Pi fonts to embellish headlines, such as putting a *plum* (that's what the design is called in typography) on either side of ornate text, as shown in Figure 20.33.

Your use of Pi fonts should be limited. Pi fonts can perk up a menu or a flyer; however, overusing these fonts can make your layout look like mail that was postmarked several times from Mars. Pi fonts are possible because typefaces are actually tiny programs that contain vector information and are decoded by a display system such as Adobe Type Manager. Technically, there is no difference between the information in a picture font and a Roman font, for example. Usually, it is best to work with Pi fonts in drawing programs such as Illustrator, XARA, or Photoshop because you usually need to scale the pictures on-the-fly. Desktop publishers (DTP) and word processors don't scale fonts with as much ease as art programs.

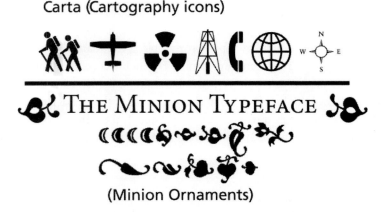

Figure 20.33   Pi fonts are particularly useful for people who design or use photography, but are not skilled with a drawing program.

These are just a few of the many classifications of typefaces. To complicate or organize matters (depending on your point of view), most classifications can be divided into many subclassifications.

Now that you are able to classify typefaces, what are some general rules that can help you use fonts with good design sense? Read on!

Type Design Basics

The following list of design basics is in no way complete, nor are these basics cast in stone so that they cannot be broken. But they *will* help get you started in the right direction when you're using type in your designs.

Consider the Technical Constraints

"What technical constraints? If the font is on my computer, I can use it, right?" Well, not without compromising good design. There are two limitations worth mentioning: the characteristics of the font and your intended output.

The thickness of the lines that make up the letters can determine what point size to use and what not to use. For example, some serif fonts have very thin lines that are part of each letter's design, and at a small size, these lines can virtually disappear, leaving your text looking terrible and making it difficult to read. An example of this is a font called

20

Premiere Liteline that absolutely will not print to a 300 dpi printer; the stems in the font are that delicate. On the other hand, some fonts don't reveal their beauty until they are seen at a large point size. Opus is a good example of a font that looks best large because the end of each stroke that comprises each character is convex—unlike almost all other fonts.

The other limitation concerns your document's output. If you plan to print your document, be aware that some fonts look good only at a high dpi (dot per inch), whereas other fonts look quite good at any dpi. For example, a font named Bergamo looks best above 300 dpi, whereas a different font named Futura looks good at both low and high resolution. What should you look for when determining the lowest acceptable dpi for a particular font? Look for loss of detail in the finer areas of the characters. The characters in some typefaces have very thin strokes in the design. If these thin strokes are no longer visible at your working dpi, choose a different font.

Tip

You get what you pay for *Hinting* is a property of a typeface. Again, typefaces are actually a collection of vectors inside a tiny runtime program. Hinting is not always added to a font; it is a process by which the font (program) describes itself as having bolder characteristics at small point sizes.

Shareware fonts typically do not have hinting because typeface design programs are either $4,000 or $29—at least those next to the water balloons at the checkout stand.

Often, investing in a quality family of typefaces pays off in the long run. Adobe, URW, ITC, and MonoType all have the reputation for selling quality fonts.

Paper is another consideration. Thinner, more detailed fonts tend to look lousy on standard copy paper but print very nicely on high grade, glossy stock. Heavier fonts, like Franklin Gothic, hold up well on just about any paper.

On the other hand, if you do not intend to print your document, but plan to keep the text in electronic format (PDF, the Web, for example), sans serif fonts are much easier to read on the computer screen than serif fonts. You can test this concept for yourself the next time you are working in your word processing program. Here's how: Type two identical sentences, each on a separate line. Make one sentence a serif font (such as Times New Roman) and the other sentence a sans serif font (such as Arial or Helvetica). Determine which sentence is easier to read. Next, zoom out until one of the sentences is almost too difficult to read, but the other sentence is quite legible. Guess which font wins? The sans serif font. If you have a Web site, it would be a good idea to change any text at small point sizes to a sans serif font during your next update.

Tip

> **Using Microsoft's fonts**   Microsoft has helped Web designers become more creative with typeface layouts.
>
> If you've purchased a Microsoft program lately or upgraded MS Explorer, you will find some new TrueType fonts on your system, such as Georgia, WebDings, and Trebuchet MS. Why are we being gifted with fonts? Microsoft is seeding the Web; eventually, everyone will own these fonts, which are more legible and fancier looking than the default Times New Roman in browsers. Even today, right now, sites are being designed with these fonts included.
>
> Check out your installed fonts. You might be pleasantly surprised!

Know the Typefaces

If youv will be working with type, you should know which fonts you have, and you should know your most-used or favorite fonts like the top of your mouse.

Here are some questions you should ask yourself when getting to know a font:

- Does this font look good at any point size? Does it lose its detail as it gets smaller?
- How readable is this font in paragraph text?
- Does this font use more (or less) horizontal space than other fonts at the same point size?
- Does the font look darker or lighter at small sizes?

Support Your Message

Type should help communicate and support your message, not overwhelm it. The reader's attention should be drawn to what you are communicating, and not to the font you think looks really cool.

For example, if you are creating an image as an advertisement for an upcoming accountants' meeting, your font choice should be somewhat conservative in design. On other hand, if you are designing an ad for a rock concert, you can easily use a decorative font to help convey your message.

The standard wedding invitation is a good example of the font supporting the message. Elegant or script typefaces are used almost exclusively for wedding invitations because of their warm, personal design (the Gothic sans serif font Bernhard Fashion is creeping into invitations). An example of the contrast between supportive and nonsupportive fonts for a wedding invitation is shown in Figure 20.34.

20

Figure 20.34   Which font supports the message for this wedding invitation? You're kidding, right?

Now that we've laid the foundation of good type design, it's time to move on to our next topic: how Photoshop's Type tools relate to real-world assignments in typography.

Okay, gang, let's fire up Photoshop and put all this typeface theory into practice. Our main tools in the next section will be the Character and Paragraph palettes. You also can display the palettes by picking them from the Window menu.

Using Type

Type is *always* measured in *points*, and there are 72 points per inch.

You might think it's odd that type isn't measured in inches or millimeters, but when you think about it, many things have their own sizes. A bucket of water, a flagon of mead, a fortnight, a metric liter—you get the idea. The true size of any given font is coded into the font file. Some fonts look smaller at 72 points (1") than others because the font creator has left a given amount of headroom space for the font. So, at 72 points, the capital letters might be only 50 points. Besides this extra padding that prevents the font leading from being too tight, foreign accent marks usually go above characters, and the accents make up the difference between the capital character and a true measurement of 72 points being exactly 1". Figure 20.35 gives you an example showing the true height.

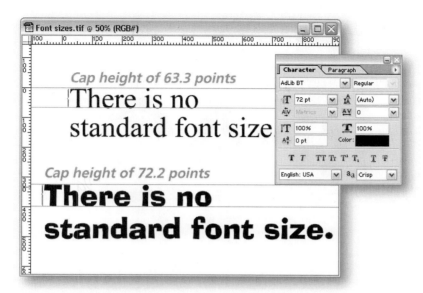

Figure 20.35   Even though you enter the same point size for two different fonts, there's no guarantee that their size will be consistent.

This first set of steps helps you size things up:

Creating 5" Type

1. Open the 2-face.psd document from the Examples/Chap20 folder on the companion CD.

2. Right-click (Macintosh: hold Ctrl and click) the title bar of the document, and choose Canvas Size. In the Canvas Size dialog box, middle Anchor should be chosen by default. You want to expand this canvas, leaving the logo at the far left, so click the anchor to the left of the middle square. Then enter **20 inches** for Width and **6 inches** for Height, and click on OK.

3. Choose the Type tool from the toolbox, and click the menu icon to view the Character and Paragraph palettes. Click on the Left align text icon on the Paragraph options. In the Character palette, choose Arial as the font, set the Style to Bold, and set point size to 360 points. Press **D** for default colors (black should be the foreground color). Click in the new document, and type **2FACE**, as shown in Figure 20.36. Press Ctrl(⌘)+Enter(Return) to commit the text to a layer.

Figure 20.36   The height of the logo is about 5 inches. If 72 points equal an inch, 360-point type should theoretically be the same height as the logo.

Insider

> You need some guides to help judge the bottom and top spacing for the text height. These guides will aid in the following steps. Here's how to create the guidelines:

4. Press Ctrl(⌘)+R to display the rulers. Click in the top ruler, drag a guide down, and position it at the lowest edge of the logo. Drag another guide from the top ruler, and position it at the highest edge of the logo (peek ahead at Figure 20.37 to see where the guides have been placed). Press the Ctrl(⌘) key to toggle to the Move tool, and position your text near the logo so that the lower edge of the text is aligned with the bottom guide.

5. With the text layer as the active layer, scrunch the width of the text by typing **50%** in the Horizontal scale option on the Character palette (see Figure 20.37). Then press Enter (Return) to apply the change. If necessary, hold down the Ctrl(⌘)key to toggle to the Move tool and reposition the text.

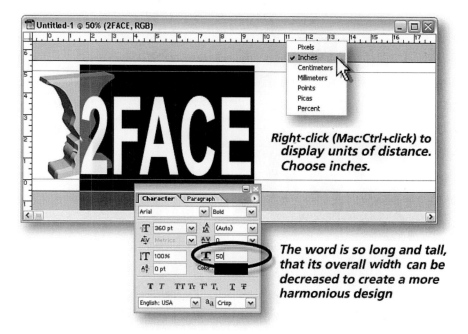

Figure 20.37   The Horizontal scale of type can be adjusted to complement and balance the vertical appearance of a design.

6. Now let's stretch the text so that it reaches the top guideline. Press Ctrl(⌘)+T to bring up the Free Transform tool. On the Options bar, click the Maintain aspect ratio icon (it's the chain icon that links width to height proportionately). Alternatively, you can hold Shift as you stretch the lettering. Click and drag the upper-right corner of the bounding box to scale the text so that it meets the upper guideline, as shown in Figure 20.38. When you're satisfied, press Enter (Return) to apply the transformation. Press Ctrl(⌘)+R to toggle the rulers off.

7. (Optional) On your own, polish off the assignment by selecting a different font to give the logo a new look and feel. See Figure 20.39 for inspiration.

20

Press Ctrl (⌘)+T to beckon the Free
Transform box, click the link button, and
then drag away from the text.

Figure 20.38   Click the Maintain aspect ratio icon and resize the text. Press Enter (Return) when finished, or click the check mark on the far-right side of the Options bar. (Clicking the "no" sign, next to the check mark, is equivalent to pressing the Esc key and cancels out any changes.)

Figure 20.39   With a little more polish (using the Adobe Viva font), we're done.

Ascenders and Descenders

In the preceding section, you learned that choosing the same size type in different type-faces might display type that looks dramatically different in size, depending on whether the font designer added leading within the characters. Ascenders and descenders are *additional* characteristics that affect the way same-sized typefaces appear. Type is also measured from the bottom of the *descenders* to the top of the *ascenders*.

Descenders are the bottoms of lowercase letters that fall below the *baseline* (or the bottom of most letters). The only letters that have descenders are *g, j, p, q,* and *y*. Ascenders are the tops of lowercase letters that rise above the *x-height*. The letters with ascenders are *b, d, f, h, k, l,* and *t*.

The *x-height* of a typeface is simply the height of the lowercase *x*. Typefaces with a small x-height, such as Bodoni, look smaller than typefaces with a large x-height, such as Caecilia. Most lowercase letters are the same height as the lowercase *x* (with the exception of letters with ascenders or descenders). Figure 20.40 illustrates these points clearly.

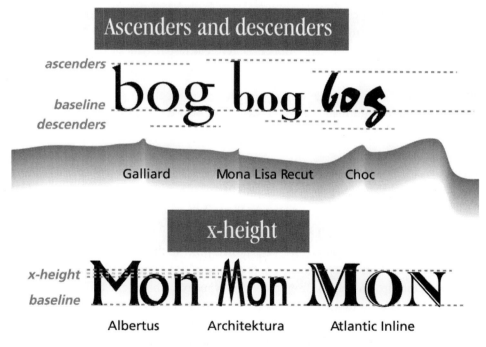

Figure 20.40   Different fonts can appear larger simply based on the measured distance from the descenders to the ascenders. X-height can play a factor in this illusion, too.

20

Vertical and Transparent Type

When one of the Text tools is active, you can type text at any time simply by clicking in a document window and typing. You also have the option to drag a marquee selection with the Type tool before typing. This way, you can create a text box for the type. When you use a text box, the type automatically wraps (when there's more than one line of text) within the confines of the box. If you need to resize the box, you use the handles on the bounding box to do the trick. In addition to resizing, you also can rotate the box.

You'll find four Type tools on the Toolbox flyout menu. The Horizontal Type tool and Vertical Type tool will create text (as their name implies) either in a horizontal or vertical direction. These tools also automatically generate their own layer on the Layers palette.

The two remaining text tools on the Toolbox flyout are the Horizontal Type Mask tool and Vertical Type Mask tool. Like the first two tools listed on the flyout, these tools lay text in a horizontal or vertical direction, respectively. Unlike the other toolbox tools, however, the Horizontal Type Mask and Vertical Type Mask tools do not create their own text layer. Instead, they create a selection of the text on the current active layer. This selection then can be used to fill another selection with a color, a gradient, or anything you might care to use as fill. You can think of the result as rasterized text, since this text can no longer be edited after you've accepted or committed the "masked" text to make it a selection.

Now that we've run through the differences of the Text tools available to you, let's try another assignment to put some of these tools to work:

Vertical Type

1. Load the Kibbutz font from the Examples/Chap20 folder on the companion CD, or use your own heavyweight font. In Photoshop, open the Hotel.tif file from the Examples/Chap20 folder on the companion CD.

2. Press **D** for default colors. Press **X** to switch white to the foreground color. Choose the Vertical Type tool from the toolbox, and open the Character palette from the Options bar (or from the Window menu). Choose the Kibbutz font (or any heavyweight font), and set the font size to around 90 pt. If necessary, return the Horizontal scale back to 100%. Click at the top of the empty sign area in the image, and type **HOTEL** (all uppercase letters). Press Ctrl(⌘)+Enter(Return) to commit the text to a layer.

Insider

When using the Vertical Type tool, you can shift the orientation of the individual letters by simply clicking on the arrow in the upper-right corner of the Character palette and choosing the Standard Vertical Roman Alignment option from the flyout menu. This will toggle the rotation of the individual characters so that they appear either vertically or horizontally (one above the other).

3. You need to tighten up the spaces between characters to make the letters fit the sign. With the text layer active, adjust the tracking on the Character palette to **–200**, as shown in Figure 20.41. Remember, this value sets the character space between letters, even though they are stacked vertically. Press Enter (Return) to commit the change.

Figure 20.41   The letters don't fit within the hotel's sign; there is too much space between the characters. Tighten the space by adjusting the tracking. A negative number brings characters closer together, and a positive number increases the distance between the characters.

4. With the text layer still active, you can adjust text size to find the magic number that makes this text appear as though it were made for the sign in this image (70 pt seems to work well). Press Enter (Return) to commit any changes made in the Character palette. If necessary, hold down the Ctrl(⌘) key to toggle to the Move tool to reposition the text. From any point in your work flow, you can always

20

turn text on its sides. Press Ctrl(⌘)+T to use the Transform tool and rotate the text, as shown in Figure 20.42. Holding the Shift key while rotating constrains rotation to 15° increments.

Hold Shift to constrain Free Transform Rotate to 45 degree increments

Figure 20.42   Ctrl(⌘)+T enables you to rotate text with the Transform tool. You can also choose the orientation for the text. Press Enter to exit the Transform tool and apply changes. Press Esc to cancel the Transform tool, along with the changes you've made.

Insider

The goal of this assignment is to help you become comfortable with the Text tool features. So experiment a little on your own with the text. We're goofing around with the finished results in Figure 20.43 because, hey, magazines use vertical text, too.

5. If you would like to experiment with a glow for your text, try this trick: Click the Add a layer style icon at the bottom of the Layers palette, and choose Outer Glow. In the Layer Style dialog box, click the color swatch to choose a color for your glow (maybe sample a green for the glow color from the Hotel sign frame from the document image). Play with the sliders, especially the Spread and Size sliders, until the results look appealing. By contrast, Figure 20.44 shows what you can do with the right font for the right occasion. We used an Image Club Graphics font called Neon, rasterized the text (Layer, Rasterize, Type), and used the Free Transform Distort tool to finesse the shape of the text. Then a Gaussian Blur was applied to a color fill behind the neon (another method to obtain an Outer Glow effect).

Figure 20.43   *Onnnnly* kidding! This sign doesn't look right.

Fills for Text

One of the great things about Photoshop is its built-in flexibility. If you can imagine a design concept, you can find a way to make it happen in Photoshop. When you're designing text, thinking of it as more than text will help you with your design. When you're creating text in Photoshop, chances are that the text is more than just letters that form words; text here is art and, as such, is an important part of your overall design.

But with all designs—and text is no exception—you should not lose sight of the power of simplicity. The effects you can create for text can be wild and zany, but many times the simplest of ideas can be the most effective. Just the right font with the right color may be all you need to complete the look you're after. If you need something fancier, you may find a style in the Styles palette that gives you just the look you want.

20

Figure 20.44   A perfect example of how an unusual font can suddenly become "just the right font" for the right situation.

Here's a quick exercise to acquaint you with color and style experimentation:

Color with Style

1. Press Ctrl(⌘)+N to open a new document (Windows users can hold Ctrl and double-click in the workspace). Make a 400-pixel square document, 72 ppi, RGB Color, and click on OK. Press **D** for default colors (black should be the foreground color).

2. Choose the Horizontal Text tool from the toolbox. Make sure the Character palette is open, and use the Kibbutz font loaded in the preceding exercise (or any heavyweight font). The font size or tracking isn't important. Because this is just practice, go ahead and set the font size to 170 pt. Set the tracking to 100 so that some space is added between letters.

3. Click near the left center of the document window, and type the word **FILL**. Press the Ctrl(⌘) key to toggle to the Move tool if you want to reposition the text in the center of the document window. Press Ctrl(⌘)+A to highlight all the letters. Now here's a little trick that many people forget to use: Press Ctrl(⌘)+H to hide the reverse coloring that occurs when you highlight the text. You can now

view the normal color of the text even though you have the text highlighted. Click the Color swatch located on the Character palette, and choose a new color. You can see the color fill update live on the text (because we are no longer captive to that pesky highlighting problem). After you find a color you like, click on OK (see item 2 in Figure 20.45). Press Ctrl(⌘)+Enter(Return) to commit the text.

4. Now, click the Styles tab to view the Styles palette (or go to the Window menu and choose Styles). Click the triangle at the upper-right corner of the Styles palette to see the context menu for this palette. Adobe has provided you with some cool choices for styles. You should see a list of these styles on the menu, one of which is titled Text Effects 2. Choose this one, and click on OK to replace your current set. Don't worry. You can get your current set back by choosing Reset Styles from the same menu when you're done.

5. Item 1 in Figure 20.45 shows that we have chosen the Double Turquoise Border style. Your text layer should still be active on the Layers palette, so simply click this style to apply the style to your text. That's it.

Have fun experimenting with other styles. After applying a style, you will see a list of the layer effects that make up the style. This list appears under the layer on the Layers palette. You can double-click any effect and tweak the settings in the Layer Effects dialog box to change that effect. These changes affect only the layer to which you have applied the style and don't change the original style.

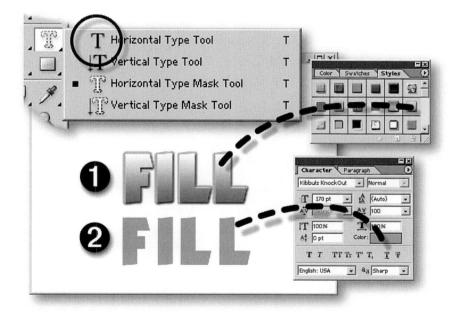

Figure 20.45   Applying a new fill or a specific style is easy.

20

Hmmmm… Now, how about the Type Mask tool? Like I said before, enough theory. Let's jump into another quick exercise to try out this tool:

Mask Type

1. Open the Rose Granite.tif image from the Examples/Chap17 folder on the companion CD. Use Kibbutz as the font (or any heavyweight font) at 300 points, and set the tracking back to 0. Press Enter (Return) to set any changes made in the Character palette. Choose the Horizontal Type Mask tool (not the Vertical). Click in the document window, and type the word **FILL** (all capital letters). Everything appears as Quick Mask (filled with a red tint color). If you do not understand Quick Masks, check out Chapter 5, "Harnessing the Power of Selections." If necessary, hold down the Ctrl(⌘) key to toggle to the Move tool, and reposition the text to the center of the document window.

2. Hmmm, the tracking in the font is off, causing two of the letters to appear too close together. Highlight the letter after which you need to add space; in this case, highlight the letter *I* and change Tracking to –25 (see Figure 20.46).

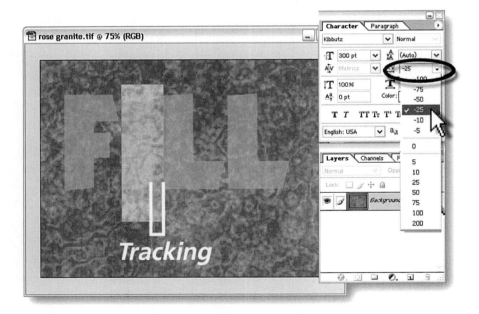

Figure 20.46   You can adjust tracking on an individual character basis.

Note

> **Just a reminder**   When you're working with the Text Mask tools, you need to make all text adjustments before the text is committed. Why? Because unlike the "normal" Text tools, no text layer will be available with editable text (no going back once the text is committed). With the Text Mask tools, once the text is committed, the font information becomes a selection and is no longer editable text.

3. You can press Ctrl(⌘)+Enter(Return) to change from Quick Mask mode to a selection, or as soon as you choose a tool other than the Type Mask tool, the Quick Mask text becomes a selection marquee. You have no special layer here, so there's no way to save this except as a channel. To help compensate for this, however, click on the Create a new layer icon at the bottom of the Layers palette. Choose the Brush tool from the toolbox, and pick a weird brush (the Chalk 60-pixel brush is chosen in Figure 20.47). On the Options bar, set a low Flow (7%), and choose a light color to make a rough, chalky design as you paint in the word-as-selection. If you prefer, press Ctrl(⌘)+H to view the text without the "marching ants." Don't forget that the selection is only hidden, but still active. When you're finished, press Ctrl(⌘)+D to deselect the selection.

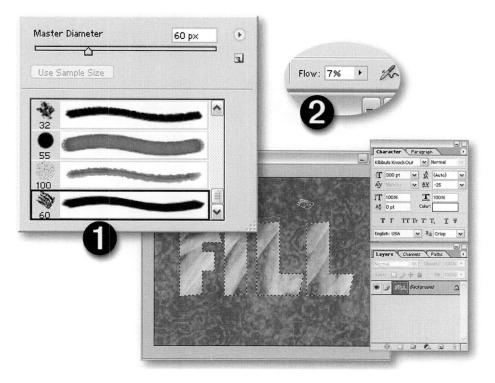

Figure 20.47   Paint across the selection to add finishing touches to a text selection created with a Type Mask tool.

4. (Optional) Click the Add a layer style icon at the bottom of the Layers palette, and choose Bevel and Emboss. In the Layer Style dialog box, choose Pillow Emboss from the Style drop-down list at the top of the dialog box options. Click on OK. On the Layers palette, play with the Fill slider. Notice that if you lower the fill, the color of the text becomes transparent, but the Pillow Emboss effect is still visible.

Picking Extended Characters

How do you enter something like a cents symbol? For Window users, a good place to start is the Character Map (found under Programs, Accessories, System Tools). I actually like having a shortcut to this little utility on my desktop because I frequently use it to see what kind of unusual characters might exist within a particular font. The character choices are especially abundant now that most Adobe products ship with Open Type Fonts (these font files have an .otf file extension). The Mac OS uses the Art Director's Toolkit. Here's a brief exercise to show how you can use these utilities to help type unusual characters that are not displayed on your keyboard:

Typing Extended Characters

1. Open the Two_cents.tif file from the Examples/Chap17 folder on the companion CD. As you can see in Figure 20.48, you need to type **2¢** at the bottom of this image.

Figure 20.48   We need to add the text *2¢*. The number 2 is easy enough, but what about the ¢ symbol?

2. Windows users, go to the Start menu and choose Programs, Accessories, System Tools, Character Map. In the Character Map dialog box, locate and choose the symbol you need. Most standard fonts will display these characters, whereas shareware fonts and Pi fonts will probably not have a cents symbol at all. When you click the character, the extended keyboard command for the cents symbol is displayed in the lower-right corner of the Character Map dialog box. At the bottom right of Figure 20.49, you can see that if you hold down the Alt key while you type **0162** (this number must be typed using the numeric keypad area of the keyboard), the result will be a cents symbol. You also can double-click the symbol to place it in the Characters To Copy box. Then click the Copy button. Back in Photoshop, you can paste the symbol into the document using the Text tool.

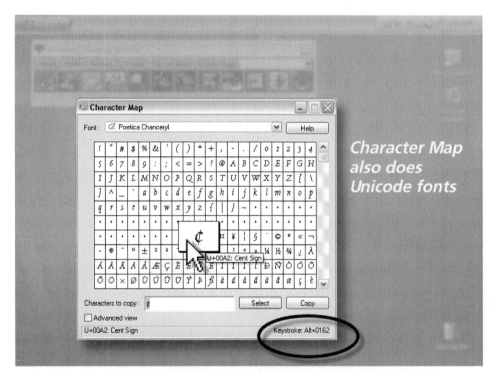

Figure 20.49   In Windows, use the Character Map to locate the character, and use either the Character to copy option or note the extended keyboard command for typing the character.

3. The Mac OS X, shown in Figure 20.50, licenses the Art Director's Toolkit, which does what Character Map does and more.

20

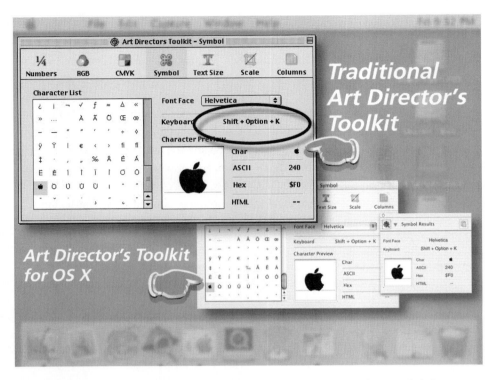

Figure 20.50   Use the Art Director's Toolkit on the Mac OS to access the extended characters.

4. Pick a foreground color for your text. Choose the Horizontal Text tool from the toolbox. Choose a font and font size, and type **2**. Then either choose Ctrl(⌘)+V to paste the character, or hold down the Alt(Opt) key while typing **0162** to type the cents symbol. If the symbol doesn't appear, the font you chose may not support that symbol. Hey, then choose another font that *will*. See Figure 20.51 for the finished image. Don't forget to press Ctrl(⌘)+Enter(Return) to commit the text to a layer.

Suggested Reading

Here are a few good resources for more information about using type:

- Sean Cavanaugh is the author of *Digital Type Design Guide*—this author's favorite book on type. On Sean's Web site, you'll find lots of very useful information, fonts at 100% off the regular price, a bookstore, and links to some of the best type-oriented sites.

- Another good book you should buy on the new age of electronic typesetting is *The Computer Is Not a Keyboard* (Peachpit Press), a thin (about $10) feature-packed book that starts you thinking about using text and typefaces instead of the left-justified, carriage return typewriter. It was written by Robin Williams (no, *she* is *not* the comedian).

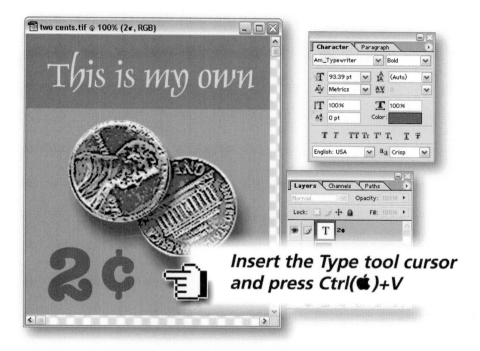

Figure 20.51   Finito. Makes cents to me!

Summary

You've taken a Photoshop-sized tour of typefaces and of basic design using type, and put some of that knowledge to practical use.

Just as you use imaging to communicate ideas to your viewers, text is certainly another obvious way to communicate. You would do well to perfect your skills in effectively using type. And that means practice, observe, study, and read books on the topic. Besides, when you create a wonderful image that also needs text, you surely want to strengthen your image by using that text in a professional way.

In the next chapter, you'll see how to bring all this fancy text and images and charts and more into the physical world. Printing your work can be simple or difficult, depending on the occasion and need. We'll take a trip through different kinds of printers, the anatomy of a dot of ink, and all the stuff that constitutes *output* (using Photoshop).

C h a p t e r 21

Output

What's written here is a lecture cleverly disguised as a reference guide, which is cleverly disguised as a chapter. Specifically, a chapter on output. We tend to use the term *output* these days because hard copy isn't

In this chapter, you'll learn

- How Photoshop uses interpolation in output
- How halftone output represents continuous tone images
- How PostScript manages halftoning and image resolution
- How to choose the right printing options
- How to record to film with Photoshop

necessarily rendered to paper. You can print to film, glossy paper, T-shirt transfers—there are oodles of ways you can get an image off your monitor and onto something in the physical world.

Throughout this chapter, I'm going to hand you tools in the guise of math formulas and nuggets of information that will do the following things:

- Give you the confidence that your printing skills are top-notch.
- Give you the straight story on many of the parameters surrounding the action of output, not the myths floating around that cause you headaches and make your work look crummy.

Let's begin with a simple term that you will hear more and more often as you gain experience with both personal and commercial printing. That word is *interpolation.*

Interpolation Means "Interpretation"

Interpolation is such a neat-sounding word, isn't it? Many of us have a vague notion (within context) of what interpolation means, but you need to understand *precisely* what it means when you're using it on your work.

Interpolation, in computer graphics, is an application's *interpretation* of what something should look like, especially when it does not have sufficient data to carry out your request. Interpolation is always an *averaging* process of some kind. For example, suppose that you have a color image that is 4 pixels wide and 4 pixels high. You want the image to be twice the size: 8 pixels by 8 pixels.

No program on earth will create the new image using sensitivity and artistic talent. The reason is obvious: Computers have neither talent nor intuition; these are human qualities. This is why *you* run the computer, and not the other way around!

When you resize an image up or down, Photoshop searches for data to help support the application's decision on how the resized image will look. You determine how extensively Photoshop uses interpretation—how much Photoshop searches to come up with new data for the image.

Bicubic Interpolation

Bicubic interpolation is the most sophisticated and elegant of Photoshop's resizing methods. This method also requires the most processing power, although in 2004, you probably will not notice even the slightest lag while Photoshop interpolates because our computers are so powerful. Figure 21.1 shows an image that is 4 pixels high and 4 pixels wide (outstanding art, it's not), with 2 horizontal and 2 vertical pixels containing a color. I've drawn imaginary grids on the images to help you visualize what's going on here.

The bottom of Figure 21.1 shows what you can expect from Photoshop when you command it to use bicubic interpolation (the default interpolation method) to make this artwork 8 pixels wide by 8 pixels high.

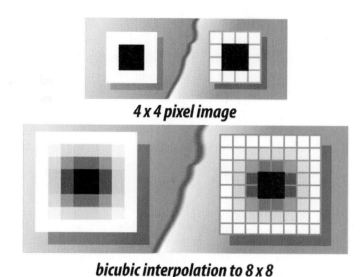

4 x 4 pixel image

bicubic interpolation to 8 x 8

Figure 21.1   By default, Photoshop uses bicubic interpolation to resize an image or an image area.

What you can conclude from bicubic interpolation is that

- The resizing of the art makes the component pixels in the new image appear a tad fuzzy.

- Photoshop makes a smooth transition between background color and foreground color. This effect is particularly important when you work with images whose *pixel count* (the number of pixels in the image) is far greater than the pathetic 16-pixel total we are looking at here.

Okay, so how did Photoshop come up with the intermediate pixels and pixel colors to "fill in" the gap caused by resizing the neighboring pixels? The term *bicubic* here means that Photoshop "looked" in the horizontal, vertical, and diagonal directions, beginning with each pixel and then scouting outward. The new pixels are an *average* of the original pixel color and the original pixel's *neighboring* pixel color. Photoshop performs a weighted average of the pixel and its neighbors along three directions and fits the new pixel between the original pixel and its neighbor.

Note

> **Specifying weighted averages**   When you command Photoshop to use Bicubic Smoother or Bicubic Sharper, you are simply specifying that the weighted average will go toward more contrast (Bicubic Sharper) or less contrast (Bicubic Smoother).

Artistically speaking, you probably want to use bicubic interpolation all the time, whether increasing or decreasing an entire image or a selection. When an image is resized to be smaller, perhaps for display on a Web page, bicubic interpolation makes the new image somewhat fuzzy, too. This happens because you're commanding Photoshop to toss away pixels from the original artwork, and Photoshop must reassign the remaining pixels an average of the original colors at any given point. And this ain't easy, because, again, machines and applications are very poor at guessing. They do the next best thing, which is called *averaging*!

Bilinear Interpolation

When you're making an image larger or smaller, you can also use *bilinear interpolation*. Bilinear interpolation is less processor-intensive than bicubic because it does less examining of pixels before creating or deleting them. However, you probably won't notice a difference in speed if you're using a processor that meets the minimum requirements for Photoshop CS.

The result of bilinear averaging (as shown in Figure 21.2—go peek ahead) might not be obvious with very small images, as my now-famous 8-by-8 pixel artwork demonstrates. However, the new pixels and/or new pixel colors in an image on which you've used bilinear interpolation will not be as faithful to the original image because you commanded Photoshop to perform a decent, but not thorough, investigation to come up with data to be averaged.

Note

> **Whenever there is blurring, use sharpening to correct any fuzziness**   Okay, so this "wisdom" is not all that profound, but you should make it standard operating procedure that whenever you make a dramatic change in the number of pixels in an image, a trip to Photoshop's Sharpen filters is the smartest course of action. Not only is it easier to use the Sharpen command to fake restoring the focus of a large image made smaller, but you also can use it to repair the focus of a small image made larger through interpolation.
>
> I recommend the Unsharp Mask filter at all times, except when you're creating a button or an icon for a Web page—when a 400-by-400 pixel image, for example, is reduced to 32 by 32 pixels. In this case, the Filter, Sharpen, Sharpen command produces an image that's a little exaggerated around the edges, but effectively communicates your artwork at a very small size.

From a math standpoint, the difference between bilinear and bicubic interpolation is that bilinear interpolation does not weight the average of samples it invents from existing image data, and it searches in only two directions—vertical and horizontal—to come up with new colors and/or new pixels. Qualitatively, you have no reason to change this interpolation preference in the General Preferences dialog box. Many applications out there do not even offer the option of bicubic interpolation.

Nearest Neighbor Interpolation

Nearest Neighbor interpolation is the crudest, quickest way to shrink or enlarge an image. The results of this method are so wildly inaccurate that it rightfully earns the name "*no* interpolation"! Nearest Neighbor interpolation might be of some use only if you are increasing the size of an image by an exact, whole amount such as 4 or 16 times an original's size. Using Nearest Neighbor is safer in this situation because pixels are square, and when you increase the height of an image by 2, you are also increasing the width by 2. Therefore, twice the resolution of an image file means 4 times its original size.

Can you see now that the Nearest Neighbor method performs no calculations or averaging, but merely repeats the pixel color at the edge of the original? This can lead to really ugly and inaccurate work, especially if you are increasing the size of an image by a fractional amount, or an amount that lies between two whole integers. In Figure 21.2, I increased the size of my famous 16-pixel artwork from 4 by 4 pixels to 6 by 6. As you can see, the deck was stacked: There is a 100% chance that Nearest Neighbor resampling will return an image area that is incorrect in size when a number such as 150% the original size is applied to the image. The "magic numbers" to use with Nearest Neighbor resampling are 4x, 16x, and multiples thereof.

I've spent a good deal of time running down the types of interpolation Photoshop offers, not because I want you to change your preferences, but because I want you to understand the visual results of interpolation. Photoshop is not the only thing on earth that uses interpolation; image-setting devices (printers) and film recorders use averaging processes, too, and your hard copy of an image can be nicely or ineptly rendered. Now that you understand the difference between methods, you have an important question to ask a service bureau (or tech support) that you did *not* have when you began this chapter.

21

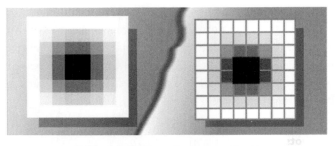

bilinear interpolation to 8 x 8

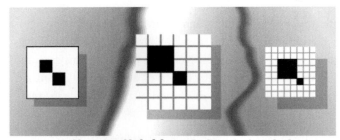

Nearest Neighbor: 4x4 to 6x6 to 8x8

Figure 21.2   Nearest Neighbor evaluation of an image to be shrunk or enlarged will usually create uneven, inaccurate image areas.

Going from Continuous Tones to Halftones

Contrary to what the name might suggest, a halftone is *not* 50% of a tone! Halftones are the lifeblood of commercial printers, and the only way you can get a continuous tone representation on paper. Continuous tones versus halftones merit a brief explanation, and then this section will get into the types of halftones that are at the designer's disposal.

What's the Difference Between Continuous Tones and Halftones?

When you look at the world, and there's a sunset with a rock in the vicinity, you'll see a subtle, *continuous* falloff of light on the rock. There's no sudden, abrupt area of tone missing, as the light gradually changes on the rock's surface. This is a *continuous tone* image because nature has every color with which to display images as the sun emits a spectrum, and your eyes are equipped to receive the parts of the spectrum that depict the rock's tones.

On the other hand, a halftone consists of precisely two colors—not exactly our sunset scene! A halftone consists of an arrangement of dots (the foreground color, usually made up of black toner) against the paper (background) color. So how do you capture photographic qualities when your output is to a laser printer? You simulate continuous tones, and this is done by the software instructing the printer to place dots of toner at different spatial intervals on the paper.

In Figure 21.3, I've created an exaggerated example of what a halftone sample looks like when compared to a continuous tone that traverses the page from black to white.

Caution

> **Dots, Dots, Dots**   Please don't bust my chops over the reality that this book is printed using dots on paper, and therefore could not possibly truly represent a continuous tone. This book is printed at 2,540 dots per inch; you can't even see the dots without a magnifying glass, and there's really no better workaround for showing you the principles of halftoning.

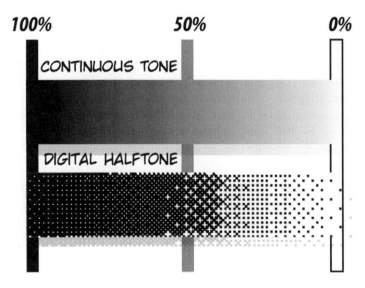

Figure 21.3   A continuous tone image makes seamless transitions between light and dark. Halftone images must rely on the density of toner dots at any given area to simulate a continuous tone.

The pattern you see in the halftone in Figure 21.3 is an exaggeration of what anyone would expect from a laser printer. I think the resolution of the halftone is something like 15 lines per inch—a resolution so coarse you could drive your new car through there and not touch the paint.

We'll get into the mystical term *resolution* shortly and demystify it. Next, let's look at how digital halftone cells help the accuracy with which a halftone image represents reality.

The Digital Halftone Cell

When you learn about halftoning, it is helpful to imagine a grid placed above your original continuous tone work. This imaginary grid helps define every inch on the image in terms of density. Suppose, for example, you have a photo of an ice cream cone against a white background. Slip a screen from a window or a door on top of the photo, and you will see something interesting happen. Pick a cell in the screen; pick it anywhere. Then, look at the tone of the photo that is framed by the cell in the screen window.

If the tone is 50% black, Photoshop and your printer will fill half an invisible, corresponding, digital screen on top of the printed page with a halftone cell that occupies 50% of the cell.

Now here's where it gets weird for a moment. In traditional printing, commercial printers have historically put a physical film screen over a photograph to make a halftoned copy. The halftones are round (usually), and each halftone dot is confined to a predetermined cell in a line of halftone dots. In Figure 21.4, you can see a digital halftone cell compared to a traditional halftone. Digital halftone cells contain square (or rectangular) dots of toner ink, but in this figure you can see how digital halftone cells closely mimic traditional coverage on a piece of paper or film. At the bottom of this figure, you can see the specific coverage amounts.

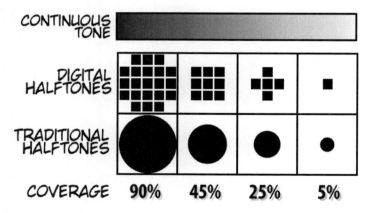

Figure 21.4   Digital halftone cells are filled with a given number of dots that, when viewed together (from a distance!), represent a specific tone.

The following section gets into PostScript technology and how it affects printing. Here are the reasons, among other things, for this excursion into the PostScript world:

- PostScript technology is the only real method of organizing toner dots (or emulsion on film) so that they truly mimic traditional, physical halftone screens.

- Because PostScript technology extends beyond merely organizing dots and into pre-press, you really should know about some math formulas (I'll do the pencil work for you in this chapter) and refer to them if you ever want to make your own camera-ready art from a personal printer for commercial ink-on-paper printing.

PostScript and Image Resolution

It's almost impossible to talk about PostScript rendering of images without talking about image resolution. Many readers have written to me in past years asking me what the input should be for a particular image, and I always have to respond with a question: What is your intended *output* for the file? It makes very little sense to choose an input resolution without first knowing whether the image is going to press, going up on the fridge, or going across the World Wide Web. Let's take a brief look at PostScript technology, and then get involved with *resolution*—both its meaning and how to calculate it.

PostScript as a Halftone Dot Shaper

Using PostScript to render a continuous tone image, you can expect the most faithful of halftone renderings possible today. Other printing technologies put different-sized dots on a page, but they are not organized in screen lines that pressmen use. In Figure 21.5, on the left is a (nearly <g>) continuous tone image of a duck. On the right is a PostScript halftone rendering of the same image. I've used only 30 dots per inch (dpi) on the PostScript duck, which is a foolishly low resolution, but it helps display the individual dots better. Can you see how every tone on the left duck has corresponding-sized dots that, together, represent the continuous tones?

Not long after the invention of the traditional, physical halftone screen, the publishing world yearned for a little more flexibility in *how* a halftone is rendered. Must a single halftone always be circular? When a screen is applied to a continuous tone image at an angle other than right angles, what do you wind up with?

To see the answer to these questions, look at Figure 21.6. Elliptical dots are being used to fill the digital halftone cells, and the screen created by Photoshop is at a 45° angle.

You might want to squint at Figure 21.6 to get a better idea of how stylized a halftone print can be when you use halftone dots that are not circular. We'll get into Photoshop's print options later in this chapter. Many interrelated factors determine the best halftone print of your work. I'll try to cover them all in the least confusing way.

The first factor in image rendering is called *resolution*. Resolution determines how your print looks and also can tell you how many samples per inch you should set your scanner to take.

21

Figure 21.5   A continuous tone image compared to a PostScript rendition of the same image.

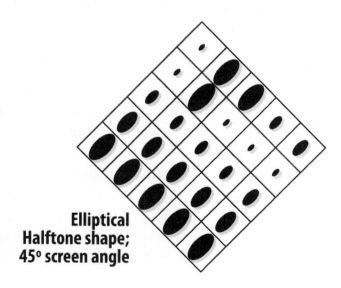

**Elliptical
Halftone shape;
45° screen angle**

Figure 21.6   Photoshop offers six different-shaped halftone dots, one of which is elliptical, plus a custom function, and any angle for the screen you choose.

Image Resolution Is a Fraction

Several accurate analogies could help you better understand the term *resolution* as it applies to computer graphics. I'm going to choose speed—specifically, the speed of a car—to help illustrate this concept.

When you measure the speed of a car, it is conveyed in one set of units over a different set of units, such as 55 miles (a unit of distance) per hour (a unit of time). Image resolution is expressed similarly: Resolution can be defined as units of data over units of distance. When someone tells you that an image is 2" by 2" at 150 pixels/inch, that person is expressing the number of pixels in an inch; this is the resolution of the image.

On the other hand, and unfortunately this happens all too frequently, if someone tells you that an image is 200 pixels by 200 pixels, she has not told you the resolution of the image at all! How many pixels per inch is this 200-by-200 pixel artwork? A pixel (short for *pic*ture *el*ement) is merely a placeholder, an entity of no fixed size that holds a color value. For example, Red: 128, Green: 214, and Blue: 78 is the best description of a pixel that anyone could come up with. But *resolution* is the expression of how *many* pixels you want per inch.

If someone tells you that an image is supposed to be 2" by 2", you need to ask her what the resolution is before you can create such an image. Conversely, if you are told that the resolution of an image is 300 ppi, you had better ask this person what are the physical dimensions of the image, as expressed in inches, picas, centimeters, or whatever.

Here's an important truth to remember when working with image dimensions:

> **Image dimensions are inversely proportional to image resolution**.
> Because a pixel is the unit of measurement for the numerator of the resolution fraction (for example, 65 pixels/inch), and because a pixel is only a placeholder, you have the flexibility of changing the size of an image by changing the resolution. And the visual information in the image will not change at all. For example, a 10" by 10" image at 100 pixels/inch can also be displayed as a 5" by 5" image at 200 pixels per inch.
>
> You can tell that no image detail has changed when you change resolution because the size of the image file remains the same (in other words, the total number of pixels doesn't change either). Keep this Profound Wisdom handy when you lay out printed work, and you will accomplish the assignment 100% correctly all the time.

Let's take a stroll through a scanner's interface and put all these nuggets of advice I'm writing into order!

21

Scanning to the Right Size

I have a fictitious assignment here that involves scanning a piece of wood to 8 1/2" by 11" with 1/4" trim around each side (so I need 9" by 11 1/2" scanned). As I mentioned in the preceding section, a pixel is a placeholder that takes up space only after you have entered it as the numerator of the resolution fraction. Now here's a key that will unlock many graphics doors for you:

> **An image expressed only in the number of pixels it contains is an absolute amount.** You learned in the preceding section that resolution is somewhat flexible: You can decrease dimensions and increase resolution, and the number of pixels will remain the same. A good way to measure images destined for the Web or other screen presentations is by the number of pixels in the image. For example, a 640 by 480 screen capture will always contain 307,200 pixels, regardless of which monitor it is displayed on.

Figure 21.7 shows a number of callouts that I'll explain shortly. What you're looking at is the TWAIN interface (a "corridor" between the scanning hardware and Photoshop, the imaging software). The piece of wood shown in the figure is a preview of the object I'm going to scan.

Let's begin examining this scanner interface based on my need for a 9" by 11 1/2" scan of some wood. First question, right? "At what resolution do you need the scan?"

I need the scan to be at 200 pixels per inch because my inkjet printer's resolution is 600 dots of ink per inch, and the guy at Epson told me that I should scan at one third the final output resolution. This is not a number that is carved in stone, but typically, for non-PostScript inkjet printers that use error diffusion as a rendering technique (which is impossible to quantify because the dots of ink are not arranged in rows), one third the output should be your scanning input.

Let's begin with explanations of the callouts:

1. **Color mode.** This feature should seem familiar; you see a Mode drop-down list every time you press Ctrl(⌘)+N in Photoshop. I've chosen RGB color here; however, sometimes you may want to scan in Grayscale, and most scanners offer this option.

Note

> **File sizes**   Grayscale mode images are one third the saved file size of RGB images. The reason for this is that RGB images have three channels of image information, while grayscale images have only one channel (brightness).

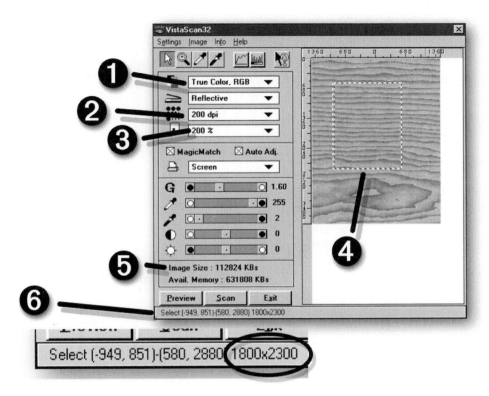

Figure 21.7   Your scanner's interface might not look like this one, but you will find the same options on most models.

2. **Resolution.** I want to get into a quarrel with scanner manufacturers because they label the resolution in *dpi* (dots per inch), and scanners are actually scanning *samples* per inch (or *pixels* per inch). A dot is *not* a pixel. I've set the resolution to 200 here because the final output to my ancient inkjet printer is 600 dpi.

3. **Scale.** Most scanners will allow you to zoom in on whatever is on the scanner's platen. Because I have a large sample of wood here, I want the scan to be 1 to 1 (100%). But if you, for example, wanted to scan a postage stamp and print it at 8 1/2" by 11", you would use the scale option to really zoom in to the stamp. Scaling does affect resolution. If you scale a scan at 200%, for example (as it is in the figure), you are scanning four times the information that you would be scanning at 100% (twice the width, twice the height).

4. **Cropping area.** Scanners enable you to pick only the portion of the sampled object you want to capture with the scan. My scanner (this is *not* shown in the figure) will tell me in pixels or in inches how large my crop box is. Generally, you choose the interface's cropping tool and then drag to select the part of the image

you want scanned. Most scanners also come with rulers in the preview window, so guesswork is not required.

5. **Image size.** This feature tells you how much RAM is needed to hold and acquire the image and is also a good indicator of what the saved file size is. You'll note in this figure that the image size is about 11MB. This means that to scan from within Photoshop, I need to have at least this amount (ideally about three times the amount) of RAM and scratch disk space available. With today's systems, this is not an issue like it used to be a few years ago.

6. **Absolute measurement.** As described earlier, the height and width of an image as measured in pixels provide an incomplete description. I have 1,800 pixels in width by 2,300 pixels in height marqueed in the preview window. What makes these numbers meaningful is that I'm scanning at 200 samples/inch. This means that 1,800/200 = 9 (inches), and 2,300/200 = 11.5 (inches).

End of story! You hit the Scan button, and in moments you can save the perfectly proportioned image to hard disk and print it later.

I've overlooked a few scanning issues in this section, such as interface options for contrast gamma control, saturation, and so on. My belief is to always "get it right in the camera" so your Photoshop correction work is not prolonged, but I've honestly never seen a scanner preview that was good enough to evaluate corrections you might make using the interface controls. If an image looks halfway decent in preview, I scan it and then use Photoshop's features to make the image perfect.

We need to put the world of resolution and the world of PostScript together now so that you have some sort of guide to follow when you're working with *your* scanner and *your* output device (not mine).

The Input/Output Chart

In Figure 21.8, I've put together a short list of scanning resolutions, the resolution of the printed work, and the expected file size of an acquired image. All these values presume that you are using PostScript technology; non-PostScript rendering technology is very difficult to measure because non-PostScript printing does not follow any of the rules of traditional screening.

When rules in science are followed, the results are totally predictable. The same is true of PostScript technology: There are rules that govern its operation, and the next section presents you with the math you need to create the best camera-ready prints.

Various Output and Input Resolutions

FOR A 4" BY 6" IMAGE AT 1:1 SAMPLING VERSUS PRINTING RESOLUTION

Resolution of Printed Work	Lines per Inch Output Device Uses	Recommended Scanning Resolution	File Size
300 dpi	45 lpi	90 to 100 samples/inch	570 KB
600 dpi	85 lpi	170 samples/inch	1.99 MB
1200 dpi	125 lpi	225 samples/inch	3.48 MB
2450 dpi	133 lpi	266 samples/inch	4.86 MB

Figure 21.8 Choose the printer resolution that most closely matches your printer, and you can see how large you should scan and what the line-screen frequency should be.

A Whole Bunch of Printing Math

Before you even consider making your own camera-ready prints, you should pay a call on the fellows who are going to make the printing plates and ask the following questions:

- What is the line-screen frequency and angle?
- What are the top-most and bottom-most tones your presses can hold?

In Figure 21.9, you can see the "times 2" rule. Commercial press houses do not measure the resolution of a halftoned image in dots. Images are measured in *lines* of dots, and the expression *lpi* (lines per inch) is relevant to your work.

Printer Line Frequency (in lpi) x 2 = Image Resolution (in pixels/inch)

Figure 21.9 Your image's resolution has to be twice the print house's line-screen frequency.

If a press house tells you that its line-screen frequency is 100 lpi, then according to the formula in Figure 21.9, you need to scan an image (or modify the resolution using Photoshop's Image, Image Size command) at 200 samples (pixels) per inch. If you do this, your halftoned image will be optimal.

21

Toner dots from a laser printer are fused to the paper; the page is instantly dry. Such is not the case with offset printing, where *ink* is rolled onto paper. Ink bleeds, and very few press houses can hold a screen that contains 100% black. The area on the printed page would be a puddle of ink. On the bright side, there is a screen limit to the lowest density of the screen (the white point): 100% white has to meet the next darker value, and the closer you keep the white point to your second brightest tone, the more even the print will look. And that point leads us to Figure 21.10.

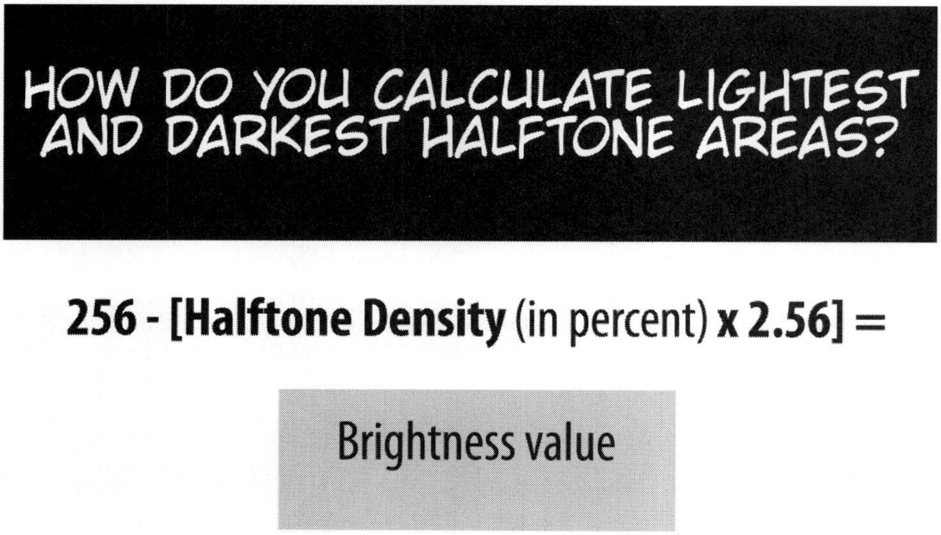

HOW DO YOU CALCULATE LIGHTEST AND DARKEST HALFTONE AREAS?

$$256 - [\textbf{Halftone Density (in percent) x 2.56}] =$$

Brightness value

Figure 21.10   Print presses are wet, and laser prints are dry. Somehow, you need to change the tonal scheme of a print so that the print house's presses don't leave a puddle of ink on your work.

When you've balanced your image to your liking, make a copy of it, and perform some tone reduction so the press house can make plates from your work. Let's say the pressman tells you that the presses can hold 10% (90% black) and 97% (3% white) on the top end of the tonal range.

Let's plug these values into the equation in Figure 21.10.

$$256 - [90 \times 2.56] = 230.4 = \textbf{25.6}$$

Great. What are you going to do with this 25.6 number? You're going to press Ctrl(⌘)+L in Photoshop to display the Levels command. Then, see where the Output Levels area is at the bottom? You type **25.6** in the left field.

Similarly,

$$256 - [3 \times 2.56] = 7.68 = \textbf{248.32}$$

You type this number in the right Output Levels field. Click on OK, save the image, print a copy, and cart it off to the print house.

Now, there is a trade-off between the number of shades of gray that a laser printer can simulate and the line frequency of the print. This issue might not be of value in your work with a commercial printer, but it does serve as an intro here for personal printing—how to optimize that image that you're going to send to your folks.

Lines/Inch Versus Shades of Gray

This section header sounds like a weird football game, doesn't it? Actually, you can do some fun stuff and even bring certain images up to print house specs if you understand the relationship between line-screen frequency and the number of tones a printer can simulate using digital halftone cells.

In Figure 21.11, you can see the equation. We'll plug some numbers into the equation shortly.

$$\frac{\text{Printer Resolution (in dpi)}}{\text{Printer Line Frequency (in lpi)}} = n^2 = \text{shades of gray}$$

Figure 21.11   You can change the number of grayscale values if you are willing to sacrifice image resolution.

Sometimes, you might want a "special effect" to enhance the visual content of a print. If you reduce the lines per inch the printer produces, you can get this effect and also increase the number of shades the printer is capable of producing. You're not changing the resolution of the printer; you're simply playing with the input.

Let's say your printer is capable of 600 dpi; a PostScript printer will output about 85 lines per inch. So let's plug these numbers into the equation:

600 (dpi)/85 (lpi) = 7.06(squared) = 49 unique shades

21

Forty-nine unique shades of black will probably not get you where you're going. Most grayscale images have almost 200 unique tones. Let's try lowering the line screen to 45 lpi (a fairly low but acceptable resolution):

$$600 \text{ (dpi)}/45 \text{ (lpi)} = 13.33\text{(squared)} = \textbf{196}$$

Whoa! Not bad! This means that practically no banding will be visible when you're representing a continuous tone image at 45 lines per inch.

Hey, how else can you make personal tack-em-on-the-corkboard prints look super-special with limited resolution and money?

PCL Printing and Error Diffusion

Because the demands of PostScript printing are higher than non-PostScript printing, we would be nuts to ignore the *alternatives* to PostScript printing.

Hewlett-Packard has a very decent Resolution Enhancement Technology that belongs to the Printer Command Language (PCL) family of rendering technologies. Every printer manufacturer has a different technology, but HP seems to hold the lead on high-fidelity, non-PostScript rendering.

On the left in Figure 21.12 is the duck created using HP printing technology at 30 dpi (to make the rendering technique visible to the eye). The results of the technology are not as elegant as PostScript printing, but the duck definitely has halftone shades across its body. The halftones are not really good enough to make a press screen, but again, these prints are for you and your family, and not the world.

On the right in Figure 21.12, you see a duck rendered using error-diffusion printing. You can do error-diffusion printing from several applications other than Photoshop, or you can actually turn an image into an error-diffusion print by using Photoshop's Image, Mode, Bitmap command and by then printing it as a normal image. Error-diffusion printing makes a soft, pleasing image using non-PostScript technology, but you absolutely *cannot* take one of these prints to a press house without getting laughed out the door! Error-diffusion prints are not rendered in lines, and they have no regard for digital halftone cells.

Mezzotints

A line of digital halftone cells is not the only way to represent continuous tones. You can use mezzotint screens as well. Mezzotinting is not as refined a printing process as PostScript, and a mezzotint image is usually highly stylized; your attention can be torn between the visual content of the image and the way the print is executed using lines, dots, and "worms" (more on this in a moment).

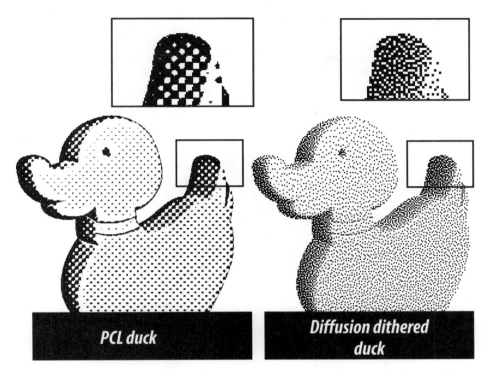

Figure 21.12   Printer Command Language and error-diffusion printing are only two of the non-PostScript methods for making an interesting personal print.

One newspaper in America refuses to use halftoned photographs of anyone; pictures of financial moguls are done using a mezzotint screen. Figure 21.13 is a cold-hearted parody of the newspaper, using a line-type mezzotint. As you can see, the screening process is quite visible, but you can make out the face of the gentleman, and the combination of the two properties is aesthetically pleasing.

Mezzotinting using *stochastic screening* produces tiny shapes that look like worms, and the patterns actually are measured in worms per inch. Figure 21.14 shows a stochastic print. Stochastic printing is all computer-generated; print houses cannot duplicate a pattern that shifts according to the input brightness of an image at any given point. To the right of the stochastic duck is a line-screen mezzotint that shows highlights going at one cut angle, and the deeper shades have a different line direction. Both images are mezzotints; the difference is that one uses stochastic screening and the other uses a line cut.

21

THE WALL STREE

' never grow up"   *Thursday, July 27th, 2004*   **$5.00**- *hey, it's 2004 now*

*Pool toy tycoon
Bob Condo*

**INFLATIO
AFFECTS
TOY TRAI**

IN A STUNNING tur
of events in the child-
ren's inflatable toy m
ket, Bob "call me Bol
Condo caused a panic
on Wall St. today whe
he announced that inr
tuhes the life blood

ATES TO BUY PANAMA

Figure 21.13   Inflation actually has a positive effect on most pool toys.

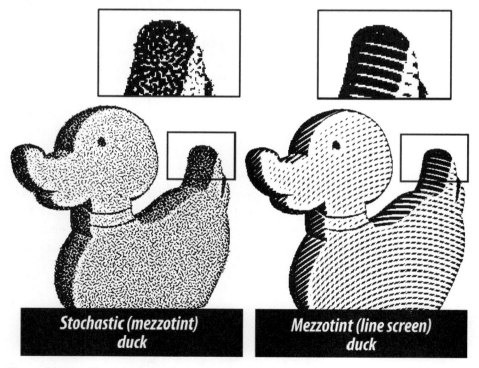

Figure 21.14   If you don't mind a pattern competing for the visual content of an image, mezzotinting could be your ticket.

After this glowing review of other screening types, particularly mezzotints, I have some good news and some bad news. The bad news is that Photoshop has a Mezzotint filter under Filter, Pixelate that doesn't come within miles of the quality effects and options Adobe's products are known for. You could not create the mezzotint effects I've shown you in the past two figures using Photoshop's Mezzotint filter.

The good news is that Andromeda Software offers a comprehensive assortment of different mezzotint screens that give you complete control over line frequency, angle, and so on. The Screens filters are available for download online at `http://www.andromeda .com`; all you need is a credit card and a fast Internet connection.

So far, we've spent a good amount of time on the fine points of printing, but not much explanation about how you print from Photoshop. Allow me to correct this oversight....

Printing Options in Photoshop

Now I'd like to cover two categories of output that are under Photoshop's roof. First, printing from Photoshop is not as effortless as, say, printing from Microsoft Word. But then again, you're printing *art* from Photoshop, while you're printing formatted text from Word—and there's a chasm of sophistication you would need to ford to bring the two application printing engines even remotely closer together.

Let's first look at how Photoshop lets you know when the resolution of a file you want to print needs tuning.

The Image Size Command: A Career-Saver

Remember the "image dimensions decrease as resolution increases" line a few pages back? Well, Photoshop is a very strict enforcer of correct image dimensions. It's a waste of paper to allow an image to be printed with clipping, just because the dimensions were not set up correctly.

Figure 21.15 shows an image I want to print. Before printing, however, I clicked on the Document Sizes area in the workspace, and a frame popped up telling me that this image will print right off the edges of my paper.

Figure 21.16 shows that when I pressed Ctrl($\mathcal{H}$)+P, to my surprise, I got my wrist slapped! Photoshop pops up a warning every time you try to print something that will run off the page.

Now, there's an easy way to make this dolphin picture print without changing a pixel of the visual content. Photoshop is capable of resampling an image, but this means you change the number of pixels, interpolation takes place, and you print a fuzzy image.

21

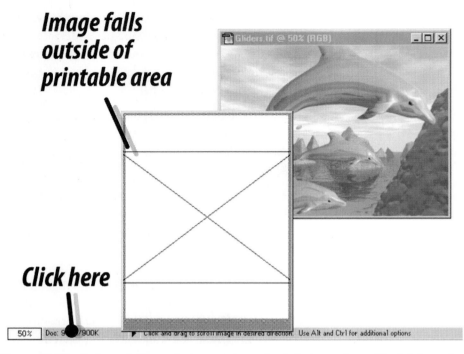

Figure 21.15   Before printing, make it a practice to check the image frame. The "x" shows the extent of the image when printed at the current dimensions and resolution.

Figure 21.16   Choose to cancel printing if you get this warning.

The solution lies in the first math formula in this chapter: If you increase the resolution of the image, you decrease the physical dimensions. Choose Image, Image Size to access the options for changing the resolution of the image. We will be resizing, and not resampling; there's an important distinction here.

What happens when you pour a quart of water into a 12-ounce glass? You get a spill, and this is sort of what happens when you decrease the dimensions of the image to the extent that the resolution is now far higher than your printer can print.

This "spill" is *okay*, though; the excess printing information is simply discarded during printing time, and you've lost perhaps 15 seconds on a print job by doing this. But I feel it's better to waste a little print spooling time than to go changing the visual content of the image forever. Check out Figure 21.17. Notice that I've decreased the dimensions so that the image will print to an 8 1/2" by 11" page. And do *not* check the Resample Image box in the Image Size command.

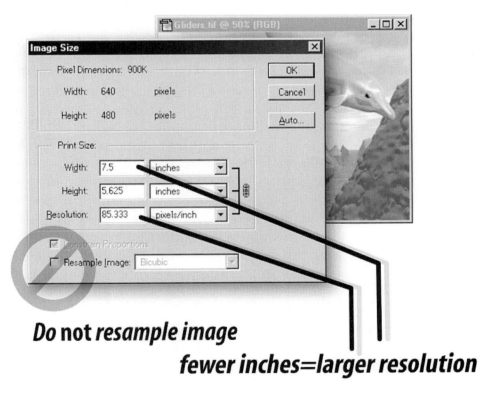

Do not resample image
fewer inches=larger resolution

Figure 21.17   Increase the resolution so the physical dimensions of the artwork will fit on a page.

21

If you're printing to a PostScript device, you will want to choose File, Print with Preview. We can't go into every printing option within the span of one chapter, but how about the two most important ones? Click the Show More Options check box, and then choose Output from the drop-down list.

In Figure 21.18, you can see the Page Setup dialog box. You probably want to click on Screen after all we've been through in this chapter on screening. From the Screen option, you get to pick the line frequency and angle, as well as the shape of the dots on the page. Also, you might want to enable Corner Crop Marks because your art might not take up the whole page, and you might want to frame your work (so that it is centered in the frame).

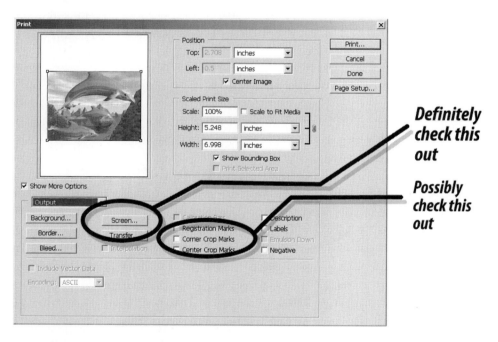

Figure 21.18   Photoshop has printing options galore, but you might need to use only a few of them.

Let's look at what you'll see when you click on the Screen button. In Figure 21.19, I make recommendations based on a grayscale image for a 600 dpi PostScript printer. For a 600 dpi printer, 85 lpi is correct, and the use of diagonal screens (such as 45°) has been a long-standing tradition among physical plate-making experts. It seems that when you run a diagonal screen, folks are less likely to notice the individual dots of ink. Try running a 90° screen on a print, and you'll see what I mean.

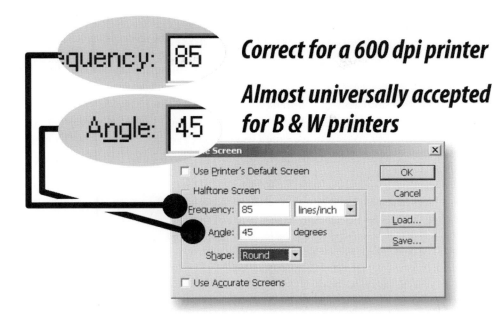

Figure 21.19   Use these settings for a 600 dpi PostScript printer.

Ah, at last we arrive at my favorite part of Photoshop imaging. It's called *film recording*, and it might or might not even involve Photoshop, unless the service bureau you use owns Photoshop. Film recording is sort of the opposite process to scanning. With film recording, you're taking a digital image and turning it into a 35mm slide (or other film format). The results are breathtaking, and the steps you need to know are just around the corner.

Film Recording

Film recording from digital media is not a new process. If you hear a lot about it these days, it's simply because the price of film recorders has come down so much that if you have two grand in your pocket, you could own a decent film recorder. Film recording has been fed by PowerPoint users for the past decade, but increasingly, fine artists have taken to putting images on a slide. It's an eminently portable medium, and the colors are usually to die from!

Steps to Film Recording

Pick up the telephone book, and find a *slide service bureau*. Regular service bureaus do imagesetting work and set type and do layouts, but it's the slide service bureau that owns the expensive machinery that will turn your Photoshop work into a pocket-sized wonder. You can expect to pay around $8 per slide, and if you have a lot of work, you might negotiate a discount.

The first step to film recording your work is to make certain that the image has the correct *aspect ratio*. Fine—what's an aspect ratio? Your image is going from data on a disk to a 35mm slide, let's say. Chances are pretty good that your image does not have the 3:2 aspect ratio that belongs to a 35mm slide. And a service bureau is not responsible for adding a background or creatively cropping your image. You don't want this to happen, the service bureau doesn't exactly welcome a request for clairvoyance, and whipping your image into the proper aspect ratio is really very simple.

To give you an example of the best way to discover how far off you are with the image, press Alt(Opt)+click on the Document sizes area of the workspace, as shown in Figure 21.20. My wind-up toy picture isn't even close to having a 3:2 aspect ratio.

Figure 21.20   You decide how your image is turned into film. Try to make it easy on the service bureau, and invest some time in making the proportion the same as 35mm film.

In my opinion, the easiest way to format an image properly is to add a background to both the horizontal and vertical aspect of the image. In Figure 21.21, you can see the fail-safe method for picking out a background color that will not clash with the image. You press Alt(Opt)+click with the Eyedropper tool to pick up a background color that already exists in the image. How much more harmonious can you get?

Figure 21.21   Alt(Opt)+click over a neutral area of the image to set the background you'll soon create.

Now, let's pay another trip to the Image Size dialog box. This time, we are deliberately going to change the dimensions with absolutely no regard to the resulting resolution of the file. Why? Because film recorders don't care about image resolution—only image size, as measured in megabytes.

In Figure 21.22, the Resample Image box is unchecked. I've typed 1.7 (inches) in the Height field, and the Width field changes to 2.2 (inches). These are approximate numbers. This is good; this means that we can stop by the Canvas Size command and add to both the vertical and horizontal measurement of the image.

Choose Image, Canvas Size, and type **3** in the Width field and **2** in the Height field. Now, you have a 3:2 image (see Figure 21.23)! Click on OK.

21

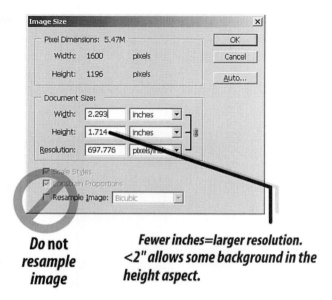

Do not resample image

Fewer inches=larger resolution. <2" allows some background in the height aspect.

Figure 21.22   Keep the Width under 3 and keep the height under 2, and then you can add background color to both aspects of the image.

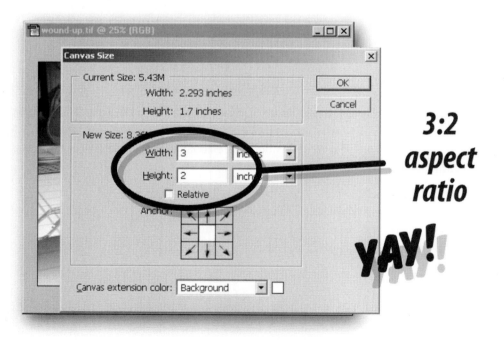

3:2 aspect ratio

YAY!

Figure 21.23   The aspect of the image is now ideal for film recording simply because you added background to the image.

When you're working with aspect ratio, remember this truth:

> **Aspect ratio follows an order: The first number is the width of the image.** When we speak of aspect ratios, the first number before the colon is the width, and the following number is the height. Therefore, a 2:3 aspect ratio is *not* the same as a 3:2. And most service bureaus would prefer that you give them a wider-than-tall image because the film recorder that's writing the film, line by line, has fewer traverses to make if the image is wide.

In Figure 21.24, you can see that I've added a little texture to the background areas of the image. You can do this too, by filling the background area with a texture. Choose the Magic Wand tool, set to a Tolerance of 1 with no antialiasing, and click in the background area to select the background border area. Then fill the area with a pattern (you can choose from plenty of pattern tiles in the BOUTONS folder on the Companion CD), or add texture through the Filter, Texture, Texturizer filter.

Figure 21.24   Get the image onto a Zip disk, and truck it on over to your slide service bureau.

I never really mentioned what is a good image size for film recording. I've had 900KB images written to slides, and the subject matter was simple enough that the lack of image information wasn't noticeable. After experimenting for about a year with my slide service bureau, I've found that a 4.5MB image renders pretty well to film, 12MB is noticeably better, and 18MB will get you the best image you could imagine.

21

Here's a secret: Most Raster Image Processors (RIPs, the software that enables a film recorder to render to film) will interpolate an image that is smaller than 18MB or so. This means that unless your image is 18MB, do not perform any interpolation by yourself with Photoshop. Interpolation once is bad enough, but if it happens twice to your image before it is recorded, the resulting 35mm slide might be fuzzy.

Summary

I hope you now know why I didn't call this chapter "Printing." There are more ways of getting your data onto hard copy than you can shake a stick at. This chapter covered three methods: camera-ready for commercial printing, personal printing, and film recording. By the time this book comes out, I'm sure there will be a score of other output devices that'll make your work take its rightful place as art in the many fields that require graphics.

The following chapter takes you beyond physical output and into the Wonderful World of the Web. Ever wonder how to create an animation? How about one of those slick Web page buttons that changes when you hover over it? Get ready to put your designs into motion in the pages to follow!

Part VII

Working for the Web with ImageReady

Chapter 22

Animations and Rollovers

The World Wide Web is the place where media converges: Sight meets sound, animation meets static graphics, and buttons respond to your cursor movements. It should come as no surprise, then, that

In this chapter, you'll learn

- Guidelines for creating animations with Photoshop
- How to use masks to animate dissolving text
- How to use displacement maps to create animations
- How to create and animate a seamless texture
- How to create simple rollovers with ImageReady
- How to slice images with Photoshop

Photoshop, the preeminent resource for still image editing, also can play a hand in creating other media types. Photoshop is especially useful for this purpose when teamed with its partner ImageReady. In this chapter, you'll see how to create stunning graphics that move when your audience visits your site and appreciates your work!

Animation with Photoshop

To those who see Photoshop as a tool to edit static images, using Photoshop to create animation might seem like using a backhoe to flip a pancake. However, when used in tandem with ImageReady, Photoshop is actually an *excellent* tool for creating short animations for the Web. In this chapter, you get first-hand experience in making three different kinds of exciting, dynamic GIF animations for a Web site. For each animation, you use Photoshop to create the graphics that compose the animation and then switch over to ImageReady to assemble the images into a compact, eye-catching file.

In the sections that follow, you'll have the opportunity to learn how to make text dissolve before your very eyes. Then you'll move on to using Photoshop's largely overlooked displacement mapping capability to create a sequence of images for use in a GIF animation. Then you'll learn how to animate seamless tiling textures to create a scene of fog drifting by your porthole window.

But before we start creating a specific animation, let's look at a list of do's and don'ts to follow when you create Web animation.

When you are approaching an animation project, keep these guidelines in mind:

- **Minimize the dimensions** of the animation, by animating only what you have to. Don't try to animate the whole screen. Several small animations on a page work much better than one huge, "undownloadable-in-your-lifetime" animation.

- **Limit the number of colors** you use. Just as with non-animated GIFs, the fewer colors you use, the smaller the file size.

- **Keep file sizes as small as possible.** Whenever you work with animation—Web animation in particular—keeping finished file sizes as small as possible is of paramount importance. Large animations download slowly, play jerkily, and annoy viewers so much that they will frequently start muttering unkind things about your family while they frantically click on the Stop button or a link to any other site they can find.

As you work your way through the chapter, you will see how to put these guidelines into use.

Creating Animated Dissolving Text

In movies and on TV, one of the classic visual special effects used to get your attention or to signal a change of scene is the *dissolve*. In a dissolve, the image simultaneously breaks up into small pieces and fades. Dissolves are very effectively used in all kinds of multimedia, Web, and video projects.

The fundamental concepts and processes that go into making a dissolve animation are universal; only the details differ from project to project and medium to medium. Once you've had a chance to get your feet wet creating the GIF animation we've lined up for you, you'll be able to approach with confidence almost any animation project that involves something melting away into nothingness.

Using Masks to Create Dissolves

Consider this chapter a *learning* experience. Do not adjust your dial, and read on to the first assignment. In this exercise, you'll create six masks that will be used to generate the dissolve effect. Of course, you can create as many or as few steps as you want, but six will be enough to get the dissolve effect across visually, without adding inordinately to the saved file size.

Beginning a Dissolve-Type Animation

1. Open the Dissolve.psd image from the Examples/Chap22 folder on the companion CD, and save it to your hard disk using the same name and file type. Double-click the Hand tool to maximize the view of the file in Photoshop.

Insider

> If you right-click (Macintosh: hold Ctrl and click) on the title bar and choose Image Size, you'll notice that the image is 190 by 56 pixels by 72 pixels per inch in resolution. We've purposely kept the dimensions small to ensure that the finished animation will download quickly. Click Cancel to close the Image Size dialog box.
>
> A quick look at the Layers palette shows two layers: the Background layer and a layer named Window. The Background layer contains a texture with a gray rectangular shape in the middle. The space occupied by the Background layer will contain an animation of dissolving text that you will create. The dissolving text animation will be framed by the static Window artwork on the Window layer.

2. First, you need to create channels for the different stages of the dissolve effect. Click the Channels tab to view the Channels palette. Notice that besides the Red, Green, and Blue channels, there's already an additional channel called Screen, which you will use a little later. Hold down the Alt(Opt) key, and click the Create a new channel icon at the bottom of the Channels palette. Name the channel **Base** in the New Channel dialog box, and press Enter (Return) to create the new channel (see Figure 22.1).

22

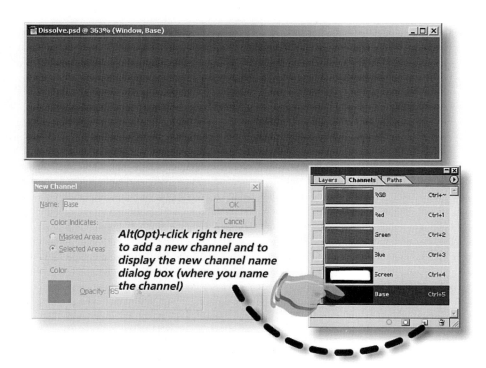

Figure 22.1   Add a channel called Base to the Dissolve image. In the New Channel dialog box, two options are listed in the Color Indicates portion: Selected Areas and Masked Areas. The resulting new channel will either appear all white or all black, depending on which of these options is chosen. Don't be concerned if your new channel does not look exactly like the one shown here.

3. With the Base channel as the active channel in the image window, choose Edit, Fill and choose 50% Gray from the Use drop-down menu. Click on OK to fill the channel with a neutral gray.

4. Choose Filter, Noise, Add Noise. Enter **100** for the Amount with a Gaussian Distribution, and check the Monochromatic option (see Figure 22.2). This noisy pattern will serve as the basis for the dissolve effect.

5. Make a copy of the Base channel by holding down the Alt(Opt) key while dragging the Base channel to the Create a new channel icon at the bottom of the Channels palette. Name the new channel **Phase 1** and click on OK.

6. Repeat step 5 to make five more copies of the Base channel. Name the new channels **Phase 2** through **Phase 6**. When you're finished, you should have six phase channels (see Figure 22.3).

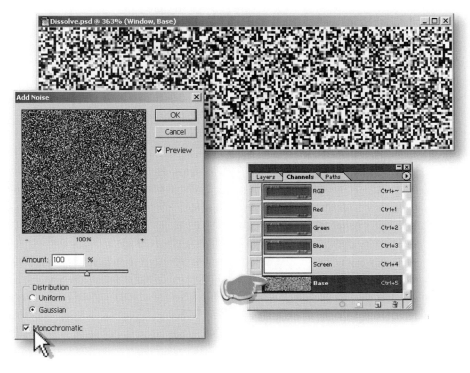

Figure 22.2 Add noise to the Base channel. This is the basis for the dissolve effect.

Insider

It is very important that the channels for each phase come from the same Base channel. If you apply the Add Noise filter to each channel separately, the dissolve effect will not work.

7. Click on the Phase 1 channel. Now, open the Threshold command (Image, Adjustments, Threshold). Change the Threshold Level to **36**, and click on OK to apply the setting to the Phase 1 channel. Repeat this process for channels Phase 2 through Phase 6, applying Threshold levels of **72**, **108**, **145**, **181**, and **218**, respectively.

At this point, you should have seven new channels: the Base channel and six channels named Phase 1 through Phase 6. The channels should look similar to the channels shown in Figure 22.4. As you can see, each channel has a different random distribution of black pixels.

22

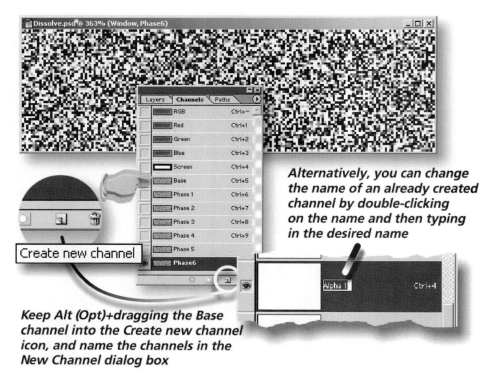

Alternatively, you can change
the name of an already created
channel by double-clicking
on the name and then typing
in the desired name

Create new channel

Keep Alt (Opt)+dragging the Base
channel into the Create new channel
icon, and name the channels in the
New Channel dialog box

Figure 22.3   Create six duplicate channels from the Base channel by Alt(Opt)+dragging the
Base channel into the Create new channel icon on the Channels palette.

8. Click on the Layers tab to view the Layers palette. Click on the Background layer
   to make it the active layer. Press **D** for the default colors, and then press **X** to
   switch white to the foreground. Choose the Type tool from the toolbox. Choose a
   bold plain font such as 20-point Arial Black. Click in the document, and type
   (in all caps) **PHOTOSHOP**. If you can't see all the text, hold down the Ctrl(⌘)
   key to toggle to the Move tool and center the text. When you're finished typing,
   press Ctrl(⌘)+Enter(Return) to commit the text to a layer.

9. On the Layers palette, right-click (Macintosh: hold Ctrl and click) on the text
   layer, and choose Rasterize Layer from the context menu (see Figure 22.5).

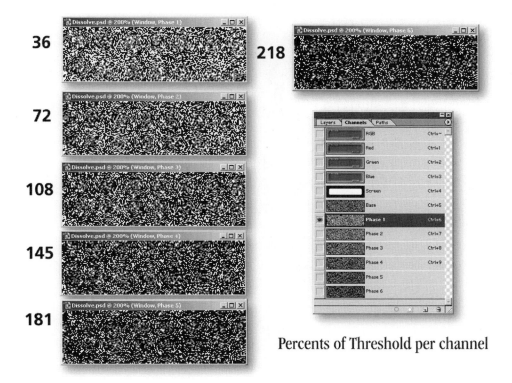

Percents of Threshold per channel

Figure 22.4   The distribution and frequency of black pixels in each channel changes as the value of the Threshold command is increased for each successive channel

10. Press Ctrl($\mathcal{H}$)+A to select all, press Ctrl($\mathcal{H}$)+X to cut, and then press Ctrl($\mathcal{H}$)+V to paste. These editing moves center the rasterized text on the layer.

11. Click the Background layer, and then press Ctrl($\mathcal{H}$)+Shift+N to create a new layer. Change the Name in the New Layer dialog box to **Phase 1**, and click on OK. Now, press Ctrl($\mathcal{H}$)+Alt(Opt)+4 to load the Screen Channel as a selection.

12. Click the Foreground Color swatch (on the toolbar) to open the Color Picker, and change the Foreground color to R:**60**, G:**60**, B:**140**. Click on OK. Press Alt(Opt)+Delete(Backspace) to fill the selection with the Foreground color. Press Ctrl($\mathcal{H}$)+D to deselect.

13. Click the PHOTOSHOP (text) layer title on the Layers palette, and press Ctrl($\mathcal{H}$)+E to merge down to the Phase 1 layer (see Figure 22.6).

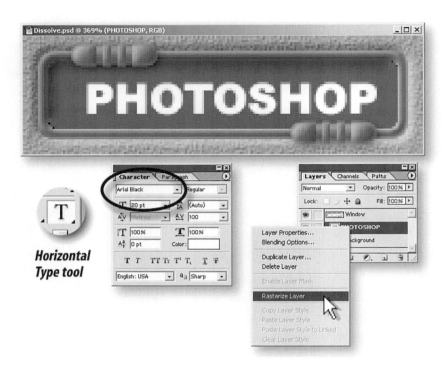

Figure 22.5   Create the text and then convert it to pixels using the Rasterize Layer command.

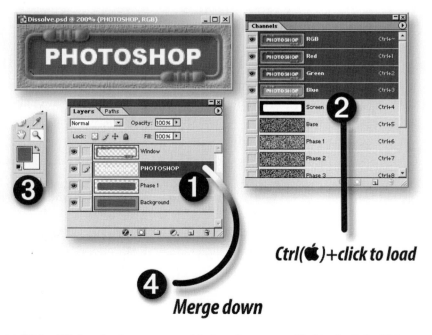

Figure 22.6   Fill the selection marquee with the color you specified in the Color Picker.

14. Alt(Opt)+drag the Phase 1 layer to the Create a new layer icon at the bottom of the Layers palette to make a duplicate layer and display the New Layer dialog box. Name the duplicate **Phase 2**. Click on OK.

15. Repeat this process five more times, naming the duplicates **Phase 3**, **Phase 4**, **Phase 5**, **Phase 6**, and **Phase 7**. When you are done, the Phase 7 layer should be above the Phase 6 layer, which in turn should be above the Phase 5 layer, and so on (see Figure 22.7).

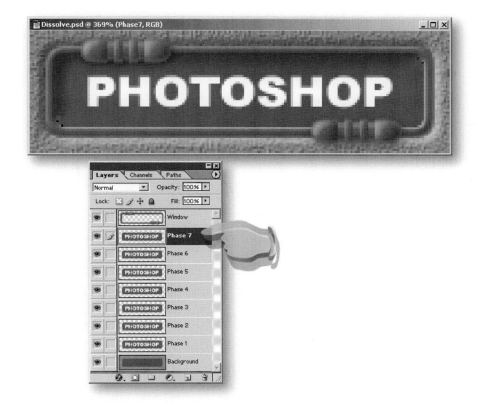

Figure 22.7 When finished creating the duplicates, you should have layers through Phase 7.

16. Press Ctrl(⌘)+S; keep the file open.

Take a breather for a moment; you've done a lot!

Ready to continue?

Continuing to Create a Dissolve-Type Animation

1. Return to the Channels palette. Delete the Screen channel and the Base channel by dragging them to the trash icon. Deleting these two channels allows you to use keyboard shortcuts to load all the Phase channels as selections.

2. Go back to the Layers palette, and click the Phase 1 layer title to make it the active layer. Press Ctrl(⌘)+Alt(Opt)+4 to load the Phase 1 channel as a selection for the Phase 1 layer. Press the Delete (Backspace) key (see Figure 22.8). Press Ctrl(⌘)+D to deselect (turn off the visibility for Phase 2 through Phase 7 layers if you would like to view the results).

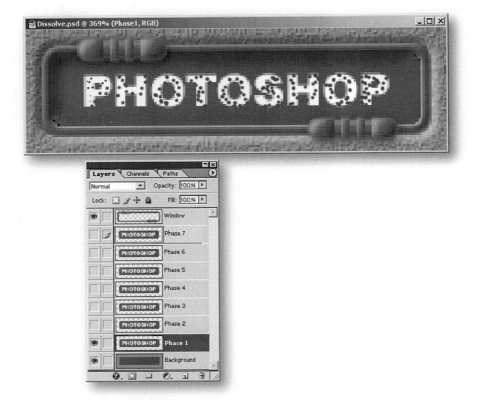

Figure 22.8   Load a channel without even seeing it on the Channels palette by using the keyboard shortcut.

3. Click on the Phase 2 layer. Press Ctrl(⌘)+Alt(Opt)+5 to load the Phase 2 channel for the Phase 2 layer. Press Delete (Backspace).

4. Continue by choosing the Phase 3 layer and loading the Phase 3 channel by pressing Ctrl(⌘)+Alt(Opt)+6. Repeat this process for each of the Phase layers;

when you reach the Phase 6 layer, you will be pressing Ctrl(⌘)+
Alt(Opt)+9 to load the Phase 6 channel (see Figure 22.9). Each time, delete the
contents within the selection. Notice that you don't have to deselect each time
you move on to the next layer; the new selection *replaces* the previous selection.
Now you have everything you need to create the animation.

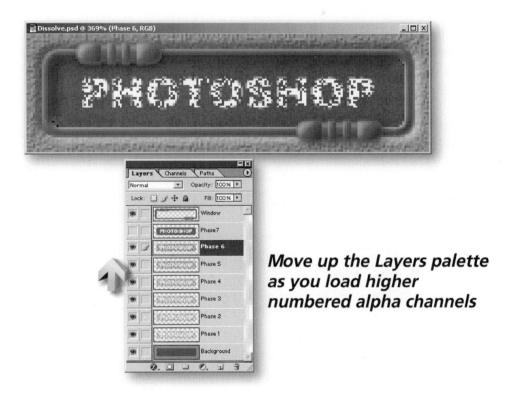

Figure 22.9   Work your way up the layers—and the saved selections—to delete different parts
of each layer.

   5. Press Ctrl(⌘)+S; keep the file open.

Compiling Your Work in ImageReady

It's time now to harness the compiling power of ImageReady. You can jump to
ImageReady (from Photoshop) simply by clicking on the Edit in ImageReady icon on
the bottom of the toolbox or by pressing Ctrl(⌘)+Shift+M. The Photoshop file you
were working on is automatically brought into ImageReady. If your system doesn't have
a terrific amount of RAM, you might choose to close Photoshop and open ImageReady
to conserve resources.

In any event, with the Dissolve.psd file opened in the ImageReady workspace, let's run down the technique for putting the layers into motion:

Animating the Dissolve Effect

1. With ImageReady opened, the Animation palette and Layers palette are all that will be needed. If either the Animation or Layers palette isn't visible, choose it from the Windows menu, or use the hot keys shown in Figure 22.10. On the Layers palette, make all the Phase layers invisible by clicking on their eye icons to hide the icons. The first frame, which automatically appears on the Animation palette, should show the Background layer and the Window layer.

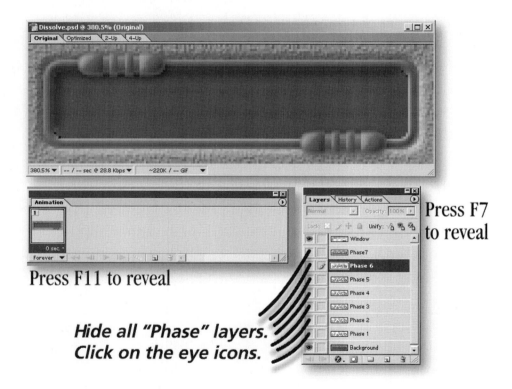

Figure 22.10   Hide the layers by clicking the eye (visibility) icons.

2. Click the Duplicates current frame icon at the bottom of the Animation palette (it looks like a page icon). This duplicates the selected frame of animation. Now, turn on the visibility of the Phase 1 layer. Notice the second frame on the Animation palette now reflects the change you made on the Layers palette.

Insider

> The key to understanding the ImageReady Animation palette is to know that the currently selected frame displays the current state of the document window. In other words, the contents of the visible layers are reflected in the current frame of the animation, as pointed out in Figure 22.11.

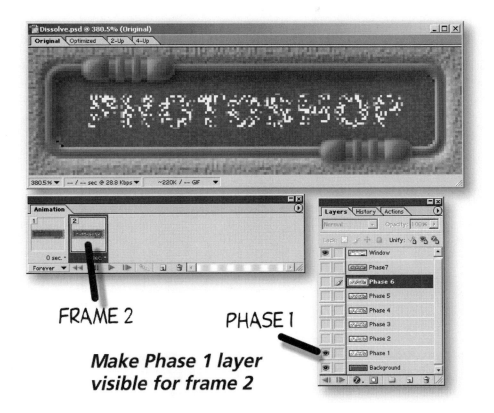

Figure 22.11   The top visible layer is shown in the current frame on the Animation palette.

Caution

> **Organize yourself**   It's easy to inadvertently mess up your animation in ImageReady. If you are not careful, you can select and change the wrong frame in the Animation palette. For that reason, it's best to have your layers well organized and clearly named before you get to the animation stage. The more tinkering you have to do, the more likely it is that you will accidentally mess things up. You can easily make corrections unless you delete layers you need, but animation is time-consuming enough as it is— so make it easy on yourself and get organized.

3. Make sure the second frame is selected, and click the Duplicates current frame icon on the Animation palette to duplicate the second frame. Then, with the third frame on the Animation palette highlighted, turn on the visibility of the Phase 2 layer. You don't need to bother with the Phase 1 layer because the contents of the Phase 2 layer cover the contents of the Phase 1 layer.

4. Repeat this process until you have eight frames in your animation. On the eighth frame, the Phase 7 layer should be visible.

Each time you create a new animation segment during this process, you need to select the last frame you created when adding a new frame from the Layers palette. This means, for example, that to generate the next frame, you would choose frame 3, click the Duplicates current frame icon (the button with the page icon on it) at the bottom of the Animation palette to duplicate the frame, and then make the Phase 3 layer visible. Then you would continue on to create frame 4, and so on (see Figure 22.12).

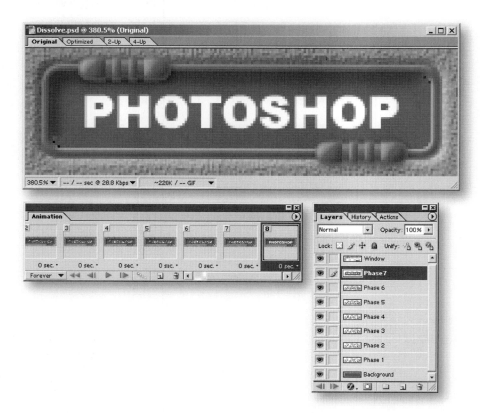

Figure 22.12   The animation at this point includes eight frames and eight configurations showing what is visible on the Layers palette.

Take a breather, get a cold beverage from the ice box, and don't change anything!

Round and Round We Go: Creating Animation Loops

To create an animation that loops—that begins again at the ending point—we must now add the frames currently on the Animation palette to the palette in reverse order. This process is sort of like inflating and deflating a balloon. And there should be no surprises for you, because we're only reverse-ordering and adding to the palette in the same way you built the beginning half of the animation.

Let's get to it!

Reversing the Dissolve Effect

1. Choose frame 8 on the Animation palette, and click the Duplicates current frame icon at the bottom of the Animation palette. Click the eye icon to toggle off the visibility for the Phase 7 layer. As you can see, we're not reversing the process yet; this is a pause in the animation. You're now going to make the Phase layers invisible sequentially as you add frames to the animation.

2. Make each successive Phase layer invisible as you add frames, as shown in Figure 22.13. For example, create the next frame by clicking frame 9 and clicking the Duplicates current frame icon. Then, turn off the visibility for the Phase 6 layer. Continue this procedure until you arrive at frame 14, where the Phase 1 layer should still be visible. You won't create a frame 15 because the animation will loop back to frame 1 after frame 14.

3. Now choose frame 8 on the Animation palette, click the Selects frame delay time arrow (the tiny arrow just below the thumbnail), and choose Other from the pop-up menu. Enter **3** in the Set Frame Delay dialog box, as shown in Figure 22.14, and click on OK. You've just set the frame delay for frame 8 to 3 seconds. Therefore, when the animation reaches frame 8, it will be displayed for 3 seconds before moving on. Choose frame 1, and change its Frame Delay to 3 seconds, too.

4. You're finally ready to export the animation. Choose Save Optimized As from the File menu. Name the animation and save it to your hard disk. View the animation with a browser or any utility you have that can preview GIF animations. You can save changes to the file if you want to keep the file on your hard disk and close ImageReady.

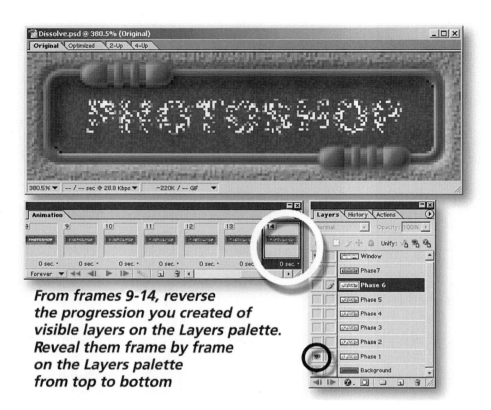

From frames 9-14, reverse
the progression you created of
visible layers on the Layers palette.
Reveal them frame by frame
on the Layers palette
from top to bottom

Figure 22.13   To make a looping animation, have the last frame make a transition to the first frame.

When you play the animation, it should pause on the first frame for a few seconds. Then the word *PHOTOSHOP* should appear gradually over a blue background. Next, the animation should pause for a few seconds while the word is fully visible. Finally, the text and blue background should dissolve out of view and loop back to start all over again.

It's worth noting that ImageReady does an excellent job of optimizing this animation. You might expect this animation to have a large file size. The GIF format uses a compression scheme that works best when there are contiguous strings of pixels with the same color. With the dissolve effect, the pixels aren't scattered all over the frame; instead, many pixels remain static from one frame to the succeeding frame, which makes compression easier and results in more manageable file sizes.

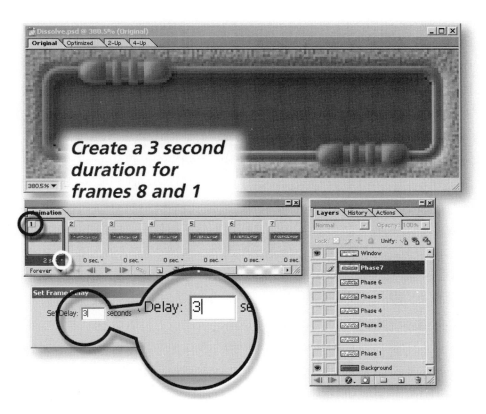

Figure 22.14 Create short pauses in the animation by increasing the display length for frame 1 and frame 8 to 3 seconds.

ImageReady employs *interframe transparency optimization* on the frames. Basically, only the pixels that have changed from one frame to the next are visible on each frame. The rest of the pixels are turned invisible. This allows the GIF format to compress the animation down to just under 15KB.

You might see this using a GIF animation utility, such as GIF Movie Gear (www.gamani.com). In Figure 22.15, most of the frames are almost entirely gray (which is the color for transparency in GIF Movie Gear). Only the pixels that have changed from the previous frame are visible. ImageReady makes all the other pixels on that frame invisible automatically.

22

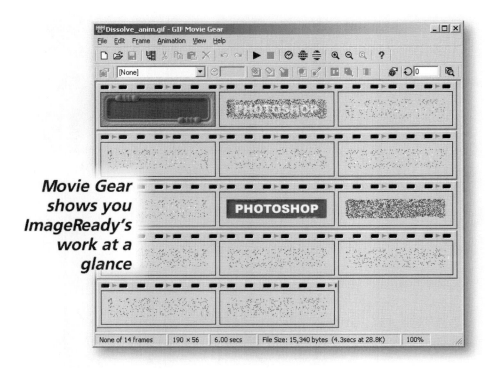

Movie Gear shows you ImageReady's work at a glance

Figure 22.15 ImageReady compresses an animation file so that pixels that appear onscreen more than once appear in the file *only* once.

The key to the dissolve animation is the Threshold filter. You created a base noisy texture and then used Threshold to set high contrast at six points along the grayscale from 1 to 255 (Threshold goes from 1 to 255, not 0 to 255 like the Levels command does). Essentially, you leveraged the unique characteristics of the Threshold filter after the results of the Noise filter to create an animation effect. There are many such vertical (unique, seldom fully used) commands in Photoshop; you simply need a book such as this one to point out the "back streets"! For example, the Displace filter will be used in a novel way in the following section.

Creating a Bulging Pipe Animation

Most of us who have ever watched a cartoon have seen Popeye or some other totally malleable character squeeze through a pipe—the humorous aspect being that metal pipes usually don't give way and take on a bulge for sailors real or imagined.

Because a cartoon is a form of animation, there's no reason a bulging pipe cannot be a GIF animation.

You just have to know a little about displacement mapping to displace the ordinarily unyielding form of a pipe.

Using Displacement Maps for Special Animations

In the steps coming up, you'll use a file from the companion CD, and learn how to seize some of the power of the Displace command, admittedly a command that in all Photoshop books gathers a little dust. You simply need to see the results to get hooked. Check out Figure 22.16. The comedy mask is *bent*, according to the tones in a displacement map.

Figure 22.16   Now *this* is a funny picture of a comedy mask!

The left image is an original, undistorted version. Each copy of the image has been distorted using the displacement maps to the right of them. In both examples, the Displace filter was set to Horizontal 70% and Vertical 0%. Since the example at top used the displacement map with white that gradually turns into medium gray, the image was displaced to the left. Conversely, the example at bottom moves from black to gray, so the image is distorted to the right. Had the Displace filter been set to Horizontal 0% and Vertical 70%, the image that used the white-to-gray displacement map would have been distorted upward, and the image that used the black-to-gray displacement map would have been distorted downward.

Digging into the Whys and Wherefores of Displace

Any non-layered Photoshop file can be used as a displacement map, which means that anything that is flattened and has the `*.PSD` tag is fair game for displacing another, different image. The key to using the Displace filter is to understand how it uses displacement maps. The Displace command works according to the brightness values in displacement maps, as you saw a small example of in Figure 22.16. A value of white (255) corresponds to the maximum positive displacement, which translates to up vertically and/or left horizontally. A value of black (0, zero) corresponds to the maximum negative displacement which translates to down vertically and/or right horizontally.

So, brightness values that are 129 or higher result in displacement up and/or to the left, and brightness values of 127 or less result in displacement down and/or to the right. A value of 128 results in no displacement.

Because displacement maps use only brightness information, it's a good idea to create them using black, white, and grayscale tones in RGB mode. Keeping the image in RGB mode is usually a good idea because many of Photoshop's filters don't work in grayscale mode. Because judging how colored images will convert to grayscale can be difficult, it's usually best to work with grayscale colors.

The Displace filter enables you to either stretch a displacement map to fit your image or tile the map to fit your image. Using a displacement map that is the same size as the image is the best choice and renders either of the options inconsequential. To create a bulging animation or any other distortion animated effect with the Displace filter, you create the displacement at the same size as the image upon which you will use it.

So, if you're ready to have some fun and create some fun for others, without further ado, here's how to begin the bulging pipe effect:

Getting Started Using the Displace Command

1. Open the Bulgepipe.psd image from the Examples/Chap22 folder on the companion CD, and save it to your hard disk using the same name and file type. Notice that this file has three layers.

   The top layer is called Top Pipe Drop Shadow, underneath that layer is a layer named Pipe, and beneath that is the Background layer. You will be creating an animation by distorting the visual contents of the Pipe layer.

22

Insider

First, you need to make a displacement map to use with the Displace filter. The image we'll use for this sample file is 180 pixels square. You can view this information if you right-click (Macintosh: hold Ctrl and click) the title bar of the Bulgepipe.psd file and choose Image Size.

2. Press Ctrl(⌘)+N to open a new document, and make it a 180-pixel square RGB document (72 ppi). Select Fill from the Edit menu, and choose 50% Gray from the Use drop-down menu. Save this file as a Photoshop (PSD) file, and call it **Bulgedmap.psd**.

3. Now, we need to do a little setup. Press Ctrl(⌘)+R to toggle on the rulers. Make sure the Snap option is on in the View menu. If it is not on, select it or press Ctrl(⌘)+Shift+; (semicolon) to toggle it on. Finally, double-click either ruler to display the Units & Rulers preferences. Change the Rulers units to pixels, as shown in Figure 22.17.

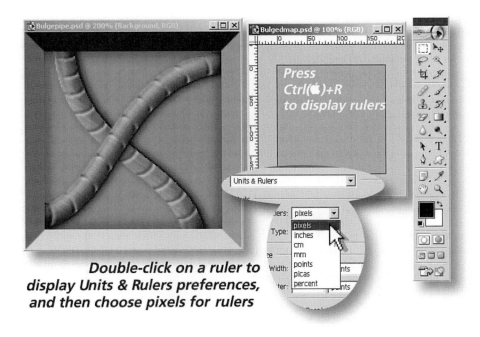

Figure 22.17   Choose pixels as the unit of measurement for Photoshop's rulers.

4. Press Ctrl(⌘)+Shift+N to open the New Layer dialog box. Name the layer **White**, and click on OK. Hold down the Shift key, drag a vertical guide from the vertical ruler, and position the guide at 90 pixels. Next, hold down the Shift key,

and drag a horizontal guide from the horizontal ruler down to 90 pixels. Save the file, and name it **DispMapBase.psd**. Keep Photoshop open.

Creating Displacement Map Visual Content

Now, it's time to apply brightness values to the current image. Watch (um, I mean "find out") how easy this is to accomplish now that guides are at your command....

Toning the Displacement Map

1. Choose the Elliptical Marquee tool from the toolbox. Make sure your Info palette is visible. If not, click the Info tab, or choose Window, Info. Using the intersection of the guides as a starting point, place the cursor crosshair on this intersection. Hold down the Shift+Alt(Opt) keys, and drag a circular selection (to make the circular selection, drag outward from the center point). Make the circle selection approximately 130 pixels in diameter. You can see this information in the lower-right corner of your Info palette, which will display the Width and Height in pixels as you drag. The measurement does not have to be exact, but the circular selection should *not* be so large that it fills the entire document (see Figure 22.18).

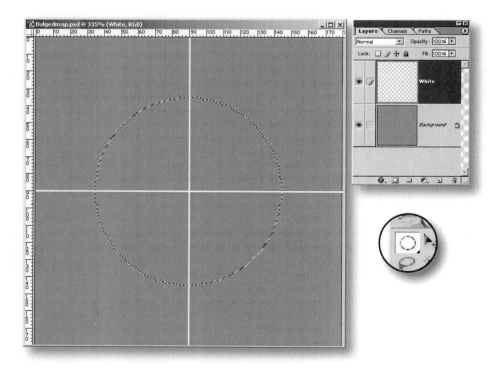

Figure 22.18   Create a circular selection in the middle of the image window, about 130 pixels across.

2. Choose Feather from the Select menu, or right-click (Macintosh: hold Ctrl and click) and choose the Feather command from the context menu. Change the Feather amount to 10 pixels, and click on OK to apply the feathering, which softens the edges of the image area. Press **D** (for default colors). Press Ctrl(⌘)+Delete(Backspace) to fill the selection with white background color. Press Ctrl(⌘)+D to deselect.

3. On the Layers palette, Alt(Opt)+drag the White layer to the Create a new layer icon, and name the new layer **Black**. Press Ctrl(⌘)+I to invert the non-transparent areas on the Black layer. At this point you should have three layers in your document: the Background layer filled with solid gray, the White layer, and the Black layer, as shown in Figure 22.19.

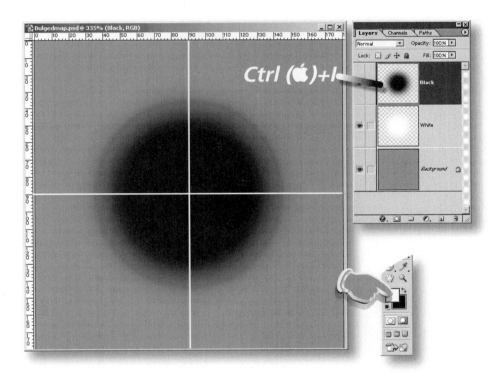

Figure 22.19 Choose the Invert (*not* Inverse) command to reverse the tonal chroma of the non-transparent contents of the Black layer.

4. The Black layer should be the active layer. Press **V** to switch to the Move tool, and drag the black fluffy ball to the bottom right so that only the upper-left quarter of it is visible (the rest is cut off by the edges of the document). Optionally, you can hold down the Shift key as you drag to constrain movement to a perfect 45° angle.

5. Click the White layer to make it active, and hold down the Shift key while dragging the white circle to the bottom–left corner so that the upper-right quarter of the ball is visible (see Figure 22.20).

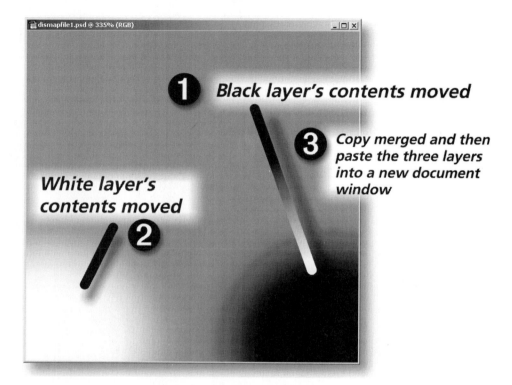

Figure 22.20   Make a flat copy of your work so far. Guess what this file will be used for.

6. Press Ctrl(⌘)+A to Select All. Choose Edit, Copy Merged. Press Ctrl(⌘)+D to deselect.

7. Press Ctrl(⌘)+N to open a new document, and click on OK to accept the default options in the dialog box. (Photoshop senses the size and other attributes of the image information on the Clipboard and will display this size information automatically in the New Document dialog box.) Press Ctrl(⌘)+V to paste the image in the document. Press Ctrl(⌘)+E to merge down—a good shortcut to remember. Save this file as a Photoshop (PSD) file, and call it **dismapfile1.psd**.

Insider

You have created the first of a series of *displacement maps* for the animation. For the rest of the displacement maps, you'll move the White and Black layers in the DispMapBase.psd file progressively upward.

8. Click the title bar of the DispMapBase.psd document to make it the current editing document in the workspace. On the Layers palette, the White layer should be active. Click the link column next to the Black layer to link the White layer to the Black layer. With the Move tool still active, hold down the Shift key, and press the up arrow on your keyboard five times. Each time you press the up arrow, you nudge the White and Black layers up 10 pixels; five presses moves them up 50 pixels. Release the Shift key and then hit the down arrow five times. This moves the White and Black layers down 5 pixels (the single strokes without holding Shift), for a total move of 45 pixels.

9. Press Ctrl(⌘)+A to Select All, and then press Ctrl(⌘)+Shift+C to Copy Merged. Press Ctrl(⌘)+D to deselect. Press Ctrl(⌘)+N to open a new document, and click on OK. Press Ctrl(⌘)+V to paste. Press Ctrl(⌘)+E to merge down. Save this file as a Photoshop (PSD) file, and call it **Dismapfile2.psd**.

10. Repeat this process three more times, naming the files **Dismapfile3.psd**, **Dismapfile4.psd**, and **Dismapfile5.psd**. Now you have all the displacement maps you need to create the animation. Check out Figure 22.21. You can close these displacement files at this point, but leave the Bulgepipe.psd file open.

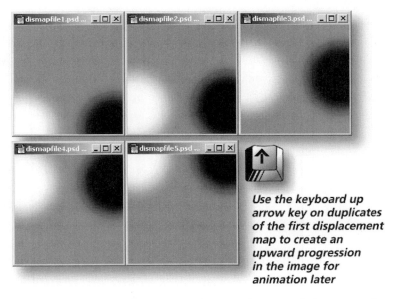

Use the keyboard up arrow key on duplicates of the first displacement map to create an upward progression in the image for animation later

Figure 22.21   You will move these colored layers upward, creating the movement that will correspond to the bulge in the pipe for the animation.

11. Click the title bar of the Bulgepipe Photoshop file to make it active. On the Layers palette, Alt(Opt)+drag the Pipe layer to the Create a new layer icon to

make a copy of this layer. Name the copy **Bulge 1** and click on OK. Choose Filter, Distort, Displace. Set the Horizontal scale to 10 and the Vertical scale to 0.

Insider

As long as a displacement map is the same size as the current image, it doesn't matter whether you choose Stretch To Fit or Tile from the Displacement Map options. As long as the displacement map is the same size as the image, it usually won't matter whether you choose Wrap Around or Repeat Edge Pixels for the Undefined areas.

22

12. Click on OK, and you will see the Choose a Displacement Map dialog box. Navigate and select the dismapfile1.psd file you created earlier, and click the Open button. Make the Pipe layer invisible (by clicking the eye icon to the far left of this layer) to make it easier to see the results (see Figure 22.22)!

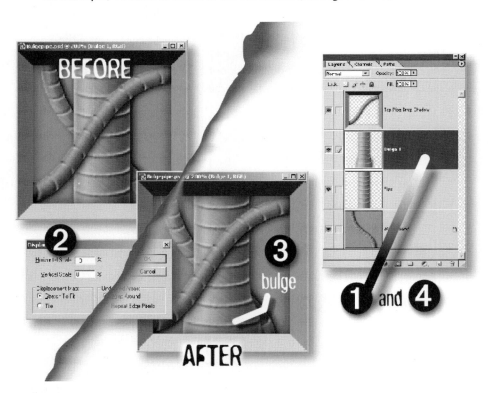

Figure 22.22   The applied displacement map creates a bulge effect in the lower portion of the pipe.

13. Create four more copies of the Pipe layer, and drag them above the Bulge 1 layer. Rename them **Bulge 2**, **Bulge 3**, **Bulge 4**, and **Bulge 5**, and place them in stacked order: Bulge 5 above Bulge 4, Bulge 4 above Bulge 3, and so on.

14. Now go through and apply the Displace filter to each layer using the corresponding displacement map in each case. For example, click the Bulge 2 layer to make it active, apply the Displace filter using the dismapfile2.psd file; click the Bulge 3 layer, use the dismapfile3.psd file, and so on (see Figure 22.23). Now you have everything you need to create an animation.

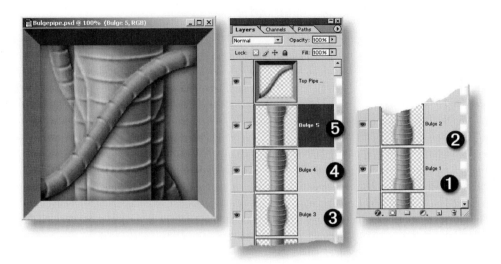

Five layers, each with a different bulge point

Figure 22.23   You now have a progression upward of the bulge in the pipe, and the PSD file is now ready for ImageReady. Um, you don't want to *know* what the bulge in the pipe really is....

15. Press Ctrl(⌘)+S to save. Press Ctrl(⌘)+Shift+M to open ImageReady. The file you were working on is automatically brought into ImageReady. Now all you need to create the animation is the Animation palette and the Layers palette. If one or both of the palettes aren't visible, choose them from the Window menu. On the Layers palette, toggle the visibility for all the Bulge layers by clicking their eye icons. The Pipe layer visibility should be turned on (make sure the eye icon is showing for this layer).

16. Click the Duplicates current frame icon at the bottom of the Animation palette to duplicate the selected frame—in this case, frame 1. Now turn on the visibility of the Bulge 1 layer, and turn off the visibility of the Pipe layer. Repeat this process by clicking the Duplicates current frame icon, turning on the visibility of the Bulge 2 layer, and then turning off the visibility of the Bulge 1 layer. Each time you create a new frame, turn on the visibility of the next Bulge layer, and then turning off the visibility of the previous Bulge layer (see Figure 22.24). Why? Because otherwise you would be able to see a bulge on an underlying layer.

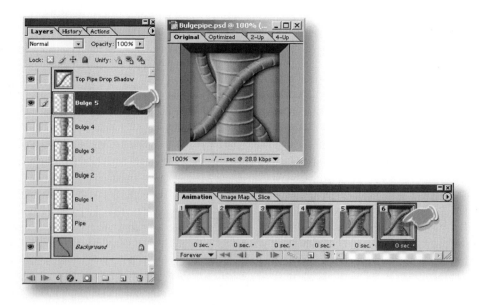

Figure 22.24   Progress up the Layers palette, making the previous layer invisible, as you add frames to the Animation palette.

When you're finished, you should have six frames in the Animation palette. The first frame should show the Pipe layer, and the remaining five frames should show each of the Bulge layers in sequence.

17. Choose frame 1 on the Animation palette, and click the tiny arrow (called the Selects Frame Delay Time arrow) just below the small thumbnail. Select Other from the pop-up menu. Enter **3** in the Set Frame Delay dialog box, and click on OK. Now repeat this step for frames 2 through 6, and change the frame delay to 0.1 second. You've just set the frame delay for frame 1 to 3 seconds. This means that there will be a three-second pause at the beginning of the animation and every time it loops. We changed the frame delay for the rest of the frames to 0.1 second so that the sequential bulge frames won't go so fast that you can't see the movement (see Figure 22.25).

Now you're ready to export the animation. Choose Save Optimized As from the File menu. Name the animation, and save it to your hard disk. View the animation with a browser or any utility you have that can preview GIF animations.

The animation should start with a short pause followed by a bulge in the pipe that will animate upward and then repeat every 3 seconds. When you look at the animation using a GIF animation utility such as GIF Movie Gear (www.gamani.com), you can see that, once again, ImageReady has optimized the animation to show only the pixels that change from frame to frame (see Figure 22.26).

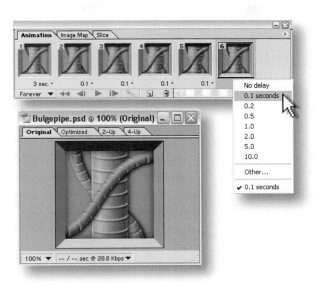

Figure 22.25   Give the poor pipe a rest at frame 1. The other frames carry the motion and should be set to 0.1 second.

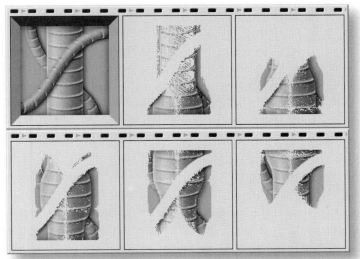

Optimizing= ImageReady only writes pixels that change from frame to frame into the GIF animation

Figure 22.26   Once again, ImageReady intelligently discards redundant visual information to make a really compressed file.

Animated Fog/Scrolling Texture

We'll make this section a *trilogy* of special effects animations with our "rolling fog over the ocean" trick. The railing is just to your right in case you get seasick....

For this animation, you'll look at two useful techniques: creating a fog texture and animating a seamless texture. A *seamless texture* is one that has been created so that its left side is a continuation of its right side, and its bottom edge is a continuation of its top edge. So regardless of how much you offset the seamless tile, the tile looks whole and has no creases running through it. Creating an animation from any seamless texture is fairly easy. Photoshop includes seamless texture generators; among them (and those you will use) are the Clouds and Difference Clouds filters.

Getting Your Hands on Some Clouds

The first step in creating this animation is to generate a seamless tile with the Difference Clouds or Clouds filter. The Difference Clouds and Clouds filters automatically generate seamless tiles if the file size is 512 pixels. (Tip: The Adobe engineer who created the Clouds effects made the fractal texture, the clouds, terminate and repeat at 128 pixels, and 512 is a multiple of 128).

The Difference Clouds filter is a little more versatile than the plain Clouds Filter, Render effect. For example, you can apply the Difference Clouds filter multiple times and create an effect that progresses in a geometric fashion, while the Clouds filter simply exchanges the previous application of the command with a new rendering of clouds.

C'mon. Let's get started:

Creating Seamless Tiling Clouds

1. Press Ctrl(⌘)+N to open a new document. In the New dialog box, make the dimensions a 512-pixel square RGB, 72 dpi document (peek ahead at Figure 22.27). Click on OK. Press **D** to set the default colors of black and white. Choose Filter, Render, Difference Clouds or Clouds. Now you have a seamless tile that you can resample to any size that you want. In fact, let's begin the next step by resizing the texture.

2. Choose Image, Image Size, and resize the file to 140 pixels square (make sure the Constrain Proportions option is checked). Click on OK. On the Layers palette, Alt(Opt)+drag the Background layer to the Create a new layer icon, and title the new layer **Fog**.

3. Click on the Background layer to make it the active layer. Click on the foreground color, and choose a nice rich medium blue color (R:**0**, G:**0**, B:**255**). Click on OK. Press Alt(Opt)+Delete(Backspace) to fill the Background layer with the

blue color. Next, select the Fog layer and change the Blend mode to Lighten. At this point, the texture looks like light clouds on a sunny day, but as you will see, you can easily convert the effect to fog (see Figure 22.27).

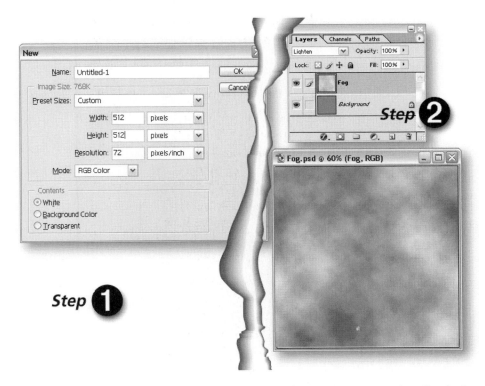

Figure 22.27   Create an image whose dimensions enable you to create a seamless Clouds tile. Then resize the image (we'll explain why shortly).

4. Open the porthole.psd image from the Examples/Chap22 folder on the companion CD, and save it to your hard disk using the same name and file type. Double-click on the Hand tool to maximize the view of the file in Photoshop. The porthole.psd file has two layers: the Background layer, which contains simple artwork for a sky/ocean scene, and the Porthole layer, which contains artwork that looks like a porthole and provides a hole looking through to the Background layer. The Channels palette contains a channel named Window, which you'll use shortly.

5. Click on the Background layer of the porthole.psd document to make sure it is the active layer. Position both documents in the workspace so that you can view them both. Click on the title bar of the document you created earlier in step 1 (to make it the active document). Hold down the Shift key, and drag the Fog layer from the Layers palette into the porthold.psd document. This action will

center and position the Fog layer into the porthole.psd document between the Background and Porthole layers. The Fog layer should already be set to the Lighten blending mode since the attributes of the layer also transferred when we dragged the layer into the porthole document (see Figure 22.28).

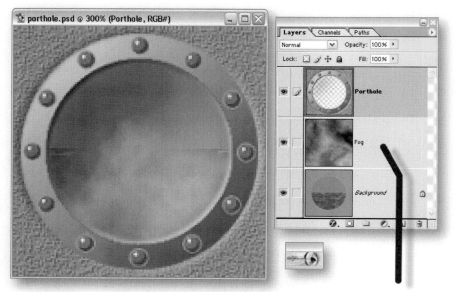

Figure 22.28   The layer you copy from the original window needs to be in Lighten blending mode so the viewer can see its effect on the Background layer.

6. Press Ctrl(⌘)+A to Select All. Press Shift+Ctrl(⌘)+C to Copy Merged. Press Ctrl(⌘)+N to open a new document. The dimensions of the new image should default to 140 pixels wide and high. Change the Name field to **Fog_anim**. Click on OK. Press Ctrl(⌘)+V to paste. Double-click the Layer 1 title, rename the layer **Fog 1**, and press Enter (Return) to set the new name. Save the file as a Photoshop (.psd) document (see Figure 22.29).

7. Click on the porthole.psd title bar to make this the active document again. The selection should still be active; you don't need to deselect until later. The Fog layer on the Layers palette should still be the active layer; if not, click on it to make it active. Choose Filter, Other, Offset. Change the Horizontal to 14 and Vertical to 0 in the Offset fields. Make sure that the Wrap Around option is checked, and click on OK to apply the transformation. Press Shift+Ctrl (⌘)+C to Copy Merged (you can copy, since there is an active selection). Click

on the Fog_anim.psd document to make this the active document in the work-space. Press Ctrl(⌘)+V to paste. Rename the new layer **Fog 2** (see Figure 22.30).

Figure 22.29 Create a new image, and then use the Copy Merged command to copy a com-

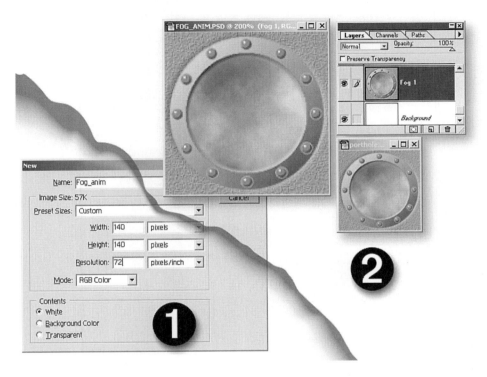

posite of the porthole scene to the new window.

8. Click the porthole.psd title bar to make it the active document. The Fog layer should still be the active layer. Press Ctrl(⌘)+F to reapply the Offset filter (without opening the dialog box, since this will apply the last filter used). Press Shift+Ctrl(⌘)+C to Copy Merged. Make the Fog_anim.psd document the active document in the workspace, and press Ctrl(⌘)+V to paste. Rename the new layer **Fog 3**.

9. Repeat the preceding step seven more times. Each time, press Ctrl(⌘)+F with the Fog layer selected in the porthole.psd file. Then Copy Merged, and paste into the Fog_anim.psd file. Rename the layers sequentially. For instance, the next layer in the Fog_anim.psd document should be Fog 4 and so on. When you're finished, you should have 10 layers named Fog 1 through Fog 10, as shown in Figure 22.31.

22

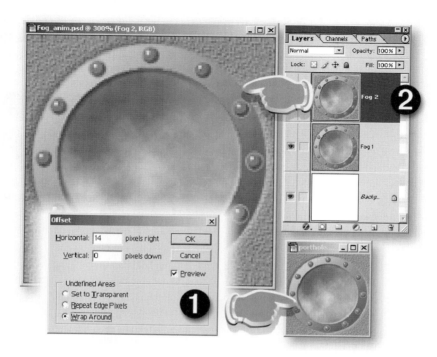

Figure 22.30   Use the Offset command to make the fog roll across the porthole.

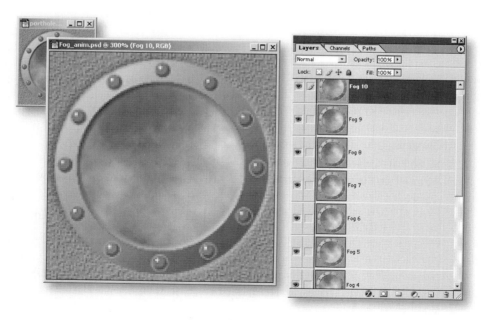

Figure 22.31   The Offset amount is 14. There are 10 frames. If you do the math, 10×14 = 140, you'll find that it's the exact width of the image window. It looks like the fog will seamlessly repeat a full cycle in 10 frames, at least from where I'm sitting.

10. With the Fog_anim.psd document active, press Ctrl(⌘)+S to save. Now press Ctrl(⌘)+Shift+M to open ImageReady. The file you're working with is automatically brought into ImageReady. Again, all you need to create the animation is the Animation palette and the Layers palette.

11. Toggle the visibility off for every layer except the Fog 1 layer. Click the Duplicates current frame icon at the bottom of the Animation palette to duplicate the selected frame of animation—in this case, frame 1. Now make the Fog 2 layer visible, as shown in Figure 22.32.

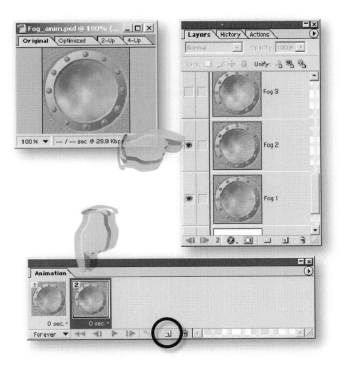

Figure 22.32   Replace the view by one layer every frame to make an animation of wafting fog.

12. Repeat the process from the preceding step by selecting frame 2, clicking the Duplicates current frame icon on the Animation palette to duplicate the frame, and then, with the newly created frame 3 selected, making the Fog 3 layer visible. Repeat for the various layers, each time duplicating the last frame and turning on the visibility for the next Fog layer. When you're done, you should have 10 frames. On frame 10 you will make the Fog 10 layer visible. Keeping track of the layers should be easy because the frame number should match the number on the Fog layer. This means that the Fog 4 layer should be on frame 4, the Fog 5 layer should be on frame 5, and so on (see Figure 22.33).

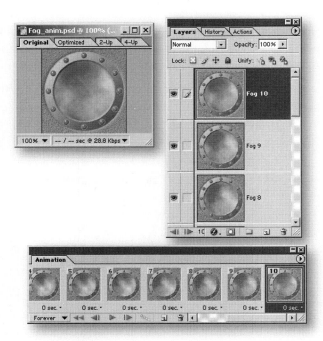

Figure 22.33   Assign each layer to the animation frame to which its number corresponds.

13. Select frame 1 in the Animation palette, click the Selects frame delay time arrow (the tiny arrow just below the small thumbnail), and choose 0.1 Seconds from the pop-up menu. Assign frames 2 through 9 the same duration. Setting each frame to 0.1 second keeps the animation from running so fast that you can't see the fog.

14. Now you're ready to export the animation. Choose Save Optimized As from the File menu. Name the animation, and save it to your hard disk. View the animation with a browser or any utility you have that can preview GIF animations.

The animation (and the seamless cloud texture) will loop continuously. After a loop or two, you will find it hard to determine which frame is at the beginning and which is at the end.

Photoshop and ImageReady make a great combination for creating GIF animations. We've looked at only a few possibilities, but they demonstrate that Photoshop has plenty of potential for creating animations and that creating animations with ImageReady is simple. Also, it's great to know that ImageReady will do an excellent job of optimizing the animation when you're ready to export.

Post Script (Pun Intended)

You might want to look into the Filter, Liquify command as a means for distorting frames. If you use this filter, you must stop adding new frames at some point and then reverse the remaining frames until you've "ping-ponged" the total animation. The reason is that the Liquify filter doesn't have a multiple undo feature. Check out Figure 22.34, and see what a lousy thing we've done to one of our relatives!

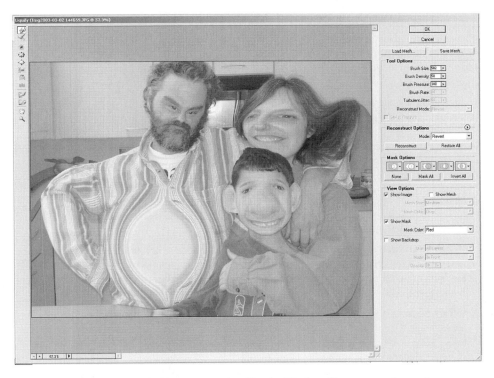

Figure 22.34 The Liquify filter is somewhat like the Displace filter, except the results are messier. And funnier.

Okay, now that you've gotten a taste for a little animation, what say we strike a little further into the unknowns of Photoshop and wrest the rollover capability from its bowels? C'mon, you'll have a lot of fun designing stuff that not only animates, but also does so to a visitor's cursor movements. Rollovers are just like animations (sort of) and they're fun, they're now, and you need to master 'em to get with the Web site crowd!

ImageReady, Photoshop, and Rollovers

Before programs like ImageReady were available, Web designers who wanted a highly graphic side with slick rollovers had to hand-code and optimize everything. This process could take upwards of 5 to 15 hours depending on the complexity and the designer's attention to detail. With ImageReady, these same tasks can take a fraction of the time to accomplish. Once you are familiar with the process, you could easily optimize a Web interface in as little as 20 minutes. (If you need a short course in rollovers, image slices, and optimization, see the sidebar titled "A Rollover Primer.")

It's important to bear in mind that ImageReady's HTML scripting capabilities are limited. For instance, you cannot use ImageReady to create a dynamic scrollable text field, pop-up menu, or dynamically expanding menu. You cannot even create rollovers inside ImageReady whose frames themselves animate, but we'll look at a simple technique to create an animated rollover.

So what can you do in ImageReady? Basically, you can slice up an image/interface and create both simple rollovers and multi-region rollovers. ImageReady also allows you to create image maps and animations (as you've seen); plus, you can optimize imagery in ImageReady.

A Rollover Primer

What is/am/are a rollover? A rollover is usually a button you find on a Web page that reacts to your cursor. You put your cursor over a rollover, and the rollover's message changes. You click down on a rollover, and a different appearance might be evident with the rollover, depending on how ambitious the rollover's creator is.

What is an image slice? ImageReady has the capability to slice an image into two or more image fragments, for the purpose of downloading the total image more quickly and to optimize each slice according to the amount it needs optimizing. For example, a blue sky with a single cloud in it might lend itself to a lot of optimization of the simple blue sky (slices), but less optimization to capture the intricacies of the cloud.

What is optimization? Optimization is the reduction of an image file's saved size so that it can be passed through the Web more quickly. Optimizing generally includes getting rid of some of the image's original visual information, either clumsily (typical of GIF) or more elegantly (such as JPEG compression). *Dithering*—the placement of colors next to each other so that at a distance they suggest a third color—can also be used to "fake" some of the colors that are missing from the optimized file.

Preparing an Interface for ImageReady

Typically, you will begin to prepare for working with ImageReady about the time you've finished designing your latest interface masterpiece in Photoshop. At that point, you will often have numerous layers, including possibly lots of layer styles, maybe some Adjustment Layers, and so on.

Usually, the best strategy is to prepare your file for working with ImageReady while you're still in Photoshop. There are several reasons for this approach. First, ImageReady's approach to creating animation frames and rollovers is essentially to take a picture of the current visible state of the document. This means that good layer management will help make the process in ImageReady much easier and less prone to error.

ImageReady is also a system resource hog. If you're running other applications, ImageReady often won't even open when you launch it from Photoshop. With the exception of the ability to create rollovers and animations, Photoshop is significantly more capable than ImageReady. So, usually it's a good idea to take the time to do all your preparation in Photoshop before switching to ImageReady.

So, we'll start our examples at the point where an interface has been completed and is ready to be sliced, diced, and optimized.

Note

> **Photoshop Web Foundry**   The interface featured in the following example is from Photoshop Web Foundry, a collection of more than 120 customizable interfaces from Eyeland Studio (`www.eyeland.com`).

The starting file on the companion CD has been reduced from 44 layers to 10 layers. In comparison to the process of reducing the layers in that image, the work we do in ImageReady will be almost an afterthought, a walk in the park, a bowl full of cherries, and a plethora of other brutal speed-oriented clichés. We'll be in and out of ImageReady in minutes.

Tip

> **Using ImageReady**   Relative to Photoshop, ImageReady is basically a plug-in that takes up way too many system resources. We want to treat it like a plug-in. We want ImageReady to do its job, and then we want to get out and get our system resources back.

Creating Image Slices

Before we start hacking away at our image with the Slice tool, we should discuss a few issues worthy of note (and perhaps a bit of soapboxing for good measure). First, why are we slicing in Photoshop instead of ImageReady? Simple. Because we *can*.

Photoshop is not as limited as ImageReady. It has more and better filters and the full contingency of bitmap editing features, whereas ImageReady is stripped down. So, if we stay in Photoshop, we're less likely to have to bounce back and forth if we need to do a Gaussian blur or something.

Note

> **Slicing using which program?**   Aside from the aforementioned issues, there's really no good reason to slice in Photoshop rather than ImageReady. The fact is that which one you use is a matter of preference. In reality, it's a bit odd that Adobe put the Slice tool inside Photoshop but not the Rollover or Animation palette. Having the Slice tool in Photoshop is sort of like having a plate full of pancakes without butter or maple syrup. It's nice to be able to have more functionality in Photoshop, and it's nice to be able to slice in Photoshop rather than in ImageReady, but ultimately we still have to go over to ImageReady. Is it just me, or is it time to put that horse out to pasture? Anyway, for now, let's work with what we've got.

22

Optimizing Slices

Now let's talk about optimization. There are really two kinds of optimization. You can optimize the files so that they download quicker over the Internet, and you can optimize the time it takes you to generate your Web interface. Usually, deadlines don't really allow you to spend gobs of time shaving off a few extra kilobytes so that your Web page will download a fraction of a second faster. On the other hand, it's worth taking a few seconds to consider the ramifications of sloppy slicing.

When we slice an image, we're usually doing so for one of three reasons: to integrate rollovers, to integrate animations, or to optimize the file size of an image by combining JPEG and GIF images. We will talk about combining JPEG and GIF images later. For now, let's talk about slicing for integrating rollovers and animations.

A rollover is implemented with at least two images (with JavaScript, you can create rollovers with multiple images, but that's beyond ImageReady's capability). Every time you create a slice for a rollover, you are specifying an area that will have twice the download requirements. In other words, two images will have to be downloaded for that area instead of one.

For the sake of optimization, therefore, we usually want to make the slices as small as possible. The smaller the slice, the less pixel information we are doubling up on. Put another way, a couple of 100 by 100 images will usually download faster than a couple of 200 by 200 images.

On the other hand, we don't want to make the slices so small that it is hard for the site's visitors to find and click on the buttons. So we really just want to minimize the size of the slices, rather than make them so small that they are unusable.

Setting the Guides

In the exercise in this section of the chapter, you will often see the instruction to hold down the Shift key when positioning the guides. Holding down the Shift key positions the guides at the intersection of pixels. If you do not have the Shift key down when you position a guide, the guide could end up in the middle of pixels, as shown in Figure 22.35.

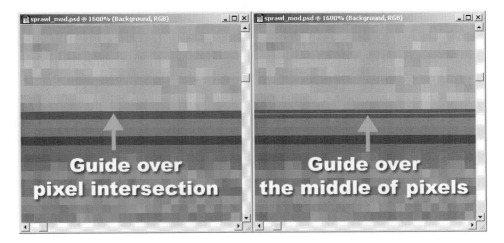

Figure 22.35   The document on the left shows a guide positioned at the intersection of the pixels, while the guide in the document on the right is positioned over the middle of the pixels.

The problem with guides being placed in the middle, rather than at the intersection, of the pixels is that this can result in imprecise selections and slices (see Figure 22.36). Selections and slices automatically snap to the intersection of pixels. If you have Snap to Guides turned on as well, you may not get the snap you want. A selection or slice tends to snap to the intersection of pixels that is closest to the guide. So, for best results, hold down the Shift key when placing the guide to avoid any confusion.

The position of the guide may not seem like a very big problem when your image is zoomed out, but it can result in your slices or selections being off by 1 pixel, which can cause a big problem later. If you notice that things don't quite line up when you're exporting your final interface, this is most likely the problem.

Now, on with the work at hand. Usually, being as consistent as possible is important. If you have a series of buttons on your Web site, all with a similar shape and size, you should make your slices so that they are all the same size and shape whenever possible. Photoshop's guides are a big help for keeping slices consistent. They also help optimize your time because they make creating slices quite literally a snap.

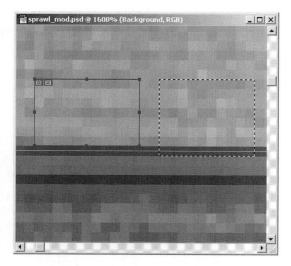

Figure 22.36   The slice on the left snapped to the pixel intersection above the guide. The selection on the right automatically snapped to the intersection of pixels that occurred below the guide.

In our example, though, the buttons are not all the same size and shape. Nevertheless, we can set up the slices so that each button behaves in a similar fashion. So let's get started already:

Setting the Guides

1. Open the Sprawl_mod.psd file from the Examples/Chap22 folder on the companion CD. Press Ctrl(⌘)+R to toggle on the rulers. Open the View menu, and make sure the Snap option is checked (see Figure 22.37). If it is not, select it to turn it on. You also can use the Ctrl(⌘)+Shift+; (semicolon) key combination to toggle the Snap option on and off.

2. Press **Z** to switch to the Zoom tool, and click twice over the Home button to zoom in a little. Press **V** to switch to the Move tool. Press and hold the Shift key while you click inside the horizontal ruler, and drag a guide down from the ruler. Position the guide just below the black line (on the inside of the top portion) of the Home button (see Figure 22.38).

Insider

I can already begin to see how we're going to optimize our slices. We are going to define all the button slices inside the blue bars that help surround the button. We'll do this for every button. Each slice for each button will be set up in a consistent fashion so that once visitors see how one button works, they will know how all the other buttons work.

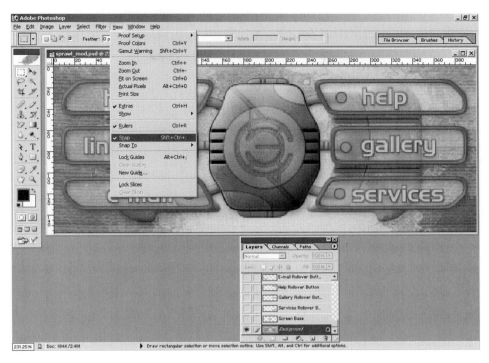

Figure 22.37   Toggle on the rulers, and make sure the Snap option is enabled.

3. (Optional) This image contains a lot of blue, which is also the default color for the guides. If you would like to change the color of the guides to make them easier to see, press Ctrl(⌘)+K to view the Preferences dialog box, and choose Guides, Grid & Slices from the top drop-down menu. Change the color for Guides (I used a Light Red). While you're there, notice also that the default Line Color for slices is also Light Blue. Try choosing Yellow for the Slices Line Color (see Figure 22.39).

4. Hold down the Shift key, and drag a guide down from the horizontal ruler. Position the guide just below the black line on the inside of the bottom portion of the Home button. Add four more horizontal guides (two each for the Links and E-mail buttons) by positioning the guides as described in step 2. Position the guides just below the black line on the inside top of the button and just above the black line on the inside bottom of the button (see Figure 22.40).

When you're finished, double-click the Hand tool to zoom out. Notice that the guides you've positioned for the Home, Links, and E-mail buttons are also perfectly positioned for the Help, Gallery, and Services buttons. Ain't symmetry grand?!

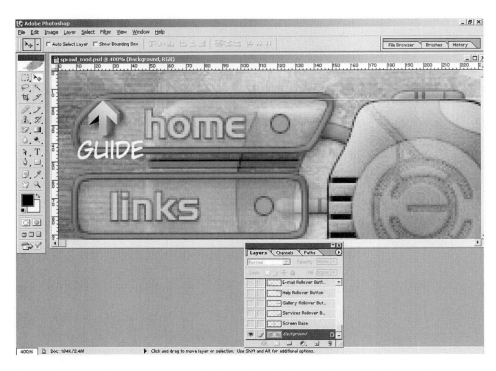

Figure 22.38   Place a horizontal guide just below the black outline within the inside top portion of the Home Button.

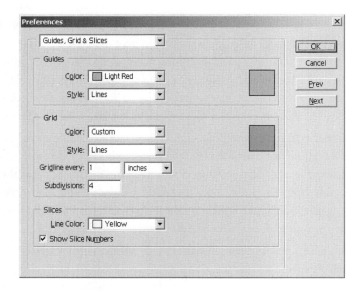

Figure 22.39   Edit Preferences to change the Guides and Slices Line Color options so that the guides will be easier to see.

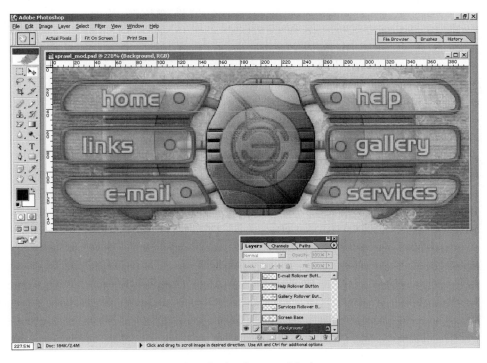

Figure 22.40   Position horizontal guides for the rest of the buttons.

5. Now you need to place two more horizontal guides for the center screen area. Press **Z** to switch to the Zoom tool, and click twice in the center of the interface to zoom in on this area. Now Shift+drag two horizontal guides from the horizontal rulers, and place one on the top of the circle and one on the bottom, as shown in Figure 22.41.

6. Now we need to place the vertical guides. Describing where to position the vertical guides is a little difficult, so we'll use pixel coordinates. To make sure that your rulers are using pixels as the unit of measurement, right-click (Macintosh: hold Ctrl and click) inside one of the rulers, and choose Pixels. You also can adjust the unit of measurement by choosing Edit, Preferences, Units & Rulers, as shown in Figure 22.42.

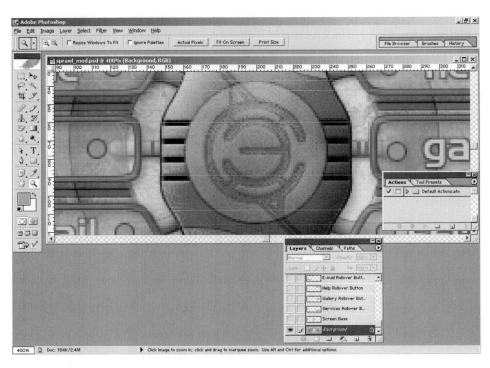

Figure 22.41   Place horizontal guides at the top and bottom of the circle for the center screen.

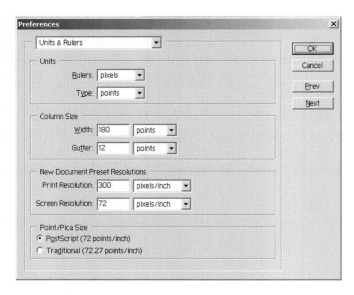

Figure 22.42   Ensure that the units for your rulers are set to pixels.

7. Now you need to position eight vertical guides. To do this, you can drag each guide out from the vertical ruler and place it in the correct position, but you'll use an alternative method to simplify the process. Choose View, New Guide. In the New Guide dialog box, choose Vertical Orientation, and type **11 px** for position. Click on OK. Repeat the View, New Guide command to position the remaining Vertical guides at the pixel coordinates 133, 147, 160, 239, 252, 266, and 387 (as shown in Figure 22.43).

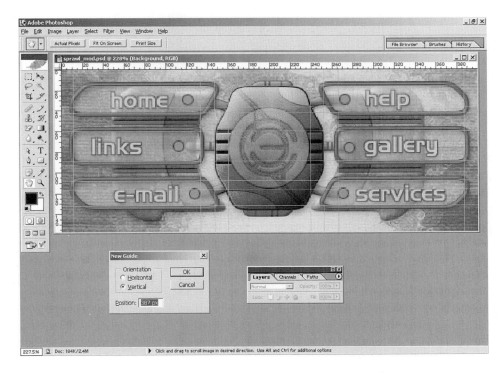

Figure 22.43   Place eight vertical guides using the View, New Guide command. These guides help isolate the buttons and central screen area.

Making the Slices

Now that all the guides are set, you're finally ready to slice:

Slicing the Image

1. Choose the Slice Select Tool from the Slice tool flyout menu on the toolbox. At the far right of the Options bar is a toggle switch for Show Auto Slice and Hide Auto Slice. This may seem counter-intuitive, but if the button reads Show Auto Slice, the Auto Slice layer is hidden. If it says Hide Audio Slice, the Auto Slice

layer is visible. You want the Auto Slice layer to be visible, so click the button if necessary to turn on the feature (the button should read Hide Auto Slice).

2. Now, choose the Slice tool from the toolbox. Using the Slice tool with the guides, draw a slice for the Home button. Start at the intersection of the guides at the upper left of the Home button, and end at the intersection of the guides at the lower right of the Home button (see Figure 22.44).

Notice that several slices adjacent to the slice for the Home button are automatically generated. A gray flag appears in the upper-left corner of auto-generated slices. Slices you create have a blue flag. If you switch to the Slice Select tool and try to select one of the auto-generated slices, you will see that you cannot select it. You can select only slices you create. You can, however, "promote" an auto-generated slice to a "user slice" by selecting Promote to User Slice from the Options bar when the Slice Select tool is active or when you right-click (Macintosh: hold Ctrl and click) on the gray slice flags.

Figure 22.44   Draw a slice over the Home button.

3. Right-click (Macintosh: hold Ctrl and click) on the blue flag in the upper-left corner of the slice you just created, and choose Edit Slice Options. In the Slice Options dialog box, change the name to **Home** and enter a URL. Click on OK (see Figure 22.45).

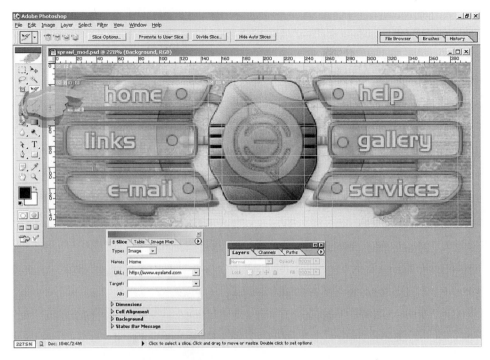

Figure 22.45   Change the name of the slice to Home and add a URL.

Insider

You also can open to the Slice Options dialog box from the Options bar when the Slice Select tool is active. Simply click to choose the active slice, and then click the Slice Options button on the Options bar. For the purpose of this exercise, enter any URL in the Slice Options dialog box. When preparing images for your own Web site, you should insert the Web site URL for the link that applies to the active slice for this section of the Slice Options dialog box.

Note

Take advantage of your options   If you leave the Name field showing the default slice name in the Slice Options dialog box, the result will be many slices generated with the document filename and some appended nonsense. When you enter your own slice names, you have the benefit of being able to easily identify the slices again later. Photoshop or ImageReady will use those slice names as the filenames. If you leave the URL field blank, nothing will happen when the user clicks the button. The Target field is used when you are working with HTML frames. The rest of the fields are not important unless you want to add Alt tags. The Slice Options dialog box also gives you the option of sizing and positioning the slice numerically, using the fields in the Dimensions section.

4. With the Slice tool still active, create slices for each of the buttons and for the screen area, as shown in Figure 22.46. Right-click (Macintosh: hold Ctrl and click) the flags in the upper-left corner of each slice, and choose Edit Slice Options to give each slice a name that corresponds to the button name and a URL. Name the screen area slice **Screen**. Do not add a URL to the Screen slice, however. The screen area will not be a button, and it will not have a rollover event assigned to it.

    Notice that the Links and Gallery buttons are not as wide as the rest of the buttons. Do not make the slices for the Links and Gallery buttons as wide as the slices for the other buttons.

Figure 22.46   Create the remaining slices, and use the Slice Options dialog box to change the name for each slice.

5. Press Ctrl(⌘)+Shift+S to save the file to your hard disk using the same filename. Keep the file and Photoshop open for the next exercise.

Creating Rollovers

Now you're finally ready to move into ImageReady. Before you launch ImageReady, be sure to save the document (Ctrl(⌘)+S). Because ImageReady and Photoshop use resources heavily (when launched together), it is always wise to save the file so that nothing is lost if resource levels become a problem. All that aside—it's just good practice in general to save your work frequently.

Now let's create some rollovers:

Creating the Rollovers

1. With the sprawl_mod.psd document still open, press Ctrl(⌘)+Shift+M to launch the document in ImageReady. Choose the Slice Select tool from the toolbox. Click the Home button slice to make it the active slice. Click the tab to view the Slice palette. If the palette is not open, go to the Window menu and choose Slice (see Figure 22.47).

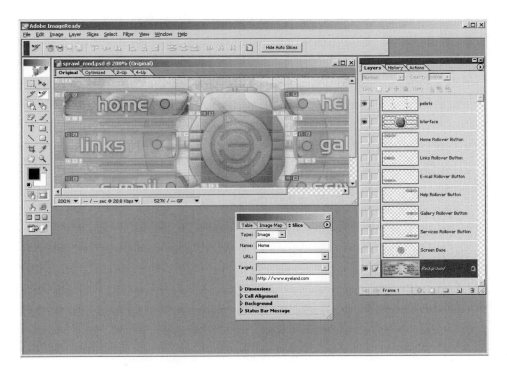

Figure 22.47   Open the interface in ImageReady, and view the Home slice information using the Slice palette. Notice that the slice information you entered in Photoshop appears in ImageReady, just the way you entered it. You also can edit the slice information in ImageReady and see the changes reflected when you jump back to Photoshop.

2. Click the Web Content tab to view the Web Content palette (or choose Window, Web Content). Scroll down to the Home slice.

22

Insider

Notice that the names used in the Web Content palette are those that were set previously in the Slice Options in Photoshop. Here is another great reason for taking the time to name your slices: The default names would be far less descriptive. Additionally, the thumbnails in the Web Content palette are usually too small to tell one similarly shaped button from another, so naming the slices really does help.

3. With the Home slice selected in the Web Content palette, click the Create rollover state icon at the bottom of the palette (next to the trash icon). A new thumbnail named Over is appended to the Home slice in the Web Content palette. Click the Over for the Home slice. Now turn on the visibility for the Home Rollover Button layer in the Layers palette (see Figure 22.48).

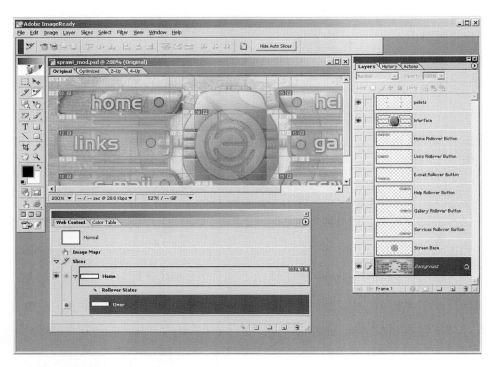

Figure 22.48   Add a rollover state to the Home slice layer, and turn on the Home Rollover Button layer visibility.

That's it! You just created a rollover state for the Home button. ImageReady basically reflects on the Over state of a button any changes you make in the Layers palette. In fact, the program does this not just for the Home slice alone, but also reflects the changes made to the Layers palette in any other slices as well. For instance, if you're working on the Over state for the Home slice and make a change to the Screen slice in the Layers palette, both slices will be changed on rollover. That is how you get your multi-slice rollover.

Editing and Optimizing the Slices

We have a problem. Have you noticed it yet? Some of the layer contents on the Layers palette are covering the changes you need to make in the screen slice area. We set up this scenario on purpose to illustrate how to make edits for situations like this in ImageReady. This little detour is unfortunately indicative of how things tend to work when you're doing a real job. No matter how much you prepare in Photoshop, sometimes problems crop up. Fortunately, ImageReady can handle most of the basic edits that you might need to do. Let's fix the problem:

Handling Basic Edits

1. Select View, Show, Slices to temporarily hide the slices. Press Ctrl(⌘)+ Shift+; (semicolon) to toggle off the Snap option. On the Layers palette, turn off the visibility for all the layers except the Interface layer. Click the Interface layer to make it the active layer. Then double-click the layer title and type **Central Platform** to rename this layer. Press Ctrl+J to duplicate the layer. Rename the duplicate layer by double-clicking on the layer title and typing **Button Bars** (see Figure 22.49). Turn off the visibility for the Central Platform layer. The Button Bars layer should still be active; if not, click on it to make it the active layer.

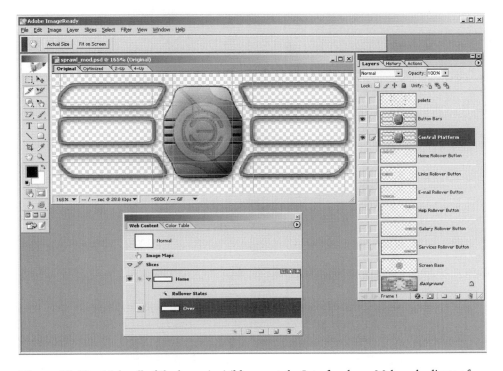

Figure 22.49   Make all of the layers invisible except the Interface layer. Make a duplicate of the Interface layer and rename the duplicate Button Bars and rename the Interface layer Central Platform.

2. Choose the Polygonal Lasso tool from the toolbox. Make a selection around the center screen object on the Button Bars layer. (Be careful to include the shadow for the center artwork, but exclude the button bars and their shadows.) The selection should be close to the left edge of the center object (to avoid the button shadows) and farther away from the right and bottom edge of the center object (to include the shadow for the center object). Press Backspace (Delete) to delete this center object selection from the Button Bars layer (see Figure 22.50). Press Ctrl(⌘)+Shift+I to invert the selection. Click the Central Platform layer to turn on the visibility and make it the active layer; then press Delete (Backspace) to delete the selection from the Central Platform layer. Press Ctrl+D to deselect. If you turn off the visibility for the Button Bars layer, you should see only the center object on the Central Platform layer.

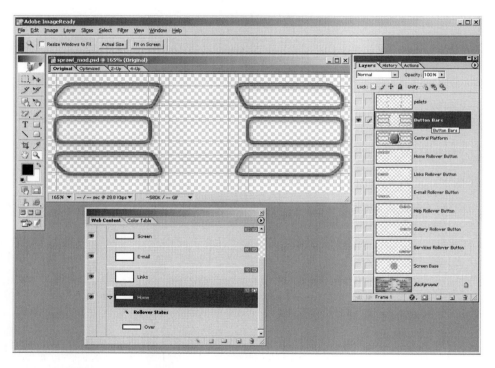

Figure 22.50   Delete the central component on the Button Bars layer.

3. Drag the Central Platform layer below the Screen Base layer. The Over state should still be active on the Web Content palette. On the Layers palette, turn on the visibility for the Background, Central Platform, Screen Base, Home Rollover Button, Button Bars, and Pellets layers (leave the visibility off for all other layers, as shown in Figure 22.51).

Insider

Now the Over state of the Home button reflects a change both on the Home button itself and over the screen area. Although you can't see any indication of it in the Over thumbnail, you've just implemented a multi-slice rollover. When we export the interface, ImageReady will generate the HTML/JavaScript code so that both the Home slice and the Screen slice will change when someone rolls over the Home button.

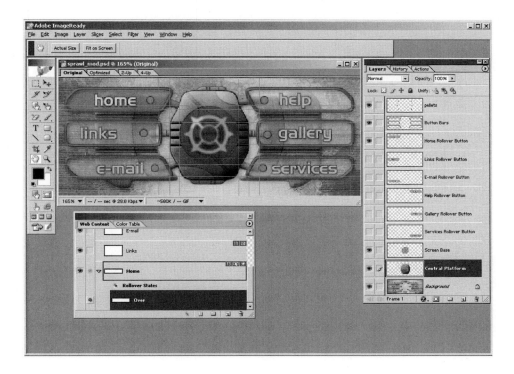

Figure 22.51 Return the visibility to the desired layers for the Home Over state on the Web Content palette.

4. Choose View, Show, Slices to toggle on the view of the slices. Press Ctrl(⌘)+Shift+; (semicolon) to toggle on the Snap option again.

5. Click Links in the Web Content palette. Click the Create rollover state icon at the bottom of the Web Content palette. With the Over state thumbnail active for the Links slice, turn on the visibility for the Links Rollover Button and Screen Base layers (see Figure 22.52).

Insider

You've created the rollover for the Links button. Notice that when you went from the Over state for the Home slice to the Links slice in the Web Content palette, the layers changed. ImageReady automatically reverted the visibility of the layers according to the way they were set for each slice or Over state. This makes it very easy for you to check your work. You can go back through the Over states for each slice and make sure that you have set up each Over state correctly.

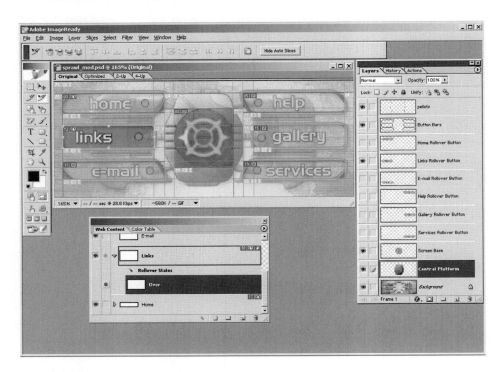

Figure 22.52   Select the Links slice, add a rollover state, and turn on the visibility to the Links Rollover Button and Screen Base layers.

6. Repeat step 5 for all the remaining button slices. Click the slice title in the Web Content palette, add an Over state, and then turn on the visibility of the Screen Base layer and the Rollover Button layer that corresponds to the slice title. For example, to create the Over state for the Services slice, click the Services slice in the Web Content palette. Click the Create rollover state icon at the bottom of the Web Content palette. With the Over thumbnail active for the Services slice, turn on the visibility for the Services Rollover Button and Screen Base layers (see Figure 22.53).

When you're finished, each slice that corresponds to the six buttons should have an Over state assigned to it in the Web Content palette. This process should be very simple. It's here where all the work in preparing a file pays off. You don't need to wade through a bunch of layers to create the rollover effects. These layers are clearly named and easy to track, so you can identify the layers to turn on easily.

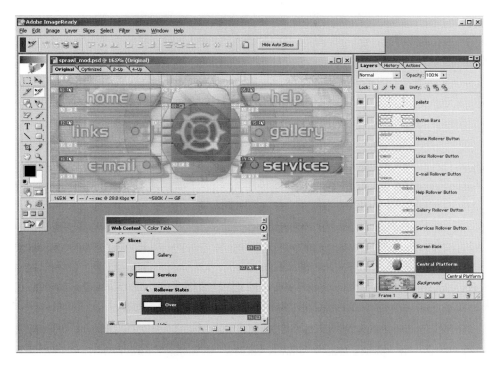

Figure 22.53   Create Over states for each of the slices that correspond to the buttons.

7. Let's optimize the file sizes of the slices so that they will all download faster. Click the Optimize tab to view the Optimize palette (or choose Window, Optimize). With the Slice Select tool active, click the Home slice. Click on the Optimized tab near the top of the main document title bar (see Figure 22.54).

Choosing a Format

When a slice is selected, the Optimize palette shows you the image settings for that slice. In this case, the image setting defaulted to GIF format. This format is great for solid colors, but for more photographic images or images like our sample interface, JPEG compresses much better.

Before you change the image settings for the Home slice to JPEG, let's determine whether switching to JPEG will make a difference.

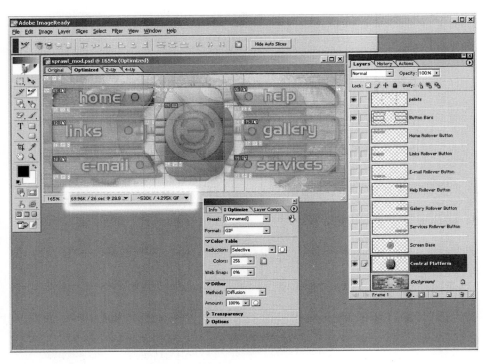

Figure 22.54   Open the Optimize palette, and switch to the Optimized tab. The status bar also provides information about the file and the current slice.

If you clicked on the Optimized tab near the top of the document window, the status bar at the bottom of the document window displays information about the file and the image slice (refer to Figure 22.54).

The first section on the left is merely the current Zoom level for the document. The second section tells you ImageReady's best guess as to what the total file size will be for all the images in this interface when the image is exported (and the slices and rollovers are generated). Notice that ImageReady estimates that this file will be 69.96KB with the current image settings.

Furthermore, this tab tells you approximately how long it will take for these images to download for a target connection rate. ImageReady uses 28.8Kbps as the default setting (for the average connection rate), but these days 56.6Kbps is probably a more accurate average.

Finally, over to the right, is another Image Information box that provides information about the selected image slice. The first number is an approximation of the overall *unoptimized* file size. The second number to the right is the "optimized" file size. You should pay attention to this number when you change the image setting for the slices. Notice in

Figure 22.54 that the Home button's slice size is 4.295KB when it is set to GIF format. Let's use the information in the status bar to help make the choice:

Defining a File Format for the Rollover

1. With the Home slice still selected, change the image settings from GIF to JPEG in the Optimize palette and compare the file sizes. You can see that ImageReady's default JPEG settings are excellent, so you can leave those settings at their default options.

    Now look at the far right Image Information box, and notice that the slice's size dropped from 4.295KB to only 1.895KB. Changing the image to JPEG cuts the files down to less than half their earlier size.

2. On your own, click the remaining slices, and change the GIF option for each one to JPEG in the Optimize palette. Using the Slice Select tool, click one of the auto-generated slices, and change it from GIF to JPEG. ImageReady will automatically convert all the other auto-generated slices to JPEG.

When you are done, look at the middle Image Information box. Notice that ImageReady now estimates the final total file size at 32KB: this is a savings of more than 50% from the original estimate of 69.96KB. As you can see, optimizing images for download over the Internet is extremely easy in ImageReady.

If you have a target size that you need to hit (let's say, for example, a client tells you the overall download needs to be less than 50KB), just adjust the image settings for the images, and monitor the Image Information boxes until you reach the size you need. When you've achieved the desired size, you're done. There is a little problem with this approach that you need to keep in mind, however. In these figures, ImageReady actually fails to account for the rollover images. What you are actually getting is information on only the default states of all the slices. The only way to accurately determine the overall download requirements for the page is to export the interface and check the results yourself.

Exporting and Testing the Interface

Now all that is left for you to do is to export the interface and test it out. Here's how:

Checking Out the Interface for Real

1. Choose File, Save Optimized As, and save the interface to your hard drive. You will see a progress bar as ImageReady goes through and processes the files (which includes generating the HMTL and JavaScript code). Everything is saved to your hard drive.

22

2. When ImageReady is done, find and open the HTML file that was generated so that you can preview the interface in a browser. Roll over the buttons and see how they work. Every time you roll over a button, the title should change color, and you should see the central screen area reflect a change.

3. You can preview the code in your current browser by opening the View menu and choosing Source. You can also press Ctrl(⌘)+Alt(Opt)+P from inside ImageReady to preview the code in a browser. When you do this, ImageReady shows you both the interface and the HTML/JavaScript code (see Figure 22.55).

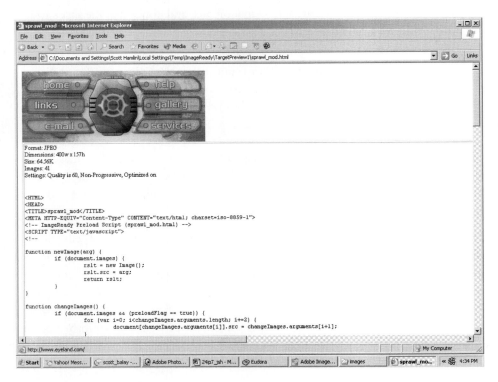

Figure 22.55   Using the preview in a default browser shows the interface and the HTML/JavaScript code.

Summary

As you've seen in this chapter, good preparation in Photoshop makes working in ImageReady almost an afterthought. ImageReady is capable of doing a lot of what Photoshop can do; but when you're working in ImageReady, you want to focus on what it does best—rollovers, animations, image maps, and so on. Take the time to set things up correctly in Photoshop because Photoshop offers a more robust feature set for the actual designing aspect of your graphics. After you set things up, you can focus on creating rollovers and optimizing image slices. Then you can export the results and easily be done with the ImageReady side of preparing files for the Web.

Let's take a further look at this image optimizing stuff as it relates to your personal Web site or your email attachments. Just turn the page!

Chapter 23

Optimizing Your Images for the Web and Email

If we look at the word *optimal* and all its sub-variants, we are led to believe that optimizing anything—an image file, a yo-yo, your housecat—makes that thing the very

In this chapter, you'll learn

- How the GIF file format differs from the JPEG format
- How to use GIF optimization options
- How to optimize JPEG images
- All about the JPEG 2000 file format
- Fast facts for using the Portable Network Graphic (PNG) format

best (of whatever it is). However, *optimization* is a nebulous term when it comes to Photoshop, ImageReady, and the files these Adobe products handle. Optimization, in the Adobe vernacular, means "making the very best-looking picture, using the fewest pixels, or making the smallest file size." If this definition seems confusing, just read along in this chapter, and we'll show you how to make the best-looking image to post or email, while making it the smallest (in file size) you possibly can.

The Lowdown on GIF

Surely by now you've been confronted with a choice: When you want to save to the Web, do you choose the GIF or JPEG file format? You won't find a lot of material written on the qualitative difference between the two formats, so this chapter is probably a really good place to unravel the mystery.

GIF: Indexed Color

As explained in Chapter 0, "Answers to the Most Important Imaging Questions," the format of a GIF image is limited with respect to the number of colors it can hold, and as a result, the colors are palletized (indexed). They are indexed in a color table (which is stored in the header of the image file) for quick loading into, say, a Web page. GIF is not a new file format, and frankly, most of the interest in this file format is that it can display one out of the maximum 256 unique colors as transparent. The other novelty with the GIF format is that you can create animations (GIF can hold multiple images within a single file and then play them back in succession). But is GIF really the best file format for displaying the Mona Lisa or the sum total of your labors on an image (GIFs are usually made from *copies* of more color-capable work)?

It depends.

GIF was actually created years ago to meet the demands of subscribers to CompuServe and other online services who wanted to see robust color images that were fairly large (remember, a 15-inch monitor was considered "large" only 10 years ago!) and would download to their machines within their lifetime. And thus GIF was born. Today, we also have JPEG, a much more "color-realistic" file format for the Web, and even the Portable Network Graphic (PNG) format, which is still a distant third place file format because the leading Internet browser, Microsoft Explorer, doesn't support it.

File Formats and the Law

Besides lack of support, legal hassles are also a good way to prevent technology for viewing Web media from reaching people. For years, using the GIF file format has been dicey because UniSys holds the patents to the compression algorithms (the "recipe" for making the file format) and semi-regularly makes noises to the effect that companies such as Adobe must pay a royalty for including the GIF format in its software.

Additionally, the future of JPEG 2000, a version with much more sophisticated compression algorithms—and better color—than the version we use today, is up in the air. At least one company, like UniSys, claims the patent rights on the compression and periodically threatens to collect royalties on programs that use JPEG 2000 compression, the product (artwork) of such compression, or both.

For the moment, it's cool to use GIF and JPEG 2000. But 2000 is not going to get the support it needs to become another player in the online artwork compression follies until manufacturers can rest assured that the file format is free and not subject to a royalty surcharge.

The lesson, dear reader? It's not always technology itself that holds up the computer design progress.

Photos That Compress Well with GIF

Now back to GIF. Yup, it's cool to use GIF when you want to send a photo of your newborn across the nation, but not every photo is right for this format. GIF is a good choice for compressing photos with these qualities:

- **Limited colors.** Because GIF is limited to 256 colors, it is good if the original has limited colors. A picture of a peacock with a 13-scoop ice cream cone throwing confetti into a psychedelic light show would not make a good original image for the GIF engine in Photoshop to color reduce to only 256 unique colors. Now, a poster (a graphic, not a photo) of your newborn (who probably has fewer than 25 unique colors in his or her face), a car, a resort—images that have strong graphic edges and composition but a limited palette—are best.

- **High-frequency images.** Huh? A high-frequency image is one that has contrasting colors from pixel to pixel. A low-frequency image, in contrast, has a smooth and low color transition between pixels, such as an ocean wave or a sunset. We naturally think of low-frequency images as having few colors because the colors in the image are mostly of the same hue. In reality, though, a sunset is packed with unique colors because there are so many color transitions in the same hue going on. Low-frequency images display banding when you attempt to make a GIF copy of them. *Banding* is the awkward, chunky-looking arrangement of slices of an image that is the result of the file format not having enough colors to display them all.

So, it's important to choose the image you want to post or email by evaluating its visual qualities. After you've chosen an image and determined the best format for compressing it, you're ready to optimize the image. ImageReady offers a slew of options as to how you want your GIF image optimized, and now is as good a time as any to start covering them.

GIF Optimization Options

Let's run down the options for your GIF-to-be, as they appear on the Optimize palette in ImageReady. Check out Figure 23.1.

23

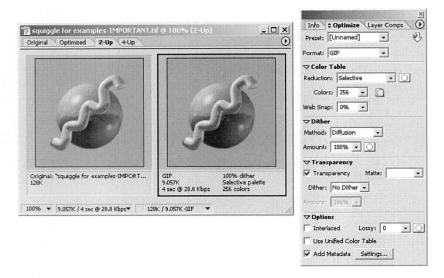

Figure 23.1   The Optimize palette, extended.

As mentioned earlier, you need to build a color table for a GIF image because the image is limited to 256 maximum colors. To start learning about this process, launch Photoshop and open Squiggle.tif from the Examples/Chap23 folder on the Companion CD as a test image. Press Ctrl(⌘)+Shift+M to jump over to ImageReady, and click on the 2-Up tab on the image window so you can see what the proposed optimization will look like; you'll also be able to see how the file size will be reduced. Make sure you have the Optimize palette (Window, Optimize) in view as we discuss the Color Table options from this palette.

Color Table Optimization

The list of preset optimizations can be a bit cryptic without some definition. Let's tackle the presets one by one:

- **Perceptual.** The human eye is more sensitive to certain colors than others. Perceptual creates a color table that appears brilliant, appealing to the eye by drawing from those colors to which we have greater optic sensitivity.

- **Selective.** This preset is the default option for optimization. It produces a color table that contains colors that are the most faithful to the original image. Perceptual might produce images whose colors are more pleasing to the eye, but not as accurately translated from the original as the Selective process.

- **Adaptive.** Adaptive is a weird one. This process creates a color table consisting of colors in the spectrum that most commonly appear in the target image. This is not to say that the color table will be the most accurate—the Selective option does that. Instead, the Adaptive option creates a color table that favors the pre-ferred spectrum of colors in the original. Say you have a picture of a blue sky with a lot of picnickers on a green turf. The Adaptive color optimization will favor blue and grass green and limit the various colors that the picnickers might be wearing.

- **Restrictive (Web).** Years ago Netscape established a palette of colors that are "Web safe"—colors that will be displayed with consistency from one monitor to the next. Primarily, this palettization technique is useful for avoiding dithering (more on dithering shortly) when the image is displayed using an 8-bit color palette. Although useful for establishing conformity and ensuring that colors are displayed as intended, Web palettization can also lead to larger saved file sizes than other techniques.

- **Custom.** This preset uses the current color table. The custom palette is not updated when you make changes to the image.

- **Mac OS.** The Mac OS uses this color table when creating Hundreds of Colors images. The palletized colors are unique to the Mac OS both in content and in color ordering within the color table of an image indexed using this scheme. A Mac OS palletized image might not look correct when viewed on a Windows machine.

- **Windows.** Like the Mac OS scheme, this option orders and formulates colors according to the Windows OS indexed color table. These images might not look correct when viewed on the Mac OS.

Recommendation? Stick to Selective, Perceptual, or Adaptive, in this order, for the bulk of your optimization work.

Now let's look at the other options in the Optimize palette.

Number of Colors, Channel Influence, and Web Snap

Look at Figure 23.2 for a visual reference of the stuff we're going to cover here:

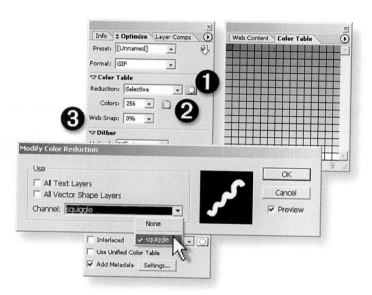

Figure 23.2   More options are available in the Color Table Area of the Optimize palette.

- Next to callout 1, note the icon that looks suspiciously like a mask. Yup, if you want to have ImageReady produce a color table that is heavily influenced by only a specific area of the image, here's your chance. To use this option, you first create an alpha channel in the image where you want ImageReady to search for the color table. Next, you click on the icon and then choose the channel (or text or vector shape layer) that you want to isolate. The pink squiggly shape was isolated in this example; consequently, the color table for the image will be built based on the pixels described by the alpha channel selection.

- The Colors drop-down menu, shown next to callout 2, is the place where you can determine how many colors will be in the color table. The cute little icon to the right of the drop-down will produce the color table visually if you click on it. The color table window is shown to the right in this figure. The fewer colors you use, the coarser the resulting image will look; but as you will note at the bottom of the image window, you save on overall file size, and sometimes that's important. If, for example, you type **Hi, mom!** using a solid color against a solid background, with antialiasing, the image has perhaps 15 unique colors, and it would be wasteful to define a color table with more colors than that.

Oh, yes, because there's a drop-down for the number of colors, you can type any number you like in there (as long as that number doesn't exceed 256).

- Callout 3 calls your attention to Web Snap (closely related to Web Crackle and Web Pop). Seriously, this dynamic control helps you determine how closely colors are assigned in the color table that are Web Safe colors. Unless you're building a Web Safe site, you may never need to use this control.

On top of this miasma of palettes and boxes is the Modify Color Reduction dialog box. This is the place where you decide whether the contents of an alpha channel are protected or exposed to the same amount and type of color reduction (optimization) as the area outside the alpha channel.

Dithering

Dithering is a method of visually smoothing out the appearance of an image that has a very small color table. You've seen the effect before: A dithered image sort of looks as though you're viewing it through bathroom shower glass (see Figure 23.3).

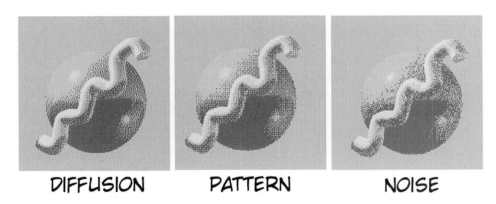

Figure 23.3   ImageReady offers three different types of dithering.

You can choose from among three different types of dithering in ImageReady:

- **Diffusion.** This is perhaps the most visually appealing of dither types, and it is the only type that allows you to control the amount of dithering. This type of dithering also enables you to use a channel to direct the amount of dithering at any particular location within the image.

- **Pattern.** To use this dither type is a matter of taste; I don't like it. The visual effect is that of a doily or some other forced, obvious pattern.

- **Noise.** Noise dithering yields an image that appears to have resulted from a fountain pen explosion or something.

Advice? Try to use dithering as little as possible. When you have a limited color palette, your choice is a trade-off between dithering and solid fields of color that most likely don't represent your original art very well.

Transparency

As mentioned earlier, the GIF file format enables you to display one of its 256 colors as transparent. In the Transparency section of the Optimize palette, these options are available:

- **Matte.** This is the color, within the color table of the selected image, that is dropped out. Click on the drop-down button and make your choice. You can also choose Other and then choose from the Color Picker, a nice feature.

- **Dither.** As with image dithering itself, transparency dithering enables you to avoid harsh edges along a transparent image.

Options

In the Options area of the Optimization palette, you can find options for metadata and other neat stuff. Let's run through the list of options in this area:

- **Interlaced.** Interlacing is a process by which the image streams to your monitor, as opposed to being delivered in one large chunk. The advantage of interlacing is that you know that the image is downloading; you're not waiting patiently while a possible broken link on a Web page is just sitting there. However, the disadvantage is that not all browsers and applications know how to read an interlaced GIF; the image could look ultra-funky when you attempt to view it after downloading it.

Insider

My opinion on interlacing? Internet connections are becoming so fast these days that the need for interlacing is dwindling to the point where it's more of a possible annoyance to the receiver than an expeditious courtesy.

- **Lossy.** This option controls how much compression you use on the image. The GIF compression algorithm allows for great amounts of compression at the price of image quality. Check the right pane in the 2-Up view of your image to see what this setting does.

Insider

The channel icon, when clicked, enables you to choose a pre-saved image area to apply greater amounts of Lossy compression.

- **Use Unified Color Table.** We need to go back to Chapter 22, "Creating Animations and Rollovers," to better explain this option. You can use GIF images as rollover buttons on a Web page; to do so, you need to save a file with multiple images. In this situation, a Unified color table is probably a good thing; you're saving all the images within the file to a single color table spec. Visually, saving the file this way prevents the rollover button from "popping" when the visitor to your site hovers over the button.

- **Add Metadata.** This option enables you to tag the image with text. This feature is handy if you want others to be able to identify your work online.

That's pretty much the show for the GIF file format. Now let's move on to a more capable file format.

Optimizing JPEG Images

Years ago, a need was seen for an image file format that produces more lifelike, photographic images. The Joint Photographic Experts Group (JPEG) was formed to create standards, and today, we have a choice between GIF and JPEG when creating Web pages and emailing files to friends and family.

Unlike GIF, JPEG is a lossy compression file format. That is, image data that you might never see anyway is cast out of the image when the file is created. The Experts Group decided that the human eye is less sensitive to changes in tone than in color, and so by averaging tones, a "well-compressed" JPEG image can show little or no data loss over the original.

Figure 23.4 shows the Optimize palette in ImageReady when we decide on JPEG as the optimization type.

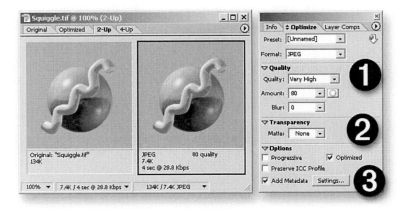

Figure 23.4   The options for JPEG compression.

Quality

Callout 1 in Figure 23.4 identifies the Quality area. You have a number of Quality choices, from Low to Maximum, but you probably don't want to "shop" for compression options in this way. Instead, use the slider next to the Amount label. Next to this pop-out slider, you'll also find a channel icon that enables you to pick a channel out of the original image and apply more compression to just the area in the image that corresponds to that channel.

Also in the Quality area is the Blur option. Why would you want to blur an image? Simple. JPEG compression causes artifacting at high compression levels, and blurring is an effective way of diminishing the appearance of these artifacts. In Figure 23.5, you can see that the edges are corrupted around two different colored areas in the image. Admittedly, this example uses high compression settings, but it's just an example of how things tend to go using high JPEG compression. Try watching the 2-up image as you slide the Amount to a lower number approaching 0 (zero), and you will see artifacting first-hand. Also, some "blocking" happens in areas of similar tones; this effect might not happen often, but, again, blurring helps to disguise such nasty artifacts.

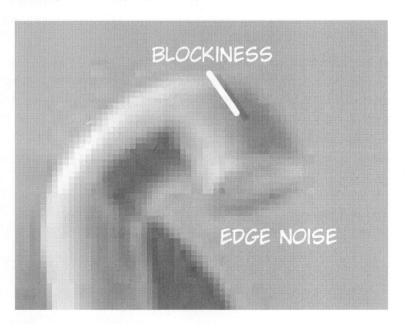

Figure 23.5   An example of JPEG "artifacting."

Transparency

JPEG was designed as an extensible standard, one that could adopt extra features as they were invented. Transparency is not recognized by all browsers and programs that can display images, but ImageReady and Photoshop support this feature. Callout 2 back in Figure 23.4 marks the Transparency options in the Optimize palette: You have your choice of a Matte (show through) color, and perhaps in the future, more programs will be able to recognize this nicely.

Options

The Options area of the Optimize palette, marked by callout 3 in Figure 23.4, includes a lot of new stuff for us to cover, including these options:

- **Progressive.** Like the Interlaced option for GIF images, Progressive is a method for sending streaming data for the JPEG image format. The advantage of using this method? The image starts building immediately onscreen. The disadvantage to using Progressive (as I'm sure you've guessed already) is that not all browsers or applications can read a progressive JPEG.

- **Optimized.** This is a good option to use. Using this option results in virtually no compatibility problems. Turning it on ensures that your image is tightly compressed and complies with all the JPEG compression standards.

- **Preserve ICC Profile.** As shown in other chapters, some image browsers can use an International Color Consortium (ICC) profile to color-correct an image. In general, including this information doesn't hurt.

- **Add Metadata.** Again, this option is used for tagging text to an image. You don't need to add metadata unless you want the world to know the creator and any other special keyword phrases that pertain to the image.

You would think that the JPEG story was over after you filled out the Optimize palette's options, but it's really not. Let's look at the grandson to JPEG, JPEG 2000, in the following section.

JPEG 2000

JPEG 2000 is a file format that's built for the future. Inevitably, then, some of its options might seem confusing. This section is included in this book to dispel misconceptions about using this futuristic file format. Let's say it again, though, before we start: JPEG 2000 is not supported by very many applications and browsers. You would be doing the graphics community a favor by writing a note to Microsoft encouraging the company to support the standard. Eventually, the standard *will* catch on, and having the big boys such as Adobe Systems behind the idea only speeds up the process.

Installing the JPEG 2000 Plug-In

Before you can use the JPEG 2000 plug-in, you have to install it; it's not installed by default like other Photoshop filters. Fortunately, this process is an easy one: Just drag the plug-in from the installation disk to C:\Adobe\Photoshop CS\Plug-Ins\Adobe Photoshop Only\File Formats (see Figure 23.6).

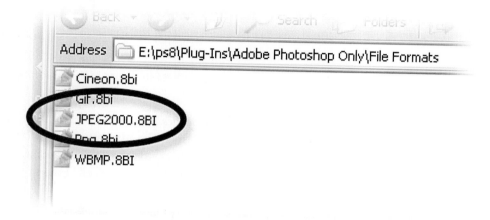

Figure 23.6   Put the plug-in here, if you've installed Photoshop to your E drive. Otherwise, find the location of Photoshop and drop the filter in the File Formats folder.

Restart Photoshop, and then open the file that you want to save as a JPEG 2000 image. Choose File, Save As, and choose JPEG 2000 from the Format menu. Specify a filename and location, select saving options, and click Save, which opens the JPEG 2000 dialog box. You will most likely want to use the .jp2 file extension, a la Myfile.jp2.

> **Note**
>
> **Saving your alpha channel**   You can save an alpha channel along with a JPEG2000 file.

The following sections describe the options, as laid out in Figure 23.7. These options include JPF Settings (callout 1), Optimization (callout 2), Advanced (callout 3), Metadata Format (callout 4), and Color Settings Format (callout 5).

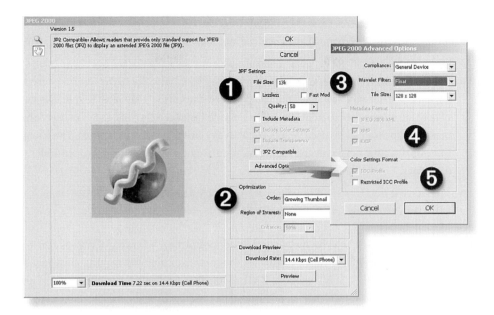

Figure 23.7   The options you have to choose from when saving to JPEG 2000 file format.

JPF Settings

Look at where callout 1 is located in Figure 23.7. The JPF Settings options are the place where we start working with JPEG 2000. These options include

- **File Size.** You can enter a value here to set the final saved size of the image. The value in the Quality text box will adjust to the best quality for the file size you enter.

- **Lossless.** If you choose the Lossless check box, the Quality slider is dimmed.

- **Fast Mode.** File size control is disabled when you choose this option. Basically, Fast Mode is standard JPEG 2000 encoding without other, more advanced options we'll describe in a moment.

- **Include Metadata.** You can choose to save all that nice file stuff you may have entered in the file browser when this file was selected.

Advanced Options

If you click on Advanced Options, you move into the special pop-up box identified by callout 3. Note that you may never need to access these options, though, because they are *very* special:

- **Compliance.** General Device compliance is usually the only option available, and it's a good one. You want the most different Web readers to be able to access (display) the file.

- **Wavelet Filter.** A *wavelet* is a type of encoding that basically turns an image into a fractal so that you can scale the image more smoothly. This setting specifies the *type* of numbers (coefficients) used to encode the file. Selecting the Lossless compression option automatically sets the Wavelet Filter option to Integer. The Float filter option may sharpen the image but could cause it to adopt noise around the edges.

- **Tile Size.** When low-quality values are used to optimize images smaller than 1,024 by 1,024 pixels, using the largest tile size produces better results.

Callout 4 marks an area that includes the Metadata Format Advanced Options (grayed out in Figure 23.7). It is here that you can set the metadata type for tagging your image. JPEG2000 XML is JPEG 2000–specific XML data; this option is available only if the image file contains this data. XMP is File Info data, and EXIF is digital camera data.

Callout 5 marks the Color Settings Format options. You use these options to select the Color Settings Format to include in the image file. The ICC Profile option, the default, includes the full ICC profile specified in the Save As dialog box. You might want to use this option if you intend to send the image to be printed. It maintains color consistency. The Restricted ICC Profile option is intended for use in portable devices such as cell phones and PDAs.

Optimization and Download Preview

Let's back up for a moment and look at the Optimization goodies near callout 2. The first of these is the Order option. Order is the way the pixels onscreen are going to build to arrive at the finished image. You have three choices:

- **Growing Thumbnail.** This is perhaps the coolest option for display. Click on Preview to see what I mean. The image begins small and then spirals out to the full-sized image.

- **Progressive.** This is a "streaming data" type resolution of the image. It is displayed as a crude bitmap at first and then resolves to full resolution.

- **Color.** This is a novel effect; the image is displayed almost immediately in black and white and then resolves into full color.

Suggestion? Use whatever effect you think will draw the most attention, remembering, of course, that you can only email JPEG2000 files; the Web doesn't support them yet.

The Region of Interest option refers to whether you want to give download priority to an area described in an alpha channel. For example, the Squiggle image has an alpha channel describing the squiggle; this area would resolve first.

Finally, you can preview how quickly or slowly your image will resolve by choosing a transfer rate from the drop-down box and then clicking Preview.

It's our hope that widespread adoption of JPEG2000 will happen to the extent that it eventually is acknowledged as a Web object natively supported by browsers. It's really a versatile, progressive (pardon the pun) image file format.

Not to Forget PNG!

To wrap up our roundup of Web file formats, it's only fair that we devote a little space here to a sparsely used but robust file format: the Portable Network Graphic (or PNG). PNG is a gift to the graphics world; its runtime is free, and you'll never be charged a license for using it. It was created as a response to the GIF file format licensing I mentioned earlier.

About the only bad news about PNG is that it is not supported by the major browsers. This may change in time. In the meantime, PNG is a wonderful, lossless format that can be used as an interchange between programs that understand PNG, for swapping and working with alpha channels. To see some of PNG's Optimization options, check out Figure 23.8.

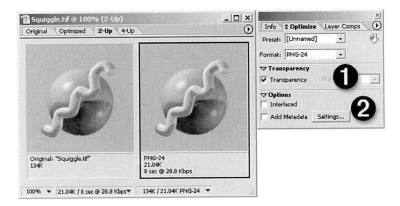

Figure 23.8   The PNG Optimization features.

There are basically two kinds of PNG: an 8-bit version with a 1-bit mask (similar in configuration to a GIF image) and a 24-bit image with an 8-bit mask. The options for the 8-bit PNG are so similar to GIF that I'll simply refer you to that section for definitions of Dither, Color Table, and so on.

PNG 24-bit, as shown by callout 1, offers these Transparency options:

- **Transparency.** You can choose whether or not to use transparency. Disabling transparency saves on overall file size.
- **Matte.** You also have your selection of matte color (color that drops out when viewed). Choose from the Web Safe palette, or choose any color at all from the Color Picker.

The options near callout 2 include the following:

- **Interlaced.** PNG supports the capability to send its data as streaming, so there is a "build" of the image the moment the image is displayed.
- **Add Metadata.** PNG supports metadata for tagging your images with text information within the file's header.

The really nice thing about PNG is that it is lossless. Additionally, you can obtain quite good compression using PNG, almost as good as JPEG, given a specific type of picture. Alas, we designers need to rally and ensure that JPEG2000 and PNG are accepted by Microsoft and other purveyors of Web browsers!

Summary

We've completed the survey on file formats that you can use to either email or post images on the Web. As you can see, at present, JPEG is the lingua franca of the Web for high-quality images, and designers commonly turn to GIF for animations and very small images that have an equally small color palette.

Choosing the right format for email and Web posting is only part of working smarter in Photoshop—which is a not-too-clever segue into the next part of our book. Want to see 10 really neat tricks you can perform in no time that'll enhance your work? The answers are only but a page or two away!

Part VIII

Working Smarter and Quicker in Photoshop

Chapter 24

Ten Photoshop Tricks

Hey, by now you've probably noticed that every chapter has a project, several techniques are outlined to accomplish a grand goal, and the chapter is about 26 pages

In this chapter, you'll learn

- How to use Photoshop to firm up your subject's neckline
- How to create images from text
- How to work with an image's color palette using practical techniques
- How to edit image areas with "fringed" edges using hands-on techniques
- How to make a photo look like a painting
- How to create a seamless fractal tiled image
- How to put a bronze figure inside a person's clothing
- How to use Adobe Dimensions with Photoshop
- How to fix a frightening photo with Photoshop
- How to retouch a drop shadow you've added to an image

long. Well, right now might be a good time to break stride and concentrate on *little* gems of techniques that don't belong to a *specific* assignment.

And yes, this chapter *could* have been called "11 Photoshop Tricks" or "9.7 Photoshop Tricks," but 10 seemed like a comfortable number, that's all!

Before we begin, I have a confession to make: *Yessss*, I used programs *other* than Photoshop (gasp) to create some of the tricks in this chapter. Not to worry—you'll get the gist of a trick or an effect without spending an extra dime. Perhaps you'll be so awestruck by program X or Y that you'll actually want to buy it, and if that's the case, make sure you recommend where you found the trick (hint: in this book) to a friend or twelve.

Trick 1: Getting Rid of a Wattle

First of all, it might be useful to define *wattle*. This term, which my wife learned from my mother-in-law, describes slack flesh that descends from one's chin to the neck. In Figure 24.1, you can see what I mean. If you're a Hollywood actor or somehow sneaked to the front of the gene pool (or if you're under 20), you probably have a connection between your jawline and your neck that can be described by a T-square—a perfect (don't you hate 'em?) 90-degree angle. For the rest of us, we have to be content with the image at the right. Let's send a distress call to Photoshop post haste!

The technique to follow is applied to a *front* view of a person with a wattle. Here's how it's done:

Firming Up a Jawline

1. Open the Wattle.tif image from the Examples\Chap24 folder on the companion CD.

2. Press **Q** to enter Quick Mask mode. Choose the Brush tool and a soft round brush (a 21-pixel brush may work well in this instance). Paint over the area identified in Figure 24.2 with the Quick Mask tint.

3. Press **Q** to switch back to Standard Editing mode. Depending on your Quick Mask settings, you may see a selection around the border edges of the document. If this is the case, press Ctrl(⌘)+Shift+I to invert the selection. Press Ctrl(⌘)+Alt(Opt)+D and choose a Feather radius of 3 (pixels). Click on OK.

4. Right-click (Macintosh: hold Ctrl and click) over the thumbnail icon on the Layers palette, and choose Layer via Copy. The copied area is on the current editing layer.

Example of an unwanted Wattle

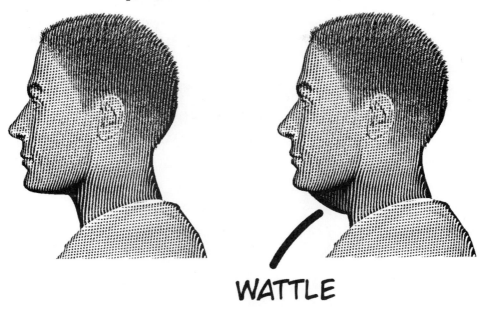

WATTLE

Figure 24.1   Waxing wistful about wattles.

Figure 24.2   This is the area where the wattle exists.

5. Press Ctrl(⌘)+L to go to the Levels command. Visibly darken the layer; for this assignment, adjust the black slider to the right until the Input Levels reading is around 36, and then adjust the midpoint slider also toward the right until the Input Levels reading is around 0.93. Click on OK to apply the tone change (see Figure 24.3).

Figure 24.3   The result—a less noticeable wattle.

6. Blur the layer a little. Choose Filter, Blur, and then Blur.

7. Press Ctrl(⌘)+S. Save the image to your hard disk if you like. Or better still, get out a picture of your own now that features a wattle and un-wattle it.

Neat, huh? You ain't seen *nuthin'* yet....

Trick 2: Creating an Image Out of Text

I'm sure you've seen this effect before: a black-and-white high-contrast image is made up of text or symbols. A couple of hard-to-find plug-ins can do this (I believe that Alien Skin Software has one), but wouldn't it be cool to be able to create the effect yourself?

Materials needed (and provided on the companion CD) are a black-and-white photo and a text file. On the companion CD, we included a copy of the Gettysburg Address and a public domain picture of Abraham Lincoln. If you want to use your own photo, you should know that the Lincoln picture has been filtered, and you should filter your photo, too. I posterized the Lincoln picture to about six levels.

Ready to build a picture of Lincoln from the Gettysburg Address?

Creating a Textual Image

1. Open Gettysburg Address.txt from the Examples\Chap24 folder on the companion CD. The file should open in a standard text editor program; make sure Word Wrap is turned on in the text editor program (go to the Format menu, and Word Wrap should be checked).

2. Press Ctrl(⌘)+A to select all the text. Press Ctrl(⌘)+C to copy the text to the Clipboard. Exit the text editor.

3. In Photoshop, open the Lincoln.tif image from the Examples\Chap24 folder on the companion CD.

4. Click the Create a new layer icon at the bottom of the Layers palette to create a layer above Lincoln. Press **D** for the default colors (black will be the foreground color; and white, the background). Press Ctrl(⌘)+Delete (Backspace) to fill the new layer with white.

Insider

> Press Alt(Opt)+Delete (Backspace) to fill with the foreground color, and Ctrl(⌘)+Delete (Backspace) to fill with background color. These shortcuts save you the time and keystrokes required to switch the background color to the foreground.

5. Choose the Type tool, and make sure the Options bar shows black as the selected text color. Drag a marquee selection that encompasses the entire image. This method of making a marquee selection before placing the text will ensure that the text wraps properly throughout the entire document.

6. You should see a blinking cursor inside the marquee selection. Press Ctrl(⌘)+V. The text will plop into the image window.

7. Now, to make an effective "text as photo" composition, the font needs to be dense, the leading needs to be tight, and the point size needs to be larger than average. In Figure 24.4, you can see that I took out the paragraph breaks and chose Compacta as the font at 40 points with 42-point leading. And the paragraph alignment is Center text. Do something like this with one of your own bold typefaces, and use the Character palette (Window, Character) to make similar adjustments.

Figure 24.4 Try to leave as little whitespace as possible when formatting the text.

8. Merge the text with the white layer. Just for reference here, Figure 24.5 shows the picture of Lincoln you'll be using.

9. To ease confusion, rename the layer with text **Gettysburg Address**, and rename the layer with the picture of Lincoln, well, **Lincoln**.

10. Choose Image, Calculations. In the Source 1 field, specify Gettysburg Address. In the Source 2 field, specify Lincoln. Check the Invert check box for Lincoln. For the Blending field, choose Subtract, and for the Result field, choose New Channel (see Figure 24.6). Click on OK to apply the calculations.

Figure 24.5 This photo will become a textual image.

Insider

When you're working in the Calculations dialog box, you can also choose other options from the Result drop-down menu. The option you choose will determine where the results will be displayed. The selection you made in step 10 will place the results in an alpha channel that you can view from the Channels palette. But if you prefer to have the results in a new document window, choose New Document from the Result drop-down menu instead and then continue with step 11.

Insider

If you chose New Channel from the Result drop-down menu as instructed in step 10, the result will be displayed on the Alpha 1 channel on the Channels palette. Click on the Channels tab to view the Channels palette (or choose Window, Channels), and then click on the Alpha 1 channel to make sure it is the active channel before performing the next step.

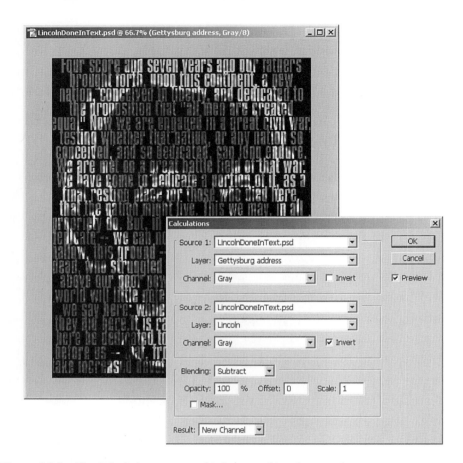

Figure 24.6   The Calculations command is key to making the textual image.

11. Press Ctrl(⌘)+I to invert the tonal scheme of the image. Now, depending on the font and font size you used, the image might need a little more contrast for you to clearly see the image of Lincoln. Press Ctrl(⌘)+L to display the Levels command, and then drag the White Point slider to the left until you see something like that shown in Figure 24.7.

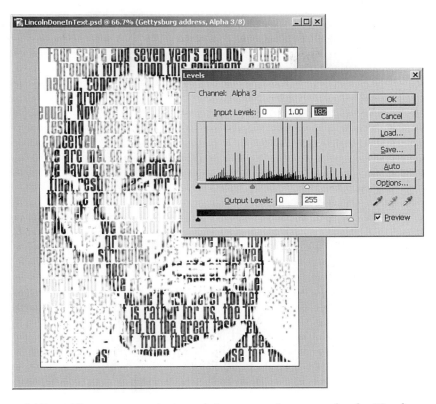

Figure 24.7   Adding contrast to the image helps sort out the tones and makes Lincoln more visually prominent.

I2. Save the image to your hard disk, get some text and a black-and-white image of your own, and try this example with different fonts.

Figure 24.8 shows the finished image. The trick here is to make sure that the text you use covers as much of the photo as possible.

Figure 24.8   The finished image.

Two down and eight to go. Let's see what other trouble we can get into!

Trick 3: Borrowing an Image's Color Palette

Actually, you'll learn how to *steal* an image's colors in this exercise because the word *borrowing* strongly suggests that you will put something *back* when you're done.

Okay, here is the scenario: First, you cannot copyright or trademark the use of certain colors. You can get in a lot of trouble borrowing corporate colors for your own logo, but I'm talking about a beautiful autumn day or, in the case of this example, a poster that uses such nice colors together that you would like to sample and repurpose the color combination.

Palletizing the colors in an image is easy. The hard part is knowing what to do with the colors when you're done! Gradients can command attention by using a color "set" like you create in this exercise, and frankly, there's a lot of mediocre black-and-white art—at least in *my* shoebox under the bed—that could get some new life pumped into it by the application of an interesting color palette.

Sampling and Downsampling a Bunch of Colors

I'm going to make this trick as simple and as ideal and as unrealistic as possible because I want you to understand what's going on and not necessarily how I set up the trick. So, suppose that the Getaway.psd image has the colors you want neatly located on a layer. Here's how the tune goes:

Copying and Downsampling Colors

1. Open the Getaway.psd image from the Examples\Chap24 folder on the companion CD. Figure 24.9 shows the image in black and white, but check out the image file and the color section of this book to get a nice idea of the colors as they'll appear on your screen.

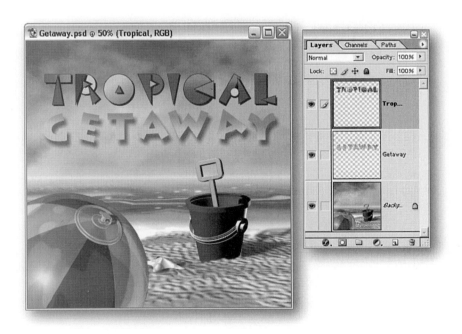

Figure 24.9   The word *Tropical* contains about 2,275 unique colors, but this number is the result of the blends between colors. Actually, the text contains only about 20 striking colors. And you *want* them!

2. On the Layers palette, right-click (Macintosh: hold Ctrl and click) on the Tropical layer, and choose Duplicate Layer. In the Duplicate Layer dialog box, under Destination, choose New from the Document drop-down menu. Click on OK, and the text appears in an image window the same size as the Getaway.psd. Crop the image.

3. Choose Image, Adjustments, Posterize. Now, I read the Photoshop documentation, and it says that the Posterize command will take as many colors as you enter in the number box, times the bits per channel. So, as you can see in Figure 24.10—you should be doing this, too—a Posterize amount of 3 will yield an image that has, um, 24 colors!

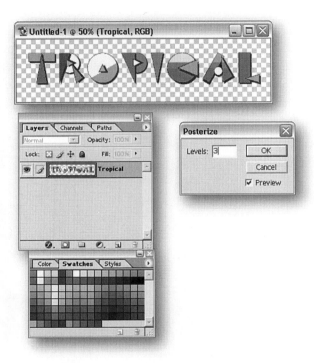

Figure 24.10   You still retain a lot of the original colors, even though some colors shift, when you apply Posterize to a 24-bit RGB image.

Note

Color sampling   I consider this the hard but more accurate way of color sampling: You start with a blank Swatches palette (provided as Blank.aco in the Chap24 folder), use the Eyedropper tool to sample a color, drop it on the Swatches palette, and then name the color. If you hold down the Alt(Opt) key when you click on an empty spot of the Swatches palette, and then name the color.

But then again, the trick here is to glom sample colors you like in one fell swoop, so these steps are legit and worth knowing.

4. Choose Image, Mode, Indexed Color. Accept the Exact setting in the dialog box, and click on OK. You might notice that the exact number of colors Photoshop reports can be anywhere from 16 to 24 or so. This technique is inexact, so the colors you wind up with depend on the color profile you have set for Photoshop. But you've still sampled a bunch of colors you like, and now it's time to save them.

5. Choose Image, Mode, Color Table, and then click the Save button to save the color table as **getaway.act** to your hard disk (remember which folder you save the file in). Click Save.

6. To load the color table, click on the menu flyout on the Swatches palette (press F6), and then choose Replace Colors. Then navigate to the getaway.act file; make sure the Files of Type at the bottom of the dialog box is set to Color Table (*.ACT), or you won't be able to see your file. Click on the getaway.act file, and click Load.

7. Press Ctrl(⌘)+S; keep the file open.

You might ask yourself, "Terrific, Gare, but now what can I do with this color table?" Glad you asked. You can now posterize a grayscale image and then apply the colors you glommed in step 5 in this exercise.

Creating a Posterized Piper

One of the wonderful things about New York City is the architecture. No two building are alike, and some of the whitestones and brownstones have gargoyles "protecting" their entranceways.

Piper.tif is an image of such architectural fine points that, sadly, no one is doing anymore except Disney resorts. I wanted to hang up the picture, but because it's a monotone, almost-grayscale image, I figured the only way to make this an undepressing wall ornament was to colorize it.

And to do that, dear reader, we'll return to this color palletization stuff:

Creating the Posterized Piper

1. Open the Piper.tif image from the Examples\Chap24 folder on the companion CD. As a grayscale image, it has 256 possible tones; but we want, let's say, only 7 tones, which we'll replace with this nifty color palette.

2. Choose Image, Adjust, Posterize, and then enter **7** in the Number field. Click on OK. This amount means 7 samples times 1 channel, or 7. In Figure 24.11, you can see a copy I made to compare the posterized piper to the original. This image isn't too bad, considering all the visual information it's lost.

Figure 24.11   These are the steps necessary for creating a color version of the posterized, grayscale piper.

3. With the posterized piper in the foreground in the workspace, choose Select and then Color Range.

4. Because the Fuzziness slider goes from 0 to 200, and you want the 7 colors you will add to be perfectly antialiased and smooth, drag the slider to 29 (about 1/7 of 200), and then click on an area of the piper. I suggest you work from dark to light (selecting the 7 tones). Click the darkest tone, and then click on OK. A selection appears. Click a color from the Swatches palette, and press Alt(Opt)+Delete (Backspace) to fill the selection with the chosen color. Press Ctrl(⌘)+D to deselect.

5. Repeat step 4 six more times, and the color palette you like will be applied to an image that *I* like!

6. Press Ctrl(⌘)+S; keep the file open.

I refuse to insult your intelligence and show a black-and-white picture of the finished color piper. Instead, check out the color gallery in this book, and it wouldn't hurt my feelings in the least if I heard some "ooooohs" and "ahhhhs"—even in my imagination.

Trick 4: Removing Fringing from Leaves

This trick involves accurately selecting the tops of trees to replace a hum-drum (Syracuse-based) sky with something more interesting. There are too many thicknesses and colors of leaves and branches to go using the Lasso tool, and other methods you probably haven't used yet will produce fringing (at least they did for *me*).

So, I brewed up this simple-to-do method for getting a better sky into a picture while maintaining 99% of the visual integrity of the surrounding treetops.

Welcome to Henderson's Mill

Henderson's Mill is one of those wonderful upstate parks where you can bring a picnic basket and eat undisturbed. I think folks chased away all the wildlife with their *own* wild lives decades ago (see Figure 24.12).

Henderson's Mill, fall 2001. Unretouched photo.

Figure 24.12 Henderson's Mill is a nice, secluded place—almost without any flies.

We snapped a few pictures, nothing interesting, to capture the trees and sky so that you can see how to separate them and then replace the sky.

Select Only What Needs Selecting

The first step to image improvement is to select only the areas that need to be selected to let the Color Range command do its thing. This means you really want to select only the treetops and a little lower to catch where the blah sky is poking through some branches.

Here's how to commence with the first step in clearing away blah sky from the nice trees:

Using the Rectangular Marquee Tool in Addition Mode

1. Open the ParkWow.tif image from the Examples\Chap24 folder on the companion CD. On the Layers palette, double-click the Background layer title, and click on OK to accept the default settings.

> **Note**
>
> **Changing zoom views**   A quick way to move an image's viewing zoom level to 30% is to enter that amount in the Zoom Level field. In Windows, this field is located at the bottom on the far left of the status bar; on the Mac, it's on the far left at the bottom image window scrollbar.
>
> After entering the zoom level amount, press Enter (Return) and life is good.

2. Choose the Rectangular Marquee tool from the toolbox, and marquee an area where trees meet monochrome sky. Hold the Shift key (this enables you to add to the current selection), and then create more rectangles until the sky looks somewhat like that shown in Figure 24.13. Add any remaining marquee selections necessary to include all the sky areas.

3. Choose Select, Color Range, and then click the Eyedropper tool into the sky, as shown in Figure 24.14. Toy with the Fuzziness slider until you think you have reached the point where the leaves are not selected, but neither do they display spindly or missing components, such as branches. In this example, I set the Fuzziness to 31.

> **Insider**
>
> Oh, yes. If looking into that dinky preview box doesn't cut it for you, you can have Photoshop lay a matte down over the image itself to show you what's going to be selected. To do this, choose Black or White Matte from the Selection Preview drop-down list in the Color Range command. You can also choose the Quick Mask option (from the same drop-down list), and a transparent red tint will appear where the selection will be. This option can be useful as well.

24

*With the Rectangular Marquee tool, hold Shift to add to the selection
and mark off the problem areas where leafy trees meet blah sky.*

Figure 24.13   Try to encompass all the "problem areas" with an additive succession of rectangular selections.

4. Click on OK to exit the Color Range command. Then delete the sky; Delete
   (Backspace) ought to do the trick. The next wise thing to do is to click the Edit in
   Quick Mask icon (or press **Q**) and see, through the Quick Mask's tinting indicator, exactly how close you came to neatly trimming away the sky from the leaves.
   See Figure 24.15, and say, "Drat!" once or twice. Okay, we are not dead on with
   separating the leaves from the sky, but that's the whole point of this trick. You
   don't try to tighten the selection; instead, you paint into the gap that the selection marquee left.

Figure 24.14   Choose the appropriate amount of fuzziness with which to select sky tones. By the way, don't worry about the black areas to the left and right top of the Color Range window. This is a variation in sky and is easily deleted later.

Figure 24.15   It's actually better to have a gap in the selection than to have the selection eat into the trees so that when you delete the sky, the treetops look like a locust-fest was there.

5. If the tinting shows the trees instead of the sky, Alt(Opt)+click on the Edit in Quick Mask mode icon to reverse what is tinted. Um, click on the Standard Editing mode button now (or press **Q**), and press Ctrl(⌘)+Shift+I to invert the selection. Go to the Channels palette, and click the Save selection as channel icon at the bottom of the palette to save the selection to a channel.

6. Get out the Brush tool, right-click (Macintosh: hold Ctrl and click), and choose the 21-pixel diameter soft-edged brush from the palette. Press Enter (Return) to hide the Brushes palette. The saved selection should still be loaded. Hold down the Alt(Opt) key to toggle to the Eyedropper tool, and click a color really close to the selection edge. Choose Darken for the painting Mode on the Options bar (better to go darker than lighter when mating a new sky with an image), and then make brisk strokes that go all the way to the edge of the selection marquee, as shown in Figure 24.16. Resample *often,* pressing the Alt(Opt) key to use the Eyedropper; the color of the treetops varies wildly from pixel to pixel!

Eyedropper sample from around here

Figure 24.16   You are filling in the areas that, through the Color Range's antialiasing feature, kept the selection you made from actually touching the treetops. In simpler terms, the gap in the selection consists of non-transparent pixels of only 3 or 4% opacity. You're driving the opacity up to an amount that looks real, in context.

7. Spend a few more minutes painting in the gap around the leaves. Now it's time for the acid test—to drop a new sky into the background. When you're satisfied with the results, press Ctrl(⌘)+D to deselect.

8. Press Ctrl(⌘)+S. Keep the file open, name it **ParkAbsurd.psd** (in Photoshop's native file format), and save it to your hard disk.

Mating the New Sky to the Treetops

Regardless of how thoroughly you think you painted the treetops, when you put in a lusher, darker sky—*drat*—the fringes of the treetops pop up again. You haven't created this image yet, but look at Figure 24.17 to see what I'm talking about. No problem, though. Here's a little secret to go along with this trick. Remember how you load an antialiased selection? You can paint the edges of the selection in RGB mode twice or even three times, and you will see that you are encroaching farther and farther out of the selection marquee. Why? Because repeated applications around an antialiased border will eventually prevail, and because the brush tips, too, are antialiased.

Move the sky into the image so you can better see the problem areas

Figure 24.17   Aha! Aha! You painted perfectly, but not enough times to mate the treetops with the sky.

Let's put the new sky into the image and then start working on this pestilence that's called image fringing:

New Sky; New Problems

1. Now, Bouton goofed again, and the sky isn't large enough for a 9MB picture, but humor me and open the DramaticClouds.tif picture from the Examples\Chap24 folder on the companion CD.

2. With the DramaticClouds.tif in the foreground, drag the Background layer title on the Layers palette into the ParkWow.psd scene. Drag Layer 1 (the clouds layer) below Layer 0 (the park layer), or press Ctrl(⌘)+[. Close the DramaticClouds.tif image without saving changes.

3. Layer 1 should still be the active layer. Press Ctrl(⌘)+T to display the Free Transform box, and then drag the sky image by the corners until it's lower than the top of the trees and extends full left and right in the image window. Press Enter (Return) to apply the transformation. Man, oh, man, that fringing is an eyesore, isn't it?

    > **Note**
    >
    > **Using the Defringe command**   Usually, you should resist the temptation to use the Layer, Matting, Defringe command. This command replaces edge pixels with pixel colors found within the selection.
    >
    > More often than not, though, unless you're working with a 10MB+ image, the Defringe command will make a mess out of the edges of a selection. The result will look like a deckled-edge book.

4. Let's spring to action! Ctrl(⌘)+click on the alpha channel you saved earlier to load the selection of the trees. If the sky is selected instead of the trees, press Ctrl(⌘)+Shift+I to invert the selection. Press Ctrl(⌘)+H to hide the selection. The Brush tool should still be active with a 21-pixel soft round brush size. Ease back on the Opacity to 74% on the Options bar for the Brush tool to give you a chance to mess with different colors before an area becomes 100% painted.

5. Keep the Mode at Darken. Get into this rhythm: Alt(Opt)+click with the Eyedropper tool close to where you want to paint. Release Alt(Opt), and then make short strokes from the trees into the sky. Naturally, your strokes will end because the selection marquee is still active, but check out Figure 24.18. Even though the image is in grayscale, you can still see that the trees blend neatly into the sky area, and that's at 200% zoom level viewing. Imagine how subtle your artistry will be at 1:1 viewing.

Figure 24.18   Keep sampling and resampling, and then make short strokes toward the edge of the selection (okay, where you *think* the edge is!).

6. Do all the retouching you can do around the treetops, and then keel over. Press Ctrl(⌘)+S; keep the file open.

Other Selection Techniques

I'd like to share one or two other moves with you because, although the image looks a lot more natural now, some things can help it along even further.

Let's work while we talk, okay?

Completing the Binding of Treetops and Sky

1. There are bound to be areas within the trees—not just the treetops—that have a blah sky in them, and if you remove these areas, the replacement sky can poke through. With the Rectangular Marquee tool, drag an area where really offensive blah sky shows through, as shown in Figure 24.19. Choose Select, Color Range, and see whether you can pick at a blah sky area with the Eyedropper tool. When you're satisfied with the Fuzziness (I used a setting of 54), click on OK and return to the scene.

**Mark off smaller areas within the trees
for use with the Color Range command**

Figure 24.19   Select the tiniest of flaws in the trees.

2. P:ck a very neutral shade of green (R:115, G:131, B:96 is good), and then press
   Alt(Opt)+Delete (Backspace) and then Ctrl(⌘)+D to deselect the marquee selection. Now, all those blah sky holes are filled with foliage.

3. You will need to load the selection again; Ctrl(⌘)+click Layer 0 on the Layers
   palette. Now, keep painting, but when you come to some twigs and some purple
   foliage in the image, sample those colors and paint with them. Remember, use
   short strokes and sample often (see Figure 24.20). Set the Brush Mode on the
   Options bar to Normal if you need to alternate colors often to achieve a more
   natural effect.

4. As mentioned in step 3, working from left to right, you will eventually hit some
   purple foliage; it was probably the outdoor lighting because plants don't usually
   grow to 40 feet tall. But respect what the camera has provided, and sample new
   colors and paint away (see Figure 24.21).

24

WORK IN PROGRESS

Figure 24.20   The painting goes quicker if you hum to yourself, "99 bottles of beer on the wall; 99 bottles of beer...."

5. Finally, with the Magic Wand tool, with Contiguous unchecked and Tolerance set to about 16, click in a blah sky area that is peeking through the trees. Doing this will drag out all the blah sky pixels because non-contiguous means "doesn't have to be neighboring to," so the whole image layer gets the treatment. Choose Select, Modify, Expand, and expand by 2 pixels. Press Ctrl(⌘)+Alt(Opt)+D to feather the selections by 2 pixels. Then, very carefully choose a bland green that will work in all selection areas, and press Alt(Opt)+Delete (Backspace) to fill the selections. Press Ctrl(⌘)+D to deselect (see Figure 24.22).

You're home free, and the picture looks terrific!

As you can see in Figure 24.23, everything at Henderson's Mill looks both pretty and plausible. And it's all because you've learned five different techniques for eliminating the fringing between original sky and treetops. We *are* a little concerned, however, about how the bumble bee landed in this figure.

Figure 24.21   Sample often, and keep the strokes short. Do I sound like a broken record? (A record was an analog music archiving device before the CD.)

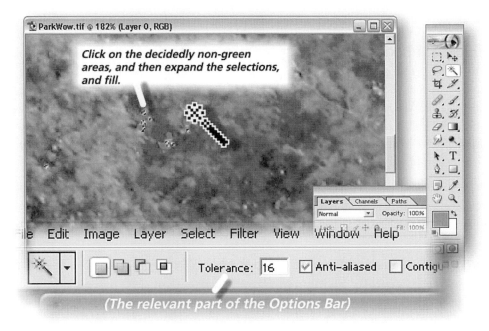

Figure 24.22   Plug up the last of the ugly holes with pleasing green, and you are finished!

24

Figure 24.23   Hey, if you wanted a "dry" book, I have plenty upstairs from college calculus.

Trick 5: Making a Painting from a Photo

This trick is at the top of my bag because it just dawned on me a week or so ago that the new Photoshop CS brushes could indeed be used in combination with the Lighting Effects filter to produce painting-like compositions from photos, models, or other photo-realistic endeavors. "Just like Painter does," I exclaimed to myself upon gleaning the similarity in approach between my idea and what Painter does in the Apply Surface Texture command.

We use a fanciful poster instead of a photograph in the steps to come because, until you get a real grasp on the technique here, you can make loved ones look hideous with a minimal amount of effort.

You Need Layers to Make Different Paint Strokes

Unlike Corel's Painter (or whoever owns Painter this week), in which you can paint and try out different brushes and then apply the resulting textures on a copy of the artwork using the Clone command, Photoshop doesn't work on clones of images. Therefore, if you want different areas to have unique textures that look like you have painted them with a real paintbrush, you need to compose your piece in layers.

Let's begin by unfolding this mysterious property that Photoshop offers:

Setting Up Your "Painting" Brush

1. Open Fat_Star.psd from the Examples\Chap24 folder on the companion CD.

2. Press Ctrl(⌘)+N to create a new document window, about 200 pixels by 200 pixels. This is where you test the flow amount of different brush tips. Choose the Brush tool, and set the Flow to 5%. If you changed the painting Mode in the preceding exercise, set the Mode back to Normal. Choose the Chalk 60-pixel "novelty" brush that's shown in Figure 24.24.

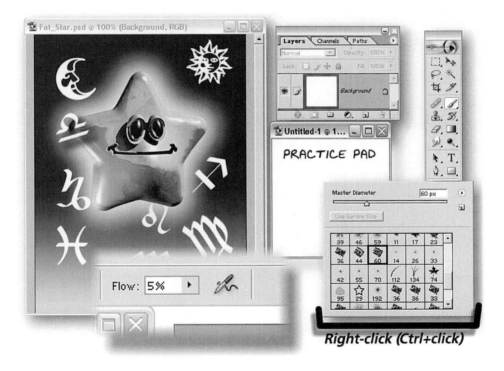

Figure 24.24   These are more or less the things you need before trying to make this silly astrology poster into a fine painting.

3. Get a feel for the brush's characteristics using the doodle pad image window. Click the Fat_Star.psd title bar to make this the active document. Click the Background layer on the Layers palette to make it the active layer.

4. Press **D** for the default colors (black should be the foreground color). Make sure that the Quick Mask option is set so that colored areas are selections; to do this, Alt(Opt)+click on the Quick Mask icon until the circle is colored and the rectangle isn't on the face of the button. Your work is in Quick Mask mode now, so here's your chance to paint all over the place. The more "character"—random, uneven strokes—the better for the finished painting (see Figure 24.25).

Make strokes all over the place, in
Quick Mask mode, on the Background layer

Figure 24.25   Knock yourself out. This is about as much fun as is legally possible!

5. Press **Q** to exit Quick Mask mode. Click the Channels tab to view the Channels palette, and click the Save selection as channel icon at the bottom of the palette to save the selection as an alpha channel. Click the Alpha 1 channel to switch your view to the alpha channel.

Insider

> You don't want this willy-nilly texture to dominate anything except the blue background. So, now you have to remove the star and the glow and the horoscope symbols from the alpha channel.

6. Ctrl(⌘)+click the Fat Star title on the Layers palette. From a view of the alpha channel, press Ctrl(⌘)+Delete (Backspace) to flood the star selection area with white (the background color). Press Ctrl(⌘)+D to deselect (see Figure 24.26).

Figure 24.26   Remove the star's silhouette from the alpha channel, and it will show no brush

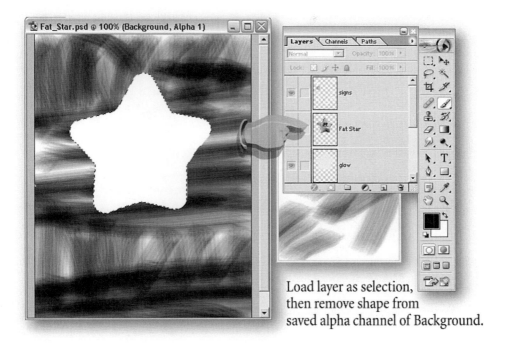

Load layer as selection, then remove shape from saved alpha channel of Background.

strokes when the Lighting Effects filter is applied.

7. Repeat step 6 with the glow layer, the signs, and especially that straggler Leo, just above the background. You can quickly select the remaining layers by Ctrl(⌘)+clicking the Leo layer, and then Ctrl(⌘)+Shift click the glow layer and signs layer to add them to the selection. Does your image look like the one in Figure 24.27?

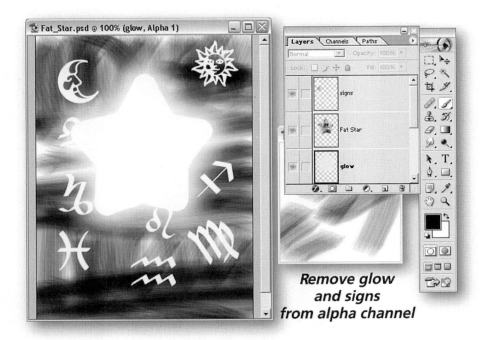

Figure 24.27   Remove all silhouettes that you don't want "paint textured."

8. Return to the Layers palette, click the Background layer to make it the current editing layer, and then choose Filter, Render, Lighting Effects. Choose Directional for the Light type and the Alpha 1 channel for the Texture Channel, as shown in Figure 24.28. The setting for the Height slider is minimal; you're making paint strokes, not trying to rival the Mariana Trench. Dispense with the fancy options below the lighting boxes (in other words, use the settings shown in the figure to keep Metallic, Shiny, and other settings minimal). Drag that point on the end of the light in the proxy window toward and then away from the center until the exposure of the proxy window looks the same as the color in the Background layer. Click on OK to apply.

9. Save your work as **Fat Star.psd** to your hard disk. Keep the file open for the next exercise.

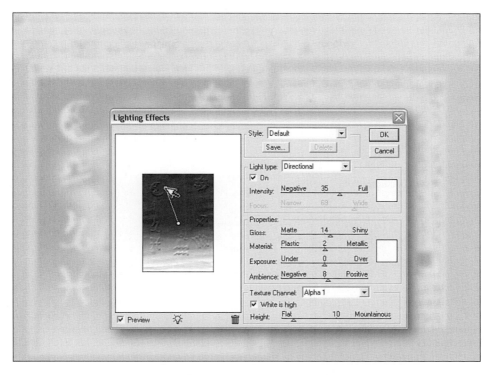

Figure 24.28   Use the Lighting Effects Texture controls to apply the paint strokes saved in an alpha channel to the Background layer.

More Fun with Pseudo-Painting

Things are going to liven up from here on out. The hero, the fat star, needs to be treated delicately simply because it is the hero of the picture and you don't want to totally demolish it with paint strokes. So, you make a copy, apply the Artistic...*wait a second*. I should be telling you this in the following *tutorial*!

When You Brush Upon a Star

1. Switch active layers on the Layers palette so that the Fat Star is chosen. Press Ctrl(⌘)+J to duplicate the star layer. The Fat Star copy should be the active layer on the Layers palette. Choose Filter, Artistic, Dry Brush; see Figure 24.29 for the settings to apply. Then click on OK to apply the Dry Brush effect and return to the workspace.

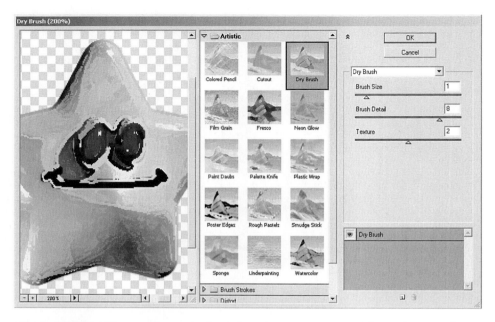

Figure 24.29   Add some preconceived artistic excitement to a copy of the star by using the Filters menu.

2. Okay, follow me closely now. You have the Brush tool selected, right? Right-click (Macintosh: hold Ctrl and click), click on the Brushes palette's flyout menu, and choose Natural Brushes. Then click on OK to replace (as opposed to adding to the current list of brushes) in the ensuing dialog box. Choose the tip near the top of the list that says "29" (pixels) on it and looks as though someone sneezed on a windshield. Crank the Flow up to 20%, and press **Q** to enter Quick Mask mode (or click on the Quick Mask icon). Make sure black is the foreground color; if it's not, press **X** to switch.

3. Ctrl(⌘)+click on the Fat Star copy layer to load the selection of the star. Paint away on the star, as shown in Figure 24.30. It helps verisimilitude (to seem more real) to paint more heavily—that is, repeat strokes more often—in the darker areas of the fat star. Use fewer strokes and perhaps leave some empty places in the fat star's lighter areas.

Figure 24.30   Paint back and forth or in any direction you might paint a star on a blank canvas.

4. Press **Q** to exit Quick Mask mode, or click on the Edit in Standard Mode icon. Save the selection as **Alpha 2** on the Channels palette, and press Ctrl(⌘)+D to deselect. Click the Fat Star copy layer in the Layers palette to make it the active layer. Then it's off to the Lighting Effects filter for texturizing, using the same settings as the preceding exercise, except that you should make Alpha 2 the Texture Channel and adjust the point in the proxy window again until the color matches the star color from the document window. Click on OK to apply settings.

5. When the fat star has been textured on the copy layer, try turning down the Opacity on this layer to achieve a blend of unfiltered and filtered versions (30% gives a subtle effect). This is a swell way to control the number of "paint strokes" after you've applied them (see Figure 24.31).

   See Figure 24.32? This image is beginning to look grand, and you don't even have to know how to use Painter!

You have the option
to mix amounts of original star
and painted, bumped copy

Figure 24.31   Just "dial up" the amount of effect you want for the finished painted star.

6. Optional: Get creative with the strokes you apply to the glow layer in Quick Mask mode (see Figure 24.33). Me? I painted back and forth around the circumference of the glow to strongly suggest the emanations are traveling outward. Go ahead and experiment using the same techniques we've applied so far.

7. Whoa, Nelly! Let's take a break for a moment to contemplate final strategies for making the horoscope signs look painted.

Insider

Be sure to return to the Brushes flyout menu (on the Brushes palette) and choose Reset Brushes before you continue with the tricks!

The horoscope signs will not withstand the radical type of filtering you've just applied to everything else. Instead, let's try a different approach and filter—so that you can make the symbols both legible and interesting.

Figure 24.32   Everything's been painted except the glow and horoscope signs.

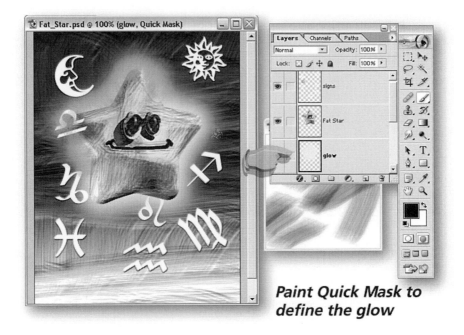

Figure 24.33   Paint in Quick Mask mode on the glow layer until you achieve the effect you want.

The Minimize Command and the Spatter Effect

The horoscope symbols are too frail to be filtered with something as strong as the Spatter Effect. You can beef up their outlines with a command that apparently very few people use: the Filter, Other, Minimize command. Contrary to its name, the Minimize command actually adds to the outline of a selection or image area.

Come. Let's do it....

Minimize, Then Spatter

1. Ctrl(⌘)+click the signs layer to load the signs as a selection, and then click the Save selection as channel icon at the bottom of the Channels palette (Alpha 3). Click the Alpha 3 channel to view this alpha channel. Press Ctrl(⌘)+D to deselect.

2. Choose Filter, Other, Minimum. Set the Radius to 2 pixels. As you can see in Figure 24.34, the symbols look beefy and can stand up to some serious distortion.

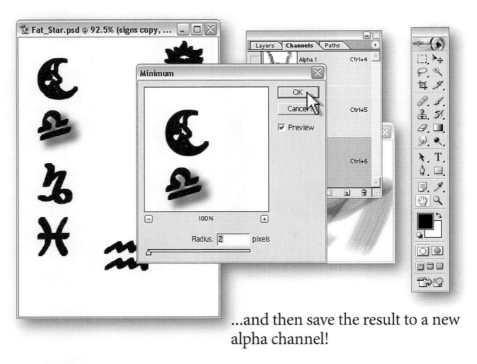

...and then save the result to a new alpha channel!

Figure 24.34   The Minimum command is sort of a combination of using Expand Selection and then filling the expanded selection.

3. Click on OK to apply the beefiness. Choose Filter, Brush Strokes, Spatter. Use the settings shown in Figure 24.35, and click on OK to apply the effect.

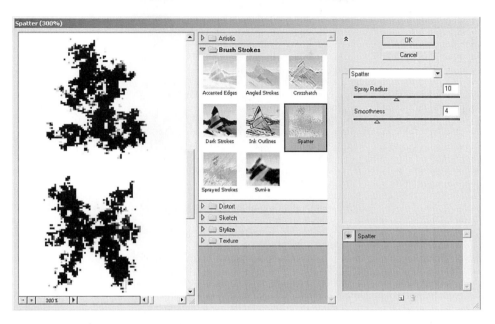

Figure 24.35   Not all artists are tidy with their strokes. Applying both straight and spattered strokes to a work makes you more of a synthetic virtuoso.

4. Ctrl(⌘)+click Alpha 3 to load the spattered symbols as a selection. Click the Layers tab to view the Layers palette. Click the Fat Star copy layer to make this layer active, and then click the Create a new layer icon at the bottom of the Layers palette to put the new layer below the signs layer. Choose a pale blue color, and press Alt(Opt)+Delete (Backspace) to fill the selection with color. Press Ctrl(⌘)+D to deselect.

5. Lower the Opacity of the signs layer so that you can see the spatter effect and still make out the symbols (around 65% might do the trick). Come to think of it, you should probably add an effect to the signs layer by clicking on the encircled *f* icon at the bottom of the Layers palette and then choosing Bevel and Emboss. Then add to the signs a Pillow Emboss from the Style drop-down list. Click on OK.

6. Repeat steps 1–5 on the Leo layer so that it doesn't feel left out. Now, look at Figure 24.36. This surely has to be one of the most robust paintings never painted!

24

Figure 24.36   Is it a painting? High art? Nope. It's Photoshop, pushed just a little!

Because this is a multi-trick chapter, we'd best move on to another thing Photoshop can do to match Painter features.

Trick 6: Creating Organic-Looking Objects Using Photoshop Filters

Fractal math, when plotted to the screen, can be an absolutely wonderful thing. There is no simple way to describe fractal math (at least not in *this* book), except to say that fractals are so complex that they cannot be plotted with a mere curve. Fractals are a seemingly random set of fluctuations that apparently cannot be represented by an equation. But many fractals *are* generated through simple mathematical equations.

Fortunately, we are artists, not mathematicians, so if you really want to make your head ache, read some of the work by Professor Ken Perlin (I mean this in a good way, Ken) at NYU who, along with Ken Musgrave (who helped re-engineer Bryce), is active on the Terragen discussion list. These men understand the self-similarity of fractals and the reasons they most often look like a coastline, a dinosaur hide, or other organic matter. And that's precisely what we're looking for in this trick: How do you make organic-looking stuff using Photoshop?

Fractals come in two types: terminating and non-terminating. We are interested in the terminating type of fractal because, more often than not, a fractal is written so as to form a seamless tile (a tile whose left and right and top and bottom edges continue the visual). And the good news is that Photoshop's Clouds and Clouds Difference filters both terminate at 128 pixels.

Note

> **What's a fractal? Really?**   Ken Musgrave probably summed up the answer to "What is a fractal?" most elegantly (and if you still have a little high school geometry left in you, like I do, it makes queer sense), to wit:
>
> "If we accept a number to the second power as a square, and a value to the third power as a cube, then fractals lie somewhere in between."

So let's start creating something that looks organic:

Creating a Seamless Fractal Tile

1. Create a New document (Ctrl(⌘)+N), 128 by 128 pixels in dimension, and RGB in color Mode. Click on OK.

2. Create an alpha channel by clicking the Create new channel icon at the bottom of the Channels palette (press F7 if the palette isn't already open onscreen). Click on the Alpha 1 channel you just created to make it the active channel.

3. Make sure your toolbox colors are black and white. Do this by pressing **D**.

4. Choose Filter, Render, Clouds. Press Ctrl(⌘)+F a few times until you think you've rendered something interesting.

Insider

> The Clouds filter generates a random fractal result each time it is used. Pressing Ctrl([@Cmd])+F merely repeats the last filter applied (in this case, the Clouds filter) and allows you to try the filter repeatedly until you have a result that appeals to you.

5. Try the Clouds Difference filter once or twice. This filter produces stronger fractal algorithms (equations) than Clouds and inverts colors every time you use it. Fortunately, only shades of black and white are used in this 8-bit grayscale alpha channel, so the result of using Clouds Difference is interesting instead of color-confused.

6. Stop applying either the Clouds or Clouds Difference filter when you arrive at something interestingly splotchy-looking (see Figure 24.37).

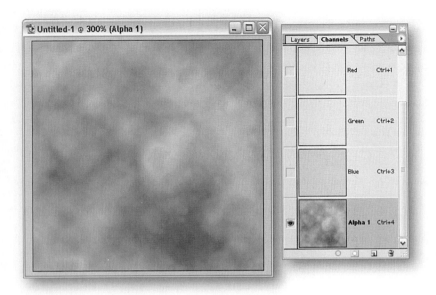

Figure 24.37   Stop brewing a fractal when you arrive at something interesting-looking.

24

7. Click on the foreground color, and pick a neutral shade (R:220, G:224, B:221). Click on the Background layer on the Layers palette to make this layer active. Press Alt(Opt)+Delete (Backspace) to fill the RGB composite channel with this color.

8. Choose Filter, Render, Lighting Effects to make bumps in the RGB composite channel by using the Texture controls. Select the Alpha 1 channel for the Texture Channel; Light type should be set at Directional. Keep the bump amount very slight, and use the directional light's point on the end of the line (in the proxy window) to make sure the image is exposed in Lighting Effects the same as the original surface color. Check out Figure 24.38. Click on OK to apply the bumps.

9. Ta-dah! You've created a seamless, tiling fractal image! Use the Define Pattern command (Edit, Define Pattern), and apply this design to a large area to prove to yourself that it has no seams. You can also drag this image into ImageReady and use GIF optimization so there are only about 14 different colors in it. Doing this will preserve 90% of the visual integrity of the image and will result in a ti*nnnnnnny* file, which means that if you use it on a Web page, download times for visitors will be courteously short (see Figure 24.39).

Ready for a mind-blower?

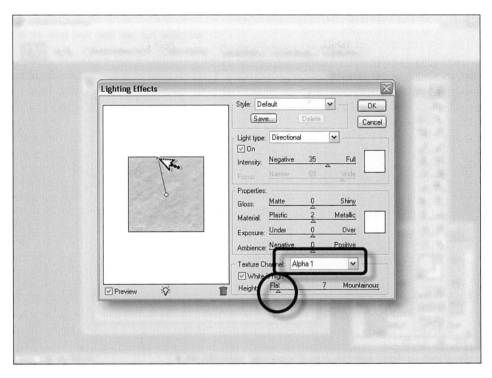

Figure 24.38   Keep the Height down to about 7%, and make all the Properties 0 (zero)—neither shiny nor metallic.

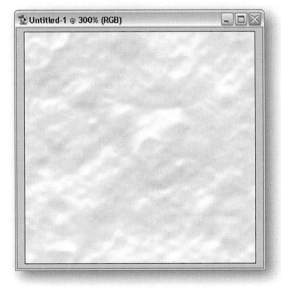

The fruits of your labor—in only a few steps!

This image will tile seamlessly. We don't know what it is, but it looks natural and organic, huh?

Try it as a JPEG or GIF as a Web page background.

Figure 24.39   The finished fractal design.

Trick 7: Creating a Bronze Guy

Don't be misled by this trick's title. You are not going to send a pale New Yorker to Fort Lauderdale for a weekend. Instead, I'm going to show you a behind-the-scenes piece of magic I created in a past *Inside Photoshop* book. You would need Poser and a modeling program such as trueSpace to complete this example.

First of all, the assignment was to remove a person from his clothing—um, so the clothing remained. This is a family book, you understand. It was a superbly surrealistic sight to see clothing marching down a road. But smart-aleck me had to improve upon the scene for the color plate section and fill this empty clothing with a sort of blobby bronze guy.

I received email out the Eudora asking me how I created the bronze-stylized character, mostly because the reflections in the bronze were accurate, and none of the readers thought I'd actually posed a bronze blob on the road.

Let's back up to the gracious Gary Kubicek, co-author of record with the *Inside Photoshop* series. In Figure 24.40, Gare was kind enough to flail his arms and legs while he walked because I knew once I'd deleted him from the clothes, the clothes themselves would have to have an indicative, forced posture. Thanks, Gare!

Figure 24.40   Gary K. thinks, "How do I let Bouton talk me into this embarrassing stuff?"

Using the photo and a lot of the Clone Stamp tool, I removed all fleshy parts, desaturated the collar (where flesh tones were reflecting off the white collar—think about that detail…the little stuff counts), and before long, a phantom Gary was trucking down the street. See Figure 24.41 for both the top and bottom halves of the trickery.

Figure 24.41   About the only thing missing here is a name tag on the inside of the shirt collar.

In the earlier book, we left the tutorial at that. But I had an interesting idea: What if I dress a Poser model in similar clothing and put bronze blobs out of his clothing to reflect the scene of the photo that had been taken long before I got this idea?

Enter Figure 24.42. This is a screen capture of the Poser figure posing in trueSpace, without its head, arms, or wallet. (trueSpace is one of those affordable modeling programs that performs accurate reflection calculations.) I set up the background with a rough photo-collage of what the surroundings in the original picture looked like, and then I colored the sky a brilliant reddish-purple, which is technically inaccurate, but it made the blobs I added look like bronze.

Figure 24.42   Setting up a simulated scene of the original enables you to create exactly the right reflections you want in the pieces to be added later.

As you can see, the reflections are not perfect, but they are close enough to fool even the most discriminating viewer. I rendered the scene once for the reflections and then a second time to create an alpha channel that would help me separate the bronze components from the background.

In Figure 24.43, Gare is back on the road, but wow, where did he go to get that tan?

I also added the shadow, based on my modeling work and the shadows that Gare's "proxy" cast in the trueSpace scene.

24

Figure 24.43   Reflections that are accurate enough to fool the casual viewer's eye can produce startling results when the whole image is presented.

Trick 8: Creating Images Using Adobe Dimensions with Photoshop CS

This trick is for folks who consider themselves to be non-artists and only dabble in Photoshop to color correct stuff. I have news for all of you: Although this next trick requires the purchase of Adobe Dimensions ($149 SMRP), there is not a step in this whole section that cannot be done blindfolded (okay, you can peek a little from beneath the blindfold).

I'm going to teach you simplicity of concept, of evocative colors, and you, too, might want to become a Post Impressionist!

Regardless of your own opinion about your results, little tutorials like these get your hands on a lot of important Photoshop features and encourage you to venture forth with your own implementation of tools with which you are experienced. Simplicity can say as much as intricacy, except simplicity is easier to create!

Doling Out the Goods from Dimensions

To me, Adobe Dimensions, which has not been updated since 1997, is sort of a wonderful utility. The program doesn't have a fraction of the modeling realism or power of, say, Maya; but then again, it costs about as much as a traffic fine, and what it does, it does excellently. Dimensions is particularly adept at plastic 3D-extruded text, by the way.

Okay, the first step is to make a weird squiggle in dimensions using the same Pen tools you find in Photoshop. What does the squiggle represent? It represents half a vase shape (see Figure 24.44).

24

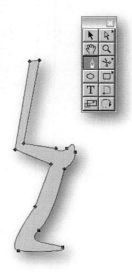

COME ON! SURELY YOU CAN DRAW THIS
SIMPLE DOODLE USING ADOBE PEN TOOLS!

Figure 24.44   This pathetic doodle is actually the makings of a vase.

In Figure 24.45, you can see that if you mirror the doodle, it indeed begins to look like a vase. And the image to the right shows that if a 2D path is swept by an infinite number of points, it becomes a 3D vase.

I hope it's obvious that you *will* participate in this adventure; we simply need to address how to use Dimensions first. The completed vase image, vase.tif, is on the companion CD.

Figure 24.45   You can easily visualize a path swept around a central vertical line becoming a vase if you have the right visualization tools!

Okay, so in Dimensions, after you've used the Revolve palette to make a vase out of the path, you can use any color you like on the vase. I used sand brown in this example. But wait, this gets better: You can select any facet of the vase with the Direct Selection tool and either color the facet or add a pattern. You can't see color in Figure 24.46, but I've made the top of the vase's body a rusty red. The body is now selected, and I'm using the Map Artwork command, which is quite a novel feature.

In Figure 24.47, you can see how Dimensions presents a facet pattern in a workspace away from the 3D image. Areas that are invisible in your current view of the vase are grayed out. All I'm doing here is making doodles and coloring them in. When I'm done, I choose Exit, and the shapes become decals on the sand brown vase.

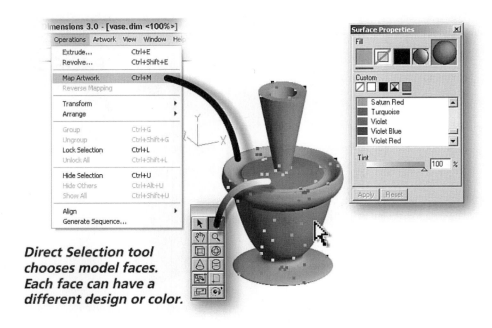

Direct Selection tool chooses model faces. Each face can have a different design or color.

Figure 24.46   Dimensions sort of irons out a 3D facet into a pattern to which you can then map artwork.

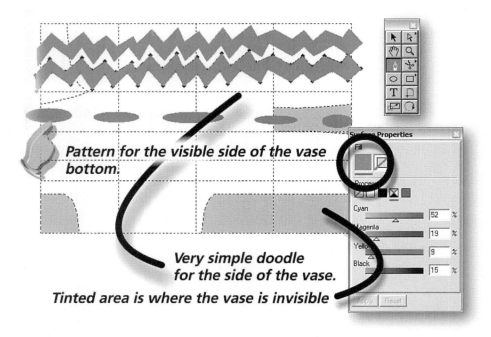

Pattern for the visible side of the vase bottom.

Very simple doodle for the side of the vase.

Tinted area is where the vase is invisible

Figure 24.47   So far, has there been anything you can't draw?

After selecting the neck of the vase, I made one more trip to the Map Artwork zone. I used Sympols, a font I created that is included on the companion CD. After exiting the zone, I'm back to a handsomely adorned vase. See Figure 24.48 for the (undemanding) application of a Sympols font character to the neck of the vase.

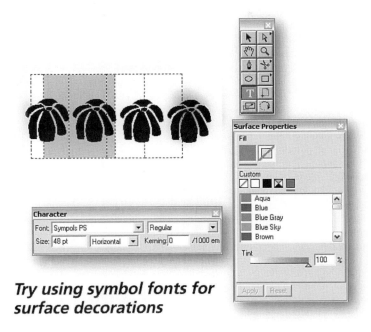

Try using symbol fonts for surface decorations

Figure 24.48   Again, I am totally confident that you can do this sort of stuff with just the little information I'm sharing here.

Back in 3D mode, I want to export a bitmap (raster) version of the vase, so I chose Dimensions. And here's a secret: There's a programming error in Dimensions. Any value to which you want to export (in pixels), you must multiply by 125% because Dimensions does not export specified sizes accurately (see Figure 24.49).

Okay, now it's your turn to put in some pixel-pushing and imitate the broad color fields and exotic tone of Gaugin's work!

Getting the Vase out of Its Background

You are going to leave the vase right there in its little window while you remove the background and embellish the image window with modest yet tasteful creations of your own. I'm not being smart here; I'm honestly trying to take the scare out of image creation.

In the following steps, you will remove the background, pull out a couple of guides, and create a ledge for the vase.

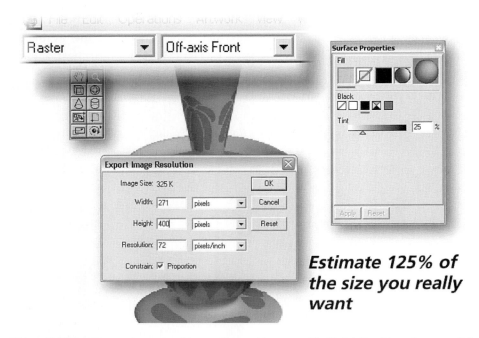

Estimate 125% of the size you really want

Figure 24.49   Export the vase to bitmap format (.bmp or .tif will do). It will render to a solid white background.

Creating a Ledge for the Vase

1. Open the vase.tif file from the Examples\Chap24 folder on the companion CD. On the Layers palette, double-click on the Background title, and rename the layer **vase.** Click on OK to apply the change. Right-click (Macintosh: hold Ctrl and click) the title bar of the document, and choose Canvas Size. In the Canvas Size dialog box, leave the middle anchor selected, and type **800** (pixels) for Width and **600** (pixels) for Height. Press **W** for the Magic Wand tool, and with Tolerance set at 32, click on the white background color. Choose Select, Modify, Expand and enter a value of **1** (pixels). Click on OK. Press Delete (Backspace) to clear the white background. Press Ctrl(⌘)+D to deselect. Press Ctrl(⌘)+R to display the rulers in the image window. This is the only way to add guides to the image window.

2. At the bottom of the Layers palette, Ctrl(⌘)+click the Create a new layer icon (when you use the Ctrl(⌘) key, Photoshop will create the new layer *below* the vase layer). Double-click the Layer 1 title, and rename this layer **Ledge**. Press Enter (Return) to apply the new name. Drag a horizontal guide out from the ruler at the top and then a vertical guide out from the ruler on the left side so they intersect about a screen inch to the left and middle of the vase. See Figure 24.50 for the precise location of the guides.

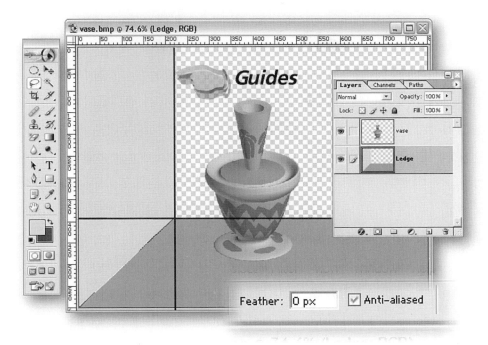

Figure 24.50   Create a primitive ledge using colors that complement the vase.

3. Create a horizontal shape using the Polygonal Lasso tool, and use the View, Snap command to keep the tool right on the guide until you make a diagonal selection segment at the left, as shown in Figure 24.50. After you've created it, color it R:130, G:134, B:226. Then create a vertical part to the ledge (also shown in Figure 24.50), and fill it with R:243, G:197, B:144. Deselect the selection.

4. With the Move tool (press **V**), drag the guides back into the rulers, and then press Ctrl(⌘)+R to hide the rulers.

5. With the Gradient tool, set the foreground color to R:0, G:51, B:124, and click on the background color to set it to R:255, G:211, B:123. Ctrl(⌘)+click on the Create a new layer icon at the bottom of the Layers palette to create a layer below the Ledge layer. Rename this new layer **Sky**. Make sure you're in Linear mode, with the Foreground to Background color gradient chosen from the Options bar. Hold the Shift key to constrain the gradient to vertical, and drag vertically in the image window, starting about 2 screen inches from the top of the window and ending at about 2 screen inches from the bottom of the window (see Figure 24.51).

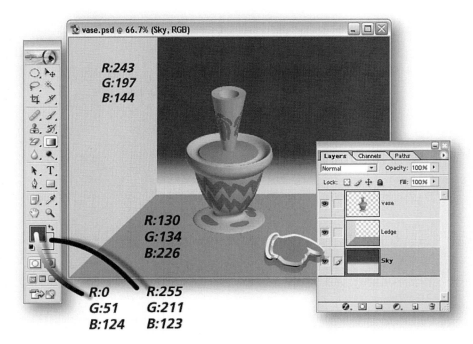

Figure 24.51   Create a sunset for the image by using the right colors and the Gradient tool in Linear mode.

6. Click the Ledge layer to make it the active layer. With the Magic Wand tool, click the vertical, peach-colored ledge area on the Ledge layer. Create an alpha channel by clicking the Create new channel icon at the bottom of the Channels palette. Click on the Alpha 1 channel you just created to make it active.

Insider

Depending on your settings, the channel you create may be filled completely with black, or it may be filled completely with white. Don't worry. Either way, the following steps will work regardless of the initial fill color.

7. Choose Filter, Render, Clouds filter to create a fractal pattern in the selected area in the alpha channel (see Figure 24.52). Return to the RGB view of the image. Do this on the Layers palette by clicking on the Ledge layer to make it the active layer. The selection marquee should still be visible.

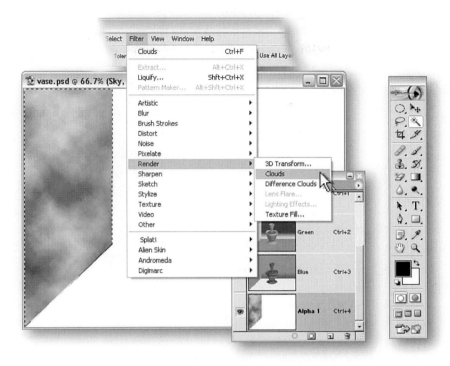

Figure 24.52   Create a texture that can then be applied to the peach side of the ledge in the design.

8. Choose Filter, Render, Lighting Effects, as you've done previously in this chapter. Set the Texture Channel to Alpha 1, and set the Height to about 12. Make sure the Light type is Directional and that the exposure is correct by twiddling with the point at the end of the source light; move it toward or away from the light origin in the proxy window until the colors in the proxy window match the colors in the document window. Click on OK to apply the Lighting Effects, and you now have a stucco ledge wall in the image. Press Ctrl(⌘)+D to deselect.

9. Click the vase layer to make it the active layer, and then with the Move tool (press **V**), drag the vase to the right of the image window.

10. Save your work to your hard disk as **Vase.psd**, and keep the file open. We *both* need a breather!

Adding some accents to the image, such as a moon and a shadow for the vase, would be cool. Again, creating these effects is *not* hard stuff.

Adding Elements to the Composition

Let's take care of creating the moon and the shadow for the vase within one set of steps. Why? Because these features are not challenging, and as you will see, they don't take that many steps.

Here's how to finish the Gaugin-type image:

Adding Finishing Touches to a Sunset Scene

1. With the vase layer as the active layer, press Ctrl(⌘)+J to duplicate this layer. Press Ctrl(⌘)+[(left bracket key) to move the vase copy layer below the vase layer.

2. Press Alt(Opt)+Shift+Delete (Backspace) to fill the shape on the vase copy layer with the foreground color. You can see on the Layers palette thumbnail that you now have a deep blue vase-shape on the vase copy layer.

3. Press Ctrl(⌘)+T to put the blue shadow in Free Transform mode. First, hold the Shift key to constrain the rotation to 15-degree increments. Then take hold of a corner on the Free Transform bounding box, and rotate the shadow by 90 degrees. If you cannot get ahold of the bounding box handle with a bent arrow cursor, right-click (Macintosh: hold Ctrl and click) and choose Rotate 90° CCW from the Context menu, or type –**90°** in the Rotate box on the Options bar.

4. After the shadow has been rotated, drag the top-center handle downward, and then drag the left-center handle to the left so the shadow is thin and long.

5. Place the cursor in the center of the Transform box, and then drag to reposition the shadow so that its base is under the vase. When you're satisfied with the effect, press Enter (Return) to accept the transformations (see Figure 24.53). As a finishing touch on the shadow, use the Lasso tool to lasso some of the areas showing past the vase's base, and press the Delete (Backspace) key to remove the unwanted parts of the shadow. Press Ctrl(⌘)+D to deselect.

6. Now, the moon. In the sky to the right of the image, use the Elliptical Marquee tool while holding Shift to make a perfect circle. Click the Quick Mask mode icon (or press **Q**), and the selection becomes a red circle.

7. Choose Filter, Distort, Glass. As you can see in Figure 24.54, a moderate Glass distortion setting makes a van Gogh–like "Starry Night" moon. By the way, Gaugin and van Gogh were both Impressionists, but Gaugin was also a Post Impressionist.

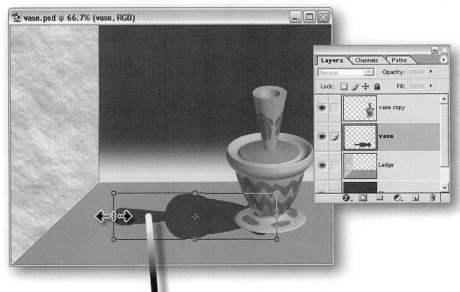

Rotate, reposition, and then Scale.

Figure 24.53   The vase shadow is a nice touch and adds geometry to the image.

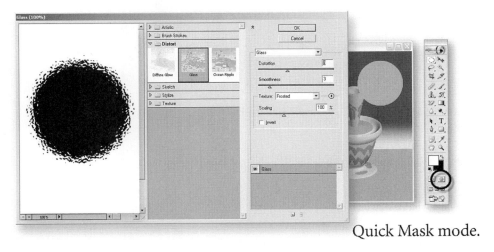

Quick Mask mode.

Figure 24.54   The Glass distortion filter creates shards out of the edges of a smooth object.

8. Click on OK to apply the filter, and then press **Q** to exit Quick Mask mode, or click the Edit in Standard Mode icon on the toolbox to make the Quick Mask into a selection marquee. Press Ctrl(⌘)+Shift+N to create a new layer, and name this layer **moon**. Click on OK.

9. To be true to Impressionism, we need an odd color for the moon to create moodiness in the image. Click on the foreground color, choose R:177, G:205, B:123 in the Color Picker dialog box, and click on OK. With the Brush tool and a 65-pixel soft round brush (Mode set to Normal, and Opacity and Flow set to 100%), paint over the selection marquee, as shown in Figure 24.55. Press Ctrl(⌘)+D to deselect when you're satisfied.

Figure 24.55   Add a touch of suspense in the image by using an unexpected color for the moon.

10. You're done! Press Ctrl(⌘)+S.

That was a walk in the park, wasn't it?

Trick 9: Coping with a Horrific Photo

(We SEE Figure 24.56 fade up in front of us.)

(We HEAR an ancient theater organ groaning out its interpretation of the song "Feelings.")

(We HEAR a guy trying to make his voice sound deep like Vincent Price's, and with far too much echo....)

Figure 24.56

Boris Gory: Good afternoon, boys and ghouls. Today we have a very scary picture. You'll want to close your eyes and scream, but you *can't*. HaHaHaHa! The picture is called "Wayne and Pam.tif."

(The scene dissolves, and you are back in front of your computer. And someone far worse than Boris Gory is speaking to you; it's Bouton.)

Bouton: If you open the Wayne & Pam.tif image from the Examples\Chap24 folder, you will indeed shriek and beg Boris Gory to come back. See Figure 24.57. Yaaaaaaaa…!

To put the record straight, my dad's friend Lou asked me if I could do something with this picture of his daughter and son-in-law. "I quit smoking. I don't have any matches," I said right before Lou punched me. Okay, okay. Apparently the photographer tripped while taking the picture and then landed on the camera. Then he developed it himself in a gas station sink.

Photoshop users say that there is no such thing as an impossible-to-fix image, but this one is stretching it!

YOU TWO DIDN'T ACTUALLY PAY
A PHOTOGRAPHER, DID YOU?

24

Figure 24.57   Some people just cannot be trusted with film.

Come along, and I'll show you what my *own* calls were for making this picture pleasant-looking—in tutorial style, of course.

Note

Flaming Pear's India Ink   You cannot finish this image without buying Flaming Pear's India Ink filter. Just so you know right now. But you will learn a lot about image filtering in this trick if you choose to read it anyhow. And you can indeed go to FlamingPear.com and download a free demo of the program so you can see what we're talking about here.

Bringing a Photo Back from Repairlessness

1. Open the Wayne & Pam.tif image from the Examples\Chap24 folder on the companion CD. I'm using two windows here to see a long view and a close-up. You can do this, too (it's only two views of the same image), by choosing Window, Arrange, New Window for Wayne & Pam.tif. Edits made to one window are made to the other.

2. Double-click on the Background layer and accept the default name in the dialog box. Click on OK. Press **Q** to enter Quick Mask mode to make a selection of Pam. With black as the foreground color and a 60-pixel hard brush, paint in Pam.

3. When satisfied with the selection, press **Q** to switch back to standard editing mode and then press Ctrl(⌘)+Shift+J to Layer via Cut. With the Move tool, move Pam up and closer to Wayne, as shown in Figure 24.58.

QUICK MASK

CROP AND
AIRBRUSH IN
LIGHT BLUE
TONE

CUT TO A NEW LAYER
AND REPOSITION

Figure 24.58   Move Pam closer to Wayne. She likes him.

4. Switch to the Crop tool and crop the picture, as shown in Figure 24.58. Click on Layer 0 to make that the active layer. Choose the Brush tool and hold down the Alt(Opt) key to toggle to the Eyedropper tool; then sample a light blue from the background of the photo. Then paint in the area where Pam used to be.

5. This is totally optional, but you might want to mask Wayne, move him to a new layer, and then put a nice sunset scene on the background layer. (A nice sunset image called Sunset.tif is located in the Examples/Chap 24 folder.) Then flatten the image.

Tip

Shifting a viewer's focus   Background detail, even that as simple as a sunset, helps to disguise editing work or flaws in the foreground.

6. Choose Image, Mode, LAB Color. On the Channels palette, choose Lightness as the current channel; then go back to the Image menu and choose Mode, Grayscale. Click on OK to the dialog box asking to discard channels. Now *this* is the way you convert color images to grayscale. In LAB mode, the grayscale information is separated from any color information (the two other channels), so there is no color influence when you convert.

7. Press Ctrl(⌘)+J to make a copy of the Background layer on the Layers palette. Choose Filter, Artistic, Poster Edges and apply the settings shown in Figure 24.59. I know—Wayne looks like he has a skin condition, but what we gain here is a strong edge detection; these folks are actually beginning to show some detail in their faces!

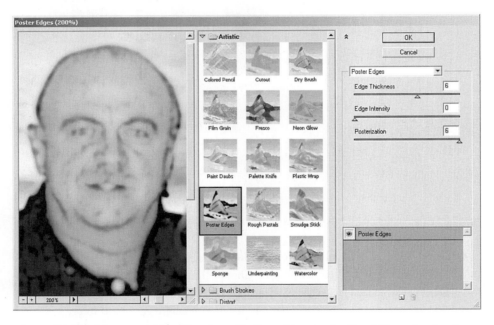

Figure 24.59   The Poster Edges filter is terrific for seeking out detail and blatantly advertising it.

Insider

It is a given that we cannot make this picture beautiful and in focus, but what we *can* do is make it beautiful and stylized—this is the aim. The colors in the picture are made up of pixels, and the nauseating focus of the picture is made up from the same pixels. Therefore, I conclude that we should work on the image in grayscale, and the finished product will be grayscale, too.

8. Using the Eraser tool with the Airbrush option turned on and a small 21-pixel soft-edge brush, start erasing with Flow and Opacity set to 100%. If you need partial erasing in any areas, change the Flow to a lower amount such as 10%. Erase away any Poster Edges dots that are just plain ugly and contribute to making this image look bad. Remember, you're only erasing something to show the original image underneath.

9. Choose Filter, Other, Maximum, as shown in Figure 24.60. In the Maximum dialog box, set the Radius to 1 pixel. This makes the heavy Poster Edges thinner and more natural looking while still helping facial detail definition.

Figure 24.60 The Maximum command takes away some of the harshness left by the Poster Edges command.

10. Blend the top copy with the Background layer. Use about 35% Opacity for the top layer, and then press Ctrl(⌘)+E to merge the layers.

11. Choose Filter, Artistic, Watercolor and use the settings shown in Figure 24.61. Then press Ctrl(⌘)+Shift+F to fade the Watercolor effect to 60%. These folks are going to look real, even if we filter the picture to the ends of the earth!

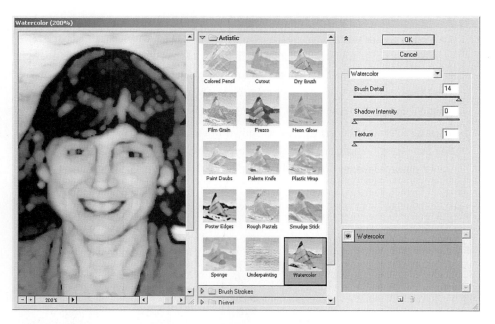

Figure 24.61   The Watercolor filter often brings out details in the shadow areas of an image, but it also creates aesthetically pleasing doodles that were never in the original photo. Have a homely client who wants to be in the Quarterly Report? Use the Watercolor filter at about 50% Opacity blended with the original base image.

12. Here's a step you cannot do without an extra purchase, but it makes all the difference to the photograph. I heartily recommend Flaming Pear's India Ink filter. It costs a whopping $15. Let's face it, you buy wedding presents for people you don't even like for more money. And you can't make a "bad" India Ink filter image. As you can see in Figure 24.62, I'm reducing the grayscale image to black or white. This also means that this image can then be enlarged with very little loss in image content.

13. Press Ctrl(⌘)+S. If you own India Ink, save the image to hard disk. If not, well, you can close the image without saving it because you probably are not Wayne or Pam.

Here we go—the "beauty pose" is shown in Figure 24.63. Didn't think this picture would ever merit a frame, eh?

Figure 24.62   Using Flaming Pear's India Ink filter is a beautiful method of reducing detail in an image but adding a sort of charm.

Making Hard Choices About Bad Images

Certainly, a massive amount of photo information has been lost to get to the Cutline version in Figure 24.63, but in this case, the color information was kah-kah; there was no way to make it contribute to the finished image. But if you examine any picture, you will notice that a flawed image usually has a characteristic missing or a characteristic that is flawed in it. You owe it to yourself to use drastic measures, when called for, to make a picture look nice. Don't waste time trying to cope. Take the route that your mind and talent tells you to take to arrive at what is usually a stylized rendition of an image.

Figure 24.63   We've come from a lousy color image to a nice, sharp black-and-white image. Who's complaining?

Trick 10: Fixing a Chopped-Off Drop Shadow

I have been putting drop shadows on everything in the *Inside Photoshop* books for years. The famous Gaussian blur drop shadow is extremely overused, starting with *PC Magazine* and ending up on both the Mac OS and Windows XP Plus! Pack interfaces. So why do I apparently succumb to peer pressure? The answer is simple: The drop shadow adds dimension, so you are not stuck reading a "flat" book for hours on end. If I get you to refocus every now and then, I've provided a valuable service and will be sending you my ophthalmologist's bill.

Seriously, there are hazards associated with drop-shadowing everything. One big hazard occurs when you apply a drop shadow, make a few editing moves, and then move a drop-shadowed image—only to discover that you've truncated the shadow. It travels abruptly from 10% gray to paper white.

Drop shadows appear to be the staple of modern printed communications. So you might as well know how to fix them when something goes amiss. Murphy's Law is alive and well in the twenty-first century!

In Figure 24.64, for example, trouble is a-brewing. The mounty picture has just had a fresh drop shadow applied. But as you can see, the shadow doesn't fade away completely before the bottom of the image.

Figure 24.64   I might get a ticket from the mounty for imprudent use of Alien Skin's Eye Candy filters!

I want you to run through this simple trick with me, so open the Mounty.tif image from the Examples\Chap24 folder on the companion CD, and follow these steps:

Fixing a Broken Drop Shadow

1. Double-click the Background layer title on the Layers palette, and click on OK to accept the defaults. Now you can move the mounty as you please.

2. As you can see, Bouton has already fouled up the picture with a drop shadow that runs off the page. Press **V** to switch to the Move tool, move the image up and to the left, as shown in Figure 24.65, and then choose Flatten Image from the Layers palette's flyout menu.

Figure 24.65   The bottom edge of the shadow is cropped off. What idiot did this?

3. With the Rectangular Marquee tool, drag a selection marquee around the bottom of the cropped shadow. Look carefully at Figure 24.66. The top of the selection should be a few pixels away from the image, and the bottom of the marquee should extend only by 3 or 4 pixels into the white area. Press Ctrl(⌘)+ Alt(Opt)+D and feather the selection by about 5 pixels. Click on OK.

4. Apply a slight amount of Gaussian blurring (Filter, Blur, Gaussian Blur), as shown in Figure 24.67. Around 4 pixels should do the trick for an image and a shadow of the sizes presented to you here. See? Instant shadow restoration?

5. You're done! Deselect the selection marquee, and save the image if you like. As you can see in Figure 24.68, the mounty is pretty happy about the repairs, too. Press Ctrl(⌘)+Shift+S if you want to save this image to your hard drive.

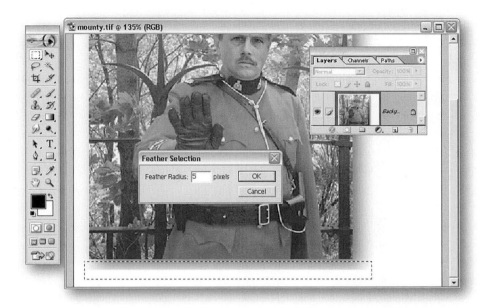

Figure 24.66   Select the "broken" part of the drop shadow, and then feather the selection.

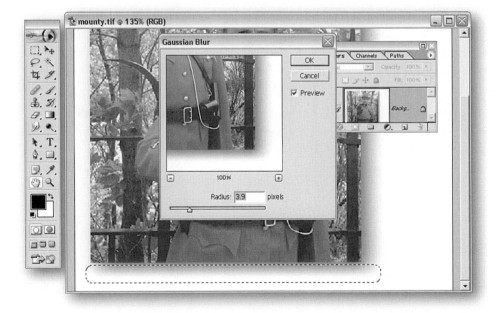

Figure 24.67   The Gaussian Blur filter restores the chopped-off drop shadow!

Figure 24.68   Drop shadows can be cropped badly, but they can also be restored in about four steps.

Grand Chapter Summary

Has this chapter seemed a little weird to you? Did you like it anyway? Well, welcome to the league of Photoshop pros. We do funky stuff all day, and ultimately, it's all in a day's work. You are forced to be ingenious at every turn, and I hope that you don't mind thinking like me at least for a little while until you get your Photoshop wings. Everything worthwhile in Photoshop is a challenge, and the impossible simply takes a little longer to do.

C h a p t e r   25

Using Photoshop with Quark, Illustrator, XARA, and Other Programs

One of the basic services that went into the

cobbling of the Mac OS and the Windows

OS was the capability for multiple applica-

tions to share documents. If the Clipboard

In this chapter, you'll learn

- From Photoshop to Quark
- From Photoshop to Illustrator
- From Illustrator to Photoshop
- From Photoshop to PageMaker
- From Photoshop to InDesign
- From Photoshop to CorelDRAW
- From CorelDRAW to Photoshop
- From Photoshop to XARA
- From XARA to Photoshop

doesn't work for this purpose, chances are that two applications support a common file type, such as TIFF or JPEG. This chapter looks at strategies for sharing documents with Photoshop and other popular applications. Chances are you own one or more of them, and chances are if you don't know how to shuffle data from and to Photoshop from other applications right now, you will by the end of this chapter!

From Photoshop to Quark

You can move an image from Photoshop into Quark in two ways: pasting from the Clipboard and using the File, Get Picture command after a frame has been created. Let's look at these methods one at a time.

Pasting from Photoshop

Object Linking and Embedding (OLE) is a Microsoft invention that is not limited to use in Windows. If you run a Macintosh and own Microsoft Word, chances are that a special instance of OLE has been installed on your system. OLE is a great way to paste from Photoshop to Quark, because after an image has been pasted, you can edit it using Photoshop. To edit it in Photoshop, you simply need to double-click on the pasted image in the Quark document. Later sections of this chapter talk more about OLE-capable applications.

You should keep in mind that there is a size limit of about 3–4MB for files you copy from Photoshop to the Clipboard. If you try to copy and paste a larger file from Photoshop into Quark, you'll receive an error message. If that happens, you'll need to copy and paste the image using the Get Picture command, which is described in the next section of this chapter.

To use OLE to copy a Photoshop image and paste it into Quark, follow these steps:

1. With your image displayed in Photoshop, press Ctrl(⌘)+A to Select, All.

2. Press Ctrl(⌘)+C to copy the image to the Clipboard if your image is on one layer; if your image has multiple layers, press Ctrl(⌘)+Shift+C to copy a merged version of all visible layers.

3. Switch to Quark and then choose Edit, Paste Special. A dialog box opens, and you have your choice of formats for the paste. As you can see in Figure 25.1, I'm choosing Paste as Adobe Photoshop Image Object. Your other choice here could be Paste As Bitmap. The quality of the image will be identical, but if you choose to paste the image as a bitmap, you won't be able to edit the image in Photoshop should you decide to do so later.

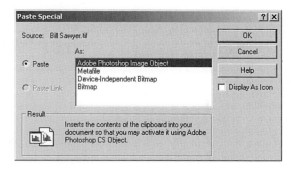

Figure 25.1   OLE at work. You can paste a small image into a Quark document as a Photoshop object and then edit the image in Photoshop later by double-clicking it.

The Get Picture Command

If you intend to use a large image in Quark, your best bet is to draw a frame and then place the imported image in it. As far as file formats go, generally, it's best to save the image as a TIFF file. Why? Because TIFF and Photoshop's native PSD format can retain resolution information, but the PSD format isn't recognized by all programs. If you save the image as a Targa file, for example, and then import it, the imported file will default to 72 pixels per inch (ppi), and the dimensions will most surely be too large for the frame. But if you use TIFF, and you specify a resolution of, say, 300 pixels per inch and a width of 3 inches, this is exactly what Quark will import.

To import a Photoshop image into a Quark document using the Get Picture command, first draw a frame around the image in Photoshop (see Figure 25.2 for a callout of the tool). Next, choose File, Get Picture, and then locate the picture on your hard disk. Choose the picture, and then in a moment it will be placed within the selected picture box.

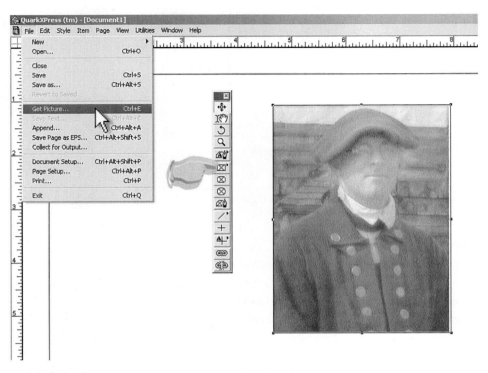

Figure 25.2   Use the Get Picture command to place an image within a picture box.

From Photoshop to Illustrator

You can actually move Photoshop data into Illustrator in three ways:

- **Edit, Paste.** The easiest way to move a small bitmap from Photoshop into Illustrator is to choose Select, All (Ctrl(⌘)+A) in Photoshop, copy the selection, and then switch to Illustrator and choose Edit, Paste. Illustrator is not an OLE server or client, so Paste Special is not an option.

- **File, Place.** To import larger bitmaps from Photoshop to Illustrator, use the File, Place command. As with Quark, your best bet is to use TIFF as the import file format (you need to make sure alpha channels have been stripped from the document if you don't want masking to occur in the target document), but Illustrator is capable of importing a wide range of bitmap file formats, from BMP to JPEG.

- **File, Open.** Photoshop has the capability to export a path as a vector-type file, the native file type of Illustrator. In Photoshop, create a path, or multiple paths, and then choose File, Export, Paths to Illustrator. Then, in Illustrator, simply choose File, Open, and open the saved file from Photoshop. The paths will need a stroke width and/or a fill, but this is a wonderful, goof-proof feature of Photoshop.

From Illustrator to Photoshop

Because Illustrator can handle both vector and bitmap information, you can export a bitmap from Illustrator right into Photoshop. To do that, you use the Edit, Paste or the Rasterize commands, depending on the type of data included in the image. I explain both methods in the following sections. One command requires that the design is already in bitmap format, whereas the other *converts* a vector design to bitmap format.

Edit, Paste

The simplest way to move a bitmap from Illustrator to Photoshop is to select it, copy it, and then go to Photoshop and choose Edit, Paste to paste the image into an open Photoshop document. If you need to open a new document, after selecting and copying the image in Illustrator, choose File, New in Photoshop (Photoshop reads the file dimensions from the Clipboard and offers up the right-sized document window), and then choose Edit, Paste. Oddly, there doesn't seem to be a Clipboard size limit when pasting from Illustrator to Photoshop, but only when pasting from Photoshop into Illustrator.

Be aware that the default Clipboard copy settings in Illustrator CS are set to copy as PDF. This means that any items copied from an Illustrator file are automatically converted to pixels when pasted into Photoshop. However, you can retain vector information when copying paths from Illustrator into Photoshop—if you simply tweak the Preference settings within Illustrator. Here's how to change the Copy As option:

1. Open Illustrator and go to the Edit menu and choose Preferences, File Handling & Clipboard.

2. On the lower portion of the File Handling Preference dialog box, you'll see two options for Copy As. Change this option from the default PDF to AICB (no transparency support); you're given two more options, Preserve Paths or Preserve Appearance and Overprints, either of which enables you to preserve the vector information when pasting into Photoshop. Select one of these options, and click on OK to exit the Preference dialog box.

3. Select a path(s) within Illustrator, and choose Edit, Copy.

4. Jump over to Photoshop, and press Ctrl($\mathcal{H}$)+V to paste. You will now see a dialog box that gives you three Paste As options: Pixels, Path, or Shape Layer.

5. Choose Paste As: Path, and the Illustrator path will appear in a document window within the workspace. You can then manipulate the path(s) using the path selection tools in Photoshop (see Figure 25.3).

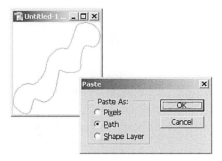

Figure 25.3   You have the option to Paste as Path from within Photoshop.

The first option (Pixels) results in rasterizing the path into a bitmap or…well…*pixels*. The second and third options preserve the path or vector information within Photoshop. If you understand how paths and shape layers work, these options might be extremely valuable to you.

Note

More Path Info   For the complete low-down on paths, check out Chapter 6, "Using the Pen Tools."

The Rasterize Command

To import Illustrator design data that consists of paths into Photoshop, you can convert paths to bitmap data before exporting the design. In Illustrator, choose Effect, Rasterize, and then choose File, Export As A Bitmap from the main menu. Then you can simply open the exported file in Photoshop.

From Photoshop to PageMaker

Importing an image from Photoshop into PageMaker is a simple process. PageMaker's importing options are almost identical to those found in Quark Xpress, as you will learn in the following sections.

Edit, Paste Special

PageMaker is an OLE client and server, so that means you can copy an image from Photoshop and then use the Edit, Paste Special command in PageMaker to import the image. You can then double-click on it and edit it in Photoshop at any point in the future. Or you can choose Paste Special, Bitmap for an unlinked/unembedded import of the image (see Figure 25.4).

Figure 25.4   You can use the Paste Special command to import images from Photoshop to PageMaker.

File, Place

To import larger images from Photoshop, use PageMaker's File, Place command, and then choose the image file you want placed in the PageMaker document. Just as a note here, including a complete copy of the image in PageMaker is usually better than linking the image. Hard drives are large these days, CDs can be burned to transport a large PageMaker document, and by including this image within the file, you never run the risk of the file becoming unlinked.

From Photoshop to InDesign

Using the File, Place command is really the only way to import a Photoshop image file into an InDesign document. But wait, you can do some fun and useful stuff with text, too. Read on!

File, Place

InDesign does not acknowledge data on the Clipboard, so a simple copy-and-paste procedure is out of the question. You need to save the file in Photoshop (to TIFF format) and then use InDesign's File, Place command to import the file. But just as a side note, you can copy and paste paths from Illustrator to InDesign.

Copying and Pasting Text

You lose the formatting, but if you need to hustle some text to or from InDesign, Photoshop can read/write the text. All you do in Photoshop is copy the text using the Type tool (to highlight the text) and then choose Edit, Copy. Then, in InDesign, you place the text cursor in the document and choose Edit, Paste (or Ctrl(⌘)+V). The other way around, you can highlight text in InDesign and copy it, and then paste it into Photoshop when the Type tool is chosen.

From Photoshop to CorelDRAW

CorelDRAW is an OLE client and server, so you can indeed paste from Photoshop to CorelDRAW. The following sections explain how.

Edit, Paste Special

You can use the Edit, Paste Special command to copy a small Photoshop image to CorelDRAW. To do so, copy a small image from Photoshop to the Clipboard, open CorelDRAW, and choose Edit, Paste Special. The dialog box that opens gives you a choice of Object types, and as with Quark and PageMaker, it's usually best to choose Adobe Photoshop Image. You can also choose Paste Special, Bitmap, but then you can't edit the image in Photoshop later because you're simply pasting the Clipboard contents with no linking or embedding (see Figure 25.5).

File, Import

For larger images, you can use the File, Import command in CorelDRAW and then import a saved file from Photoshop. Again (again, again!), TIFF is usually the best file format in which to save, but CorelDRAW can import just about any bitmap image file format.

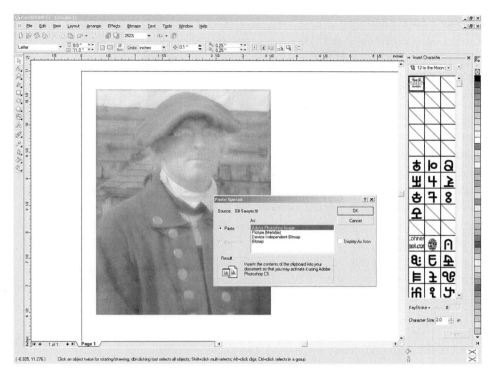

Figure 25.5   Use the Paste Special command to paste a linked Photoshop image into CorelDRAW.

From CorelDRAW to Photoshop

CorelDRAW is much like Illustrator when it comes to Import and Export options. The following sections describe the three best ways to move data from CorelDRAW to Photoshop.

Edit, Paste

You can copy an image from CorelDRAW into Photoshop using the Edit, Paste command; the process is the same as that you learned earlier in this chapter for using Edit, Paste to transfer an image from Illustrator to Photoshop. The only disadvantage to copying and pasting from CorelDRAW to Photoshop is that the resulting bitmap is aliased (it has jaggy edges). But if you just want a design as a reference in Photoshop, this is a quick and easy way to transfer the image data.

Convert to TIFF

You can easily convert a CorelDRAW design to bitmap format (choose Bitmaps, Convert to Bitmap from the main menu), and then export the resulting bitmap as a TIFF. You then just open the TIFF file in Photoshop. Pay careful attention to the resolution and color mode when you make the conversion in CorelDRAW.

Illustrator Format

CorelDRAW can export a genuine Illustrator file format. This means that you can export the design in the Illustrator format (with the *.ai file extension) and then either place it in a new Photoshop document window, or choose File, Open and rasterize the file. You cannot, unfortunately, import the CorelDRAW design as paths; it must be converted to bitmap format to be of any use in Photoshop. If you have Illustrator, another possible solution would be to open the file in Illustrator and then copy the paths (see the earlier section "From Illustrator to Photoshop," to learn more about Illustrator's Preferences, which allow paths to be preserved when you're copying into Photoshop).

From Photoshop to XARA

XARA is *sort of* an OLE client/server. And it's a Windows-only program, although it runs quite nicely over emulation on the Mac. The following sections take you through your importing and exporting options.

Edit, Paste Bitmap

No Adobe Photoshop Image Object option is available when you paste from the Clipboard into XARA from Photoshop. Your best option is to choose Bitmap from the XARA dialog box after pressing Ctrl+V. The default resolution of 96 pixels per inch is in effect.

File, Import

XARA's File, Import command, as in many other applications discussed in this chapter, is used for larger bitmaps. Use the TIFF file format to retain resolution when you import.

Import Illustrator Format

If you like, you can export Paths to Illustrator from Photoshop and then import the paths to XARA. This technique is useful if you've designed a logo or something in Photoshop and want to be able to share it with other XARA users or just want to have the flexibility of working with paths in their native format.

From XARA to Photoshop

Copying an image or design from XARA to Photoshop couldn't be easier. Here are the ways to do this:

- **Copy to the Clipboard.** If you have a bitmap image already in XARA, all you need to do is select it and press Ctrl+C. Then switch to Photoshop, open a New document, and paste the copy into the image window. You can copy an image of most any size this way.

- **Convert to TIFF.** You can convert a copy of your design to TIFF and then open it in Photoshop. Resolution and dimensions are retained.

- **Export as Illustrator.** If you want to get a design into Photoshop at any size, choose to export the design in Illustrator format. Then in Photoshop, you can choose File, Place to put the design in an existing image window, or choose File, Open and then rasterize the image to the size you need.

- **Export as PNG.** To export an image with an alpha channel in place, use the PNG file format. Photoshop recognizes PNGs, which saves you steps because you will then have a mask in place within the exported PNG file.

Summary

Whew! There are surely as many import/export options to use with Photoshop as there are applications; this chapter provided only a *brief* list of the most popular applications used with Photoshop. Basically, you should keep two points in mind as you work cross-application:

- If the target program is an OLE client, you can use the Paste Special command with files under 4MB or so. By doing this, you can edit the image using Photoshop at any point in the future.

- You can't go wrong with the TIFF file format (you need to make sure alpha channels have been stripped from the document if you don't want masking to occur in the target document). Then you just need to use an Import (or Place) command in the document to receive the image.

The next chapter, unfortunately, is our last, and it has very little to do with Photoshop and a lot to do with you, the designer. "Where do I go from here?" is a very natural question, and fortunately, we have some answers. Just turn the page.

Chapter 26

Where Do We Go from Here?

Closing Thoughts

That's right; there are definitely more pages under your left thumb than under your right. This means that *Inside Photoshop CS* must close because the publisher has run out of paper (onnnnnnly kidding, Betsy!). Seriously, though, *Inside Photoshop CS* was not the beginning of your computer graphics education—you began when you developed enough of an interest in graphics to go out and look for a book—and it is not the end of your education either. As Adobe Photoshop evolves, we will certainly be back with ongoing, fully updated versions of this book, to help you stay on top of all the software's new features and the most creative ways to use them. Until then, be sure to keep this book by your computer, and continue to use and learn from it.

Learning from Life

In the same way that you must occasionally take your face away from the monitor to catch a breath of fresh air, you should also seriously consider taking a day or two off from the computer. Go outdoors, visit a friend you respect and haven't spoken with in a while, and even stick your head into a continuing education classroom that looks interesting. The creative mind is always looking for outside stimulation: You see a beautiful scene, your mind filters it, and you eventually express what you feel about this scene, using Photoshop or even (gasp) a pencil on paper. When the creative urge strikes (and it has historically been a very strong urge), you should do two things:

- Realize firmly in your mind what the *concept* is that you are considering. It can be as commercial as a stunning graphic to sell a car, or as personal as a graphic to tell your spouse that you love her.

  A concept is an elusive thing. Many people presume, for example, that a concept is, "Okay, we get this elephant to stand on one leg next to a clothes washer." This describes what someone wants to *see* visually in a composition, but it is not the concept. Why is the elephant there? Why is the elephant next to a clothes washer? If there's no reason, there's no concept, and as we would traditionally say, it's "back to the drawing board."

  A fair example of a concept (I don't want to give away *too* many free concepts!) would be of a clown, in color, walking down an urban street that's in black and white. The picture says that there is humor amidst the cold, serious world; that's the concept. Do you see the difference between the clown and the elephant?

- Gather stock photography, but also gather stock ideas and write them down. There's a yin/yang to ideas. You give an idea life, but the idea also provokes you on an emotional level and then gives life to even more ideas. There's nothing sadder than sitting down in front of Photoshop without an idea. It's time wasted, better spent examining the geometric complexity of a flower or considering how clouds can create specific moods.

26

We, as civilized people, are so caught up in the day-to-day machinery we call a working life that we often deprive ourselves of inspiration and really good ideas. After this book is finished, I intend to mow the lawn, inspect all the flowers my spouse has planted, look at the sky, look at an insect crawling around for food—and then open Photoshop or another application and see where these impressions of life lead. To be an artist means being able to see life with the widest vision you permit yourself and then filter what you're thinking about and what you saw into a graphical composition. It doesn't get much easier than that. And don't feel intimidated about the outcome of your work, either. Simply immerse yourself in what you're creating without shame or fear of public acceptance or rejection, and gaze upon what you've done as a way of expressing yourself.

Learning How to Learn

Instinctive learning isn't easy for everyone. Schools tend to make us recite instead of invent, and we tend to be conditioned, not taught, by even the best-intentioned but often opinionated scholars. As the lead author, I feel differently about books than any other medium of communication because you, the reader, have the option of closing the book and taking a break any time you feel like it. Additionally, *Inside Photoshop CS* is a reference and tutorial above all things, so this puts me in the position of being a fellow artist second and an "information vendor" first. Hopefully, we've set a conversational tone in this book, but not at the expense of our prime goal, which is teaching.

Inside Photoshop CS is the 14th book we have written on Photoshop. Through the years, we've received mail from our friends and readers with questions (and a scattered complaint here and there). Like other artists, we depend on feedback to influence what we document and how we communicate with you, the reader. The most useful feedback we've received has been on how users approach this book.

Many readers never actually perform the tutorials; instead, they skip around in the book looking for a magic recipe or technique here and there. For many users, this approach works when they need to solve a specific problem quickly. But the most "successful" readers—the ones who have increased their overall relationship with art and increased their skill level—are the ones who found time to sit with the book for an hour or two at a time and work their way through a chapter. Like most things in life, mastery of an art comes from doing. Only through action do the principles behind the steps become tangible. If you've passed over chapters on your way to this paragraph, please invest in your own talent and work completely through a favorite chapter. Follow the steps, and then do something similar with images of your own. Make the knowledge truly yours.

Also, we should tell you that we actually *read* sometimes(!) and even a tutorial-based book has some "good stuff" lodged between the pages that might not be a formal set of steps designed to help you arrive at a finished piece. What we do when we discover a nugget of wisdom is outlined in (you guessed it) a numbered list:

Indexing a Nugget of Wisdom in a Book

1. Take out a pad of fluorescent sticky notes.

2. Detach one leaf.

3. Place it on the page in the book that contains a morsel of interest.

For all the information organized into procedures found in this book, however, please *don't* treat *Inside Photoshop CS* as a workbook. We've tried to make this book an excellent *resource* guide, and a book on art, too.

Whether you are an imaging enthusiast who simply wants to retouch photos as a pastime, a designer in a large enterprise who is forced to measure output in volume, or a fine artist who is looking for that "special something" to refine your work, you might not immediately know where you're going creatively. But we all pack toolkits for our artistic voyages, both virtual and physical. You've seen in this book that Photoshop is not only a necessary part of your computer graphics toolkit, but that it also should be located at the *top* of the toolkit, where you can reach it easily.

We have had the career privilege of never having to write about an application we do not believe in. Bringing all the examples in this book together, with the tricks, tips, techniques, and secrets, required the ability to learn correctly. But it also required an imaging program as capable as Photoshop as the vehicle of our expression. You have the right application, you have the right book (we think), so now it's simply up to you to create your own gallery of ideas.

26

Part IX

Appendices

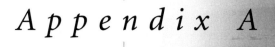

A p p e n d i x   A

The Inside Photoshop CS CD-ROM

So you're wondering what's on the CD-ROM and how to use it? Glad you asked! The short answer is, "Lots!" The long answer is found in the following pages.

Be sure to check out these sections:

- Instructions on where to get Acrobat Reader 6 if you don't already have a copy
- Descriptions of the companion CD's contents
- Information concerning special offers
- Details on what to do if you have problems with your companion CD

Instructions for Installing Acrobat Reader 6

The Inside Photoshop CS Companion CD contains a number of Adobe Acrobat PDF files. Of particular importance are the PDF files in the Textures and Fonts folders within the Boutons folder, crammed onto the CD (okay, technically, Mr. Software Specialist-guy stuffed the CD); and eGlossary.pdf, the Online Glossary. Because PDF files are so important to the CD, we want to make sure you have a copy.

If you have already installed Photoshop, Acrobat Reader is almost certainly installed. Try opening one of the files with the .pdf file extension. If your operating system complains that it doesn't know what program to use to open the file, you probably need to install a copy of Adobe Acrobat Reader. You can find a copy of Acrobat Reader in Adobe's Photoshop CS. Or, if you want to be sure that you have the newest version of this very useful, free program, jump on the Web and download it from Adobe's site at, `http://www.adobe.com/products/acrobat/readstep2.html`.

What's on the Companion CD?

We're really proud of the CD that accompanies this book. You won't believe all the goodies it contains!

The Online Glossary

In the root of the CD is the eGlossary.pdf file, an Acrobat document that is the book's Glossary. It's more than 280 pages in color, thoroughly indexed, and it provides scores of cross-references. You need Acrobat Reader 3 or later to access this file.

The Boutons Folder

In the Boutons folder, you'll find

- The Textures folder, with more than 100 images, many of them 3D. Now, as with most BoutonWare, this stuff is CharityWare, and we'll say the following just once and spare you from reading it over and over:

CharityWare is *not* Freeware or Shareware.

If you want to use a Bouton-generated piece of data (fonts or art) commercially, we ask that you donate a sum (it's up to your own conscience) to a charity or charities listed in the PDF file in a particular folder. Do your heart and someone else's life some good as you use our work that's truly from the heart.

- The Fonts folder, which is loaded with Gary David Bouton–created fonts in TrueType and Type 1 for the Mac and Windows. A lot of these fonts are better quality than commercial fonts you'd pay $30 or more for.

The Nick Curtis Folder

In the Nick Curtis folder, you'll find some one-of-a-kind, groovy, fascinating typefaces by one of the world's greatest typographers. Nick, through a special deal with us, is allowing you to play with some of his commercial fonts totally free of charge. Check out his ad in the back of the book, too.

The Examples Folder

The Examples folder has subfolders, marked Chap02, Chap20, and so on. (Please note that some chapters do not require Example files, so do not freak out if a chapter folder is "missing" from the companion CD.) When you read the examples in the chapters, you'll be asked to access something such as duck.psd from the Examples\Chap22 folder. Locating the materials you need to work through this book is a snap. Double-click on Examples, and then navigate to the folder listed in the text.

The Software Folder

In the Software folder, you'll find several subfolders that contain working demos or totally functional programs that we feel work well with Photoshop. The following sections list the programs in these subfolders. We're pretty proud of our legwork.

The Genetica Folder

Genetica is a fun and productive application that generates realistic-looking textures by using a shader tree (that is, components of the overall design are arranged in a tree-like fashion; you can move the components around until you arrive at a different tree and a remarkably different design).

The Digital Element Folder

Verdant and Aurora 2 are plug-ins for Photoshop that, respectively, produce realistic-looking trees and some spectacular skies. These splendid, useful little utilities in the Digital Element folder can be used to replace or hide unwanted areas of a photograph.

The Path Styler Folder

Path Styler takes the idea of bevel edges on a shape and refines it to high art. With this Photoshop plug-in, you can create textured shapes and typefaces, create scores of interesting bevel designs, and all you have to do is start off with a Photoshop path. Ideal for Web work!

The Power Retouche Folder

Power Retouche is a suite of filters that take some of the existing filters in Photoshop to the max. For example, you can create a true sepia tone without changing color modes. This is an exciting bundle for anyone who wants to get a little more control over some of the basic adjustments found in Photoshop, such as Hue, Contrast, and more.

The Xara Folder (Windows Only)

Xara X is a Windows-only drawing program. Wait a minute. To say it's only a drawing program is like saying the Statue of Liberty won't fit in a size 7 dress. Xara X is a fully functional, two-week, time-limited program that is highly compatible with Photoshop. It slips in and out between vectors and bitmaps with ease and precision. If you know CorelDRAW, you'll feel right at home with this state-of-the-art drawing program. In fact, all the screen annotations and the color signature in this book were generated out of Xara X. Bouton's been using this program along with Photoshop for more than five years now.

VisCheck

VisCheck isn't a "fun" plug-in, but then again, it isn't funny when your audience is color-blind and you don't know what they can see in your artwork. Be kind to the color-blind; check in with VisCheck before you post an image to the Web.

Special Offers

Finally, the publisher and the authors are out to save you some bucks with firms we've known and trust as being outstanding in their respective fields. In fact, many of our demo versions on the CD are accompanied with a discount ad in this book. How about that!??!

Happy hunting on the CD. We think you'll discover some real gems—especially the just-for-fun pineapples!

What to Do If You Have Problems with the Companion CD

For more information about the use of this CD, please review the ReadMe.txt file in the root directory. This file includes important disclaimer information as well as information about installation, system requirements, troubleshooting, and technical support.

Note

> **Technical support issues**   If you have any difficulties with this CD, you can access our tech support Web site at `http://www.sams.com`. Hint, look under the Contact Us menu.

A p p e n d i x B

The Inside Photoshop CS eGlossary

We felt it would be more convenient for our readers if the glossary to this book was done in Acrobat format with tons of links. That way, you can cruise from one topic to another in no time. All you need is Acrobat Reader, and you're all set.

First, load the eGlossary into Acrobat Reader. Then turn to page 2, where you'll see a keyboard-like page; this is your key to unlocking the wealth (see Figure B.1).

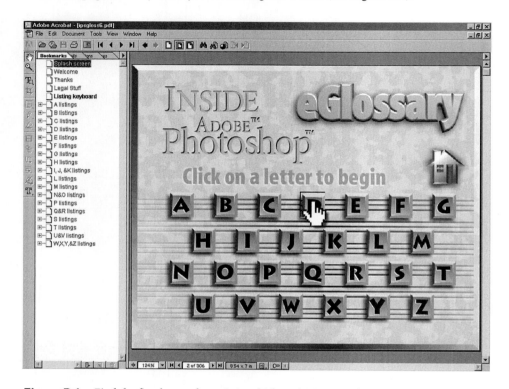

Figure B.1   Find the first letter of a topic in which you're interested, and click away.

Once you've navigated to the listings page for a letter (we're using *D* in this example), pick a topic, such as *Dithering*. Click on it, as shown in Figure B.2.

Figure B.2   Click on a topic you'd like to explore.

Now comes the neat part. Notice the callout in Figure B.3? That's a hyperlink, and if you click on it, it'll scoot you to an entirely different section of the eGlossary, expanding on the Dithering topic. The more you read and click, the more you learn and discover how interconnected the information can be.

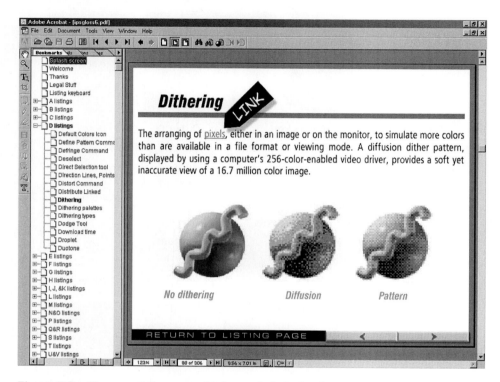

Figure B.3   Hypertext links are provided extensively in this document.

That's about it! Using the file is that simple! Have fun exploring our eGlossary, and pick up several morsels of good insights.

B

Index

E

M

Memory & Image Cache settings (Preferences dialog box), 153-154

memory cards
number of exposures per, 412
speeds, 377
transferring images to digital cameras, 377-380
automated transfer, 381-382
card readers, 379-380
manual transfer, 381
serial connections, 378
WIA Wizard, 382-383
wired connections, 378-379
wireless connections, 378-379
types, 376-377

MemoryStick (MS) memory cards, 377

Merge Down command, 62

merging
layers, 62-63
text, 797-798

metadata
GIF images, 951
JPEG 2000 images, 955
JPEG images, 953
Picture CD images, 469
PNG images, 958

mezzotints, 866-869

Microdrive memory cards, 377

Microsoft fonts, 829

midtones, 249

Minimize command, 996

mirror images, creating, 438-442

mirroring selections, 39

MMC (MultiMedia Card) memory cards, 376, 380

modifier keys, Marquee tools, 268, 273-274

Modify Color dialog box, 949

moiré patterns, 387

monitors
calibration, 84
color values, 76
ICC profiles, creating, 86-92

Move tool
Auto Select feature, 705
linked layers, 41, 798

moving
curves, 479-480
images
from CorelDRAW to Photoshop, 1039-1040
from Illustrator to Photoshop, 1035-1036
from Photoshop to CorelDRAW, 1038
from Photoshop to Illustrator, 1034-1035
from Photoshop to InDesign, 1038
from Photoshop to PageMaker, 1036-1037
from Photoshop to Quark, 1032-1033
from Photoshop to XARA, 1040
from XARA to Photoshop, 1041
layers
linked layers, 41
image areas on, 214-216

MS (MemoryStick) memory cards, 377

MultiMedia Card (MMC) memory cards, 376, 380

Multiply blending mode, 60, 203

Mystical Lighting filter (Auto F/X), 368

Mystical Tint, Tone, and Color filter (Auto F/X), 368

N

naming
alpha channels, 293
layers, 40, 177

Nearest Neighbor interpolation, 129, 853

NEF file format (Nikon), 417

negatives
film grain, 389
tips, 388
cleaning, 402
scanning, 401-403

T

U

V